Quantum Implications

Quantum Implications

Essays in honour of
David Bohm

EDITED BY
B. J. Hiley   *Birkbeck College, University of London*
F. David Peat   *Ottawa, Canada*

Routledge & Kegan Paul
London and New York

This collection first published in 1987 by
Routledge & Kegan Paul Ltd
11 New Fetter Lane, London EC4P 4EE
Published in the USA by
Routledge & Kegan Paul Inc.
in association with Methuen Inc.
29 West 35th Street, New York, NY 10001
Reprinted 1988

Set in Times
by Richard Clay Ltd
and printed in Great Britain
by Richard Clay Ltd,
Bungay, Suffolk

Library of Congress Cataloging in Publication Data

Quantum implications.
  Includes index.
  1. Quantum theory.   2. Bohm David.   I. Bohm, David.
II. Hiley, B. J. [Basil J.]   III. Peat, F. David, 1938–
QC174.125.Q34 1987   530.1′2   86–22032

British Library CIP Data also available
ISBN 0–7102–0806–5

Contents

1

General introduction: the development of David Bohm's ideas from the plasma to the implicate order

B. J. Hiley and **F. David Peat**

David Bohm was born in Wilkes-Barre, Pennsylvania, in 1917. His father ran a successful furniture business, making his way to the USA from what was then Austria-Hungary. There appears to be no physics whatsoever in the family background. Bohm, himself, became interested in science at an early age, being urged on by a fascination of finding out how things worked. By the age of eight he had already been introduced to science fiction. This fired his imagination and generated in him a deep interest in real science. But it was the nature of the real world that fascinated him most. He recalls the profound effect that a book on astronomy had on him in those formative years. He was struck by the vast order and regularity of the universe. This impressed him so much that he began to devote a great deal of time to science.

Needless to say, his father became somewhat concerned about the boy's future. Being a successful businessman, he could not imagine how anyone could make a living out of 'scientism' as he insisted on calling it. Young David took this as a challenge and using his earlier interest in redesigning mechanical devices he decided to try to make money out of inventing. He was rather proud of one invention in particular: namely, a 'dropless pitcher'. (This ingenious item had nothing at all to do with that great American sporting pastime, baseball. It was a jug or teapot that did not drip!) His principal concern now became how to make this design pay. After almost giving up in despair, he came across an advertisement in a popular science magazine offering, for the sum of $5, advice on how to exploit financially a good invention. Off went the $5 and back came some advice on how to obtain a patent. But that, of course, would cost a few hundred dollars! Would it be worth it? The answer (apparently, included in the $5!) was to do a door-to-door survey to test market demand! It was at

1

this point in his life that he determined that he would become a theoretical physicist.

As he began to study physics seriously, he was repeatedly struck by the interconnectedness of what, at a superficial glance, seemed to be totally unrelated phenomena. As he delved deeper into the sub-structure of matter and its movement, this characteristic of a rich and highly interconnected substructure became more and more apparent. Furthermore, as Bohm saw it, these deeper structures seemed to pos-sess properties which did not reflect the way physicists were talking about the behaviour of matter. In quantum mechanics, for example, it seemed that this interconnectedness was vital, yet the usual pre-sentation of the subject seemed to minimise this aspect of the phenom-ena.

In Bohm's original perception, this notion of interconnectedness was rather vague and ill-defined but with its continual reappearance in different forms, the notion slowly took shape, ultimately leading to a very radical and novel way of looking at reality. This view eventually crystallised into what he now terms the implicate order. But much was to happen before that idea eventually became clear.

The first formal indication of Bohm's departure from orthodoxy can be traced to his reformulation of quantum mechanics published in *Physical Review* in 1952.[1] But the ideas that lay behind that for-mulation seem to many to be totally against the spirit of his later work on the implicate order, so much so that they find it hard to see any connection at all. It is true that those papers were more intent on demonstrating that there was another logically coherent interpretation of the quantum mechanical formalism, other than the usual one. But it is the ideas implicit in this reformulation that have connections with the notion of the implicate order. Since there has been some interest in this connection, we have asked David to write a short article outlining what he sees as the essential relationship between the two.[2]

We would like here to present an overall sketch of the relevant background in which Bohm's ideas took shape so that the reader can appreciate the significance of the various developments in a broader context. This will also enable us to relate the various contributions to this book to the same background and so see where they fit in. By doing this we hope the book will become more than a collection of isolated contributions.

Bohm's interest in the fundamental questions of physics started at high school. Even at that early stage he was beginning to ask how the theories of physics enable one to build up an understanding of reality. At college he soon quickly became fascinated with quantum mechanics and relativity as he began to study these subjects in depth for the first time.

After graduating he began his research project under the supervision of Robert Oppenheimer. His dissertation topic involved a theoretical study of neutron–proton scattering. Yet even while working on this technical problem, he kept up his interests in fundamentals, always probing deeper into quantum theory and relativity. He remembers his long discussions with Joseph Weinberg, who had made a study of Bohr's point of view. During that period he admits to becoming a supporter of Bohr's position.

Before receiving his doctorate in 1943 from Berkeley, he moved to the Radiation Laboratory where he worked on problems connected with the later phases of the Manhattan Project. He was involved in a theoretical study of the ionisation of uranium fluoride in an electric arc which formed part of the broader study of the problems involved in the separation of ^{235}U from ^{238}U. Thus began his interest in plasma physics, to which he made some outstanding contributions.

Although much of this work was basically involved in technical problems, Bohm could not help noticing the philosophical implications. The individual particles in the plasma were highly correlated and behaved like an organic whole rather than a mechanistic system. The plasma constantly regenerated itself and surrounded all impurities with a sheath so as to isolate them completely. To understand in more detail how the plasma functioned, it was necessary to study the relation between the individual and the collective modes of behaviour. It was here that he introduced the idea of collective co-ordinates and developed a general way of handling plasmas.

When he took up the post of assistant professor at Princeton University he extended his earlier ideas to study the behaviour of electrons in metals, where quantum mechanics played an essential role. It was his innovative work in this area that established David Bohm's reputation as a theoretical physicist.

Neither of the editors knew Bohm in those days, but fortunately Eugene Gross, who was one of Bohm's first graduate students, has given a personal sketch of Bohm's thinking in the period he spent at Princeton. This is presented in the introduction to his article on 'Collective variables in elementary quantum mechanics' which appears in this volume.[3] We are particularly grateful for his contribution and find that the final paragraph to his introduction captures the feeling that many of us, students and colleagues, felt towards David Bohm: a totally unselfish man who shares his latest thoughts on many topics with his colleagues and students alike. This enthusiasm for the search for order in nature continues unabated today.

The main part of Gross's contribution is an illustration of how collective co-ordinates can provide a useful way of understanding the behaviour of different systems. He takes as examples the atom–molecule transition, the electron interacting with two lattice oscillators and ends with some remarks concerning the polaron problem. The following article is by another of Bohm's graduate students, David Pines.[4] It is a masterful review of some of the basic ideas involved in the development of plasma physics. He also outlines the role played by Bohm in developing the concepts needed to deal with the problems, and touches on the application of the random phase approximation and its use in liquid helium (^{4}He).

While still at Princeton, Bohm was asked to give a course of lectures on quantum mechanics to undergraduates and was faced with the task of presenting a clear account of the subject that had fascinated him for some time. Here was a theory that had emerged after a long struggle by many physicists to account correctly for a wide range of experimental results, which the classical theory could not even begin to explain. But the conceptual structure of this theory was very different from that of the classical theory. It implied a radical change in our outlook on reality. But precisely what were the nature of these changes did not yet seem very clear. The majority view was (and still is) that the precise nature of the conceptual changes are not important. All that was needed was to work with the self-consistent mathematical formalism, which, in some mysterious way, correctly predicts the numerical results of actual experiments.

After lecturing on the subject for three years, Bohm thought that this was not a satisfactory position to adopt so he decided to try to get a better understanding of the subject by writing a definitive textbook in which the physical aspects of the mathematics would be emphasised. Part of the task would involve clarifying Bohr's interpretation of the theory by drawing, to some extent, on Bohr's book *Atomic Theory and the Description of Nature*.[5]

It was while writing his book that he came into conflict with what eventually became known as McCarthyism. A year or so after arriving at Princeton he was called to appear before the Un-American Activities Committee, a committee of the House of Representatives. He was asked to testify against colleagues and associates. After taking legal advice he decided to plead the Fifth Amendment. A year or so later, while he was in the middle of his book, his plea was rejected and he was indicted for contempt of Congress. While awaiting trial, the Supreme Court ruled that no one should be forced to testify if the testimony is self-incriminating, provided no crime had been committed. Since no crime had been committed the indictment against Bohm was dropped.

During this period the University advised Bohm to stay away, one of the few benefits to emerge from this whole sordid affair. During his enforced isolation he was able to complete the book far sooner than he had anticipated. After that, however, with his contract at Princeton expired, he was unable to obtain a job in the USA and was advised by Oppenheimer to leave the country before the full force of McCarthyism took effect. Fortunately he had some friends in Brazil who were able to offer him a professorship in the University in São Paulo. He held this post from 1951 to 1955.

The textbook *Quantum Theory* was first published by Prentice-Hall in 1951 and is still in print today. It is generally regarded as one of the best textbooks of its day. Apart from a clear presentation of the main physical ideas lying behind the formalism, the book has the additional merit of discussing some of the more difficult aspects of the theory usually omitted from modern texts. For example it contains sections on the approach to the classical limit, the measurement problem and the Einstein, Podolsky, Rosen (EPR) paradox. The latter was of particular importance since it reformulated the EPR example in terms of correlated spin one-half systems. This discussion not only clarified the essential issues raised in the debate but also led to the suggestion of using positronium decay and optical cascades in actual experiments designed specifically to explore the consequences of EPR situations. These experiments have been significant in moving the continuing debate from what was generally regarded as a realm of speculative philosophy, or even theology, into hard physics.

All three of the above topics are still the subject of many current research papers. Indeed the contributions of Clark,[6] Leggett[7] and Penrose[8] are directly concerned with these topics. Terry Clark reports the experimental progress that his group at Sussex University have made in demonstrating quantum mechanical behaviour over macroscopic distances using SQUIDS. The aim has been to develop experimental techniques that could lead to a better understanding of macroscopic quantum mechanics and to explore a new approach to the measurement problem.

Tony Leggett presents an excellent review of the measurement problem which he believes to be a 'glaring indication of the inadequacy of quantum mechanics as a total world view'. He maps out an exploration of the likely direction in which it will break down. His discussion centres around the type of experiments discussed by Clark. By a vigorous and critical approach in these directions he hopes to provide a better understanding of how pure states can be converted into mixtures, thus connecting the microworld with our familiar classical macroscopic world. Roger Penrose examines a similar question, arguing that 'an essentially new and non-linear physical input to bring about the collapse' is needed and that this input should come from a general-relativistic gravity. He argues that the non-local nature of the collapse of the wave function could be connected with the fact that in general relativity the energy cannot be defined locally.

These types of difficulties always tend to leave an uneasy feeling that we really have not got to the bottom of quantum theory. As Gell-Mann puts it, 'Quantum Mechanics, that mysterious, confusing discipline which none of us really understands but which we know how to use.'[9] The problem is that we do not know precisely where the difficulty actually lies. It is quite clear that quantum theory is a statistical theory in the sense that the description of the individual particle can only be given in terms of a probability of it being observed at a certain point in space-time. There is no description of the individual process except in terms of its possible observation by some suitable measuring device. There is no way to understand what is happening: there is no actual fact. There is only a sequence of results of measurements, with no possibility of discussing what goes on between measurements.

This feature has led some physicists to question the existence of micro-realism. Bernard d'Espagnat has given a great deal of attention to this question in his books on the *Conceptual Foundations of Quantum Mechanics*[10] and *In Search of Reality*.[11] In the present volume he continues the discussion in a new way that involves a detailed comparison of Wheeler's point of view, which is essentially Bohrian, and that of Bell, who assumes there is a micro-reality.[12]

In classical physics, of course, any description in terms of probability can ultimately be understood in terms of ensemble averages over a well-defined individual behaviour. Here the statistical results would have their origins in a collection of well-defined individual events. Is there an underlying individual behaviour that could account for the statistical results of quantum mechanics? Of course, the individual behaviour would not be classical, but something different. The existence of such processes would not in any way detract from the present statistical theory which would still be valid and very useful in dealing with the more common situation involving many particles, such as for example in electron conduction, etc. However, if an underlying process did exist then an understanding of this process would lead to a better intuitive understanding of the quantum phenomena in general.

If such a process existed then it would require some set of parameters to specify it and traditionally these parameters have been called 'hidden', presumably because one is discussing a new, as yet unknown, process. All attempts in that direction were brought to a halt as a result of a theorem contained in von Neumann's book *The Mathematical Foundations of Quantum Mechanics*. He writes, after presenting the theorem, 'It should be noted that we need not go any further into the mechanism of the hidden parameters since we know that the established results of quantum mechanics can never be re-derived with their help.'[13] Because of the high (and justified) mathematical reputation of von Neumann, this statement, together with the various writings of Bohr, Heisenberg, Pauli, etc., gave rise to the dogma that there is no alternative. The wave function had now come to be regarded as the most complete description of the state of the system, a statement which essentially creates many of the 'problems of quantum mechanics'.

A year or two after completing his book, Bohm produced an alternative approach to quantum mechanics which he published as two papers in the *Physical Review*. They were entitled 'A suggested interpretation of the quantum theory in terms of "hidden" variables'.[1] The original purpose of these two papers was simply to show that there is, in fact, an alternative interpretation of quantum mechanics contrary to von Neumann's remarks and the prevailing view of that time. As Bohm points out in his second book, *Causality and Chance in Modern Physics*, this approach was never intended to be an ultimate definitive statement of what lies behind quantum mechanics.[14] Rather it was simply intended to point out that certain assumptions are made in the usual interpretation which turned out to be too restrictive. Indeed this alternative interpretation allows certain things to be done which in the ordinary approach are deemed to be impossible. As Bell puts it, 'In 1952 I saw the impossible done.'[15] (Some of the features of this approach had already been anticipated by de Broglie[16] in the pilot wave theory and by Madelung[17] in his hydrodynamical approach. However, both theories faced serious difficulties with many-body systems. In fact de Broglie conceded defeat by an objection raised by Pauli[18] and gave up his approach until Bohm showed how Pauli's objection could be answered.[1])

Unfortunately the physics community did not take very kindly to the appearance of this alternative view. Certainly the physicists who had contributed most to the evolution of the ordinary interpretation felt there was some fundamental flaw in Bohm's argument. Some of the early technical objections raised were quickly answered as they were based on a misunderstanding of how the approach actually worked. In fact, no sustainable technical objections against the theory have ever been made. In its primitive form, the approach gives the same statistical results as the quantum theory and therefore experiment cannot be the arbitrator. Ultimately the objections have their roots in the assumptions one makes about the nature of reality, i.e. what constitutes a set of reasonable requirements necessary for a physical theory to be acceptable?

Such a question falls outside the normal sphere of discourse of the usual physics journals and it is not surprising to find that nearly all the objections to the theory appear in books, conference reports or Festschrifts of one kind or another. What we have found remarkable is the emotional nature of the responses. For example, in his book *Physics and Philosophy*, Heisenberg tries to sustain the argument that it is logically impossible to develop an alternative point of view and starts with a quotation from Bohr: 'We may hope that it will later turn out that sometimes $2 + 2 = 5$.'[19] But exactly where the logical contradictions lie is never made clear. Again in the Born–Einstein letters, Born writes, 'Pauli has come up with an idea that slays Bohm'.[20] An examination of Pauli's article[21] in *Louis de Broglie, physicien et penseur* reveals a criticism that can only accuse the alternative approach of being 'metaphysical'; a word which nowadays, together with the word 'philosophical', is used as a derogatory euphemism to condemn a theory which doesn't fit into the common consensus. The situation has been summarised very succinctly by Bopp: 'We say that Bohm's theory cannot be refuted, adding, however, that we don't believe it.'[22]

But it is not simply a question of belief. Bohm's original intention was to show that a consistent alternative does actually exist. This, in itself, is important since it opens the possibility of exploring new ideas without being trapped into believing there is no possible alternative. As someone once aptly remarked, 'I do not know whether quantum mechanics is a beautiful building or a prison with very high walls.' With the appearance of an alternative approach at least a ray of light has appeared through those very high walls!

The emotive terms associated with these arguments led to the implicit view that to mention the term 'hidden variables' was in some sense to commit a cardinal heresy. Even today the term often provokes a sceptical, if not irrational and antagonistic, response. Bohm now admits it might have been a mistake to call his theory a 'hidden variable theory'. After all, it only uses positions and momenta, whereas the real drive for the hidden variable approach was to find 'additional' parameters to describe the underlying process.

One can sympathise with the use of the term 'hidden' in the sense that although a particle can have a simultaneous position and momentum, we still cannot measure them simultaneously. It is in this sense they were called 'hidden'. But perhaps it would be more appropriate to call the wave function ψ the 'hidden variable'[23] because, although both x and p can be measured (even though *not* simultaneously), ψ itself only shows up indirectly through the quantum potential, which is reflected only in the behaviour of the ensemble of particles. In the 1952 work the quantum potential plays a crucial role. The essential difference between classical and quantum mechanics is accounted for by this potential. We will bring these features out later.

To answer the more general criticisms of his approach, Bohm presented his own ideas in a broader context in his book *Causality and Chance in Modern Physics.*[14] This book showed that Bohm was not only a master in handling the mathematical tools used in physics but that he could also think deeply about the philosophical background implicit in the physicist's framework. The book begins by analysing the philosophy of mechanism, within which the nineteenth century physics had developed. It then goes on to discuss the usual interpretation of quantum mechanics within this context and to explain, in more general terms, the alternative approach that he outlined in his 1952 papers. Here we already see emerging, for the first time, his dissatisfaction with his 1952 papers. He stressed that his discontent was not with the logical consistency of the approach. Rather he felt that it did not go far enough and thought that it was in some way a coarse-grained view of something yet deeper underlying quantum mechanics.

In his final chapter he raised the possibility of a more general concept of physical laws that went beyond mechanism. He suggested the notion of the qualitative infinity of nature in which all theories have limitations on their domains of validity so that every theory must be qualified by its context, conditions and degrees of approximation to which they are valid. In this way scientific research can be freed from irrelevant restrictions which tend to result from the supposition that a particular set of general properties, qualities and laws must be the correct ones to use in all possible contexts and conditions and to all degrees of approximation. This was a clear signal that David Bohm was not going to be tied down by any consensus that insisted that quantum mechanics was the last word and that all that was left was to obey its rules.

Again this position was not well received in the late 1950s and early 1960s. The physics community in general had made up its mind that the earlier achievements of quantum electrodynamics, with its successful treatment of divergences through renormalisation techniques, had established the paradigm for future work. The central problem thus became one of trying to apply the same method to the weak and strong interactions in particle physics. Anyone attempting to question the conventional approach to quantum mechanics was regarded, to put it mildly, as rather odd. (In actual fact statements made at that time were often much stronger!)

The prevailing atmosphere therefore was such that development of the ideas along the lines of the 1952 paper were not pursued further. By that time Bohm had moved from Brazil via Israel to England, where he held a research fellowship at Bristol University from 1957–61. There he took on a young research student, Yakir Aharonov. Together they published a paper on what has become known as the Aharonov–Bohm (AB) effect.[24] They discovered that if one confines a magnetic field in the geometric shadow between the two slits of an electron interference device, and ensures that the electrons travel only in a field-free region, then the resulting fringe pattern is shifted, the shift being a function of the flux enclosed in the inaccessible region. Actually the effect had been discovered ten years earlier by Ehrenberg and Siday[25] at Birkbeck College, where Bohm was to be appointed in 1961 to a chair in theoretical physics. The Aharonov–Bohm paper is cited as the definitive work on the subject because of its incisiveness. The discussion goes straight to the point at issue in a very clear and simple way, a feature that has always characterised Bohm's work.

The AB effect was quite surprising and initially the work was received with some suspicion. As Weisskopf puts it, 'The first reaction to this work is that it is wrong, the second is that it is obvious.'[26] Indeed it is a direct result of application of the standard rules of quantum mechanics. It is, in fact, the first example of a gauge theory of the type which today, when generalised, seems to offer the best possibility of uniting the weak, electromagnetic and strong interactions and, it is hoped, will eventually include gravity.

In spite of the fact that there are at least four independent sets of experimental techniques verifying the existence of the AB effect, papers still appear arguing that no such effect exists. The problem arises because the vector potential plays a fundamental role in the calculations, whereas in classical physics this potential is regarded merely as a mathematical device. The classical charged particles respond only to the fields and not to the potentials.

It is a great pity that the stigma of hidden variables has stuck with Bohm. We have often been greeted by physicists with the question, 'How is David Bohm getting along with his hidden variables?' This shows a very deep misconception of what Bohm is trying to achieve and ignores completely the radical nature of his ideas. As we have pointed out before, the content of the 1952 papers was intended simply to show that there was an alternative to the accepted view. They were not intended as an end in themselves, but simply to open the way for further progress. To go beyond hidden variables one must first see exactly what novel features quantum mechanics introduces, and to do this one needs to consider Bohr's work a little more closely.

Perhaps Bohr's deepest perception was not wave-particle duality, nor complementarity, but *wholeness*. Bohr writes, 'The essential wholeness of a proper quantum phenomenon finds indeed logical expression in the circumstances that any attempt at its well-defined subdivision would require a change in the experimental arrangement incompatible with the appearance of the phenomenon itself.'[27] Remember of course that for Bohr the word 'phenomenon refers only to observations obtained under circumstances whose description includes an account of the whole experimental arrangement'.[28] This notion of phenomenon used by Bohr is different from its more customary meaning. It is based on the assumption that 'in quantum mechanics, we are not dealing with an arbitrary renunciation of a more detailed analysis of atomic phenomena, but with the recognition that such an analysis is *in principle* excluded'.[29]

The sentiments expressed in these quotations are sometimes summarised in the phrase, 'the inseparability of the observed and the observer'. If these notions are, in fact, correct then quite clearly some very deep questions as to the nature of reality are raised, as is clearly recognised by d'Espagnat.[11] Unfortunately most physicists either do not know what Bohr wrote or, if they do, they do not quite understand what he is getting at. When various quotations of Bohr's work are put to them they tend not to believe them, yet continue to defend the usual (Copenhagen) interpretation! They praise Bohr, but think like Einstein.

As we have remarked already, Bohm's early perception when he began thinking seriously about physics was to notice the interconnectedness of the process. When Bohm found Bohr was advocating an extreme form of interconnectedness, he became very fascinated with this notion and explored it with much more energy. What turned out to be rather surprising was that the quantum potential also contained a notion of wholeness, even though analysis was still possible. Thus the quantum potential approach, rather than refuting Bohr's position, actually supported it on the question of wholeness, a feature that was totally unexpected. As this is a very important feature of Bohm's ideas, we feel that we should try briefly to outline how these aspects emerge from the quantum potential approach.

One of the main difficulties in trying to understand the precise changes implied by quantum mechanics lies in the formalism itself. It is very different from that used in classical physics and consequently a comparison becomes very difficult. In order to bring the formalisms closer together we can do one of two things. (1) Either we can try to reformulate classical physics in terms of operators in Hilbert space and hence see how the intuitive classical ideas translate into the quantum formalism. Such an approach has been adopted by Prigogine and his co-workers. Perhaps the clearest introduction to their work is presented in *Physica*.[30]

(2) Or we can try to reformulate quantum mechanics in a language which is closer to that of classical physics. This is the essential feature of Bohm's approach. It is achieved in a very simple way by writing the wave function in the form:

$$\psi = R \exp (iS/\hbar)$$

By assuming ψ satisfies Schrödinger's equation one can obtain two real equations, one of which is essentially a classical equation of motion supplemented by an additional potential term (called the quantum potential). It is this additional term alone that is responsible for producing the quantum behaviour. To understand this equation you have to assume there is an underlying micro-reality in which particles have both position *and* momentum, although these cannot be measured simultaneously. The solutions of the equation of motion give rise to an ensemble of individual particle trajectories arising from various initial conditions. If the distribution of initial conditions agrees with that calculated from the initial wave function, then this ensemble will give rise to the expected probability distributions found in experiment. This is guaranteed by the second equation derived from Schrödinger's equation, which is a continuity equation corresponding to the conservation of probability.

The details of this approach are presented in the article by Vigier, Dewdney, Holland and Kyprianidis.[31] This article contains illustrations of the calculated trajectories for electrons incident on a two-slit screen (Figure 9.3, page 177). It will be immediately noticed that these trajectories are very different from those expected on purely classical reasoning. The differences arise purely from the presence of the quantum potential. The quantum potential approach therefore is not an attempt to return to classical physics. All the strange features are accounted for by the quantum potential, which is in no way like a classical potential.

Before proceeding to discuss the difference between the classical and quantum potentials we feel it is necessary to point out an essential difference between Bohm's approach and that of Vigier *et al.* which has caused some confusion. To Bohm the quantum potential arises formally from the mathematics and, in order to demonstrate the logical consistency of the whole approach, it is unnecessary to seek a deep explanation of the potential's physical origins. In fact all of the illustrations of how the quantum potential accounts for various quantum phenomena that have been carried through recently by Bohm and one of us (B. J. Hiley) [32,33,34,35] do not require any specific action of the underlying process. In all these cases there are no differences with the results predicted by the usual approach.

The advantage of the approach even in the absence of a specific underlying process is that one can obtain a sharp picture of what is involved. With the trajectories, for example, we can see clearly how the interference pattern arises. In transition processes the time of transition for a particular process is sharp. Aharonov and Albert [36] further illustrate this sharpness by raising the question of retrodiction in quantum mechanics, contrasting von Neumann's collapse postulate with the time-symmetry of the experimental probabilities. These issues are rather unclear in the usual formulation but they show how the quantum potential approach gives a much clearer picture. This feature of clarity in Bohm's approach is quite general and can be regarded as one of its advantages.

Naturally if one were to take the model as a definitive physical theory of quantum phenomena one must seek a physical explanation of its origin. But here there are a wide variety of possibilities and Vigier *et al.* have adopted a particular position in which they argue that the quantum potential has its origins in 'non-locally correlated stochastic fluctuations of an underlying covariant ether'. However, many of the examples cited in their article do not require such an assumption.

Bohm's position with regard to the underlying process is very different and depends on a much more radical approach. Both ideas stem from the recognition that the many-body approach exhibits some form of 'non-locality' and the difference arises from the interpretation of what this non-locality means. For Vigier the explanation must arise from some phase-like process in space-time; it can be regarded as a 'quasi-mechanical' explanation. For Bohm the quantum non-locality has more of an affinity with Bohr's notion of 'wholeness', which ultimately calls into question the very notion of an *a priori* given space-time manifold.

In order to provide a context in which the latter notions take meaning, we will outline some of the key developments in which the notion of quantum non-locality emerged. The first clear account of the nature of this quantum non-locality was presented by Schrödinger[37], using the usual approach of quantum mechanics. He developed the line started by Einstein, Podolsky and Rosen[38] in their well-known paper where they criticised the completeness of quantum mechanics. Schrödinger showed that there was what he called an 'entanglement relation' appearing in the quantum formalism. By this he meant that the states of the subsystems cannot be separated from each other and this implied that, for a certain class of systems, the results of a measurement of a subsystem A, spatially well-separated from its companion B, depends not only on the results obtained at B *but on what one decided to measure at B.* It is this last phrase that contradicts our usual notion of locality. *What* is done to B should not influence the result of a measurement of A, especially when they are spatially separated and are not connected through a classical potential. Thus the usual formulation of quantum mechanics showed, in the hands of Schrödinger, that some notion of non-locality is involved. As Dirac puts it, 'For an assembly of particles we can set up field quantities which do change in a local way, but when we interpret them in terms of probabilities of particles we get again something which is non-local.'[39] However, because the usual approach cannot discuss the individual actual process, the question of locality becomes rather fuzzy and these questions can be conveniently ignored.

The quantum potential approach shows quite clearly that for a certain class of wave function, particles that are separated in space with no classical potential connecting them are not really separated but are connected through the quantum potential.[40] They are, as it were, 'together yet apart'. Furthermore the quantum potential contains an instantaneous connection rather than the expected retarded connection. In some ways this is like a reintroduction of a kind of action-at-a-distance, a feature that goes against the whole historical development of physics. Einstein, of course, could not accept this way out of the paradox, insisting that 'physics should represent a reality in space-time, free from any spooky action at a distance'.[41] In view of his position, it is not surprising that he did not like the quantum potential approach.

John Bell noticed the non-locality but, rather than reject it outright, he raised the question of whether it was a particular defect of the quantum potential approach or whether it was true for any model based on locality.[42,43] By assuming a pair of particles with dichotomic variables and by proposing a simple and reasonable definition of locality, Bell was able to produce an inequality involving correlation functions which must be satisfied by a theory which is to be called 'local'. Under certain conditions quantum mechanics is found to violate this inequality, a fact that has been confirmed by a series of experiments which culminated in the work of Aspect *et al.*[44] Although the debate continues, focusing essentially on two questions:

1   whether Bell's notion of locality is too restrictive;
   and
2   whether in fact the experiments actually measure what they intend to measure;

there is a general but somewhat reluctant acceptance of the presence of some form of non-locality in quantum mechanics.

This reluctance is very understandable since the notion that all physical phenomena occur within a local reality is one of those self-evident truths that seem utterly absurd to contradict. Relativity itself, with its maximum signal velocity, has gone a long way to reinforce this notion. Even Dirac who, as we have seen, clearly recognised non-locality in quantum mechanics wrote, 'It (non-locality) is against the spirit of relativity but it is the best we can do.'[39]

No one has yet suggested a way of accounting for the results of quantum mechanics in a theory based on locality. Bohm, himself, with one of us (B. J. Hiley)[45], did propose a tentative local but non-linear theory that could in principle account for quantum non-locality, but the assumptions upon which it was based implicitly required a radical view of nature in which process rather than particles-in-interaction was taken to be fundamental. But even this approach is far from satisfactory. Some authors have noticed that one can escape from violating the Bell inequalities in quantum mechanics by allowing negative probabilities.[46] It has generally been regarded that such a notion is meaningless and amounts to replacing one difficulty by another. But it is well known that negative probabilities arise elsewhere when one tries to obtain quantum mechanical averages using phase-space distributions, so the question of negative probabilities is not restricted to the question of non-locality. Richard Feynman has thought a great deal about these problems and, indeed, has admitted to having difficulty in trying to understand the world view that quantum mechanics represents. He has always tried to narrow the problem down to particular features and explore them in depth to try to learn something new. In this volume he re-examines the notion of negative probabilities and explores its possibilities.[47]

It is thus clear that quantum non-locality is one of the most radical features of quantum phenomena and a careful discussion of its full implications is extremely important. What is its relation to Bohr's notion of wholeness? Can we learn anything more from the quantum potential approach? One important factor in the discussion is that if the quantum potential were simply a classical potential then there would, indeed, be violations of relativity and this would be strong grounds for rejecting the whole approach. But the essential point is that the quantum potential is not like a classical potential. And the pursuit of the quantum potential approach is not a question of 'jumping out of the frying pan into the fire'.[48] On the contrary, what this approach does bring out ultimately is a clearer understanding of what Bohr was referring to when he talked about 'the essential wholeness of a proper quantum phenomenon' or 'a closed indivisible phenomenon'.

It is vital to bring out these points more clearly as they are a key feature of Bohm's thinking. He actually discusses these issues in his own article, but it is our experience that people do not generally fully grasp the significance of this radical feature of the quantum potential. We therefore make no apologies for repeating the arguments here.

Unlike a classical potential, the quantum potential appears to have no point-like source. Moreover, since the field from which one derives the potential satisfies a homogeneous equation, the field is not radiated, as is, for example, the electromagnetic field. But there are two further very important differences.

1　The quantum potential does not produce, in general, a vanishing interaction between two particles as the distance between those particles becomes very large. Thus two distant systems may still be strongly and directly connected. This is, of course, contrary to the implicit requirement of classical physics, where it is always assumed that where two systems are sufficiently far apart, they will behave independently. This is a necessary condition if the notion of analysis of a system into separately and independent existent constituent parts is to be carried out. Thus the quantum potential seriously calls into question the notion that all explanations of complexity must be understood by considering independent systems in interaction with each other.

2　What is even more striking is that the quantum potential cannot be expressed as a universally determined function of all the co-ordinates of the particles. Rather it depends on the 'quantum state' $\psi(r_1 \ldots r_n)$ of the *system as a whole*. This means that even if at some time the positions and momenta of two sets of particles are the same, but they are in different quantum states, then their subsequent evolution can be very different.

All of this implies that the relationship between two particles depends on something that goes beyond what can be described in terms of these two particles alone. In fact more generally, this relationship may depend on the quantum states of even larger systems, ultimately going on to the universe as a whole. Within this view separation becomes a contingent rather than a necessary feature of nature.

This is very different from the way we perceive the macroscopic world around us, where separation seems basic. However, it is well known that when we go to low enough temperatures, bulk matter behaves very differently. Currents flow without dissipation in superconductivity, superfluids flow without viscosity, etc., but as the temperature rises, the distant correlations necessary for non-dissipation break up and the particles no longer flow without resistance. If we regard these long-range correlations as stemming from quantum non-locality, then they seem to be very fragile and can be broken quite easily, simply by raising the temperature. In fact it is this fragility that makes it impossible to send signals in EPR situations. This is another way of explaining why a conflict with relativity is by no means necessary.

But this fragility is not always the case. The binding of electrons in atoms, covalent molecular bonds, etc., are much stronger. Nevertheless these, too, can be broken, provided enough energy is supplied. This could be either in the form of heat or chemical energy. Thus it is in thermodynamic systems that separability arises. In fact there seems to be a deep connection between irreversibility and the break-up processes, but the details are not clear.

Prigogine and his group have studied the question of irreversibility in physical systems in great depth. Although most of this work has been concerned with classical systems, very wide-reaching results have been obtained, some of which have deep epistemological consequences. In his paper with Elskens, Prigogine argues that in making the transition from dynamics to thermodynamics, the introduction of irreversibility at the microscopic level implies deep changes in the structure of space-time. Here irreversibility leads to a well-defined form of non-locality in which a single point in space-time is replaced by an ensemble of points giving rise to a geometry which contains a unique time order. Their paper outlines the basic concepts that are involved in the new dynamics.[49]

This new dynamics has not yet been used to address the question of how a breakdown of the correlations discussed above can occur. Nevertheless, it seems likely that it could provide a deeper understanding of the process involved, not only in breaking the correlations, but also in establishing non-local correlations in systems that are far from equilibrium. Indeed Fröhlich has recognised such a possibility and has conjectured that in certain dielectric systems longitudinal electric oscillations may extend over macroscopic distances, giving rise to quantum non-local correlations.[50] These effects are of particular interest in biological systems and are themselves maintained in equilibrium through a constant supply of energy, i.e. they are, like all living systems, far from thermal equilibrium. But there are deeper problems for the application of quantum mechanics to biological systems. One such problem is raised by Fröhlich in this volume; namely, can there also be non-locality in time?[51]

Such questions are already implicit when we extend the notion of wholeness to relativistic quantum mechanics. Here relativity puts space and time on an equal footing so that non-locality in space suggests the possibility of non-locality in time. Such questions, in fact, have been discussed in Bohm's group but their work in this area has not been published yet. Any meaningful discussion along these lines cannot take place until the quantum potential approach has been applied to relativistic quantum mechanics. Some work, particularly by Vigier's group in Paris, has explored the Klein-Gordon[52] and Dirac[53] equations with some success. However, the Klein-Gordon equation produces difficulties even before one introduces the quantum potential ideas. Bohm has long felt that the best generalisation is through relativistic field theories. Thus in an appendix to his 1952 paper, Bohm sketches an approach to the electromagnetic field. Here the superwave function leads to a generalised Hamilton-Jacobi equation containing a super-quantum potential in addition to any classical potentials. This equation is a field equation which, when the super-quantum potential is neglected, reduces to the classical d'Alembert equation.[33]

In this approach the quantum field may be non-locally connected, so that instantaneous effects may be carried from one point of the field to another distant point. As with the non-relativistic case, it can be shown that no signal connecting distant events instantaneously is possible, provided the measurements that would detect these signals are limited by the statistical nature of the results of quantum theory.

This whole approach through the super-quantum potential offers a new way to explain the quantum properties of fields. Here the energy may spread out from one source, ultimately to focus on another as a result of the non-local non-linear terms in the super-Hamilton-Jacobi equation. Thus, a quantised field is not basically a collection of individual quanta (i.e. particles); rather, it is a dynamical structure, organised by the super-quantum potential so that it gives rise to discrete results, even though the process itself is not discrete.

The relevance of this way of interpreting the theory can be seen even more clearly in the case of an electromagnetic wave that is formed from interference of weak beams from two independent optical lasers as described by Pfleegor and Mandel.[54] The photon picture raises the unanswerable question: from which laser does the photon come? But in the super-quantum potential interpretation, there is no problem because there are no permanent photons. There is only a total field of activity arising from both lasers, organised non-linearly and non-locally by the super-quantum potential, and it is this feature that gives rise to the excitation of a single quantised transfer of energy to the detector.[35]

All of this deals with boson field systems; nothing has been done with fermion fields. The quantum potential approach itself does not include spin very happily. Bohm worked on this problem together with Tiomno and Schiller[55] during his stay in Brazil. They were able to show that it is possible to obtain a causal description of the Pauli equation. Bohm, himself, has made some comments on the application of the quantum potential approach to the Dirac equation but the details have not been worked out.[56] Cufaro-Petroni and Vigier[57] have explored a possible approach using the Feynman-Gell-Mann equation for spin-half particles but, as yet, there is no method for discussing spin-half *fields*. The first tentative steps in this direction appear in this volume in an article by John Bell.[58] He argues for the exclusion of the notion of 'observable' and the introduction of a beable whose existence does not depend on observation. If we replace the three-space continuum by a dense lattice and define a fermion number operator at each lattice point, we can regard the fermion numbers as local beables. The dynamics is replaced by a stochastic development of the fermion number configuration. Bell goes on to discuss the consequences of this model.

For many years Bohm himself never felt the need for a detailed exploration of these particular aspects of field theory. Rather he felt that the novel nature of quantum wholeness that emerged both from the quantum potential and Bohr's work required a radical re-structuring of our view of reality, and this could not be obtained simply by reworking everything in terms of the quantum potential and the super-quantum potential. He has only recently returned to these topics, essentially for two reasons.

1   There have been considerable advances in experimental techniques which have made possible an exploration of the foundations of quantum mechanics using single particles or single-atom emitters. These experiments have raised the old issues again and, with the new generation struggling to make sense of these results in terms of the usual quantum mechanics, Bohm felt that a careful and more detailed explanation of his original ideas sketched in his 1952 papers was needed.

2   Bohm has found, as he explains in his article, that it is now useful to re-examine those aspects of the super-quantum potential which offer a guide as to the limitations that must be imposed on the implicate order if it is to produce results that are not contrary to our experience of quantum phenomena.

None of this should be taken as a return to the old model. On the contrary, it is to be seen as a way of explaining the deep nature of his new view on the nature of reality that has emerged from different explorations that he has made in the last twenty years.

In order to bring these out, it is necessary to sketch how these views developed from the perception of the holistic view that quantum mechanics demanded. Since nearly all our habitual thinking involves analysis into independent entities of one kind or another interacting to form complex systems, we are faced with a very difficult problem. Do we follow Bohr and rule out any possibility of analysis in principle, thus leaving ourselves with an 'algorism' from which we calculate the outcome of given experimental situations? Do we restrict ourselves to the quantum potential approach trying to explain its origin in some deeper underlying process in space-time, as does Vigier and his group? Or can we try something else? If so, what is this something else? Where do we start?

In order to motivate a point of departure let us look at Bohr's position and try to see why he insisted on unanalysability. One strand of the argument involved what he called the 'finite quantum of action'. This notion arises from the uncertainty relation

$\Delta x \Delta p \geqq h$

where h has the dimensions of the classical action. Thus the product of the uncertainties cannot be less than this 'finite quantum of action'. Bohr took this to imply that it was not possible to make a sharp distinction between the observer and the observed. It was like a blind man with a rubber stick exploring a room. By feeling the reactions to his prodding stick he cannot obtain as sharp an image of, say, the walls of the room than he could have obtained with a rigid stick. The flexibility in the stick could not be 'calculated' away. There was an indivisible, uncontrollable and unpredictable connection between subject and object which rendered a sharp separation between the two impossible.

The second strand of the argument involved regarding 'the concepts of classical physics as refinements of the concepts of daily life and as an essential part of the language which forms the basis of all natural science'.[59]

Thus, according to Bohr, classical concepts are inherent in all logical thinking. As Bohm writes:

> Such a point of view implies that every understandable and describable aspect of experience could in principle be analysed by regarding the world as made out of various component parts, each having at any moment a definite position and a definite momentum. If we in practice do not do this in everyday life but use other concepts instead, this means only that we are approximating to the ideal of such a complete analysis.[60]

But quantum mechanics is already suggesting that such an analysis is in principle excluded. This, in turn, suggests that our desire to pinpoint precisely, say, the positions of particles is not necessary. In other words, could it not be that our insistence on the use of a Cartesian co-ordinate system to describe physical processes is at fault? After all, when we are describing the location of common objects, we resort to phrases like 'It is *on* the table' or 'It is *on* the shelves *between* two books' etc. We hardly ever use a co-ordinate system but rely very much on topological relations. Could it then be that our insistence on a co-ordinate description as opposed to a topological description is leading us to the conceptual problems in understanding quantum theory?

It was in the late 1960s that the group at Birkbeck began an exploration of topological methods. This involved excursions into the mathematical techniques of homology and cohomology. At that stage few physicists studied these mathematical disciplines, although there were notable exceptions, including John Wheeler, whose lucid explanations of cohomology for physicists were a very great help in clarifying some of the questions involved.[61] It was not difficult to show that many of the main laws of physics, such as the Hamilton-Jacobi theory, Maxwell's equations and even the Dirac equation, could be given a very simple meaning without resorting to the continuous space-time backcloth.

There was one notable exception and that was general relativity, which could not be expressed naturally in this topological language. But clearly a simple mathematical transcription was not sufficient, so Bohm began to investigate the notion of order in a more general way. One of his main investigations was to develop new principles of order that would replace those implied in the concept of continuity.[62]

One such idea was to regard the particle as a break in some background structure. Here one was exploiting the analogy of a dislocation in a crystal. Frank had already shown that an edge dislocation migrating through a crystal could be regarded as a particle having an effective mass, where the mass itself varies in the same way as mass varies in relativity, but now the speed of light is replaced by the speed of sound.[63] The fields themselves could be thought of as the stresses arising from the deformations caused by the presence of the dislocations.

Bohm wanted to abandon the traditional notion of particles and fields-in-interaction in a continuous space-time, replacing it by the notion of structure process. That is to say one analyses all physical processes structurally, using as basic building blocks structures called simplexes (analogues of lines, triangles, tetrahedra, etc.) which could be ordered, boundary to boundary, forming a structure called a simplicial complex. The failure of perfect fitting would then correspond to the presence of matter or fields.[64]

This type of approach through topo-chronology offers the possibility of being able to incorporate some notion of wholeness required by quantum mechanics. A particle could not be separated from the surrounding structure because what is called a particle is simply a break in the background structure. Furthermore, two dislocations could not be separated since they are only breaks in the same structure.

Several attempts were made to use matrix representations to describe these structures but it became very cumbersome. Indeed there have been many papers published in dislocation theory exploiting the analogies with continuum dynamics. In this volume two former research students, Peter Holland and Chris Philippidis, have exploited and generalised these ideas to show how *classical* electrodynamics can be interpreted as a theory of a continuously dislocated covariant space-time ether. One of the important features of this work is to show in detail how the particle and field are seen as structurally inseparable even in the continuum limit.[65]

But in order to get a better understanding of quantum phenomena it was the discrete structure process that offered the better prospects. However, even here the structure seems too primitive to be carried very far. Time did not seem to be naturally part of the structure. The structure changed in time but was not of time. The whole approach seemed to be in the category of what Bergson called a cinematographical outlook, a series of 'stills' with no natural flow.[66]

A vital clue on how to overcome this difficulty was provided by some experimental work on the human eye. Ditchburn had noticed that the eye was in continous vibration and that this vibration was vital in order to see.[67] To show this he fixed a mirror system to the eye so as to 'freeze' out the vibration. The result was that the eye could no longer see anything. Thus to see a line or boundary, for example, the eye must scan backwards and forwards across the line. The difference in the response in the retina as the eye crosses the line enables the brain to reconstruct the line. If the scanning is stopped, no line is seen, even though there is a static image on the retina. Thus, movement is basic to perception. But, equally, if there are no relatively invariant features for the eye to scan, then again nothing will be seen. So 'nothingness' does not mean there is nothing there; it could mean simply that there are no features that remain invariant for a sufficient length of time.

Suppose now we carry through this idea to quantum field theory where the vacuum state plays a basic role. We could argue that the vacuum state is not empty, but is in fact full of undifferentiated activity. This could then account for things like vacuum fluctuations which strongly suggest a vacuum state is far from empty. It could be full of activity that is changing so rapidly that it cannot be perceived above a certain level. Could it therefore be that the structure described by the simplicial complex is merely the relatively invariant features of the basic underlying process or activity or what we call movement? Then in order to accommodate wholeness we regard this unbroken activity as the basic notion and what our physics discusses are the quasi-stable, semi-autonomous features of this underlying holomovement.

One important feature concerning the holomovement is that it is not described in space-time but from it space-time is to be abstracted. Thus we no longer start with an *a priori* space-time manifold in order to discuss physics; rather, we construct space-time from the underlying process. It is not, as Wheeler and Hawking suggests, a progression from the continuum via fluctuations to the space-time foam; rather, it is the simplicial description of the relative invariant features of the holomovement that become the foam from which the continuous space-time is abstracted. Thus locality is no longer a primary concept but is also abstracted so that quantum non-local correlations could be explained as a remnant of the basic underlying complex. Furthermore 'staticness' is no longer a problem. The relatively invariant features can change as the underlying holomovement changes. It is like Heraclitus' candle flame dancing and flickering, giving the appearance of an autonomous entity but, in fact, being constantly renewed.

Ideas along these lines have also been suggested by David Finkelstein and we have been very stimulated by his unique way of looking at things.[68] He acknowledges being influenced by Bohm's exploration of structure process, and in his article 'All is flux'[69] he outlines some of the areas of cross fertilisation that have taken place. He too proposes a simplicial approach to quantum theory, calling his basic structures quantum simplexes. As we will see, the simplexes used to describe the holomovement are in fact algebraic and, in consequence, are quantum in origin. Thus both approaches attempt to abstract classical space-time from an essentially quantum structure.

Given the holomovement, it is now but a small step to the implicate order. We can regard the relative invariant features of the holomovement as the explicate order while that which remains in the background is the implicate order. What is missing is the notion of folding and enfolding, and that has its source in three separate and different developments.

In his book on causality and chance, Bohm had already suggested that the trajectories that emerged from the quantum potential approach were some kind of average property of a deeper process. He writes:

> Thus, we are led to a point of view rather like that suggested in section 2 in connection with the Brownian motion of mist droplets near the critical point, namely that particle-like concentrations are always forming and dissolving. Of course, if a particle in a certain place dissolves, it is very likely to re-form nearby. Thus on the large-scale level, the particle-like manifestation remains in a small region of space following a fairly well-defined track, etc. On the other hand, at a lower level, the particle does not move as a permanently existing entity, but is formed in a random way by suitable concentrations of the field energy.[70]

In view of this statement is is not surprising that the unmixing (glycerine) demonstration Bohm saw on television provided a vital stimulus in arriving at the implicate order (see Chapter 2 in this volume). In this example the folding–unfolding idea emerges very clearly.

Also from this example there appears a further principle; namely, that not everything can be unfolded together. Such an idea is already present in perception, where a set of lines can appear to give one form or another but never both together. But in physics the Cartesian notion that everything can be displayed together simultaneously has dominated, albeit implicitly, even though the appearance of quantum mechanics with its sets of commuting operators calls this into question. There is a continual drive to find models in which all aspects of the process can be 'displayed' simultaneously. In the new view it is necessary to distinguish between that which could be unfolded together (the explicate order) and that which remains enfolded (the implicate order). Surely this is the deeper truth that essentially lay behind Bohr's notion of complementarity, although it tended to become trivialised into wave-particle duality.

Perhaps the most significant stimulus for the folding–unfolding notion came from a mathematical technicality, namely, the Green's function approach to Schrödinger's equation. Feynman first pointed out that in quantum mechanics, one can use the Huygens construction to determine the wave function at a point y from the wave function at $\{x\}$, where $\{x\}$ is the set of points on a surface at a previous time. Thus:

$$\psi(y,t_2) = \int_{\text{surface}} M(x,y,t_1,t_2)\psi(x,t_1)\mathrm{d}x$$

where $M(x,y,t_1,t_2)$ is a Green's function. Pictorially this is represented in Figure 1.1. The wave function at all points of the surface S contributes to the wave function at y. Thus the information on the surface S is enfolded into $\psi(y)$. This $\psi(y)$ determines the quantum potential acting on the particle at y so that the particle reacts to the enfolded information of a set of earlier wave functions. In turn $\psi(y)$ itself gets 'unfolded' into a series of points on a later surface S' (see Figure 1.2). In this way we see that the quantum potential itself is determined by an enfolding–unfolding process.

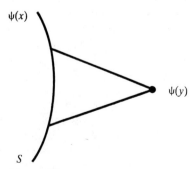

Figure 1.1

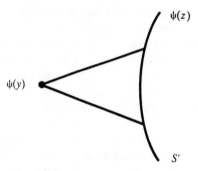

$\psi(z)$

$\psi(y)$

S'

Figure 1.2

We can now generalise this in the following way: if E and E' are two successive explicate orders, then for continuity we can argue that the enfolded E is equal to the unfolded E', i.e.:

$$EM_1 = M_2 E'$$

where M_1 and M_2 are the enfolding and unfolding elements (essentially Green's functions). Then:

$$E' = M_2^{-1} E M_1$$

If we assume:

$$M_2 = M_1 = e^{-iHt/h}$$

we find Heisenberg's form of the Schrödinger equation follows immediately.[71] It was a generalisation of arguments of this kind that led Bohm to suggest that the basic mathematics required to describe the implicate order will involve the use of matrix algebras. Furthermore, although most physicists use the Hilbert space formalism for quantum mechanics, there is an equivalent formulation in terms of matrices, where the state functions are replaced by appropriate algebraic ideals. Thus there is a common mathematical structure shared by quantum mechanics and the implicate order. All of this, and a lot more, is explained in more detail in Bohm's *Wholeness and the Implicate Order*.[72]

The notion that the space-time continuum should not be taken as basic notion had a number of advocates in the late 1960s. They included Roger Penrose, who was then a member of the mathematics department at Birkbeck College. He would often take part in the seminars run by the physics department and explained to us his idea of a 'spin network'[73] and how he was hoping the twistor would play a part in generating these ideas.[74] At about the same time we were joined by a research student, Fabio Frescura, who carried out a detailed investigation of the algebraic approach and showed that if one took the direct product of a suitable Clifford algebra and a symplectic algebra (essentially the Heisenberg algebra supplemented by the addition of a special element), one could bring about a complete algebraisation of quantum mechanics without any reference to a space-time continuum.[71,75] These algebras are essentially geometric algebras, the Clifford algebras carrying the rotational symmetries and the symplectic algebra carrying the translational symmetries. Thus they have within their structures all the required symmetry properties for abstracting the space-time continuum.

Penrose's approach through the spin network and twistors can be given an algebraic flavour once one recognises that the non-relativistic spinor is simply an ideal in the Paul Clifford algebra (C_2) while the twistor is a similar ideal in the conformal Clifford algebra (C_6). A discussion of the details of how these similarities can be exploited would not be appropriate here and more details can be found in the papers of Bohm and Hiley[76] and Frescura and Hiley.[71] The essential consequence of this approach is that the simplicial complexes used to describe structures in the holomovement are essentially algebraic and hence can be regarded as quantum in origin, as are the simplexes used by Finkelstein that we referred to earlier.

Clive Kilmister has always been very encouraging in our explorations of the algebraisation of the implicate order and his article in this volume investigates the automorphism group of C_4, the Dirac Clifford algebra, providing some simple geometric insights present in this algebra.[77] These results are quite central to the work described above. In the following paper Frescura and Hiley[78] indicate that the algebraic spinor offers a generalization of the usual approach and suggest how this can be exploited in the extension which allows the algebra to carry a structure equivalent to curvature.

We were very happy to learn that Geoffrey Chew's work using an S-matrix approach has found Bohm's implicate order a useful general scheme in which to bring out some of the features of his approach. One of us (B. J. Hiley) still vividly remembers Chew's 1963 Rouse Ball lecture 'The dubious role of the space-time continuum in microscopic physics' which was eventually published in *Science Progress*.[79] There he writes: 'but a growing number of us are reaching the conclusion that to make major progress we must stop thinking and talking about such an unobservable (space-time) continuum'. The main theme of the talk was to point out the advantages of the S-matrix over the more usual quantum field approach. (Perhaps today one could argue that the S-matrix describes various structures in the implicate order.) In the original talk the link between macroscopic space-time and the S-matrix was left as a challenge about which Chew said little except for a rather vague remark concerning the role of photons.

This work has progressed considerably since those early days and Chew explains in a very general way how the soft photons enable the macroscopic space-time to be made explicate.[80] A colleague of Chew's,

Henry Stapp, has also done a significant amount of work on questions arising from the S-matrix approach. He has also worked for a long time on the foundations of quantum mechanics and has contributed significantly to the discussions of quantum non-locality.[81] In his article he presents a simple model that incorporates lessons learned from the S-matrix.[82] He shows in detail how the classical concepts emerge from the 'soft' photons which are described by coherent states.

So far we have concentrated mainly on physics but David Bohm's interest and influence extend far beyond physics and embrace biology, psychology, philosophy, religion, art and the future of society. His contributions are not, however, made in the academic sense of someone who makes additions within the accepted, historical framework of a discipline but always in a creative way as one working from a new perspective based on the implicate order. It would be impossible even to summarise his contributions to the discussions over this wide range of topics. Rather we will let the contributors who have been influenced by him speak for themselves.

Brian Goodwin sees Bohm as working in the same tradition as the Renaissance *mage* who sought a unification between mind and nature.[83] His vision of nature as an undivided whole could well be applied to biology, Goodwin argues, where it would counteract an 'atomistic (molecular) fragmentation' in favour of an approach that emphasises the wholeness and relational order of the organism. Goodwin, in his essay, discusses how a revolution in perspective could be achieved and suggests that our current fragmentary view of the organism as divided between phenotype and genotype involved in genetic information processing be replaced by a theory of morphogenetic fields.

Robert Rosen also discusses biological systems and raises the question of the relationship of physics to biology.[84] Does biology simply require an application of the general laws of physics to complex systems or will new ideas not already present in physics be required? He argues for the latter, claiming that physics in its present form is too narrow. This is in no sense a plea to introduce ideas of 'vitalism'; rather new concepts of order will be required, a theme that has a close relationship with Bohm's own thinking. With Bohm, new orders are required within physics. These new orders incorporate 'wholeness' and here a more organic view of nature is required. Rosen suggests that the study of the behaviour of macromolecules may provide a clue as to the nature of these orders. He uses the van der Waals gas to illustrate what he has in mind and shows how this can be re-analysed in the old Aristotelian categories of causation. This leads him to suggest a novel idea that each category of causation is reflected in a logically independent aspect of system description, thus implying that it is no longer possible to think of a description purely in terms of states plus dynamical laws.

Maurice Wilkins, working at the macromolecular level in biological systems, found that the complementary aspects of symmetry and asymmetry seemed to be playing a crucial role. Again, at a different level, in DNA there seems to be a similar relationship of opposites between the precise replication of genes and the extensive rearrangement that now seems to be necessary for evolution to take place. His article[85] explores from a very general point of view how complementarity arises in a number of disciplines ranging from physics, through biology, to the visual arts. Here complementarity is taken to imply a specific interaction between the parts that gives rise to wholeness or perfection. He also asks whether any of the lessons learned can help with the problem of human conflict, a problem that concerns Maurice very deeply in this nuclear age.

In his *The Special Theory of Relativity*[86] Bohm gave considerable attention to the way in which we gain knowledge about the world. But this analysis was not carried out in a simple positivistic sense of building scientific theories out of sense data but rather in an attempt to understand how our concepts of reality grow out of the dynamic activity of perception. During the 1960s, while working with one of his students, D. Schumacher, Bohm began to give emphasis to the role of language and communication in this process; indeed he has more recently chosen to describe it in united, and hyphenated, form as perception-communication. Following Bohr, Bohm discussed the role of informal languages in scientific theories of nature and investigated what he felt to be a failure in communication between Einstein and Bohr himself.

Bohm's interest in language led to the development of what he called the rheomode, a language of communication more suited to his notions of enfolded order.[72] Alan Ford, stimulated by Bohm's writings on physics and language, has attempted to forge a connection between linguistics and category theory, the latter topic being, in Bohm's view, the first step to creating any form of order.[87] As we have already seen, Bohm's researches came to fruition in the form of the implicate or enfolded order and, more recently, generative orders. The essence of the implicate order is a form of enfoldment such that any aspect of the system enfolds and is interior to the whole. Clearly this idea of order is a far reaching one, with implications that extend far beyond current physics. Karl Pribram,[88] for his part, explains how Bohm's insights enabled him to construct a holographic theory of the brain that helped to resolve problems of non-local storage and the way in which spatial frequencies are resolved during vision. Gordon Globus acknowledges the significance of Pribram's model in changing our perspective on the brain, but attempts to go further with what he calls holonomy.[89] While the holographic approach assumes an essential *tabula rasa* into which the external environment is folded, Globus assumes that the brain contains a plenum of *possibilia*. Such an approach,

Globus feels, makes relevant the traditions of mysticism with its Godhead as well as Western research on 'altered states of consciousness'.

Bohm's work has always held a particular fascination for the artist for, while the physics may be inaccessible, Bohm's essential approach to nature is sympathetic to their nature. John Briggs[90] explores the relationships between Bohm's theories on the ultimate structure of matter and his own views on the structure of a work of art. Briggs draws attention to a particular aspect of the metaphor, which he calls a reflectaphor, in which each side reflects the other and meaning lies in a continuing reflexive movement. Through an analysis of poetry, the short story and painting, Briggs concludes that in its deepest structure a work of art is built not on explicit forms but out of numerous metaphors that are woven together in such a way that each one reflects all others. Just as each part of nature represents an enfoldment of the entire universe, so each part of a work of art reflects the whole. Clearly Briggs' approach gives insight into Bohm's contention that a unity can exist between the artistic, scientific and religious mind.

For Montague Ullman, Bohm's notions of enfolded order and the non-local nature of reality have a significant connection to dreams.[91] In his paper he analyses the creative way in which images and events are woven together in the dream and discusses its essential healing nature. Ullman also believes that dreams have a social nature and, indeed, that they have a survival value for the human race. Again there is evidence from amongst so-called primitive peoples that dreams fulfil just such a function. Here Ullman touches on one of Bohm's current interests, for it is the latter's belief that a form of true co-operation and harmonious society once existed amongst the early hunter-gatherers and such 'leadership from behind' may even be possible amongst urban society today. To what extent dreams play a role in the creative cohesion of such groups is a matter for further investigation.

This interest in dialogue and the co-operative activity of small groups is also explored by David Shainberg. Shainberg draws attention to the way in which human consciousness erects fixed barriers to the dynamic process of enfolding and unfolding that is characteristic of the implicate order. Shainberg's discussion[92] of the way in which thought seeks security by fixing the moment in endless repetitions of itself brings us close to the heart of Bohm's dialogues with the late Indian philosopher J. Krishnamurti. Bohm met Krishnamurti in the early 1960s and since that time has held a number of dialogues in which the two thinkers have explored many issues together including the nature of reality and the urgent need for a change in human consciousness.

Shainberg traces the origins of these blocks in consciousness and discusses the various approaches that individuals have adopted when made aware of such a trap. In particular he explores the nature of private meditation and a form of group dialogue in which no position is fixed but each participant is sensitive to the constant movement of thought and its tendency to seek security in fixed positions. Within such a dialogue it becomes possible for new insights to develop as relationships are constantly created anew.

The final contribution in this collection of essays takes the form of a dialogue between Renée Weber and David Bohm.[93] Renée Weber felt that the best way that she could contribute to this Festschrift was to try to get David Bohm to explain some of the philosophical ideas that arise in the implicate order. Recently Bohm has come to realise the importance of information and meaning, not only in the context of the human world, but also in the inanimate world. For Bohm meaning *is* being and meaning *is* the essence of reality. These ideas are very different from our normal way of thinking and seem to be essential in the context of wholeness. What Renée Weber does in the dialogue is to bring out the thinking that lies beyond these ideas.

David Bohm has argued that the essence of the scientific mind is the ability to see the fact no matter what it says. This fearlessness and passion of the intelligence characterises all of David Bohm's work and explains its far-reaching attraction for so many of the contributors gathered here. For reasons of space they represent only a small selection of researchers, thinkers, writers and artists who could have contributed to this volume. Clearly David Bohm's ideas have influenced a wide audience and stimulated much discussion which has helped to create new insights and lead to an essentially unified vision of nature in which artist, scientist and religious thinker are no longer divided. Even more significant, perhaps, is the hope that individuals may come together in a spirit of creative co-operation to build a world in which undivided wholeness and creative order are an essential ground.

References

1 D. Bohm, *Phys. Rev.*, **85**, 166, 180 (1952).
2 D. Bohm, 'Hidden variables and the implicate order', this volume, p. 33.
3 E. P. Gross, 'Collective variables in elementary quantum mechanics', this volume, p. 46.
4 D. Pines, 'The collective description of particle interactions: from plasmas to the helium liquids', this volume, p. 66.
5 N. Bohr, *Atomic Theory and the Description of Nature*, Cambridge University Press, Cambridge, 1961.
6 T. D. Clark, 'Macroscopic quantum objects', this volume, p. 121.
7 A. J. Leggett, 'Reflections on the quantum measurement paradox', this volume, p. 85.
8 R. Penrose, 'Quantum physics and conscious thought', this volume, p. 105.

9   M. Gell-Mann, *The Nature of Matter, Wolfson College Lectures, 1980*, Clarendon Press, Oxford, 1981.

10   B. d'Espagnat, *Conceptual Foundations of Quantum Mechanics*, Benjamin, Reading, Mass., 1976.

11   B. d'Espagnat, *In Search of Reality*, Springer-Verlag, New York, 1983.

12   B. d'Espagnat, 'Meaning and being in contemporary physics', this volume, p. 151.

13   J. von Neumann, *Mathematical Foundations of Quantum Mechanics*, Princeton University Press, Princeton, 1955, p. 324.

14   D. Bohm, *Causality and Chance in Modern Physics*, Routledge & Kegan Paul, London, 1957, p. 110.

15   J. S. Bell, *Foundations of Physics*, **12**, 989 (1982).

16   L. de Broglie, *Non-linear Wave Mechanics: A Causal Interpretation*, Elsevier, Amsterdam, 1960.

17   E. Madelung, *Z. Phys.*, **40**, 332 (1926).

18   W. Pauli, in L. de Broglie (ed.), *Non-linear Wave Mechanics: A Causal Interpretation*, Elsevier, Amsterdam, 1960, p. 174.

19   W. Heisenberg, *Physics and Philosophy*, Harper, London, 1959, p. 117.

20   M. Born (ed), *The Born–Einstein Letters*, Macmillan, London, 1971, p. 207.

21   W. Pauli, in A. Georg (ed.), *Louis de Broglie, physicien et penseur*, A. Michel, Paris, 1953.

22   F. Bopp, *Observation and Interpretation: A Symposium of Philosophers and Physicists*, S. Korner (ed.), Butterworths, London, 1957, p. 51.

23   J. S. Bell, in C. J. Isham, R. Penrose and D. W. Sciama (eds), *Quantum Gravity 2: A Second Oxford Symposium*, Clarendon Press, Oxford, 1981, p. 611.

24   Y. Aharonov and D. Bohm, *Phys. Rev.*, **115**, 485 (1959).

25   W. Ehrenberg and R. E. Siday, *Proc. Phys. Soc.*, **62**, 8 (1949).

26   V. F. Weisskopf, *Lectures in Physics III, Boulder, 1960*, eds W. E. Britten, B. W. Downs and J. Downs, Interscience, NY, 1961.

27   N. Bohr, *Atomic Physics and Human Knowledge*, Science Editions, New York, 1961, p. 72.

28   *Ibid.*, p. 64.

29   *Ibid.*, p. 62.

30   C. George and I. Prigogine, *Physica*, **99A**, 369 (1969).

31   J.-P. Vigier, C. Dewdney, P. Holland A. Kyprianidis, 'Causal particle trajectories and the interpretation of quantum mechanics', this volume, p. 169.

32   D. Bohm and B. J. Hiley, *Found. of Phys.*, **12**, 1001 (1982).

33   D. Bohm and B. J. Hiley, *Found. of Phys.*, **14**, 255 (1984).

34   D. Bohm, C. Dewdney and B. J. Hiley, *Nature*, **315**, 294 (1985).

35   D. Bohm and B. J. Hiley, *The Ontological Significance of the Quantum Potential Model*, Phys. Reports. **144**, 321 (1987).

36   Y. Aharonov and D. Albert, 'The issue of retrodiction in Bohm's theory', this volume, p. 224.

37   E. Schrödinger, *Proc. Camb. Phil. Soc.*, **31**, 555 (1935).

38   A. Einstein, B. Podolsky and N. Rosen, *Phys. Rev.*, **47**, 777 (1935).

39   P. A. M. Dirac, in J. Mehra (ed.), *The Development of the Physicist's Conception of Nature*, Reidel, Dordrecht, Holland, 1973, p. 10.

40   D. Bohm and B. J. Hiley, *Found. of Phys.*, **5**, 93 (1975).

41   A. Einstein, in M. Born (ed.), *The Born–Einstein Letters*, Macmillan, London, 1971, p. 158.

42   J. S. Bell, *Rev. Mod. Phys.*, **38**, 447 (1966).

43   J. S. Bell, *Physics*, **1**, 195 (1964).

44   A. Aspect, J. Dalibard and G. Roger, *Phys. Rev. Letts.*, **49**, 1804 (1982).

45   D. Bohm and B. J. Hiley, *Found. of Phys.*, **11**, 529 (1981).
46   W. Mückenheim, *Lett. Nuovo Cimento* **35**, 300 (1982).
47   R. P. Feynman, 'Negative probability', this volume, p. 235.
48   J. C. Polkinghorne, *The Quantum World*, Longman, 1984.
49   I. Prigogine and Y. Elskens, 'Irreversibility, stochasticity and non-locality in classical dynamics', this volume, p. 205.
50   H. Fröhlich, *Rivista del Nuovo Cimento*, **7**, 399 (1977).
51   H. Fröhlich, 'Can biology accommodate laws beyond physics?', this volume, p. 312.
52   J.-P. Vigier, *Lett. Nuovo Cimento*, **24**, 258 and 265 (1979).
53   N. Cufaro Petroni and J.-P. Vigier, *Phys. Lett.* **81A**, 12 (1981).
54   R. L. Pfleegor and L. Mandel, *Phys. Rev.*, **159**, 1084 (1967); *J. of Opt. Soc. Amer.*, **58**, 946 (1968).
55   D. Bohm, R. Schiller and J. Tiomno, *Nuovo Cimento Supp.*, **1**, 48 (1955).
56   D. Bohm, *Prog. of Theor. Phys.*, **9**, 273 (1953).
57   N. Cufaro-Petroni and J.-P. Vigier, 'A causal stochastic theory of spin $\frac{1}{2}$ fields', Institut Henri Poincaré, preprint, 1983.
58   J. Bell, 'Beables for quantum field theory', this volume, p. 227.
59   W. Heisenberg, *ibid.*, p. 55.
60   D. Bohm, *Brit. J. of the Phil. of Sci.*, **12**, 265 (1962).
61   C. W. Misner and J. A. Wheeler, *Ann. Phys.*, **2**, 525 (1957).
62   D. Bohm, *Proc. Int. Conf. on Elementary Particles*, Kyoto, Japan, 252 (1965); in *Satyendranath Bose, 70th Birthday Commemoration Volume*, Part 2, 279, Calcutta, 1964.
63   F. C. Frank, *Proc. Phys. Soc. London*, **A62**, 131 (1949).
64   D. Bohm, B. J. Hiley and A. E. G. Stuart, *Int. J. of Theoretical Phys.*, **3**, 177 (1970)
65   P. R. Holland and C. Philippidis, 'Anholonomic deformations in the ether: A significance for the electrodynamic potentials', this volume, p. 295.
66   H. Bergson, *Creative Evolution*, Macmillan, London, 1922.
67   R. W. Ditchburn, *Research*, **9**, 466 (1951); *Optica Acta*, **1**, 171 and **2**, 128 (1955).
68   D. Finkelstein, *Phys. Rev.*, **184**, 1261 (1969); **5D**, 220 (1972); **5D**, 2922 (1972); **9D**, 2231 (1974).
69   D. Finkelstein, 'All is flux', this volume, p. 289.
70   D. Bohm, *Causality and Chance in Modern Physics*, Routledge & Kegan Paul, London, 1957, p. 120.
71   F. A. M. Frescura and B. J. Hiley, *Revista Brasileira de Fisica, Volume Especial*, July, p. 49 (1984).
72   D. Bohm, *Wholeness and the Implicate Order*, Routledge & Kegan Paul, 1980.
73   R. Penrose, in E. Bastin (ed.), *Quantum Theory and Beyond*, Cambridge University Press, Cambridge, 1968.
74   R. Penrose, in J. R. Klauder (ed.), *Magic without Magic: John Archibald Wheeler*, Freeman, San Francisco, 1972.
75   F. A. M. Frescura and B. J. Hiley, *Found. of Physics*, **10**, 7 (1980).
76   D. Bohm and B. J. Hiley, *Revista Brasileira de Fisica, Volume Especial*, July, p.1. (1984).
77   C. Kilmister, 'The automorphism group of C_4', this volume, p. 267.
78   F. A. M. Frescura and B. J. Hiley, 'Some spinor implications unfolded', this volume, p. 278.
79   G. Chew, *Science Progress*, **51**, 529 (1963).
80   G. Chew, 'Gentle quantum events as the source of explicate order', this volume, p. 249.

81   H. P. Stapp, *Phys. Rev.*, **D3**, 1303 (1971).
82   H. P. Stapp, 'Light as foundation of being', this volume, p. 255.
83   B. Goodwin, 'A science of qualities', this volume, p. 328.
84   R. Rosen, 'Some epistemological issues in physics and biology', this volume, p. 314.
85   M. H. F. Wilkins, 'Complementarity and the union of opposites', this volume, p. 338.
86   D. Bohm, *The Special Theory of Relativity*, Benjamin, New York, 1965.
87   A. Ford, 'Category theory and family resemblances', this volume, p. 361.
88   K. Pribram, 'The implicate brain', this volume, p. 365.
89   G. Globus, 'Three holonomic approaches to the brain', this volume, p. 372.
90   J. Briggs, 'Reflectaphors: the (implicate) universe as a work of art', this volume, p. 414.
91   M. Ullman, 'Wholeness and dreaming', this volume, p. 386.
92   D. Shainberg, 'Vortices of thought in the implicate order and their release in meditation and dialogue', this volume, p. 396.
93   R. Weber, 'Being as meaning in the implicate order philosophy of David Bohm: a conversation', this volume, p. 414.

2

Hidden variables and the implicate order[1]

David Bohm *Birkbeck College, University of London*

I have been asked to explain how my ideas of hidden variables tie up with those on the implicate order, and to bring out in some detail how both these two notions are related. In doing this, it would perhaps be best to begin with an account of how I came to these ideas in the first place.

The whole development started in Princeton around 1950, when I had just finished my book *Quantum Theory*.[2] I had in fact written it from what I regarded as Niels Bohr's point of view, based on the principle of complementarity.[3] Indeed, I had taught a course on the quantum theory for three years and written the book primarily in order to try to obtain a better understanding of the whole subject, and especially of Bohr's very deep and subtle treatment of it. However, after the work was finished, I looked back over what I had done and still felt somewhat dissatisfied.

What I felt to be especially unsatisfactory was the fact that the quantum theory had no place in it for an adequate notion of an in-dependent actuality – i.e. of an actual movement or activity by which one physical state could pass over into another. My main difficulty was not that the wave function was interpreted only in terms of probabilities, so that the theory was not deterministic; rather, it was that it could only be discussed in terms of the results of an experiment or an observation, which has to be treated as a set of *phenomena* that are ultimately not further analysable or explainable in any terms at all. So, the theory could not go beyond the phenomena or appearances. And, basically, these phenomena were very limited in nature, consisting, for example, of events by which the state of a particle could be ascertained. From a knowledge of this state we could go to a wave function that predicted the probability of the next set of phenomena, and so on.

On thinking about what all this meant, it began to occur to me that the quantum theory might actually be giving a fragmentary view of reality. A wave function seemed to capture only certain aspects of what happens in a statistical ensemble of similar measurements, each of which is in essence only a single element in a greater context of the overall process. Though von Neumann [4] had given what purported to be a proof that to go any further would not be compatible with the quantum theory (which was already very well confirmed indeed), I still realized that mathematical proofs are based on axioms and presuppositions whose meanings are often obscure and always in principle open to question. Moreover, the theory of relativity, which was also regarded as fundamental, demanded a space-time process (e.g. one that could be understood in terms of fields) which constituted an independent actuality, with a continuous and determinate connection between all its parts. Such a process could not be treated solely as a set of fragmentary phenomena that are related only statistically.

This requirement becomes especially urgent when relativity is extended to include cosmology. It seems impossible even to contemplate the universe as a whole through a view which can discuss only in terms of discrete or distinct sets of phenomena, for in a cosmological view the observing instruments, and indeed the physicists who construct and operate them, have to be regarded at least in principle as parts of the totality. There does not seem to be much sense in saying that all these are nothing more than organized sets of appearances. To whom or to what would they appear, and of what would they be the appearances?

I felt particularly dissatisfied with the self-contradictory attitude of accepting the independent existence of the cosmos while one was doing relativity and, at the same time, denying it while one was doing the quantum theory, even though both theories were regarded as fundamental. I did not see how an adequate way to deal with this could be developed on the basis of Niels Bohr's point of view. So I began to ask myself whether another approach might not be possible.

In my first attempt to do this I considered a quantum mechanical wave function representing, for example, an electron, and supposed that this was scattered by an atom. By solving Schrödinger's equation for the wave function, one shows that the scattered wave will spread out more or less spherically. Nevertheless, a detector will detect an electron in some small region of space, while the extended spherical wave gives only the probability that it will be found in any such region. The idea then occurred to me that perhaps there is a second wave coming in toward the place where the electron is found, and that the mathematical calculus of the quantum theory gives a statistical relationship between outgoing and incoming waves.

However, to think this way requires that we have to enrich our concepts to include an incoming wave as well as an outgoing wave. Indeed, since further measurements can be made on the electron, it follows that, as the second wave spreads out, it may give way to a third, and so on. In this way, it becomes possible to have an ongoing process in which the electron is understood as an independent actuality (which will, of course, give rise to phenomena through which it may be detected). One is thus implying that the current quantum theory deals only with a fragmentary aspect of this whole process – i.e. that aspect which is associated with a single observational event.

It seems clear that at this stage I was anticipating what later became the implicate order. Indeed, one could say that ingoing and outgoing waves are enfolding and unfolding movements. However, I did not pursue this idea further at the time. What happened was that I had meanwhile sent copies of my book to Einstein, to Bohr, to Pauli and to a few other physicists. I received no reply from Bohr, but got an enthusiastic response from Pauli. Then I received a telephone call from Einstein, saying that he wanted to discuss the book with me. When we met, he said that I had explained Bohr's point of view as well as could probably be done, but that he was still not convinced. What came out was that he felt that the theory was incomplete, not in the sense that it failed to be the final truth about the universe as a whole, but rather in the sense that a watch is incomplete if an essential part is missing. This was, of course, close to my more intuitive sense that the theory was dealing only with statistical arrays of sub-processes associated with similar observational events. Einstein felt that the statistical predictions of the quantum theory were correct, but that by supplying the missing elements we could in principle get beyond statistics to an at least in principle determinate theory.

This encounter with Einstein had a strong effect on the direction of my research, because I then became seriously interested in whether a deterministic extension of the quantum theory could be found. In this connection I soon thought of the classical Hamilton-Jacobi theory, which relates waves to particles in a fundamental way. Indeed, it had long been known that when one makes a certain approximation (Wentzel-Kramers-Brillouin), Schrödinger's equation becomes equivalent to the classical Hamilton-Jacobi equation. At a certain point I asked myself: What would happen, in the demonstration of this equivalence, if we did not make this approximation? I saw immediately that there would be an additional potential, representing a new kind of force, that would be acting on the particle. I called this the quantum potential, which was designated by Q.

This gave rise directly to what I called a causal interpretation of the quantum theory.[5,6] The basic assumption was that the electron *is* a particle, acted on not only by the classical potential, V, but also by the quantum potential, Q. This latter is determined by a new kind of wave that satisfies Schrödinger's equation. This wave was assumed, like the particle, to be an independent actuality that existed on its own, rather than being merely a function from which the statistical properties of phenomena could be derived. However, I showed on the basis of further physically reasonable assumptions that the intensity of this wave is proportional to the probability that a particle *actually is* in the corresponding region of space (and is not merely the probability of our observing the phenomena involved in *finding* a particle there). So the wave function had a double interpretation – first as a function from which the quantum potential could be derived and, secondly, as a function from which probabilities could be derived.

From these assumptions I was able to show that all the usual results of the quantum theory could be obtained on the basis of a model incorporating the independent actuality of all its basic elements (field and particle), as well as an in principle complete causal determination of the behaviour of these elements in terms of all the relevant equations (at least in a one-particle system, which is as far as I had got at the time).

I sent pre-publication copies of this work to various physicists. De Broglie quickly sent me a reply indicating that he had proposed a similar idea at the Solvay Congress in 1927, but that Pauli had severely criticized it and that this had led him to give it up. Soon after this I received a letter from Pauli, stating his objections in detail. These had mainly to do with the many-particle system, which I had not yet considered seriously. However, as a result of these objections, I looked at the problem again and came out with a treatment of the many-particle system which consistently answered Pauli's criticisms. In doing this, I also developed a theory of the process of measurement which gave an objective account of this process, without the need for the arbitrary and unexplained 'collapse' of the wave function that was implied in the usual interpretation of the theory.[7]

A more detailed consideration of this extended theory led me to look more carefully into the meaning of the quantum potential. This had a number of interesting new features. Indeed, even in the one-particle system these features showed up to some extent, for the quantum potential did not depend on the intensity of the wave associated with this electron; it depended only on the *form* of the wave. And thus, its effect could be large even when the wave had spread out by propagation across large distances. For example, when the wave passes through a pair of slits, the resulting interference pattern produces a complicated quantum potential that could affect the particles far from the slits in such a way as to 'bunch' them into a set of fringes equivalent to those predicted in the usual interpene-tration of the quantum theory.[8] Thus, by admitting that, even in an 'empty' space in which there is no classical potential, the particle can be acted on by a quantum potential that does not fall off with the distance, one is now able to explain the well-known wave particle duality of the properties of matter. And by noting that this quantum potential can generally have a major effect on the particle, an effect that indeed reflects the whole environment, one can obtain a further insight into the crucially significant new feature of wholeness of the electron and its relevant experimental context, which Bohr had shown to be implicit in the quantum theory.

When one looked at the many-particle system, this new kind of wholeness became much more evident, for the quantum potential was now a function of the positions of all the particles which (as in the one-particle case) did not necessarily fall off with the distance. Thus, one could at least in principle have a strong and direct (non-local) connection between particles that are quite distant from each other. This sort of non-locality would, for example, give a simple and direct explanation of the paradox of Einstein, Podolsky and Rosen, because in measuring some property of one of a pair of particles with correlated wave functions, one will alter the 'non-local' quantum potential so that the other particle responds in a corresponding way.

Because the above response is instantaneous, however, it would seem at first sight to contradict the theory of relativity, which requires that no signals be transmitted faster than the speed of light. At the time of proposing these notions I regarded this as a serious difficulty, but I hoped that the problem would ultimately be resolved with the aid of further new orders. This indeed did happen later in connection with the application of the causal interpretation to the quantum mechanical field theory, but as this question is not relevant to the subject of the present paper, I shall not discuss it further here.[9] Meanwhile, however, I felt that the causal interpretation was affording valuable insight into a key difference between classical and quantum properties of matter. Classically, all forces are assumed to fall off eventually to zero, as particles separate, whereas in the quantum theory the quantum potential may still strongly connect particles that are even at macroscopic orders of distance from each other. In fact, it was just this feature of the quantum theory, as brought out in the causal interpretation, that later led Bell[10] to develop his theorem, demonstrating quite precisely and generally how quantum non-locality contrasts with classical notions of locality.

As important as this new feature of non-local connection is, however, the quantum potential implies a further move away from classical concepts that is yet more radical and striking. This is that the very form of the connection between particles depends on the wave function for the state of the whole. This wave function is determined by solving Schrödinger's equation for the entire system, and thus does not depend on the state of the parts. Such a behaviour is in contrast to that shown in classical physics, for which the interaction between the parts is a predetermined function, independent of the state of the whole. Thus, classically, the whole is merely the result of the parts and their pre-assigned interactions, so that the primary reality is the set of parts while the behaviour of the whole is derived entirely from those parts and their interactions. With the quantum potential, however, the whole has an independent and prior significance such that, indeed, the whole may be said to organize the activities of the parts. For example, in a superconducting state it may be seen that electrons are not scattered because, through the action of the quantum potential, the whole system is undergoing a co-ordinated movement more like a ballet dance than like a crowd of unorganized people. Clearly, such quantum wholeness of activity is closer to the organized unity of functioning of the parts of a living being than it is to the kind of unity that is obtained by putting together the parts of a machine.

If the whole is such a primary notion in the quantum theory, how do we account for our usual experience of a world made up of a vast set of essentially independent parts that can correctly be understood in terms of ordinary mechanical notions? The possibility of accounting for this is grounded in the fact that when the wave function reduces to a set of constituent factors, the quantum potential reduces to a sum of independent components. As a result, the activity of the whole reduces to that of a set of independent sub-wholes. As explained in detail elsewhere,[11] under conditions of temperature commonly found on the large-scale level, such factorization comes about in an entirely objective way, depending neither on our knowledge nor on the existence or functioning of any kind of observing or measuring apparatus. Nevertheless, more generally (especially on the small-scale level but, under suitable conditions, as for example in superconductivity, also on a larger-scale level), it is an equally objective implication of the theory that the wave function does not factorize, so that the whole cannot then be divided into independent sub-wholes.

To sum up, then, the quantum potential is capable of constituting a non-local connection, depending directly on the state of the whole in a way that is not reducible to a preassigned relationship among the parts. It not only determines an organized and co-ordinated activity of whole sets of particles, but it also determines which relatively independent sub-wholes, if any, there may be within a larger whole. I want to emphasize again how radically new are these implications of the quantum theory. They are hinted at only vaguely and indirectly by the subtle arguments of Bohr, based on the usual interpretation of the quantum theory as nothing more than a set of mathematical formulae yielding statistical predictions of the phenomena that are to be obtained in physical observations. However, by putting quantum and classical theories in terms of the same intuitively understandable concepts (particles moving continuously under the action of potentials), one is able to obtain a clear and sharp perception of how the two theories differ. I felt that such an insight was important in itself, even if, as seemed likely at the time that I proposed it, this particular model could not provide the basis for a definitive theory that could undergo a sustained development. However, a clear intuitive understanding of the meaning of one's ideas can often be helpful in providing a basis from which may ultimately come an entirely new set of ideas, dealing with the same content.

These proposals did not actually 'catch on' among physicists. The reasons are quite complex and difficult to assess. Perhaps the main objection was that the theory gave exactly the same predictions for all experimental results as does the usual theory. I myself did not give much weight to these objections. Indeed, it occurred to me that if de Broglie's ideas had won the day at the Solvay Congress of 1927, they might have become the accepted interpretation; then, if someone had come along to propose the current interpretation, one could equally well have said that since, after all, it gave no new experimental results, there would be no point in considering it seriously. In other words, I felt that the adoption of the current interpretation was a somewhat fortuitous affair, since it was affected not only by the outcome of the Solvay Conference but also by the generally positivist empiricist attitude that pervaded physics at the time. This attitude is in many ways even stronger today, and shows up in the fact that a model that gives insight without an 'empirical pay-off' cannot be taken seriously.

I did try to answer these criticisms to some extent by pointing out that the enriched conceptual structure of the causal interpretation was capable of modifications and new lines of development that are not possible in the usual interpretation.[12] These could, in principle, lead to new empirical predictions, but unfortunately there was no clear indication of how to choose such modifications from among the vast range that was possible. And so these arguments had little effect as an answer to those who require a fairly clear prospect of an empirical test before they will consider an idea seriously.

In addition, it was important that the whole idea did not appeal to Einstein, probably mainly because it involved the new feature of non-locality, which went against his strongly-held conviction that all connections had to be local. I felt this response of Einstein was particularly unfortunate, both during the Solvay Congress and afterwards, as it almost certainly 'put off' some of those who might otherwise have been interested in this approach. Although I saw clearly at the time that the causal interpretation was not entirely satisfactory, I felt that the insight that it afforded was an important reason why it should be considered, at least as a supplement to the usual interpretation. To have some kind of intuitive model was better, in my view, than to have none at all, for, without such a model, research in the quantum theory will consist mainly of the working out of formulae and the comparison of these calculated results with those of experiment. Even more important, the teaching of quantum mechanics will reduce (as it has in fact tended to do) to a kind of indoctrination, aimed at fostering the belief that such a procedure is all that is possible in physics. Thus new generations of students have grown up who are predisposed to consider such questions with rather closed minds.

Because the response to these ideas was so limited, and because I did not see clearly, at the time, how to proceed further, my interests began to turn in other directions. During the 1960s, I began to direct my attention toward *order*, partly as a result of a long correspondence with an American artist, Charles Biederman, who was deeply concerned with this question. And then, through working with a student, Donald Schumacher, I became strongly interested in *language*. These two interests led to a paper[13] on order in physics and on its description through language. In this paper I compared and contrasted relativistic and quantum notions of order, leading to the conclusion that they contradicted each other and that new notions of order were needed.

Being thus alerted to the importance of order, I saw a programme on BBC television showing a device in which an ink drop was spread out through a cylinder of glycerine and then brought back together again, to be reconstituted essentially as it was before. This immediately struck me as very relevant to the question of order, since, when the ink drop was spread out, it still had a 'hidden' (i.e. non-manifest) order that was revealed when it was reconstituted. On the other hand, in our usual language, we would say that the ink was in a state of 'disorder' when it was diffused through the glycerine. This led me to see that new notions of order must be involved here.

Shortly afterwards, I began to reflect on the hologram and to see that in it, the entire order of an object is contained in an interference pattern of light that does not appear to have such an order at all. Suddenly, I was struck by the similarity of the hologram and the behaviour of the ink drop. I saw that what they had in common was that an order was *enfolded*; that is, in any small region of space there may be 'information' which is the result of enfolding an extended order and which could then be unfolded into the original order (as the points of contact made by the folds in a sheet of paper may contain the essential relationships of the total pattern displayed when the sheet is unfolded).

Then, when I thought of the mathematical form of the quantum theory (with its matrix operations and Green's functions), I perceived that this too described just a movement of enfoldment and unfoldment of the wave function. So the thought occurred to me: perhaps the movement of enfoldment and unfoldment is universal, while the extended and separate forms that we commonly see in experience are relatively stable and independent patterns, maintained by a constant underlying movement of enfoldment and unfoldment. This latter I called the *holomovement*. The proposal was thus a reversal of the usual idea. Instead of supposing that extended matter and its movement are fundamental, while enfoldment and unfoldment are explained as as particular case of this, we are saying that the implicate order will have to contain within itself all possible features of the explicate order as potentialities, along with the principles determining which of these features shall become actual. The explicate order will in this way flow out of the implicate order through unfoldment, while in turn it 'flows back' through further enfoldment. The implicate order thus plays a primary role, while the explicate order is secondary, in the sense that its main qualities and properties are ultimately derived in its relationship with the implicate order, of which it is indeed a special and distinguished case.

This approach implies, of course, that each separate and extended form in the explicate order is enfolded in the whole and that, in turn, the whole is enfolded in this form (though, of course, there is an asymmetry, in that the form enfolds the whole only in a limited and not completely defined way). The way in which the separate and extended form enfolds the whole is, however, not merely superficial or of secondary significance, but rather it is essential to what that form *is* and to how it acts, moves and behaves quite generally. So the whole is, in a deep sense, *internally* related to the parts. And, since the whole enfolds all the parts, these latter are also internally related, though in a weaker way than they are related to the whole.

I shall not go into great detail about the implicate order [14,15] here; I shall assume that the reader is somewhat familiar with this. What I want to emphasize is only that the implicate order provided an image, a kind of metaphor, for intuitively understanding the implication of wholeness which is the most important new feature of the quantum theory. Nevertheless, it must be pointed out that the specific analogies of the ink drop and the hologram are limited, and do not fully convey all that is meant by the implicate order. What is missing in these analogies is an inner principle of organization in the implicate order that determines which sub-wholes shall become actual and what will be their relatively independent and stable forms. Indeed, in both these models, the order enfolded in the whole is obtained from pre-existent, separate and extended elements (objects photographed in the hologram or ink drops injected into the glycerine). It is then merely unfolded to give something similar to these elements again. Nor is there any natural principle of stability in these elements; they may be totally altered or destroyed by minor further disturbances of the overall arrangement of the equipment.

Gradually, throughout the 1970s, I became more aware of the limitations of the hologram and ink droplet analogies to the implicate order. Meanwhile, I noticed that both the implicate order and the causal interpretations had emphasized this wholeness signified by quantum laws, though in apparently very different ways. So I wondered if these two rather different approaches were not related in some deep sense – especially because I had come at least to the essence of both notions at almost the same time. At first sight, the causal interpretation seemed to be a step backwards toward mechanism, since it introduced the notion of a particle acted on by a potential. Nevertheless, as I have already pointed out, its implication that the whole both determines its sub-wholes and organizes their activity clearly goes far beyond what appeared to be the original mechanical point of departure. Would it not be possible to drop this mechanical starting point altogether?

I saw that this could indeed be done by going on from the quantum mechanical particle theory to the quantum mechanical field theory. This is accomplished by starting with the classical notion of a continuous field (e.g. the electromagnetic) that is spread out through all space. One then applies the rules of the quantum theory to this field. The result is that the field will have discrete 'quantized' values for certain properties, such as energy, momentum and angular momentum. Such a field will act in many ways like a collection of particles, while at the same time it still has wave-like manifestations such as interference, diffraction, etc.

Of course, in the usual interpretation of the theory, there is no way to understand how this comes about. One can only use the mathematical formalism to calculate statistically the distribution of phenomena through which such a field reveals itself in our observations and experiments. But now one can extend this causal interpretation to the quantum field theory. Here, the actuality will be the entire field over the whole universe. Classically, this is determined as a continuous solution of some kind of field equation (e.g. Maxwell's equations for the electromagnetic field). But when we extend the notion of the causal interpretation to the field theory, we find that these equations are modified by the action of what I called a super-quantum potential. This is related to the activity of the entire field as the original quantum potential was to that of the particles. As a result, the field equations are modified in a way that makes them, in technical language, non-local and non-linear.

What this implies for the present context can be seen by considering that, classically, solutions of the field equations represent waves that spread out and diffuse independently. Thus, as I indicated earlier in connection with the hologram, there is no way to explain the origination of the waves that converge to a region where a particle-like manifestation is actually detected, nor is there any factor that could explain the stability and sustained existence of such a particle-like manifestation. However, this lack is just what is supplied by the super-quantum potential. Indeed, as can be shown by a detailed analysis,[6,7] the non-local features of this latter will introduce the required tendency of waves to converge at appropriate places, while the non-linearity will provide for the stability of recurrence of the whole process. And thus we come to a theory in which not only the activity of particle-like manifestations, but even their actualization, e.g. their creation, sustenance and annihilation, is organized by the super-quantum potential.

The general picture that emerges out of this is of a wave that spreads out and converges again and again to show a kind of average particle-like behaviour, while the interference and diffraction properties are, of course, still maintained. All this flows out of the super-quantum potential, which depends in principle on the state of the whole universe. But if the 'wave function of the universe' falls into a set of independent factors, at least approximately, a corresponding set of relatively autonomous and independent sub-units of field function will emerge. And, in fact, as in the case in the particle theory, the wave function will under normal conditions tend to factorize at the large-scale level in an entirely objective way that is not basically dependent on our knowledge or on our observations and measurements. So now we see quite generally that the whole universe not only determines and organizes its sub-wholes, but also that it gives form to what has until now been called the elementary particles out of which everything is supposed to be constituted. What we have here is a kind of universal process of constant creation and annihilation, determined through the super-quantum potential so as to give rise to a world of form and structure in which all manifest features are only relatively constant, recurrent and stable aspects of this whole.

To see how this is connected with the implicate order, we have only to note that the original holographic model was one in which the whole was constantly enfolded into and unfolded from each region of an electromagnetic field, through dynamical movement and development of the field according to the laws of classical field theory. But now, this whole field is no longer a self-contained totality; it depends crucially on the super-quantum potential. As we have seen, however, this in turn depends on the 'wave function of the universe' in a way that is a generalization of how the quantum potential for particles depends on the wave function of a system of particles. But all such wave functions are forms of the implicate order (whether they refer to particles or to fields). Thus, the super-quantum potential expresses the activity of a new kind of implicate order. This implicate order is immensely more subtle than that of the original field, as well as more inclusive, in the sense that not only is the actual activity of the whole field enfolded in it, but also all its potentialities, along with the principles determining which of these shall become actual.

I was in this way led to call the original field the first implicate order, while the super-quantum potential was called the second implicate order (or the super-implicate order). In principle, of course, there could be a third, fourth, fifth implicate order, going on to infinity, and these would correspond to extensions of the laws of physics going beyond those of the current quantum theory, in a fundamental way. But for the present I want to consider only the second implicate order, and to emphasize that this stands in relationship to the first as a source of formative, organizing and creative activity.

It should be clear that this notion now incorporates both of my earlier perceptions – the implicate order as a movement of outgoing and incoming waves, and of the causal interpretation of the quantum theory. So, although these two ideas seemed initially very different, they proved to be two aspects of one more comprehensive notion. This can be described as an overall implicate order, which may extend to an infinite number of levels and which objectively and self-actively differentiates and organizes itself into independent sub-wholes, while determining how these are interrelated to make up the whole.

Moreover, the principles of organization of such an implicate order can even define a unique explicate order, as a particular and distin-guished sub-order, in which all the elements are relatively independent and externally related.[16] To put it differently, the explicate order itself may be obtainable from the implicate order as a special and de-terminate sub-order that is contained within it.

All that has been discussed here opens up the possibility of con-sidering the cosmos as an unbroken whole through an overall im-plicate order. Of course, this possibility has been studied thus far in only a preliminary way, and a great deal more work is required to clarify and extend the notions that have been discussed in this paper.

References

1   This article is an extension and modification of a talk, D. Bohm, *Zygon*, **20**, 111 (1985).
2   D. Bohm, *Quantum Theory*, Prentice-Hall, New York, 1951.
3   N. Bohr, *Atomatic Physics and Human Knowledge*, Science Editions, New York, 1965.
4   J. von Neumann, *Mathematical Foundations of Quantum Mechanics*, R. T. Beyer (trans.), Princeton University, Princeton, New Jersey, 1955.
5   D. Bohm, *Phys. Rev.*, **85**, 166 (1952).
6   D. Bohm, *Phys. Rev.*, **85**, 180 (1952).
7   See reference 6; see also D. Bohm and B. J. Hiley, *Foundations of Physics*, **14**, 255 (1984), where this question is discussed in more detail.
8   For a detailed treatment of this point, see C. Philippidis, C. Dewdney and B. J. Hiley, *Nuovo Cimento*, **B52**, 15 (1979).
9   For a further discussion of this point, see reference 7.
10 J. Bell, *Rev. Mod. Phys.*, **38**, 447 (1966); see also *Foundations of Physics*, **12**, 989 (1982).
11 D. Bohm and B. J. Hiley, *Foundations of Physics*, **14**, 255 (1984).
12 D. Bohm and J.-P. Vigier, *Phys. Rev.*, **96**, 208 (1954).
13 D. Bohm, *Foundations of Physics*, **1**, 359 (1971).
14 D. Bohm, *Foundations of Physics*, **3**, 139 (1973).

15   D. Bohm, *Wholeness and the Implicate Order*, Routledge & Kegan Paul, London, 1980.
16   D. Bohm, 'Claremont Conference', in *Physics and the Ultimate Significance of Time*, ed. David R. Griffin, State University of New York Press, Albany, 1986.

3

Collective variables in elementary quantum mechanics

Eugene P. Gross　*Department of Physics, Brandeis University*

In the present article I discuss some features of the use of collective co-ordinates in two systems with a small number of degrees of freedom. In both cases the utility of collective coordinates is connected with the validity of an adiabatic approximation. The two examples are pedagogical in nature, but are perhaps appropriate in a volume honoring David Bohm, who has made major contributions to the theory of collective coordinates. First, however, I present some personal reminiscences of the days when I was a student of David Bohm.

My first recollection is of a seminar given in 1946 by David Bohm, shortly after he arrived in Princeton as an assistant professor. The subject was plasma physics. The talk was divided into three parts. The first part dealt with the plasma as a distinct state of matter, with an organization different from the solid, liquid and gas. The charge screening and lack of velocity locking was emphasized. The second part had to do with the widespread occurrence of plasmas in discharge tube physics, in astrophysics and in chemistry. He touched on the connection with microwave space-charge devices. Particular attention was paid to plasma oscillations and the frequent occurrence of in-stabilities. The third part dealt with metals viewed as quantum plas-mas. The main tool of analysis was the linearization of the equations of motion for products of creation and annihilation operators by means of the random phase approximation.

I was then looking for a thesis advisor. In his low key fashion, Dave Bohm had opened up a vast panorama. It was clear that an enormous range of problems had to be explored. The intertwining of conceptual and practical problems was very appealing and exciting. How lucky to have the possibility of doing a thesis which was much more than doing the simple next step in an ongoing research program. I worked hard on my notes, and wrote up the lecture very carefully. I gave them to Dave and was taken on as a student.

We spent a tremendous amount of time together. There are advan-tages to having a bachelor as a mentor. We spent some time at the blackboard, but mainly talked. Then Dave wrote things down on paper. But even more vivid in my memory are the very long walks through Princeton, with numerous stops for coffee. Dave developed ideas and responded to questions and criticisms. What was remarkable was that one could do theoretical physics without a blackboard and without pencil and paper. After returning to the office it seemed that the mathematics just settled into place, with significant results coming quickly.

I slowly realized that there was a hidden background. Dave had been an assistant to W. R. Smythe and had done essentially all of the difficult problems in *Static and Dynamic Electricity*. He had written papers on the theory of high energy accelerators and on the velocity distribution of electrons in nebulae. There was several years of total involvement with the behavior of plasmas in magnetic fields, in connection with his work for the Manhattan Project. These papers were written with his characteristic lucidity. The physical descriptions stand out and control the mathematical analysis. All of this work was germane to our research on the classical kinetic theory of plasmas and beams. There is undoubtedly more background that I am not aware of.

Dave was also deeply concerned with quantum problems. He thought about many-electron problems and superconductivity. He was at work on his text on quantum theory. He reformulated the theory of measurement in quantum mechanics. Most of all, he was fascinated by Bohr's ideas on the role of complementarity in describing nature.

The problem of the divergences in quantum electrodynamics was very much on people's minds. Dave worked on self-oscillations of finite-sized particles and on Kramer's theory of non-relativistic electrodynamics. His lectures on advanced quantum mechanics dealt with electrodynamics. He gave much thought to the hypothesis of a minimum length in physics and to reconciling relativity and quantum mechanics for structures of finite extent. Along with other physicists such as Bohr, he felt that a really radical change in physical ideas was needed. Instead, Schwinger's program of starting with the full Maxwell-Dirac Lagrangian, insisting on manifest covariance, and quarantining the divergences, represented a different kind of radical change. Feynman's introduction of diagrams freed the imaginations of theoretical physicists to deal with what had been depressingly complicated formalisms in quantum field theory and many-body physics.

In the light of this rich background, it is now less surprising to me that one could do physics by talking. The use of analogy is very powerful when there is a well-defined mathematical basis for the analogies. Still, I continue to marvel at Dave's extraordinary manner of expressing ideas and of constructing coherent intellectual structures. It made possible communication with non-physicists, who appreciated Dave's ability to explain the fundamental ideas of physics. Indeed, this sometimes became ludicrous. I recall a social evening where, tongue in cheek, he constructed an elaborate and 'convincing' theory of the existence of ghosts and devils.

The reconciliation of collective and individual aspects of behavior in many-body theory, and of wave and particle aspects in quantum theory, moved to the forefront of Dave's thoughts. He was not satisfied with the equations-of-motion approach to many-body theory. He felt that a description was needed that dealt with collective and individual aspects simultaneously. This led to the successful auxiliary variable theory of Bohm and Pines.[1] A beautiful account of the ideas is found in Dave's later (1956) Les Houches lectures.[2]

He continued this work with T. Staver and D. Salt, and extended the description in his papers with G. Carmi.[3] The ideas of these later papers have not been sufficiently appreciated by physicists.

On the problem of the foundations of quantum theory, his analysis of the Einstein, Podolsky, Rosen thought experiment gave rise to his causal reformulations. He continued this work in Brazil, Israel and England. The role of non-locality emerged. This culminated in the celebrated and startling Aharonov–Bohm analysis of electromagnetic potentials in quantum theory. It now occupies an important position in the physical foundations of gauge theories.

There is another aspect. It was the non-competitive atmosphere in which Dave did his work. I recall an incident. In our first paper on plasma oscillations we had independently discovered the phenomenon of Landau damping. We used an orbit-tracing approach and considered the low collision frequency limit. It was used to understand particle trapping and the limitations of the linear theory. I came upon a copy of the *Journal of Physics* containing Landau's solution of the linearized Vlasov equation.[4] Due to wartime dislocations it arrived in Princeton after a delay of a year. I rushed to show it to Dave, who was in the shop constructing a frame for a hi-fi set. He was not at all perturbed at being scooped and simply admired the elegance and incisiveness of Landau's paper.

Broader philosophical questions were often discussed in the numerous conversations that Dave had with me and others. I had taken courses in mathematical logic from A. Church and pressed its claims on Dave. We talked about the relation to dialectical modes of thinking. I recall a conversation in the graduate student library at Princeton. It had a copy of the *Catholic Encyclopedia*. We looked at the article on the Holy Trinity, and noted how similar the language was to that of Bohr. However, nothing came of an attempt to generalize Bohr's notion of wave-particle duality. Dave was always concerned with the philosophical problem of obtaining adequate concepts and modes of thinking to make sense of our experience. He has continued this with his explorations of the notions of implicate and explicate order.

Finally, I can only use old-fashioned language to describe his impact on me and others. Dave's essential being was then, and still is, totally engaged in the calm but passionate search into the nature of things. He can only be characterized as a secular saint. He is totally free of guile and competitiveness, and it would be easy to take advantage of him. Indeed, his students and friends, mostly younger than he is, felt a powerful urge to protect such a precious being. Perhaps the deep affection of his many friends helped to sustain him in the difficult years of the early 1950s.

1 Atom-molecule transition

(a) Introduction

As the first example of the use of collective coordinates, consider a three-particle system, with two of the particles having the same mass M and the other particle a mass m. The Hamiltonian is:

$$H = \frac{\vec{p}^2}{2m} + \frac{\vec{p}_1^2 + \vec{p}_2^2}{2M} + V(\vec{q} - \vec{q}_1) + V(\vec{q} - \vec{q}_2) + U(\vec{q}_1 - \vec{q}_2)$$

The Hydrogen molecular (two center) ion corresponds to the attractive:

$$V(r) = -e^2/r$$

between an electron (mass m) and the nuclei (mass M).

$$U(r) = +e^2/r$$

is the nuclear repulsion, and $M \gg m$.

The H$^-$ ion is the atomic (one center) case where m is the mass of the proton and M is the mass of the electrons. The potential energies are the same. This is the opposite limit of the same Hamiltonian, i.e. $M \ll m$.

One can choose one of the masses (say m) to set the scale of energy. For example we can choose a Bohr radius $a_\text{B} = \dfrac{\hbar^2}{me^2}$ and the energy unit $\dfrac{me^4}{\hbar^2}$. Then the spectrum depends on the ratio m/M. It is interesting that there is a drastic change in the spectrum as the single parameter m/M is varied. The diatomic molecule is a highly organized system.[5] We have a well-defined structure of the atomic, vibrational and rotational low levels whose energies are in the ratio 1, $1/\sqrt{M}$ and $1/M$. In the atomic limit $m \gg M$, the H$^-$ ion has only a ground state that is 3/4 eV below the continuum. We would like to understand the concepts that are needed to describe this transition of the level structure.

Cases where the mass ratio is not so extreme do occur in nature, e.g. μ mesic atoms and molecules. In nuclear physics there are also three-body problems where all the masses are comparable, but the potential energies are different. We expect the level variation with m/M to be smooth.

To proceed we need a suitable set of new coordinates. Guided by the physics of the molecular limit we choose:

$$\vec{R} = \frac{m\vec{q} + M(\vec{q}_1 + \vec{q}_2)}{m + 2M}, \quad \vec{r} = \vec{q} - \left(\frac{\vec{q}_1 + \vec{q}_2}{2}\right), \quad \vec{y} = \vec{q}_1 - \vec{q}_2$$

Here $\vec{R}$ is the center of mass of the system as a whole, and is a collective coordinate. (Frequently a collective coordinate is a one-body additive function of the original coordinates.) $\vec{r}$ is a coordinate of the lone particle relative to the center of mass of the nuclei:

$$\frac{\vec{q}_1 + \vec{q}_2}{2}$$

$\vec{y}$ is the relative coordinate of the two nuclei.

Introducing the reduced mass of the electron:

$$\frac{1}{\mu} = \frac{1}{m} + \frac{1}{2M}$$

the Hamiltonian takes the form:

$$H = \frac{\vec{p}_R^2}{2(m + 2M)} + \frac{\vec{p}_r^2}{2\mu} + \frac{\vec{p}_y^2}{M} + V\left(\frac{\vec{y}}{2} - \vec{r}\right) + V\left(\frac{\vec{y}}{2} + \vec{r}\right) + U(\vec{y})$$

The center of mass motion is clearly separated, i.e. $\vec{R}$ is an ignorable coordinate. This expresses the rigorous translation invariance of the Hamiltonian, i.e. that it is unchanged when there is a common displacement of the original coordinates.

In atomic theory, the standard coordinates for the discussion of the effects of the finite nuclear mass on atomic spectra are:

$$R = \frac{m\vec{q} + M(\vec{q}_1 + \vec{q}_2)}{m + 2M}, \quad \vec{x}_1 = \vec{q}_1 - \vec{q}, \quad \vec{x}_2 = \vec{q}_2 - \vec{q}$$

Since $\vec{q}$ is the coordinate of the heavy particle (mass m) and $\vec{q}_1$ and $\vec{q}_2$ the coordinates of the electrons (mass H), it is natural to measure the position of the light particles (mass M) relative to the heavy particle (mass m). Then:

$$H = \frac{p_R^2}{2(m + 2M)} + \frac{\vec{p}_{x_1}\vec{p}_{x_2}}{m} + \frac{p_{x_1}^2 p_{x_2}^2}{2}\left(\frac{1}{m} + \frac{1}{M}\right) + V(\vec{x}_1) + V(\vec{x}_2)$$
$$+ U(\vec{x}_1 - \vec{x}_2)$$

Again the center of mass motion is clearly separated. We identify the term:

$$\frac{\vec{p}_{x_1}\vec{p}_{x_2}}{m}$$

as a perturbation which comes into play when $\frac{m}{M} \gg 1$ but not infinite.

We will introduce still another set of coordinates. In the first description we had:

1   a good center of mass coordinate $\vec{R}$ for the system as a whole;

2   a center of mass coordinate $\frac{\vec{q}_1 + \vec{q}_2}{2}$ for the two-particle subsystem.

In the second description we used only the first center of mass coordinate. There are other problems where one can't introduce acceptable collective coordinates of either kind. In the three-particle system consider:

$$\vec{Q}_1 = \vec{q}_1 - \vec{q}, \ \vec{Q}_2 = \vec{q}_2 - \vec{q}, \ \vec{Q} = q$$

with the canonical momenta:

$$\vec{P} = \vec{p} + (\vec{p}_1 + \vec{p}_2), \ \vec{P}_1 = \vec{p}_1, \ \vec{P}_2 = \vec{p}_2$$

Then:

$$H = \frac{1}{2m}[\vec{P} - (\vec{P}_1 + \vec{P}_2)]^2 + \frac{P_1^2 + P_2^2}{2M} + V(\vec{Q}_1) + V(\vec{Q}_2) +$$
$$U(\vec{Q}_1 - \vec{Q}_2)$$

the $\vec{Q}$ coordinates are directly expressed in terms of original coordinates and the motion of a center of mass is not introduced. The Hamiltonian still involves the total momentum $\vec{P}$, and $\vec{Q}$ is an ignorable coordinate, so the translational invariance finds an appropriate expression. This description is also satisfactory for the $m/M \gg 1$ atomic limit.

The different coordinate choices correspond to different pictures that are used in obtaining an understanding of the behavior of the system. Usually no single description is best in the entire parameter space m/M.

(b)   The semi-oscillator model-molecular limit

To analyse the qualitative features of the m/M transition, it is useful to first examine a 'semi-oscillator' model. The attractive potential is replaced by an oscillator potential:

$$V(x) = \frac{K\vec{x}^2}{2}$$

where K is a stiffness coefficient. We lose some important feature of the actual systems, since the oscillator attraction always holds the particles together. The model does not have ionized, i.e. continuum, states, apart from the center-of-mass continuum states.

The intrinsic part of the Hamiltonian separates in the $\vec{y}$ and $\vec{r}$ variables. We have:

$$H_{\text{int}} = \frac{p_R^2}{2\mu} + Kr^2 + \frac{p_y^2}{M} + K\left(\frac{\bar{y}}{2}\right)^2 + U(|\bar{y}|)$$

First consider the additional approximation of neglecting the repulsion, i.e. $U(y) = 0$. The spectrum is:

$$E = \left(n_x + n_y + n_z + \frac{3}{2}\right)\sqrt{\frac{K}{M}} + \left(v_x + v_y + v_z + \frac{3}{2}\right)$$

$$\sqrt{2K\left(\frac{1}{m} + \frac{1}{2M}\right)}$$

where the $n_x \ldots, v_x \ldots$ are integers (including zero). Since each of the sub-Hamiltonians is rotation invariant, we have alternative descriptions in terms of principal, angular momentum and azimuthal quantum numbers. These are important in discussing perturbations of the systems by external electric and magnetic fields.

In the molecular limit ($M \gg m$) there is a triply-degenerate high-frequency branch represented by v_x, v_y, v_z, proportional to $\dfrac{1}{\sqrt{m}}$ and with a weak dependence on m/M. The n_x, n_y, n_z branch is proportional to $\dfrac{1}{\sqrt{M}}$ and is low frequency.

In the atomic limit ($m \gg M$) the branches coalesce and are described by the single frequency $\sqrt{\dfrac{K}{M}}$.

Next, consider the effects of the repulsion $U(q_1 - q_2)$ between the M particles. The modes of frequency:

$$\sqrt{2K\left(\frac{1}{m} + \frac{1}{2M}\right)}$$

are unaltered. This is the only place that the mass m enters. These modes are high frequency in both the molecular and atomic limits, with a minimum at $m = 2M$.

The branches corresponding to n_x, n_y, n_z in absence of the repulsion are now described by the rotation invariant Hamiltonian:

$$H_2 = \frac{p_y^2}{M} + K\left(\frac{\eta}{2}\right)^2 + U(\eta). \ \eta \equiv |\bar{y}|$$

An appropriate set of quantum numbers is the angular momentum l with a $(2l + 1)$ azimuthal degeneracy. The radial function $R_{v,l}(\eta)$ are also characterized by a principal quantum number v. They obey the equations:

$$-\frac{1}{\mu}\left\{\frac{d^2}{d\eta^2} + \frac{2}{\eta}\frac{d}{d\eta} - \frac{l(l+1)}{\eta^2}\right\}R_{v,l}(\eta) + \left\{\frac{K\eta^2}{4} + U(\eta)\right\}R_{v,l}(\eta)$$
$$= E_{v,l}R_{v,l}(\eta)$$

We find the vibration-rotation spectrum from this equation. One first considers the case $l = 0$. The potential energy $\dfrac{K\eta^2}{4} + U(\eta)$ is positive and has a minimum at:

$$\eta^* = \left(\frac{2e^2}{K}\right)^{1/3}$$

when $U(\eta) = e^2/\eta$. Expanding about this point the energy is:

$$\frac{3}{4}K\eta^{*2} + \sqrt{\frac{3KM}{M4}}(\eta - \eta^*)^2 + \ldots$$

In the large M limit asymptotic analysis shows that one can ignore the half range of η coordinate and the boundary condition at $\eta = 0$.

For $l = 0$ one then has a one-dimensional harmonic oscillator and thus a vibrational spectrum $(v + 1/2)\sqrt{\dfrac{3K}{M}}$ with a vibrational quantum number v. The frequency is $\sqrt{\dfrac{3K}{M}}$, i.e. proportional to $\dfrac{1}{\sqrt{M}}$. The rotational spectrum is roughly estimated by taking $\eta = \eta^*$ in the term $\dfrac{l(l+1)}{M\eta^2}$. This gives a moment of inertia $\dfrac{M\eta^{*2}}{2}$. Thus the electronic, vibrational and rotational separations are in the ratios $1, \dfrac{1}{\sqrt{M}}, \dfrac{1}{M}$.

This is a crude first approximation. It rests on the fact that, for $M \gg 1$, the minimum η^* is far from the origin, i.e. $\eta^*\sqrt{M} \gg 1$. A more precise analysis of the $R_{v,l}$ equation yields a theory of the vibration-rotation interaction. If one moves away from the molecular limit to the transition region, where M and m are comparable, we get increasing distortion and modification of the spectrum. The analysis appears to be complicated but feasible, provided one does extensive computer calculations. The results should be similar to standard analysis using Morse potentials.

(c) Semi-oscillator model-atomic limit ($m \gg M$)

Let us return to the standard coordinates used in the discussion of the effect of nuclear motions on atomic spectra. Since $m/M \gg 1$ we look on the term:

$$\frac{\vec{p}_{x_1}\vec{p}_{x_2}}{m}$$

as a perturbation.

For high Z two-electron atoms the interelectronic repulsion can also be treated by perturbation theory. The starting point is then an independent particle description with hydrogenic wave functions and with the reduced masses $\left(\dfrac{1}{M} + \dfrac{1}{m}\right)$. An even better starting point is the Hartree-Fock independent particle description.

However, when Z is reduced so that one reaches the helium atom ($Z = 2$), this description is not very good. One needs wave functions that, even in the fixed nucleus limit, give a more accurate account of the correlated motion of the electrons. It is necessary to classify the levels into para and ortho-helium. The Pauli principle requires that the wave functions are antisymmetric under combined interchange of space and spin coordinates of the electrons. The perturbations arising from the finite nuclear mass give differential shifts of the energy levels..

By the time one reaches the H^- ion ($Z = 1$) the independent electron description is completely inadequate. If one does not have the extreme situation $m/M \gg 1$, the fact that the momenta are coupled leaves us with an unclear picture of the behavior. For the semi-oscillator model the description in terms of $\vec{R}$, $\vec{r}$, and $\vec{\eta}$ coordinates appears to be better in the intermediate situation, since the complications are transferred to the $\vec{\eta}$ coordinates alone, i.e. one has a one-body problem. But this is not true for the actual $V(r) = -e^2/r$ problem.

(d)   The H_2^+ -H^- transition-actual potential

To solve the molecule problem for the H_2^+ case where $V(r) = -\dfrac{e^2}{r}$ we have the adiabatic (Born-Oppenheimer) approximation.[6] We look for the electronic wave functions for fixed nuclear coordinates. In the $\vec{r}$, $\vec{y}$ descriptions:

$$\left\{\frac{\vec{p}_r^2}{2\mu} + V\left(\frac{\vec{y}}{2} + \vec{r}\right) + V\left(\frac{\vec{y}}{2} - \vec{r}\right)\right\}\psi_v(\vec{R}|\vec{y}) = \varepsilon_v(\vec{y})\psi_v(\vec{r}|\vec{y})$$

This is a two-center problem with the parameter $\vec{y} = \vec{p}_1 - \vec{q}_2$ only involving the nuclear coordinates. It separates in elliptical coordinates. In the simple adiabatic approximation $\varepsilon(\vec{y})$ enters as part of the potential for the nuclear wave functions $\chi_{v,n}$ $(\vec{y})$;

$$\left\{\frac{p_y^2}{M} + \varepsilon_v(\vec{y}) + U(\vec{y})\right\}\chi_{v,n}(\vec{y}) = E_{v,n}\chi_{v,n}(\vec{y})$$

where n corresponds to additional quantum numbers for the rotation vibration spectrum (l and $ml = -l, \ldots 0, \ldots l$). In fact ε_v depends only on the absolute value $\eta = |y|$, as does $U(\vec{y}) = e^2/\eta$. For the semi-oscillator model:

$$\varepsilon_N(\eta) = \left(v_x + v_y + v_z + \frac{3}{2}\right)\sqrt{\frac{2K}{\mu}} + K\left(\frac{\eta}{2}\right)^2$$

and the adiabatic approximation is exact.

In the actual H_2^+ molecular ion the electronic wave function is governed by a potential that is $\dfrac{-2e^2}{\eta}$ when $\eta \to 0$. So the $\varepsilon_v(\eta \to 0)$ are hydrogenic levels for $Z = 2$ with a reduced mass μ.

On the other hand, for large nuclear separations we have a spectrum which is $1/4$ of the $\eta \to 0$ spectrum. So the $\varepsilon_v(\eta)$ curve is slowly varying and proportional to $\dfrac{mM}{m + M}$. The potential for the nuclear wave function also involves $U(\eta) = e^2/\eta$ which $\to \infty$ as $\eta \to 0$ and to 0 as $\eta \to \infty$. If we fix the units so that $m = 1$, we see that we lose the minimum as $M \to 0$, i.e. in the atomic limit. In addition the adiabatic approximation has broken down by the time $M \sim 1$.

Of course in the atomic region it is better to proceed by doing the perturbation analysis with the appropriate set of coordinates.

It is clear that the destruction of the highly organized level structure as m/M decreases occurs in a very non-uniform manner. Even in the extreme molecular limit the large quantum number rotational and vibrational states merge into the continuum. As m/M is reduced, only the lowest states retain identity. They are still satisfactorily described in terms of the collective coordinate. Finally all of these disappear and one is left with the H^- ion. In the present problem, where there are only a few degrees of freedom, all of these properties emerge from rather simple familiar mathematical equations. There is nothing really surprising, but perhaps we obtain a more explicit understanding of the strengths and limitations of the use of collective coordinates. A very important point is that the failure to satisfy the boundary condition at $\eta = 0$ becomes very serious as one moves away from the domain where the collective coordinate yields a good approximation. We would like to emphasize that, while it may be possible to give a theory of the ground state energy valid over the entire m/M range, it is much more difficult to give an account of the level structure.

2   Electron interacting with two-lattice oscillators

(a)   Introduction

As a second example of the use of collective coordinates, consider the Hamiltonian:

$$H = \frac{p^2}{2M_1} - g(q_e \cos kq_1 + q_0 \sin kq_1) + \frac{p_e^2 + p_0^2 + q_e^2 + q_0^2}{2} - 1$$

An electron interacts with two oscillators of wave vector k. Units are chosen so that the common mass and frequency of the oscillators as well as $\hbar$ are unity. This Hamiltonian comes from the polaron problem in a standing wave description. We single out a single pair of wave vectors. By scaling the coordinate so that $q = kq_1$ and $M = (M_1/k^2)$ we have a two-parameter dependence of the energy levels on M and g. In addition the levels depend on the total momentum of the system. We would like to understand the way the low-lying level structure depends on these parameters.

We can describe the system in terms of a pair of travelling waves by introducing new Hermitian coordinates:

$$q^\pm = \frac{q_e{}^\pm p_0}{\sqrt{2}}, \, p^\pm = \frac{p_e{}^\pm q_0}{\sqrt{2}}$$

and creation and destruction operators by:

$$a_\pm = \frac{q^\pm + ip^\pm}{\sqrt{2}}, \, a_\pm^\dagger = \frac{q^\pm - ip^\pm}{\sqrt{2}}$$

It is convenient to put:

$$a_+ \equiv a, \, a_- \equiv b$$

Then:

$$H = \frac{p^2}{2M} - \frac{g}{2}(a + b^\dagger)e^{iq} - \frac{g}{2}(a^\dagger + b)e^{-iq} + a^\dagger a + b^\dagger b$$

This is a more familiar form for a particle-field Hamiltonian. It has the total momentum G as an exact constant of motion:

$$G = p + (a^\dagger a - b^\dagger b)$$

In the standing wave description the constant of motion is:

$$G = p + (q_e p_0 - q_0 p_e)$$

Still another description takes note of the degeneracy of the oscillators. One can introduce polar coordinates Q, φ by:

$$q_e = Q \cos \varphi, \, q_0 = Q \sin \varphi$$

The phase φ will play the role of a collective coordinate for the two-oscillator subsystem. We have:

$$H = \frac{p^2}{2M} + D(Q) - \frac{1}{2Q^2}\frac{\partial^2}{\partial\varphi^2} + \frac{1}{2}Q^2 - 1 - gQ \cos(q - \varphi)$$

where:

$$D(Q) = -\frac{1}{2}\left(\frac{\partial^2}{\partial Q^2} + \frac{1}{Q}\frac{\partial}{\partial Q}\right)$$

The constant of motion is:

$$G = p - i\frac{\partial}{\partial\varphi}$$

For this system there is no natural center-of-mass coordinate for the system as a whole. The collective coordinate representation is useful in the strong coupling domain.

When the interaction is turned off ($g = 0$), the spectrum has a continuous free particle part plus integer excitations. Thus:

$$E_0 = \frac{p^2}{2M} + n_e + n_o = \frac{p^2}{2M} + (n_a + n_b)$$

in the first two descriptions.

When the mass M is sent to infinity we have a fixed-source problem, i.e. two displaced oscillators. All levels are shifted downward by an amount g^2. The Q, φ description is unnatural in the fixed-source limit.

The coordinates that we use provide the basis for the language that is needed to describe the behavior. Different coordinates lead to different pictures of the motion.

It is useful to classify the levels in terms of the exact constant of motion. This leads to still other coordinate choices.

In the running-wave description we introduce new variables by the canonical transformation:

$$A = ae^{iq}, B = be^{-iq}$$

$$p' = p + (a^\dagger a - b^\dagger b), q' = q$$

The number operators are $n_a = a^\dagger a$, $n_b = b^\dagger b$, $N_A = A^\dagger A$, $N_B = B^\dagger B$. Then:

$$G = p'$$

$$H = \frac{1}{2M}(G - (N_A - N_B))^2 + N_A + N_B - \frac{g}{2}(A + A^\dagger + B + B^\dagger)$$

Let us consider the case where $G = 0$. Elementary perturbation theory gives for the spectrum to order $\frac{1}{M}$:

$$E(N_A, N_B) - E_0(N_A, N_B) = -\frac{g^2}{2} + \frac{g^2}{4M}(1 + N_A + N_B)$$

$$E_0(N_A, N_B) = \left(\frac{N_A - N_B}{2M}\right)^2 + N_A + N_B$$

This displays the level structure in the weak coupling and heavy source limit. The higher levels are shifted upward more than the lower levels.

We would like to find the level structure in other domains of the parameter space.

The constants of motion can be introduced in other descriptions. With the rotation:

$$q'_e = q_e \cos q + q_0 \sin q$$

$$q'_0 = -q_e \sin q + q_0 \cos q$$

$$p' = p + (p_0 q_e - q_0 p_e), \quad q' = q$$

we find:

$$H = \frac{1}{2M}\{p' - (p'_0 q'_e - q'_0 p'_e)\}^2 - gq'_e + \frac{p_e'^2 + p_0'^2 + q_e'^2 + q_0'^2 - 1}{2}$$

Finally going to polar coordinates, we have for $p' = 0$:

$$H = -\frac{1}{2M}\frac{\partial^2}{\partial(\varphi')^2} - gQ' \cos \varphi' + D(Q') + \frac{Q'^2}{2} - 1 - \frac{1}{2Q^2}\frac{\partial^2}{\partial\varphi'^2}$$

The wave functions are periodic in φ or φ', but q ranges from $-\infty$ to $+\infty$. In these coordinate systems it is impossible to violate translation invariance.

One can set up the secular equation for the amplitudes in terms of the non-interacting basis functions. For example insertion of:

$$\Psi = \sum_{N_A}\sum_{N_B} C(N_A, N_B/G)\frac{(A^\dagger)^{N_A} (B^{\dagger +})^{N_B}}{\sqrt{N_A!} \sqrt{N_R!}}\Phi_0$$

in the Schrödinger equation gives a five-term difference equation for the coefficients C. The problem is simple enough so that for given values of g and M one can truncate the equations and find the level scheme to desired accuracy. This is indeed what Devreese and Evrard have done.[7] However one does not obtain insight into the behavior in the domain $g \gg 1$, $g\sqrt{M} \gg 1$. This is the region where collective variables come into play and where a systematic strong-coupling expansion is possible.

(b)   The adiabatic approximation

We discuss the problem using the collective phase coordinate φ but we do not introduce the constant of motion explicitly.

The idea of the adiabatic approximation is that when $M \ll 1$ one first sets up the equation for the electronic surfaces, i.e.:

$$\left\{-\frac{1}{2M}\frac{\partial^2}{\partial q^2} - gQ \cos (q - \varphi)\right\}\psi_v(q|Q,\varphi) = \varepsilon_v(Q)\psi_v(q|Q,\varphi)$$

with Q and φ as parameters. This is the Mathieu equation. The ε_v are independent of φ and the wave functions depend only on $q - \varphi$. For an extended-zone scheme the spectrum is put into correspondence with the free-particle spectrum. The lowest state is periodic in $(q - \varphi)$.

The total wave function is now approximated by the product function:

$$\psi_v(q - \varphi|Q)\Phi_n^v(Q,\varphi)$$

One looks for a band associated with the nuclear (i.e. oscillator) motions

Consider the lowest electronic state. Then $\varepsilon_0(Q)$ forms part of the potential for the oscillator function. It obeys:

$$\left\{ D(Q) + \frac{1}{2}Q^2 + \varepsilon_0(Q) + T_{00}(Q) - 1 - \frac{1}{2Q^2}\frac{\partial^2}{\partial\varphi^2} \right\}\Phi^{(0)}(Q,\varphi)$$

$$= E\Phi^{(0)}(Q,\varphi)$$

where:

$$T_{00}(Q) = \frac{1}{2}\int \left[\frac{\partial\psi_0}{\partial Q}(q - \varphi|Q) \right]^2 dq$$

This is the 'extended' Born-Oppenheimer approximation. It results simply by making a variational ansatz of the product form and then varying ψ_0 and $\Phi^{(0)}$ independently.

Now we have a number of auxiliary problems within the framework of the adiabatic approximation. None of them can be solved exactly. By asymptotic analysis of the Mathieu equation we can represent $\varepsilon_0(Q)$ in the form:

$$\varepsilon_0(Q) = -qQ\left\{ 1 - \frac{1}{2\sqrt{gQM^*}} + \frac{1}{32}\frac{1}{gQM^*} + \dots \right\}$$

$$\frac{1}{M^*(Q)} \equiv \frac{1}{M} + \frac{1}{Q^2}$$

Asymptotic analysis also yields:

$$T_{00}(Q) = \frac{1}{64Q^2}\left(\frac{3M + Q^2}{M + Q^2} \right)^2$$

In the next step we study the vibrations and rotations corresponding to each electronic level. We will examine only the lowest electronic band, i.e. $v = 0$. Introduce:

$$\Phi_{v,m}^{(v)} = \frac{1}{\sqrt{Q}}R_{v,m}^{(v)}(Q)\frac{e^{im\varphi}}{\sqrt{2\pi}}$$

Here $m = 0, \pm 1, \ldots$ and v is a vibrational quantum number. Note that the product functions:

$$\psi_v(q - \varphi|Q)\Phi_{v,m}^{(v)}$$

are translation invariant, i.e. exact eigenfunctions of G. We find for the radial functions:

$$\left(-\frac{1}{2}\frac{\partial^2}{\partial Q^2} + U(Q) + \frac{m^2}{2Q^2} - \frac{1}{8Q^2}\right)R_{v,m}^{(0)}(Q) = E_{v,m}^{(0)}R_{v,m}^{(0)}$$

where:

$$U(Q) = \varepsilon_0(Q) + \frac{Q^2}{2} - 1 + T_{00}(Q)$$

We locate the minimum of the potential energy. In first approximation it is at $Q^* = g$, so that the leading term in the total energy is $-\frac{g^2}{2}$. In the next approximation:

$$\bar{Q} = q\left\{1 - \frac{1}{4g\sqrt{M}}\left(1 + \frac{1}{8}\frac{1}{g\sqrt{M}}\right)\right\}$$

One sees that the terms T_{00}, $\frac{m^2}{2Q^2}$, $-\frac{1}{Q^2}$ are all of order $\frac{1}{g^2}$, so the m dependent levels are separated by $\frac{1}{g^2}$.

The elementary strong-coupling theory requires $g \gg 1$, $g\sqrt{M} \gg 1$. Then the minimum is far removed from the origin and the Q range can be taken to be $-\infty$ to $+\infty$. The frequency of the vibration is shifted from 1 to $1 - \frac{1}{16g\sqrt{M}}$. Thus the energies of the states corresponding to the lowest electronic band are:

$$E_{v,m}^{(0)} = -\frac{g^2}{2} + \frac{1}{2}\frac{g^2}{g\sqrt{M}} - \frac{1}{16M} - \frac{1}{2} + 0\left(\frac{1}{g\sqrt{M}}\frac{1}{M}\right)$$
$$+ \left(v + \frac{1}{2}\right)\left(1 - \frac{1}{16g\sqrt{M}}\right) + \frac{m^2}{2g^2}$$

The constant term $-\frac{1}{2}$ is interesting. It corresponds to the removal of the zero point energy of one of the oscillators. It always occurs in an explicitly translation invariant theory. We have again found that the adiabatic (strong coupling) theory based on collective variables has a rich spectrum.

The conclusion is the same that we drew from the three-body problem. Even if the adiabatic approximation is accepted, the systematic strong coupling expansion is not exact. R. E. Langer[8] studied the radial equation for a rotating harmonic oscillator. This analysis leads to $(\log g)/g^2$ terms in the analysis energy spectrum. The adiabatic approximation breaks down first for the higher electronic states and for fast moving particles.

In more general theories that introduce collective variables it is usually impossible to perform the inverse transformation. The regularity conditions on the wave functions are defined in terms of the original variables and imply conditions on the wave functions expressed in terms of the new collective variable. In our simple model they are the periodicity in φ and the behavior at $Q = 0$. Any of the systematic schemes for working in the collective description uses wave functions that are, strictly speaking, inadmissible because they violate the conditions. It is usually impossible to do much about this.

(c)   Transition theories

Let us now ask whether one can find an analytic theory that goes from strong to weak coupling, e.g. fixed, variable g. From the point of view of adiabatic theory we imagine solving the Mathieu equation and the vibration equation for any g and M. It is however clear that non-adiabatic effects prevent one from going to the weak coupling limit with a single-product wave function. On the other hand a simple perturbation calculation (which is easily made variational) using all the adiabatic states should be adequate. This is of course quite complicated. However, one need not have all the details of the strong coupling limit. Consider the translation invariant product function:

$$\psi_0(q - \varphi|\bar{Q})\Phi^{(0)}(Q,\varphi)$$

where $\bar{Q}$ is a suitable average, defined by a variationally calculation. One can define an orthonormal set of excited states and proceed to a complete transition theory. We have not worked out details, but presumably the level scheme will transform smoothly. The main reason for the failure of Hamiltonian transition theories for the polaron to show a smooth transition is the failure to use manifestly translation-invariant wave functions. We are using translation-invariant states for the two-oscillators model.

On the other hand it is interesting that a transition theory for this problem (for the ground state) can be made with ideas that come from the $M \to \infty$ limit. These ideas are intermediate coupling theory or Bloch-Nordsieck transformations and variants of a generalized harmonic approximation. The wave functions are very different from those involved in using extensions of strong coupling approaches.

Consider the problem of determining the ground state energy in the manifestly translation-invariant representation q'_e, q'_0 that is natural in the weak-coupling and fixed-source limit. We dilate the odd-parity oscillator coordinate by introducing:

$$q_0' = Q_0/\sqrt{\Omega_0}$$

Take the expectation value with a wave function:

$$\left(\frac{1}{\pi}\right)^{1/4} \exp\left[-\frac{Q_0^2}{2}\right]$$

This gives a quadratic Hamiltonian for the even-parity oscillator. Introduce a dilation and displacement by:

$$q_e' = \sqrt{1 + \frac{1}{2M\Omega_0}}\left\{Q_e + \frac{q}{1 + \frac{\Omega_0}{2M}}\right\}$$

Taking the expectation value with a wave function:

$$\left(\frac{1}{\pi}\right)^{\frac{1}{4}} \exp\left[-\frac{Q_e^2}{2}\right]$$

we find the ground-state energy:

$$E_G \leqslant \frac{\Omega_e}{2} - \frac{g^2}{2}\frac{1}{(1 + \Omega_0/2M)} + \frac{1}{4}\left(\Omega_0 + \frac{1}{\Omega_0}\right) - \frac{1}{4M} - 1$$

where:

$$\Omega_e^2 = \left(1 + \frac{1}{2M\Omega_0}\right)\left(1 + \frac{\Omega_0}{2M}\right)$$

Next we vary E_G with respect to Ω_0 to find the minimum. It is most convenient to express the resulting condition as:

$$g^2 = M\left(1 + \frac{\Omega_0}{2M}\right)^2\left(\frac{1}{\Omega_0^2} - 1\right)\left(1 + \frac{1}{2M\Omega_e}\right)$$

For given M we let Ω_0 range between 1 and 0, compute Ω_e, and find the appropriate value of g^2.

In the weak coupling limit $\Omega_0 \to 1$, $\Omega_e \to 1 + \frac{1}{2M}$ and we find the intermediate coupling theory result:

$$E_0 \to -\frac{g^2}{2}\frac{1}{\left(1 + \frac{1}{2M}\right)}$$

The strong coupling limit is $g \gg 1$ for fixed M. Then:

$$\Omega_0 \to \frac{M}{g\sqrt{M}}, \quad \Omega_e^2 \to \frac{g\sqrt{M}}{2M^2}$$

The static shift goes from $-\dfrac{g}{1 + \dfrac{1}{2M}}$ to g. The ground-state energy has the expression:

$$E_0 = -\frac{g^2}{2} + \frac{g}{2\sqrt{M}} + \frac{1}{2}\left(\frac{g\sqrt{M}}{2M^2}\right)^{1/2} - \frac{1}{4M}$$

The first two terms agree with the adiabatic theory. The other terms disagree. The adiabatic theory is of course the correct theory for strong coupling.

This type of extension of the weak coupling theory connects to the leading term in strong coupling. In a polaron theory with a fixed lattice cut-off, one reaches the strong coupling limit with a normal mode transformation and a suitable linear shift in the oscillator variable. The mechanism is the same, i.e. the static shift of modes of wave vector k goes from $\dfrac{g}{1 + k^2/2m}$ at weak coupling to g for sufficiently large g and wave vector k less than the fixed cut-off. This means that the dynamic coupling of long wavelength lattice modes to the electron (represented by the normal mode transform) suppresses the recoil denominator of perturbation theory. On the other hand, for given g, sufficiently short-wave modes couple as in perturbation theory. In the polaron theory without a lattice cut-off, all modes up to a wave vector $k \sim g^2$ couple classically, i.e. without a recoil denominator. This explains why the strong coupling energy for the polaron goes as $-g^4$ rather than as $-g^2$ for the two-mode theory.

This type of transition theory for the ground-state energy is not very accurate. If the theory is extended to a study of the entire level scheme, the results are poor in the strong coupling domain. Feynman's path integral calculation of the ground-state energy can also be done for the two-mode model. It gives more accurate results, but it is not a theory of the level structure. On the other hand it would be desirable to have a theory that gives an account of the spectrum on the transition region. At present only the adiabatic theory, based on collective variables, gives the spectrum in the strong coupling region. Within the Hamiltonian scheme, one can probably go to weaker couplings by taking into account the non-adiabatic effects. It would be worthwhile to extend the path integral approach to a theory of the structure of the low-lying levels.

3 Polaron problem

We add a few remarks on the use of collective coordinates in the polaron problem. Consider the particle field Hamiltonian:

$$H = \frac{p^2}{2M} + \int D(\vec{x} - \vec{q})\varphi(x)d\vec{x} + \frac{1}{2}\int (\pi^2 + \varphi^2):d\vec{x}$$

with:

$$[\varphi(\vec{x}), \pi(\vec{y})] = i\hbar\vec{\delta}(\vec{x} - \vec{y})$$

The field $\varphi(x)$ corresponds to an optical branch, i.e. constant frequency for all field oscillators. The source function is:

$$D(x) = g/|x|^2$$

The constant of motion is:

$$\vec{G} = \vec{p} - \int \pi(\vec{x})\vec{\nabla}\varphi(\vec{x})d\vec{x}$$

but there is no good associated collective coordinate. In the weak coupling or heavy source limit it is useful to introduce the Jost transform.

$$\vec{p}' = \vec{p} - \int \pi(\vec{x})\nabla\varphi d\vec{x}, \; \varphi'(x) = \varphi(\vec{x} - \vec{q}), \pi'(x) = \pi(\vec{x} - \vec{q}), \vec{q}' = \vec{q}$$

This is the analogue of the coordinates introduced in the atomic limit and in the weak coupling limit for the two-mode problem.

In the strong coupling limit collective coordinates can be introduced by writing:

$$\varphi(x) = \sum_{v \neq 1,2,3} Q_v X_v(\vec{x} - \vec{R})$$

Here we have an orthonormal set $X_v(x)$. Three of the field oscillators are deleted and replaced by the three $\vec{R}$ collective coordinates. These can be fixed by imagining that one can solve:

$$\int \varphi(x)X_\alpha(x - R)d^3x = 0, \quad \alpha = 1,2,3$$

for $\vec{R}(\varphi)$. The X_α are three (essentially p-wave) functions. This is an idea due to Pekar. It makes possible a strong coupling adiabatic theory which can be carried through without explicitly solving for $\vec{R}$. (See the detailed study by the author.[9])

However $\vec{R}$ is not really a good collective coordinate globally. One sees this by examining the elementary soluble fixed-source problem ($M \to \infty$) for a field $\varphi(x)$. The solution with the coordinates Q_v and $\vec{R}$ is ridiculously complicated. Nonetheless it gives a good strong coupling theory of the low-lying states when $M \ll 1$.

This type of theory can also be done by introducing $\vec{R}$ as extra coordinates and imposing three auxiliary conditions on the wave function. This is the adiabatic theory of Bogolyubov and Tyablikov.[10] It is similar in spirit and predates the collective coordinate theories of

Bohm and Pines and of Zubarev for the more difficult electron gas problem. As applied to the polaron it shares the difficulties and successes of the more explicit Pekar theory.

It is well known that Feynman has given a beautiful path integral theory of the polaron ground state and effective mass.[11] It connects the weak and strong coupling limits and has been used to calculate the mobility, optical absorption and other properties. However, it does not give an account of the strong coupling level structure. In the light of the analysis of the present paper, it is not likely that one will obtain a simple account of the breakdown of the level structure as one proceeds from strong to weak coupling. However, it is an interesting challenge to extend the path integral approach to deal with this type of problem.

References

1   D. Bohm and D. Pines, *Phys. Rev.*, **92**, 607 (1953).
2   D. Bohm in *The Many Body Problem: Cours donné à l'école d'été de physique théorique*, eds. C. De Witt and P. Nozières, Dunod, Paris, 1959, p. 401.
3   D. Bohm and G. Carmi, *Phys. Rev.*, **133A**, 319 and 332 (1964).
4   L. D. Landau, *J. Phys. USSR*, **5**, 71 (1941).
5   W. R. Smythe, *Static and Dymanic Electricity*, McGraw-Hill, New York, 1939.
6   H. Bethe and E. E. Salpeter, *Quantum Mechanics of One and Two Electron Atoms*, Springer Verlag, Berlin, 1957.
7   J. Devreese and M. Evrard, *Phys. Lett.*, **11**, 178 (1949).
8   R. E. Langer, *Phys. Rev.*, **75**, 792, (1949).
9   E. P. Gross, *Ann. of Phys.*, **99**, 1 (1976).
10 N. N. Bogolyubov and S. V. Tyablikov, *ZETF*, **19**, 256 (1949).
11 R. P. Feynman, *Phys. Rev.*, **97**, 660 (1955).

4

The collective description of particle interactions: from plasmas to the helium liquids

David Pines   *University of Illinois at Urbana-Champaign*

Introduction

A plasma, for the physicist, is not a jelly-like substance. It is a gas containing a very high density of electrons and ions. The name 'plasma' for such a gas was coined by the late Irving Langmuir in the course of his theoretical and experimental investigations of gas discharges at General Electric Research Laboratories during the 1920s. In a gaseous discharge, such as one finds in a fluorescent light, only a minute fraction of the atoms present are ionized, that is disassociated into positive ions and electrons; none the less a study of the motion of the ions and electrons shows that many new and interesting phenomena can take place. In most highly-ionized gases, such as one finds in the ionosphere (the layer of free ions and electrons present toward the top of our atmosphere), the motion of the electrons and ions is, in fact, organized to a remarkable extent. The organization takes two forms, neither of which is characteristic of ordinary dilute gases made up of neutral atoms. First, a given particle, ion or electron, does not move independently of its neighbors. Rather, such a particle is always accompanied by a cloud of other particles, which move along with it in such a way as to screen out the electric field produced by its charge. Second, the electrons carry out long-wavelength, high-frequency oscillations, which involve the coherent motion of many thousands of particles. Langmuir's studies of the possibilities for organized behavior in such a system led him to believe that here was a new state of matter – neither solid, liquid or gas. He called it plasma.

A handful of physicists were occupied in studying the behavior of plasmas in the period before the Second World War. For the most part such investigations could be classified as basic research; in other words, physicists studied plasmas out of a sense of curiosity as to their behavior. During the war the size of that group increased somewhat; one of the methods of obtaining separated isotopes of uranium, the so-called calutron, invented at the University of California at Berkeley, involved the use of highly ionized arc sources, i.e. plasmas. Also toward the end of the war, and in the years immediately following it, physicists began to be interested in plasmas as possible devices for the production and amplification of electromagnetic waves in the microwave region. Thus in 1950, at the time I received my PhD degree from Princeton University under David Bohm for a thesis entitled 'The role of plasma oscillations in electron interactions,' there were likely no more than a hundred physicists in this country and abroad who were, in one sense or another, working on plasmas. Some were electrical engineers, working on electron vacuum tubes; some were still concerned with gaseous discharges. Others were astrophysicists, interested not so much in the ionosphere as in the plasma of charged particles which surround the sun, or that very dilute plasma which makes up all of inter-planetary and intergalactic space. Bohm and I were interested in plasmas for yet another reason – as offering a clue to a fundamental understanding of the behavior of electrons in metals.

Today the number of physicists engaged in working on plasmas is in the thousands. There is a Plasmas Physics Division of the American Physical Society; it boasts some 2,000 members and represents only a modest fraction of the physicists and electrical engineers in the United States interested in such problems. This hundred-fold growth in plasma research has been due primarily to the launching of large-scale programs designed to harness the power liberated in the fusion of light atoms at high temperatures. Such attempts at controlled thermonuclear fusion involve the use of plasmas. At the temperatures at which a thermonuclear reactor might operate, the matter within would be a plasma; moreover, the screening action of plasmas permits one to envisage the possibility of a thermonuclear reactor with its interior at millions of degrees centigrade and its walls at room temperature.

Interest in plasmas grew, too, because theoretical physicists came to recognize that an idealized model for a plasma represents a particularly simple, and often soluble, example of a many-body problem. The many-body problem is one of the problems of principal concern to the theoretical physicist today. It may be formally defined as 'a study of the behavior of systems in which the simultaneous presence and interaction of many particles markedly alters their isolated individual behavior.' Less formally, we could describe it as a study of all condensed systems and most gases – that is liquids, solids, plasmas and not-too-dilute gases. The kinds of many-body problems the physicist is interested in range from the behavior of metals to the motion of nucleons in the nucleus and the interior of neutron stars. They comprise the greater part of chemistry, solid-state physics and nuclear physics.

The theoretical physicist who works on a many-body problem such as the plasma would seem, at first sight, to be faced with an insuperable handicap. How can someone who is unable to solve precisely any problem involving the interactions between three bodies hope to solve one involving millions of billions of particles? The theorist's first reaction is to make a virtue of necessity; to hope and expect that just this feature – the large number of particles – will make life simple again. In part it does, in that it makes possible a statistical description of the average behavior of the system; furthermore, the fluctuations about that average behavior are small. However, the use of a statistical description is not in itself enough; the problems under consideration are still too complicated to be understood in precise mathematical detail.

In any approach to understanding the behavior of complex systems, the theorist must begin by choosing a simple, yet realistic, model for the behavior of the system in which he is interested. Two models are commonly taken to represent the behavior of plasmas. In the first, the plasma is assumed to be a fully ionized gas; in other words, as being made up of electrons and positive ions of a single atomic species. The model is realistic for experimental situations in which the neutral atoms and impurity ions, present in all laboratory plasmas, play a negligible role. The second model is still simpler; in it the discrete nature of the positive ions is neglected altogether. The plasma is thus regarded as a collection of electrons moving in a background of uniform positive charge. Such a model can obviously only teach us about electronic behavior in plasmas. It may be expected to account for experiments conducted under circumstances such that the electrons do not distinguish between the model, in which they interact with the uniform charge, and the actual plasma, in which they interact with positive ions. We adopt it in what follows as a model for the electronic behavior of both classical plasmas and the quantum plasma formed by electrons in solids.

In this article I shall try to put in historical perspective the key physical ideas and mathematical approaches which David Bohm and I used in our development of a collective description of electron interactions in metals during the period 1948–53. This work led to the identification of quantized plasma oscillations as the dominant long-wavelength mode of excitation of electrons in most solids. It justified the application of the independent electron model to the low-frequency motion of electrons in metals, and made possible a consistent and accurate calculation of metallic cohesion. I shall then describe briefly how the extension of those ideas to systems of strongly interacting neutral particles, the helium liquids, has, some thirty years later, enabled us to understand effective particle interactions, elementary excitations and transport in the helium liquids. As a result we now possess a unified picture of excitations and transport in both charged and neutral strongly-interacting quantum many-body systems.

From classical to quantum plasmas

Consider a classical plasma; one in which the density and temperature of the electrons are such that their motion may be treated according to the laws of classical mechanics. As we have mentioned, such an electron system displays a high degree of organization, which is manifested in both its screening action and in the coherent high-frequency oscillations known as plasma oscillations. Here we have our first glimpse of the quite different electronic behavior resulting from the many-body character of the problem. We begin with a gas of individual electrons, each of which behaves in isolation as a free particle. We bring the electrons together in a uniform background of positive charge to form the plasma, with, say, an average density of 100 billion electrons per cubic centimeter. We find that as a consequence the electrons no longer behave simply as independent particles; their mutual interaction leads them to screen out any charge disturbance and to carry out the plasma oscillations.

To understand the screening aspect of the plasma, let us imagine that we have established an imbalance of charge distribution over some region in its interior. We might try to do this by trying to build an artificial cage for the electrons out of the uniform positive charge, since the latter has opposite sign to that of the electrons and so attracts them. If we have an equal density of electrons and positive charge, we have overall charge neutrality in our cage. Now we put more electrons into the cage, building up an excess of negative charge. The electrons then experience a strong mutual repulsion, due to their Coulomb interaction. Their reaction will be a violent one. The excess electrons resent the artificial cage into which they have been put, and lose no time in breaking out. They may accomplish their cage-break with ease, because the energy to finance it comes readily from the strong repulsive interaction. As a consequence, any imbalance in the overall charge distribution is unstable, and the electron system will quickly return to the equilibrium state of charge neutrality.

What we have been describing is the suppression of density or charge fluctuations in the plasma by the Coulomb interactions. The Coulomb interaction is remarkable in that the suppression is so efficient, extending over large distances in such a way that even quite long-range density fluctuations are sharply reduced. (In other words, even though we construct a very large cage, a slight imbalance in charge will not be tolerated.) The screening action of the plasma occurs because of the availability of many highly-mobile free electrons, which move so as to cut down and screen out any strong electric fields within its interior.

We have been discussing screening in a macroscopic way; it is also present at the microscopic level. Any given electron in the plasma may, after all, be regarded as producing an imbalance of charge in its immediate neighborhood; its field, therefore, will also be screened out by the motion of the other particles. We may say that the electron thus acts to polarize the plasma; when it moves it is accompanied by a polarization cloud of other particles. The polarization cloud alters the motion of the electron slightly; most important it acts to screen out its field at long distances.

The plasma oscillations come about in the following way. Let us return to our example of the charge imbalance over a given region. When the electrons burst forth from their cage, in general too many electrons will leave, so that within the cage there is now too much positive charge for the number of electrons contained within. The cage then becomes a trap, pulling electrons back in to establish charge neutrality. In fact, too many will come in once more, then go out, back in, etc., corresponding to an oscillation in the density of electrons about the equilibrium position of charge neutrality. In this fashion a plasma oscillation is born. The oscillation is a longitudinal oscillation since the electron density changes in the direction of motion of the wave. It thus corresponds to a sound wave, and does indeed resemble the oscillations observed in a slab of jelly or plasma. The frequency of the oscillations is nearly constant. It is proportional to the electron charge and to the square root of the electronic density. For our plasma of 100 billion electrons per cubic centimeter the frequency of plasma oscillation is in the microwave range.

Thus far we have discussed only the organized aspects of the plasma behavior. These are the aspects which are revealed to us if we study the plasma with coarse-grained observational tools, which give us information only about what is going on over long distances. Were these the only instruments we had available we might conclude that the plasma is a liquid rather than a gas, since it possesses a stable equilibrium state about which it carries out organized oscillations. Such would no longer be the case when we increase the resolving power of our microscope and study what is going on at distances comparable to or slightly larger than the average spacing between the electrons. For such distances the screening action of the plasma is no longer perfect; strong electric fields can and do exist. Further, the organized oscillations are no longer possible, and one merely observes the random effects expected from a gas of individual particles. The plasma is therefore capable of displaying both organized collective behavior, brought about by the forces between the particles, and individual particle behavior, of the kind expected if there were no forces between the particles.

We have argued that the organized behavior of the plasma is of considerable interest. What, however, makes the plasma a particularly interesting object of study is its schizophrenic behavior; depending on the stimulus, it will display either collective or individual particle behavior of the kind we have discussed. One such stimulus is a probe which transfers momentum and energy to the system in a measurable way. In principle we could think of accomplishing the momentum transfer by striking the plasma with a hammer. In practice we might use a charged particle as our probe. We then ask what is the transfer of energy which goes with a given momentum transfer. If we had only a gas of free, non-interacting electrons, the energy transfer would be proportional to the momentum transfer and to the velocity of the electron which received the impact. For a low-momentum probe, therefore, the energy transfer is correspondingly low. The interaction between the electrons alters the situation markedly. The energy transfer in the plasma will be proportional to the frequency of the plasma oscillation and very nearly independent of the momentum, for a small transfer of momentum. The energy transfer is much larger than that obtaining in a gas of non-interacting electrons. We see that the characteristic excitation energy is increased by the Coulomb interactions. Because many electrons are coupled together by the long range of this interaction, as a group they can take up much more energy than would be possible if they acted as individual, uncoupled particles. If, now, we continue to increase the momentum transfer associated with our probe, we eventually reach a point at which this is no longer the case. The momentum transfer to an individual particle yields an energy transfer which becomes comparable with that produced by the collective motion induced by the Coulomb interaction. We have arrived at the region for a transition from collective to individual particle behavior; in such a transition region the system will display a mixture of individual particle and collective behavior which will in general be quite difficult to describe in detail. When we consider a yet higher momentum transfer, we find that the behavior is simple once more, for now the system displays only individual particle behavior, and the effects associated with the interaction between the electrons become unimportant.

Actually the behavior of a plasma is still more subtle than I have indicated. Not only are there regions in which we might say it exhibits primarily wave-like behavior, or primarily particle-like behavior, but within a given regime the two forms of excitation are coupled together. Thus there is a transfer of momentum and energy from the plasma waves to those single particles which move in such a way as to be resonantly coupled to them; we say then the plasma oscillations are damped. Moreover, when a single particle in the plasma moves sufficiently rapidly, it will excite a plasma wave in the form of a wave behind it, in much the same way that a ship leaves a wake which marks its path. At any time, then, waves decay into particles and particles excite waves; such processes continue until the plasma reaches thermal equilibrium, at which time there exists a balance between the two phenomena.

Our discussion of the dual aspects of classical plasma behavior has been intended to prepare the way for a description of the developments which took place in the theory of electron interaction in solids during the decade 1950–60. As we mentioned earlier, the plasma serves as a useful prototype for the other many-body problems, notably for the motion of electrons in solids. This possibility was first recognized by David Bohm at Princeton University in the late 1940s. Bohm had worked on gaseous discharges during the war at the University of California Radiation Laboratory, and came to the conclusion that the plasma offered real possibilities for an improved understanding of the theory of metals. His belief was based on the fact that in a metal, as in a plasma, one dealt with a high density of nearly-free electrons moving in the field of positive ions. One might accordingly hope to describe the metal as a plasma of very high density by replacing the positive ions by a uniform distribution of positive charge. There were two apparent obstacles to the development of a theory of metals based on the plasma. The first was that the density of electrons in a metal is some ten billion times larger than that found in gas discharges. As a result the electrons can no longer be described by the laws of classical mechanics, but must be treated by a theory based on quantum mechanics. We call such a plasma a quantum plasma. Second, the ions in a gas discharge are free to move, while those in a metal oscillate about fixed positions in a lattice. Their equilibrium positions form a periodic array which defines the crystal structure of the lattice. As a result it is no longer clear whether the model in which the influence of the positive ions is replaced by a uniform positive charge will be a realistic model for metallic behavior. Such a simplified model will certainly miss the important role that the periodicity of the ions has upon the electron motion. The question is whether such an omission would prove disastrous to the physical predictions of the theory.

The theory of metals circa 1948

We can better appreciate the situation if we review the status of the theory of metals as of 1948, the year I began my thesis research with Bohm. Shortly after the advent of quantum mechanics, in the period 1928–31, a number of physicists, notably Sommerfeld, Bloch and Wilson, developed a theory of the motion of electrons in metals which had at its basis a one-electron model. In this model primary attention was paid to the motion of a single electron in the periodic field of the ions. The many-body character of the problem was allowed for only in a simple, statistical sense. Thus each electron was assumed to move quite independently of all the other electrons, and explicit correlations in the positions of the electrons brought about by the Coulomb interaction were completely ignored. The one-electron model was chosen, then, to emphasize the role played by the periodic potential of the ions in determining the electron motion. The predictions of the theory turned out to agree well with experiment in a wide variety of instances, including the electrical and thermal conductivities, specific heat and magnetic properties of metals.

Despite the good agreement with experiment, theoretical physicists were not completely happy with the independent-electron model. First of all, they could not understand why it worked so well. Moreover, it did not yield a satisfactory result for one of the most basic physical quantities, the binding energy of electrons in the metal. That it did not do so was scarcely surprising, since the neglect of correlations in the particle positions meant that the electrons, in this description, would have an appreciable chance of being close together. Such close encounters, in turn, added a large positive energy arising from the Coulomb repulsion of the electrons. The energy so added was sufficiently large that most metals, in this approximation, would not be stable, but would disintegrate into individual atoms. The stability of metals therefore had its origin in the correlations brought about by the Coulomb interactions, and it was necessary to devise a method for taking these into account.

The success of the independent-particle model would lead one to suspect that these interactions could easily be included, since they would appear to be only a small perturbation on the motion of the electrons. (Otherwise, why would the electrons behave as if so nearly free?) As things turned out, however, they could not. The first attempts to calculate correction terms led to answers which no longer agreed with experiment for just those properties for which the independent-electron model worked so well. Attempts at a further improvement in the theory, within the framework of regarding the mutual electron interaction as a small perturbation, were even less successful. The answers thereby obtained were infinite – a strong hint to the theoretical physicist that his formulation of the problem was not a consistent one.

Looking back on the situation, we might decide that we were not surprised at this turn in events. We have already seen that in the plasma the Coulomb interactions do modify the motion of the electrons considerably and lead to considerable organization in the overall electronic behavior. We should therefore not expect that a theory of electron motion in metals which virtually ignores these interactions could succeed. We then find that, despite its impressive initial successes, the independent-electron model does not work, and for just the reasons which might have led us not to adopt it in the first place – the interactions between the electrons proved too strong.

Viewed in this light, the attempt to make a plasma theory of metals seems a little less foolish. In a sense such a theory is complementary to the one-electron theory. In the former theory, the interaction between the electrons is viewed as the determining factor for the electronic behavior, while the influence of the periodic potential of the ion cores is regarded as a relatively small effect. In the latter, the situation was simply reversed; the periodic potential of the ions was taken into account, the intereactions being regarded as weak.

The collective description of electron interaction in metals

The plasma theory of metals was developed by Bohm and the writer during the years 1948–53. Its genesis was the classical plasma, and its results may be easily understood in terms of the concepts we have already introduced for that system, plasma oscillation and screening. The theory was based on our recognition that, just as in the classical case, the Coulomb interaction between the electrons gave rise to plasma oscillations. We felt the oscillations played a decisive role; our problem was how to construct a theory of metals in which their existence was explicitly recognized. Because in the conventional mathematical formulation the only variables which appear are those which describe the motion of single electrons, it was necessary, first, to find the collective variables which described plasma waves, and, second, to devise a mathematical formulation in which both collective and individual particle variables appeared. In other words, we had first to invent a new language and second to find a way to apply that language to the problem at hand.

The clues essential to the development of our theory came from two directions: from an analysis of the behavior of transverse electromagnetic waves in a quantum plasma; and from a direct examination of the behavior of longitudinal density fluctuations in the quantum plasma. We found that if we constructed a description of longitudinal electric waves which was the longitudinal counterpart of the conventional treatment of the transverse electromagnetic wave, we could, in a suitable approximation, solve the resulting problem and obtain a collective mode, the plasma oscillation, which had a dispersion relation (i.e. dependence of its frequency on the wavelength of the oscillatory mode) which was identical to that we were able to calculate directly from the quantum-mechanical equation of motion for the fluctuations in the plasma density. We arrived in this way at two independent ways of constructing a collective description of the quantum plasma: one was an explicit construction of a combination of particle coordinates which would oscillate collectively; the other was based on a formal problem which appeared, at first sight, to be quite different from that with which we had started, in that there was present at the outset a collection of waves in interaction with the electrons. The coordinates of the wave field were chosen as a vehicle for describing the quantum plasma oscillations; the number of such coordinates we introduced and the way in which these interacted with the individual electrons was chosen in such a way as to render the resulting problem soluble.

In both approaches we were able to see that at very long wavelengths the collective behavior must dominate, and that the major consequence of the long-range part of the Coulomb interaction between the electrons was to give rise to collective modes, the plasma oscillations. In both approaches, too, we could see that at short wavelengths the system would behave as a collection of individual particles which interacted only weakly. The approach in which wave field coordinates were introduced explicitly was in many ways the more powerful one, in that we could specify quite easily the transition from collective to individual-particle behavior, and determine explicitly the resulting interaction between the particles once the part of the Coulomb interaction responsible for the collective modes had been taken into account. It possessed the further advantage that the collective modes (the plasma oscillations) and the individual electrons were treated on an equal footing; it possessed the disadvantage that it appeared that we had over-described the system by introducing too many degrees of freedom. We therefore had to devise arguments as to how a set of subsidiary conditions, which related the field coordinates to the particle coordinates, might automatically be satisfied. Our inability to come up with a simple mathematical proof that these subsidiary conditions could, in fact, be satisfied (put another way, would not cause any difficulties and could safely be ignored) delayed our publication of this formulation by some three years. It caused us to devise several other approaches to the problem (such as a method of self-consistent fields for calculating plasma oscillations which I included in my thesis) before we had sufficient confidence in our physical intuition to write up our results for publication as the third in our series of papers dealing with the description of electron interaction.

The success of the collective description hinged on two factors. First of all, the new problem had to be easier to solve than the old. There was no point in inventing a new 'model' problem for a plasma if it were to be plagued by the same difficulties present in the original one. Second, it was important to show that the solution of the new electron *and* wave field problem was, in fact, equivalent to a solution of the original problem of interacting electrons only. Our expectations for the theory proved, in time, correct in both respects.

It was possible, by a series of mathematical transformations, to relate the coordinates which were introduced to describe the wave field to the collective variables developed to describe the plasmons.

Moreover we could, within a well-defined method of approximation, decouple completely the plasma waves from the electrons so that the long-wavelength plasmons represented an independent well-defined excitation mode of the system. The model was thus an 'independent plasma wave' model, in contrast with the independent electron model discussed above. The introduction and isolation of the plasma waves served to redescribe almost completely the long-range part of the electron–electron interaction. What remained was a screened inter-action with a quite short range, of the order of the average spacing between the electrons.

Herein lay the beauty and the utility of the approach. It explicitly recognized at the outset the novel feature introduced by the long range of the Coulomb interaction, the high-frequency plasma waves. Once these were properly accounted for, what was left was comparatively simple to understand and treat mathematically; namely a collection of individual electrons interacting via a short-range interaction. Indeed, this was just what was required to put the 'one-electron' model of metals on a more satisfactory footing. Because of the short range of the effective particle interaction, the mathematical divergences which had haunted previous attempts at constructing a consistent treatment of an electron interaction were no longer present. It was therefore pos-sible to apply perturbation theory to compute the way the interaction between the electrons altered the ground-state energy of the system. Such a calculation led directly to a calculation of the cohesive energy of electrons in metals; it was found that simple metals were now stable, and that the binding energies calculated theoretically were in good agreement with those observed experimentally.

Next, it was possible to compute the effect of electron interaction on the motion of a single electron. What one finds thereby is a *quasi-particle*; that is, a particle whose motion resembles that of a free electron, but differs from it in that its various physical properties are somewhat altered as a consequence of the electron–electron interac-tion. A simple physical picture of a quasi-particle is that of an electron plus its associated screening cloud of other particles. The alteration in the electron's physical properties are then to be attributed to the pres-ence of that co-moving screening cloud. Thus, the independent plasma-wave model leads directly to an independent quasi-particle model. The calculated quasi-particle properties were, for the most part, in good quantitative agreement with experiment.

Plasmons

The plasma theory of metals predicted the existence of a quite new effect, the excitation of plasma waves by fast electrons passing through a metal. In this process the quantum character of the plasma waves plays an essential role. According to the laws of quantum mechanics, the energy in a given plasma-wave mode can change only in discrete amounts, or quanta. It is therefore convenient to go over from a wave description of the plasma oscillations, in which one thinks of waves with a frequency v and wavelength λ, to a particle description, in which one specifies the plasma wave mode by the number of quanta present, of energy, hv, and momentum, h/λ, where h is Planck's constant.

The basic quantum of plasma oscillation we shall call a plasmon. Because the frequency of the plasma oscillations is high, the energy of a plasmon turns out to be rather large. It ranges from about 6 electron volts to 25 electron volts, and is always greater than the energy that the most energetic single electron in the metal possesses. As a result, plasma oscillations will not be internally excited in metals because no internal electron can transfer to the plasma waves the energy required to excite a single plasmon. Such excitation could, however, occur when a charged particle which has energy large compared to that of a plasmon passes through a metal. In fact, as Conyers Herring pointed out to us in the early stages of our investigation, the basic experiments which confirmed our prediction of the existence of plasma oscillations in metals had already been carried out some years earlier. The relevant experimental data had thus been obtained; all that was required was our interpretation of it in terms of plasmon excitation.

The experiments had been carried out by two German physicists, Ruthemann and Lang, in the early 1940s. Their experimental arrangement was quite simple. They fired electrons through a thin metallic foil and measured the energy of those electrons emerging almost undeflected by the foil. Similar experiments on the reflection of electrons by metal surfaces had been carried out some years earlier by the Swedish physicist, Rudberg. The Ruthemann-Lang experiment required a careful measurement of the energy of both the incident electrons and those emerging from the foil, since the incident electrons had an initial energy some hundred times larger than the energy transferred to the foil. What was surprising about their experimental results was the sharpness with which the energy transfer to the metallic electrons took place in the case of certain metals, notably aluminum and beryllium. Thus the characteristic energy-loss spectrum for Be and Al consists of several comparatively narrow lines, in multiples of a basic loss quantum, approximately 19 eV for Be and 15 eV for Al. When we attempted, in the simplest possible fashion, to interpret this data as plasmon excitation, we received a delightful surprise. The energy transfers were just those to be expected for plasmon excitation, provided we regarded the outermost, or valence, electrons in each metal as free.

Such good agreement between experiment and the simplest plasma theory was most heartening, and yet it was also a little puzzling. Consideration of electrical conductivity and allied experimental phenomena shows that in this latter class of experiments the outermost electrons cannot all be regarded as free. During the next few years, many more such characteristic-energy-loss experiments produced results that agreed closely with the predictions from this simplest version of our model, including semi-metals such as Bi and Sb, semiconductors such as Si and Ge, and compounds ranging from ZnS to SiO_2 and mica. For these materials, too, the outermost electrons could not be regarded at first sight as making up a free-electron plasma. The puzzle is related to the question we raised earlier – that of whether our replacement of the periodic potential of the positive ions by a uniform positive charge was a realistic model for metallic behavior. For it is just the influence of the periodic potential which gives rise to the distinction between metals, semiconductors and insulators, and which further causes the outermost electrons in metals like aluminum and beryllium to seem far from free.

The explanation was provided by Neville Mott during the Tenth Solvay Congress in Brussels in 1954. Mott pointed out that it does make a difference whether we discuss the electrical conductivity of a solid or its possible plasma behavior. When we talk about the electrical conductivity we are asking a low-frequency question of the electrons; that is, a question in which the field of the positive ions, which gives rise to comparatively low-frequency effects, may be expected to play an important role. On the other hand, in discussing electron energy losses, we are asking a question of the electrons at a frequency of the order of magnitude of the free-electron plasma frequency for the outermost electrons. This frequency is typically quite high compared to the characteristic frequency associated with the influence of the periodic ionic potential on the electrons. As a result the electrons in responding at such a high frequency essentially pay no attention to the fact that there is a periodic ion field acting. They are moving too fast to feel the effect of the positive ions, or, to put it another way, they move so fast that they cannot distinguish between the ions in a periodic array and a uniform positive charge of equal overall density.

Mott argued that in aluminum and beryllium, in particular, one should expect to find a plasma frequency which is high compared to the characteristic periodic potential frequencies, so that plasma oscillations at the free-electron frequency should occur. As we have seen, such is indeed the case. One may easily extend these considerations to other solids. One finds that plasma oscillations at nearly the free-electron plasma frequency should be a quite general property of solids, since the frequencies that lead to a distinction between metals, insulators and semiconductors are usually all low compared to the plasma frequency.

By 1956 both the theoretical arguments and the experimental evidence for plasma oscillations as the dominant long-wavelength mode of excitations in most solids had progressed to the point that at the Maryland Conference on quantum interactions of the free electron I proposed the term 'plasmon' to describe the associated quantum of elementary excitation, and could demonstrate that characteristic-energy-loss experiments provided information on plasmon energies, lifetimes and dispersion, as well as the critical wave vector beyond which plasmons could no longer be regarded as well-defined elementary excitations (an effect usually arising from the decay of plasmons into single-pair excitations). In 1957 Robert Ritchie proposed the existence of surface plasmons associated with the waves of charge bound at a vacuum–solid interface, and subsequent experiments provided ample evidence for the existence of these excitations as well. Indeed, with the increasing sophistication of both electron energy-loss techniques and vacuum techniques, plasmons are now often used as a diagnostic tool to study oxidation and the electronic structure of new materials.

Finally, it should be pointed out that, just as was the case for the classical plasma, there is a continual transfer of momentum and energy between the plasmons in a solid and quasi-particles; as a consequence the plasmons possess a finite lifetime, which depends on the quasi-particle spectrum of the solid under consideration. None the less, that lifetime is sufficiently long in most solids that the plasmons are observed, and the plasmon joins the quasi-particle as a well-defined elementary excitation.

The random phase approximation

The basic approximation which Bohm and I made, both in our studies of the equations of motion of density fluctuations and in our collective description of plasma waves plus single particles, we called at first the plasma approximation. We later changed the name to random phase approximation (RPA). The latter name better described what we were doing, which was to neglect the couplings between density fluctuations or plasma waves of different wavelengths, because such coupling involved the sum over an exponential term with randomly varying phases; a sum which would, on average, vanish, and which was small compared to the terms of order, the number of particles, N, which we kept in our description. In this approximation, which we were able to justify rigorously in the limit of long wavelengths (where all the difficulties with the perturbation theory treatment of the Coulomb interaction arose), the plasma modes could be decoupled from the individual electrons; what remained was a system of electrons interacting via a short-range interaction, a system which *was* amenable to a perturbation-theoretic treatment.

The random phase approximation has subsequently been widely used in many-body problems, ranging from studies of oscillations of particles in the outer shells of atoms to the behavior of quark matter. The first of its many applications in nuclear physics came in work which my student, Mel Ferentz, and I carried out on a derivation of the giant dipole resonance in nuclei from the basic nucleon–nucleon interaction. (Because Ferentz developed other interests, only a brief account of this work was published, in a 1953 letter to the *Physical Review*, written in collaboration with Murray Gell-Mann, who had suggested to us a useful way of going from oscillations in nuclear matter to finite nuclei; our approach therefore had little impact on the nuclear physics community until it was reinvented by G. E. Brown and M. Bolsterli some seven years later.) It has proved so useful because, like the Hartree and Hartree-Fock approximations, it is relatively straightforward to apply. More importantly, it is the lowest-order systematic approximation which enables one to test whether well-defined collective modes might appear; where these do appear, they are treated on an equal basis with the single-particle modes.

In all versions of the RPA, the collective behavior arises as a result of the influence of the average self-consistent field of the other particles on the motion of a given particle. Viewed from this perspective, the RPA can be considered as a time-dependent mean-field theory. It appeared in three very different guises in the course of work done during the period 1956–8, a period of especially intense theoretical activity on the quantum plasma. Murray Gell-Mann and Keith Brueckner used diagrammatic techniques, similar to those employed by Richard Feynman in field theory, to carry out a calculation of the correlation energy and specific heat that was exact in the high-density limit, while John Hubbard used a similar approach to show how the results that Bohm and I had obtained could be directly derived from perturbation theory, and went on to develop an alternative approach to the calculation of the correlation energy at metallic electron densities which yielded results similar to those we had obtained earlier. Although plasma oscillations nowhere appeared in the calculations of Gell-Mann and Brueckner, Keith Brueckner, K. Sawada, N. Fukuda and Robert Brout subsequently developed yet another approach, involving a new set of collective modes, and then showed that the Gell-Mann and Brueckner approach contained them implicitly. Further, their calculation was equivalent to applying the random phase approximation for all momentum transfers, rather than simply the low-momentum transfers for which Bohm and I had introduced it.

The circle was closed when Philippe Nozières and I were able to prove that the low-momentum-transfer part of the correlation energy calculated using the Bohm-Pines collective description gave results identical to those of Gell-Mann, Brueckner and Hubbard, and to demonstrate the way in which the random phase approximation breaks down if one attempts to use it for large-momentum transfers at metallic electron densities, a point which had always been emphasized by Bohm and myself. As Nozières and I subsequently remarked:

> The development, frequent independent rediscovery, and gradual appreciation of the random phase approximation for the electron gas . . . offers a useful object lesson to the theoretical physicist; it both illustrates the splendid variety of ways that can be developed for saying the same thing, and it suggests the usefulness of learning more than one 'language' of theoretical physics, and of attempting the reconciliation of seemingly different but obviously related results.

The helium liquids

Liquids made up of the isotopes of helium, helium-3 and helium-4, are unique in nature. No matter what the temperature to which they are cooled (at atmospheric pressure), their liquid form is preserved. The physical origin of this behavior is the quantum-mechanical zero-point motion of the low-mass individual atoms, which is so large as to overcome the physical effects responsible for the solidification of all other liquids at sufficiently low temperatures. The helium liquids are true quantum liquids, in that one must simultaneously take into account the strong interaction between the individual atoms and the underlying quantum statistics which the atoms as a whole must obey. Thus, although the particle interactions in ^{3}He and ^{4}He are essentially the same, and although neutron and X-ray scattering experiments show that the microscopic structure is quite similar, ^{3}He, which obeys Fermi-Dirac statistics, and ^{4}He, which obeys Bose-Einstein statistics, behave quite differently at temperatures low compared to the 'quantum' temperatures, 3–4 K, at which the de Broglie wavelength of a particle becomes comparable to the inter-particle spacing. Thus at 2.19 K, ^{4}He exhibits a phase transition from its 'normal' phase to a new 'superfluid' phase in which its viscosity is essentially unmeasurable, while the corresponding phase transition for ^{3}He occurs only at temperatures in the millikelvin range.

Soon after our initial work on the quantum plasma (which, because the electrons possess charge and obey Fermi-Dirac statistics, is a charged Fermi liquid), David Bohm and I sought to apply our approach to understanding the spectrum of density fluctuations in neutral quantum liquids. We were particularly interested in superfluid ^{4}He, whose spectrum Landau had shown would consist of phonons, a long-wavelength sound-like mode, and rotons, an excitation found at wavelengths comparable to the inter-particle spacing. We ran into difficulties because we were not able to devise a way of dealing with the short-range, but very strong, repulsion between the helium atoms. In the random phase approximation the restoring force for an oscillation at a given wavelength is the corresponding Fourier transform of the bare particle interaction; for liquid ^{4}He the restoring force, as calculated in the random phase approximation, is unphysically large.

Theoretical work during the 1950s strongly suggested that the physical origin of the restoring force responsible for the elementary excitation in liquid ^{3}He and ^{4}He was closely tied to quantum statistics. Feynman showed how, starting from a ground state described by a condensate (the macroscopically-occupied single-quantum state responsible for the superfluid behavior of liquid ^{4}He, the existence of which is a natural consequence of the Bose-Einstein statistics obeyed by the ^{4}He atoms), one could derive the phonon–roton spectrum proposed by Landau, which was then measured directly in neutron-scattering experiments at the end of the decade. Landau, in his Fermi liquid theory, showed that for very long wavelengths and low temperatures, a Fermi liquid such as ^{3}He would be expected to possess a *zero-sound* mode (subsequently found experimentally by John Wheatly) as a result of restoring forces directly tied to the interaction between quasi-particles. Collective modes in the helium liquids thus appeared to be quite different from the long-wavelength plasma modes, which are *not* sensitive to quantum statistics. Because the plasma frequency is extremely large compared to those of the single-particle modes, it is not influenced by whether the underlying single-particle spectrum is that of a normal metal, a superconductor or a high-temperature classical Maxwell–Boltzmann gas of the same density.

This picture of the helium liquids began to change in 1965, after David Woods, in a neutron-scattering experiment, found that in superfluid liquid ^{4}He comparatively high-energy (~ 8 K) phonons not only displayed essentially no change in energy between $T = 0$ and $T = 2.19$ K but remained a well-defined elementary excitation of normal liquid ^{4}He, with comparatively little shift in energy, up to temperatures near 4 K. Hence such excitations did not depend for their existence on the presence of a condensate. I therefore concluded in 1965 that the physical origin of the phonon–roton excitation in liquid ^{4}He and the zero-sound mode in liquid ^{3}He was not to be found in the quantum statistics obeyed by the individual atoms, but rather in the strong (and quite similar) particle interaction. I used linear response theory to show how one could describe that restoring force phenomenologically, and hence generalize the random phase approximation for the Bose liquid, ^{4}He, and extend Landau's theory to higher temperatures and wavelengths for the Fermi liquid, ^{3}He. I argued that the restoring forces responsible for the phonon–roton spectrum of ^{4}He must be very nearly the same as those responsible for zero sound in ^{3}He, and suggested that it should prove possible to observe zero sound in ^{3}He as a well-defined elementary excitation at temperatures and wavelengths for which Landau's Fermi liquid theory would clearly not be applicable.

The key to that explanation (and prediction) was the idea that the restoring force for the collective modes in both helium liquids should be derived from an effective phenomenological pseudopotential, rather than the bare-atom potential which Bohm and I had used in our application of the random phase approximation to neutral quantum liquids. Subsequently, my student, Charles Aldrich, and I developed a detailed physical model for the configuration space pseudopotentials responsible for these collective modes, a model in which the very strong, almost hard-core, repulsive bare-atom interaction would, as a consequence of short-range particle correlation, be replaced in the liquid by a soft-core repulsion, while the long-range part of the bare-atom interaction would be essentially unchanged on going from the gas to the liquid. We calculated in 1974 and 1975 the phonon–roton spectrum for liquid ^{4}He and the expected zero-sound spectrum for ^{3}He. We obtained agreement with experiment for the excitation spectrum of ^{4}He, while our predicted detailed dispersion curve for zero sound in ^{3}He was confirmed the following year in experiments carried out at the Argonne reactor by Kurt Sköld, Charles Pelizzari, R. Kleb and G. Ostrowski. Sköld and his collaborators then went on to show that, in accord with my 1965 prediction, the measured zero-sound energy spectrum scarcely changed as the ^{3}He sample was warmed up from 0.04 K (where the ^{3}He is a well-defined Fermi liquid for which Landau's theory is applicable) to 1.28 K (where the Fermi surface is no longer well-defined and Landau's theory does not apply).

Thus, some twenty-five years after Bohm and I had first proposed that strong particle interaction could, in neutral systems, give rise to a distinct collective mode, analogous to the plasma oscillation of a charged quantum liquid (and ten years after I had defined the circumstances under which this might come about, and demonstrated its applicability to liquid ^{4}He), this idea was found to apply to liquid ^{3}He. It has, moreover, proved possible to develop a unified theory of excitations and transport in both ^{3}He and ^{4}He based on the pseudopotential which Aldrich and I had constructed.

We may therefore conclude that the key to understanding strongly interacting many-body systems, be they plasmas or the helium liquids, is to take into account at the outset the very strong restoring forces responsible for the existence of well-defined collective modes; what remains are a collection of nearly independent quasi-particles whose effective interactions can be described by scattering amplitudes which are related to the restoring forces responsible for the collective modes. We may thereby understand the nature of the collective modes, the transition from collective behavior to single-particle-like behavior and the interactions between the 'residual' quasi-particles on the same basis for both classical and quantum plasmas and for the quantum and semi-classical helium liquids ^{3}He and ^{4}He. The vision which Bohm and I shared of a unified collective descriptive of particle interaction in both charged and neutral strongly-interacting many-body systems has thus been realized.

Afterword

The alert reader may have noticed changes in style and level of presentation as the article unfolds. The disparities are not accidental. The first part of the article is based on an unpublished chapter of a book I began to write in the mid-1960s. In this chapter I had hoped to describe for the layman how theoretical physicists actually work, how a unified theory develops out of the interplay between physical concepts and mathematical calculation between theory and experiment, and between theorist and theorist. I found the task difficult, if not impossible, and put the book aside. The second part of the article represents a present-day attempt on my part to give the interested reader a sense of recent related developments in the helium liquids and is based in part on an article, 'Elementary excitations in quantum liquids,' which appeared in the November 1981 issue of *Physics Today*.

It gives me great pleasure to contribute this article to a Festschrift which honors David Bohm, who taught me so many of the concepts I have described herein. As teacher, collaborator and friend, David Bohm introduced me to the primacy of physical ideas and physical intuition in physics; he taught me the importance of examining a given problem from many different perspectives, and of using whatever mathematical techniques are needed to test physical ideas. I am grateful for his initial guidance not only in doing theoretical physics. but in a way of working as a theoretical physicist.

The support of the National Science Foundation, through grant NSF DMR82-15128 during part of the preparation of this manuscript, is gratefully acknowledged.

5

Reflections on the quantum measurement paradox

A. J. Leggett   *University of Illinois at Urbana-Champaign*

Abstract

Consideration of the classic measurement paradox of quantum mechanics raises the question: What is the relationship between acceptable theories of the physical world at different levels? It is suggested that it is similar to the relationship between maps of different types and that, while theories at different levels need not be derivable from one another, they must at least be mutually consistent in their predictions. The relationship between quantum mechanics, in its standard interpretation, and classical physics fails this test. Existing attempts to resolve the measurement paradox are briefly reviewed, and it is suggested that one avenue has been insufficiently explored; namely, the possibility that the *complexity* of a physical system may itself be a relevant variable which may introduce new physical principles. Possible reasons for this lacuna are discussed, and it is pointed out that some of the relevant questions are now within the reach of an experimental test.

In this essay I shall try to defend three claims. The first is that the classic quantum measurement paradox, so far from being a non-problem, is a sufficiently glaring indication of the inadequacy of quantum mechanics as a total world-view that it should motivate us actively to explore the likely direction in which it will break down. The second is that, as a consequence of ingrained reductionist prejudices and perhaps to some extent of sociological factors, we may have been looking in precisely the wrong direction. And the third is that we are already at the threshold of some very significant experiments in what just might turn out to be the right direction. The third claim is one which I have discussed rather extensively elsewhere, so I will deal with it here rather briefly, without much technical detail.

Let us remind ourselves briefly what the quantum measurement paradox is all about. A quantum-mechanical system drawn from an ensemble in a pure state is, according to the axioms as presented in most textbooks, most completely characterized by a wave function ψ, which may or may not be an eigenfunction of any particular quantity we wish to measure on it. Suppose it is not, and that the quantity in question is described by an operator $\hat{A}$ with eigenfunctions φ_i and eigenvalues a_i. Then in the standard way we write ψ as a linear combination of the φ_i (the structure of the theory guarantees that this can always be done):

$$\psi = \sum_i c_i \varphi_i \qquad [1]$$

and the prediction is then that, if the measurement in question is actually performed, the probability of obtaining the result a_i is $|c_i|^2$. Once the result a_i has been obtained, the system must be assigned (in the case of an 'ideal' measurement) to a new ensemble whose wave function is φ_i. However, it is *not* correct to think of the description [1] as implying that before the measurement the system was already in some (unknown) one of the ensembles whose wave functions are φ_i (i.e., in technical language, that its density matrix corresponded to a 'mixture' of the φ_i). To demonstrate the incorrectness of this conclusion (or rather its incompatibility with the usual interpretation of quantum mechanics) it is sufficient to consider the results of a measurement of some quantity $\hat{B}$ which fails to commute with $\hat{A}$. In general the 'mixture' description will predict a result quite different from that which one would expect on the basis of the pure-state wave function of equation [1].

There are, of course, a number of well-known thought-experiments which illustrate this feature of quantum mechanics, of which the best-known is probably the classic Young's slits experiment. In this case the operator $\hat{A}$ in effect has eigenvalues corresponding to passage through one or the other of the two slits in the first screen, and the quantity $\hat{B}$ is the position of arrival at the detecting screen. (Or more precisely the operator which evolves into this under the time evolution of the system; see reference 1, equation [4.4].) Actually, an even more spectacular experiment has been carried out in real life recently using a neutron interferometer.[2] In this experiment a beam of spin-polarized neutrons was split into two beams, well separated from one another in space; the spins of the neutrons in one beam were flipped and the beams then allowed to recombine. By blocking off one beam at a time it was possible to examine the properties of the other at the point of recombination, and in this way it was explicitly established that the spin properties of the complete ensemble (the recombined beams) were quite different from those of the mixture of the two sub-ensembles (the separated beams). Since the average flux of neutrons was low enough that the probability of two being close enough to affect one another's dynamics was totally negligible, this experiment provides rather spectacular confirmation of the conclusion that one should not think of the neutron as 'being in' one or other beam until it has actually been measured to be so.

So, crudely speaking, even in situations where a measurement will reveal a microscopic system to have one of a set of possible values of a variable, quantum mechanics forbids us to conclude that it actually *had* that value before the measurement was made. This picture is no doubt paradoxical (in the original meaning of the term, 'against expectation') and might lead us to *guess* that we will some day obtain a more intuitively pleasing description, but in itself it is not obviously internally inconsistent, nor does it lead in any obvious way to any discrepancy with our everyday view of the macroscopic world – *provided* that we are prepared to accept the notion of 'measurement' as given from outside the theory. Indeed, Bohr,[3] and with greater sophistication Reichenbach,[4] were able to develop an interpretation of the quantum-mechanical formalism which is consistent within its self-imposed limits precisely by postulating a radically different ontological status for microscopic entities such as electrons or neutrons and the macroscopic apparatus which performs the measurement. In the words of a famous quotation from Bohr: 'Atomic systems should not even be thought of as possessing definite properties in the absence of a specific experimental set-up designed to measure these properties.' On the other hand, Bohr also maintains that in order to secure unambiguous communication of our results, we *must* describe the macroscopic apparatus and its behavior in the language of classical physics (in which, of course, the apparatus must possess definite properties). Thus, it is the act of measurement that is the bridge between the microworld, which does not by itself possess definite properties, and the macroworld, which does. Indeed, according to most textbooks it is the act of measurement which causes the 'collapse of the wave function' from a linear superposition into an eigenstate of the measured quantity. Thus, the concept of measurement is, *prima facie* at least, absolutely central to the interpretation of the quantum-mechanical formalism.

Now, the problem is not that quantum mechanics itself provides no criterion for when a measurement has taken place. That would not necessarily matter if we could find some criterion elsewhere (and, as we shall see, some alleged resolutions of the measurement paradox do in effect try to do just this). The problem is that quantum mechanics *absolutely forbids* a measurement to take place, if by a 'measurement' is meant a process which has the features ascribed to it in the standard textbook account. This statement needs some amplification. The point is that, if we believe (as most physicists at least implicitly seem to) that quantum mechanics is a universal theory, then it applies not only to single atoms and molecules but to arbitrarily large and complex collections of them, and in particular to the special collections which we have chosen to use as measuring devices (photographic plates, Geiger counters, etc.). So, although it is not obviously *necessary* to describe these objects, and their interaction with the microsystems whose properties are to be measured, in explicitly quantum-mechanical terms, it is at any rate *legitimate* to do so. Let us then initially (for the sake of simplicity of exposition only) assume that the measuring device starts in an initial state which is represented by a quantum mechanical wave function Ψ_0. As before, we suppose that the property of the microscopic system which is to be measured is represented by a quantum-mechanical operator $\hat{A}$ with eigenfunctions φ_i and eigenvalues a_i. Suppose, first, that a particular microsystem entering the apparatus is drawn from an ensemble whose quantum state is represented by the wave function φ_i. Then, if we are to be able to read off the value of a_i from the behavior of the macroscopic measuring device, the interaction between the microsystem and the device must induce the latter to make a transition into a different state, with a wave function we shall label Ψ_i. (It is possible that one (but no more than one) of the Ψ_i is identical to Ψ_0, in which case we speak of a 'negative-result' measurement. This feature in no way affects the general argument.) Moreover, the different states Ψ_i must be not only mutually orthogonal but also distinguishable by purely macroscopic measurements (e.g. inspection with the naked eye). (A discussion (considerably more sophisticated than the above one, cf. below) of how some common measuring devices fulfil this condition is given in reference 5.) At the end of the measurement process the 'universe' (system plus apparatus) is in a pure state χ which (for an 'ideal' measurement) is a product of φ_i and Ψ_i, i.e.:

$$\varphi_i\Psi_0 \rightarrow \varphi_i\Psi_i \equiv \chi_{un}^{(i)} \qquad [2]$$

The properties of the 'universe' are, as we have noted, *macroscopically* different for the different values of i. Now, what happens in the case that the microsystem was drawn from an ensemble whose quantum state is the linear superposition [1]? Quite irrespective of the details of the systems involved, it is a general feature of the quantum-mechanical formalism that if, under specified conditions, an initial state $\chi_i^{(0)}$ evolves into a final state χ_i, then a given superposition $\Sigma c_i\chi_i^{(0)}$ will evolve into the corresponding superposition of final states, i.e. into $\Sigma c_i\chi_i$. Thus, from [2], we have:

$$\left(\sum_i c_i\varphi_i\right)\Psi_0 \rightarrow \sum_i c_i\varphi_i\Psi_i \equiv \sum_i c_i\chi_{un}^{(i)} \qquad [3]$$

The right-hand side of [3] is a linear superposition of states of the universe possessing *macroscopically different* properties. If we interpret a linear superposition at the macroscopic level in the same way as we

have learned to do at the microlevel, then the only possible interpretation of [3] is that the macroscopic state of the universe is not
well-defined until some *further*, unspecified, 'measurement' is performed. In other words, the notion of 'measurement' has on closer
inspection dissolved before our eyes; there is no magic ingredient in
the process of interaction of a microsystem with a measuring device
which could lead to the reduction of the wave packet postulated in
the standard textbook discussions of the axioms of quantum mechanics.

It is necessary to remark that the above discussion of the quantum-
mechanical description of the measurement process is, of course, quite
naive. In the first place, in real life we rarely if ever know enough
about the initial state of the apparatus to assign to it a single pure
quantum-mechanical state, and would need in practice to describe it
by a density matrix; the final state of the universe would therefore
also be described by an appropriate density matrix. Secondly, the case
where the state of the microsystem is unchanged by its interaction
with the measuring device ('ideal' measurement) is the exception rather
than the rule, and the description of the final state may have to be
modified to allow for this. Thirdly, the measuring device is in practice
itself an open system which interacts with outside influences such as
the vacuum electromagnetic field, and the 'universe' which is described
by the superposition [3] (or the appropriate density-matrix generalization) contains many other such degrees of freedom. These are
technical details which do not (at least in the present author's opinion)
in any way blunt the force of the paradox, and will not be discussed
here. (For a conclusive refutation of the conjecture that taking account
of the first feature would resolve the paradox, see reference 6. The
second feature has never to my knowledge been exploited in any
alleged resolution. The third, which has, is discussed by implication
below.)

The quantum measurement paradox, then, consists in the fact that
an extrapolation of the quantum-mechanical formalism to the scale of
the macro-world leads under certain circumstances to a description,
namely equation [3], which is *prima facie* quite incompatible with
the commonsense everyday picture we have of the world around us.
In a nutshell, in quantum mechanics events don't (or don't necessarily)
happen, whereas in our everyday world-view they certainly do: the
Geiger counter does or does not fire; the photographic plate is or is
not blackened at a definite point; and so on. So the first question we
might ask ourselves is: Why should we find this state of affairs even
surprising, let alone intellectually intolerable? To answer this question
it is necessary to make a digression and investigate what we expect of
those conceptions of the world around us which we are prepared to
dignify by the name of scientific 'theories.'

The relationship between 'the external world' (however that notion may be conceived) and what we human beings may say or think about it is of course one of the oldest problems in philosophy, and the particular sets of thoughts which have come to constitute the subject-matter of the natural sciences as we know them today have no claim to exemption from the rigorous philosophical questioning to which their less technical counterparts are regularly subjected.[7] While most professional scientists, including the present author, lack the competence (and for that matter the time) to pursue such an analysis in detail, it is clear that their reactions to questions such as the ones raised by the measurement paradox will be determined by their (often implicit) perception of the basic functions of language in general and scientific language in particular. So it is appropriate that I should try to make explicit at this point the prejudices with which I myself approach this subject.[8]

I would suggest that a helpful way of looking at scientific theories is not as something totally divorced from the everyday language in which we describe our experience, but as an extension of its resources; that, at least in those aspects of language which we would normally be happy to call 'factual description,' we are trying in some crude sense to build for ourselves and others *maps* of the world; and that this 'map-making' function of language is made much more precise and explicit in the language developed in modern scientific theories. This no doubt sounds not only unoriginal but naive; and indeed, so long as we take the concept of a 'map' as equivalent to that of a 'picture,' it is a view which has deservedly and repeatedly been shot through with holes by successive generations of philosophers. But let us for a moment experiment with the idea of taking the notion of a 'map,' as such, deadly seriously. In that case it is obvious after a moment's thought that a map is certainly *not* equivalent to a picture. What kinds of maps do we know? There are Ordnance Survey (or USGS) maps; there are the road maps put out by the motoring organizations; there are maps prepared for military use; there are demographic maps; maps of the city subway system; and so on. What do they have in common? In the first place, a negative feature; a map is *not* a picture of anything. (On looking down from a low-flying plane, one does not see contour lines twisting around the hillsides, nor does the red or brown with which Ordnance Survey maps mark the roads designated as A- or B-class by the UK Ministry of Transport bear any relation to the actual color of the road.) Indeed, while many maps (e.g. Ordnance Survey or military maps) do bear a metric or at least a topological correspondence to the objects they describe, even this feature is not essential; the maps of the London Underground (subway) system displayed in the stations are certainly not metrically accurate, and (as far as I remember) maps of Charles de Gaulle airport do not show the complicated topology of the connecting tubes in detail. Why do we, nevertheless, regard these as adequate and useful maps? Quite simply, because they fulfil the basic function of a map, which is to convey, in the form of a visual *gestalt*, an amount of information adequate to permit us to plan whatever activity we had in mind (the ascent of a mountain, a car journey to Scotland, an airport security operation, or whatever it was). Since different kinds of maps have different functions, it is not surprising that they have little in common, except for being two-dimensional displays (though in future we may no doubt get used to holographic maps). Mountaineers do not usually complain because their map fails to show the names of roads, nor do London subway travellers complain that, if you believe the wall maps, all subway lines travel in one of only eight directions; both maps are perfectly adequate for the particular purpose for which they are intended. It would be totally ridiculous to complain that a map of one kind is somehow inadequate because it is not in one-to-one correspondence with a map of a quite different kind. There is not and could not be any 'ultimate map.'

Now, I would like to suggest that in many cases, where two different types of scientific theory apparently cover the same subject-matter and are not obviously reducible to one another (as for example in the case of statistical mechanics and thermodynamics) we should view their relationship as resembling that of two different types of map of the same area; that is, they are different because they are trying to answer different types of question, but they are not therefore mutually incompatible. I believe that this type of relationship between theories at different 'levels' (to use a rather question-begging word) is much more common in science generally, and even in physics, than one would think if one reads either most physics textbooks or most philosophers of science. For example, most textbooks of solid-state physics give the impression [9] that the whole goal of the subject is to solve Schrödinger's equation for a collection of, say, 10^{23} nuclei and associated electrons, and that any models which we may build at an intermediate or macroscopic level (for example, the Drude model of electrons in metals, the Debye model of an elastic continuum, the Landau-Fermi liquid theory, and so on) are rather regrettable props which are in essence attempts to cover up our inability to do this by giving approximately valid solutions to the problem. Popular as this way of thinking may be among solid-state physicists, I believe that it is totally mistaken. In the first place, even if we could solve the appropriate Schrödinger's equation for an arbitrary, specified set of boundary conditions, we should never be able to apply the solution since we should in practice never be able to determine these boundary conditions with sufficient accuracy. Secondly, and far more importantly, what would be the value in having a complete and exact solution anyway? We should be rather in the position of the ancient Babylonians, who had (or so it is said) an elaborate system of recipes which enabled them to predict astronomical phenomena with a high degree of accuracy, but without any unifying principle or anything which we could call a model. Such a solution would by itself in no way help us to predict qualitatively new phenomena, for it would not identify for us the qualitatively important features of the physical situation. That is precisely what the intermediate-level models of condensed-state physics are all about; they are attempts (and, to the extent that they survive, successful attempts) to grasp the *relevant* features of the physics and to present them in the form of a mental *gestalt*. They are *not* 'approximations' to the microscopic solution of the problem, any more than the London Transport subway map is an 'approximation' to a 6-inch Ordnance Survey map of the same region.

If the relationship between scientific theories, or descriptions, at different levels is not one of derivability, then does it make sense to impose any constraints at all on one description in relation to the other? Clearly it does. At the very least, we need the constraint of *consistency*; that is, it should not be possible to derive results from one description which are clearly in contradiction to those derived from the other. It is, actually, an implicit recognition of this requirement which is responsible for much of the current output of theoretical work in condensed-matter physics, though with the ironical aspect that most of the authors of this work are under the impression that they are doing something quite different. Take, for example, the case of a clearly macroscopic law of physics such as Ohm's law. There must be literally hundreds of papers in the literature which aim (or claim to aim) to 'derive' Ohm's law from microscopic considerations. Yet, if the word 'derivation' is taken literally (in the sense, say, in which it would be understood by a pure mathematician) they all fail utterly. They can claim success, to one degree or another, only if by 'derivation' is meant a procedure which is familiar to all working physicists but, oddly enough, little studied by philosophers of science, in which what one actually does is to show that there exists a series of not implausible auxiliary assumptions which, when added to the microscopic description, will make it explicitly compatible with the required macroscopic result. (In the case of a 'derivation' of Ohm's law, such assumptions might for example relate to the cancellation of off-diagonal elements of the density matrix, to the irrelevance of the exact shape of the sample, and so on.) In other words, what this kind of work is really seeking to demonstrate is not derivability but *compatibility* of the models used at the microscopic and macroscopic (or intermediate) levels. Indeed, it is to my mind no accident that some of the most important theorems in the history of physics have actually been *in*compatibility theorems, e.g. the Bohr-van Leeuwen theorem on the inexplicability of atomic diamagnetism within the framework of classical statistical mechanics, or the famous theorem of Bell on the incompatibility of the predictions of so-called local hidden-variable theories with those of quantum mechanics.

After this rather lengthy digression, let us return to our original subject, the quantum measurement paradox. Viewed in the light of the above remarks, the paradox resides not in the fact that the quantum and classical descriptions of the state of the macroscopic world are not *derivable* one from the other, but in the fact that they are, *prima facie, incompatible.* To put it crudely, in appropriate circumstances quantum mechanics not only fails to assert that macroscopic events (clicking of a counter, etc.) occur, but positively asserts that they *don't* occur; whereas our ordinary everyday language, which we naturally think of as embodying our direct experience, asserts with equal firmness that they do. It is as if we had two maps of quite different type but both guaranteed by their makers to represent topological features accurately, in one of which a certain road crosses a certain river while in the other the two never get close together. In that case we would certainly say that one of the two maps must be a bad one. Yet already there is a difficulty with the analogy. In the case of the maps, we could *prove* that one map (at least) was a bad one, because under suitable circumstances it would lead us demonstrably to mis-plan our route; that is, its badness would have practical consequences. What makes the quantum measurement paradox, by contrast, so uniquely elusive is that, as we shall see below, in a certain sense it appears to have no *observable* consequences. It is no doubt precisely this feature which allows most professional physicists to dismiss it from their consciousness.

It is now over fifty years since the quantum measurement paradox first made its appearance recognizably in the literature [10], and in the intervening half-century numerous 'solutions' have been discovered and (much more frequently!) rediscovered. We may classify these attempts into two broad groups, which are distinguished by whether or not they accept the formal validity of the extrapolation of quantum mechanics to systems of arbitrary size, complexity, etc., including if necessary the human brain. In the category which in effect refuses to do so, the best-known 'solution' is probably the Copenhagen interpretation as formulated by Bohr, and, with some differences, Heisenberg; this in effect lays down by fiat that the macroscopic world, including our preparation devices, measuring instruments, etc., *must* be described in classical terms, on the grounds that otherwise we should have no possibility of communicating with one another. While this is no doubt a strong argument, the Copenhagen interpretation as such totally evades the real question, which is *how* the quantum-mechanical description at a microscopic level becomes converted into a classical one at the macroscopic level, even (presumably) in cases of the type described above, where a literal extrapolation of the quantum mechanical formation would lead to a quite non-classical account of the macroscopic world. It seems to the present author that in so far as this question is addressed at all in the writings of Bohr and Heisenberg, it is answered only by implicitly assuming that there really is a *qualitative* distinction between the microscopic and macroscopic levels of reality, and in particular that there comes some point on the apparent continuum where one can say that the quantum-mechanical description simply stops (in effect, when one can apply the standard textbook 'measurement axioms'). But, as numerous detailed examinations of specific measurement procedures have made clear (see for example references 5, 11, 12), and as we discussed earlier, the physics involved in 'measurement' is no different from any other kind of physics, and there seems no point at which it is natural to invoke the violent discontinuity of description which the Copenhagen interpretation would seem to require; nor is it helpful (though it is no doubt true) to remark that in most real-life situations it will not matter *where* the 'cut' is introduced, so long as it occurs somewhere. It is the very *legitimacy* of the cut, not its precise position, that is at issue.

A much more radical approach to the measurement problem is the 'mentalistic' solution espoused by Wigner[13] and some other physicists, which holds that the quantum-mechanical description should be applied right up to the macroscopic level and that the occurrence of specific macroscopic events is a consequence of an interaction of human consciousness with the physical world which cannot be explained within the framework of the laws of physics itself. (This view should be sharply distinguished from a version of the 'statistical' interpretation (see below) in which the quantum-mechanical state vector is a description not of the physical world itself but of our information concerning it, and therefore changes discontinuously when we acquire new information. In this latter approach there is no question of a *causal* interaction between 'consciousness' and the physical world.) In the absence of further amplification of this idea, and in particular of specific experimental predictions, it seems rather difficult to comment meaningfully on it, except perhaps to remark that the very meaning of 'consciousness' is itself the subject of furious controversy among philosophers, psychologists and others, and that it may be somewhat dangerous to 'explain' something one does not understand very well by invoking something one does not understand at all!

There is, however, a more conservative way of trying to involve the phenomenon of consciousness in the problem; namely, by speculating that, while it should be possible in principle (even if not very useful) to describe the physical environment associated with the phenomenon (e.g. the human brain) without bringing in any extra-physical ingredient, the laws of physics themselves might have to be substantially modified when one deals with systems with the incredibly high degree of complexity and organization which is necessary to sustain even life, let alone consciousness. In particular, one might speculate that the basic principles of quantum mechanics, and in particular the principle of superposition, might break down for such highly organized systems. This hypothesis is actually a special case of a more general possibility which I return to below, so I will defer discussion of it for the moment.

Let me now turn to those 'solutions' of the quantum measurement problem which accept the universal applicability of the quantum formalism. The most conservative of these is probably the so-called 'statistical' interpretation (for example reference 14) according to which the formalism is merely a description of our information about the system in question, or more precisely about the ensemble from which it is drawn, and says nothing about the actual state of any particular object, even at the macroscopic level. In this interpretation the description [3] of the final state of the 'universe' after a measurement has been made merely gives us statistical information about the distribution of results obtained in a long series of trials using identical pieces of apparatus and identical initial conditions, *and nothing more*; the question 'In what macroscopic state is this particular apparatus on this particular occasion?' is one which simply does not lie within the competence of quantum mechanics to answer. The formalism is simply a calculus for predicting, from given macroscopic initial conditions, the probability of various macroscopic outcomes. This interpretation, while no doubt internally self-consistent, has the very unpleasant feature that under certain conditions it makes it impossible, even in principle, to give a quantum-mechanical description of the state of a particular macroscopic object; since the theory is claimed to be the most fundamental description of the world which we now have and, according to many physicists, which we are ever likely to get, this seems rather a high price to pay.

If the statistical interpretation is the most modest of the interpretations of quantum mechanics as a universal formalism, the most ambitious is surely the Everett-Wheeler [15] 'relative state' interpretation (often known, since its popularization by de Witt [16], as the 'many-worlds' interpretation). This interpretation in effect takes a number of simple and unexceptionable theorems of the formal quantum theory of measurement (e.g. the theorem that if, under suitably 'ideal' conditions, the same microscopic quantity is measured successively by two different macroscopic instruments, the probability of getting two different results is zero) and superposes on them a novel metaphysical superstructure. The wave function, it is claimed, describes particular macroscopic objects, not ensembles, and is never 'reduced' by a measurement, even at the level of human consciousness; thus the universe is never 'really' in a particular macroscopic state at all but is forever in a linear superposition of macroscopically different states. The apparent violent contradiction with our 'commonsense' view of the macroscopic world is argued away by claiming that, because of the formal theorems mentioned above, we would never know of the existence of the branches of the wave function which correspond to outcomes we have not observed, and that all physically observable phenomena would be the same as if the measurement *had* reduced the wave function. The problem that bothers critics of the Everett-Wheeler interpretation is *not* (contrary to what many advocates of this interpretation seem to believe) that they are unaware or dubious of the formal theorems on which it relies, but that they see, quite literally, no meaning in the metaphysical superstructure; in the words of Ballentine [17], 'Rather than deny that a state vector can be a complete model of the real world, Everett and de Witt choose to redefine the real world so that a state vector (like [3]) can be a model of it.' In particular, the Everett-Wheeler interpretation seems totally unable to give an account of my subjective consciousness, on any particular occasion, of observing a particular outcome; to say that this consciousness is fallacious, even if a meaning can be attached to the words, is not an explanation!

The line of approach to the quantum measurement problem which is probably most favored by the majority of working physicists, and which I will therefore from now on refer to as the 'orthodox' resolution of the problem, goes roughly as follows. Let us agree that the technically correct description of the state of the universe following a measurement is a linear superposition of the form of equation [3], or something similar. Nevertheless, it is argued, it will be impossible in real life to distinguish between the experimental predictions made by equation [3] (supplemented, of course, by the standard measurement axioms) and those made by a classical 'mixture' description, in which the universe is simply assigned a probability:

$$p_i = |c_i|^2$$

of being in the macroscopic state $\chi_{un}^{(i)}$. In more technical language, it is claimed that the off-diagonal elements of the density matrix in a representation corresponding to the macroscopically distinguishable states i are unobservable in any realistic experiment, and that therefore the technically correct density matrix, which has elements:

$$\rho_{ij} = c_i^* c_j$$

may be safely replaced by the one corresponding to the mixture, namely:

$$\rho_{ij} = |c_i|^2 \delta_{ij}$$

A variant of this approach, which is more or less equivalent, is to point out that realistic measurements are never carried out on 'the universe' as a whole, but only on some finite part of it (e.g. the macroscopic measuring apparatus), and that after any appreciable time any macroscopic system will have interacted sufficiently with its environment that by itself it is no longer characterized by a pure state;

in fact, the *reduced* density matrix corresponding to the system by itself will indeed be of the 'mixture' form $|c_i|^2\delta_{ij}$. In either version, the argument then goes on to claim that since the correct quantum mechanical description is equivalent (or equivalent for all practical purposes) to a classical mixture description, there is no conceptual problem in interpreting it, and in particular no paradox in the fact that we observe, in any given experiment, a definite result; this is no more puzzling, it is claimed, than the fact that we have to describe a die which has been thrown but not inspected in terms of probabilities, despite the fact that we know very well that it must in fact be in a definite state which inspection will reveal.

This 'solution' to the quantum measurement paradox (which seems to be rediscovered, and re-published, in some variant or other about once a year on average) seems to the present author, and many others, to be no solution at all. To be sure, if its only point is to reassure the working physicist that in interpreting his experiments he may apply the standard measurement axioms at any time after the macroscopic apparatus has been triggered, without the risk of error, then the argument is unexceptionable. But as a solution of the *conceptual* problem it is a non-starter; if taken seriously, it confuses the (usually justified) assertion that the correct quantum mechanical description (supplemented, of course, by the measurement axioms) will give the same *experimental predictions* as a classical description in which the system is in a definite state, but our information is such that we can only talk in terms of probabilities, with the assertion that the macroscopic system actually *is* in a definite state. The latter statement is in transparent violation of the interpretation of the quantum formalism as applied at the microscopic level, so unless one is prepared either to modify the interpretation discontinuously somewhere on the way from the microworld to the macroworld, or to embrace the full-blooded 'statistical' interpretation (see above), the argument seems internally inconsistent. In fact, it only looks plausible at all because of a fundamental ambiguity in the interpretation of the density-matrix formalism (see the discussion in d'Espagnat [18], section 7.2). To repeat: the conceptual (as distinct from the practical) problem is not whether at the macroscopic level the universe (or the macroscopic apparatus) behaves *as if* it were in a definite macroscopic state, but whether it *is* in such a state.

Must we, then, resign ourselves to forever living with a violent conceptual paradox in our most successful, and most cherished, theory of the physical world? Not necessarily. There is one possible chink in the reasoning which leads to the paradox which is so obvious that it is really rather surprising that in the debates of the last fifty years or so it has attracted so little attention. It is quite simply that the assumption that the laws of quantum mechanics apply to macroscopic, complex and possibly highly-organized systems of matter, in the same way as they do to microscopic objects such as elections and atoms, is just that: an *assumption*, for which at the time of writing there is no direct and little circumstantial evidence. Perhaps the easiest way to see this is to note that the only time that the average physicist ever needs to write down a wave function of the type [3] is precisely when he is discussing the quantum measurement paradox; in his ordinary working life, be he a theorist or an experimentalist, he never needs to deal with superpositions of macroscopically different states[19], and hence never produces any evidence either for or against their existence. In other words, *there is simply no convincing evidence that macroscopic superpositions of the type [3] exist in nature.* It is therefore quite conceivable that at the level of complex, macroscopic objects the quantum mechanical superposition principle simply fails to give a correct account of the behavior of the system. One alternative possibility, for example, is that as more and more particles are involved in the linear superposition it gradually and continuously evolves into one or other of its branches, the probability of its ending up in a particular branch being determined by random factors in such a way that in an ensemble of experiments the statistical predictions of the quantum measurement axioms are verified. However, once one decides that the formalism is not sacrosanct, there are clearly many other schemes which could be considered, any of which would preserve the predictions of the quantum formalism at the microlevel while allowing the occurrence of definite events at the macrolevel. It is needless to add that any concrete proposal of this type would require us to introduce new physical laws which are not contained in the quantum formalism itself and which, while important at the macrolevel, would presumably have negligible effect at the level of one-, two- or few-particle systems. For some suggestions as to a possible definition of the property which discriminates cases in which these laws would be important or unimportant, see reference 1, section 3.

Why are physicists as a community so reluctant to consider even the possibility of such a solution to the quantum measurement paradox? I believe that the answer is to be sought on a number of different levels. At the most technical level, there seems to be a widespread belief that all solutions of this type have already been refuted by theory or experiment or both. This is quite simply a misconception. As regards theory, the only theoretical consideration which would invalidate such a proposal is simply the demand that the quantum formalism should apply universally, which merely begs the question; theorems of the von Neumann type[20], which in effect simply state that the notion of objective properties cannot be incorporated *within* the quantum formalism, are clearly irrelevant in this context. As regards experiment, the often-repeated claim that experiment has shown beyond reasonable doubt that 'quantum mechanics works at the macroscopic level' (or 'applies to macroscopic systems') embodies a fundamental confusion. I have discussed this point in considerable detail in reference 1, and will merely summarize the conclusion here. Even the most spectacular of the so-called 'macroscopic quantum phenomena' (Josephson effect, flux quantization, etc.) in themselves give no evidence at all for the existence of the states of the general form [3] which are necessary to establish the quantum measurement paradox, nor does the detailed agreement (such as it is) between the quantum-mechanically calculated and the observed properties of macroscopic systems (binding energies, excitation spectra, etc.) yield any more evidence in this direction. In the technical language introduced in reference 1, all these phenomena can be, and routinely are, explained in terms of the properties of states with 'disconnectivity' of the order of 1, 2, or at most a few, while the state described by equation [3] has typically a disconnectivity of order 10^{23}. There simply is no direct experimental evidence, at the time of writing, that such states actually exist.

A second reason for reluctance to consider the possibility outlined above lies at a more philosophical level. With few exceptions (who include David Bohm[21]), scientists of the last 300 years or so have been deeply committed to a form of reductionism which holds, in effect, that the behavior of a complex system of matter must be simply the sum of the behavior of its constituent parts. Whether it is actually profitable to *describe* it in these terms is, of course, a different question, and it seems to me that it would be perfectly consistent to subscribe to this kind of 'weak' reductionism while nevertheless accepting the validity and desirability of higher-level descriptions; in terms of the map-making analogy developed above, this would be like claiming that it would in principle be possible to make a perfect and complete map which would describe in minute detail every last topological feature, but that there is no practical purpose for which it would be useful to do so. What is essential to 'weak' reductionism in the sense referred to is the assumption that the experimental behavior of a complex system such as a solid, a biological organism or the human brain could 'in principle' be completely predicted if one knew the laws which describe the behavior of the individual atoms (or nucleons, or quarks...) which compose it and also the relevant initial conditions on the equations. (Whether one could in practice ever know all these things is, again, a different question.) What is *excluded* by this assumption is the possibility that there are new physical laws which appear *only* at the level of complex systems, so that the result of a solution of (let us say) Schrödinger's equation for the 10^{23}-odd electrons and nuclei composing a small biological organism might give results which are not only practically useless but are actually *wrong*. To put it another way, such a prejudice excludes *a priori* the possibility that complexity is itself a relevant variable which may require the laws of physics to be modified or generalized, in the same way as high velocities require relativity theory and small distances (or high energies) require quantum mechanics.

As a matter of history, the reductionist prejudice has of course had spectacular success. The behavior of gases has been analyzed in terms of the constituent molecules, that of molecules in terms of atoms, that of atoms in terms of the nucleons and electrons composing them, that of nucleons in terms of quarks, and so on. Certainly, there is no particular reason to believe that there is any special new ingredient which has to be added to quantum theory at the level of small or even large molecules which is not already present at the lower levels; if anything, the often spectacular agreement between theory and experiment leads to the opposite conclusion. Moreover, while the situation regarding bulk systems of condensed matter is inevitably less clearcut (in that totally rigorous and exact calculations in terms of the microscopic constituents are not usually available, even with the power of today's computers) there seems no strong reason to believe that, *as regards the one- and two-particle correlations* which are essentially all (or nearly all) that experiment usually measures, a quantum-mechanical calculation based on Schrödinger's equation as applied to the constituent electrons and nuclei will give misleading results. (As discussed above, it is quite a different question whether the results will be *useful*.) However, this situation is not one which we should regard as totally obvious *a priori*; a scientist from Mars, unconditioned by 300 years of reductionist science, might well find it a rather remarkable feature of our current understanding of the world. In any case, the fact that the reductionist assumption does apparently hold (or at any rate does not obviously fail) for the rather coarse features of the quantum formalism which are reflected in the calculation of one- and two-particle correlations is no evidence at all that it will continue to hold for the much more subtle features of the formalism which lead to the measurement paradox; as discussed in detail in reference 1, failure at a certain level of 'disconnectivity' would preserve all the well-established existing agreements between theory and experiment while removing the paradox. The prejudice that no such failure will occur is no doubt the simplest and (were it not for the measurement paradox) the most elegant assumption, but we have no *a priori* guarantee that nature will continue to entertain us with simple behavior as she has seemed to do in the past!

Finally, it may not be totally fanciful to seek part of the explanation at what we might call the sociological or political level. It is commonly believed that the 'fundamental' areas of research in physics are elementary-particle physics and cosmology, and that all other areas, in particular the physics of condensed matter, are 'derivative.' Clearly the prevalence of this belief, not merely among the physics community itself but among the general public, is extremely useful to those who seek hundreds of millions of dollars or pounds of public money to build the next round of high-energy accelerators, since it enables them to argue not only that particle physics and cosmology are 'fundamental' areas of scientific research (which they unarguably are) but that they are the *only* such fundamental area, and that advances in other areas of science (or at any rate other areas of physics) will not qualitatively change our world-view in the way that may come out of investment in these areas. Were it to become seriously envisaged that the physics of complex matter need not be, in all respects, reducible to that of its constituent parts, this argument might perhaps be examined a little more sceptically; one might begin to ask, in fact, for the actual evidence that pushing back the frontiers of physics in the direction of the very small or the very large will in the end change our basic understanding of the world in a way more fundamental than an equivalent thrust in the direction of the very complex.

Apart from the three reasons mentioned above, there is, I believe, a fourth reason why many physicists, while admitting the possibility in principle of a solution to the measurement paradox of the type envisaged, regard the question as not particularly interesting; namely, they believe that the question of the existence of such a solution is in principle not accessible to experimental resolution. At first sight some of the remarks made above would seem to lead precisely to this conclusion, since, as I have pointed out, the average experimentalist or theorist, in his everyday work, never comes within a mile of a wave function of the 'dangerous' type, i.e. equation [3]. In fact, merely by accepting what I have called the 'orthodox' resolution of the measurement paradox area, one in effect commits oneself to the belief that, at least in the context of a realistic measurement, it will always be impossible in practice to see any effects of the interference between the different macroscopic states $\chi_{un}^{(i)}$ (and hence, *a fortiori*, to test the hypothesis that the true description at the macroscopic level is *not* of this type). It is evidently this belief which most physicists feel justifies them in relegating questions about the validity and consistency of quantum mechanics at the macroscopic level to the realm of the 'philosophical' (which, in the loose usage of the physics community, appears to mean just about anything which at the moment cannot be subjected to direct experimental test).

In the days of the original controversies about the interpretation of the quantum formalism, in the first few decades of its existence, such a belief was no doubt well justified. In the 1980s, however, I believe that the question looks a good deal more complex. What has changed the situation qualitatively in the last decade or two is our ability to produce in the laboratory systems where there is a genuine hope of attaining the conditions where not only does quantum mechanics predict that the state is a linear superposition of macroscopically different states, but where the consequences of such a description are different, in an experimentally testable way, from the consequences of other types of assumption such as the scheme suggested above, in which already by this stage the system has evolved into a definite macroscopic state. I have discussed the conditions necessary to attain this state of affairs, and the systems which are the most promising candidates for it, in detail elsewhere[22], and will here merely review briefly what seems to be the experiment most likely to be feasible. One takes a superconducting ring closed by a Josephson junction ('rf SQUID') and imposes on it a controlled external magnetic flux. The system will then respond by generating currents which circulate in such a way that the total trapped flux, φ, is different from that applied externally; in thermal equilibrium it will choose a value of φ which makes its free energy $F(\varphi)$ a local minimum. This allows (at least) two different kinds of experiments. In one kind (known in the literature as 'macroscopic quantum tunnelling' or MQT) one traps the flux in a metastable minimum and tries to detect its 'escape' into a more stable minimum by a quantum tunnelling process. In the other ('macroscopic quantum coherence' or MQC) one chooses the value of the externally imposed flux so that $F(\varphi)$ has two *degenerate* minima which are separated by an energy barrier; the situation then resembles that found in the ammonia molecule, and one looks for the coherent oscillations between the two states which are the analog of the ammonia inversion resonance. The point of both kinds of experiment is that by any reasonable criterion the states which are connected by the process of tunnelling through the potential barrier are *macroscopically different* (in particular, a macroscopic number of electrons circulate clockwise or counter-clockwise in the two states respectively). Thus, observation of the quantum-mechanically predicted behavior should constitute at least circumstantial evidence (cf. below) that the quantum formalism still works for such macroscopic superpositions, and conversely failure of the predictions might suggest the hypothesis that at the macroscopic level quantum mechanics needs to be replaced or supplemented by physical laws of a qualitatively different type.

At the time of writing a number of experiments on MQT have already been done, though most of these are on a system (a so-called current-biassed junction) which is related but not identical to the one described above (for a review see references 22 and 23). Most of these experiments have found a tunnelling behavior which is at least qualitatively consistent with the quantum-mechanical predictions. However, it is difficult to assess to what extent they *exclude* alternative hypotheses. The MQC experiment, if it can be done, should be much more informative in this respect. In fact, it can be shown[24] that, provided suitable values of the parameters can be attained, the behavior predicted by quantum mechanics in this experiment is in conflict with the conjunction of two very basic 'commonsense' assumptions about the macroscopic world, namely that a macroscopic system which has available to it two macroscopically different states:

1   must always 'actually be' in one state or the other:
     and

2   can in principle be detected to be so with arbitrarily small effect on the state or its subsequent macroscopic dynamics.

Thus the MQC experiment would discriminate definitively between quantum mechanics and any theory of the alternative class discussed above which proposed to replace it at the level of a macroscopic superconducting device or below.

Although this experiment of course could not refute (or confirm) alternative theories which predicted a deviation from quantum mechanics only at the level of systems more complex, or more highly organized in (say) a biological sense, than the rather crude system formed by a superconducting device, I believe nevertheless that a clearcut result in either direction would constitute a very important input into discussions of the quantum measurement problem. A result in conflict with quantum mechanics would (after all the loopholes in theory and experiment had been plugged!) obviously throw the whole question back into the melting-pot. A result in accordance with the quantum predictions would no doubt at first sight be less spectacular; however, I believe that it should make us even more sceptical about the 'orthodox' resolution of the paradox. For if in this (admittedly very special) case the linear superposition of two *macroscopically* different states can be shown *experimentally* not to be equivalent to a classical mixture of these states, then it becomes that much less plausible to argue that in all other cases, where we have no direct experimental evidence to the contrary, the pure state has by some magical process been converted into a mixture (or, rather, has been converted into a definite but unknown macroscopic state). At the very least, it would force advocates of this resolution to specify with considerably more precision than has been done in the past exactly what aspects of the 'macroscopic' nature of the system they believe are relevant to the process in question.

Although the above ideas are different in detail from those promoted by David Bohm, I believe they are very much in the spirit of his approach to physics, and in particular of his long-standing concern with the fragmentation of our world-view imposed by the orthodox interpretations of quantum mechanics. It is a pleasure to dedicate this essay to him on the occasion of his retirement and to wish him many more happy years of scientific activity.

Acknowledgment

This work was supported through the MacArthur professorship, endowed by the John D. and Catherine T. MacArthur Foundation at the University of Illinois.

References

1   A. J. Leggett, *Prog. Theor. Phys. Supplt*, **69**, 80 (1980).
2   J. Summhammer, G. Badurek, H. Rauch, U. Kischko and A. Zeilinger, *Phys. Rev.*, **A27**, 2523 (1983).
3   N. Bohr, *Essays 1958–62 on Atomic Physics and Human Knowledge*, Interscience, New York, 1963.
4   H. Reichenbach, *Philosophic Foundations of Quantum Mechanics*, University of California Press, Berkeley and Los Angeles, 1944.
5   A. Daneri, A. Loinger and G. M. Prosperi, *Nucl. Phys.*, **33**, 297 (1962); *Nuovo Cimento*, **44B**, 119 (1967).
6   E. P. Wigner, *Am. J. Phys.*, **31**, 6 (1963).
7   Cf. T. S. Kuhn, in *Criticism and the Growth of Knowledge* (I. Lakatos and A. Musgrave, eds), Cambridge University Press, Cambridge, 1970, p. 231.
8   The discussion which follows has been much influenced by conversations over the years with Aaron Sloman (who is, however, in no way to blame for its inadequacies).
9   For example, G. Weinreich, *Solids: Elementary Theory for Advanced Students*, John Wiley and Sons, New York, 1965, pp. 98–9.
10 E. Schrödinger, *Die Naturwissenschaften*, **23**, 844 (1935).
11 D. Bohm, *Quantum Theory*, Prentice-Hall, New York, 1952, part VI.
12 K. Gottfried, *Quantum Mechanics*, Benjamin, New York, 1966.
13 E. P. Wigner, in I. J. Good, (ed.), *The Scientist Speculates – An Anthology of Partly-Baked Ideas*, Heinemann, London, 1961.
14 L. E. Ballentine, *Rev. Mod. Phys.*, **42**, 358 (1970).
15 H. Everett III, *Rev. Mod. Phys.*, **29**, 454 (1957); J. A. Wheeler, *ibid.*, **29**, 463 (1957).
16 B. S. de Witt, *Physics Today*, April, 1971, p. 36.
17 L. E. Ballentine, *Found. Phys.*, **3**, 229 (1973).
18 B. d'Espagnat, *Conceptual Foundations of Quantum Mechanics*, 2nd ed., W. A. Benjamin Inc., Reading, MA, 1976.
19 An exception to this statement is a proposal by V. R. Chechetkin (*Fiz. Nizk. Temp.*, **2**, 434 (1976); translation, *Sov. J. Low Temp. Phys.*, **2**, 215 (1976)) for a new type of wave function for the ground state of an anisotropic superfluid. However, it has been shown by S. K. Yip, *Phys. Letters*, **105A**, 66 (1984), that the proposed state is in fact not the ground state of the system in question.
20 J. Von Neumann, *Mathematical Foundations of Quantum Mechanics*, Princeton University Press, Princeton, 1955, Chapter 5.
21 D. Bohm, *Wholeness and the Implicate Order*, Routledge & Kegan Paul, London, 1980.
22 A. J. Leggett, in A. M. Goldman and S. A. Wolf (eds), *Percolation, Localization and Superconductivity*, Plenum Press, New York, 1984 (NATO ASI Series B, *Physics*, V, 109).
23 R. de Bruyn Ouboter, in S. Kamefuchi (ed.), *Proc. Intl. Symposium on the Foundations of Quantum Mechanics*, Japanese Physical Society, Tokyo, 1984.
24 A. J. Leggett and Anupam Garg, *Phys. Rev. Letters*, **54**, 857 (1985).

6

Quantum physics and conscious thought

Roger Penrose *Mathematical Institute, Oxford*

There can be few physicists who have delved as deeply into the philosophical implications of their subject as has David Bohm. It is therefore with some trepidation that I am paying my respects to him on the occasion of his retirement with an attempt of my own to relate questions of philosophy to those of the foundations of physics. The viewpoint that I am putting forward here attempts to relate questions that have been two of Bohm's major interests over the years; namely, a possible breakdown of quantum mechanics on a macroscopic scale and the physical basis of conscious thought. It must be evident to the reader that in both these topics I am venturing into dangerously speculative territory. Moreover others more expert that I (such as Wigner [1], as well as Bohm [2] himself) have put forward strongly-reasoned views which relate these topics. Yet I do feel that my own viewpoint is both well worth describing and sufficiently different from these others that the reader may find something of value here. But my account must necessarily be somewhat truncated, for reasons of space and of time. It is my intention to expand these thoughts at much greater length elsewhere.

1 Problems with quantum theory

Let me begin by expressing my personal worries and beliefs about the quantum theory. First, let it be said without reservation that the basic scheme, for all its philosophical difficulties, is an extraordinarily beautiful mathematical structure. The strength of the theory (and here I refer to standard non-relativistic quantum theory, not to quantum field theory) lies not just in the unbelievable range and accuracy of its physical predictions, but also in the mathematical elegance of its formalism.

It is here that I have always had difficulties with most hidden-variable theories. To me, it is no help just to improve upon the underlying philosophy of quantum mechanics by the introduction of hidden variables if the price to be paid is the sacrifice of this mathematical elegance. Yet it must also be emphasized that, in my view, the standard theory is indeed quite unsatisfactory philosophically. Like Einstein and his hidden-variable followers, I believe strongly that it is the purpose of physics to provide an *objective* description of reality.

However, I do not regard *indeterminacy*, in the ordinary sense of that word, as being necessarily objectionable. We have become accustomed, through classical physics, to a picture of the world whose future evolution is completely determined by data on an initial Cauchy hypersurface. Yet I find nothing *a priori* appealing about the idea. We know from results of general relativity (Penrose[3], Hawking and Ellis[4]) that there are otherwise seemingly acceptable space-times for which no Cauchy hypersurface exists. More serious are two other objections. In the first place, the *accuracy* with which one needs to know the initial data in order to be certain about the qualitative development of a system is absurdly unreasonable (Born[5], Feynman *et al.*[6]) and easily swamped by quantum uncertainties (if that is not begging the question). In the second place, there is always the problem of deciding *what* initial data one should be choosing. It seems to me to be of little value to know that there is *some* initial data containing all information if one has no rules for determining what that initial data is allowed to be or likely to be.

Considering things on the ultimate universal scale, one needs, it would seem, some theory to tell us how the universe actually started off, or at least which provides probability values for the different possible initial data sets. But if it is the latter, it seems to me that one is not really better off than with a non-deterministic theory. I see no reason to be happier about feeding probabilities into the universe's initial state than peppering them throughout the space-time, as is done in the standard interpretation of quantum mechanics. If, on the other hand, the initial state is to be determined *uniquely* by some new principle, then we have the problem of understanding the extreme complication and curious interplay between precisely-operating physical laws on the one hand, and the presence of apparent total randomness on the other. The picture is not an entirely hopeless one, however. One is beginning to become accustomed to the great mathematical complication, variety and apparent randomness that can arise with very simple and precise mathematical transformations, especially where iterative procedures are involved (cf. Ott[7] and references therein). So perhaps all the complication, variety and apparent randomness that we see all about us, as well as the precise physical laws, are all exact and unambiguous consequences of one single coherent mathematical structure.

Such a view I would call *strong determinism*. My guess is that Einstein[8] was hinting at such a possibility in his famous remark 'What I'm really interested in is whether God could have made the world in a different way; that is, whether the necessity of logical simplicity leaves any freedom at all.' Perhaps this view would represent the ultimate 'optimistic' attitude to the goals of science. Yet strong determinism is quite unlike ordinary determinism. There is not now any question of the future state being determined by data on an initial Cauchy hypersurface. The entire future (and past) is simply fixed by theory once and for all!

I do not propose to take sides on this grandiose issue. We are clearly extremely far from such a 'theory', even if eventually a viewpoint of that kind were to turn out to be 'correct'. My immediate purpose in bringing such matters up is largely to point out that, strong determinism aside, it seems no worse to feed probabilities into the theory 'peppered' throughout the space-time than to feed them all into the initial conditions. I shall return to strong determinism later.

At this point I should make mention of the many-worlds types of viewpoint[9, 10, 11]. Here one may be allowed a form of 'strong determinism without determinism'. The totality of all possible universes may be thought of as a single structure – the *omnium* (this terminology was suggested to me by Peter Derow) – and one might take the view that it is the omnium that is completely fixed by mathematical rules. The probabilities (or randomness) now arise owing to the uncertainties involved in the question of where one finds oneself located within the omnium. This 'location' involves not only one's spatiotemporal location within a particular universe branch, but also the selection of that particular branch itself.

Unsatisfied though I am by such a world-view, I do not have any really fundamental objection to pictures of this general kind. One problem I do have with them, however, is that the continual branching of the world and the threading of my own consciousness through it would seem to result in my becoming separated from the tracks of consciousness of all my friends. This is what I have referred to as the 'zombie' theory of the world[12]. It seems to me that one needs a respectable theory of consciousness before the many-worlds view can hang together as a physical theory and as a viable interpretation of quantum mechanics. This strikes me as a tall order at the present time. I shall have more to say about the many-worlds viewpoint later.

Let us now consider what the standard formalism of quantum mechanics has to say about the evolution of the world. Taking this formalism at its face value, we have a state vector $|\psi>$ which evolves for a while according to the completely deterministic Schrödinger equation. (If preferred, one could of course use the Heisenberg picture instead, in which case the state itself is considered not to evolve in time. The distinction is not important for my purposes. The two pictures are completely equivalent, but I feel that, at least for a non-relativistic discussion, the Schrödinger picture is less confusing.) Then, at odd times, when an 'observation' is deemed to have been made, the Schrödinger-evolved state vector is discarded and replaced by another, which is selected in a random way, with specific probability weightings, from among the eigenvectors of the operator corresponding to the observation. As has been argued on innumerable occasions, this is a wholly unsatisfactory procedure for a fundamental description of the 'real world'. There are, of course, very many different attitudes to the resolution of this problem, and it is not my purpose here to enter into a discussion of all of them, but some brief remarks will be in order.

In the first place, it is often argued that $|\psi\rangle$ itself should not be regarded as giving an objective description of the world (or of part of it) but as providing information merely of 'one's state of knowledge' about the world. This view I really cannot accept. Quite apart from the question as to who the 'one' might be in this statement (and the 'one' is surely not me!), it seems to me to be perfectly clear that there is (if we accept standard quantum mechanics) a completely objective meaning to $|\psi\rangle$ – at least to the *ray* determined by $|\psi\rangle$ in the Hilbert space (so that uncertainty $|\psi\rangle \mapsto e^{i\theta}|\psi\rangle$ is not of significance). For we can, in principle (according to the theory), set up a measurement defined by the operator:

$$Q = |\psi\rangle\langle\psi|$$

and find that $|\psi\rangle$ (assumed normalized: $\langle\psi|\psi\rangle = 1$) is the *unique* state (up to phase) corresponding to the eigenvalue unity for Q. This $|\psi\rangle$ is distinguished from all other states by the fact that it yields the value unity with certainty for the measurement Q. This is an entirely objective property, so we conclude that (if the theory is correct) the property of being in state $|\psi\rangle$ is, indeed, completely objective.

In practice, however, it may well turn out that the actual performing of the measurement Q is quite out of the question and it is in such circumstances that I would myself begin to doubt that $|\psi\rangle$ actually describes 'reality'. (There are situations, in the context of relativity or in connection with time-symmetry considerations, where the 'reality' of $|\psi\rangle$ seems to lead to a paradox; cf. Penrose [12]. I am not concerned with such matters here, but such 'paradoxes' are part of my own doubts about the complete validity of the quantum formalism.) To reject the objective view requires a denial of one of the fundamental tenets of quantum theory: any (bounded) Hermitian operator, such as Q, represents a measurement that could in principle be made.

So it seems to me that one must take it that in quantum mechanics the state vector *is* actually intended to represent 'reality'. The trouble comes, of course, when a measurement is made for which $|\psi>$ is *not* in an eigenstate. Now $|\psi>$ jumps non-deterministically into some new state – this is state-vector *reduction*. Because of this lack of determinism it is not possible to consider such behaviour as resulting from the Schrödinger evolution of some larger system which includes the apparatus configuration as part of the state. (Some attempts have been made to pin the blame for this indeterminism on a lack of knowledge about the environment, the claim being that when this random environment is taken into account, Schrödinger evolution might hold always. I have not yet found these attempts to be very believable and I shall ignore this possibility in the discussion which follows.) So it seems that quantum mechanics asserts two quite distinct types of evolution: deterministic Schrödinger evolution and state-vector reduction.

If we accept that state-vector reduction is a real physical process – and the physical objectivity of the state vector itself seems to imply this (leaving the many-worlds viewpoint aside) – then we may ask: at what stage does such a reduction take place? Again there are different views. Perhaps it occurs quickly and spontaneously at some level just not quite reached by experiments designed to detect violations in Schrödinger evolution. Or perhaps it is delayed until the latest allowable moment, as the results of the observation finally enter the mind of some *conscious* observer (Wigner[1]). As we well know (von Neumann[13]) either view, or any other viewpoint according to which the reduction takes place at some intermediate stage between these two extremes, is equally and completely compatible with all the experiments.

This frustrating and beautiful fact is, at one and the same time, among the greatest strengths and the most disturbing weaknesses of the theory. It is such a strength because it enables the theory to operate – as it does with such extraordinary accuracy and power – without our needing to have the remotest idea of what 'actually' takes place during the reduction process. This strength is also the theory's weakness, since for that very reason it offers us almost no clue as to what is physically going on during reduction. Moreover, it leads us into endless arguments about 'interpretation' where strange (and, to my mind, highly questionable) philosophy is often invoked to lull one into thinking that no new physical theory is needed to explain the details of the actual physics of reduction.

The reader will realize that I am expressing a very personal view here, and that much more discussion and open-mindedness is required than I have allowed myself in the foregoing remarks. However, my purpose here is not to be open-minded but to make some suggestions, so I hope that the reader will continue to bear with me and, instead, take upon himself or herself this burden of open-mindedness. I wish to make some comments concerning the place to look for a new physical theory of reduction, and then to make a speculative suggestion as to how this might ultimately relate to the phenomenon of consciousness. In bearing with me, the reader must, as a first step, be prepared to envisage that there is indeed a real physical process of reduction, where the Schrödinger equation and linearity are presumably both violated and where determinism may perhaps be violated also.

It may seem that, as I am suggesting a connection with consciousness, I propose to follow the Wigner[1] extreme, where reduction takes place only at the level of conscious thought. In fact I am not at all happy with that viewpoint and my suggestions with regard to reduction will be quite different. I share the discomfort of many others that the 'Wigner view' seems to imply a markedly different physical behaviour in our own small corner of the universe from that which would be taking place almost everywhere else, in the absence of local conscious observers to keep things under control. Of course, von Neumann again comes to the aid of that viewpoint to ensure that no contradiction with actual observation (by conscious beings) occurs. Or so it would seem. In any case, I personally find such a lop-sided picture of a *real* physical universe too unattractive to be believable.

Alternatively, as quite a number of physicists now seem to argue, perhaps one should go *beyond* Wigner and say that reduction fails to take place, even at the level of consciousness. This leads us, instead, to Everett's many-worlds picture. It seems that the main motivation behind this idea is the understandable desire for economy and uniformity of description. Rather than having to have two seemingly incompatible modes of evolution for the universe – Schrödinger's equation and reduction – is it not more economical and unified to settle just for the former and discard the latter? A faith in the elegance of Schrödinger linearity and the strong experimental support for Schrödinger evolution are among the arguments put forward for this view, but in my opinion both arguments are somewhat misconceived. Linearity seems elegant only when one has not seen an even more attractive, essentially non-linear, generalization. (Compare the analogy of Newtonian gravity and general relativity.) And the unquestionably impressive experimental support that quantum theory continues to have is *not* for the Schrödinger evolution of a quantum state. It is for that absurd concoction of Schrödinger evolution on the one hand and state-vector reduction on the other which defines the standard Copenhagen interpretation. That is where the support lies and it is *that* with which we must come to terms in our attempts toward an improved theory.

2 Quantum gravity and reduction

What we seek, I am therefore claiming, is a new theory, presumably non-linear and possibly non-deterministic, which:

1 is extremely accurately approximated, for reasonably small or simple systems, by a Schrödinger-evolving state vector; and

2 accords closely, for systems which are large or complicated, with reduction and with the standard replacement of probability amplitudes by the probabilities of actual alternative outcomes. (See Pearle [14, 15, 16] for a very serious concrete proposal of this kind.)

In various other places [17, 18] I have put forward arguments to support my own viewpoint that the essential new and non-linear physical input should be general-relativistic gravity, together with certain considerations about the second law of thermodynamics and the apparently strongly time-asymmetric constraints on the structure of space-time singularities. I do not wish to repeat the details of my (rather roundabout) argument here. My latest thinking on this question is being presented elsewhere [19] and I refer the interested reader to that source for more details. In my opinion there are indeed strong grounds for believing that for a quantum gravity theory to have any chance of real success it must incorporate among its important features a precise and objective theory of state-vector reduction. (A different line of thought, also leading to the conclusion that state-vector reduction is a gravitational phenomenon, had earlier been put forward by Károlyházy [20]; see Károlyházy, Frenkel and Lukács [21] for an up-to-date account of these ideas; cf. also Komar [22].)

There are various reasons for thinking that the structure of quantum mechanics may well have to be modified in the context of general relativity. One of these concerns the choice of variables with respect to which the process of 'quantization' is to be conducted. In the standard non-relativistic (or special-relativistic) quantization procedure one has the canonical variables x^a, p_a of position and momentum which are made into non-commuting operators and whose (canonical) Poisson bracket relations are replaced by (canonical) commutators. It would not be valid to apply this quantization procedure instead to some other variables $\tilde{x}^a$, $\tilde{p}_a$, obtained from x^a and p_a by an arbitrary canonical transformation, again replacing the canonical Poisson bracket relations of $\tilde{x}^a$ and $\tilde{p}_a$ by canonical commutators. It might, for example, be the case that $\tilde{x}^a$ is related to x^a by some arbitrary co-ordinate transformation, with canonical conjugate $\tilde{p}_a$ correspondingly chosen, and then the canonical quantization procedure will not in general apply to $\tilde{x}^a$ and $\tilde{p}_a$. What distinguishes the standard (x^a, p_a) from the more arbitrary $(\tilde{x}^a, \tilde{p}_a)$ (cf. Komar [23]) is its direct relation to the symmetry group of flat space-time, so that p_a indeed represents the standard (conserved) energy-momentum concept.

It will be noted that this selection principle for 'preferred' canonical variables will not work in a curved space-time. This is a much more immediate problem than the daunting difficulties involved in trying to quantize the gravitational field itself, since it arises already when gravity is simply taken to be an unquantized background field. Thus, even at this simplified level, the standard quantum-mechanical procedures run into difficulties. One does not, in fact, have any clear rules for a quantizing procedure, in the general case. When one is asked the question of whether the incorporation of space-time curvature into physics in any way affects the general framework and rule of procedure of quantum mechanics, one is forced to reply (if truthful) that one does not even know what the rules are, in a general curved-space setting!

It seems that in curved space, one must resort to some 'patchwork' formalism and, at best, much of the compelling elegance of quantum mechanics is removed. It has become fashionable to argue that, in view of the abounding difficulties that have been encountered in attempts to quantize general relativity, one should replace that theory by some other which might more willingly submit to being forced into the linear framework of standard quantum theory. Yet it is not often suggested that the quantum framework might itself be forced to yield. I would not dispute that some changes in classical general relativity must necessarily result if a successful union with quantum physics is to be achieved, but I would argue strongly that these must be accompanied by equally profound changes in the structure of quantum mechanics itself. The elegance and profundity of general relativity is no less than that of quantum theory. The successful bringing of the two together will never be achieved, in my view, if one insists on sacrificing the elegance and profundity of either one in order to preserve intact that of the other. What must be sought instead is a grand union of the two – some theory with a depth, beauty and character of its own (and which will be no doubt recognized by the strength of these qualities when it is found) and which includes both general relativity and standard quantum theory as two particular limiting cases.

This is all very well, the reader is no doubt thinking, but what relevance has the extremely weak phenomenon of even classical gravity – let alone the absurdly tiny and quite undetectable 'quantum corrections' that one anticipates would result from a quantum gravity theory – to the commonplace phenomenon of reduction? Whether one contends that reduction occurs early or late in the chain of alternatives – whether reduction has already physically taken place with the track in a cloud chamber or mark on a photographic plate, or whether it is delayed until it affects the state of a human brain – in either case only tiny amounts of energy are involved, by the standards of gravitation theory. Yet it is my contention that it is this link with gravity which effects the apparent change in rules that takes place with reduction. When two states of differing energy distribution are linearly superposed, the slightly differing space-time geometries that these energy distributions produce (according to general relativity) must also be superposed. This is not clearcut matter since, as we have seen, the geometry is not just a 'physical state' but is something essentially involved in the very determination of the 'procedure of quantization' (cf. foregoing remarks concerning x^a, p_a and $\tilde{x}^a$, $\tilde{p}_a$). It is hard to see how 'quantization procedures' are to be superposed.

I would contend, therefore, that when two geometries involved in a linear superposition become too different from one another – in some yet-to-be-determined precise sense – then linear superposition fails to hold, and some effective non-linear instability sets in, resulting in one or the other geometry winning out, the result being *reduction*. However, the criterion for deciding when such an instability becomes operative cannot depend solely on the energies or masses involved. The masses involved in cloud chamber droplets, or relevant collections of silver iodide molecules in a photograph, or configurations in a brain, would appear to be very tiny – apparently tinier than the Planck-Wheeler mass of 10^{-5} g which seems to characterize the scale of quantum gravity – which, in turn, might perhaps be smaller than the total electron mass involved in a *coherent* quantum state for a large superconducting coil. Some care will be needed in deciding upon the precise measure of mass-energy distribution difference that is needed to trigger off the instabilities of reduction.

My earlier arguments[17, 18] have emphasized the time-asymmetric role of entropy in reduction and the gravitational origin (via time-asymmetry in space-time singularity structure) of the second law of thermodynamics. For an overall consistency of the physics involved, it is argued that gravity ought also to be critically relevant to the quantum-mechanical reduction process. But it is gravity in its role of providing a *gravitational entropy* that enters. In the early stages of the universe (at the big bang) the entropy content of the matter was high. The second law arises because, at the singularity, something constrained the entropy of *gravity* to be extremely low, whereas the potential for entropy *content* of (conformally) curved space-time was enormously high.

As the universe evolves, this unused potential of gravitational entropy is gradually taken up (clumping of gas into stars, etc.) and is directly or indirectly taken advantage of by systems requiring a low entropy reservoir (e.g. plants making use of degradable photons from the sun, which is a hot spot in the sky by virtue of its gravitational clumping). The ultimate high value of entropy for a gravitationally clumped object is achieved by the black-hole state. This entropy can be given in precise terms by the Bekenstein-Hawking formula (cf. Wald[24]) and we find that for an ordinary black hole, resulting from the collapse of, say, a ten solar-mass star, the entropy per baryon is some twenty orders of magnitude larger than even the seemingly huge value of 10^8 or so (taking units with Boltzmann's constant as unity) for the thermal black-body radiation left over from the hot big bang.

Even when this maximum entropy value is not achieved, the gravitational entropy can be quite sizable, though as yet no precise determination of this entropy has been suggested. In a rough way, we can say that this entropy is intended to estimate (the logarithm of) the number of quantum states that go to make up a given classical geometry. Such an entropy measure would have to be very much a non-local expression. But this is not surprising in general relativity, where even energy must be given by a non-local expression (cf. Penrose and Rindler[25]).

The idea is that, for 'reduction' to take place, we must be in a situation where, such as in the localization of a photon on a photographic plate, the lowering of entropy that this 'reduction' would seem to entail must be at least compensated by a corresponding increase in the gravitational entropy, this gravitational entropy being higher for clumped localized energy distributions than for those which are spread out more uniformly. (This cannot be just the 'quantum-mechanical entropy', which remains at zero so long as one uses a pure-state description, but is some more 'commonsense', though somewhat ill-defined, entropy concept which increases as more and more degrees of freedom become involved. I am grateful to P. Pearle for illuminating discussions concerning this. Quantum reduction must be a non-local process, and the hope is that this non-locality can be matched with the non-locality involved in the gravitational entropy concept.

It will be clear to the reader that there is much speculation and lack of precision in this picture. (For more clarification, see Penrose[19].) But my purpose here is not to spell out in detail how the reduction procedure might work (which I cannot do, not having a proper theory) but merely to attempt to persuade the reader of the plausibility of there being *some* new physical process going on which has a perfectly objective character, even though we do not understand how this process works in detail. I would certainly anticipate, however, that the process is likely to defy any meaningful local description in ordinary space-time terms. But any speculation involved in the 'details' of this process will, I suppose, pale to insignificance by comparison with the speculative aspects of what I have to suggest in the next section – where I turn to what will (at first) seem to be a totally different topic!

3   Concerning the physics of conscious thought

There has been a great deal of discussion in recent years – since the emergence of modern high-speed computers – of the question as to whether human thought can be adequately understood in terms of computational algorithms. There is a rather prevalent school of belief (cf. Hofstadter[26]) which maintains that an algorithm (or perhaps the end-product of an algorithm) is itself all that 'counts' in determining whether 'thoughts', or even 'conscious feelings', have been achieved during the implementation of that algorithm. According to this view, the actual physical nature of the device which carries out the algorithm is of no consequence. The point of view is a strongly 'operationalist' one and springs, to a large extent, from a well-known and penetrating discussion due to Turing[27], according to which an experimenter has to decide, merely by means of questions and answers (transmitted impersonally with, say, keyboard and display screen), which of two 'subjects' is a human being and which is a computer, the computer having been programmed to imitate human responses as closely as possible. This has become known as the 'Turing test', and the point of view to which I have referred ('strong AI') would maintain that once a computer has satisfactorily passed this test (i.e. has become able to imitate human responses closely enough to be able to 'fool' a perceptive experimenter), then all the normal terms such as 'thought', 'understanding', 'awareness', 'happiness', 'pain', 'compassion', 'pride', etc., could be as meaningfully and as truthfully applied to the computer as to the human subject.

I do not believe that it would be strongly disputed that computer technology (both at the hardware and software ends) is some good way from attaining this avowed goal. Nevertheless, at a much more restrictive level, there are already computer programmes which can respond to extremely simple types of stories in the English language. The computer can provide answers to elementary but slightly indirect questions about the story, these answers seeming to indicate some very primitive 'understanding' of the content of the story by the computer. However, Searle[28] has argued impressively that answers of this sort need in no way imply that any kind of 'understanding' has actually been achieved by such a mechanism since, in place of the electronics of the computer, one could use human beings blindly following instructions and they need have no inkling of the 'meaning' of the story in order to carry out these instructions successfully.

It seems to me to be clear that in this essential respect Searle is correct and we have no reason to apply such a word as 'understanding' to the operations of a mechanism, electronic or otherwise, of this kind. It appears that Searle is willing to concede that at some stage computers (of present-day type, but improved in speed, storage capacity and logical design) may be able to pass the Turing test proper (let us say, by 100 years from now) but that we would still have no reason to attribute to them such human qualities as I have mentioned. Most particularly, we would have no reason to attribute to them any form of conscious awareness. Thus, according to Searle, the actual physical material and detailed construction of a 'computer' (i.e. the 'hardware') may, for such qualities, be of 'crucial' importance.

My own personal view is very much in sympathy with this, though it remains what I believe to be a highly significant difference. I would agree that the actual *physical* construction of the proposed 'thinking device' is likely to be crucial, but not merely with regard to the appropriateness of such terms as 'conscious awareness'. I think that the physical (or biological) nature of the 'device' is likely to be crucial also in determining the effectiveness of its very operation. I would contend that the evolutionary development, through natural selection, of the ability to think consciously indicates that consciousness is playing an *active* role and has provided an evolutionary advantage to those possessing it. For various reasons I find it hard to believe that conscious awareness is merely a concomitant of sufficiently complex modes of thinking – and it seems to me clear that consciousness is itself *functional*.

People behave quite differently while in the states of full conscious awareness from when they are not properly conscious of what they are doing (such as while daydreaming, sleepwalking or in a state of epileptic 'fugue'). Indeed, if consciousness had no operational effect on behaviour, then conscious beings would never voice their puzzlement about the conscious state and would behave just like unconscious mechanisms 'untroubled' by such irrelevancies! Moreover, I am very much aware that, in my own thinking, there are certain kinds of problem for which conscious appraisal is essential, whereas there are others – those which are 'automatic', there being a clearly defined algorithm which I have previously learnt (like walking or driving a car in very familiar circumstances) – for which conscious action is not needed.

Why do some kinds of thinking seem to 'need' consciousness while others seem not to? What is the crucial distinction between tasks that require (or at least benefit from) conscious thought and those that appear to have no real use for it? I do not suppose that very clear answers to these questions can be given at present, but at least there seems to be something very suggestive about the kind of terminology that most readily springs to mind. Terms such as 'automatic', 'following rules mindlessly', 'programmed' and even 'algorithm' seem appropriate for various kind of mental processes that are not necessarily accompanied by conscious awareness. These are the kind of activities that most closely accord with the actions of computers as we presently understand them. On the other hand, 'common sense', 'judgment of truth', 'understanding' and 'artistic appraisal' are among the terms one might use to describe mental activities that can seemingly be carried out effectively only when consciousness is present. For these, one is much more in the dark in attempting to imitate human thinking with computers. It seems not unnatural to suggest, therefore, that unconscious mental processes (perhaps such as can be carried out by the cerebellum) may indeed be effectively imitated by computers which do not differ in principle from those already in existence, but that conscious thinking may be essentially 'non-algorithmic' in its nature and qualitatively different from that which can in principle be carried out by such computers.

The matter is perhaps not so clearcut as this, however. In the first place it is evident that many unconscious ingredients are present in our artistic appraisals, in our studied judgments and in our common sense. Though we form our judgments with consciousness as an apparently necessary ingredient, we do so by bringing together innumerable factors of logic, experience and prejudice, a good proportion of which we are probably not aware. Perhaps conscious appraisals are no less algorithmic in nature than unconscious, 'automatic' actions, but are simply incomparably more complicated and subtle in their operation – as many would argue. Perhaps, then, consciousness is simply a concomitant of these higher-level and more sophisticated – but still algorithmic – operations of mental machinery.

This is a view that gains support from the kind of picture that is now most commonly presented for the essential workings of the brain. A complicated network of neurones and synapses is envisaged, where electrochemical signals propagate, indulging in elementary 'logical' switching processes – apparently similar to those of an electronic computer, though with a probabilistic ingredient. This all seems to be something that could be imitated closely by a computer, at least in principle. The additional probabilistic ingredient would seem to present no real problem. Computers can, after all, easily generate sequences of numbers which to all intents and purposes behave as random sequences. Or, if preferred, (effectively) random sequences can be produced by suitable *physical* processes (e.g. decays of radioactive atoms) which could easily be additionally incorporated into the computer.

In any case – apart from the fact that the storage capacity is finite rather than being unlimited – is one not simply providing an instance of a *Turing machine*? Any computational procedure whatever (in the normal sense of that term) comes under the heading of a procedure attainable by a Turing machine. To perform a computation, one is using a piece of physical apparatus, so the common argument goes, be it a human brain or an electronic computer or whatever, which is subject to the normal physical laws. These laws are of the usual deterministic type (classical, or else Schrödinger, time-evolution) or entirely probabilistic (state-vector reduction) and, as it would seem at first sight, are of the type which could be carried out by a Turing machine (with a limited store) with, if need be, an additional random input.

However, the question of computability, with ordinary deterministic laws, is not quite so straightforward as it might seem. Indeed, according to Pour-El and Richards[29,30], there is one sense in which evolving even so simple a deterministic system as the wave equation in flat space can be regarded as a non-computable procedure. But this particular sense is probably not the appropriate one in the present context. As they point out, sufficiently smooth solutions of the wave equation are indeed quite adequately computable from initial data (say by means of the Kirchhoff formula) and the same may be basically true also of the other main deterministic equations of physics, even though there will be the problems of stability, etc., that I mentioned in section 1.

On the other hand, there is a critical assumption built into this discussion that the operative physical laws are indeed of the type referred to, where deterministic classical (or Schrödinger) evolution is maintained, except where punctuated by the random procedure of state-vector reduction. As I have been arguing in the earlier sections, one needs some replacement for this unhappy combination, the evolution and reduction being seen as approximations to some more accurate and precise grand scheme. It seems to me to be quite on the cards that this sought-for grand scheme contains an effectively *non-computable* time-evolution. It would be my view that the brain in its conscious state (or the 'mind'?) is able to harness these effects and make use of whatever subtleties are involved at that delicate borderline between linear Schrödinger evolution and the apparent randomness of reduction, thereby achieving effects far beyond those attainable by the ordinary operations of algorithmic computers.

Non-computability of some kind seems also to be a necessary ingredient of strong determinism. If one could compute the full space-time state of the universe, one could in principle compute one's own future. Then, of course, one might simply choose to do something different – an incompatibility with the feeling of free will.

These ideas are, of course, matters of considerable speculation, as present physical and physiological understandings go. Yet there are very many instances where biological systems have been able to make extraordinarily effective use of subtle physical or chemical effects. Surely the greatest of evolution's achievements, the development of conscious awareness, must have needed to call upon physical processes even more profound and delicate than any we have yet understood. Any world in which minds can exist must be organized on principles far more subtle and beautifully controlled than those even of the magnificent physical laws that have so far been uncovered. At least, that is my own very strong opinion.

Added in proof

I am now of the opinion that the criterion for 'reduction' referred to in Section 2 should not be phrased as though it referred to a 'gravitational entropy' but rather to a 'longitudinal graviton number'. See the postscript in reference 19 for further clarification.

References

1   E. P. Wigner, 'Remarks on the mind-body question', in I. J. Good (ed.), *The Scientist Speculates*, Heinemann, New York, 1961; also in J. A. Wheeler and H. Zurek (eds.), *Quantum Theory and Measurement*, Princeton Univ. Press, Princeton, NJ, 1983.
2   D. J. Bohm, *Wholeness and the Implicate Order*, Routledge & Kegan Paul, 1980.
3   R. Penrose, *Revs. Mod. Phys.*, **37**, 215–20 (1965).
4   S. W. Hawking and G. F. R. Ellis, *The Large Scale Structure of Space-Time*, Cambridge Univ. Press, Cambridge, 1973.
5   M. Born, *Nature*, **119**, 354 (1927).
6   R. P. Feynman, R. B. Leighton and M. Sands, *The Feynman Lectures on Physics*, Vol. III, Addison-Wesley, Reading, Mass., 1965.
7   E. Ott, 'Strange attractors and chaotic motions of dynamical systems', *Revs. Mod. Phys.*, **53**, 655–71 (1981).
8   A. Einstein, letter to Ernst Straus; cf also A. Pais, *Subtle is the Lord . . .*, Oxford Univ. Press, Oxford, New York, 1982.
9   H. Everett, '"Relative state" formulation of quantum mechanics', *Revs. Mod. Phys.*, **29**, 454–62 (1957).
10   B. S. DeWitt and R. D. Graham (eds.), *The Many-Worlds Interpretation of Quantum Mechanics*, Princeton Univ. Press, Princeton, NJ, 1973.
11   D. Deutsch, 'Three connections between Everett's interpretation and experiment', in R. Penrose and C. J. Isham (eds.), *Quantum Concepts in Space and Time*, Oxford Univ. Press, Oxford, 1985.
12   R. Penrose, 'Singularities and time-asymmetry', in *General Relativity: An Einstein Centenary Survey*, S. W. Hawking and W. I. Israel (eds.), Cambridge University Press, Cambridge, 1979.
13   J. von Neumann, *Mathematical Foundations of Quantum Mechanics*, Princeton Univ. Press, Princeton, 1955.
14   P. Pearle, *Phys. Rev.*, **D13**, 857 (1976).
15   P. Pearle, *Phys. Rev.*, **D29**, 235 (1984).
16   P. Pearle, 'Models for reduction', in C. J. Isham and R. Penrose (eds.), *Quantum Concepts in Space and Time*, Oxford Univ. Press, Oxford, 1985.
17   R. Penrose, 'Singularities and time-asymmetry', in S. W. Hawking and W. Israel (eds.), *General Relativity – An Einstein Centenary Survey*, Cambridge Univ. Press, Cambridge, 1979.
18   R. Penrose, 'Time-asymmetry and quantum gravity', in C. J. Isham, R. Penrose and D. W. Sciama (eds.), *Quantum Gravity 2*, Oxford Univ. Press, Oxford, 1981.
19   R. Penrose, 'Quantum gravity and state-vector reductions', in R. Penrose and C. J. Isham (eds.), *Quantum Concepts in Space and Time*, Oxford Univ. Press, Oxford, 1985.
20   F. Karolyhazy, *Nuovo Cimento*, **A42**, 390 (1966).
21   F. Karolyhazy, A. Frenkel and B. Lukacs, 'On the possible role of gravity in

the reduction of the wave function', in C. J. Isham and R. Penrose (eds.), *Quantum Concepts in Space and Time*, Oxford Univ. Press, Oxford, 1985.

22   A. B. Komar, *Int. J. Theor. Phys.*, **2**, 157.

23   A. B. Komar, 'Semantic foundation of the quantization program', in M. Bunge (ed.), *Studies in the Foundations, Methodology and Philosophy of Science, Vol. 4, Problems in the Foundations of Physics*, Springer-Verlag, Berlin, 1971.

24   R. Wald, *General Relativity*, Chicago Univ. Press, Chicago, 1984.

25   R. Penrose and W. Rindler, *Spinors and Space-Time, Vol. 2; Spinor and Twistor Methods in Space-Time Geometry*, Cambridge Univ. Press, Cambridge, 1986.

26   D. R. Hofstadter, *Gödel, Escher, Bach: an External Golden Braid*, Harvester Press, Hassocks, Sussex, 1979.

27   A. M. Turing, 'Computing machinery and intelligence', *Mind*, **59** (1950); also in A. T. Anderson (ed.), *Minds and Machines*, McGraw-Hill, New York, 1978.

28   J. R. Searle, in D. R. Hofstadter and D. C. Dennett (eds.), *The Mind's I*, Harvester Press, Hassocks, Sussex, 1981.

29   M. B. Pour-El and I. Richards, *Adv. in Math.*, **39**, 215–39 (1981)

30   M. B. Pour-El and I. Richards, *Adv. in Maths.*, **48**, 44–74 (1983).

7

Macroscopic quantum objects

T. D. Clark *School of Mathematical and Physical Sciences, University of Sussex*

I first met David Bohm in the early spring of 1976. At the time I had the idea that, given suitable experimental conditions, certain kinds of superconducting circuits should display manifestly quantum mechanical behaviour over macroscopic length scales. I hoped that such circuits would provide a new experimental vehicle for investigating quantum mechanics. David Bohm was, and is, one of the great authorities on the foundations of quantum mechanics so it seemed natural that I should seek his advice. I found him very approachable and he listened with great patience to my attempts to explain my still rather rudimentary physical views of these circuits. His encouragement then was a great morale booster for our group at Sussex. Eventually we were able to justify that encouragement. We now have superconducting circuits roughly a centimetre across which behave as single quantum objects. I would like to think that in due course these circuits will be of use in testing some of David Bohm's remarkable ideas concerning the nature of quantum mechanics.

The superconducting state

In 1956 Cooper[1] demonstrated that the existence of an arbitrarily small net attractive interaction between the conduction electrons of a metal leads inevitably to the formation of states of bound pairs of electrons. Subsequently Bardeen, Cooper and Schrieffer[2] showed that such an attractive interaction could indeed exist in a metal. Pairs of electrons can interact attractively via the lattice ions. This attractive interaction is maximised when the pairing process occurs between electrons of opposite momenta and spin. Although single electrons are fermions, paired electrons can be treated as bosons. These Cooper-pair bosons can, through Bose-Einstein statistics, occupy a single quantum state extending over a macroscopic distance. In this state, which we identify with superconductivity, all the electron pairs have the same centre of mass momentum. It is useful to consider the creation of the superconducting state in terms of pair overlap. The electron–lattice–electron interaction which leads to the formation of Cooper pairs is very weak and only has observable consequences at low temperatures. The very small binding energy means on average the paired electrons are a large distance apart, roughly 10^{-5} cm in a typical superconductor. Compared with a single electron in a normal metal, an electron pair in a superconductor occupies a large volume. However, it can only do so by co-existing in that same volume with approximately 10^6 other pairs[3]. Obviously there exists a large overlap of the wave functions of the Cooper pairs. This dictates that the phases of these wave functions should be locked together over macroscopic length scales. This macroscopic phase coherence, which forces different points in a superconductor to have built-in phase relations, has far-reaching consequences.

Multiply connected superconductors

One consequence of macroscopic phase coherence in superconductors appears to be that a state which is, in principle, many-bodied can be represented by a 'single particle' wave function, i.e. a single macroscopic wave function for a very large number of particles. This can be written as[4]:

$$\Psi = |\Psi|e^{i\varphi} \qquad [1]$$

The concept of a macroscopic single-particle wave function describing the correlated behaviour of a very large number of superconducting pairs leads directly to the requirement for lossless diamagnetic screening currents to flow in the surface region of a superconductor in the presence of an external applied magnetic field[5]. The characteristic distance over which external magnetic fields are screened in a superconductor is known as the London penetration depth (λ_L)[6].

With the simple wave function [1] in mind, it is instructive to consider the case of a superconducting ring with a thickness large compared with λ_L. In order to keep the wave function single-valued at every point within the ring the phase (φ) of the wave function [1] must change by zero or integer $(n) \times 2\pi$ along a path around the ring inside the bulk superconductor. This integer n is known as the winding number of the superconducting ring.

Given the single-particle wave function [1] and the quantum-mechanical probability current density equation expressed in terms of an effective charge of $2e$, an effective mass of twice the electronic mass (m_e) and the vector potential $\vec{A}$ of any ambient magnetic field $\vec{B}$:

$$J_p = -\frac{i\hbar}{4m_e} [\Psi^* \left(\nabla - \frac{2ie}{\hbar}\vec{A}\right)\Psi - \Psi\left(\nabla + \frac{2ie}{\hbar}\vec{A}\right)\Psi^*] \tag{2}$$

it is easy to show[3] that if the above phase-quantisation condition holds, then any magnetic flux (Φ) threading the ring must be quantised as:

$$\Phi = n\Phi_0 \tag{3}$$

where $\Phi_0 = h/2e$ is the superconducting flux quantum.

Flux quantisation in thick superconducting rings is now a very well established experimental fact[7]. As a phenomenon, however, it is of limited use since, for the case of a uniformly thick ring, the flux state can only be changed by warming the ring through its superconducting transition temperature, followed by cooling in a different ambient magnetic field. Fortunately another method exists for changing flux states which avoids this tedious procedure.

In 1962 Josephson invented what is now known generically as the superconducting weak link[8]. In its simplest form the weak link consists of a tapered constriction roughly a few hundred angstroms across at its narrowest section. This corresponds closely to the penetration depth λ_L in a superconductor. With dimensions as small as this, it is relatively easy for magnetic flux to leak across the weak link and, as we have shown[9,10], this leakage takes place as a quantum mechanical process. Thus, in this context, we can consider a weak link as a device which couples together quantum mechanically different flux states of a superconducting ring.

From the above discussion it is clear that the integer ($n\Phi_0$, $n = 0, \pm 1, \pm 2 \ldots$) flux states exist in a quantum mechanical sense as macroscopically different states of a thick superconducting ring. These states, which have no classical analogue, are a consequence of the macroscopic quantum behaviour of the ring. In describing the behaviour of the thick ring it is useful to define the total included flux, which must be quantised as $n\Phi_0$, in terms of an externally applied magnetic Φ_x so that:

$$n\Phi_0 = \Phi_x + \Lambda I_s \tag{4}$$

where Λ is the geometric inductance of the ring and I_s is the superconducting diamagnetic screening current flowing in the ring.

The magnetic energy storage in the ring is just:

$$W_n = \Lambda I_s^2/2 \tag{5}$$

so from [4]:

$$W_n = (n\Phi_0 - \Phi_x)^2/2\Lambda \tag{6}$$

Thus we can write a time-independent Schrödinger equation for the thick ring:

$$W_n D_n = E_n(\Phi_x) D_n \qquad [7]$$

where D_n is the amplitude for the ring to be in the $n\Phi_0$th flux state. As can be seen from Figure 7.1, the energies $E_n(\Phi_x)$ are a set of intersecting, but non-connecting, parabolas. Since for a thick ring there exists no mechanism for coupling different n states together, no transitions can occur between these parabolas, even at the points where they cross one another. The situation changes radically when a weak link is included in the ring. In this case two limiting regimes can be discerned, depending on the strength of the coupling between integer flux states provided by the weak link. We will consider each in turn.

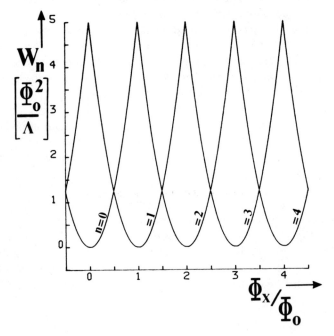

Figure 7.1   Plot of external magnetic flux (Φ_x) dependent energy levels for a thick superconducting ring with trapped flux 0, Φ_0, $2\Phi_0$ ... $n\Phi_0$.

The flux mode regime – weak coupling between nearest-neighbour flux states of a superconducting weak link ring

It is convenient to consider a thick superconducting ring incorporating a weak link constriction as an inductor Λ enclosing a weak link capacitor C, as shown in Figure 7.2(a). In this model it is assumed that charge can move through the weak link in integer units of $q = 2e$ and flux can move across the weak link in integer units of Φ_0, both processes being quantum mechanical in nature. For this weak link ring treated as a single macroscopic quantum object, the canonically conjugate variables are the magnetic flux Φ threading through the ring and $C\dot{\Phi}$, effectively the charge at the weak link[11]. Thus:

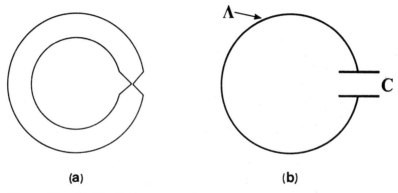

(a) (b)

Figure 7.2 (a) Idealised representation of a weak link ring. (b) Leaky inductor/capacitor circuit model of a weak link ring.

$$[\Phi, C\dot{\Phi}] = i\hbar \qquad [8]$$

which implies the uncertainty relation:

$$\Delta\Phi.\Delta(C\dot{\Phi}) \geqslant \hbar \qquad [9]$$

The role of these conjugate variables can best be explained by example. Let us again consider the thick superconducting ring. Here, the flux is extremely well defined and localised at discrete values of $n\Phi_0$. To see what has happened to the charge we can imagine making a cut across the ring of infinitely narrow section (Figure 7.2(b)) such that $C \to \infty$. It follows that charge on either side of this cut must be ill-defined since quantum-mechanical pair transfer processes $(0, \pm q, \pm 2q \ldots \pm Nq)$ can occur across the cut up to extremely high order in N. This is equivalent to saying that macroscopic screening supercurrents can flow in the ring. Thus, from a quantum-mechanical viewpoint, as implied by [9], precise quantisation of flux in units of

$\Phi_0 = h/2e$ will only be observed in circumstances where charge can be completely delocalised around the ring; that is, for the case of the thick superconducting ring.

Rigid quantisation of flux cannot be maintained when a weak link constriction is incorporated in the ring since, by definition, this constriction is made small enough in section to allow quantum-mechanical coupling between different flux states of the ring. For a relatively large cross section constriction we can arrange for nearest neighbour coupling $[n\Phi_0 \rightarrow (n \pm 1)\Phi_0]$ to be dominant. If we assume that the matrix element for this nearest neighbour coupling is $\hbar\Omega/2$, where $\Omega/4\pi$ is the quantum-mechanical frequency for the transfer of Φ_0 bundles of flux across the weak link, then, for small Ω, we can write a matrix equation for all such nearest-neighbour couplings of the form:

$$W_n D_n - \frac{\hbar\Omega}{2}(D_{n+1} + D_{n-1}) = E(\Phi_x)D_n \qquad [10]$$

which yields the Φ_x-dependent ground-state energy of the weak link ring.

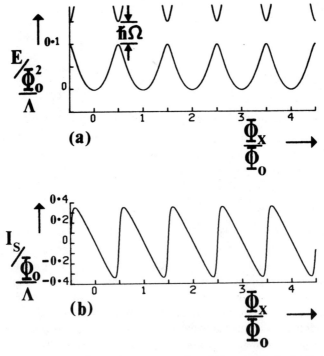

Figure 7.3   (a) Ground-state energy band E versus Φ_x in the flux mode shown for $\hbar\Omega = 0.05\Phi_0^2/\Lambda$. (b) Screening current dependence $-dE/d\Phi_x$ versus Φ_x for the ground-state energy band (a).

In Figure 7.3(a) we show the ground-state energy, periodic in Φ_0, as a function of Φ_x, computed using a small value of Ω ($\hbar\Omega = 0.05\Phi_0^2/\Lambda$). As can be seen, the introduction of a weak link into the ring creates a splitting at the crossing points of the energy parabolas in Figure 7.1. It can also be seen that for small Ω coupling between adjacent flux states is only important close to the maxima in E versus Φ_x, at which points an amplitude superposition (e.g. $n\Phi_0 \rightleftharpoons (n + 1)\Phi_0$) exists between these macroscopically different quantum-mechanical states of the ring. In any one of the almost parabolic sections between these maxima the flux state of the weak link ring is rather well defined and localised about a particular value of $n\Phi_0$. As implied by [9], this requires that the weak link constriction is large enough in cross-section to accommodate a macroscopic screening current; that is, quantum-mechanical pair-charge transfer processes $\pm Nq$ can take place through the weak link up to very high order in N. This is demonstrated very clearly in Figure 7.3(b), where the screening super-current ($<I_s> = -dE(\Phi_x)/d\Phi_x$) is plotted as a function of the external applied flux Φ_x, as calculated from the ground-state energy $E(\Phi_x)$ of Figure 7.3(a). The screening current response $I_s(\Phi_x)$, shown in Figure 7.3(b), is necessarily the sum of harmonics [12] such that:

$$I_s(\Phi_x) = -dE(\Phi_x)/d\Phi_x = \sum_{m=1}^{\infty} I_m \sin (2\pi m\Phi_x/\Phi_0) \qquad [11]$$

In terms of the uncertainty relation [9], if the flux threading the ring inductor is relatively well defined about discrete values of $n\Phi_0$, the charge on the weak link capacitor must be a superposition of a large number of integer pair-charge states. This is clearly not in the limit of weak link behaviour, as defined by Josephson [8], where only nearest-neighbour superpositions ($Nq \rightleftharpoons (N \pm 1)q$) are considered. In the 'flux mode' limit (small Ω, $n\Phi_0 \rightarrow (n \pm 1)\Phi_0$ couplings) we can therefore treat the charge Q as continuous (i.e. no longer discrete) and write a wave function in terms of an angular displacement $\theta = 2\pi Q/q$ as:

$$\Psi(\theta) = \sum_n D_n e^{-in\theta} \qquad [12]$$

which, from [1], yields for the ground-state energy a Schrödinger equation of the form:

$$(1/2\Lambda)[i\Phi_0(\partial/\partial\theta) - \Phi_x]^2\Psi(\theta) - \hbar\Omega \cos \theta\Psi(\theta) = E(\Phi_x)\Psi(\theta) \qquad [13]$$

We note, first, that [13] is not the Schrödinger equation, based on the Josephson definition of weak link behaviour, which has been used previously to calculate the properties of weak link rings operating in the flux mode regime [10], and, second, that [13] contains just one cosine in the potential.

Equations [10] and [13] yield only the ground-state energy. To find the weakly-excited states we must consider the quantised oscillator modes of the weak link ring. If the effective capacitance of the weak link is C then these oscillator modes are created at a frequency:

$$\omega_c = 1/(\Lambda C)^{\frac{1}{2}} \tag{14}$$

Thus, neglecting the zero-point energy, we can introduce a new energy (from [6]):

$$W_{n,m}(\Phi_x) = \frac{(n\Phi_0 - \Phi_x)^2}{2\Lambda} + m\hbar\omega_c \tag{15}$$

If, in the flux-mode limit, flux can move in or out of the ring in units of Φ_0 while at the same time the photon number can change from m to m', with coupling $C_{mm'}$, the matrix equation for all possible nearest-neighbour flux-state couplings now becomes:

$$W_{n,m}D_{n,m} + \frac{\hbar\Omega}{2}\sum_{m'} C_{mm'}[D_{n+1,m'} + D_{n-1,m'}] = E_\kappa(\Phi_x)D_{n,m} \tag{16}$$

where:

$$C_{mm'} = \sum_{r=0}^{\min\{m,m'\}} (m!m'!)^{\frac{1}{2}} [r!(m-r)!(m'-r)!]^{-1}\lambda^{(m+m'-2r)} \tag{17}$$

λ is a dimensionless parameter, and the combinatorial factors arise because photons are identical bosons.

The energies calculated from [16] form a set of bands in Φ_x space, with periodicity Φ_0 and band number κ. It can be seen that n and m are no longer good quantum numbers and are replaced as such by the band number κ. The ground state and first two excited state energy bands ($E_\kappa(\Phi_x)$ versus Φ_x, $\kappa = 1$, 2 and 3) are shown in Figure 7.4 for a choice of small Ω and ω_c ($\hbar\Omega = 0.05 \ \Phi_0^2/\Lambda$, $\hbar\omega_c = 0.078 \ \Phi_0^2/\Lambda$) and $\lambda = 0.5$. The effect of the ring-oscillator mode photons is to create ever more complex band patterns as the band number κ is increased. Again, the expectation value of the macroscopic screening super-current flowing around the ring is just:

$$\langle I_s(\Phi_x)\rangle_\kappa = -dE_\kappa(\Phi_x)/d\Phi_x \tag{18}$$

and the ring magnetic susceptibility for a particular band is given by:

$$\chi_\kappa(\Phi_x) = \Lambda d\langle I_s(\Phi_x)\rangle_\kappa/d\Phi_x \tag{19}$$

Observation of the flux-space band structure of a weak link ring – quasi-static method

Although it is apparent that an observation of flux-space energy bands, examples of which are given in Figure 7.4, would constitute incontrovertible evidence for the operation of quantum mechanics on the macroscopic level, the actual experimental techniques required to make such an observation have turned out to be very demanding in terms of electronic technology. The principal technical problem is easy to appreciate. We are dealing with an electronic device, the weak-link ring, which displays quantised energy levels with separations of a few hundred GHz. In order to probe this energy level structure electronically the measurement system (i.e. the electronics external to the weak link ring) noise temperature must be reduced to ~ few K over a large band-width (nominally DC to 10^{12} Hz). Fortunately, with modern liquid-helium cooled electronics, based on gallium arsenide (GaAs) devices, this is now a perfectly practicable proposition.

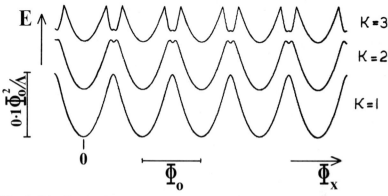

Figure 7.4   Energy bands E_κ versus Φ_x for the ground state and first two excited states ($\kappa = 1$, 2 and 3) of a superconducting weak link ring with $\hbar\Omega = 0.05\Phi_0^2/\Lambda$, $\hbar\omega_c = 0.078\Phi_0^2/\Lambda$ and $\lambda = 0.5$.

The experimental techniques we have devised to look at flux-space band structure do not require transitions to be made between bands. Instead, we have been able to use very low energy methods which allow us, in effect, to monitor the first and second derivatives of a particular band energy as a function of Φ_x, while the weak link ring remains in this band. This can be achieved because the quantum object (the weak link ring) can be made larger than the measurement apparatus to which it is coupled. In this section we describe a quasi-static technique which allows us to monitor the in-band magnetic susceptibility $\chi_\kappa(\Phi_x)$, proportional to the second derivative $d^2E_\kappa(\Phi_x)/d\Phi_x^2$ of the band energy.

Consider, first, a coil inductor, of inductance L_t, at a generalised temperature T. For convenience electronically, this inductor is narrow-banded by means of a capacitor connected in parallel. If the centre frequency of this tuned (tank) circuit is ω_R, such that $\hbar\omega_R \ll k_BT$, then the magnetic flux noise in the inductor, integrated over the band pass of the tank circuit, is just:

$$\langle|\Delta\Phi_t|^2\rangle = k_B T L_t \qquad\qquad\qquad\qquad [20]$$

If the tank circuit inductor is coupled to the weak link ring through a mutual inductance M_{ts}, such that, as usually defined, the coupling coefficient between tank circuit and ring is:

$$K_{ts} = [M_{ts}^2/L_t\Lambda]^{\frac{1}{2}}$$

then the flux noise in the inductor is now given by[9,10]

$$\langle|\Delta\Phi_t|^2\rangle = k_B T L_t[1 + K_{ts}^2\chi_\kappa(\Phi_x)] \qquad\qquad [21]$$

In practice we always measure a mean-square noise voltage across the tank circuit. From [18], [19] and [21] this is given by:

$$\langle|\Delta V_t|^2\rangle \simeq \omega_R^2 k_B T L_t[1 - K_{ts}^2\Lambda d^2 E_\kappa(\Phi_x)/d\Phi_x^2] \qquad [22]$$

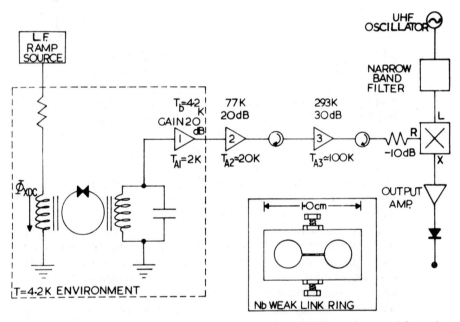

Figure 7.5   Block diagram of the UHF (430 MHz) receiver used for noise spectroscopy (magnetic susceptibility) experiments.

The extremely low noise receiver we use to monitor such voltage fluctuations is shown in block form in Figure 7.5. For technical reasons concerned with the fabrication of transistors and diodes which can operate effectively at liquid helium temperatures, we have chosen 430 MHz as the centre frequency for this receiver. Using state-of-the-art microwave GaAs field-effect transistors (GaAs FETs) and variable-capacitance diodes, we have been able to achieve an in-band noise temperature at the tank circuit of a few K; that is, comparable with the condensed-matter temperature of the weak link ring (4.2 K). The receiver consists of a chain of three UHF amplifiers, operating at temperatures of 4.2 K, 77 K and room temperature ($\simeq 300$ K), respectively. Each amplifier has electronically-adjustable matching networks, incorporating GaAs varactor diodes, on the input and output. The power gain and approximate in-band noise temperature of each amplifier stage is given in Figure 7.5. As can be seen, UHF circulators are provided for in-band isolation (40 dB) between the second- and third-stage amplifiers and the third-stage amplifier and the UHF mixer. Broad-band attenuation is provided between each amplifier stage (not shown) and between the third-stage amplifier and the mixer. Very careful attention is paid in this receiver system to properly terminating, in a broad-band sense, the output terminal of the mixer. Without due care being taken over this detail, we find that the noise temperature of the receiver can easily increase by an order of magnitude. In addition, we arrange for both the cryogenically-cooled and room-temperature receiver electronics to be extremely well-shielded electromagnetically, effectively from ~ 1 Hz upwards. As a further precaution against unwanted external noise being injected into the tank circuit (and hence the weak-link ring), all active devices used in the receiver system (e.g. GaAs FETs and GaAs diodes) are powered by very-low-noise FET-based power supplies, operated from car batteries. This combination of broad-band (roughly a few MHz to >3 GHz) reverse isolation, very-low-noise amplifiers and effective electromagnetic shielding and power-supply noise-reduction techniques leads to an all-up broad-band receiver-noise temperature at the tank circuit of approximately a few K. In practice this receiver-noise temperature is only maintained if we use an extremely stable UHF local oscillator, with a few parts in 10^{10} frequency stability.

The experimental method used by us to monitor the magnetic susceptibility χ_κ of the weak link ring is very simple. We adjust all the matching stages and GaAs FET gate-bias voltages in the UHF amplifier chain for minimum noise temperature. We then plot the mean-square noise voltage $\langle |\Delta V_t|^2 \rangle$ developed in the tank circuit as a function of a very-slowly-varying external applied flux, Φ_{XDC}. Typically, this flux will increase (or decrease) by one flux quantum over a time scale of 10 to 30 seconds. The UHF-receiver output is displayed in a small bandwidth (DC to a few Hz) on a standard X-versus-time plotter. Susceptibility patterns extending over 10 to 20 Φ_0 of external bias flux, both positive and negative, are then plotted over time periods of up to 10 minutes.

In Figures 7.6(a), 7.6(b) and 7.6(c) we show noise-voltage data for the ground state and first and second excited-state bands ($\kappa = 1, 2$ and 3) taken using a niobium point-contact weak link constriction ring[9,10]. As Φ_{XDC} is changed it can be seen that these susceptibility patterns, which are observed on a larger static noise-voltage background, repeat themselves with Φ_0 periodicity. Experimentally, these

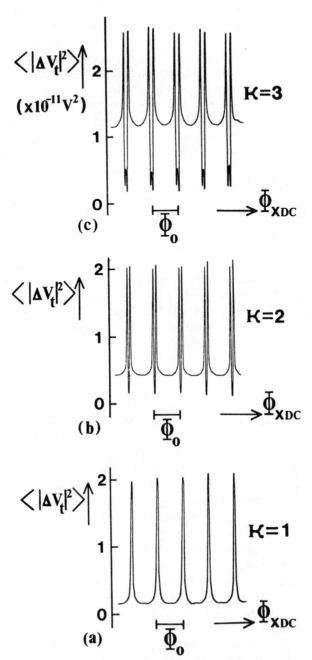

Figure 7.6   Experimental noise $\langle|\Delta V_t|^2\rangle$ spectroscopy patterns (band-magnetic susceptibilities) for the ground state ($\kappa = 1$) and first two excited state ($\kappa = 2$ and 3) flux-space bands; receiver centre frequency is 430 MHz; post-detection bandwidth is DC to a few Hz and $T = 4.2$ K; periodicity $= \Phi_0$. Scale for the mean square voltage shown in units of 10^{-11} V^2.

susceptibility patterns display no hysteresis; that is, when Φ_{XDC} is reversed, even over large ranges in bias flux, these patterns super-impose up themselves. This must be the case if the weak link ring is maintaining itself in a single band. Within the practical limitations imposed by our existing UHF receiver system, we find that the weak link ring can remain stably in a particular band for a period as long as 10 minutes, although this time may be much shorter (~ 30 seconds). A transition is then made to an adjacent band. We assume that such transitions are caused by the absorption or emission of millimetre wave photons of energy comparable to the separation between the low-lying weak link ring bands ($\simeq \hbar\omega_c$). Even with all the care we have taken in shielding, isolation and low-noise amplification, and given the poor coupling configuration of the weak link ring to millimetre-wave radiation, the stability of the ring in these first few energy bands is remarkable.

In Figures 7.7(a), 7.7(b) and 7.7(c) we show the theoretical best-fit band-susceptibility patterns for the ground state and first two excited states of the ring. This best fit is achieved for $\hbar\Omega = 0.05\Phi_0^2/\Lambda$, $\hbar\omega_c = 0.078\Phi_0^2/\Lambda$ and $\lambda = 0.5$. The energy bands corresponding to the magnetic susceptibilities of Figure 7.7 have already been presented in Figure 7.4. The correspondence between the experimental and theoretical susceptibility patterns is striking. We note that quite substantial changes in $\lambda(0.5 \pm 0.2)$ have little effect on the theoretical suscepti-bility patterns of Figure 7.7 For each pattern $\hbar\omega_R \ll \hbar\Omega$ and $\hbar\omega_c$ which means that we can observe the ring in one of its eigenstates without causing a transition between states. This is a direct consequence of the essential measurement apparatus; that is, the tank circuit, being smaller than the quantum object, the weak link ring. In a practical arrangement the tank-circuit coil inductor is actually placed inside the weak link ring[13]. As far as we are aware, this non-invasive probing of a single-quantum mechanical object by a macroscopic apparatus constitutes a radical departure from conventional approaches to the problem of measurement in quantum systems. In this context it is apparent from the susceptibility patterns of Figure 7.6 that, using non-invasive measurement techniques, it is perfectly practicable to observe a macroscopic quantum object in an amplitude superposition of macroscopically different states. For the case of the weak link ring of Figure 7.6, these macroscopically different states are the quantised magnetic-flux states which we deliberately do not choose to measure. This, therefore, provides one experimental retort to the often-posed paradox of Schrödinger's cat[14], although, of course, a supercon-ducting weak link ring is an extraordinarily coherent object compared with a room-temperature cat.

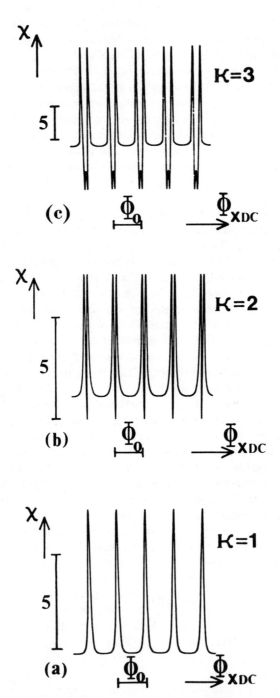

Figure 7.7   Theoretical $\kappa = 1$, 2 and 3 in band magnetic susceptibility patterns (a), (b) and (c) calculated from [16] using $\hbar\Omega = 0.05\Phi_0^2/\Lambda$, $\hbar\omega_c = 0.078\Phi_0^2/\Lambda$ and $\lambda = 0.5$. Susceptibility scale for each band as indicated.

Observation of the flux-space band structure of a weak link ring – dynamical method

The circuit shown as a block diagram in Figure 7.5 can form the basis for a particular version of the well-known AC-biased superconducting quantum interference device (SQUID) magnetometer [13]. The only requirements for turning this system into a SQUID magnetometer are, first, that a high-frequency (AC) current I_{IN} be injected into the tank circuit from an external current source and, second, that this current source be frequency- and phase-locked to the local oscillator source. AC in this context is generally taken to mean a frequency range from a few MHz to roughly 0.5 GHz. The system now operates as a phase-sensitive detector (PSD) at the frequency of the AC input. The response of the coupled weak link ring-tank circuit combination to the injected current I_{IN} is monitored via the AC voltage V_{OUT} developed across the tank circuit. In a PSD SQUID magnetometer the phase difference between V_{OUT} and I_{IN} can be adjusted by means of an AC phase shifter incorporated into the local oscillator arm of the system. In simple AC-biased SQUID magnetometers the PSD system is dispensed with and the amplified SQUID signal V_{OUT} is displayed directly after diode detection [15,16].

When a high-frequency current is injected into the tank circuit a high-frequency magnetic flux is generated in the tank-circuit coil. This flux couples to the weak link ring, which in response sets up a circulating screening supercurrent. If we know the form of this screening current, that is, its dependence on the external flux with the weak link ring in a particular energy band, it is possible to calculate quantum mechanically the dynamical (V_{OUT} versus I_{IN}) characteristics of the ring–tank circuit combination. This requires that the current I_{IN} be amplitude-modulated so that its peak amplitude increases linearly with time. In a practical magnetometer I_{IN} cannot increase without limit, so a triangular amplitude modulation is invariably adopted. The frequency of this amplitude modulation is always kept very small compared with the AC carrier frequency.

To take one example, the quantum-mechanical expression for the rf cycle average in-phase V_{OUT} versus I_{IN} characteristic (V_{OUT} at zero phase with respect to I_{IN}) with the ring operating in a single-flux mode band (Ω small) is given by [17]:

$$\bar{V}_{OUT}(\text{in phase}) = Q\omega_R L_t [I_{IN} \sin^2 \delta + \frac{\mu}{\pi}\int_{-\pi}^{\pi} d\zeta \cos \zeta \langle I_s(\Phi_x^{tot}, \zeta)\rangle] \quad [23]$$

where I_s is the Φ_x-dependent screening current in a given flux mode band, Q is the quality factor of the unloaded tank circuit, and $\mu = M_{ts}/L_t$. For a static applied flux Φ_{XDC} and an AC flux Φ_{XAC} coupled to the ring, the argument of the screening current $\langle I_s\rangle$ is

$$\Phi_X^{\text{tot}} = [\Phi_{\text{XDC}} + \mu\Phi_{\text{XAC}}(\zeta)],$$

where $\mu\Phi_{\text{XAC}}$ is the flux felt by the ring due to the rf current in the tank circuit. The interaction between the tank circuit and the ring renormalises the impedances of both, changing Λ to $\Lambda_r = \Lambda(1-K_{ts}^2)$ and shifting the resonant frequency of the tank circuit from ω_R to $\omega_r = \omega_R(1-K_{ts}^2)^{-\frac{1}{2}}$. In [23] δ is the phase of the unrenormalised tank circuit impedence at frequency ω_r.

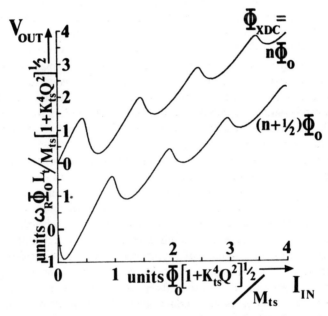

Figure 7.8   Theoretical dynamical flux mode in phase V_{OUT} versus I_{IN} characteristics calculated from [16] and [23] for: (a) $\Phi_{\text{XDC}} = n\Phi_0$; and (b) $\Phi_{\text{XDC}} = (n + \frac{1}{2})\Phi_0$.

In Figures 7.8(a) and 7.8(b) we show the ground-state flux-band dynamical characteristics for the two DC flux states ($\Phi_{\text{XDC}} = n\Phi_0$ and $\Phi_{\text{XDC}} = (n + \frac{1}{2})\Phi_0$) with the weak link ring ground-state ($\kappa = 1$) energy band as given in Figure 7.4 ($\hbar\Omega \doteq 0.05\Phi_0^2/\Lambda$, $\hbar\omega_c = 0.078\Phi_0^2/\Lambda$ and $\lambda = 0.5$). In this calculation we have used a value of $K_{ts}^2Q = 1.58$ which is very typical for the inductances (Λ, L_t and M_{ts}) and quality factor found in practical AC-biased SQUID magnetometers[13]. The screening current $\langle I_s \rangle$ used in this calculation is shown in Figure 7.3(b). The effect of the DC flux Φ_{XDC} is to shift the origin for the amplitude modulated AC flux, Φ_{XAC}. For the $\Phi_{\text{XDC}} = (n + \frac{1}{2})\Phi_0$ state this leads to a cusp in V_{OUT} appearing at the origin in I_{IN}, corresponding to the weak link ring biased on one of the maxima in E versus Φ_X (Figure 7.3(a)).

In Figures 7.9(a) and 7.9(b) we show experimental lowest band in phase V_{OUT} versus I_{IN} characteristics for an ultra-low-noise SQUID magnetometer, operating at 430 MHz, with an amplifier chain frequency bandwidth of 50 MHz, and based on the circuit of Figure 7.5. This magnetometer uses a niobium point-contact constriction weak-link ring[13,15] which is maintained at a helium bath temperature of 4.2 K. The effect of changing the DC bias flux from $n\Phi_0$ (Figure 7.9(a)) to $(n + \frac{1}{2})\Phi_0$ (Figure 7.9(b)) is:

1   to invert the triangular features in the characteristic; and

2   to create a cusp feature in V_{OUT} at the current origin following closely the theoretical characteristics of Figure 7.8.

Although the features displayed in the V_{OUT} versus I_{IN} characteristics of this very high performance magnetometer are roughly triangular in shape, as is to be expected if the flux transitions in the weak-link ring take place quantum mechanically, the more familiar SQUID 'steps' are easily recovered[18]. This can be achieved in two ways. First, if the frequency bandwidth of the UHF SQUID electronics is restricted sufficiently, the higher harmonics associated with the triangular features are lost and all that can be seen experimentally are positively-sloped steps. Second, if noise of sufficient amplitude is injected into the tank circuit the triangular features are again washed out into steps. This arises because, from an electrical-circuit model viewpoint, these noise fluctuations create jitter in the times at which flux transitions occur in any particular cycle of the externally generated AC flux[19]. It is noteworthy that within the quasi-classical treatment of the AC-biased SQUID magnetometer, where quantum mechanical flux transition processes are not taken into account, the concept of a shunt resistor R, in parallel with the weak link supercurrent channel, has to be introduced in order to generate these step features[20,21]. Thus, in this treatment the dynamical behaviour of the weak link ring is described in terms of a quasi-classical non-linear equation of motion:

$$C \cdot \frac{d^2\Phi}{dt^2} + \frac{1}{R}\frac{d\Phi}{dt} = \frac{-dU}{d\Phi}(\Phi,\Phi_x) \tag{24}$$

where the potential is:

$$U(\Phi,\Phi_x) = \frac{(\Phi - \Phi_x)^2}{2\Lambda} - \frac{I_c\Phi_0}{2\pi}\cos(2\pi\Phi/\Phi_0) \tag{25}$$

I_c is the 'critical current' of the weak link (that is, the current required to drive the link normal) and Φ is the included flux in the ring.

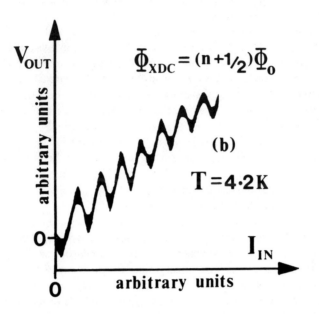

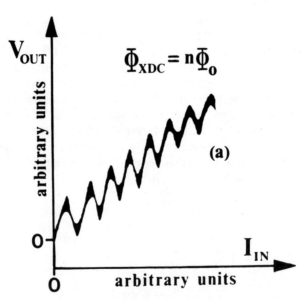

Figure 7.9   Experimental in phase V_{OUT} versus I_{IN} characteristics for a flux mode 430 MHz bias SQUID magnetometer at T = 4.2 K for: (a) $\Phi_{XDC} = n\Phi_0$; and (b) $\Phi_{XDC} = (n + \frac{1}{2})\Phi_0$. Amplifier chain bandwidth 50 MHz, rf amplitude modulation frequency 100 kHz.

The resistively-shunted junction (RSJ) model, where the shunt resistor R acts as a Nyquist noise source, has played a very important role in the development of weak link physics[22]. However, from the viewpoint of weak link rings, this electrical-circuit model really only parameterises the limitations in the performance of the SQUID magnetometer electronic system. The normal dissipation occurs in the finite Q-tank circuit and this is included in the quantum mechanical expression [23] for the magnetometer V_{OUT} versus I_{IN} characteristic.

It is worth comparing the lowest-band dynamical characteristics of Figure 7.9 with the experimental susceptibility patterns of Figure 7.6. Again, we are making a radically different kind of measurement on a single-quantum object simply because this object is larger than the classical circuit measurement apparatus. In this dynamical experiment we monitor the screening current in the weak link. We do not, at any time, make a measurement to decide which macroscopically different flux state the ring is in. What we are seeing in both the SQUID magnetometer and susceptibility experiments is the effect of a macroscopic quantum object on a classical measurement apparatus while this object – the weak link ring – remains in an eigenstate of the system.

The charge mode regime – coupling between all possible flux states of a superconducting weak link ring

We have seen that it is possible to incorporate a weak link in a thick superconducting ring so that, to lowest order, quantum transitions are only made between nearest-neighbour flux states of the ring $[n\Phi_0 \rightarrow (n \pm 1)\Phi_0]$. This requires that macroscopic screening currents should be able to flow around the ring and, as we have pointed out, this cannot correspond to the Josephson limit of weak link behaviour. We now consider the conjugate mode of a superconducting weak link ring, where the link is small enough in cross-section to couple all possible flux states of the ring together; that is, couplings $n\Phi_0 \rightarrow (n, \pm 1, \pm 2, \pm 3 \ldots)\Phi_0$ are allowed up to very high order in the number of flux quanta transferred. The ring is now in an amplitude superposition of all possible flux states so that the flux in the ring is extremely ill-defined. From the uncertainty relation [9] this implies that charge, in units of $q = 2e$, should become well defined (localised) at the weak link. This limit, which we shall term the 'charge mode', constitutes the macroscopic quantum-mechanical state of a weak link ring conjugate to the flux mode described by the matrix equations [10] and [13]. By comparison with the quantised flux states of a superconducting ring, we can imagine the weak link capacitor possessing instantaneous polarisation states of different integer $(N)q$

charge, where $N = 0, \pm 1, \pm 2 \ldots$ etc., from which we can build up a matrix description of the charge mode by analogy with [10]. If we assume

1   to lowest order, only weak nearest neighbour $Nq \rightarrow (N \pm 1)q$ coupling between the localised pair-charge states on the weak link capacitor need be considered;

2   an amplitude A_N for the weak link to be in the Nq^{th} polarisation state;

3   a quantum-mechanical transition frequency between these polarisation states of $v/4\pi$; and

4   an energy storage on the weak link capacitor of:

$$W_N = Q_{\text{tot}}^2/2C \qquad [26]$$

where:

$$\begin{aligned} Q_{\text{tot}} &= N_q - C\dot{\Phi}_x \\ &= N_q + Q_x \end{aligned} \qquad [27]$$

Given that Q_x is the displacement charge on the capacitor, so that:

$$W_N = (N_q + Q_x)^2/2C \qquad [28]$$

then the matrix equation for all nearest-neighbour couplings is just:

$$W_N A_N - \frac{hv}{2}(A_{N+1} + A_{N-1}) = E(Q_x)A_N \qquad [29]$$

For relatively small values of hv (compared with q^2/C), equation [29] yields a ground-state 'charge band' in displacement charge (Q_x) analogous to the flux-space (Φ_x) ground-state band of Figure 7.3(a) [23,24]. This ground-state charge band, calculated from [29] for $hv = 0.05q^2/C$, is shown in Figure 7.10(a). The screening voltage for this band, defined as:

$$\langle V_x(Q_x) \rangle = dE(Q_x)/dQ_x \qquad [30]$$

with electric susceptibility:

$$\chi_e(Q_x) = -Cd\langle V_x(Q_x) \rangle/dQ_x \qquad [31]$$

is shown in Figure 7.10(b).

By analogy with the screening current in the flux mode (equation [11]), the screening voltage response on the weak link capacitor, due to an externally generated Q_x, is the sum of harmonics:

as is obvious from Figure 7.10(b).

Again, by analogy with [12] and [13], in this charge mode limit (small v, $Nq \rightarrow (N \pm 1)q$ couplings) we can treat the flux Φ as continu-

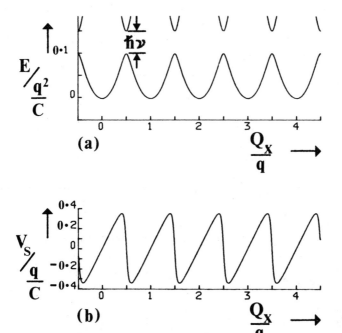

Figure 7.10 (a) Ground-state energy band E versus Q_x in the charge-mode shown for $\hbar\nu = 0.05q^2/C$. (b) screening voltage dependence dE/dQ_x versus Q_x for the ground-state energy band (a).

ous (no longer discrete) and write a wave function in terms of an angular displacement $\alpha = 2\pi\Phi/\Phi_0$ as [25,26]:

$$\Psi(\alpha) = \sum_N A_N e^{iN\alpha} \qquad [33]$$

which generates, through [29], a Schrödinger equation for the ground state in this charge mode of the form:

$$1/2C[-iq(\partial/\partial\alpha) + Q_x]^2\Psi(\alpha) - \hbar\nu \cos \alpha\Psi(\alpha) = E(Q_x)\Psi(\alpha) \qquad [34]$$

When Q_x is set to zero, [34] is just the quantum mechanical form of the well-known Josephson pendulum equation [8,10,24]. As with [13], equation [34] contains just one cosine in the potential. This cosine, together with the magnetic energy storage term $(\Phi - \Phi_x)^2/2\Lambda$, constitute the potential adopted in the quasi-classical description of a superconducting weak link ring, as given by [24] and [25]. We can rewrite [34] explicitly in terms of flux, including a magnetic energy storage term and, again, with $Q_x = 0$, as [27,28]:

$$\left[\frac{-\hbar^2}{2C}\cdot\frac{\partial^2}{\partial\Phi^2} + \frac{(\Phi - \Phi_x)^2}{2\Lambda} - \hbar v \cos\left(2\pi\frac{\Phi}{\Phi_0}\right)\right]\Psi(\Phi) = E(\Phi_x)\Psi(\Phi) \quad [35]$$

It is possible to solve [35] to yield energy levels $E_\kappa(\Phi_x)$, $\kappa = 1,2,3\ldots$, and magnetic susceptibilities:

$$\chi_\kappa = -\Lambda d^2 E_\kappa(\Phi_x)/d\Phi_x^2$$

which correspond to the patterns shown in Figure 7.6, for a particular choice of v^{10}. Now, from a quantum mechanical viewpoint [34], and hence [25], can only be arrived at by assuming an amplitude superposition of all possible flux states of the ring; that is, in the charge mode or the Josephson limit of weak link behaviour. This is a contradiction in terms since flux-mode descriptions, either quantum mechanical (equations [10] and [13]) or quasi-classical (equations [24] and [25]) are concerned with the situation where the flux states of a weak link ring are relatively well-defined about the values $n\Phi_0$ ($n = 0, \pm 1, \pm 2 \ldots$ etc.) and macroscopic screening supercurrents can flow around the ring. From our previous arguments a better description of a flux-mode weak link ring should develop, starting with charge-mode equation [34], if we introduce higher harmonics into the potential. Our trial 'flux mode' Schrödinger equation then takes the form:

$$\left[\frac{-\hbar^2}{2C}\frac{\partial^2}{\partial\Phi^2} + \frac{(\Phi - \Phi_x)^2}{2\Lambda} - \hbar\sum_{\eta=1}^{\infty} v_\eta \cos\left(\frac{2\pi\eta\Phi}{\Phi_0}\right)\right]\Psi(\Phi) =$$

$$E(\Phi_x)\Psi(\Phi) \quad [36]$$

We are now actively investigating solutions of [36].

Observation of the charge space band structure of a weak link ring – dynamical method

The analogy between equations [10] and [29], which yield, respectively, the ground-state energy bands in external flux and displacement charge space, leads directly to an experimental method for investigating the charge-band behaviour of a weak link enclosed by a superconducting ring. In the charge-mode limit we can treat the ring simply as an inductive element to couple a time-dependent magnetic flux across the weak link. We can then use a SQUID magnetometer system as we have already described (Figure 7.5) to probe charge-band behaviour dynamically. Assuming that the weak link is operating in a single charge mode band, the quantum mechanical expression for the rf cycle average in phase V_{OUT} versus I_{IN} characteristic is given by [17,29]:

$$\bar{V}_{OUT} = Q\omega_R L_t \left[I_{IN} \sin^2 \delta - \frac{\mu}{\Lambda_r \omega_r \pi} \int_{-\pi}^{\pi} d\zeta \sin \zeta \langle V_s(Q_x^{tot}, \zeta) \rangle \right] \qquad [37]$$

Here, L_t, δ, ω_R, ω_r and μ have the same meanings as in [23]. The coupling coefficient is, as before:

$$K_{ts} = [M_{ts}^2 / \Lambda L_t]^{\frac{1}{2}}$$

V_s is the Q_x-dependent screening voltage in a given charge band (see [30]), with an argument:

$$Q_x^{tot} = -C[\dot{\Phi}_x + \mu \dot{\Phi}_{XAC}(\zeta)]$$

where $-C\dot{\Phi}_x$ is the static bias displacement charge corresponding to the magnetic flux Φ_x in [23]. As in this flux-mode dynamical expression, the coupling of the quantum mechanical weak link ring to the dissipative external-circuit oscillator mode of the tank circuit is taken into account rigorously in the charge-mode equation [37].

Examination of [23] and [37] shows that a scaling factor of $\omega_R \Phi_0 : q/C$ exists between the flux mode and the charge mode. Thus, although for $\Omega = v$ both [23] and [37] yield precisely the same features in the ground-state band V_{OUT} versus I_{IN} characteristics, the scale of these features in voltage and current are very different. For example, with $C = 10^{-15}$ F [10,30] and $\omega_R/2\pi$ in the 10 to 100 MHz

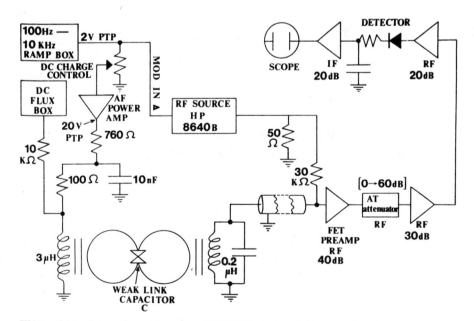

Figure 7.11 Large dynamic range rf SQUID electronics system for charge-mode dynamics with diode detector and static-bias displacement-charge subcircuit shown.

range, this sets the charge-mode features (that is, triangles) approximately 100 to 1,000 times larger in voltage and current than the conjugate flux mode features.

Charge-mode effects have only been observed very recently [29,31] and the experimental problem in their realisation appears to have been one of scale, as we have just described. We have, in fact, found it very easy to set up niobium point contacts with small enough cross sections $(\leq \lambda_L)$ [29] to exhibit charge-mode behaviour. However, the standard arrangement of AC-biased SQUID electronics [13,18,30] lacks the dynamic range required to observe this behaviour. In practice the dynamic range of both the input rf current source and the output amplifier stages of the SQUID system must be increased by a factor

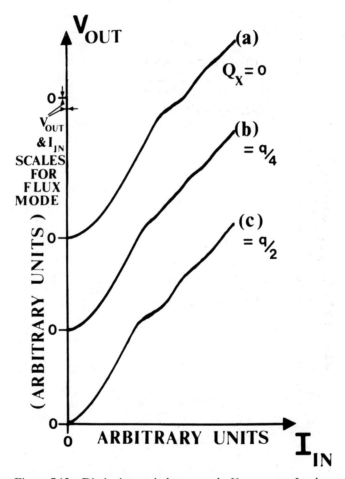

Figure 7.12   Diode detected charge-mode V_{OUT} versus I_{IN} characteristics for: (a) $Q_x = -C\Phi_x = 0$; (b) $Q_x = q/4$; and (c) $Q_x = q/2$, with $T = 4.2$ K, $\omega_R/2\pi = 30$ MHz and flux-mode scalings as indicated.

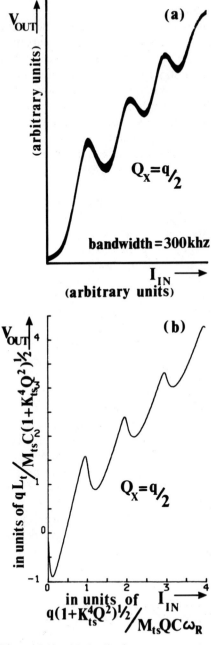

Figure 7.13 (a) Radio frequency ($\omega_R/2\pi = 30$ MHz) in phase V_{OUT} versus I_{IN} charge mode characteristic for $Q_x = q/2$ plotted at $T = 1.5$ K showing ground-state behaviour. (b) Theoretical in-phase V_{OUT} versus I_{IN} charge-mode characteristic for $Q_x = q/2$ calculated from [29] and [37] with $\hbar v = 0.05 q^2/C$.

of up to 1,000. The design of a SQUID electronics system, developed for charge-mode work, is shown in block form in Figure 7.11. This electronics is set up for diode detection but can easily be rearranged to become a phase-sensitive system. The static bias displacement charge $(-C\dot\Phi_x)$ is provided by means of the 3 μH coil coupled to the weak link ring.

In Figure 7.12(a), (b) and (c) we show charge-mode characteristics for $Q_x = -C\dot\Phi_x$ set at 0, $q/4$ and $q/2$, respectively [29,31]. The scale corresponding to flux mode features is as indicated. The niobium point contact, set in a two-hole niobium block [15], is of the usual mechanically-stabilised and thermally-oxidised variety [13]. The actual adjustment of the point contact weak link is made *in situ* in the cryostat at 4.2 K. The weak link ring is coupled to an rf tank circuit at 30 MHz. The output signal from this tank circuit is amplified and then diode detected. This detection technique is well known to be noisy [13,30,31]; it also provides no phase information. The outcome is that the triangular features predicted by [37] are washed out into steps [19,31]. Even so, knowing the inductance (3 μH) of the static-bias displacement-charge coil and the amplitude and modulation frequency of the current input to this coil, we can estimate the capacitance C of the weak link [29,31], provided the charge mode periodicity in Q_x space is $q = 2e$. For a range of input current modulation frequencies we find C (average) $= 1.1 \times 10^{-15}$ F. We have used this technique, at various cryostat temperatures, to determine the capacitance of a whole series of charge-mode limited point-contact weak link. We find capacitances ranging from a few $\times 10^{-16}$ F to a few $\times 10^{-15}$ F.

In Figure 7.13(a) we provide one example of what can be achieved in terms of V_{OUT} versus I_{IN} charge-mode characteristics using a well-defined low-noise phase-sensitive detection system, again operating at an rf frequency $(\omega_R/2\pi)$ of 30 MHz, but this time at a cryostat temperature of 1.5 K. The characteristic shown corresponds to a static-bias displacement-charge of $q/2$. In Figure 7.13(b) we show the in-phase V_{OUT} versus I_{IN} characteristic calculated from [37], assuming that the weak link is operating in the ground-state charge band. Here, $Q_x = q/2$, $K_{ts}^2 Q = 1.58$ and $h\nu = 0.05q^2/C$, as shown in Figure 7.10(a). The expression [37] predicts a spike at the origin of the $Q_x = q/2$ characteristic in Figure 7.13(b). This appears not to be resolved in Figure 7.13(a) (cf. Figure 7.9(b) for the $(n + \frac{1}{2})\Phi_0$ flux-mode characteristic) but the origin does move up and down weakly and periodically on the V_{OUT} axis with changing Q_x.

Charge-mode effects in a normal ring containing a superconducting weak link

Although we have chosen to consider the canonically conjugate roles of magnetic flux and charge in a thick superconducting ring containing a weak link, this quantum mechanical description can be carried over to the case of a superconducting weak link enclosed in a normal metal ring. The concept still holds that for small enough cross sections flux can be transferred quantum mechanically back and forth across the weak link in units of $\pm\Phi_0$, $\pm2\Phi_0$ ... $\pm n\Phi_0$. Thus equation [29], which yields the ground-state charge-band energy, is not dependent on the weak link being contained within a superconducting ring. Magnetic flux is still confined when the ring is normal, at least on a time scale short compared with the circuit time constant of the ring (Λ/R, where R is the resistance of the normal section).

We have started to investigate the rf behaviour of niobium point-contact weak links incorporated in normal copper rings. We find that these hybrid rings, operated at frequencies between 17 and 30 MHz, display perfectly good SQUID charge mode V_{OUT} versus I_{IN} character-istics which are split in the usual way by a static bias displacement charge (Q_x). We have not observed flux mode behaviour in these hybrid rings. The obvious difference between the normal copper and superconducting niobium ring devices is that for the former the Q_x-bias cannot be generated by currents of too small a modulation frequency. When the inverse of this frequency becomes comparable with Λ/R, the time-dependent bias flux Φ_x, which is required to generate Q_x, simply leaks out through the copper ring and does not cut across the weak link.

As an example of the behaviour of hybrid rings we show in Figure 7.14 the result of our first attempt to monitor directly the ground-state charge band of the superconducting niobium weak link. We plot the mean square noise voltage across the tank circuit coupled to the ring as a function of increasing bias displacement charge with no rf current drive applied to the tank circuit and, from [31], observe the second derivative pattern $d^2E(Q_x)/dQ_x^2$ versus Q_x with the weak link operating in the ground-state band. This is the charge mode analogue of the noise spectroscopy technique used to plot the flux-mode magnetic susceptibility ($d^2E_\kappa(\Phi_x)/d\Phi_x^2$, equation [19], Figures 7.6 and 7.7) as a function of external applied flux Φ_x. The susceptibility spikes in Figure 7.14, which were recorded using a linearly increasing and decreasing (triangular modulation) Q_x at a frequency of 3 kHz, are somewhat truncated in height due to band-width limitations in the charge-mode receiver system. Nevertheless, the power of the noise spectroscopy technique and the correspondence between flux-mode and charge-mode susceptibility data (Figure 7.6(a) and Figure 7.14) are obvious.

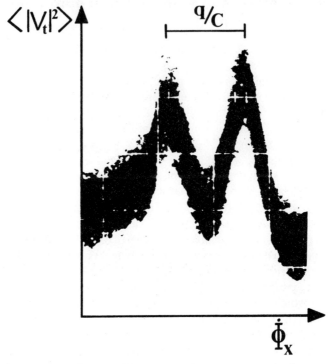

Figure 7.14   Plot of mean square noise voltage $\langle |\Delta V_t|^2 \rangle$ as a function of linearly increasing $V_x = -\dot{\Phi}_x$; triangular modulation frequency to generate Φ_x set at 3 kHz; frequency band-pass for measurement 10 kHz to 100 kHz; $T = 1.5$ K; periodicity $= q/C$.

Conclusions

We have attempted to provide a systematic description of weak link ring devices treated as single macroscopic quantum objects. We have demonstrated that within this description even these simple objects display a remarkably rich macroscopic quantum-mechanical structure. However, the usefulness of these devices in any future study of quantum mechanics itself, and its relationship to relativity, is an area still to be explored.

Acknowledgments

I would like to thank my friends and fellow researchers at the University of Sussex, Drs R. J. Prance, J. E. Mutton, H. Prance and T. P. Spiller for making all this work possible. I am also grateful to Dr R. Nest of the University of Copenhagen for his much appreciated collaboration with us and to Professor A. Widom of Northeastern for his unique contribution to this subject. Our special thanks to Dr J.

Gallop of the National Physical Laboratory, Teddington, for keeping our spirits up in hard times.

References

1 L. N. Cooper, *Phys. Rev.*, **104**, 1189 (1956).
2 J. Bardeen, L. N. Cooper and J. R. Schrieffer, *Phys. Rev.*, **108**, 1175 (1957).
3 A. D. C. Grassie, *The Superconducting State*, Sussex University Press, 1975, p. 30.
4 R. P. Feynman, *Statistical Mechanics*, Benjamin, Reading, Mass., 1972, p. 304.
5 M. Tinkham, *Introduction to Superconductivity*, McGraw-Hill, Kogakusha, 1975, p. 59.
6 F. London and H. London, *Proc. Roy. Soc.* **A149**, 71 (1935).
7 W. L. Goodman, W. D. Willis, D. A. Vincent and B. S. Deaver, *Phys. Rev.*, **B4**, 1530 (1971).
8 B. D. Josephson, *Phys. Lett.*, **1**, 251 (1962).
9 R. J. Prance, J. E. Mutton, H. Prance, T. D. Clark, A. Widom and G. Megaloudis, *Helv. Phys. Acta*, **56**, 789 (1983).
10 J. E. Mutton, R. J. Prance and T. D. Clark, *Phys. Lett.*, **104A**, 375 (1984).
11 A. Widom, *J. Low Temp. Phys.*, **37**, 449 (1979).
12 A. Widom, T. D. Clark and G. Megaloudis, *Phys. Lett.*, **76A**, 163 (1980).
13 A. P. Long, T. D. Clark and R. J. Prance, *Rev. Sci. Instrum.*, **51**, 8 (1980).
14 E. Schrödinger, *Naturwissenschaften*, **23**, 807 (1935).
15 A. H. Silver and J. E. Zimmerman, *Phys. Rev.*, **157**, 317 (1967).
16 L. Solymar, *Superconductive Tunnelling and Applications*, Chapman & Hall, London, 1972, Chapter 14.
17 T. P. Spiller, J. E. Mutton, H. Prance, R. J. Prance, T. D. Clark and R. Nest, 'Quantum mechanical flux band dynamics of a superconducting Weak Link Constriction Ring', Phys. Lett. **115A**, 125 (1980).
18 A. P. Long, T. D. Clark, R. J. Prance and M. G. Richards, *Rev. Sci. Instrum.*, **50**, 1376 (1979).
19 J. E. Mutton, R. J. Prance, T. D. Clark and A. Widom, 'Influence of noise on the voltage versus current characteristics of an AC-biased SQUID magnetometer', in M. Savelli, G. Lecoy and J. P. Nougier (eds), *Noise in Physical Systems and 1/F Noise*, Montpellier, France, May, 1983, Elsevier Science Publishers BV, 1983.
20 J. Kurkijärvi, *J. Appl. Phys.*, **44**, 3729 (1973).
21 A. Barone and G. Paterno, *Physics and Applications of the Josephson Effect*, John Wiley, New York, 1982, Chapter 13.
22 *Ibid.*, Chapter 6.
23 A. Widom, G. Megaloudis, T. D. Clark, H. Prance and R. J. Prance, *J. Phys.*, **A.15**, 3895 (1982).
24 A. Widom, G. Megaloudis, T. D. Clark, J. E. Mutton, R. J. Prance and H. Prance, *J. Low Temp. Phys.*, **57**, 651 (1984).
25 J. Callaway, *Quantum Theory of the Solid State* (Academic Press, 1976), p. 681.
26. P. G. de Gennes, *Superconductivity of Metals and Alloys* (Benjamin, New York, 1966), p. 118.
27 A. J. Leggett, 'Quantum tunnelling and noise in SQUIDS', *Sixth Int. Conf. on Noise in Physical Systems*, National Bureau of Standards Special Publication 614, Library of Congress Catalog Number 81, 600084, p. 355.

28   W. den Boer and R. de Bruyn Ouboter, *Physica*, **98B**, 185 (1980).
29   H. Prance, R. J. Prance, J. E. Mutton, T. P. Spiller, T. D. Clark and R. Nest, 'Quantum duality in SQUID rings and the design and operation of a quantum mechanical voltmeter', published in the *Proceedings of the 1985 European Physical Society Condensed Matter Conference*, Berlin, March 1985 (*Fest-körperprobleme – Advances in Solid State Physics*, Vol. XXV).
30   R. J. Prance, A. P. Long, T. D. Clark, A. Widom, J. E. Mutton, J. Sacco, M. W. Potts, G. Megaloudis and F. Goodall, *Nature*, **289**, 543 (1981).
31   R. J. Prance, T. D. Clark, J. E. Mutton, H. Prance, T. P. Spiller and R. Nest, *Phys. Letts.*, **107A**, 133 (1985).

8

Meaning and being in contemporary physics

Bernard d'Espagnat *Laboratoire de Physique Théorique et Particules Elémentaires, Orsay, France*

1 Introduction

Anybody who intends to ponder on the foundations of contemporary physics and who feels a need for a starting point should read in parallel two remarkable recent articles by Wheeler [1] and Bell [2]. No experience can show more clearly than this the fact that the foundation problem does not simply merge into what we normally call physics. For, in this latter field, we never get the impression that two mutually incompatible standpoints are both valid, whereas this is just the queer feeling that can easily emerge from the experience in question. Indeed, although the contents of these two articles are mutually exclusive, the articles themselves are so persuasive that we must think hard before we find an acceptable way not to take up unreservedly – at the same time – the views expressed by both of them.

This thinking adventure differs from day-to-day physical research also in the fact that it calls for no recourse to highbrow mathematics or to long sets of elaborate formulae. It essentially consists in trying to bring some more light into the question of the implicit views, assumptions, concepts and the like that tacitly underlie our way of thinking and that make us agree in succession with the arguments of each article. In other words it makes us aware of the force of Einstein's assertion that what is most basic in physics is not the mathematics but rather the set of the underlying concepts.

It is of course clear that David Bohm ranks first among the physicists of our generation who illustrated through their example the deep truth of Einstein's maxim. Many of us – including the present writer – were awakened from a kind of 'dogmatic slumber' (to take up

Kant's words) by reading his 1952 papers. But most certainly (as his later work shows) Bohm would, more emphatically than anybody else, advise us not to just jump from one dogma to another. This is why we feel entitled to dedicate to him the discussion presented here.

In a way, the first of the quoted articles (although the developments of the present paper are inspired by the two authors quoted, we are quite far from giving here a mere transcription of what they assert; hence their responsibility is not in the least involved in any statements given here which would be unpalatable to the reader) may be considered as an explication of the main ideas of the Copenhagen group or, more precisely, of a way in which these ideas may be given manifest internal consistency. As is well known, some of the most significant of these ideas were left in a not-completely-explicit and even somewhat ambiguous stage by their authors. Moreover, some of them were obliterated to some extent by the considerable development of the quantum formalism. This is because this formalism was essentially rooted in Dirac's and von Neumann's works and laid therefore – compared to the Copenhagen views – a greater emphasis on the notion of a (microscopic) quantum state (or equivalently on that of a state preparation procedure) and correspondingly a smaller emphasis on the consideration of the experimental conditions under which such and such a particular proposition (bearing on a physical system) can be tested. Because he neither shuns nor conceals behind general statements the most baffling consequences of the undiluted Copenhagen views, Wheeler gives us in his recent articles (and particularly in the one quoted) extremely valuable clues as to what the basic ideas are, on which the view in question should be anchored if we want them to be non-ambiguous and to constitute a fully self-consistent set.

As for the Bell article, it offers both a concise and extremely clear description of what requirements a theory of independent reality can reasonably be expected to fulfill and the basic outline of a quantum field theory which, in line with Bohm's 1952 papers, actually satisfies them. As already stressed, Wheeler's and Bell's conceptions and conclusions, as to 'what the world is' and as to our relationship with whatever may be called reality, are opposite and mutually exclusive. This, in a way, is fortunate because a challenge is thereby presented to us. Each of these two articles should help us to discover what in the other one are the apparently obvious ideas that we too quickly took for granted.

2   A view of Wheeler's article

It is not the case that every physicist who considers himself as being a supporter of the Copenhagen views will necessarily agree with the content of Wheeler's article. In the opinion of many among these scientists, the Copenhagen views are based on the assertion that the 'classical' or 'macroscopic' objects and events exist in some absolute sense which is in no need of being defined. Indeed, trying to define it, or even trying to speak about it, would (so they think) be idle talk. Or if it is not, if such a task is not entirely meaningless, at least it is one which, in their opinion, can and should be entirely left to the philosophers. They *then* claim that we should not try to speak of the quantum objects by themselves and that any valid description of the quantum phenomena must be anchored on the notion of these obviously existing objects and events (and in particular on the two closely related notions of 'complete experimental set up' and of 'conditions of observation' so often appearing in Niels Bohr's works). Such a conception may conveniently be called macro-objectivism; and we may then assert that many theoretical physicists identify the Copenhagen view with a special case of macro-objectivism.

Now, macro-objectivism is a view which works very well in practice but which meets with conceptual difficulties that are actually quite serious. The most conspicuous of these is that it seems unavoidable to consider macroscopic objects as ultimately composed of microscopic, i.e. quantum, ones. And one of the notions which one was trying to discard, namely the notion of quantum objects existing in some absolute sense independently of the conditions of observation, seems thereby to be inescapably creeping back. Closely related with this difficulty is the one that macro-objectivism seems to require a rather sharp distinction to be made between classical and quantum objects (and events), whereas physics proper does not seem really to give us any clue as to how such a distinction could be made objective in any sense that would be in harmony with the basic ideas of, precisely, macro-objectivism. Admittedly irreversibility has – at least as regards events – been considered by many authors as a good candidate for playing the role of a criterion in that respect. But, again, it seems difficult to define irreversibility in a way which would make no reference whatsoever, not even an implicit one, to the limitations of the abilities of the community of observers. In fact, the proposals that have been made along these lines do not seem to comply with the requisites that, for consistency, a macro-objectivist must have in mind when he considers an 'objective' macroscopic event. An alternative possibility, namely the idea that quantum mechanics should only be an approximate theory, remains open. But it is not substantiated by any experimental fact and it would be quite a new thing if a momentous scientific change were initiated neither by new findings nor by new theoretical developments but just by considerations that can well be called philosophical about the nature of reality.

Under these conditions it seems that whoever wants to 'remain faithful' to the letter of the Copenhagen conception should preferably not identify the latter with macro-objectivism. Moreover it seems that he will thus remain closer to the real spirit of the Copenhagen founding fathers. In his book *Physics and Philosophy*, Heisenberg, for instance, considers that a statement 'can be made objective' if we may consistently claim that its content does not depend on the conditions under which it can be verified. And when he then defines several varieties of realism, he dismisses as meaningless any 'metaphysical realism' (this is the expression he used) that would not reduce either to what he calls practical realism or to what he calls 'dogmatic realism'; that is, to a conception asserting that most or, respectively, all of our meaningful statements about the material world can be 'made objective', in the sense just specified. Now what is most significant in this standpoint of Heisenberg is not the distinction he makes between practical and dogmatic realisms (although this, of course, is important too). It is the very fact, first, that this author does *define* what he calls objectivity and realism instead of considering that these are primary concepts and, second, that he defines them by referring to what can actually be done. By choosing to define these terms and to define them in this way, Heisenberg in fact makes *verification* the primary concept; that is, he chooses as a primary concept in science one which basically refers to the actions of *men*. This choice has implications which are in fact so momentous that most of the physicists who consider themselves as agreeing with the Copenhagen viewpoint seem somehow not to have dared taking them quite fully into account.

This however is not the case with John Wheeler. In Wheeler's paper the ultimate referent is 'meaning', a concept for which Føllesdal's definition 'Meaning is the joint product of all the evidence that is available to those who communicate' is taken. Another key word of this paper is 'phenomenon'. However let us not be abused by the fact that in current scientific language the word 'phenomenon' is very often understood as just signifying a type of event taking place within a reality whose concept is tacitly understood as being *the* ultimate referent. Wheeler's sentence 'no phenomenon is a phenomenon until it is an observed phenomenon' very clearly dismisses this 'commonsense' view. Indeed his 'phenomena' should be understood in the etymological sense (which is also the one in which Kant used the word); namely, 'what is observed and about which an agreement gets established amongst the community of all people in their right mind'. It is important to stress that in Wheeler's paper there is no primary concept other than these two (or just 'meaning' if we consider that 'phenomenon' refers to 'meaning'). In particular, we shall not understand this article if we consider that there is another primary concept, namely 'reality', tacitly underlying it. The article in question makes no use of such a concept but if it did there is no doubt that reality would be defined relative to one of the aforenamed two concepts or to both – again, just as is the case in Kant's work. Consequently, Wheeler urges us 'to abandon for the foundation of existence a physics hardware located "out there" and to put in instead a "meaning" software located who knows where'.

There is no point in reviewing Wheeler's article further, except to notice that the qualitative ambiguities and difficulties mentioned above are of course removed by such a drastic approach. In particular it is clear from the whole content of this paper that its author does not give any basic status to the concept of irreversibility. (He does mention the notion of an 'irreversible act of amplification' however, but it seems that he considers it as a mere 'potential' phenomenon, unless it is 'put to use' to make the meaning.) For example, the splitting of a uranium nucleus, though it is called irreversible, could be undone in principle. It then would not count as a phenomenon. Indeed, if we are right, his way of solving the well-known quantum riddle 'How is it possible that mere information (that is, "software") should in some cases (e.g. that of the Schrödinger cat) modify the real state of macroscopic things (hardware)?' is as follows. He answers by just denying to this postulated hardware any existence of its own. This way of solving the problem will be analysed and discussed in the next section.

3 A dividing line: modal logic (necessity, counterfactuality)

It is well known that in order to make explicit and to formalize our familiar (valid or invalid, this is another question) way of thinking a number of logicians considered that they had to supplement 'ordinary' logic (and in particular its most elementary part, namely the propositional calculus) by introducing the notions of 'necessity' and of 'possibility', for which 'ordinary' logic has no symbol. This gave rise to the so-called 'modal logic', the need of which, although it is questioned by some, is made plausible by the observation that in ordinary logic the relation 'if – then' (called 'material implication', symbol $\supset$) does *not* actually play the role it is intuitively expected to play. For example it does not make it possible to identify the definition of the word *magnetic*, applied to some object x, to the sentence 'If small iron specks are in the vicinity of x, they get attracted', for according to ordinary formal logic this sentence is true, in particular, whenever it is the case that no small iron specks are in the vicinity of x, whatever substance x is composed of ... One way of removing this difficulty (it is not the only way, see below) is obviously to introduce a new relation, called 'strict implication' or 'entailment' and reading 'if – then necessarily'. We can then define 'magnetic' – and more generally all the properties that can be identified to dispositional terms (aptitudes) – by sentences of the form 'If small iron specks are in the vicinity of x, then necessarily they are attracted.'

Should all the properties of material objects be, in the last analysis, considered as 'dispositional terms'? This is a debatable point but it seems that the choice of a positive rather than a negative answer is the less 'metaphysical' option since, at least, it defines properties through a reference to experience. Unquestionably – and this is particularly obvious in quantum physics – we do not have any direct knowledge that an object has or does not have a given property. To gain such a knowledge we must make a measurement; so that it seems appropriate to identify a property of an object with an aptitude this object has of inducing a given definite result when subjected to a definite test (measurement). This observation has the consequence that if we choose the strict implication procedure for defining the dispositional terms, then it is the whole realm of all the properties of objects (including even their very existence) that must be defined this way.

This is not the proper place for describing the details and in particular the formalism of this method (see, for example, reference 3 and the references given in reference 4). Let it be mentioned however that, in order to define in a precise way the notion of strict implication, modal logic has to introduce the notion of 'possible situations' (or, as they are often called, 'possible worlds') differing from the actual situation (or 'world'), and has to specify that the implication under study holds not only in the actual situation but also in all these possible situations. When applied to the definition of properties this method obviously implies that measurements which, actually, are *not* done, should be considered. For example, if it is asserted that a photon has some definite momentum **p**, because it has been so prepared, what is meant, according to this method, is that if a measurement (of the photon momentum), which actually is not made, *were* made with the help of some appropriate instrument (which *actually* is not present) it would give result **p**. For that reason the strict implications considered here may also be called 'counterfactual implications'. But one point should be stressed. We must specify what the set is of all the 'possible situations' used in the definition. Technically this set is sometimes called the 'sphere of accessibility' associated with the actual situation under study. Clearly a great many physically conceivable situations should not be included in it. In classical physics, for example, if we want to counterfactually define the fact for a system to have some given energy, quite obviously we must exclude from the corresponding sphere of accessibility all the conceivable physical situations in which the system in question interacts with other systems in such a way that its 'energy' is not definable. When – explicitly or, more often, implicitly – we try to apply this procedure of definition to quantum mechanics (see section 4 below), the restrictions we must impose on the sphere of accessibility are even more stringent (to avoid misunderstandings, let it be mentioned right away that the thus-obtained description of quantum mechanics is nevertheless nearer to von Neumann's than to Bohr's views).

It should be observed that the counterfactual implication method here under study is a mere explication of a process which quite naturally and spontaneously takes place in our mind when we speak of properties of systems, including their very existence. In fact (and in this section this is the first point we want to make) our usual notion of a reality 'existing out here' is essentially based on our unconscious use of the counterfactual method. My car really exists since, even when I lie in my bed at night, I *could* (though I do not) look through the window and see it parked in the street. Consequently we assert here that counterfactuality is at the root of the (almost universally held) world-view that may be called 'physical realism'.

Now the second main point we want to make is that the Copenhagen view can (and probably should) be understood as not making any use of counterfactual implications whatsoever, and that Wheeler's approach indeed makes no use, not even an implicit one, of the implications in question. The possibility of defining 'properties' without any resort to counterfactuality is technically known (to the epistemologists) as the 'partial definition' procedure. For brevity let us simply note here that if this alternative is chosen then, properly speaking, a system S may have property A only when the experimental set-up is such as to allow for a measurement of A. Otherwise the sentence 'S has property A' is 'worse than false', for it is simply meaningless. Although a few isolated sentences of the Copenhagen founding fathers seem to refer to a kind of macro-objectivism which, in turn, would tacitly refer to counterfactuality in the macroscopic domain, it remains true that in the microscopic domain, at least, the method of partial definition of properties is actually the one which is in agreement with the 'hard core' of the Copenhagen standpoint (and, in particular, with the substance of Bohr's reply to Einstein). It can be considered that in Wheeler's article – in which no sharp distinction between these two domains is made and in which the notion of a hardware 'reality out here' is banned, as we saw – even the physical properties of the macroscopic objects are supposed to be defined by this man-centred method (it is man centred because in it the instruments can only be defined as the 'things' that serve to measure).

At this stage we can draw a provisional conclusion, which is that Wheeler's standpoint, although it is most baffling (except to some followers of Kant), cannot nevertheless be rejected right away on technical grounds since a method (the partial definition procedure) does indeed exist for defining properties (and therefore for doing physics) without having to rely conceptually on the pair counterfactuality–physical realism. Moreover we understand somewhat more precisely the root of our vague feeling that this conception *is* baffling. It lies in the fact that we are not used to defining properties (and existence) by the partial definition method. As we said, without being even aware of the fact, we always conceive of them as though they were defined by the counterfactual method.

The best way we have of grasping how and to what extent a given conceptual approach removes the conceptual difficulties raised by quantum physics is to look at the way in which the approach in question can help solve the central riddle of this physics, which – again – may be formulated as follows. While it is conceivable that a measurement may modify a small object, the idea that a measurement of the co-ordinates of the moon may grossly affect these co-ordinates should be avoided at all costs. Similarly we should avoid at all costs being trapped into the conclusion that the fact of ascertaining where the pointer of an instrument lies (thus 'making a measurement' of this position, either with the naked eye or with some second instrument) may in some cases 'do something' appreciable to this physical quantity. But in the Schrödinger cat paradox (in which, for simplicity, we may replace the cat by a pointer) how is it possible to avoid the conclusion in question? How is it possible to remove the simple objection which reads 'After we look the pointer has a given definite position. Before we look it has not. Hence by looking we "do something" to the pointer'?

This is not the proper place for discussing whether or not any of the numerous attempts at building up a 'quantum measurement theory' succeeded in solving this riddle. What is of immediate interest to us is whether and how the two mutually exclusive views adopted by Wheeler and Bell, respectively, succeed in doing so. Bell's view is discussed below, but we may right away make the qualitative remark that, since this author accepts the notion of 'hidden variables', his prospects of removing the difficulty seem at first sight to be quite good. At first sight, on the contrary, since Wheeler does *not* accept the 'hidden variables' notion, his prospect of removing the objection looks bad.

But we claim the thesis can be upheld that this is just an appearance. Again, the objection seems insuperable to us because, without being even aware of the fact, we systematically think in terms of a counter-factually-defined reality (here the reality of the wave function; that is, the reality of the state in which the object-plus-pointer composite system was prepared or happened to be). If we are really willing to take the major conceptual step that the Copenhagen founding fathers, somewhat ambiguously perhaps, invited us to take and that Wheeler, frankly rejecting this ambiguity, explicitly claims we *should* take – that is, if we give up altogether any idea of a knowable hardware reality existing *per se* out here – then the very basis of the objection disappears. It just has no meaning to say, for example, that 'before we look the pointer has no definite position'. To understand why this is so we may compare the complex situation under study with a simpler one. For example, let us replace the whole composite system (measured quantum system *plus* apparatus) by a spin one-half particle P and let us replace the fact of looking at the pointer by that of measuring its spin component S_z. In the case in which the preparation procedure consisted in passing P through a Stern-Gerlach device directed along $0x$, we then normally tend to say that before the measurement P has an S_x which has a definite value so that S_z can have no definite value on P. But actually, if we decide to define properties exclusively by means of the partial definition method, we cannot even assert the premise since P is not associated with an apparatus capable of measuring S_x. Be it only for this reason, we then cannot derive from the axioms of quantum mechanics any falsification of the assertion that before the measurement S_z already has some definite but unknown value.

Of course, this argument can be carried over in a straightforward way to the actual problem under study. Hence we are right in asserting it is only the fact of the human mind spontaneously not following the partial definition method and tacitly thinking instead in terms of a counterfactually defined 'external reality' that gives to the objection under study the appearance of being valid. In fact it is not. Its validity is restricted to the 'elementary' conceptual description of quantum mechanics which we hinted at above, and which counterfactually defines the state of the system before measurement. To repeat: if we hold fast to the prescription of using exclusively the partial-definition procedure we cannot meaningfully say that we 'do something' to the pointer by looking at it (and we cannot say either that we are acting on the past by inducing it to 'have taken' a definite position when it interacted with the quantum system).

Remark

This conclusion can also be reached by criticizing – in the objection under study – the use made of the phrase 'after we look, the pointer has a definite position' for establishing the role of the observer as a cause. At least, this is true if we accept the definition of the (controversial) notion of cause which restricts its use to the case of events that, although they may just happen in nature without any involvement of man, nevertheless can *also* be induced by man's free will. This definition [5] reads: 'If A is such an event and if it is the case that event B takes place (after A) in all the cases in which we made A to happen, and does not take place in the cases in which we refrained from doing so, then A is the cause of B.' To apply this definition to our problem we must, of course, say that A is the fact of looking at the pointer. But what is B? B (the effect) cannot be that the pointer co-ordinate takes a value within a given interval (say, between 4 and 5 on the scale) since it is not true that in all the cases in which we do look we observe that special result. Hence the effect can only be 'the pointer has *some* definite position' (by opposition to 'the pointer has a given definite position'). But in ordinary formal logic the sentence 'the pointer has some definite position' is a mere tautology. It can acquire a non-tautological meaning only through a resort to modal logic (a V ā is a tautology but $\square$ a V $\square$ ā is not, where $\square$ a means 'necessarily a'). Hence in the approach considered here (no modal logic accepted) it is false to say that this sentence only became true when we looked.

Is it claimed here that Wheeler's approach removes all the conceptual difficulties of quantum physics? Certainly not. In fact the present author, for one, pointed out[6] that non-local indirect measurements of the EPR variety raise difficult questions in the partial definition approach; and, more generally, Wheeler himself warns us that what he is trying to do is mainly to indicate a direction, and that major difficulties still remain to be settled. Our purpose in this section is merely to point out the way in which, within the approach in question, a particular – but puzzling – question can be settled.

4   Some comments on Bell's views

Before leaving (for the time being at least) Wheeler's article, it is appropriate to mention a highly illuminating analogy therein contained. It consists in comparing the work of the scientific community to a very peculiar type of the well-known game of guessing a word by asking a group of friends questions such as 'Is it an animal?' 'Is it blue?', and so on. We say 'a very peculiar type' because, in the analogy proposed by Wheeler, the friends of the guesser have decided not to choose a word in advance. Everyone could answer as he pleased, with the only proviso being that he had to have a word in mind compatible with all the previous answers. As Wheeler points out, we used to think of the electron as having a definite position, whether we observe it or not, just as the guesser thinks the word exists in his friends' minds even before he starts asking questions. The analogy consists in the fact that both these ideas are wrong. And it is clear from the whole context – in the quoted article – that the analogy is supposed to hold just as well for a pointer position as for an electron position.

In this analogy the guesser obviously corresponds to the scientist. But to what, may we ask, do the guesser's friends correspond? Wheeler answers: 'They play the role that "nature" does in the typical experiment.'

Now, up to this point we were happy. We were somehow in the state of mind of a student who reads a textbook in mathematics or physics; who grasps the transitions from one equation to the next; who sometimes, for better understanding, makes explicit for his own use some intermediate calculations that the writer left implicit; and who, apart from this, has no questions and no worry. But now, with this word 'nature' appearing just in this role which Wheeler assigns to it, suddenly a – highly non-technical but all the same highly worrying – question does appear. For is not physics the science of nature? Is it not true that its aim is to try to know at least some features of nature itself? But then how can we escape the following remark? The just-recalled analogy – the fitness of which we do not question – shows just the contrary. It shows that, if Wheeler is right, the scientist actually does no more increase his knowledge of 'nature' than the guesser increases his knowledge of his friends. They both build up a knowledge, but just not that one.

Does this objection destroy our previous opinion that Wheeler's argument is strong? Not at all, but nevertheless, and particularly if we recently read some of the very explicit statements (presumably inspired in part by David Bohm and at least consonant with important ideas of the latter) contained in some of Bell's articles (see, for example, reference 7), we must be specially receptive to the objection in question; for in several of these texts Bell's views link up with those of Einstein in that they both consider that a satisfactory physical theory should tell us about *what is*, instead of endlessly playing with such concepts as observables, measurements, state preparation procedures, and so on.

In a number of classical, very general, assertions of philosophy (such as 'ideas can only be related to ideas', and so on) some may see grounds for *a priori* rejecting this requirement. But such arguments do not look binding since, as we saw, a technically respectable means – namely counterfactual implication – exists for defining the properties of at least the macroscopic objects (and their existence as well) in such a way that, although the definitions do involve man's experience, nevertheless the reality of their described union may without any contradiction be considered as independent of man's mind.

On the other hand, as soon as this latter view (commonsense realism) is accepted as regards the macroscopic objects it is, as we saw, difficult to reject the requirement that it should be extended to physics in general. Indeed, so natural is this requirement that most of the physicists (including even quantum theorists) who have not given special attention to these problems implicitly believe that somehow it is fulfilled as regards contemporary physics.

If we try to follow these lines explicitly, *a priori* two possible ways seem to be open for our query. One of them is to try to dispense with supplementary (or 'hidden') variables; the other is not to exclude the existence of the latter. It may be said that the first way is the one which is followed by most physicists (without them always being fully aware of it). It consists (commonsense realism again) in systematically using the counterfactual implication method of definition, in extending it, therefore, also to the properties of the *quantum* systems, and in trying to avoid the well-known conceptual difficulties (two-slits experiment and so on) by restricting in some suitable way the relevant sphere of accessibility. Technically this is achieved by specifying that the sphere of accessibility corresponding to (a given value of) a given property of the system does not include possible situations ('worlds') in which an instrument capable of measuring a quantity incompatible with the property in question is associated to the system. Practically, this way of thinking leads very directly to the view that the quantum states (as described by state vectors) are 'physically real' in the sense explained in the foregoing section.

The advantages of this conceptual approach (which we may call the conventional one, since it is in the minds of so many working physicists) lie in its formal simplicity and in its practical efficiency. Nevertheless, its inconveniences are serious. First of all it should be noted that it does not entirely fulfill the Einstein-Bell requirement as defined above, since it defines a property by means of a sphere of accessibility, the specification of which incorporates the use of the man-centred concept of an instrument. But even if this special difficulty can be removed, other ones remain. As soon as the state vector is considered as being 'physically real', the Schrödinger 'cat paradox' reappears. In a sense it may be said that the whole content of the so-called 'quantum measurement theory' (or 'theories') is nothing but an effort to remove this paradox. But, as we briefly noted above, it seems that the price these theories have to pay for success is always the same. It consists in making somewhere (preferably at some not-too-conspicuous place) some reference to the practical inability of mankind at making particularly difficult measurements. Hence these theories cannot be said to satisfy the Einstein-Bell requirement.

Another inconvenience of the conceptual approach under study was pointed out by Aharonov and Albert[8]. These authors could show that in quantum theory there exist *some* non-local physical quantities that are measurable in principle, at least in the restricted sense that it can be checked whether or not the physical system under study is in an eigenstate of the considered quantity. Moreover, the measurements in question are non-demolition measurements; that is, they leave the system in this state. They can thus be repeated as often as desired. The point then is that we can monitor such a non-local eigenstate (that is, we can continuously check that the system still is in it) in any referential we choose. Under these conditions an ordinary local measurement of some other quantity pertaining to the system cannot reduce the state other than on the hyperplane defined by the time of this measurement in this chosen referential (any other assumption would lead to a contradiction between two sets of predictions which are both verifiable in the referential in question). Hence the collapse of the quantum state cannot be considered as being a covariant process. This does not imply a violation of relativity conceived of as an operational theory since, as several authors including the quoted ones have shown, relativistic causality *in this sense* is not violated. However it would imply a violation of this same relativistic causality – but now conceived of in a realistic sense – if we were to assume that the non-local state under consideration is 'physically real' (in the sense made precise by the counterfactual method) *and* is reduced by the ordinary measurement considered above (the Everett approach, in which no collapse takes place, is thereby immune to this criticism). Now the necessity of reducing the state vector upon measurement has always been viewed as an unpleasant feature of the conception discussed here that state vectors of micro-systems are, by themselves, elements of reality. But now we see that this necessity implies the existence of an actual *contradiction* between such a conception and relativity, also understood in some realistic sense. We are therefore confronted, within this conception, with a difficulty which can no more be reduced to the status of a mere 'unpleasant feature'.

A difficulty complementary to the one just described emerges if we choose to remove the latter by just deciding that no state vector reduction ever appears, for we then are led to one or other of the different versions of the Everett theory. And these versions all have features (such as superposition of macroscopically distinct states of consciousness, multiplication of universes and so on), the discussion of which must, for the sake of brevity, be omitted here but the acceptance of which is, at any rate, a heavy price to pay for regained consistency.

If we have all these difficulties of the conventional approach in mind, we are well prepared to listen to Bell's assertion that 'professional theoretical physicists ought to be able to do better', and to appreciate his proposal for doing so in the spirit of the de Broglie-Bohm version of non-relativistic quantum mechanics. This is of course not the proper place for describing the thus-obtained theory. Let it just be mentioned that it works and that it is free from the following defects which mar the conventional approach: necessity of dividing the world into two parts, 'system' and 'instrument'; absence, in the mathematics, of any clue telling us what is 'system' and what is 'instrument'; and, correspondingly, the non-existence of any objective criterion distinguishing, among the natural processes, those which have the special status of 'measurements'. Moreover, the fact that theories of the de Broglie-Bohm type have supplementary variables (supplementary means, here, present in addition to the state vector) entails of course that the 'Schrödinger cat' paradox is far less acute there than in the conventional approach. In its gross features at least, the objective state of the pointer was the same before we looked as it is after we did.

5 Veiled reality?

The first of the conclusions to be derived from this comparison between Wheeler's and Bell's approaches is, I think, that as regards self-consistency and definiteness (absence of ambiguity) both are far superior to what we called the 'conventional approach'. Moreover, the foregoing analyses show that these superiorities stem from the fact that the conventional approach applies ill-defined rules for specifying the cases in which counterfactual implication should be used in the definition of properties. By contrast, both Wheeler's and Bell's approaches have clearcut prescriptions in that respect. In fact, Wheeler's answer is 'never' and Bell's answer implicitly is 'always, unless of course the alleged property under consideration is but a secondary quality, not to be taken into account in the formulation of the basic rules of physics'. In his theory, many of the observables of ordinary quantum mechanics are in fact reduced to this low status of secondary qualities, but the positions of the particles – or, more precisely, the numbers of fermions at any point in space – are not, and in the last analysis we must indeed consider that these quantities are there implicitly defined, just as in classical physics, through the counterfactual implication method (since, at any rate, it is clear they are not defined through the partial definition method). This is why we may say that Bell's approach is openly in agreement with physical realism, while Wheeler's approach is openly not (and the conventional approach makes unsuccessful efforts at trying to make us believe it is).

Shall we then choose between these two theories and, if so, which one of them will have our preference? If we were pure positivists (and if pure positivism could actually be consistently maintained, a hypothesis which now seems doubtful) we would have to choose Wheeler's, or, more precisely (but this specification is important), we would have to choose Wheeler's approach while at the same time refraining, in our comments concerning it, from any allusion to what he calls 'nature' in the quotation commented on above. This is because, as we observed, the entity which he designates there by this name (the name 'independent reality' would be a more precise one since the word 'nature' has many different interpretations) cannot be operationally defined and is in fact unknowable in his theory; and strict positivism has idealist connotations in that it instructs us to deny any meaning to such entities. Since Wheeler's allusion to this independent reality is merely incidental we feel we would not thereby substantially deviate from his views. Nevertheless, if we are neither pure positivists nor pure idealists we can hardly dispense with the notion of a reality which somehow is more than just a 'product' of man's mind. But, as already noted, we may then be seriously worried by the unknowability of 'nature' (of independent reality) in Wheeler's approach. For that reason we may, at first sight, be tempted to choose Bell's theory.

However, along with their nice formal approaches, all the theories of this type also have well-known drawbacks. One of these is their lack of predictive power as regards original experimental results. Another, and probably more serious, one has to do with relativistic covariance and corresponds in fact to the Aharonov-Albert difficulty in the conventional approach. As Bell himself points out, although his theory agrees with the observable predictions of (operational) relativity theory, 'it relies heavily on a particular division of spacetime into space and time', a fact we can express by saying that, in this theory, relativistic covariance has, for a realist, the low status of a mere appearance. Correlatively it implies the presence of non-observable but nevertheless existing non-local influences (non-separability).

Now, an important point is that such non-local features do not constitute just a particular defect of this special theory, of which we could hope other 'realistic' theories to be free. The well-known Bell theorem shows indeed that any theory which correctly reproduces some elementary (and experimentally well verified) quantum predictions and in which reality ('matter, things') is considered as being in spacetime (so that it views spacetime as existing independently of ourselves) *must* have the very peculiar non-local features in question. These, however, are worrying in two respects. First, in spirit at least (not in the equations), they somehow run counter to the very assumption (of space and time embedding of reality) on which the theory is based. Indeed it would seem that the basic motivation for constructing a theory such as Bell's, in which the positions of things are considered as being 'more real' than anything else, is that we do observe things as occupying definite positions in space and that we consider our theory will be simplest if it allows us to interpret this as corresponding to reality instead of just being an appearance. But then, the fact that in the theory under study:

1   we find highly non-local influences and fields (in particular the 'beable' $|t>$); and
2   these influences and fields 'manage' to be completely *unobservable* except in highly sophisticated indirect ways;

certainly constitutes both a surprise and a disappointment since, to a large extent, it re-introduces in the relationship between observation and reality that very 'distance' that we tried to suppress.

And, of course – this is the second point – surprise and disappointment are even amplified by the (related) fact that relativistic covariance is, in this theory, just an appearance. For, again, it seems to be in the spirit of this approach to try to identify as much as possible appearances and reality (or, in a more philosophical language, phenomena and reality) and, at this point, the result obtained is the contrary (some physicists[9] claim they can reconcile relativity with a variety of superluminal action at a distance but it is doubtful[10] that the type of action they consider can account for the correlations observed in the EPR experiments).

Under these conditions, although we cannot disprove Bell's theory, we may be justified in suspecting that after all there is perhaps a sign of some great truth in the mismatch between the quantum rules and the notion of locality; a mismatch that keeps showing up in various aspects of physics. If this were the case, it would mean that we are wrong when we believe the notions we have of space, of time, of spacetime, of the positions of things and of events, are faithful descriptions of features possessed by independent reality.

This is not a view that I, for one, would have taken *a priori*. In other words, methodologically I am not a Kantian. But, *a posteriori*, I feel somehow forced, by the foregoing analyses, to take up a standpoint, some features of which are not very far from some views expressed by Kant. More precisely, I think we should make a sharp distinction between empirical reality – the set of the phenomena – and independent reality. Empirical reality is all to which we have a strictly cognitive access. Kant would have said 'It is in space and time but this is essentially because space and time are the ways we have of describing our experience.' Modern physicists tend to say instead 'It is in spacetime', and the followers of Einstein point out that, since spacetime is not an *a priori* mode of our sensibility, the very fact that physics forces us to this assertion shows that spacetime is real, quite independently from us. I do not go as far as this. In view of the results of the foregoing discussion I feel inclined to consider that even spacetime (and locality, and events and so on) is a notion that owes much to the structure of our mind and that independent reality is in no way embedded in it. However, the argument of the Einsteinians remains impressive. Notions such as that of spacetime and everything that goes with it are not primitive modes of thought. They therefore must have come to us from somewhere, and it is natural to think that they reflect something of independent reality. But, again, in view of the foregoing analyses, it seems that they reflect this 'something' in such a distorted way that it is impossible for mankind to reconstruct with full clarity, from such a poor information, what independent reality 'really is'. In short, independent reality is – and will remain – veiled to us.

Again, within this conception, empirical reality is all that is scientifically (i.e. precisely) knowable. Basically, it is what our present-day quantum physics describes for us. Now, if this is true, a question arises as to whether, within the realm of this empirical reality, which after all corresponds to the whole of our scientific experience, such difficulties as the Schrödinger cat paradox, non-separability and the rest are not still present. If they are, and if they remain as acute as when the distinction between empirical and independent reality is not made, then this distinction should be considered as useless and therefore as irrelevant.

The answer to this last question is that to some extent these difficulties are still there but that they are *not* as acute as they were before. In its strict form, for example, non-separability is merely the assertion that the principle of separability is not valid, and this principle cannot even be formulated in terms of empirical reality alone since it makes references to the 'objective states' of the systems. Within a description of physics centred on the partial definition method it is replaced by a kind of indivisibility between system and instrument which is also non-local in some cases, but this non-locality is then hardly more surprising than the very restriction to the partial definition method in which we saw that a consistent description of empirical reality may be based.

Similarly, as we saw, the central conceptual difficulty of quantum physics, which is 'How can we avoid being forced to say that it is the observer, when he looks at the pointer, who fixes it up in one definite macro-state?', can be removed in principle just by giving up what we called the 'conventional approach' and its dual reference to the partial definition method and to the counterfactual implication method of definition. In particular the difficulty disappears (at least as long as only local measurements are considered) in the approach (to which we believe that Wheeler holds fast) which consists in defining properties and states exclusively by means of the partial definition method and which therefore allows no counterfactual interpretation whatsoever to be given of the so-called 'initial state' of the system (or, in better words, of the state preparation procedure to which this system was subjected). On the other hand, as we said, the indirect, non-local measurements of the EPR type raise, in this approach, some problems of their own[6] that can hardly be considered as being solved and that could, therefore, create some doubts concerning the internal consistency of any 'physics of the phenomena'. This comes in addition to the difficulty that empirical reality is of course the one we have to deal with both in scientific and ordinary life. Especially in ordinary life, we are so accustomed to think of macroscopic systems in terms of the counterfactually defined properties they have that we find it extraordinarily difficult to think of them and of their properties within the exclusive framework of the partial definition approach.

It is at this stage that I consider that the notion of independent reality (even of an unknowable one) may help us. For example, although – for the above described reasons – I do not 'believe' in Bell's description of independent reality (in the sense that I would not swear it is true), I must observe that it is a contradiction-free model of what could conceivably be. And the mere existence of one such self-consistent possibility makes it clear that some (knowable or unknowable but at least contradiction-free) structures of independent reality may 'produce' the observed features of empirical reality so correctly predicted by quantum physics. It shows therefore that the meaning-centred approach of empirical reality which is so characteristic of modern physics is, at least, not hopelessly inconsistent. But it shows this under the condition that empirical reality, even if it is final *for us* – due to the limited powers of human mind – is not considered as the ultimate thing. This, I think, backs up my conception that a distinction between empirical reality and a knowable *or unknowable* independent reality is relevant [11].

To those readers who would consider that this way of thinking is too peculiar to be respectable, I would like to point out that a somewhat similar one was used a long time ago by Epicurus, when he tried to convince his contemporaries that the phenomena could be accounted for rationally, without referring to a pandemonium of deities and of good and evil spirits. At the time of Epicurus an enormous number of simple questions could not be answered scientifically and in the course of showing that deities were unnecessary Epicurus therefore had to point out that we must sometimes make specific hypotheses. For example, concerning the respective sizes of the earth and the sun he advocated the choice of the more natural assumption, which is of course that the sun is smaller, and he stressed that, qualitatively at least, it is possible to explain many phenomena this way without having recourse to the notions he did not like. Now, clearly he was too daring in putting forward the idea that the sun is smaller than the earth, as we might perhaps be too daring if we claimed that Bell's theory is correct. But we shall understand this philosopher somewhat better if we observe that the point he really wanted to make was just that at least one solution to his problem could be consistently thought to exist (my thanks are due to Miss Anne Richard for drawing my attention to this aspect of Epicurus' assertion). It is a similar idea I am trying to convey here. Let it be pointed out moreover that Epicurus' argument would be considered as correct even if a decision as to which one of the two heavenly bodies is larger finally turned out to lie outside human intellectual abilities, and that the analogy with what I have in mind concerning the present problem would then be even closer.

References

1   J. A. Wheeler, 'Bits, quanta, meaning', in the Caianiello Celebration volume, A. Giovannini, M. Marinaro, F. Mancini and A. Rimini (eds), to be published.
2   J. S. Bell, 'Beables for quantum field theory', this volume, p. 227.
3   B. d'Espagnat, *In Search of Reality*, Springer, New York, 1983.
4   B. d'Espagnat, 'Nonseparability and the tentative descriptions of reality', *Physics Report*, **110**, 201 (1984).
5   G. H. von Wright, *Causality and Determinism*, Columbia University Press, New York, 1974.
6   B. d'Espagnat, *Epistemological Letters*, **22**, 1 (1979).
7   J. S. Bell, report to Istituto Italiano per gli Studi Filosofia, Amalfi, 11 May 1984.
8   Y. Aharonov and D. Z. Albert, *Phys. Rev.*, **D21**, 3316 (1980); **D24**, 359 (1981).
9   J.-P. Vigier, *Lett. Nuovo Cimento*, **29**, 467 (1980); *Astron. Nachr.*, **303**, 55 (1982).
10 A. Shimony, *Proc. Int. Symp. Foundations of Quantum Mechanics*, Tokyo, 1983, p. 225.
11 B. d'Espagnat, *Une incertaine réalité*, Gauthier-Villars, Paris, 1984. English translation forthcoming, Cambridge University Press, 1987.

9

Causal particle trajectories and the interpretation of quantum mechanics

J.-P. Vigier, C. Dewdney,
P. R. Holland and **A. Kyprianidis**   *Institut Henri Poincaré.*

1   Introduction

The fundamental disagreement between Bohr and Einstein at the 1927 Solvay conferences concerned not only the interpretation of quantum mechanics but also general philosophical orientations as to the nature of physical theory. Although these two aspects of the debate can never be fully separated, it is clear that, since quantum mechanics is after all a theory about the behaviour of matter, specific claims of the various interpretations can be more or less adequate in the face of experimental evidence, and even shown to be false in certain cases[1,2].

In relation to this debate perhaps the greatest significance and contribution of Bohm's causal interpretation of quantum mechanics[3] is that it not only exposes the arbitrary philosophical assumptions underlying the claims of the Copenhagen interpretation but also brings into relief the essentially new content of quantum mechanics, which is reflected in different ways in Bohr's interpretation. Indeed the claim that the quantum formalism itself requires us not only to abandon the quest for explanation of quantum phenomena but also the concepts of causality, continuity and the objective reality of individual micro-objects, is shown to be false. However the existence of the single counter-interpretation proposed by Bohm constitutes sufficient grounds for rejecting the absolute and final necessity of complementary description and indeterminacy, along with the inherent unanalysable and closed nature of quantum phenomena.

This in itself was a major contribution, but further than this, since the possibility of alternative interpretations is not ruled out, specific models may be proposed which allow a space-time description of individual micro-events and the possibility of a deeper understanding, perhaps leading to an approach which transcends current perceptions.

Although the causal interpretation has in effect been in existence since the very beginnings of quantum mechanics, in the form of the pilot-wave model proposed by de Broglie, it has not been widely adopted in the physics community, perhaps for reasons more ideological and metaphysical than physical, and many people remain ignorant of it.

In this contribution we wish to reconsider Bohm's interpretation in the light of recent developments and to return to the question of the interpretation of quantum mechanics. In particular we examine the adequacy of the Copenhagen interpretation (CIQM), the causal stochastic interpretation (SIQM – an extension of Bohm's original approach) and the statistical interpretation in accounting for quantum interference phenomena and quantum statistics. We further demonstrate that the assumption of the existence of particle trajectories entails the elimination of negative probabilities from quantum mechanics.

Such phenomena are at the heart of quantum mechanics and interference experiments were crucial in the early stages of the Bohr–Einstein debate, in which the discussion was centred on the two-slit experiment. In fact they have become of central concern once again since the recent neutron interferometry experiments present more strikingly the same puzzling behaviour, and offer wider possibilities to examine the adequacy of the various interpretations. However, let us consider first the three interpretations of the two-slit experiment.

2   Interpretation and the two-slit experiment

(i) Bohr and the Copenhagen interpretation

Although several versions of this approach to quantum mechanics exist, the most consistent and coherent version was formulated by Bohr.[4] For Bohr science is only possible through unambiguous communication of results. A necessary condition for this is that a clear distinction be possible between subject and object (system and instrument). The concepts and language of classical physics automatically entail such a distinction and we have to communicate within its framework. If in any situation the subject/object distinction can be made in alternative ways, then the descriptions arising are to be termed complementary rather than simply contradictory. Bohr regarded complementarity as a general relationship evident in all areas of knowledge. The similarity between diverse domains regarding complementary description was not based on a more or less vague analogy, but on a thorough investigation of the conditions for the proper use of our conceptual means of expression. Complementarity, then, is not derived from quantum mechanics; it simply has a well-defined application in this area of knowledge where the existence and indivisibility of the quantum of action implies the unanalysability of the interaction between system and instrument. The placing of the division between system and instrument becomes arbitrary and unambiguous communication impossible. From Bohr's philosophical position the only possibility is to retreat to the classical description of the results of experiments. Their classical nature is taken as given, but then quantum phenomena become hermetically sealed. The fundamental unit for description in these terms is then the whole 'phenomenon' constituted by the system and experimental apparatus which together form an indivisible and unanalysable whole. Altering a part of the apparatus in order to define more closely the quantum process, by elucidating a conjugate quantity, simply produces a complementary phenomenon. In this view, 'There is no quantum world, there is only an abstract quantum physical description'[5].

Quantum mechanics only concerns the statistical prediction of the results of well-defined experiments and nothing more; it represents an ultimate limit to our knowledge. The wave function ψ is the most complete description of an individual state; it is merely a probability amplitude which states the odds on various results and is subject to instantaneous changes during measurement. If some preparation device (source, shutter, collimator) is designed to produce a wave packet, then all we can say is that the wave packet represents the fact that a single particle has a probability of appearing at a position x given by $|\psi(x)|^2$, if a measurement is made. Until such a time it is not legitimate even to conceive of a particle, let alone its properties.

In the specific case of the two-slit experiment (see Figure 9.1), what happens between source and screen when interference is observed cannot be described, even in principle. In fact the quantum system, detected at the plate, cannot even be said to have an existence in the usual sense. There is no possibility of defining the process giving rise to the interference pattern. Either we design an apparatus to observe interference, and hence the wave properties of matter, and forgo the

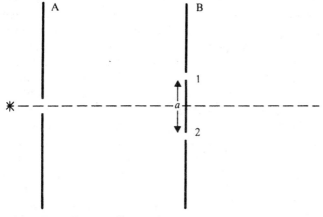

Figure 9.1 The two-slit experiment

description in terms of space-time co-ordination, or we design an incompatible arrangement to determine more closely the space-time motion, particle properties, and forgo the possibility of observing interference. The two are complementary phenomena.

When Einstein[6] proposed a *gedanken* experiment which would enable the path of the particle to be determined by measuring the momentum it transfers to the slits, Bohr argued that if a screen is to be used in this way then its own momentum must be controlled with such a precision that by application of the uncertainty relations its position becomes uncertain by an amount sufficient to destroy the interference. It is a curious fact that in order to arrive at this conclusion Bohr must assume rectilinear particle trajectories between source and slits and slits and screen. The quantum object behaves classically whereas the macroscopic slit system behaves quantum mechanically. Indeed, to be consistent it must be said that the screen actually has no position; its existence has become 'fuzzy', not that its definite position is just unknown. Greenberger[7] has shown in detail how the interaction with such a 'fuzzy' object (in the neutron case) destroys the coherence of the overlapping wave functions.

In proscribing the possible in quantum physical description, Bohr has ruled out explanations in terms of determinate individual physical processes taking place in space and time. This is not the task of physics; the quantum theory is just an algorithm for predicting results and its theoretical entities need no interpretation. In this way, by epistemological re-definition, Bohr can avoid all the problems and paradoxes which arise when an attempt is made to provide the formalism and its rules with a physical interpretation in terms of the behaviour of matter. In Bohr's view the 'observer' plays no more special a role in quantum mechanics than in any other area of knowledge, and his or her consciousness of a given situation has no special effect. This is the core of Bohr's position and the unambiguous basis of the Copenhagen interpretation. Many other versions of the Copenhagen interpretation exist and these have led to extended discussions as a result of attempting to provide a physical, or psychophysical, interpretation of the entities and laws of quantum mechanics, in terms of which the phenomena and the interphenomena may be described and explained. These should really be distinguished from Bohr's position, which does not constitute a physical interpretation in the usual sense.

In the following we separate Bohr's position from those versions of CIQM which attempt to interpret the formalism physically.

(ii) The statistical interpretation

As emphasized by Ballentine[8], the statistical interpretation is to be distinguished from the Copenhagen interpretation. He asserts that the wave function simply represents an ensemble of similarly prepared systems and does not provide a complete description of an individual system: 'In general, quantum theory predicts nothing which is relevant to a single measurement.'[8]

The interpretation of a wave packet is that, although each particle has always a definite position r, each position is realized with relative frequency $|\psi(r)|^2$ in an ensemble of similarly-prepared experiments. It follows that each particle has a well-defined trajectory, but its specification is beyond the statistical quantum theory; probabilities arising in the predictions of the theory are to be interpreted as in classical theory.

In the two-slit experiment this means that each particle in fact goes through one or other of the slits. Clearly the interference of particles is something new in quantum theory which this model must reproduce. If the particle goes through one or other of the slits, the two possibilities are in principle distinguishable; we should write a mixture instead of a pure state and the interference disappears. In order to explain the persistence of interference in this interpretation Ballentine refers to the work of Duane[9] in 1927, more recently revived by Landé[10]. The result is obtained by considering the possibilities for momentum transfer between the individual particle and the screen containing the slits. The matter distribution of the screen is Fourier analysed into a 'three-fold infinity of sinusoidal elementary lattices of spacings $l_1, l_2, l_3 \ldots$ and amplitude $A(l_i)$'. According to an extension of the Bohr-Sommerfeld quantum conditions, each such lattice is capable of changing its momentum in the direction of the periodicity only by amounts;

$$\Delta p_i = h/l_i$$

The intensity of an l component in the harmonic analysis is proportional to the statistical frequency of the corresponding momentum transfer. Thus each particle does not simply interact locally with the screen but non-locally with the matter distribution of the screen as a whole. Now a change in this matter distribution, e.g. closing a slit, results in an instantaneous change in the components of the harmonic analysis and thus in a corresponding change in the possible momentum transfers, resulting in a single-slit distribution of intensity. We are bound to ask what, in this analysis, determines which of all the possible momentum transfers actually occurs in the individual particle's passage. There is no answer and so individual events are inherently statistical.

It is not clear in this model why the matter distribution consisting the screen should be Fourier analysed but not the matter distribution which constitutes the particle. The screen is, after all, made of particles. The physical status of the Fourier components which exist with certain amplitudes is also unclear. Einstein originally denied that the wave function gives a complete description of an individual because he saw that this assumption contradicted the notion of locality[11]. If we assign the wave function only a meaning in a statistical ensemble and resort to the above arguments to explain interference and diffraction, then clearly non-locality is introduced, but in a way which is not intuitively clear.

If we reconsider Einstein's modification of the two-slit experiment in this model then we see that the meaning of the uncertainty in the position of the slits, resulting in the loss of interference, is to be interpreted differently. In each experiment the screen has a definite position (this position has a statistical dispersion in the ensemble, Δx) and so in each individual case the particle is forbidden to land in the positions of the minima of the pattern. (This incidently is a definite prediction for the outcome of an individual experiment, in contradiction to Ballentine's statement above.) However, because the position of the maxima and minima in each case is different, in the ensemble interference is lost – a different explanation to that of the Copenhagen interpretation but with the same results.

The statistical interpretation claims to be a minimal interpretation which removes the 'dead wood' of the Copenhagen interpretation. However, nothing is gained in the understanding of the quantum world and the mysteries remain complete.

(iii) The causal interpretation

This interpretation was originally proposed by de Broglie[12] and independently by Bohm[3]. It has recently been extended by Vigier[13] to include a sub-quantum Dirac ether as an underlying physical model.

In fact it is the only known interpretation of quantum mechanics in terms of which all quantum effects can be explained on the basis of causal continuous motions in space and time. The quantum mechanical description of an individual through the wave-function is held to be incomplete in the sense of Einstein. The description may be supplemented with real physical motions of particles, without ambiguity or contradiction, but in a manner which introduces severely non-classical features. Bohr's epistemological position is set aside and the task of physics is held to consist not only of the attempt to predict the statistical frequency of results in ensembles but also to provide explanations and descriptions of the individual processes between source and detection. No problems arise in the analysis of 'phenomena' into constituent parts, as the essential feature of their unity is now manifested by the quantum potential which arises from the non-locally correlated stochastic fluctuations of the underlying covariant ether (see Introduction). The quantum potential exhibits radically new properties. In the single-particle case its form depends on the state of the system as a whole, a feature which is the analogue of its non-local character in the many-body system[14].

Clearly if we consider that individual particles really exist in the interphenomena between source and screen and follow determinate trajectories, then the motion of each particle must be inextricably linked with the structure of its environment. Any change in the apparatus affects the whole ensemble of possible trajectories. This undivided connection is mediated by the quantum potential which arises as an extra potential term in the Hamilton-Jacobi-like equation, which may be derived by substituting $\psi = Re^{iS/\hbar}$ in the Schrödinger equation and separating the real and imaginary parts, as Bohm did in 1952. In addition to the Hamilton-Jacobi equation:

$$-\frac{\partial S}{\partial t} = \frac{(\nabla S)^2}{2m} + V - \frac{\hbar^2}{2m}\frac{\nabla^2 R}{R} \qquad [1]$$

one finds a continuity equation with $P = R^2$:

$$\frac{\partial P}{\partial t} + \nabla \cdot \left(P\frac{\nabla S}{m} \right) = 0 \qquad [2]$$

R and S are interpreted as the amplitude and phase of the real ψ field. The possible real average motions of a particle may be represented by trajectories derived from the relation that the particle momentum is given by:

$$\bar{p} = \nabla S \qquad [3]$$

In the many-body case, particle motions are correlated by the quantum potential in a non-local way, although in the scalar case this action at-a-distance does not give rise to any special problems. Even in the relativistic case, where non-locality may be thought to conflict with the requirements of relativistic causality, it can be shown that this connection is mediated superluminally, yet causally, and cannot lead to any results conflicting with the predictions of special relativity[15,16].

An exact calculation has been carried out in detail by Philippidis *et al.*[17] in the causal interpretation of the one-particle Schrödinger equation description of the two-slit experiment. Here we represent the form of the quantum potential and the associated trajectories in Figure 9.2 and Figure 9.3 respectively. The intensity distribution at the screen depends on the density of trajectories along with their occupation probability, and of course agrees in the Fraunhoffer limit with that expected from the usual considerations.

The precise form of each trajectory is sensitive to changes in variables describing the particle's environment. The distribution of trajectories demonstrates that each particle travelling in the apparatus

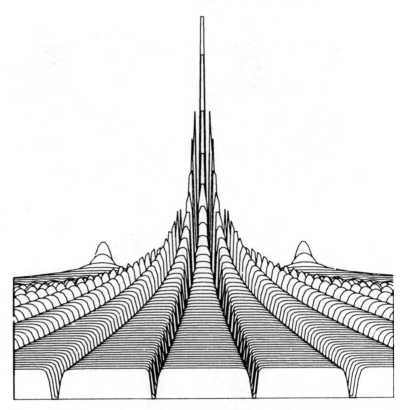

Figure 9.2   The quantum potential for two Gaussian slits viewed from a position on the axis beyond screen B.

'knows about' or responds to the global structure of its environment (e.g. the presence of two slits, not one) and so exhibits a wholeness completely foreign to mechanistic models in classical conceptions.

The quantum potential approach provides a way of understanding the feature of the quantum wholeness of phenomena emphasized by Bohr. Yet we are not required to relinquish the attempt to explain the interphenomena in terms of space-time co-ordination and causal connection simultaneously.

The unity of system and environment, so clearly demonstrated in the double-slit trajectories, is then revealed as the essentially new non-classical feature of quantum mechanics. Of course the single-particle description is an abstraction and this unity is really a reflection of the non-local character of the correlations that arise in the many-body case. The non-separability of quantum systems had been emphasized by Schrödinger[18] and Einstein, Podolsky and Rosen[11] in 1935. That such non-local correlations exist can no longer be doubted, as the

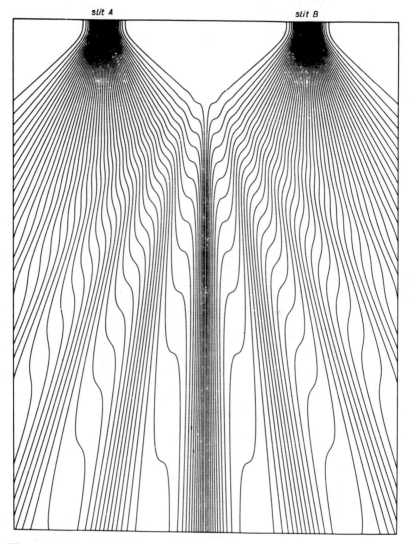

Figure 9.3 Trajectories for two Gaussian slits with a Gaussian distribution of initial positions at the slits.

results of Aspect's experiment demonstrate[19]. Indeed these experiments find a perfectly causal explanation through the quantum potential[20].

Reconsidering Einstein's modified two-slit experiment, the explanation of the loss of the interference pattern upon path determination in an ensemble of results is similar to that of the statistical interpretation, but now with precisely-definable individual particle trajectories determined by the quantum potential. None of the trajectories crosses the line of symmetry (a point confirmed by Prosser, who calculated lines of energy flow in the electromagnetic case[21]) and this is a new macroscopic prediction.

(iv) Wave-packet collapse

In the Bohr–Einstein debate, Bohr was able to defend the complementarity principle by showing that attempts to use detailed energy or momentum conservation in individual processes to determine particle trajectories more closely requires a change of the experimental arrangement which results in a loss of interference and the wave aspect. Bohr never referred to wave-packet collapse in these arguments. However, many of his supporters did and the concept is associated with his interpretation. Using the concept of wave-packet collapse to provide a physical interpretation of the quantum formalism is contrary to the spirit of Bohr's epistemological position. Nevertheless the argument is often put in the following way in CIQM. The introduction of a device capable of determining through which slit a particle passes induces a collapse of the wave function in the apparatus and a consequent loss of interference. Such a collapse follows from the assumption that the wave function provides a complete description of an individual system. In fact it is an hypothesis added to the quantum formalism and not an integral part of that formalism, although this is not the impression given in most texts. Arguments demonstrating the redundancy of this *ad hoc* postulate in quantum theory have existed for a long time.

Bohm, followed more recently by Cini[22], have argued that wave packet collapse does not correspond to any objective real physical change in the state of a system. By including the interaction with the measuring device in the quantum description, it can be shown that the interference between the components of a pure state is destroyed as a result of the interaction between the system and the macroscopic instrument, which is in effect irreversible. That is, there are no observable differences between the description of the composite in terms of the pure-state density matrix with vanishing interference terms and that in terms of the mixture density matrix (with wave-packet collapse). If we find out which component of the pure state is actualized in the process, the others may be disregarded as they can have no further influence on the behaviour of the system after the (irreversible) interaction with the macroscopic instrument has taken place. Wave-packet collapse is now simply a matter of convenience. The physical interpretation of individual quantum processes in terms of particle trajectories excludes the necessity of introducing wave packet collapse.

Consider the general case of particle interference with two wave functions ψ_I and ψ_{II} (this could be a two-slit experiment with ψ_I from slit 1 and ψ_{II} from slit 2 or an interferometer with ψ_I in path 1 and ψ_{II} in path 2). Also let the wave function of an apparatus introduced only in path II be φ_i initially and φ_f finally, then we have:

$$\Psi_i = \varphi_i\psi_I + \varphi_i\psi_{II} \rightarrow \Psi_f = \varphi_i\psi_I + \varphi_f\psi_{II} \qquad [4]$$

If, through its functioning the states, φ_i and φ_f become orthogonal then interference is destroyed:

$$\Psi_f^+\Psi_f = \varphi_i^+\varphi_i\psi_I^+\psi_I + \varphi_f^+\varphi_f\psi_{II}^+\psi_{II} \qquad [5]$$

and the system (neutron, photon, electron) acts as a particle that goes either on path I or path II. Observation of the measuring instrument merely tells us which alternative took place and thus we replace Ψ_f by $\varphi_i\psi_I$ or $\varphi_f\psi_{II}$. This is a collapse of the wave function which simply represents a change of our knowledge and does not correspond to any real physical changes in the state of the system. If φ_i and φ_f are not orthogonal then interference persists:

$$\Psi_f^+\Psi_f = \varphi_i^+\varphi_i\psi_I^+\psi_I + \varphi_f^+\varphi_f\psi_{II}^+\psi_{II} + \varphi_i\psi_I\varphi_f^+\psi_{II}^+ + \varphi_f\psi_{II}\varphi_i^+\psi_I^+ \qquad [6]$$

and the system acts as a wave in both paths.

If by observing the apparatus we could still in fact determine the path of the particle, then in CIQM the act of observation would have to cause real physical changes in the particle's state as a consequence of a wave-packet collapse, since, if neutrons, electrons and photons are conceived as *particles* that go one way or the other, equation [6] should reduce to equation [5].

Thus CIQM concludes that all measurements capable of determining the particle's path imply orthogonality of the apparatus wave functions initially and finally. In SIQM, determination of particle path need not imply orthogonality of apparatus wave functions in order to exclude the intervention of consciousness in physical processes. What appears as a 'pseudo-collapse' is the action of a macroscopic measuring device which makes the interference terms negligible, as is consistently shown by Cini in a detailed application of the time-dependent Schrödinger equation to the interaction between a system and a measuring device. Thus there is no *a priori* impossibility of path determination and persisting interference; one has only to find an appropriate measuring device that during an interaction with the micro-system does not undergo a change to an orthogonal state, i.e. preserves the interference terms, and still offers a possibility to decode this small quantum-number change. The use of SQUIDS and no-demolition measurements could be considered in this context.

The possibility to go beyond CIQM was known to Bohm, in his original paper[3], albeit in a different context. He remarks, in relation to the loss of interference properties on measurement: 'In our interpretation, however, the destruction of the interference pattern could in principle be avoided by means of other ways of making measurements.'

3   Neutron interferometry

We propose now to take up these questions in relation to another specific quantum interference situation, neutron interferometry[23]. Neutron interferometry has the advantage that it reproduces the double-slit configuration with massive particles and introduces new possibilities for interaction through the neutron spin, thus essentially altering the situation.

(i)   Spatial interference

To this purpose consider the experimental arrangement of Figure 9.4 with both spin flippers turned off. A simple calculation shows[24] that if an originally spin-up polarized beam $\psi = |\uparrow_z>$ enters the interferometer, it is subdivided in two partial beams $\psi_I = e^{i\chi}|\uparrow_z>$ and $\psi_{II} = |\uparrow_z>$ that successively recombine and yield an intensity interference behind the interferometer modulated with the phase shift factor χ:

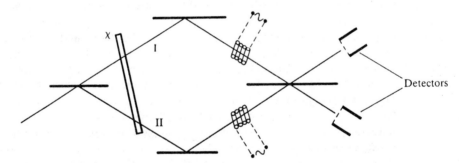

Figure 9.4   The neutron interferometer with a spin-flip coil in each arm.

$$I = (\psi_I + \psi_{II})^+(\psi_I + \psi_{II}) = 2(1 + \cos \chi) \tag{7}$$

while the polarization remains in the z-direction, i.e.:

$$P = (0,0,1) \tag{8}$$

Let us now turn to consider the interpretation of the results. For Bohr, the concept of the interphenomena cannot be unambiguously applied; the phenomenon is unanalysable. All we can do is calculate the interfering probability amplitudes associated with each path through the apparatus. Neutron paths and 'neutron waves' are equally ambiguous for Bohr. He states that descriptions in terms of photons and electron waves have the same ambiguity as other pictorial descriptions of the interphenomena; only the classical concepts of material particles and electromagnetic waves have an unambiguous field of application. However, if we wish to discuss the interphenomena we must set Bohr's position aside (as in fact most physicists actually do). Then a clear choice exists between two possible explanations. Either:

1   we say the neutron does not exist as a particle in the interferometer; or
2   we say the neutron actually travels along path I *or* II only, but is influenced by the physical conditions along both.

(a) The CIQM   Suppose, with the usual interpretation of the quantum formalism, a particle were actually to travel along one path, then the existence of the other would be irrelevant and interference cannot occur. Interference arises not from our lack of knowledge of the path but from the fact that the neutron does not have one. Any attempt to reveal the particle between source and detector induces a wave-packet collapse, i.e. localizes the particle in one beam, and interference effects disappear. The wave and particle nature of matter are complementary aspects. Since in this view the neutron is not to be conceived of as a particle before detection localizes it, questions concerning which beam a given neutron enters at the region of superposition cannot be formulated and the question of explanation is summarily closed.

(b) The causal stochastic interpretation   If, contrary to the usual interpretation outlined in (a), we believe with Einstein[25] and de Broglie[12] that neutrons are particles that really exist in space and time, then Rauch's statement, ruled out in the CIQM, can be made; namely that: 'At the place of superposition every neutron has the information that there have been two equivalent paths through the interferometer, which have a certain phase difference *causing the neutron* to join the beam in the forward or deviated direction'[26].

It is then possible to suggest physical models to explain the causation of individual events, a non-existent option in CIQM. In the SIQM neutrons can be thought of as particles accompanied by waves simultaneously; the particle travels along one path through the interferometer whilst its real wave is split and travels along both. The waves interfere in the region of superposition and give rise to a quantum potential which carries information concerning the whole apparatus and determines the particle trajectories. The changing phase relations between the waves in I and II lead to a changing quantum potential structure that determines which beam each individual neutron enters according to its initial position in the wave packet and phase shift χ. The detailed explanation provided for the two slit experiment and square potential phenomena[27] may be easily extended to this case. The details may be found in reference 28; here we simply represent the form of the effective potential (quantum potential plus classical barrier) and the associated trajectories. The results of the numerical calculation show that varying the phase shift factor χ between 0 and 2π produces the correct type of interference figure. When $\chi = 0$, π, the effective potential (quantum + classical), as shown in Figure 9.5, is symmetric about the barrier centre. A series of violent oscillations develops on each side of the barrier potential. These arise when the incident wave interferes with the combination of its own reflected wave and the in-phase transmitted wave from the other side. Figure 9.6 shows the associated trajectories.

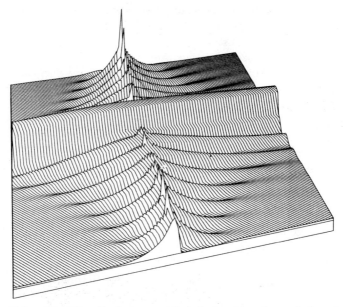

Figure 9.5   The effective potential at the last 'set of crystal planes' with phase shift π. Corresponding to region $x = 0.6$ to $x = 0.9$, $T = 4.0$ to $T = 12.0$ on trajectory plot.

With $\chi = \pi/2$ the situation is very different. In this case the quantum potential oscillations are greatly reduced on one side of the potential barrier, in the region where the density of trajectories is large, and this allows the particles to be transmitted (see upper section of Figure 9.7). In the lower section notice that the quantum potential oscillations are enhanced and occur at an earlier time, ensuring that all the trajectories constituting beam II are reflected (Figure 9.8). Those constituting beam I now enter the potential barrier and emerge after the reflection of those in beam II, both forming the single emerging beam. In this case the reflected wave from beam I is (almost completely) cancelled by the anti-phase transmitted wave from beam II.

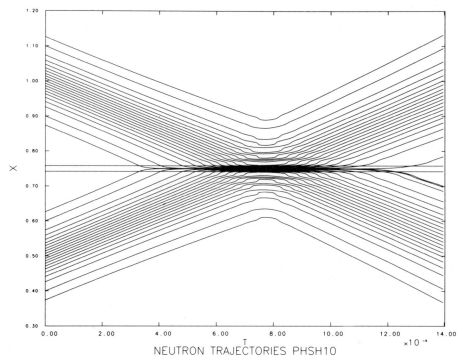

Figure 9.6   Trajectories associated with $\chi = \pi$.

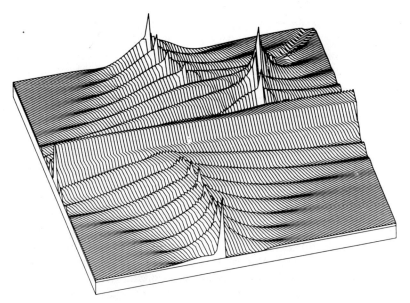

Figure 9.7   The effective potential at the last 'set of crystal planes' with phase shift $\pi/2$.

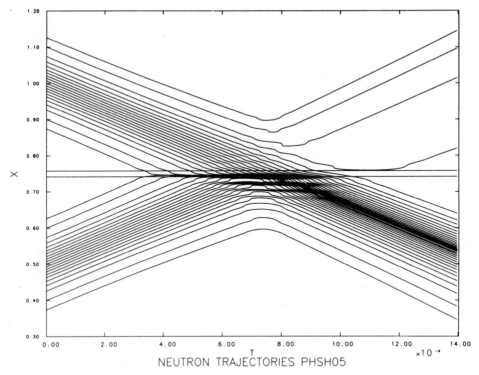

X

NEUTRON TRAJECTORIES PHSH05

Figure 9.8   Trajectories associated with $\chi = \pi/2$.

When $\chi = 3\pi/2$ the situation is essentially reversed (see Figures 9.9, 9.10), all the trajectories and any neutron emerging in the upper section. The few trajectories which do not follow the others come from the extreme tails of the packets and so have very low probability; here they represent the effect of a finite potential width.

(ii)   Time-dependent spin superposition

Now according to Badurek *et al.*[29] a completely different physical situation arises in the case of the time-dependent superposition of linear spin states using a radio-frequency spin-flip coil. Indeed, 'in that case the total energy of the neutrons is not conserved'. The detailed experimental arrangement can be schematically represented as follows. The incident neutron beam containing one neutron at a time is subsequently divided into beams I and II. On beam I acts a nuclear phase shifter represented by the action of a unitary operator $e^{i\chi}$ on ψ. Beam II is subjected to the following combination of magnetic fields:

1   a   static   magnetic   field   in   the $+z$ direction $B = (0,0,B_0)$;

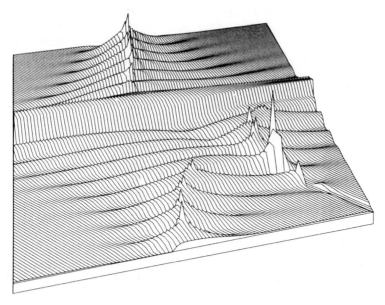

Figure 9.9   Effective potential with phase shift $\chi = 3\pi/2$.

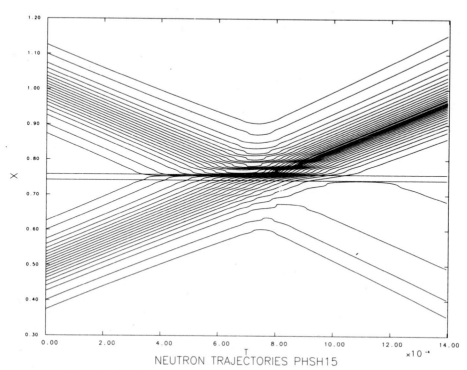

NEUTRON TRAJECTORIES PHSH15

Figure 9.10   Trajectories associated with $\chi = 3\pi/2$.

2   a radio-frequency time-dependent magnetic field $B = (B_1 \cos \omega_{rf}t,$ $B_1 \sin \omega_{rf}t, 0)$ rotating in the xy plane with a frequency ω_{rf} obeying the resonance condition, $\hbar\omega_{rf} = 2\mu B_0$, where μ is the magnetic moment of the neutron, i.e. it yields exactly the Zeeman energy difference between the two spin eigenstates of the neutron within the static field.

Neutrons passing through such a device (a spin flipper) reverse their initial $+z$ polarization into the $-z$ direction, by transferring an energy $\Delta E = 2\mu B_0$ to the coil whilst maintaining their initial momentum

The wave function in beam I after passing through the phase shifter is:

$$\psi_1 = e^{i\chi}|\uparrow_z\rangle = e^{i\chi}\binom{1}{0} \tag{9}$$

The corresponding wave function in II after the coil should be written:

$$\psi_{II} = e^{i\frac{\Delta E_t}{\hbar}}|\downarrow_z\rangle = e^{i\frac{\Delta E_t}{\hbar}}\binom{0}{1} \tag{10}$$

since the rf-coil is shown to be almost 100 per cent efficient[30].

Let the wave function of the coil initially be φ_i and finally be φ_f. Then initially the wave function of the whole (neutron and coil) is:

$$\Psi_i = \varphi_i(a\psi_1 + b\psi_{II}) \tag{11}$$

and the final state is:

$$\Psi_f = \varphi_i a\psi_1 + \varphi_f b\psi_{II} \tag{12}$$

and the condition for the observation of interference is $\varphi_i \approx \varphi_f$; that is, the state of the coil is virtually unaltered and no measurement in the usual sense takes place. Then:

$$\Psi_f = \varphi_i(a\psi_1 + b\psi_{II})$$

and intensity:

$$I = \Psi_f^+\psi_f = 2$$

with polarization:

$$\bar{p} = (\cos(\omega_{rf}t - \chi), \sin(\omega_{rf}t - \chi), 0) \tag{13}$$

entirely in the xy plane. These are the well-known results of Badurek *et al.*[29] which are experimentally verified.

(a) The Copenhagen interpretation Now how are these results encompassed within the CIQM? The observation of interference implies the wave aspect; hence the particle cannot even be said to exist during the time between emission and absorption in the detector. A particle cannot exist in one beam (or pass through one slit in the double-slit experiment) and take part in interference. However in order to describe the functioning of the coil we must use the complementary localized particle aspect. The energy transfer that takes place giving rise to the change of ψ_{II} is described by Rauch in terms of photon exchange between the neutron and the field in the coil. Thus the neutron is conceived as a particle in one beam to explain energy transfer and simultaneously as a wave existing in both to explain interference. The complementarity of wave and particle descriptions is broken; both aspects must be used simultaneously in one and the same experimental arrangement. Complementary description is thus incomplete, or can energy be exchanged with a probability wave?

(b) **The causal stochastic interpretation** In the SIQM we use the Feynman–Gell–Mann equation for spin half-particles as a second-order stochastic equation for the collective excitations of the assumed underlying covariant random vacuum, Dirac's ether[31,32]. A spin half-particle is conceived as a localized entity surrounded by a real spinor wave due to perturbation of the vacuum. While the particle really travels one way (path I or II), the spinor wave propagates in both paths. In path II the interaction with the rf spin-flipper inverts the spinor symmetry of the wave while in path I the initial state is maintained. What happens in the interference region can be now represented by the action of a spin dependent quantum potential Q and a quantum torque τ which can be shown to produce a time-dependent spinor symmetry in the xy plane. The particle travelling, for example, in path I is constrained by the spinor symmetry in the interference region and its $+z$ spin is twisted into the xy plane by the quantum torque. If it travels along path II it suffers an additional spin inversion due to the rf coil, yielding this energy to the coil while in the intersection area its $-z$ spin is twisted again to the xy plane. Consequently, a coherent picture is established which accounts for both particle and wave aspects.

(iii) Measurement and time-dependent spin flippers

Now, Badurek *et al.*, who performed the experiment, have stated: 'This experiment has shown explicitly that the interference properties of beams can be preserved even when a real energy exchange takes place, which is intuitively a measurement'[29]. But does it constitute a measurement? The situation must be analysed carefully.

Clearly if the functioning of the coil is a measurement in the quantum mechanical sense, then φ_i would be orthogonal to φ_f and interference would disappear. The reasons for considering such an interaction as a quantum measurement process are the following. First, there is an energy exchange taking place unidirectionally from the passing neutron to the rf-circuit, since the energy of the initial state differs by ΔE from that of the final state. This energy exchange, if decoded and extracted from the resonator circuit, could reveal the passage of the neutron. Second, this energy transfer in the form of a photon transition establishes a one-to-one correspondence between the change of the neutron's spin state from spin up to spin down.

If φ_i and φ_f are not orthogonal, then interference and spin superposition persist, but in order to demonstrate the coexistence of particle path and interference some means must be found to decode the small quantum number change involved between φ_i and φ_f.

If, in spite of the non-orthogonality of φ_i and φ_f, the particle path could be observed, then in CIQM the act of observation itself (i.e. our knowledge) would have to destroy the interference terms (wave-packet collapse), whereas this is not ruled out *a priori* in the quantum potential approach, in which particle path and interference are not exclusive and the wave function of the apparatus does not provide a complete description of an individual apparatus. Within the quantum potential approach one could consider, as we have suggested, the possible adaptation of quantum non-demolition measurements to detect the passage of a neutron.

Does the possibility exist of detecting the passage of a neutron from the energy it transfers to the rf coil? For Bohr the question of an individual energy transfer to the coil when it is part of the interferometer set-up cannot arise, as this amounts to an attempt to subdivide the experiment. Actually changing the experiment to allow the detection of the energy transfer results in a complementary phenomenon in which interference would not be observed. In the quantum potential approach there is no contradiction between energy transfer and interference. Consider the following possibilities.

1   If the single energy transfer is detectable with certainty by inspecting the coil's state, then its final state must not overlap with the initial state. However the addition of a single photon to the field in the coil does not, even under the most favourable assumptions concerning the state of this coil, lead to any observable change (consider the field to be in a coherent state, for example).

2   If it is possible, by introducing a superconducting quantum interference device (SQUID)[33], to detect the exchange of a single photon, then according to the usual application of the quantum formalism the implied orthogonality of SQUID states destroys the interference. This experiment, if performed, would, if interference is not observed, confirm the non-separability of neutron and SQUID states. If on the other hand interference persists, then the experiment would contradict quantum non-separability; the SQUID state would be decoupled from the neutron state.

3   If a single energy transfer is not detectable, can some device be added that stores the individual unidirectional energy transfers eventually leading to a detectable amount? Is so then this energy can only have come from the passage of individual neutrons

through the coil, which implies that each individual neutron actually travels along one or the other of the paths through the interferometer *and* takes part in interference.

(iv)   Energy conservation and the double-coil experiment

Consider now the situation with two time-dependent rf coils, one in each beam[34]. In this proposed experiment the doubts raised by Badurek *et al.*[29] concerning the phase-number uncertainty do not apply at all[34], since the resulting interference pattern is stationary. No theoretical objection arises for a possible detection of single photon transitions in the field of the rf spin flipper on this count.

Ignoring all common phase factors, the wave functions of the superposed beams are:

$$\psi_1 = e^{i\chi}|\downarrow_z\rangle \tag{14}$$

$$\psi_{11} = |\downarrow_z\rangle \tag{15}$$

with polarization:

$$P = (0,0,-1) \tag{16}$$

and:

$$\Psi_f^+\Psi_f = 2(1 + \cos\chi) \tag{17}$$

Spatial interference is recovered. The results of this single apparatus are:

1   each emerging neutron has lost an energy ΔE; its spin is now 'down' in the guide field;

2   each neutron takes part in interference.

In order to explain the measured loss of energy, the neutron must pass as a particle through one or the other coil and exchange a photon with the field. In the quantum potential approach this is consistent with the observation of interference; in a description based on wave/particle duality it is not, as both particle (loss of energy) and wave (interference) properties must be manifest simultaneously in one and the same experimental arrangement.

A measurement of the polarization of the neutron behind the interferometer reveals that each neutron has suffered a spin flip. Each emerging neutron has lost an amount of energy ΔE where $\Delta E = 2\mu B$ represents the Zeeman splitting. If energy is to be conserved this energy must have gone to one or other of the coils. This is only possible if the neutron passes as a particle through one or other and gives an indivisible photon of energy $E = \hbar\omega_{rf} = \Delta E$ to the rf-field. The spatial interference can only be explained by assuming that the neutron does not pass through one or other of the coils.

Since here both interference and spin direction can be measured simultaneously, according to CIQM the neutron actually travels path I or II and at the same time does not exist as a particle at all.

In the Bohr–Einstein debate the application of particle momentum conservation in individual events always led to the consistency of CIQM. Here the energy conservation leads to the inconsistency of CIQM, since wave and particle aspects must be used together to explain the observed results. If it is insisted in CIQM that neutrons do not travel one way or the other in this experiment, no energy can be transferred to the coils and then there is no conservation of energy in individual events. Further, if a statistical ensemble of individual neutron passages is considered, we see that, even there, there is no conservation of energy in CIQM when the interference is observed.

We are confronted by a stark alternative. Either:

1   we renounce any possibility of describing what happens in the neutron interferometry experiments; there exists then no possibility of explaining quantum phenomena, not even in terms of a wave/particle duality which only leads to ambiguity; individual quantum phenomena are in principle and irreducibly indeterminist in character and there can be no form of physical determinism appropriate in the quantum domain; or

2   we adopt the quantum potential approach as the only known consistent manner in which the quantum world can be conceived and explained in terms of a physically determinist reality; then, even if the quantum potential approach is not taken as the finally satisfactory description of quantum mechanical reality, it at least shows in a clear way the features that such a description must entail.

Consider the question of energy conservation in a more general way in SIQM and CIQM. In CIQM, as emphasized by Bohr, we may only consider the energy of a system to be definite when the system is in a stationary state. The system may only be in a stationary state in the absence of perturbing forces, such as those necessarily introduced in a measuring process. Such interactions are necessary to localize the system in order to allow a space-time description. Thus, in a transition between stationary states, energy conservation can be applied to the initial and final states but this excludes the conditions necessary for a space-time description. Bohr would say that when we are in a position to speak of space-time location there can be no question of energy conservation and, when energy conservation can be applied, the concepts of space-time co-ordination lose their immediate sense.

In SIQM a stationary state means the particle energy given by $\partial S/\partial t$ is a constant. The quantum potential is time independent and the particle's motion is conservative in that:

$$\frac{(\nabla S)^2}{2m} + Q = -\frac{\partial S}{\partial t} = \text{constant}$$

The particle can gain or lose kinetic energy at the expense of quantum potential energy. For example in an S state of an H atom, the particle is stationary with energy E, this energy being held as quantum potential energy whilst the quantum force $-\nabla Q$ balances the Coulomb force $-\nabla V$. In a different example, when ψ is a plane monochromatic wave, the particle energy is a constant since the quantum potential vanishes. A more complex case is that of the double-slit experiment discussed above.

For stationary states and systems which undergo changes between them, conservation of energy may be established in both SIQM and CIQM, but SIQM can also provide a space-time description.

The case in which Ψ is a superposition of stationary states is rather different, as discussed by Bohm[3,35] and de Broglie[12,36]. Consider the state:

$$\Psi = \sum_K C_K \psi_K \qquad [18]$$

where Ψ is a sum of stationary states with energy E_k.

In CIQM we simply say that the energy of the individual system is not well defined but that upon measurement the value E_n will be found with probability $|C_n|^2$. Thus any individual process that includes (as part of its initial or final state) a superposition of states of different energy cannot be described in terms of energy conservation. If we insist that infinite plane waves represent an excessive abstraction and the more realistic description of a free particle is a wave packet or superposition of plane waves of different momenta, then we are led to conclude that energy conservation cannot be applied even to the motion of an individual free particle. The particle, in so far as it exists in CIQM, has potentially all the energies E_k with probabilities $|C_k|^2$.

In SIQM a particle represented by a superposition of stationary states with different energies has a well-defined energy at each moment (dependent on its initial position) in the wave packet but this energy is continuously variable with time. (However, the mean particle energy averaged over the ensemble is equal to the usual quantum mechanical result for the energy operator.) The variation of energy is due to the influence of the quantum potential which fluctuates with time. Thus in a wave-packet representation of the free particle we find that energy is not conserved for an individual particle since $\partial S/\partial t \neq$ constant.

Let us reconsider from this point of view the neutron interferometer experiment with one rf-coil in path II. Before entering the interferometer the neutron has a well-defined energy E corresponding to $|\uparrow_z\rangle$. On leaving it is a superposition of states of different energy $E(\uparrow_z)$ on path I and $(E - \Delta E)(\downarrow_z)$ on path II. Thus the spin can be found in the xy plane, by the measurement procedure described above, clearly demonstrating the principle of spin superposition (interference), i.e. the state is not a mixture of $\uparrow_z$ and $\downarrow_z$. However this interference observation requires us to relinquish the possibility of a description in terms of energy conservation. The attempt to apply energy conservation would require the use of a definite spin state in the guide field; that is, the state would have to be either $\uparrow_z$ or $\downarrow_z$ (a mixture). In that case energy conservation could apply in individual processes since superposition and interference is lost. A neutron in beam *I* with $\uparrow_z$ retains its original spin energy whilst one beam II exchanges ΔE with the coil. Thus we may choose to measure the *z* component of the spin and apply conservation of energy or observe the superposition and deny energy conservation. The two are complementary.

A similar situation exists in the two-slit experiments. If we wish to consider conservation of momentum of an individual electron, then it must be described as passing through one slit or the other in order to exchange momentum. If it passes through one slit, or the other, then interference is not possible.

In SIQM the particles have definite positions, momenta, energy and spin at all times, their associated (spinor) waves producing interference properties through the action of the (spin-dependent) quantum potential. In the neutron interferometer experiment described above there are then two possibilities depending on the path taken at the first crystal plane when interference is observed, i.e.:

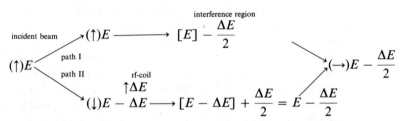

If we choose to measure the *z* component no superposition effects can be observed and energy is conserved on both paths.

If interference is observed then a neutron which travels in path I has an overall loss of energy $\Delta E/2$ while a neutron which travels path II has an overall gain of energy of $\Delta E/2$ (ΔE transfer to coil). Thus for SIQM, in an ensemble, energy is conserved when interference occurs. This is *not* the case in CIQM. Also in SIQM when we include the possibility of energy exchange with the ether, through the action of the quantum torque which rotates $\uparrow_z$ and $\downarrow_z$ to $\rightarrow_{xy}$ it is seen that energy may be conserved even in the individual case.

In general we see that in CIQM there is no possibility of recovering energy conservation in non-stationary situations; indeed, individual processes have no real independent existence.

Such a possibility does exist in SIQM if we assume that the particle exchanges energy with the sub-quantum Dirac ether. Indeed the recovery of conservation of energy in real individual processes is a strong reason for accepting the existence of such an ether.

We should note that the prediction of variable or non-constant energy made by SIQM does not contradict any experimental results of quantum mechanics. Indeed all the results of quantum mechanics can be reproduced by SIQM. Thus, as Bohm points out, when describing the scattering of a particle wave-packet by an atom whilst the interaction is still taking place and the wave packets overlap the particle and atomic electron energies fluctuate violently and it is only when the packets separate that the energies obtain a constant value. The corresponding feature in CIQM is given by the uncertainty relations $\Delta E \Delta t > \hbar$, and the energy of each system can only become definite after a sufficient time has elapsed to complete the scattering.

Thus the prediction of the existence of variable energies in SIQM does not contradict any result of quantum mechanics. In fact the SIQM can provide detailed information concerning the energy variation along well-determined trajectories in space-time in particular experimental situations. CIQM simply does not deny the possible existence of such energies if they are measured. The implication of this is that SIQM can make predictions which do not contradict CIQM but, in going beyond what CIQM allows to be possible, in the sense of being more precise, clearly demonstrates its incomplete character. In particular, some effects in non-linear optics experiments, i.e. the ejection of a photo-electron[37], photo-ionization of a gas[38] and fluorescence[39], occur even when the laser frequency is in fact below the necessary threshold for the process (provided the beam is put in a non-stationary state by focusing or by creation of a pulse). These effects can be interpreted in both CIQM and SIQM. However, by providing a detailed description of the individual trajectories and particle energies involved, SIQM can make testable predictions which are not possible in CIQM. In SIQM it is possible to predict at which points the particles of increased energy will be found and hence exactly where the effects should be observed[40]. If such predictions can be confirmed the CIQM would be shown to be incomplete in the original sense of Einstein.

4 Quantum statistics

In orthodox theory the wavelike density fluctuations of collections of like particles are described using Bose-Einstein or Fermi-Dirac statistics based solely on the notion of indistinguishability and the symmetry or antisymmetry of the wave function. However any interpretation of quantum mechanics which asserts the existence of individual particle trajectories is faced with a problem when the question of quantum statistical behaviour arises. Brillouin[41] had already in 1927 considered this problem. He argued that even if particles are identical *a priori*, it is easy nevertheless to distinguish them by their history. He then finds the auxiliary assumptions that enable quantum statistics to be obtained with distinguishability of elements. When the elements are assumed to be independent classical statistics result, in order to obtain quantum statistics some correlation between the distinguishable elements must be assumed. Further, as has been more recently emphasized by Feynman[42], no classical model with local interactions between the elements can ever reproduce all the results of quantum mechanics. This represents a serious problem in the statistical interpretation, and in SIQM.

In the derivation of the formulae of classical statistics with distinguishability, the assumption that the elements are free between random local collisions and that each distinct state has equal probability leads, for N elements distributed among M available discrete states, to the result that the probability of a set of occupancies $\{n_i\}$ $i = 1 \ldots M$ is proportional to the number of distinct configurations corresponding to $\{n_i\}$:

$$P\{n_i\} = M^{-N} N! / n_1! \ldots n_M!$$ [19]

However, Tersoff and Bayer[43] have shown that Bose-Einstein statistics can be recovered with distinguishable particles if the assumption of equal probability distribution among available states is replaced by that of arbitrary probability weighting. It has also been shown[44] that such an arbitrary probability weighting is a natural consequence of the causal interpretation. In this interpretation the assumption of random local collisions and independent particles no longer holds. The average motions of N particles given by:

$$V_K^\mu = \frac{1}{m} \partial_K^\mu S \quad (K = 1 \ldots N)$$ [20]

are determined from the non-local action at-a-distance quantum potential:

$$Q = \sum_K \frac{\hbar}{2m} \frac{\Box_K R}{R} = \sum_K Q_K$$ [21]

This potential acts instantaneously in the centre of mass rest-frame and also implies that the interaction is causal (since the individual Hamiltonians $H_k = \frac{1}{m} P_k^\mu P_{k\mu} + Q_k$ satisfy the causality constraints $\{H_k, H_j\} = 0$) so that all colliding particles are permanently correlated and can *never* be considered free. This implies that each individual state is not identical with all others, so that we should attribute to each one a different probability weighting ω_i of course requiring $0 \leqslant \omega_i \leqslant 1$ and $\sum_{i=1}^{M} \omega_i = 1$. This weight depends on all former possible different real subquantal random motions in phase space, so that the total statistics results from an averaging over all possible ω_i in all possible configurations. Thus we should write:

$$P\{n_i\} = A_V\left[\frac{N!}{n_1!\ldots n_N!}(\omega_1)^{n_1}\ldots(\omega_M)^{n_M}\right]$$

$$= \int_0^1\ldots\int_0^1 d\omega_1\ldots d\omega_M\frac{N!}{n_1!\ldots n_M!}(\omega)^{n_1}\ldots(\omega_M)^{n_M}$$

$$\delta\left(1 - \sum_{i=1}^M \omega_i\right) \quad [22]$$

which, as shown by Tersoff and Bayer[43], leads to the Bose-Einstein result:

$$P\{n_i\} = \frac{N!(M-1)!}{(N+M-1)!} \quad [23]$$

Fermi-Dirac statistics can also be reproduced[45] in a similar way with the constraint that $n_i = 0$ or 1.

As an illustration we now show in a particular physical situation how the individual motions of particles under the influence of the many-body quantum potential lead to different statistical results according to the type of wave function assumed[46]. The causal interpretation of quantum statistics can thus be shown to provide an intuitive understanding of quantum statistical results (in terms of correlated particle motions), classical statistics arising as a special case when the particles are not correlated by the quantum potential. The case examined here is the following. Consider a harmonic oscillator potential:

$$V = \frac{kx^2}{2} = \frac{m\omega^2 x^2}{2}$$

and construct, by solving the Schrödinger equation, a wave-packet solution[35]:

$$\psi(x,t) = \exp(-i\omega t)\exp\left[-\frac{1}{2}(x - x_0\cos\omega t)^2\right]\exp$$

$$\left[\frac{i}{2}\left(x_0^2\frac{\sin 2\omega t}{2} - 2xx_0\sin\omega t\right)\right] \quad [24]$$

This wave-packet solution is non-dispersive and, depending on the time parameter t, defines in the causal interpretation a set of possible trajectories for a particle located at the position x, where x_0 is the centre of a wave packet.

Now consider the case of two particles, one in each of the wave packets $\psi_A(x_1,t)$ and $\psi_B(x_2,t)$ in the harmonic oscillator potential. The packet $\psi_A(x_1,t)$ is assumed to be centred at x_0 and, in order to simplify the calculations, the packet $\psi_B(x_2,t)$ centred at $-x_0$.

It is clear that, depending on the assumed statistics (MB, BE or FD), three wave functions can be written. These are:

$$\varphi_{MB} = \alpha_{MB}\psi_A(x_1,t)\psi_B(x_2,t) \tag{25}$$

$$\varphi_{BE} = \alpha_{BE}[\psi_A(x_1,t)\psi_B(x_2,t) + \psi_B(x_1,t)\psi_A(x_2,t)] \tag{26}$$

$$\varphi_{FD} = \alpha_{FD}[\psi_A(x_1,t)\psi_B(x_2,t) - \psi_B(x_1,t)\psi_A(x_2,t)] \tag{27}$$

where the αs are renormalization constants to be determined by the condition $\iint\varphi dx_1 dx_2 = 1$. A standard quantum mechanical calculation yields the mean squared separation of the particles and it can be shown that the mean squared separation of the particles is in the BE case decreased and in the FD case increased with respect to the MB case.

In SIQM individual pairs of trajectories can be calculated from suitable initial positions in the wave packets and the results are shown in Figure 9.11. This figure provides us with the basic physical features of the process. The MB particles, being independent, possess trajectories that cross one another. They propagate undisturbed and produce no interference. This is not the case for BE or FD particles. They do not cross but form interference patterns in which the two particles are on the average closer together in the BE case than in the FD case.

The correlation effects mediated by the quantum potential between the two particles determines their physical behaviour and conditions their different statistical averages of physical variables or observables. This can be easily understood in the SIQM, where particles obeying quantum statistics are constantly submitted to the stochastic random motions of the underlying subquantal medium, the Dirac ether. The symmetric or antisymmetric character of the system's wave function is a consequence of the existence (or not) of local repulsive gauge fields and not a first quantum mechanical principle.

Thus it can be seen that MB statistics (and independence) arise as a special case of the more general quantum statistics (and correlation) when the many-body quantum potential is separable in the particle variables.

5   Negative probabilities

We have seen how accepting the physical idea of particle trajectories in the quantum domain can lead to the formulation of new physical questions which one would not be led to on the basis of the CIQM. We end this paper by discussing an interpretative problem raised by relativistic quantum mechanics, namely the mathematical existence of negative probability density and negative energy solutions to second-order wave equations, which, as in all other quantum processes, we argue can only be coherently treated by assuming the real physical existence of paths. Indeed, this is an important issue in the SIQM since the very existence of paths in space-time implies positive pro-

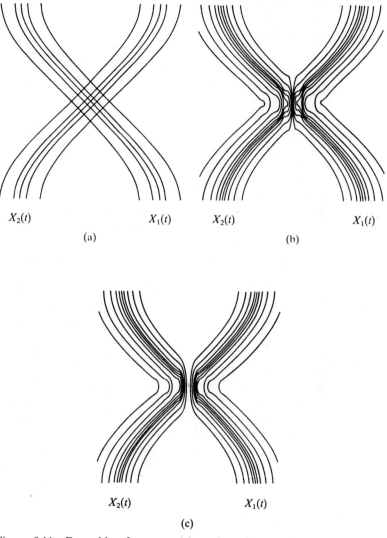

Figure 9.11 Ensemble of two particle trajectories $x_1(t)$, $x_2(t)$ with initial positions such that $x_2(0) = -x_1(0)$ and a concentration of particle trajectories around the packet maxima. (a) Maxwell-Boltzman (b) Bose-Einstein (c) Fermi-Dirac.

bability distributions and, moreover, in accordance with Einstein's basic principles, all material drift motions should be timelike and propagate positive energy forward in time.

It is sometimes erroneously stated that the only way out of the problem of negative probability solutions to the Klein-Gordon (KG) equation is to reject the first quantized formalism in favour of second quantization. In fact, this is not so and it is possible to show by a

Hamiltonian method due to Feshbach and Villars[47,48] that for certain well-behaved external potentials the KG solutions may be split into positive and negative energy parts associated respectively with positive and negative probability.

To see this, let us start from the charged scalar wave equation:

$$(D_\mu D^\mu - m^2)\psi = 0 \tag{28}$$

where $D_\mu = \partial_\mu - ieA_\mu$, e and m are the charge and mass of the particle moving in the external field A_μ, the metric has the signature $(-+++)$ and the units are chosen so that $\hbar = c = 1$. [28] may be expressed in the form:

$$i\dot\Psi = H(e)\Psi \tag{29}$$

where Ψ is a two-component wave function and H is a 2×2 matrix Hamiltonian. One can show that for the inner product

$$<\Phi,\Psi> = \int \Phi^* \sigma_3 \Psi d^3x = \int j^0 d^3x$$

where:

$$j^\mu = \psi^*(i^{-1}\overleftrightarrow{\partial^\mu} - ieA^\mu)\psi \tag{30}$$

is the conserved current, the mean value of H in any state is positive: $<\Psi,H\Psi> > 0$. It follows that, with $H\Psi = E\Psi$, the space of solutions of equation [29] splits into two disjoint subsets: $\{E > 0, <\Psi.\Psi> > 0\}$ and $\{E < 0, <\Psi,\Psi> < 0\}$. The latter subset of solutions may be mapped into positive-energy positive-probability anti-particle solutions by means of the charge conjugation operation:

$$\Psi \rightarrow \Psi^c(x) = \sigma_1 \Psi^*(x)$$

since from equation [29]:

$$H(-e)\Psi^c = -E\Psi^c \text{ and } j_0^c = -j_0$$

Thus, within the CIQM, one can show formally how, for stationary states, the signs of energy and integrated probability are correlated and that negative probability solutions may be physically interpreted. Note though, that the local values of probability density may become negative and that such motions remain interpreted. We shall now show how in the causal interpretation we are able to prove a stronger result than that just given, and in a way which is technically easier and physically clearer. Our approach extends some brief remarks of de Broglie[49] concerning this problem.

Substituting $\psi = e^{P+iS}$, where P, S are real scalars, in [28] yields the Hamilton-Jacobi and conservation equations:

$$(\partial^\mu S - eA^\mu)(\partial_\mu S - eA_\mu) = -M^2 \tag{31}$$

$$\partial_\mu j^\mu = 0 \tag{32}$$

where

$$M^2 = m^2 - \Box P - \partial^\mu P \partial_\mu P$$

is de Broglie's variable rest mass and:

$$j^\mu = 2e^{2P}(\partial^\mu S - eA^\mu)$$

is the current (equation [30]).

The assumption of the SIQM is that the KG particle has a drift velocity

$$u^\mu = dx^\mu/d\tau$$

where τ is the proper time along paths parallel to j^μ. In terms of the momentum $P^\mu = \partial^\mu S - eA^\mu$, $u^\mu = M^{-1}P^\mu$ with $u_\mu u^\mu = -1$, from equation [31].

Defining a scalar density $\rho = Me^{2P}$ we may express equation [32] in the form[50]:

$$\frac{D\rho}{D\tau} \equiv \partial_\mu(\rho u^\mu) = 0$$

From this it follows that along a line of flow:

$$\omega Me^{2P} = K \tag{33}$$

where ω is a volume element of fluid and K is a real or pure imaginary constant (which, however, varies from one drift line to another). If on an initial spacelike surface the motion is timelike, then from equation [31] M is real and so is K. Now, in the rest frame, $u^0 E = M$ where the particle energy $E = \partial^0 S - eA^0$. It follows that if initially the motion is future-pointing, with $E > 0$, then $M > 0$ which implies $K > 0$ (since $e^{2P} > 0$ and $\omega > 0$ always) and we see from equation [33] that the timelike and positive energy character of the motion is preserved all along a trajectory. Moreover, the sign of the probability density $j^0 = 2e^{2P}E$ is correlated with the sign of E and will remain positive along a line of flow if the initial motion has $E > 0$.

Identical arguments lead to an association of past-pointing negative-energy motions with negative probability densities and this coupling is preserved along a line of flow if initially $E < 0$. Such solutions may be mapped on to positive energy, positive probability density anti-particle solutions by the charge conjugation given above: $\psi^c = \psi^*$.

These results, proved in the rest frame, evidently remain valid under orthochronous Lorentz transformations.

We have thus succeeded in separating the solutions to the causal

KG equation into two disjoint subsets $\{E > 0, j^0 > 0\}$ and $\{E < 0, j^0 < 0\}$ and shown that the causal laws of motion prevent the development of one type of solution into the other. This reasoning holds for all external fields A_μ which maintain the timelikeness of the momentum P^μ. Should the external potential be strong enough, pair creation may occur and the separation of the solutions breaks down. In addition, we assume that the initial motion is associated with a wave packet so that the initial total probability is unity. This is an important point, since de Broglie[12] has shown how, with a plane KG wave incident on a partially reflecting mirror, superluminal motions apparently occur in the region of the Wiener fringes. It seems that these unphysical motions are a consequence of the excessive abstraction implied by the use of plane waves.

It is emphasized that we have only been able to overcome the difficulty of negative probabilities by assuming that particles possess well-defined space-time trajectories, and that they are subject to action by the quantum potential (contained in M). With these assumptions, we can immediately associate the sign of particle energy with the sign of local probability density, an energy moreover which is well-defined and continuously variable for all possible particle motions (and not just for stationary states). The initial character of these motions is preserved for all time by the Hamilton-Jacobi and conservation equations.

If one accepts that the quantum mechanical formalism is complete then one must accept Feynman's statement[51] that there is no way of eliminating negative probabilities from the intermediate stages of, for example, an interference calculation. The problem of their physical interpretation then cannot be avoided.

However, if one accepts the introduction of trajectories in the description, then our demonstration above shows how the positive character of probability is preserved at every stage of the calculation. The association of positive probabilities with positive energy is of course in accordance with the principles of relativity theory.

We note finally that, although our discussion here has been confined to a single KG particle[52], our method may be applied to the elimination of negative probabilities from the theory of the many-body KG system, the spin-1 Proca equation, and the spin-$\frac{1}{2}$ Feynman-Gell-Mann equation[53].

Finally, we wish to stress that the causal interpretation does not reinstate the mechanistic classical world view. Particles may be described as possessing definite values of physical variables but these variables depend, through the quantum forces arising from the quantum potential and torque, on the whole quantum state which includes the influence of the environment.

The lessons of Bohm's work are clear. We can adopt Bohr's idealist epistemology and deny the very possibility of analysing what happens within quantum phenomena, such as neutron interference. However we should then be consistent and refuse to speak of the quantum world as if it actually exists. The only other known alternative, which is capable of reproducing all the results of quantum mechanics in terms of a physically determinist reality, is the non-classical causal interpretation. Far from returning to classical mechanics it shows exactly how radical a revision of our concepts quantum mechanics entails. Even if it is not taken as a fully satisfactory description of quantum mechanical reality, it at least shows in a clear way the features that such a description must entail. The interpretations of Bohr and of de Broglie-Bohm-Vigier both emphasize that the fundamentally new feature exhibited by quantum phenomena is a kind of wholeness completely foreign to the post-Aristotelean reductionist mechanism in which all of nature in the final analysis consists simply of separate and independently existing parts whose motions, determined by a few fundamental forces of interaction, are sufficient to account for all phenomena. The difference arises in the methods for dealing with the situation. One thing however is clear; the organization of nature at the fundamental level is far more complex than mere mechanistic models can encompass. The ghost cannot be exorcized from the machine.

Conclusion

Throughout this contribution we have discussed various 'interpretations' of the quantum formalism, and what has emerged is that the problem is not simply one of interpreting the same results in various ways. In fact there are good reasons for the argument that CIQM and SIQM are essentially different theories between which a choice can be made in a no arbitrary manner. Moreover:

1   They have different ontologies since the real existents are different. In SIQM individual processes are real, take place in space and time and have well-defined properties. In fact SIQM can account for all the quantum properties of matter, including all the so-called paradoxes, within this framework without conflicting with the requirements of special relativity. Further it does this in terms of a model which is immediately intuitively clear and which allows a visualization of the actual processes taking place.

2   All events occurring in space and time can be attributed to material causes which are also processes taking place in space-time, albeit non-locally. In CIQM the behaviour of matter is irreducibly indeterminate; for example, *nothing* causes the decay of an unstable nucleus.

3   In some versions of CIQM the behaviour of matter depends on the cognizance of observers. Such a possibility does not exist in

SIQM in which the material world has an existence independent of the knowledge of observers.

4   Since SIQM allows a description of the causation of individual events, it enables a deeper analysis and understanding of phenomena with the possibility of developing more penetrating theories of these events which CIQM shrouds in mystery by the dogmatic insistence in the absolute and final character of complementarity and indeterminacy.

5   The possibility exists in SIQM to make testable predictions which go beyond, by being more precise, but nevertheless do not contradict those of quantum mechanics.

6   Complementarity is inadequate in the description of time-dependent neutron interferometry and requires the renunciation of energy conservation in interference situations, whereas the description of SIQM is consistent and apparent non-conservation of energy may be explained through the possibility of energy exchange with the ether.

Acknowledgements

The authors C. Dewdney, P. R. Holland and A. Kyprianidis wish to thank the Royal Society, the SERC and the French government respectively for financial support which enabled the work reported here to be completed, and the Institut Henri Poincaré for its hospitality.

References

1   A. Garuccio, A. Kyprianidis, D. Sardelis and J.-P. Vigier, *Lettere al Nuovo Cim.*, **39**, 225 (1984).

2   A. Garuccio, V. Rapisarda and J.-P. Vigier, *Phys. Lett.*, **90A**, 17 (1982).

3   D. Bohm, *Phys. Rev.*, **85**, 166, 180 (1952); *Phys. Rev.*, **89**, 458 (1953); *Causality and Chance in Modern Physics*, Routledge & Kegan Paul, London, 1951; *Wholeness and the Implicate Order*, London, 1980; D. Bohm and J.-P. Vigier, *Phys. Rev.*, **96**, 205 (1954); D. Bohm and B. J. Hiley, *Found Phys.* **5**, 93 (1975).

4   N. Bohr, *Atomic Physics and the Description of Nature*, Cambridge University Press, 1934; *Atomic Physics and Human Knowledge*, Random House, New York, 1958; *Essays 1958–1962 on Atomic Physics and Human Knowledge*, Random House, New York, 1962.

5   N. Bohr, *op. cit.*, 1934.

6   A. Einstein, in Schilpp (ed.), *Albert Einstein: Philosopher Scientist*, Harper Torchbooks, New York, 1959.

7   D. M. Greenberger, *Rev. Mod. Phys.* **55**, 4 (1983).

8   L. E. Ballentine, *Rev. Mod. Phys.*, **42**, 358 (1970).

9   W. Duane, *Proc. Natl. Acad. Sci.*, **9**, 153 (1923).

10   A. Landé, *Am. J. Phys.*, **33**, 123 (1965); **34**, 1160 (1966); **37**, 541 (1969).

11   A. Einstein, R. Podolsky and N. Rosen, *Phys. Rev.*, **47**, 777 (1935).

12   L. de Broglie, *Non Linear Wave Mechanics*, Elsevier, 1960.

13   J.-P. Vigier, *Astr. Nachr.*, **303**, 55 (1982) and references therein.

14   D. Bohm and B. J. Hiley, *Found Phys.*, **5**, 93 (1975); **12**, 1001 (1982).

15   P. Droz-Vincent, *Phys. Rev. D.*, **19**, 702 (1979); *Ann. IHP*, **32**, 377 (1980).
      A. Garuccio, A. Kyprianidis and J.-P. Vigier, *Nuovo Cim.*, **B83**, 135 (1984);
      C. Dewdney, P. H. Holland, A. Kyprianidis, and J.-P. Vigier, *Phys. Rev.
      D.*, **31**, 2533, 1985.
16   D. Bohm and B. J. Hiley, *Found Phys.*, **14**, 255 (1984).
17   C. Philippidis, C. Dewdney and B. J. Hiley, *Nuovo Cim.*, **52B**, 15 (1979).
18   E. Schrödinger, *Proc. Camb. Phil. Soc.*, **31**, 555 (1935).
19   A. Aspect, P. Grangier and G. Rogier, *Phys. Rev. Lett.*, **47**, 460 (1981);
      49, 91 (1982).
20   J.-P. Vigier and N. Cufaro-Petroni, *Phys. Lett.*, **93A**, 383 (1983); *Lett.
      Nuovo Cim.*, **26**, 149 (1979); D. Bohm and B. J. Hiley, *Found. Phys.*, **11**,
      529 (1981).
21   R. Prosser, *Int. J. Theo. Phys.*, **15**, 3 (1926).
22   D. Bohm, *Quantum Theory,* Prentice Hall (1951); M. Cini, *Nuovo Cim.*,
      73B, 27 (1983).
23   H. Rauch, *Proc. Int. Symp. Foundations of Quantum Mechanics*, Tokyo,
      1983, 277; S. A. Werner and A. G. Klein in D. H. Price, K. Sköld (eds),
      Neutron Scattering, Academic Press, 1984, and references therein.
24   G. Eder and A. Zeilinger, *Nuovo Cim.*, **34B**, 26 (1976).
25   A. Einstein, *Proc. Congrès Solvay*, 1927.
26   H. Rauch, Tokyo, *Proc. Int. Symp. Foundations of Quantum Mechanics*,
      1983, 277.
27   C. Dewdney and B. J. Hiley, *Found. Phys.*, **12**, 27 (1982).
28   C. Dewdney, 'Particle trajectories and interference in a time dependent
      model of neutron single crystal interferometry', *IHP*, preprint (1985).
      Phys. Lett., **109A**, 377, 1985.
29   G. Badurek, H. Rauch and J. Summhammer, *Phys. Rev. Lett.*, **51**, 1015
      (1983).
30   B. Alefield, G. Badurek and H. Rauch, *Zeit. Phys. B.*, **41**, 231
      (1981).
31   P. A. M. Dirac, *Nature*, **168**, 906 (1951); **169**, 702 (1952).
32   N. Cufaro-Petroni, P. Gueret and J.-P. Vigier, *Phys. Rev. D.*, **30**, 495
      (1984); *Nuovo Cim. B.*, **81**, 243 (1984).
33   H. J. Park, *Nuovo Cim. B.*, **55**, 15 (1980).
34   C. Dewdney, A. Garuccio, A. Kyprianidis and J.-P. Vigier, *Phys. Lett.*,
      104A, 325 (1984); L. de Broglie, *Wave Mechanics, the First Fifty Years*,
      Butterworths, London, 1973.
35   D. Bohm, *Quantum Theory*, Prentice Hall, (1951).
36   L. de Broglie, *Compt. Rend.*, **183**, 447 (1926); **184**, 273 (1927); **185**, 380
      (1927).
37   E. M. Logothetis, and P. L. Hortman, *Phys. Rev.*, **187**, 460 (1969); G.
      Farkas, I. Kertesz, Z. Naray and P. Vargo, *Phys. Lett.*, **21A**, 475 (1962);
      E. Panarella, *Lett. Nuovo Cim.*, **3**, 417 (1972).
38   E. Panarella, *Phys. Rev. Lett.*, **33**, 950 (1974); *Found Phys.*, **4**, 227 (1974).
39   E. Panarella, *Found Phys.*, **7**, 405 (1977).
40   C. Dewdney, M. Dubois, A. Kyprianidis and J.-P. Vigier, *Lett. Nuovo
      Cim.*, **41**, 177 (1984); C. Dewdney, A. Garuccio, A. Kyprianidis and J.-P.
      Vigier, *Phys. Lett. A.*, **105**, 15 (1984).
41   L. Brillouin, *Ann. der Phys.*, **1**, 315 (1927).
42   R. P. Feynman, *Int. J. Theo. Phys.*, **21**, 612 (1982).
43   J. Tersoff, and D. Bayer, *Phys. Rev. Lett.*, **50**, 8 (1983).
44   A. Kyprianidis, D. Sardelis, and J.-P. Vigier, *Phys. Lett.*, **100A**, 228
      (1984).
45   N. Cufaro-Petroni, A. Maricz, D. Sardelis and J.-P. Vigier, *Phys. Lett.*,
      101A, 4 (1984).

46   C. Dewdney, A. Kyprianidis and J.-P. Vigier, *J. Phys. A.*, **17**, L741. (1984).
47   H. Feshbach and F. Villars, *Rev. Mod. Phys.*, **30**, 24 (1958).
48   V. A. Rizov, H. Sazdjian and I. T. Todorov, 'On the relativistic quantum mechanics of two interacting spinless particles', Orsay preprint (1984).
49   L. de Broglie, *The Current Interpretation of Wave Mechanics*, Elsevier, Amsterdam, 1964.
50   F. Halbwachs, *Théories relativistes des fluides à spin*, Gauthier-Villars, Paris, 1960.
51   R. P. Feynman, 'Negative probability', this volume, p. 235.
52   N. Cufaro-Petroni *et al.*, *Phys. Lett.*, **106A**, 368 (1984).
53   N. Cufaro-Petroni *et al.*, *Lett. Nuovo Cim.*, **42**, 285 (1985); P. R. Holland *et al.*, *Phys. Lett.*, **107A**, 376 (1985); P. Gueret *et al.*, *Phys. Lett.*, **107A**, 379 (1985).

10

Irreversibility, stochasticity and non-locality in classical dynamics

Ilya Prigogine and *Université Libre de Bruxelles and*
Yves Elskens *Center for Statistical Mechanics and Thermodynamics, University of Texas at Austin*

It is a privilege to contribute to this volume honouring David Bohm. There is no need to enumerate his basic contributions to modern theoretical physics; these are well known to the scientific community. What is however unique about David Bohm is his deep involvement in epistemological problems. In this perspective, there is probably no single concept more fundamental than time in its connection with cosmology. As Karl Popper beautifully writes [1]: 'There is at least one philosophic problem in which all thinking men are interested. It is the problem of cosmology: the problem of understanding the world – including ourselves, and our knowledge, as part of the world.'

1 The problem of time

It is interesting to recall that one of the deepest analyses of the concept of time is due to Aristotle [2,3] and dates back twenty-three centuries. Aristotle's analysis, as developed in his *Physics*, is very subtle, and introduces the idea of a radical polarity in time; the celebrated definition of *Physica* iv, 219a–b says that time is something connected with motion, *in the perspective of the earlier and the later*. This can lead to divergent interpretations; the distinction of the earlier and the later may be an objective feature of the cosmos, or it may be due to the counting activity of the 'soul'. We then have two different viewpoints: one which unites us with the universe; and one in which it is man who introduces time in a timeless universe. This problem is still with us. However, the reconceptualisation which physics is presently undergoing places the problem in a new perspective.

It is well known that the formulation of modern science by Isaac Newton occurred in a period of absolute monarchy, under the sign of an Almighty God, 'suprême garant' of rationality. The Western concept of 'law of nature' can simply not be separated from its judicial and religious resonances; the ideal of knowledge is patterned according to the omniscience we may ascribe to a Ruler. For Him, there would be no distinction between past and future. Therefore, in this perspective, in which the scientist represents the human embodiment of a transcendental vision, Time could indeed only be an illusion, in the words of Einstein[4].

However, the atemporal world of classical physics was shaken by the industrial revolution. One of the greatest intellectual novelties[5,6] of that period was the formulation of the laws of thermodynamics by Rudolf Clausius in 1865: 'Die Energie der Welt ist constant. Die Entropie der Welt strebt einem Maximum zu.' In this view the world has a history. But beware: this history is a history of decay, of degradation; a history expressed by the increase of entropy.

At present, physics is in search of a third time, reducible neither to repetition nor to decay. One of the major developments of this century is associated with the study of non-equilibrium systems. We have already mentioned the second law of thermodynamics, which expresses the increase of entropy for isolated systems. For a long time, the interest of thermodynamics was limited to equilibrium systems; today, interest shifts to non-equilibrium systems interacting with their surroundings through an entropy flow. Let us emphasise an essential difference with the description of classical mechanics. In thermodynamics we are dealing with 'embedded' systems; interaction with the outside world through entropy flow plays an essential role. This immediately brings us closer to objects like towns or living systems, which can only survive because of their embedding in their environment.

The inclusion of dissipation leads to a drastic change in the concept of stability. If some foreign celestial body approached the earth, this would lead to a modification of the earth's trajectory, which would remain for ever; conservative dynamical systems have no way to forget perturbations. This is no longer the case when we include dissipation; a damped pendulum will reach a position of equilibrium, whatever the initial perturbation. We can now also understand in quite general terms what happens when we drive a system far from equilibrium. The 'attractor' which dominated the behaviour of the system near equilibrium may become unstable, as a result of the flow of matter and energy which we direct at the system. Non-equilibrium becomes a source of order; new types of attractors, more complicated ones, may appear, and give to the system remarkable new space-time properties (in phase space).

We cannot go further into these questions, which are now the subject of an extensive literature[7,8,9,10]. Let us only mention that, because of the constructive role of irreversibility, we need to reappraise the role of irreversibility on the fundamental level, be it classical or quantum.

Here a confrontation with the traditional point of view becomes unavoidable. Indeed, the conventional viewpoint is that the fundamental laws of physics being symmetric with respect to the time-reversal transformation, there can be no fundamental physical basis for oriented time. The appearance of irreversibility in physical processes and the related 'arrow of time' are only the result of statistical averaging (or 'coarse graining'), which is necessitated not by any objective aspect of physical phenomena but simply to take into account our ignorance (or lack of interest) of the exact dynamical state of the system. Thus Born, for instance, asserts[11] that 'irreversibility is a consequence of the explicit introduction of ignorance into the fundamental laws'. This would make a chemical or biological structure the outcome of our personal ignorance, which is paradoxical.

However, the difficulties in introducing irreversibility on the fundamental level are obviously very serious, as they lead us to question the meaning of trajectories in the case of classical dynamics, as well as the relevance of fundamental theorems such as the Liouville theorem[12,13]. In this note, we want to emphasise that, in spite of such difficulties, the programme initiated by Boltzmann 100 years ago can now be rigorously worked out for well-defined classes of unstable dynamical systems.

As a result, we now begin to decipher the message of the second law of thermodynamics: we are living in a world of unstable dynamical systems (in a sense to be specified later); moreover, our physical world has a broken temporal symmetry. There exist classes of initial conditions which are admissible while their time-inverse is not. To some extent these considerations apply also to quantum theory and relativity; for lack of space we limit ourselves here to classical systems.

Probably the most fascinating aspect involved in the transition from dynamics to thermodynamics is the deep change in the structure of space-time which the introduction of irreversibility requires on the microscopic level. Irreversibility leads to a well-defined form of *non-locality*[14,15] in which a point is replaced by an ensemble of points according to a new space-time geometry determined by the inclusion of the privileged arrow of time. We cannot hope to present a extensive account in this paper, but we intend to describe some of the basic concepts involved in this new approach to dynamics.

It is interesting to note that the need to go beyond the dynamical concepts, to include among the fundamental notions those of randomness and irreversibility, has been recognised recently by various authors in all fields of physics[16,17,18,19]. It is also the direction which our group is pursuing for more than two decades[20], but the novelty of the subject required for forging of appropriate mathematical tools and framework, which were not available at the start[7,21,22].

2 Classical and modern dynamics

Classical dynamics rests on the notion of *trajectories in phase space*. If we let $\omega = (\omega_1 \ldots \omega_n) \in \Gamma$ describe the state of a physical system, the system's evolution is represented by a one-to-one mapping:

$$S_t : \omega(0) \mapsto S_t \omega(0) = \omega(t) \tag{1}$$

from Γ to itself. For Hamiltonian systems, and more generally for flows, the mapping S_t is *invertible*: $S_t^{-1} = S_{-t}$ is also defined as a one-to-one mapping of Γ onto itself; the present configuration $\omega(0)$ uniquely defines all the past and future configurations $\omega(t)$, $-\infty < t < \infty$.

Modern analysis developed an alternative approach to classical dynamics with the description of the system's state by a set of symbols s, taking values in an 'alphabet' Σ according to the following rule. Let us first choose a partition $\mathscr{P}$ of Γ, i.e. a set of subsets P_s, $s \in \Sigma$, covering Γ, such that $P_s \cap P_r = \varnothing$ if $s \neq r$. Then we say that a state ω is described by a symbol s if $\omega \in P_s$ (s is a 'coarse-grained' description of ω). If we make sequential observations, say at every time $t \in \mathbb{Z}$, the system's evolution defines the sequence $\mathbf{s} = (s_t)$, $t \in \mathbb{Z}$, of the successive symbols for the successive states $\omega(t)$. Then the dynamics of S_t induces on the sequence $\mathbf{s}$ a *symbolic dynamics* in the form of a 'shift' mapping:

$$\sigma_t : \Sigma^{\mathbb{Z}} \to \Sigma^{\mathbb{Z}} : \mathbf{s} = (s_n) \mapsto \sigma_t \mathbf{s} = (s_{n+t}) \tag{2}$$

This description expresses clearly the reversibility of classical mechanics: the sequence (s_n) exists once and for all, and the flow of time leads to a mere relabelling of the symbols s_n.

In the study of complex systems, involving many degrees of freedom, a description of the system's state by a single point ω in phase space is unrealistic. We thus resort with Gibbs to a statistical description, by a probability measure $\mathrm{d}\mu = \rho(\omega)\mathrm{d}\omega$ over Γ. The physical interpretation of this *ensemble* (through this paper, when speaking of the classical ensemble theory of Gibbs, we do not refer to Gibbs invariant ensembles – which play a fundamental role in the statistical mechanics of ergodic systems[7,23] – but rather to his presentation[24] of the concept of an ensemble as a collection of systems: this presentation takes no account of time asymmetry) is an assembly of identical systems with the same macroscopic properties; the evolution of the ensemble is induced by the microscopic motion as:

$$\rho_t(\omega) = U_t^* \rho_0(\omega) = \rho_0(S_{-t}\omega) \tag{3}$$

If the mapping S_t is invertible, the evolution operators $U_t^*, -\infty < t < \infty$, form a *unitary group*:

$$U_t^* U_t = 1, \quad U_t^* U_r^* = U_{t+r}^* \tag{4}$$

This Koopman description of the dynamics in terms of distribution functions or ensembles evolving by the action of the operator U_t^* is only a *formal* extension of the microscopic view of points moving on trajectories in phase space, as the action of U_t^* is conjugate to the point transformation S_t on Γ. Moreover, for Hamiltonian systems in canonical co-ordinates, *Liouville's theorem* states that:

1   the evolution operator U_t^* preserves the measure $d\omega$:

$$\int_A d\omega = \int_{S_{-t}A} d\omega \tag{5}$$

$$U_t^* 1 = 1$$

2   for any measure $\rho(\omega)d\omega$ and function $f(x)$:

$$\int_\Gamma f(U_t^* \rho(\omega)) d\omega = \int_\Gamma f(\rho(\omega)) d\omega \tag{6}$$

In particular, the Boltzmann *H*-functional:

$$H[\rho] = \int_\Gamma \rho \ln \rho \, d\omega \tag{7}$$

is constant in time. However, while the volume (the 'measure') of sets in phase space is preserved, their shape may be highly deformed or they may even fragment (see Figure 10.3 below). This deformation or fragmentation gives the appearance of an approach to equilibrium – where all points would be uniformly distributed in the phase space. But this is only an appearance, as $H[1] = 0$, whereas for any non-equilibrium distribution:

$$H[U_t^* \rho] = H[\rho] > 0 \tag{8}$$

In the classical view, the world is thus similar to a museum in which information is stored once and for all. Time could then be compared to a patient demolition of artefacts into pieces, which are preserved and could be used to reconstruct the artefacts in full detail.

For nearly three centuries after Newton, classical dynamics appeared as a closed method enabling one to compute whatever physical quantity from first principles and well-defined initial data. This holds true, but only for a limited class of dynamical systems, for the recent developments in dynamics show (see examples in section 3) that 'many' dynamical systems are unstable; in such systems, each region of phase space (whatever its size) contains many diverging trajectories, so that the assimilation of a finite region of phase space (however small) to a single point becomes ambiguous [22].

In this context, it is interesting to recall the classification of dynamical systems recently proposed by Ford, Eckhardt and Vivaldi [25,26]:

1   for 'algorithmically (A-)integrable' systems, the action of S_t is coherent enough for the trajectory of a point to be computable with arbitrary precision over any time lapse quite easily from prescribed initial data; the orbits of neighbouring points are (marginally in general) stable; examples of such systems include all analytically integrable systems, 'rational' planar billiards, etc.;

2   to the opposite, 'Kolmogorov' (K-) systems exhibit a complex behaviour of individual trajectories, like exponential divergence, to the effect that no finite algorithm (including its data) can reliably compute the motion of phase points sensibly faster than the dynamics itself; systems of this kind include geodesic flow on surfaces with negative curvature, hard spheres in three dimensions, the planar Lorentz gas model, etc.

The essential difference between the two classes is that the concept of 'the phase-space trajectory of the system' is operational in A-integrable systems and useless in Kolmogorov systems. It becomes therefore natural to look for a formulation of dynamics which eliminates for the K-systems the unobservable concept of a trajectory. One may expect that this elimination would also permit us to include in the frame of dynamics the concept of irreversibility; accordingly, we consider that the natural theoretical framework for unstable dynamical systems is a theory of semi-groups rather than groups.

The main object of this paper is to provide an elementary presentation of this transition from dynamical groups to semi-groups in the framework of statistical mechanics and ergodic theory. Before showing this construction, let us give two simple examples of K-systems.

3   The baker transformation and the hard-point gas

To clarify the mathematical properties involved in this discussion, let us introduce two simple K-systems. We first consider the baker transformation of the unit square [27]: on the phase space $\Gamma = [0,1[\times [0,1[$, we define the mapping $S_1 : \Gamma \to \Gamma : (x, y) \mapsto (x', y')$ where (see Figure 10.1):

$$\begin{cases} x' = 2x \ (\text{mod } 1) \\ y' = (y + 2x - x')/2 \end{cases} \qquad [9]$$

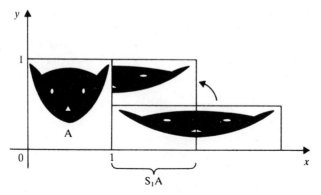

Figure 10.1 The baker transformation of the unit square is a piecewise linear, area-preserving mapping.

This mapping is invertible, and it preserves the measure $d\omega = dx \, dy$. As it expands along the x-direction by a constant factor 2, neighbouring points diverge exponentially in time, so that the value of $S_t(x, y)$ can be computed to a number N of binary digits only from data giving x with $N + t$ digits. Hence, according to the classification of section 2, this system is not A-integrable and is a K-system. In particular, it has a finite Kolmogorov-Sinai invariant h_K. (The K–S invariant (or entropy) gives the rate at which an algorithm, required to give a specified precision at time t, must grow as $t \rightarrow \infty$. In the case of the baker transformation one finds $h_K = \ln 2$.)

A symbolic description of the baker model is provided by the partition $\mathscr{P} = \{P_0, P_1\}$ with alphabet $\Sigma = \{0,1\}$, and P_0 (resp. P_1) is the left (right) half of the square. It is easily seen that the symbolic sequence (s_t), $t \in \mathbb{Z}$, corresponding to a point $\omega = (x, y)$, is given by the binary expansions:

$$x = \sum_{t=0}^{\infty} \frac{1}{2^{t+1}} s_t$$

$$y = \sum_{t=-\infty}^{-1} 2^t s_t$$

[10]

The measure $dx \, dy$ translates on the sequence space $\Sigma^{\mathbb{Z}}$ into a Bernoulli measure $B(1/2, 1/2)$, i.e. the probability measure for which all symbols s_t of a sequence $\mathbf{s}$ are independent and $P(s_t = 0) = P(s_t = 1) = 1/2$ for any t. The baker dynamical system is therefore said to be (isomorphic to) a *Bernoulli shift* – which is the simplest realisation of K-systems.

For a more physical example [28], consider the one-dimensional lattice of integers $\mathbb{Z}$. Each 'site' of $\mathbb{Z}$ can accommodate at most one 'particle' with velocity $+1$ and one 'particle' with velocity -1 (we exclude states where two particles would have the same position and velocity). The particles are distributed, at time $t = 0$, according to the Bernoullian rules (with $0 < \gamma < 1$):

1   no odd site is occupied by a particle;

2   at any even site, there is a probability γ^2 for finding two particles (with opposite velocities), $\gamma(1 - \gamma)$ for finding only a particle with $v = +1$, $\gamma(1 - \gamma)$ for only a particle with $v = -1$, and $(1 - \gamma)^2$ for no particle at all;

3   the sites' occupations are independent.

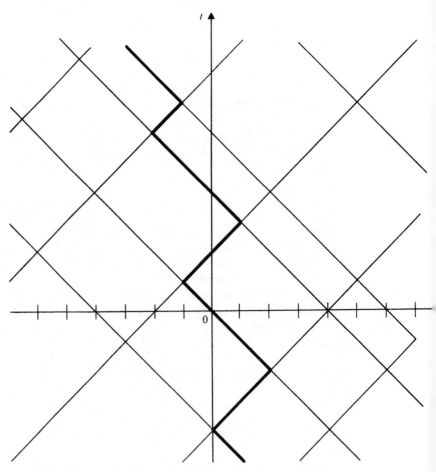

Figure 10.2   If we embed the hard-point model in a continuous space-time, the motion of a typical particle (thick line) is a succession of free flights, with instantaneous velocity reversals at collisions. In the model, collisions can only happen at integer instants.

The system's state is determined from the initial data of all particles' positions and velocities $(x_k, v_k)(0)$.

Let $x_k(t)$ denote the position of a particle, labelled k, at time t. Each particle moves freely at constant velocity until it meets another particle – in which case it reverses its velocity (see Figure 10.2). The motion of particle k is thus completely specified by the data of its initial position $x_k(0)$ and velocity $v_k(0)$, along with a sequence $(C_k(t))$, $t \in \mathbb{Z}$, where $C_k(t) = -1$ (resp. $+1$) if the particle suffers a collision (resp. no collision) at time t.

It can be shown that the motion of a single particle (say $k = 0$) for all times $-\infty < t < \infty$, determines completely the initial data $(x_k(0), v_k(0))$, $k \in \mathbb{Z}$, and hence the motion of all particles for all times. Besides, the evolution of the sequence $C_0(n)$, $n \in \mathbb{Z}$, under the dynamics S_t reduces to a shift $\sigma_t C_0(n) = C_0(n - t)$. The Bernoullian distribution of initial positions and velocities translates in this picture to a Bernoulli distribution $B(\gamma, 1 - \gamma)$ for the sequence $C_0(n)$, $n \in \mathbb{Z}$, on $\{-1, +1\}^{\mathbb{Z}}$ and an independent distribution $P(v_0(0) = -1) = P(v_0(0) = +1) = 1/2$. In particular, if $\gamma = 1/2$, the use of $x_0(0)$, $v_0(0)$ and $C_0(n)$, $-\infty < n < \infty$, maps our lattice gas model onto the abstract baker model. The hard-points model is also a K-system, and the explicit determination of a particle's trajectory during a lapse (t) requires an information about initial data of 'incoming particles' over a spatial interval with length $(2t)$.

Examples of unstable dynamics appear today in many fields of physics. In celestial mechanics, for instance (the paradigm of classical mechanics!), a statistical approach has facilitated the study of the parabolic restricted three-body problem [8,29], and of the distribution of asteroids in the solar system [30], for which orbital perturbation methods prove insufficient.

These examples illustrate the inadequacy of the concept of a trajectory for unstable dynamical systems. For such systems it proves impossible to verify by a computer experiment the validity of Liouville's theorem or the invariance of Gibbs' *H*-functional over arbitrary time intervals. Classical dynamics thus appears as an idealisation which cannot be reached experimentally, be it in 'real world' experiment or through a computer experiment. Furthermore, the breakdown of classical mechanics occurs on an *intrinsic* time scale (inversely proportional to the K–S entropy or the Lyapunov exponents), which can only decrease if in addition computational errors are taken into account.

One of the reasons for introducing a new conceptual frame at the basic level of description of dynamics is to develop methods able to deal with real-world situations without introducing unobservable concepts (such as initial data known with infinite precision) in the theoretical scheme. In this sense, our approach follows the trails of quantum theory and relativity.

4   Irreversibility and probability

Boltzmann's pioneering work in statistical physics is based on his relation:

$$S = k_B \log P/P_0 \qquad [11]$$

for the entropy S of a macroscopic state with probability P. The appearance of this concept of probability in the context of deterministic dynamics can only have two possible causes: it may result from our *ignorance* of some relevant variables or functions; or from the actual *inadequacy* of the fundamental concepts of classical dynamics. The analogy with the problem of 'hidden variables' in quantum theory, to which David Bohm has so much contributed, is obvious.

For time-dependent phenomena, a basic probabilities description may be formulated in terms of Markov processes. These are characterised by a transition operator W_t^* acting on densities $\rho(\omega)$ over Γ:

$$\tilde{\rho}_t(\omega) = W_t^* \tilde{\rho}_0(\omega) \qquad [12]$$

whose kernel is given by transition probabilities. The transition operators W_t^* for a Markov process form a semi-group:

$$W_0^* = 1, \; W_t^* W_r^* = W_{t+r}^* \quad (t \geqslant 0, r \geqslant 0) \qquad [13]$$

Most physical Markov chains have a single invariant probability measure $\tilde{\rho}_{eq}(\omega)$:

$$W_t^* \tilde{\rho}_{eq} = \tilde{\rho}_{eq} \qquad [14]$$

Let $\tilde{\rho}_{eq} = 1$ for simplicity. Then the action of W_t^* on a non-equilibrium distribution $\tilde{\rho} \neq 1$ relaxes it towards equilibrium, as measured in a natural norm $\|-\|$:

$$\lim_{t \to \infty} \| W_t^* \tilde{\rho} - 1 \| = 0 \qquad [15]$$

$$\lim_{t \to \infty} \int_\Gamma \tilde{\rho}_t(\omega) \ln \tilde{\rho}_t(\omega) d\omega = 0 \qquad [16]$$

Thus Markovian processes *contract* the discrepancies between the non-equilibrium function $\tilde{\rho}$ and the invariant equilibrium function 1, whereas classical dynamics does not damp non-equilibrium discrepancies but only hides them by mixing pieces of phase space more and more intimately as time proceeds (see Figure 10.3); the *relaxation* to equilibrium (equations [15] and [16]) can only be obtained by means of a *non-local* description of the system's evolution.

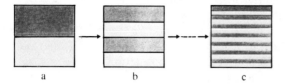

Figure 10.3 The illusion of approach to equilibrium for $t \to \infty$ in the baker model is caused by the fragmentation of the region supporting the non-equilibrium density ρ in ever smaller pieces and by the ever more intimate mixing of high-density and low-density pieces over the whole phase space. (a) The initial density ρ_0 is uniform over the upper half of the square. (b) Its first image under the transformation. (c) Its third image under the transformation.

5 Non-equilibrium ensembles and the second principle in statistical physics

The fundamental problem in the microscopic description of irreversible phenomena is thus mathematically expressed as the passage from a one-to-one dynamical system $(\Gamma, d\mu, S_t)$ to a non-local Markov process $(\Gamma, d\mu, W_t)$. Clearly, such a passage cannot follow from a universal construction, as we expect it to be possible for K-systems but not for integrable systems. Moreover this breaking of locality can only occur at the level of distribution functions. We thus associate with any distribution function $\rho(\omega)$ over Γ another distribution function:

$$\tilde{\rho} = \Lambda \rho \qquad [17]$$

obtained from ρ by a *linear deformation.*

The deformation operator Λ *depends on the dynamics* as to ensure that:

$$w\text{-lim}_{t \to \infty} \tilde{\rho}_t = 1 \qquad [18]$$

under the actual evolution of the system. The evolution of $\tilde{\rho}$ itself must also be consistent with the deterministic evolution of ρ as imposed by the dynamics S_t; this implies an intertwining relation:

$$W_t^* \Lambda = \Lambda U_t^* \qquad [19]$$

between the unitary operator U_t^* and the contracting operator W_t^*, describing the system's evolution in its two representations:

$$\rho_t = U_t^* \rho_0$$
$$\tilde{\rho}_t = W_t^* \tilde{\rho}_0 \qquad [20]$$

The role of Λ in the transition from deterministic to Markovian dynamics deserves more physical considerations. First, such a deformation is meaningful only for dynamically unstable systems, in which the notion of a trajectory is inadequate; this suggests that Λ must be *non-local*, which validates the introduction of the probability concept into

dynamics. Second, it must guarantee the decay of distribution functions to equilibrium in the future, with no restrictions on their past
behaviour; Λ must *break the dynamics' symmetry under time-reversal*.
We shall return to these points in sections 7 and 8 after presenting an
explicit construction of such a deformation.

Transformation operators, leading from classical or quantum
mechanics to Markov processes, were first introduced in 1973 by
our group[31,32] in connection with kinetic theory, but there the
large number of degrees of freedom causes supplementary complications[21,13]. We therefore restrict ourselves in this paper to situations
first considered by Misra, Courbage and one of us (I. Prigogine),
where the mathematical construction can be worked out with full
rigour[33,34].

6   Markov processes equivalent to deterministic dynamics

For K-systems, non-local deformation operators can be constructed
naturally as follows. The phase space of a K-system can be partitioned
in a family $\mathscr{P} = \{P_s\}$, $s \in \Sigma$, of disjoint subsets, which:

1   is 'generating': two points ω, ω' almost surely visit different cells
for at least one moment in their motion;

2   has 'trivial tail': the motion of a point $\omega(t)$ across the partition's
cells for $t > T$ bears no correlation, as $T \to \infty$, with its motion
across the cells for $t < 0$.

This characteristic enables one to construct an operator $\mathscr{T}$ conjugate
to the evolution operator[35,22]:

$$U_t^* \mathscr{T} U_t = \mathscr{T} + t\mathbb{1} \tag{21}$$

which is interpreted as an internal time or *age* operator on the Hilbert

space $\mathscr{H}^\perp$ of functions with vanishing sum $\left(\int_\Gamma \varphi(\omega) \, d\omega = 0 \right)$.

The existence of an age operator also yields an orthonormal basis
$\{\varphi_{ti}\}(-\infty < t < \infty, i \in I)$ of $\mathscr{H}^\perp$, in which any distribution function in
L^2 admits a unique decomposition:

$$\rho(\omega) = 1 + \sum_{ti} a_{ti}\varphi_{ti}(\omega)$$

$$\tag{22}$$

$$a_{ti} = \int_\Gamma \rho(\omega) \, \varphi_{ti}(\omega) \, d\omega$$

In terms of eigenfunctions:

$$\mathscr{T} \varphi_{ti} = t\varphi_{ti} \tag{23}$$

$$U_r^* \varphi_{ti} = \varphi_{t+r,i} \tag{24}$$

The coefficients a_{ti} express how much the non-equilibrium distribution function $\rho(\omega)$ differs from the equilibrium 1, to the extent that can be determined in observing the system through the partition $\mathscr{P}$ for times $\tau \leqslant t$. A non-equilibrium ensemble is thus equivalently described by a phase-space distribution $\rho(\omega)$ or by an infinite sequence (a_{ti}), $-\infty < t < \infty, i \in I$. With this decomposition, the evolution of ρ under the unitary group [3] becomes a shift mapping:

$$U_t^*\rho = 1 + \sum_{ni} a_{n-t,i}\varphi_{ni} \qquad [25]$$

and the L^2-distance between ρ and the equilibrium distribution remains constant:

$$\|U_t^*\rho - 1\|^2 = \|\rho - 1\|^2 = \sum_{ni} a_{ni}^2 \qquad [26]$$

The classical view of decay to equilibrium as the effect of the mixing of trajectories in phase space (see Figure 10.3) is realised by the square-integrable distribution functions, as for them

$$\lim_{t \to \pm\infty} a_{ti} = 0 \qquad [27]$$

but it necessarily holds equally well for the future and the past evolutions. There is no room for an intrinsically irreversible evolution of distribution functions in the classical description.

On the other hand, the L^2-distance may decay to zero under a non-unitary evolution. Consider the deformed distribution function:

$$\tilde{\rho} = 1 + \sum_{ni} \tilde{a}_{ni}\varphi_{ni}$$
$$\tilde{a}_{ni} = \lambda(n)a_{ni} \qquad [28]$$

with coefficients $1 \geqslant \lambda(t) \geqslant 0$. In operator language, we define:

$$\tilde{\rho} = \Lambda\rho$$
$$\Lambda = \lambda(\mathscr{T}) + P_0 \qquad [29]$$

where $P_0\rho = \int_\Gamma \rho(\omega)d\omega$, and λ is a prescribed function. The deformation (equations [28] and [29]) associates a semi-group of transition operators W_t^* to the unitary evolution group U_t^*, in the form:

$$W_t^* = \Lambda U_t^*\Lambda^{-1} \qquad [30]$$

$$W_t^*\tilde{\rho} = \Lambda U_t^*\rho = 1 + \sum_{ni} \frac{\lambda(t + n)}{\lambda(n)} \tilde{a}_{ni}\varphi_{n+t,i} \qquad [31]$$

Then the squared distance

$$\|W_t^*\tilde{\rho} - 1\|^2 = \sum_{ni} \left(\frac{\lambda(t + n)}{\lambda(n)} \tilde{a}_{ni}\right)^2 \qquad [32]$$

is a decreasing function of t if $\lambda(t)$ is decreasing, and it vanishes for $t \to \infty$ if $\lambda(t)$ does. We actually require that $\lambda(t)$ decrease monotonically from $\lambda(-\infty) = 1$ to $\lambda(+\infty) = 0$, and that it be log-concave ($\lambda(t + n)/\lambda(n)$ is a non-increasing function of n, for any t). A genuine form for this function is $\lambda_c(t) = \min(1,c^t)$ with $0 < c < 1$; the constant c depends on the dynamics under consideration. This exponential decrease of $\lambda(t)$ for $t \to \infty$ plays an important role in the physical interpretation of the operator Λ, which we discuss in the next section.

The meaning of the profile function $\lambda(t)$ is easily derived from the simple example:

$$F_0\rho = \tilde{\rho} = 1 + \sum_{t \leqslant 0} a_{ti}\varphi_{ti} \tag{33}$$

i.e.:

$$\lambda_0(t) = 1 \text{ if } t \leqslant 0, \ \lambda_0(t) = 0 \text{ if } t > 0 \tag{34}$$

In this case, for any non-equilibrium ensemble, one observes only the coefficients a_{ti} for $t \leqslant 0$ and not a_{ti} ($t > 0$). As the initial conditions on $\tilde{\rho}$ involve all the experimental knowledge on the ensemble, no reference to idealised data such as Dirac distributions (for which all coefficients a_{ti} are needed with a precision *inaccessible* at initial time) can be made in our formulation.

However, the choice $\lambda(t) = \lambda_0(t)$ in equation [33] is particular as the resulting deformation $\Lambda = F_0$ is not invertible; in general, $\lambda(t) > 0$ $\forall t$, so that Λ^{-1} is defined densely over L^2. Both Λ and W_t^* are non-local operators, because the functions $\Lambda\rho$ and $W_t^*\tilde{\rho}$ are computed through the coefficients a_{ti}, which depend on the values of ρ over the whole phase space and whose values affect $\Lambda\rho$ and $W_t^*\tilde{\rho}$ over the whole Γ.

7 Geometrical aspects of the Λ-transformation

The construction and the action of Λ-deformations are best presented for dynamical systems satisfying Anosov's conditions, like our two examples[27,36]. For simplicity, we only discuss the baker model.

The baker transformation (equation [9]) contracts all vertical segments by a factor 2 and dilates horizontal ones by the same factor. Therefore, two points ω, ω' differing only by their ordinates move along converging trajectories, but the slightest difference in their abscissae would make them diverge exponentially. For any point ω, one defines the contracting (stable) and dilating (unstable) fibres (see Figure 10.4):

$$\hat{X}_n^s(\omega) = \{\omega' \in \Gamma : s_j = s'_j \ \forall j \geqslant n, \ s_{n-1} \neq s'_{n-1}\}$$
$$\hat{X}_n^u(\omega) = \{\omega' \in \Gamma : s_j = s'_j \ \forall j \leqslant n, \ s_{n+1} \neq s'_{n+1}\} \tag{35}$$

where (s_i), $i \in \mathbb{Z}$, is the doubly infinite binary sequence associated to ω

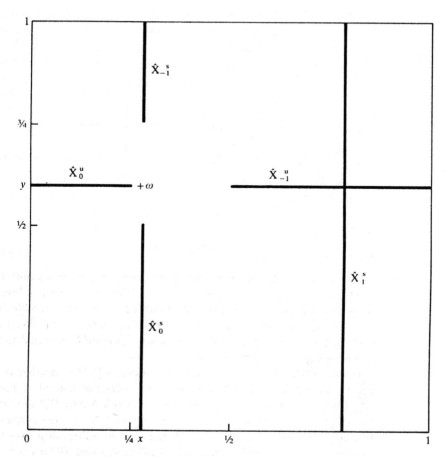

Figure 10.4 Some components of the contracting and dilating fibres of a point in the baker model.

by equation [10]. These fibres form the stable and unstable manifolds of ω:

$$X^s(\omega) = \{\omega' \in \Gamma : \lim_{t \to \infty} d(S_t\omega, S_t\omega') = 0\}$$

$$X^u(\omega) = \{\omega' \in \Gamma : \lim_{t \to -\infty} d(S_t\omega, S_t\omega') = 0\}$$

[36]

It can be shown[37] that the age eigenfunctions for this dynamical system are constant along contracting fibres:

$$\forall n \leqslant -t, \forall \omega' \in \hat{X}^s{}_n(\omega) : \varphi_{ti}(\omega') = \varphi_{ti}(\omega)$$

[37]

and take values in the finite set $\{+1, -1\}$. Thus, given a distribution function $\rho(\omega)$, a Λ-transformation disperses the weight carried by each point over its contracting fibres[14]. This is natural, since the points of a contracting fibre share the same behaviour for increasing time.

The radical change in scope, which our theory introduces, is best realised by studying the entropy functional [38,39]:

$$\Omega[\rho] = -H[\tilde{\rho}] = -\int_{\Gamma} \tilde{\rho}(\omega) \ln \tilde{\rho}(\omega) d\omega \qquad [38]$$

which measures the amount of information contained in the non-equilibrium distribution $\tilde{\rho}$ in comparison with $\rho_{eq} = 1$. It is easily seen [34] that, under the action of the semi-group W_t^*, the entropy $\Omega[\rho_t]$ increases with time t towards its equilibrium value like a macroscopic entropy. In this context, the second law of thermodynamics appears as a *selection principle*, excluding ensembles with an infinite (negative) entropy like a Dirac distribution $\delta_D(\omega, \omega_0)$ or a distribution $\rho^s(\omega, \omega_0)$ supported by the contracting fibres of the point ω_0. These distributions (though not belonging to L^2) are admitted by the classical extended Gibbs-Koopman formalism and do not decay to equilibrium.

On the other hand, a classical coarse-graining [40,24] would replace δ_D or ρ^s by a distribution uniform over a finite cell of phase space, whose points generally belong to different stable manifolds; the asymptotic evolution of the coarse-grained ensemble is then very different from that of the original one. As we see, the classical coarse-grained ensemble's approach to equilibrium results from the mixing of images of the partition's cells (see Figure 10.3) and does not follow from a definite *dynamical scheme*, since it corresponds to no group or semi-group description [41].

We would like to add a few more technical remarks. We already saw that the action of Λ-transformations on phase-space distributions is non-local. This non-locality can be expressed in a more precise way for systems like Anosov's [27] where one introduces a metric over the phase space and the instability is characterised by *Lyapunov exponents*, which measure the rates of exponential divergence of trajectories along all directions; for a metric adapted to the dynamics, the stronger the instability, the shorter the typical distance between the points (for an 'infinitely strong' instability, all points would be mixed instantaneously). The interval of time over which the motion can be predicted is inversely proportional to the Lyapunov exponents; they are also related to the K–S entropy. For the baker example, the Lyapunov exponents are $\sigma_{\pm} = \pm \ln 2$, associated to the horizontal and vertical directions at each point.

For these dynamical systems, our theory suggests [36] the definition of a distance (adapted to the topology) such that for any $\omega \in \Gamma$, $\omega' \in \hat{X}^s_n(\omega)$, $n < 0$:

$$d(\omega, \omega') \sim e^{-|n\sigma|} \qquad [39]$$

with $\sigma = h_K$. An interesting consequence of introducing this distance is that the Λ-transformation, which remained to some extent arbitrary, can now be completely specified as we find that $\lambda(t)$ is then

$$\lambda(t) = \min (1, e^{-\sigma t}) \qquad [40]$$

The Λ-transformation acts as an effective cut-off for non-equilibrium states on a time-scale $\sim 1/\sigma$. For the hard-point model, this is just the collision time-scale.

8 The fundamental entities of dynamics

The development of modern dynamics invites us to reconsider the traditional view that the microscopic description of irreversible phenomena should be justified by our ignorance of the exact microscopic states of physical systems. To the opposite, it is the very property of instability in dynamical systems as realised in Kolmogorov flows that leads to the construction of Markov chains, with their probabilistic and time-irreversible character. The statistical ensembles on which these Markov chains act differ radically from Gibbs ensembles, because of their non-locality and their broken temporal symmetry leading the system to equilibrium in the future.

Indeed, the classical ensembles admit as a particular case the Dirac distribution, and the unitary group propagates it in time, following a single trajectory in phase space. In contrast, our Markovian equations do not propagate Dirac distributions and, as we saw, do not even admit them for initial conditions. In this sense, the basic objects of (unstable) dynamics are no longer phase points and trajectories, but extended distribution functions with broken time-symmetry evolving under non-local semi-group relations.

For Anosov systems, the instability of the dynamics is expressed by the appearance of new geometrical structures in phase space, relating the temporal concepts of past and future to the spatial ones of contracting and dilating manifolds. The flow of time, which was often considered as a macroscopic notion that eluded the microscopic laws of nature, here appears as intrinsically determined by the (microscopic phase-space) directions along which the instabilities manifest themselves, e.g. by non-zero Lyapunov exponents.

The example of abstract K-systems shows how deeply dynamics is changed when instability is taken into account in the theoretical framework. We expect that similar considerations hold in general relativity and quantum physics, whose traditional formulations do not distinguish between stable and unstable systems. As this distinction is now universally accepted in the frame of the phenomenological description of nature, the solution to the fundamental problems encountered by these theories today should come from the incorporation of new concepts in their formulation, as the ones discussed in this paper[42,43,44].

Acknowledgments

The authors are indebted to their colleagues for many fruitful discussions, especially with M. Courbage, S. Martinez, B. Misra, G. Nicolis, L. E. Reichl and E. Tirapegui.

I. Prigogine thanks the Robert A. Welch Foundation for sponsoring this research. Y. Elskens gratefully acknowledges the support of the Instituts Internationaux de Physique et de Chimie, fondés par E. Solvay, and of the Belgian National Fund for Scientific Research.

References

1   K. Popper, *The Logic of Scientific Discovery*, London, Hutchinson, 1960, p. 15.

2   Aristotle, *The Physics*, tr. P. H. Wicksteed and F. M. Cornford, London, Heinemann, 1929 (2 vols).

3   M. Heidegger, *Die Grundprobleme der Phänomenologie*, Frankfurt am Main, Klostermann, 1975; part two, *passim*.

4   A. Einstein and M. Besso, *Correspondance* (tr. P. Speziali), Paris, Hermann, 1972, p. 538.

5   R. Clausius, 'Ueber verschiedene für die Anwendung bequeme Formen der Hauptgleichungen der mechanischen Wärmetheorie', *Ann. Phys. Chem.*, **125**, 353–400 (1865).

6   I. Prigogine and I. Stengers, *La Nouvelle Alliance*, Paris, Gallimard, 1979.

7   J. P. Eckmann and D. Ruelle, 'Ergodic theory of chaos and strange attractors', *Rev. Mod. Phys.*, **57**, 617–56 (1985).

8   C. W. Horton, L. E. Reichl and V. G. Szebehely (eds.), *Long-Time Prediction in Dynamics*, New York, Wiley-Interscience, 1983.

9   G. Iooss, R. H. Helleman and R. Stora (eds.), *Chaotic Behaviour of Deterministic Systems* (Les Houches, 1981), Amsterdam, North-Holland, 1983.

10   G. Nicolis and I. Prigogine, *Self-Organisation in Non-Equilibrium Systems*, New York, Wiley, 1977.

11   M. Born, *Natural Philosophy of Cause and Chance*, Oxford, Clarendon Press, 1949, p. 72.

12   R. Balescu, *Equilibrium and Non-Equilibrium Statistical Mechanics*, New York, Wiley-Interscience, 1975.

13   O. Penrose, 'Foundations of statistical mechanics', *Rep. Prog. Phys.*, **42**, 1937–2006 (1979).

14   S. Martinez and E. Tirapegui, 'A possible physical interpretation of the Λ-operator in the Prigogine theory of irreversibility', *Phys. Lett.*, **110A**, 81–3 (1985).

15   B. Misra and I. Prigogine, 'Irreversibility and non-locality', *Lett. Math. Phys.*, **7**, 421–9 (1983).

16   J. Ford, 'How random is a coin toss?', *Phys. Today*, **36**, 40–7, April, 1983.

17   O. Penrose, *Foundations of Statistical Mechanics*, Oxford, Pergamon, 1970.

18   R. Penrose, 'Singularities and time-asymmetry', in S. Hawking and W. Israel (eds), *General Relativity*, Cambridge University Press, 1979, pp. 581–638.

19   J. A. Wheeler and W. H. Zurek (eds.), *Quantum Theory and Measurement*, Princeton University Press, 1982.

20 I. Prigogine, *Non-Equilibrium Statistical Mechanics*, New York, Wiley-Interscience, 1962.

21 J. L. Lebowitz, 'Exact results in non-equilibrium statistical mechanics: where do we stand?', *Suppl. Prog. Theor. Phys.*, **64**, 35–49 (1978).

22 I. Prigogine, *From Being to Becoming*, San Francisco, Freeman, 1980.

23 Y. G. Sinai, 'Gibbs measures in ergodic theory', *Russian Math. Surveys*, **27**, 4, 21–69, July–August, 1972.

24 J. W. Gibbs, *Elementary Principles in Statistical Mechanics*, Woodbridge, Connecticut, Ox Bow Press, 1981, p. 5.

25 B. Eckhardt, J. Ford and F. Vivaldi, 'Analytically solvable dynamical systems which are not integrable', *Physica*, **13D**, 339–356 (1984).

26 J. Ford, 'How random is a coin toss?', in reference 8 pp. 79–92.

27 V. Arnold and A. Avez, *Problèmes Ergodiques de la Mécanique Classique*, Paris, Gauthier-Villars, 1967.

28 Y. Elskens, 'Nonunitary deformations and hydrodynamic limit in the one-dimensional hard-point gas', to be published.

29 T. Petrosky, 'Chaos and cometary clouds in the solar system', *Phys. Lett.* **117A**, 328–32 (1986).

30 J. Wisdom, 'The origin of the Kirkwood gaps: a mapping for the asteroidal motion near the 3/1 commensurability', *Astron. J.*, **87**, 577–93 (1982).

31 I. Prigogine, 'The statistical interpretation of non-equilibrium entropy', *Acta Phys. Austr. Suppl.*, **X**, 401–50 (1973).

32 I. Prigogine, C. George, F. Henin and L. Rosenfeld, 'A unified formulation of dynamics and thermodynamics', *Chemica Scripta*, **4**, 5–32 (1973).

33 S. Goldstein, B. Misra and M. Courbage, 'On intrinsic randomness of dynamical systems', *J. Stat. Phys.*, **25**, 111–26 (1981).

34 B. Misra and I. Prigogine 'On the foundations of kinetic theory', *Suppl. Prog. Theor. Phys.*, **69**, 101–10 (1980).

35 B. Misra, 'Non-equilibrium entropy, Lyapunov variables, and ergodic properties of classical systems', *Proc. Natl Acad. Sci. USA*, **75**, 1627–31 (1978).

36 Y. Elskens and I. Prigogine, 'From instability to irreversibility', *Proc. Natl. Acad. Sci. USA*, **83**, 5756–60 (1986).

37 B. Misra, I. Prigogine and M. Courbage, 'From deterministic dynamics to probabilistic descriptions', *Physica*, **98A**, 1–26 (1979).

38 M. Courbage, 'Intrinsic irreversibility of Kolmogorov dynamical systems', *Physica*, **122A**, 459–82 (1983).

39 S. Goldstein and O. Penrose, 'A non-equilibrium entropy for dynamical systems', *J. Stat. Phys.*, **24**, 325–43 (1981).

40 P. Ehrenfest and T. Ehrenfest, *The Conceptual Foundations of the Statistical Approach in Mechanics* (tr. M. Moravcsik), Ithaca, New York, Cornell University Press, 1959.

41 R. C. Tolman, *The Principles of Statistical Mechanics*, Oxford, University Press, 1962.

42 J. Géhéniau and I. Prigogine, 'The birth of time', *Found. Phys.*, **16**, 437–43 (1986).

43 C. George, F. Mayné and I. Prigogine, 'Scattering theory in superspace', *Adv. Chem. Phys.* **61**, 223–99 (1985).

44 I. Prigogine and C. George, 'The second law as a selection principle: the microscopic theory of dissipative processes in quantum systems', *Proc. Natl Acad. Sci. USA*, **80**, 4590–4 (1983).

11

The issue of retrodiction in Bohm's theory

Y. Aharonov and **D. Albert** *Tel Aviv University and University of South Carolina*

Bohm's pathbreaking hidden variable theory of 1952[1] is often accused of artificiality and inelegance, and doubtless it is guilty of both. But to make such accusations, and to leave it at that, is to entirely miss the point. What Bohm was after in his theory was not elegance and not naturalness; Bohm's intentions were simply to produce a theory which, *whatever* its other characteristics, had *logically clear foundations*. It is for that clarity which Bohm's theory is highly and rightly praised.

We should like to point to one very straightforward example of that logical clarity here, one which is related to an ancient debate within quantum mechanics, and to some recent work of ours[2,3,4]. It concerns the question of retrodiction.

The question of retrodiction might be posed like this. Can we know more of *the past history of a quantum-mechanical* system than we can in principle predict about its future? Or, more time-symmetrically and more precisely, like this. Can we know more of quantum-mechanical systems within the interval *between* two complete measurements than can in principle be known about the past or the future of any single complete measurement?

The conventional quantum-mechanical answer, the answer which follows from von Neumann's non-time-reversal-symmetric collapse postulate, is 'No.' That postulate dictates that the quantum state of any system at any time is determined (via the equations of motion) entirely by the result of the most recent complete measurement of that system. *Upcoming* measurements, whatever they may be (according to this view), determine nothing whatever about the state of the system *now*; they, rather, produce information about the state of the system *subsequent* to their execution.

On the other hand, the probability that a given experiment, carried out within the interval between two other complete measurements on the same system, will produce a given result, is known to depend *symmetrically* on the results of the measurements at the beginning and at the end of that interval (see references 2–4). Albeit that all this can be derived from the non-time-symmetric formalism, the time-symmetry of the experimental probabilities suggests that the *correct* underlying description of the quantum-mechanical systems ought to be time-symmetric as well; that the results of experiments on *both* ends of a given time-interval ought to be regarded as producing information about the system *within* that interval.

This question, the reader is doubtless aware, has been and continues to be the subject of a long convoluted and mirky debate; but, within Bohm's theory (and this is the point of the present note), this question can be posed and answered definitively, and with stunning clarity. Can we know more of the past than of the present or the future? Bohm's answer is yes. A very simple example will suffice to make the point.

Suppose that a small impenetrable box is located at the point x_1, and that another such box is located at the point x_2. A single-particle system is prepared at time t_0 in the state:

$$|x_1\rangle + |x_2\rangle \equiv |\alpha\rangle; A|\alpha\rangle = \alpha|\alpha\rangle$$

(where $|x_1\rangle$ is a state wherein the particle is located within the box at x_1, etc.) by means of a measurement of some complete set of commuting observables A at that time, and that at some later time t_2 the particle is found to be in the box at x_2.

According to the conventional quantum-mechanical account, the state of such a particle as that within the interval $t_0 < t < t_2$ is $|x_1\rangle + |x_2\rangle$, and its position (within that interval) is undefined. The fact that any measurement of X within that interval would with certainty have produced the result $X = x_2$ has a very different explanation, within this account, than the fact that any measurement of A within that interval would with certainty have produced the result $A = \alpha$. According to the retrodictive (or, rather, the time symmetric) picture of references 2–4 both A and X are well-defined within the interval ($A = \alpha$ and $X = x_2$ there); within that picture it is in some sense the case that either of *two* quantum states (or, in some other sense, *both* of them) can be associated with the particle within that interval.

Within Bohm's account, all this is splendidly clear and definite. The quantum state, the *wave-function* of the particle within the interval $t_0 < t < t_2$, is certainly and unambiguously $|x_1\rangle + |x_2\rangle$, and the *position* of the particle is clearly and unambiguously x_2 (it is hoped, by the way, that the reader will find this somewhat perplexing; and this perplexity will serve as the reader's invitation to become familiar with Bohm's brilliantly clear, if inelegant and artificial, theory).

It ought to be pointed out that there will in general be many particulars about which Bohm's picture and the time-symmetric retrodictive one do *not* agree; but there is at least one profound generality about which they surely *do*: more can be known of the pasts of quantum systems than of their futures.

Acknowledgments

This work was supported in part by the National Science Foundation grant number PHY 8408265.

References

1   D. Bohm, *Phys. Rev.*, **85**, 166 (1952).
2   Y. Aharonov, P. G. Bergmann and L. Lebowitz, *Phys. Rev.*, **134**, B 1410 (1964).
3   Y. Aharonov and D. Z. Albert, *Phys. Rev.*, **24**, D 223 (1984).
4   D. Z. Albert, Y. Aharonov and S. D'Amato, *Phys. Rev. Lett.*, **54**, 5 (1985).

12

Beables for quantum field theory

J. S. Bell   *CERN*

1   Introduction

Bohm's 1952 papers[1,2] on quantum mechanics were for me a revelation. The elimination of indeterminism was very striking. But more important, it seemed to me, was the elimination of any need for a vague division of the world into 'system' on the one hand, and 'apparatus' or 'observer' on the other. I have always felt since that people who have not grasped the ideas of those papers (and unfortunately they remain the majority) are handicapped in any discussion of the meaning of quantum mechanics.

When the cogency of Bohm's reasoning is admitted, a final protest is often this: it is all non-relativistic. This is to ignore that Bohm himself, in an appendix to one of the 1952 papers[2], already applied his scheme to the electromagnetic field. And application to scalar fields is straightforward[3]. However, until recently[4,5] to my knowledge, no extension covering Fermi fields had been made. Such an extension will be sketched here. The need for Fermi fields might be questioned. Fermions might be composite structures of some kind[6]; but they also might not be, or not all. The present exercise will not only include Fermi fields, but even give them a central role. The dependence on the ideas of de Broglie[7] and Bohm[1,2], and also on my own simplified extension to cover spin[8,9,10] will be manifest to those familiar with these things. However, no such familiarity will be assumed.

A preliminary account of these notions was entitled 'Quantum field theory without observers, or observables, or measurements, or systems, or apparatus, or wave-function collapse, or anything like that'. This could suggest to some that the issue in question is a philosophical one. But I insist that my concern is strictly professional. I think that conventional formulations of quantum theory, and of quantum field theory in particular, are unprofessionally vague and ambiguous.

227

Professional theoretical physicists ought to be able to do better. Bohm has shown us a way.

It will be seen that all the essential results of ordinary quantum field theory are recovered. But it will be seen also that the very sharpness of the reformulation brings into focus some awkward questions. The construction of the scheme is not at all unique. And Lorentz invariance plays a strange, perhaps incredible, role.

2   Local beables

The usual approach, centred on the notion of 'observable', divides the world somehow into parts: 'system' and 'apparatus'. The 'apparatus' interacts from time to time with the 'system', 'measuring' 'observables'. During 'measurement' the linear Schrödinger evolution is suspended, and an ill-defined 'wave-function collapse' takes over. There is nothing in the mathematics to tell what is 'system' and what is 'apparatus'; nothing to tell which natural processes have the special status of 'measurements'. Discretion and good taste, born of experience, allow us to use quantum theory with marvellous success, despite the ambiguity of the concepts named above in quotation marks. But it seems clear that in a serious fundamental formulation such concepts must be excluded.

In particular we will exclude the notion of 'observable' in favour of that of '*be*able'. The beables of the theory are those elements which might correspond to elements of reality, to things which exist. Their existence does not depend on 'observation'. Indeed observation and observers must be made out of beables.

I use the term '*be*able' rather than some more committed term like 'being'[11] or 'beer'[12] to recall the essentially tentative nature of any physical theory. Such a theory is at best a *candidate* for the description of nature. Terms like 'being', 'beer', 'existent'[11-13], etc., would seem to me lacking in humility. In fact 'beable' is short for 'maybe-able'.

Let us try to promote some of the usual 'observables' to the status of beables. Consider the conventional axiom: the probability of observables $(A, B \ldots)$, if observed at time t, being observed to be $(a, b \ldots)$ is:

$$\sum_q |\langle a, b \ldots q | t \rangle|^2 \tag{1}$$

where q denotes additional quantum numbers which together with the eigenvalues $(a, b \ldots)$ form a complete set.

This we replace by: the probability of beables $(A, B \ldots)$ at time t *being* $(a, b \ldots)$ is:

$$\sum_q |\langle a, b \ldots q | t \rangle|^2 \tag{2}$$

where q denotes additional quantum numbers which together with the eigenvalues $(a, b \ldots)$ form a complete set.

Not all 'observables' can be given beable status, for they do not all have simultaneous eigenvalues, i.e. do not all commute. It is important to realise therefore that most of these 'observables' are entirely redundant. What is essential is to be able to define the positions of things, including the positions of instrument pointers or (the modern equivalent) of ink on computer output.

In making precise the notion 'positions of things' the energy density $T_{00}(x)$ comes immediately to mind. However, the commutator

$$[T_{00}(x), T_{00}(y)]$$

is not zero, but proportional to derivatives of delta functions. So the $T_{00}(x)$ do not have simultaneous eigenvalues for all x. We would have to devise some new way of specifying a joint probability distribution.

We fall back then on a second choice – fermion number density. The distribution of fermion number in the world certainly includes the positions of instruments, instrument pointers, ink on paper ... and much much more.

For simplicity we replace the three-space continuum by a dense lattice, keeping time t continuous (and real!). Let the lattice points be enumerated by:

$$l = 1, 2 \ldots L$$

where L is very large. Define lattice point fermion number operators:

$$\Psi^+(l)\, \Psi(l)$$

where summation over Dirac indices and over all Dirac fields is understood. The corresponding eigenvalues are integers:

$$F(l) = 1, 2 \ldots 4N$$

where N is the number of Dirac fields. The fermion number configuration of the world is a list of such integers:

$$n = (F(1), F(2) \ldots F(L))$$

We suppose the world to have a definite such configuration at every time t:

$$n(t)$$

The lattice fermion numbers are the *local* beables of the theory, being associated with definite positions in space. The state vector $|t\rangle$ also we consider as a beable, although not a local one. The complete specification of our world at time t is then a combination:

$$(|t\rangle, n(t)) \tag{3}$$

It remains to specify the time evolution of such a combination.

3 Dynamics

For the time evolution of the state vector we retain the ordinary Schrödinger equation:

$$\mathrm{d}/\mathrm{d}t \, |t\rangle = -iH \, |t\rangle \tag{4}$$

where H is the ordinary Hamiltonian operator.

For the fermion number configuration we prescribe a stochastic development. In a small time interval $\mathrm{d}t$ configuration m jumps to configuration n with transition probability:

$$\mathrm{d}t \, T_{nm} \tag{5}$$

where:

$$T_{nm} = J_{nm}/D_m \tag{6}$$

$$J_{nm} = \sum_{qp} 2 \, Re \, \langle t|nq\rangle\langle nq|-iH|mp\rangle\langle mp|t\rangle \tag{7}$$

$$D_m = \sum_q |\langle mq|t\rangle|^2 \tag{8}$$

provided $J_{nm} > 0$, but:

$$T_{nm} = 0 \quad \text{if} \quad J_{nm} \leqslant 0 \tag{9}$$

From equation [5] the evolution of a probability distribution P_n over configurations n is given by:

$$\mathrm{d}/\mathrm{d}t \, P_n = \sum_m (T_{nm}P_m - T_{mn}P_n) \tag{10}$$

Compare this with a mathematical consequence of the Schrödinger equation [4]:

$$\mathrm{d}/\mathrm{d}t \, |\langle nq|t\rangle|^2 = \sum_{mp} 2 \, Re \, \langle t|nq\rangle\langle nq|-iH|mp\rangle\langle mp|t\rangle$$

or:

$$\mathrm{d}/\mathrm{d}t \, D_n = \sum_m J_{nm} = \sum_m (T_{nm}D_m - T_{mn}D_n) \tag{11}$$

If we assume that at some initial time:

$$P_n(0) = D_n(0) \tag{12}$$

then from equation [11] the solution of equation [10] is:

$$P_n(t) = D_n(t) \tag{13}$$

Envisage then the following situation. In the beginning God chose three-space and one-time, a Hamiltonian H, and a state vector $|0\rangle$. Then She chose a fermion configuration $n(0)$. This She chose at random from an ensemble of possibilities with distribution $D(0)$ related to the already-chosen state vector $|0\rangle$. Then She left the world alone to evolve according to equations [4] and [5].

It is notable that, although the probability distribution P in equation [13] is governed by D and so by $|t\rangle$, the latter is not to be thought of as just a way of expressing the probability distribution. For us $|t\rangle$ is an independent beable of the theory. Otherwise its appearance in the transition probabilities (equation [5]) would be quite unintelligible.

The stochastic transition probabilities (equation [5]) replace here the deterministic guiding equation of the de Broglie-Bohm 'pilot wave' theory. The introduction of a stochastic element, for beables with discrete spectra, is unwelcome, for the reversibility (I ignore here the small violation of time reversibility that has shown up in elementary particle physics; it could be of 'spontaneous' origin, and, moreover, PCT remains good) of the Schrödinger equation strongly suggests that quantum mechanics is not fundamentally stochastic in nature. However I suspect that the stochastic element introduced here goes away in some sense in the continuum limit.

4 OQFT and BQFT

OQFT is 'ordinary' 'orthodox' 'observable' quantum field theory, whatever that may mean. BQFT is de Broglie-Bohm beable quantum field theory. To what extent do they agree? The main difficulty with this question is the absence of any sharp formulation of OQFT. We will consider two different ways of reducing the ambiguity.

In OQFT1 the world is considered as one big experiment. God prepared it at the initial time $t = 0$, and let it run. At some much later time T She will return to judge the outcome. In particular She will observe the contents of all the physics journals. This will include of course the records of our own little experiments – as distributions of ink on paper, and so of fermion number. From equation [13] the OQFT1 probability D that God will observe one configuration rather than another is identical with the BQFT probability P that the configuration *is* then one thing rather than another. In this sense there is complete agreement between OQFT1 and BQFT on the result of God's big experiment– including the results of our little ones.

OQFT1, in contrast with BQFT, says nothing about events in the system in between preparation and observation. However adequate this may be from an Olympian point of view, it is rather unsatisfactory for us. We live in between creation and last judgment – and imagine that we experience events. In this respect another version of OQFT is more appealing. In OQFT2, whenever the state can be resolved into a sum of two (or more) terms:

$$|t\rangle = |t, 1\rangle + |t, 2\rangle \tag{14}$$

which are 'macroscopically different', then in disregard for the Schrödinger equation, the state 'collapses' somehow into one term or the other:

$|t\rangle \rightarrow N_1^{-1/2} |t, 1\rangle$ with probability N_1 [15]

$|t\rangle \rightarrow N_2^{-1/2} |t, 2\rangle$ with probability N_2

where:

$$N_1 = |\langle t, 1|t, 1\rangle| \quad N_2 = |\langle t, 2|t, 2\rangle|$$ [16]

In this way the state is always, or nearly always, macroscopically unambiguous and defines a macroscopically definite history for the world. The words 'macroscopic' and 'collapse' are terribly vague. Nevertheless this version of OQFT is probably the nearest approach to a rational formulation of how we use quantum theory in practice.

Will OQFT2 agree with OQFT1 and BQFT at the final time T? This is the main issue in what is usually called 'the quantum measurement problem'. Many authors, analysing many models, have convinced themselves that the state vector collapse of OQFT2 is consistent with the Schrödinger equation of OQFT1 'for all practical purposes'[14]. The idea is that even when we retain both components in equation [14], evolving as required by the Schrödinger equation, they remain so different as not to interfere in the calculation of anything of interest. The following sharper form of this hypothesis seems plausible to me: the macroscopically distinct components remain so different, for a very long time, as not to interfere in the calculation of D and J. In so far as this is true, the trajectories of OQFT2 and BQFT will agree macroscopically.

5   Concluding remarks

We have seen that BQFT is in complete accord with OQFT1 as regards the final outcome. It is plausibly consistent with OQFT2 in so far as the latter is unambiguous. BQFT has the advantage over OQFT1 of being relevant at all times, and not just at the final time. It is superior to OQFT2 in being completely formulated in terms of unambiguous equations.

Yet even BQFT does not inspire complete happiness. For one thing, there is nothing unique about the choice of fermion number density as basic local beable; we could have others instead, or in addition. For example the Higg's fields of contemporary gauge theories could serve very well to define 'the positions of things'. Other possibilities have been considered by K. Baumann[4]. I do not see how this choice can be made experimentally significant so long as the final result of experiments are defined so grossly as by the positions of instrument pointers or of ink on paper.

And the status of Lorentz invariance is very curious. BQFT agrees with OQFT on the result of the Michelson-Morley experiment, and so on. But the formulation of BQFT relies heavily on a particular division of space-time into space and time. Could this be avoided?

There is indeed a trivial way of imposing Lorentz invariance[4]. We can imagine the world to differ from vacuum over only a limited region of infinite Euclidean space (we forget general relativity here). Then an overall centre of mass system is defined. We can simply assert that our equations hold in this centre of mass system. Our scheme is then Lorentz invariant. Many others could be made Lorentz invariant in the same way; for example, Newtonian mechanics. But such Lorentz invariance would not imply a null result for the Michelson-Morley experiment ... which could detect motion relative to the cosmic mass centre. To be predictive, Lorentz invariance must be supplemented by some kind of locality, or separability, consideration. Only then, in the case of a more or less isolated object, can motion relative to the world as a whole be deemed more or less irrelevant.

I do not know of a good general formulation of such a locality requirement. In classical field theory, part of the requirement could be formulation in terms of differential (as distinct from integral) equations in three-plus-one-dimensional space-time. But it seems clear that quantum mechanics requires a much bigger configuration space. One can formulate a locality requirement by permitting arbitrary external fields and requiring that variations thereof have consequences only in their future light cones. In that case the fields could be used to set measuring instruments, and one comes into difficulty with quantum predictions for correlations related to those of Einstein, Podolsky and Rosen[18]. But the introduction of external fields is questionable. So I am unable to prove, or even formulate clearly, the proposition that a sharp formulation of quantum field theory, such as that set out here, must disrespect serious Lorentz invariance. But it seems to me that this is probably so.

As with relativity before Einstein, there is then a preferred frame in the formulation of the theory ... but it is experimentally indistinguishable[19, 20, 21]. It seems an eccentric way to make a world.

References

1 D. Bohm, *Phys. Rev.*,, **85**, 166 (1952).
2 D. Bohm, *Phys. Rev.*, **85**, 180 (1952).
3 D. Bohm and B. Hiley, *Foundations of Physics*, **14**, 270 (1984).
4 K. Baumann, preprint, Graz (1984).
5 J. S. Bell, report to Istituto Italiano per gli Studi Filosofici, Amalfi, 11 May, 1984.
6 T. H. R. Skyrme, *Proc. Roy. Soc.*, **A260**, 127 (1961); A. S. Goldhaber, *Phys. Rev. Lett.*, **36**, 1122 (1976); F. Wilczek and A. Zee, *Phys. Rev. Lett.*, **51**, 2250 (1983).
7 L. de Broglie, *Tentative d'Interpretation Causale et Nonlineaire de la Mechanique Ondulatoire*, Paris, Gauthier-Villars, 1956.
8 J. S. Bell, *Rev. Mod. Phys.*, **38**, 447, (1966).
9 J. S. Bell, in Isham, Penrose and Sciama (eds), *Quantum Gravity*, Oxford, 1982, p. 611 (originally TH.1424-CERN, 27 Oct 1971).

10   J. S. Bell, *Foundations of Physics*, **12**, 989 (1982).
11   A. Shimony, *Epistemological Letters*, Jan. 1978, 1.
12   B. Zumino, private communication.
13   B. d'Espagnat, *Physics Reports*, **110**, 201 (1984).
14   This is touched on in references [15] and [16], and in many papers in the anthology of Wheeler and Zurek [17].
15   J. S. Bell, *Helvetica Physica Acta*, **48**, 93 (1975).
16   J. S. Bell, *International Journal of Quantum Chemistry: Quantum Chemistry Symposium*, **14**, 155 (1980).
17   J. A. Wheeler and W. H. Zurek (eds), *Quantum Theory and Measurement*, Princeton University Press, 1983.
18   J. S. Bell, *Journal de Physique*, Colloque C2, suppl. au no. 3, Tome 42, p. C2–41, mars 1981.
19   J. S. Bell, in M. Flato *et al.* (eds), *Determinism, Causality, and Particles*, Dordrecht, Holland, D. Reidel, 1976, p. 17.
20   P. H. Eberhard, *Nuovo Cimento*, **46B**, 392, (1978).
21   K. Popper, *Foundations of Physics*, **12**, 971, (1982).

13

Negative probability

Richard P. Feynman   *California Institute of Technology*

Some twenty years ago one problem we theoretical physicists had was that if we combined the principles of quantum mechanics and those of relativity plus certain tacit assumptions, we seemed only able to produce theories (the quantum field theories) which gave infinity for the answer to certain questions. These infinities are kept in abeyance (and now possibly eliminated altogether) by the awkward process of renormalization. In an attempt to understand all this better, and perhaps to make a theory which would give only finite answers from the start, I looked into the 'tacit assumptions' to see if they could be altered.

One of the assumptions was that the probability for an event must always be a positive number. Trying to think of negative probabilities gave me a cultural shock at first, but when I finally got easy with the concept I wrote myself a note so I wouldn't forget my thoughts. I think that Prof. Bohm has just the combination of imagination and boldness to find them interesting and amusing. I am delighted to have this opportunity to publish them in such an appropriate place. I have taken the opportunity to add some further, more recent, thoughts about applications to two-state systems.

Unfortunately I never did find out how to use the freedom of allowing probabilities to be negative to solve the original problem of infinities in quantum field theory!

It is usual to suppose that, since the probabilities of events must be positive, a theory which gives negative numbers for such quantities must be absurd. I should show here how negative probabilities might be interpreted. A negative number, say of apples, seems like an absurdity. A man starting a day with five apples who gives away ten and is given eight during the day has three left. I can calculate this in two

235

steps: $5 - 10 = -5$; and $-5 + 8 = 3$. The final answer is satisfactorily positive and correct, although in the intermediate steps of calculation negative numbers appear. In the real situation there must be special limitations of the time in which the various apples are received and given since he never really has a negative number, yet the use of negative numbers as an abstract calculation permits us freedom to do our mathematical calculations in any order, simplifying the analysis enormously and permitting us to disregard inessential details. The idea of negative numbers is an exceedingly fruitful mathematical invention. Today a person who balks at making a calculation in this way is considered backward or ignorant, or to have some kind of mental block. It is the purpose of this paper to point out that we have a similar strong block against negative probabilities. By discussing a number of examples, I hope to show that they are entirely rational of course, and that their use simplifies calculations and thought in a number of applications in physics.

First let us consider a simple probability problem, and how we usually calculate things, and then see what would happen if we allowed some of our normal probabilities in the calculations to be negative. Let us imagine a roulette wheel with, for simplicity, just three numbers: 1, 2, 3. Suppose, however, the operator, by control of a switch under the table, can put the wheel into one of two conditions, A, B, in each of which the probability of 1, 2, 3 are different. If the wheel is in condition A, the probabilities of 1, $p_{1A} = 0.3$ say, of 2 is $p_{2A} = 0.6$, of 3 is $p_{3A} = 0.1$. But if the wheel is in condition B, these probabilities are $p_{1B} = 0.1$, $p_{2B} = 0.4$, $p_{3B} = 0.5$, say, as in Table 13.1.

Table 13.1   *Probability table for roulette wheel with two conditions*

	Condition A	Condition B
1	0.3	0.1
2	0.6	0.4
3	0.1	0.5

We use the table in this way: suppose the operator puts the wheel into condition A 7/10 of the time and into B the other 3/10 of the time at random (that is, the probability of condition A, $P_A = 0.7$, and of B, $P_B = 0.3$.), then the probability of getting 1 is Prob. $1 = 0.7\,(0.3) + 0.3\,(0.1) = 0.24$, etc. In general, of course, if α are conditions and $p_{i\alpha}$ is a conditional probability (the probability of getting the result i if the condition α holds), we have ($p_{i\alpha} = $ Prob (if α then i)):

$$P_i = \sum_\alpha p_{i\alpha} \cdot P_\alpha \qquad\qquad [1]$$

where P_α are the probabilities that the conditions α obtain, and P_i is the consequent probability of the result i. Since some result must occur in any condition, we have:

$$\sum_i p_{i\alpha} = 1 \qquad\qquad [2]$$

where the sum is that over all possible independent results i. If the system is surely in some one of the conditions, so if:

$$\sum_\alpha P_\alpha = 1$$

then:

$$\sum_i P_i = 1 \qquad\qquad [3]$$

meaning we surely have some result, in virtue of [2].

Now, however, suppose that some of the conditional probabilities are negative; suppose the table reads so that, as we shall say, if the system is in condition B the probability of getting 1 is -0.4 (see Table 13.2). This sounds absurd, but we must say it this way if we wish that our way of thought and language be precisely the same whether the actual quantities $p_{i\alpha}$ in our calculations are positive or negative. That is the essence of the mathematical use of negative numbers – to permit an efficiency in reasoning so that various cases can be considered together by the same line of reasoning, being assured that intermediary steps which are not readily interpreted (like -5 apples) will not lead to absurd results. Let us see what $p_{1B} = -0.4$ 'means' by seeing how we calculate with it.

Table 13.2 *Probability table with negative probability*

	Condition A	Condition B
1	0.3	-0.4
2	0.6	1.2
3	0.1	0.2

We have arranged the numbers in the table so that $p_{1B} + p_{2B} + p_{3B} = 1$, in accordance with equation [2]. For example, if the condition A has probability 0.7 and B has probability 0.3, we have for the probability of result 1:

$$p_1 = 0.7\,(0.3) + 0.3\,(-0.4) = 0.09$$

which would be all right. We have also allowed p_{2B} to exceed unity. A probability greater than unity presents no problem different from that of negative probabilities, for it represents a negative probability that the event will not occur.

Thus the probability of result 2 is, in the same way:

$$p_2 = 0.7\ (0.6) + 0.3\ (1.2) = 0.78$$

Finally, the probability of result 3 presents no problem for:

$$p_3 = 0.7\ (0.1) + 0.3\ (0.2) = 0.13$$

The sum of these is 1.00 as required, and they are all positive and can have their usual interpretation.

The obvious question is what happens if the probability of being in condition B is larger; for example, if condition B has probability 0.6, the probability of result 1 is negative $0.4\ (0.3) + 0.6\ (-0.4) = -0.12$. But suppose nature is so constructed that you can never be sure the system is in condition B. Suppose there must always be a limit of a kind to the knowledge of the situation that you can attain. And such is the limitation that you can never know for sure that condition B occurs. You can only know that it may occur with a limited probability (in this case less than 3/7, say). Then no contradiction will occur, in the sense that a result 1 or 2 or 3 will have a negative probability of occurrence.

Another possibility of interpretation is that results 1, 2, 3 are not directly observable but one can only verify by a final observation that the result had been 1, 2 or 3 with certain probabilities. For example, suppose the truly physically verifiable observations can only distinguish two classes of final events. Either the result was 3 or else it was in the class of being either 1 or 2. This class has the probability $p_1 + p_2$, which is always positive for any positive P_A, P_B. This case corresponds to the situation that 1, 2, 3 are not the finally observed results, but only intermediaries in a calculation.

Notice that the probabilities of conditions A and B might themselves be negative (for example, $P_A = 1.3$, $P_B = -0.3$) while the probabilities of the results 1, 2, 3 still remain positive.

It is not my intention here to contend that the final probability of a verifiable physical event can be negative. On the other hand, conditional probabilities and probabilities of imagined intermediary states may be negative in a calculation of probabilities of physical events or states.

If a physical theory for calculating probabilities yields a negative probability for a given situation under certain assumed conditions, we need not conclude the theory is incorrect. Two other possibilities of interpretation exist. One is that the conditions (for example, initial conditions) may not be capable of being realized in the physical world. The other possibility is that the situation for which the probability appears to be negative is not one that can be verified directly. A combination of these two, limitation of verifiability and freedom in initial conditions, may also be a solution to the apparent difficulty.

The rest of this paper illustrates these points with a number of examples drawn from physics which are less artificial than our roulette wheel.

Since the result must ultimately have a positive probability, the question may be asked: Why not rearrange the calculation so that the probabilities are positive in all the intermediate states? The same question might be asked of an accountant who subtracts the total disbursements before adding the total receipts. He stands a chance of going through an intermediary negative sum. Why not rearrange the calculation? Why bother? There is nothing mathematically wrong with this method of calculating and it frees the mind to think clearly and simply in a situation otherwise quite complicated. An analysis in terms of various states or conditions may simplify a calculation at the expense of requiring negative probabilities for these states. It is not really much expense.

Our first physical example is one in which one usually uses negative probabilities without noticing it. It is not a very profound example and is practically the same in content as our previous example. A particle diffusing in one dimension in a rod has a probability of being at x at time t of $P(x,t)$ satisfying $\partial P(x,t)/\partial t = -\partial^2 P(x,t)/\partial x^2$. Suppose at $x = 0$ and $x = \pi$ the rod has absorbers at both ends so that $P(x,t) = 0$ there. Let the probability of being at x at $t = 0$ be given as $P(x,0) = f(x)$. What is $P(x,t)$ thereafter? It is:

$$P(x,t) = \sum_{n=1}^{\infty} p_n \sin nx \exp(-n^2 t) \qquad [4]$$

where p_n is given by:

$$f(x) = \sum_{n=1}^{\infty} p_n \sin nx \qquad [5]$$

or:

$$p_n = \frac{2}{\pi} \int f(x) \sin nx \, dx \qquad [6]$$

The easiest way of analyzing this (and the way used if $P(x,t)$ is a temperature, for example) is to say that there are certain distributions that behave in an especially simple way. If $f(x)$ starts as $\sin nx$ it will remain that shape, simply decreasing with time as $e^{-n^2 t}$. Any distribution $f(x)$ can be thought of as a superposition of such sine waves. But $f(x)$ cannot be $\sin nx$ if $f(x)$ is a probability and probabilities must always be positive. Yet the analysis is so simple this way that no one has really objected for long.

To make the relation to our previous analysis more clear, the various conditions α are the conditions n (that is, the index α is replaced by n). The *a priori* probabilities are the numbers p_n. The conditions i are the positions x (the index i is replaced by x) and the conditional probabilities (these do not satisfy equation [2], for we have particles 'lost' off the end of the rod, and the state of being off the rod is not included among the possibilities i) (if n then x at time t) are:

$$p_{i\alpha} \longrightarrow p_{x,n} = e^{-n^2 t} \sin nx$$

Equation [4] is then precisely equation [1], for the probabilities p_i of having result n is now what we call $P(x,t)$. Thus equation [4] is easily interpreted as saying that if the system is in condition n, the chance of finding it at x is $\exp(-n^2 t) \sin nx$, and the chance of finding it in condition n is p_n.

No objection should be made to the negative values of these probabilities. However, a natural question is: What are the restrictions which ensure that the final probability for the event (finding a particle at x at time t) are always positive? In this case they are simple. It is that the *a priori* probabilities, although possibly negative, are restricted by certain conditions. The condition is that they must be such that they could come from the Fourier analysis of an everywhere positive function. This condition is independent of what value of x one wishes to observe at time t.

In this example, the restrictions to ensure positive probabilities can be stated once and for all in a form that does not depend on which state we measure. They are all positive simultaneously.

Another possibility presents itself. It can best be understood by returning to our roulette example. It may be that the restrictions on the conditions A, B which yield a positive probability may depend on what question you ask. In an extreme example, there may be no choice for the p_α that simultaneously make all p_i positive at once. Thus, although certain restrictions may make probability of result 1 positive, result 3 under these circumstances would have a negative probability. Likewise, conditions ensuring that p_3 is positive might leave p_1 or p_2 negative. In such a physical world, you would have such statements as: 'If you measure 1 you cannot be sure to more than a certain degree that the condition is A; on the other hand it will be all right to think that it is certainly in condition A, provided you are only going to ask for the chance that the result is 3.' For such a circumstance to be a viable theory, there would have to be certain limitations on verification experiments. Any method to determine that the result was 3 would automatically exclude that at the same time you could determine whether the result was 1. This is reminiscent of the situation in quantum mechanics in relation to the uncertainty principle. A particle can have definite momentum, or a definite position in the sense that an experiment may be devised to measure either one. But no experiment can be devised to decide what the momentum is, to error of order Δp, which at the same time can determine that the position x is within Δx unless $\Delta x > \hbar/\Delta p$.

It is possible, therefore, that a closer study of the relation of classical and quantum theory might involve us in negative probabilities, and so it does. In classical theory, we may have a distribution function $F(x,p)$ which gives the probability that a particle has a position x and a momentum p in dx and dp (we take a simple particle moving in one dimension for simplicity to illustrate the ideas). As Wigner has shown, the nearest thing to this in quantum mechanics is a function (the density matrix in a certain representation) which for a particle in a state with wave function $\psi(x)$ is:

$$F(x,p) = \int \psi^*(x - y/2) \exp(-ipy)\psi(x + y/2)dy \qquad [7]$$

(If the state is statistically uncertain we simply average F for the various possible wave functions with their probabilities.)

In common with the classical expression, we have these properties.

1 $F(x,p)$ is real.

2 Its integral with respect to p gives the probability that the particle is at x:

$$\int F(x,p)dp/(2\pi) = \psi^*(x)\psi(x) \qquad [8]$$

3 Its integral with respect to x gives the probability that the momentum is p:

$$\int F(x,p)dx = \varphi^*(p)\varphi(p) \qquad [9]$$

where $\varphi(p)$ is the usual Fourier transform of $\psi(x)$. $\varphi(p) = \int e^{-ipx}\psi(x)dx$.

The average value of a physical quantity M is given by:

$$<M> = \int w_M(x,p)F(x,p)dxdp \qquad [10]$$

where w_M is a weight function depending upon the character of the physical quantity.

The only property it does not share is that in the classical theory $F(x,p)$ is positive everywhere, for in quantum theory it may have negative values for some regions of x,p. That we still have a viable physical theory is ensured by the uncertainty principle that no measurement can be made of momentum and position simultaneously beyond a certain accuracy.

The restriction this time which ensures positive probabilities is that the weight functions $w_M(x,p)$ are restricted to a certain class – namely, those that belong to hermitian operators. Mathematically, a positive probability will result if w is of the form:

$$w(x,p) = \int X(x - Y/2)e^{+ipy}X^*(x + Y/2)dY \qquad [11]$$

where X is any function and X^* is its complex conjugate. Generally, if $w(x,p)$ is the weight for the question 'What is the probability that the physical quantity M has numerical value m?', w must be of the form equation [11] or the sum of such forms with positive weights. With this limitation, final probabilities are positive.

To make the analogy closer to those previously used, we can take two systems a, b, in interaction, such that measurements on b can provide predictions of probabilities for a. Thus, using the one-dimensional case again, we have a two-point correlation function $F(x_a,p_a; x_b,p_b)$ defined via an obvious generalization of equation [7] to two variables. This corresponds to the conditional probability $p_{i\alpha}$. Then if a quantity M is measured in b, the *a priori* probabilities for various x_b,p_b are given by an appropriate $w_M(x_b,p_b)$ (the analogue of P_α in equation [1]). The probability that system 'a' has position and momentum x_a,p_a is (the analogue of P_i), then:

$$P(x_a,p_a) = \int F(x_a,p_a; x_b,p_b)w_M(x_b,p_b)dx_bdp_b$$

the analogue of equation [1]. As an example, we may take the strong correlation possible arising from the two-particle wave function $\delta(x_a - x_b)$ which is:

$$F(x_a,p_a; x_b,p_b) = \delta(p_a + p_b)\delta(x_a - x_b)$$

which means that the particles a, b, have the same position and opposite momenta so that a measurement of b's position would permit a determination of a's and a measurement of b's momentum would determine a's (to be the opposite). This particular F is entirely positive and classical in its behaviour, so that letting $w_M(x_b,p_b)$ be $\delta(x_a - b) \times \delta(p_a - Q)$ would not lead to negative probabilities directly, for equation [1] gives $P(x_a,p_a) = \delta(x_a - b)\delta(P_a + Q)$ in this case, but further use of such a P in subsequent interactions has the danger of producing negative probabilities. We have become quite used to the rules of thought and limitations of an experiment, which ensures that they never arise in quantum mechanics.

It is not our intention to claim that quantum mechanics is best understood by going back to classical mechanical concepts and allowing negative probabilities (for the equations for the development of F in time are more complicated and inconvenient than those of ψ). (The classical equations for F for a particle moving in a potential are:

$$\partial F(x,p,t)/\partial t = -p/m \cdot \partial F/\partial x + V'(x)\partial F/\partial p$$

while the quantum equations are:

$$\partial F(x,t)/\partial t = -p/m \cdot \partial F/\partial x + \int G(x,Q)F(x,p + Q)dQ$$

so instead of the momentum changing infinitesimally during an infinitesimal time, Δt, it may jump by an amount Q with probability when it is at x:

$$\Delta t G(x,Q) = \Delta t \cdot 2 \text{ Im} \int e^{iQ \cdot Y}V(x + Y/2)dY$$

which is a real, but possibly negative probability.) Rather we should like to emphasize the idea that negative probabilities in a physical theory does not exclude that theory, providing special conditions are put on what is known or verified. But how are we to find and state these special conditions if we have a new theory of this kind? It is that a situation for which a negative probability is calculated is impossible, not in the sense that the chance for it happening is zero, but rather in the sense that the assumed conditions of preparation or verification are experimentally unattainable.

We may give one more example. In the quantum theory of electrodynamics, the free photon moving in the z direction is supposed to have only two directions of polarization transverse to its motion x,y. When this field is quantized, an additional interaction, the instantaneous Coulomb interaction, must be added to the virtual transverse photon exchange to produce the usual simple:

$$(j_x j_x' + j_y j_y' + j_z j_z' - j_t j_t')e^2/q^2 \tag{12}$$

virtual interaction between two currents, j and j'. It is obviously relativistically invariant with the usual symmetry of the space j_x, j_y, j_z and time j_t components of the current (in units where the velocity of light is $c = 1$). The original starting Hamiltonian with only transverse components does not look invariant. Innumerable papers have discussed this point from various points of view but perhaps the simplest is this. Let the photon have *four* directions of polarization of a vector x,y,z,t, no matter which way it is going. Couple the time component with ie instead of e so that the virtual contribution for it will be negative, as required by relativity in equation [12]. For real photons, then, the probability of a t-photon emission is negative, proportional to $-|\langle f|j_t|i\rangle|^2$ the square of the matrix element of j_t between initial and final states, just as the probability to emit an x photon is $+|\langle f|j_x|i\rangle|^2$. The total probability of emitting any sort of photon is the algebraic sum of the probabilities for the four possibilities:

$$|\langle f|j_x|i\rangle|^2 + |\langle f|j_y|i\rangle|^2 + |\langle f|j_z|i\rangle|^2 - |\langle f|j_t|i\rangle|^2 \tag{13}$$

It is always positive, for by the conservation of current there is a relation of j_t and the space components of $\mathbf{j}$, $k_\mu j_\mu = 0$ if k_μ is the four-vector of the photon. For example, if k is in the z direction, $k_z = \omega$, and $k_x = k_y = 0$ so $j_t = j_z$ and we see equation [13] is equal to the usual result where we add only the transverse emissions. The probability to emit a photon of definite polarization e_μ is (assume e_μ is not a null vector):

$$-|\langle f|j_\mu e_\mu|i\rangle|^2/(e_\mu e_\mu)$$

This has the danger of producing negative probabilities. The rule to avoid them is that only photons whose polarization vector satisfies

$k_\mu e_\mu = 0$ and $e_\mu e_\mu = -1$ can be observed asymptotically in the final or initial states. But this restriction is not to be applied to virtual photons, intermediary negative probabilities are not to be avoided. Only in this way is the Coulomb interaction truly understandable as the interchange of virtual photons, photons with time-like polarization which are radiated as real photons with a negative probability.

This example illustrates a small point. If one t photon is emitted with a negative probability $-\alpha(\alpha > 0)$, and another t photon is emitted say independently with probability $-\beta(\beta > 0)$, the chance of emitting both is positive $(-\alpha)(-\beta) = \alpha\beta > 0$. Should we not expect then to see physical emission of two such photons? Yes, but (if these photons are moving in the z direction) there is a probability to emit z photons α and β also, and there are four emission states: two t photons with probability $+\alpha\beta$; two z photons with probability $+\alpha\beta$; the first z and second t probability $(+\alpha)(-\beta) = -\alpha\beta$ and the first t second z with probabilities $-\alpha\beta$ so again, for total emission rate only the transverse photons contribute.

Although it is true that a negative probability for some situations in a theory means that that situation is unattainable or unverifiable, the contrary is not true; namely, a positive probability for a situation does not mean that that situation is directly verifiable. We have no technique for detecting t photons which is not similarly sensitive to z photons, so that we can only always respond to a combination of them. Likewise, no direct test can be made that the two t photons are indeed present without including the additional probabilities of having z photons. The fact for example, that $F(x,p)$ is everywhere positive:

$$\left(\exp\left(-\frac{p^2/m + m\omega^2 x}{2\hbar\omega} \right) \right)$$

for the ground state of an oscillator does not mean that for that state we can indeed measure both x and p simultaneously.

As another example we will give an analogue of the Wigner function for a spin half system, or other two-state system. Just as the Wigner function is a function of x and p, twice as many variables as in the wave function, here we will give a 'probability' for two conditions at once. We choose spin along the z-axis and spin along the x-axis. Thus let f_{++} represent the 'probability' that our system has spin up along the z-axis and up along the x-axis simultaneously. We shall define the quantity f_{++} for a pure state to be the expectation of $\frac{1}{4}(1 + \sigma_z + \sigma_x + \sigma_y)$, where σ_x, σ_y, and σ_z are the Pauli matrices. For a mixed state we take an average over the pure state values. Likewise f_{+-} is the expectation of $\frac{1}{4}(1 + \sigma_z - \sigma_x - \sigma_y)$, f_{-+} is the expectation of $\frac{1}{4}(1 - \sigma_z + \sigma_x - \sigma_y)$ and f_{--} is the expectation of $\frac{1}{4}(1 - \sigma_z - \sigma_x + \sigma_y)$.

Understanding that this 'probability' can be negative, we shall train ourselves to deal with it otherwise as a real probability and thus dispense with the warning quotes hereafter. Analogously f_{+-} is the probability that the spin is up along the z-axis and down along the x-axis (that is pointing in the negative x direction). Likewise f_{-+} and f_{--} give the probability that the spin is along the negative z-axis and along the x-axis in the positive or negative sense, respectively. These are all the possible conditions so we have $f_{++} + f_{+-} + f_{-+} + f_{--} = 1$. As an example, we might have $f_{++} = 0.6, f_{+-} = -0.1, f_{-+} = 0.3$ and $f_{--} = 0.2$.

Now the probability that the spin is up along z is simply the sum of the probability that it is up along z and up along x, and the other possibility, that it is up along z but down along x; that is simply $f_{++} + f_{+-}$ or $0.6 + (-0.1) = 0.5$ in our example. The probability the spin is down along z is $f_{-+} + f_{--}$, also 0.5. In the same way the probability that the spin is along the positive x-axis, independent of its value along z is $f_{++} + f_{-+}$ or 0.9. We, of course, cannot measure simultaneously the spin in the z and in the x direction, so we cannot directly determine f_{+-} and there is no difficulty with its negative value.

These four numbers give a complete expression of the state of the system, and the probability for any other question you can ask experimentally is some linear combination of them. For example, the probability that a measurement of spin along the y-axis gives 'up' is $f_{++} + f_{--}$ or 0.8, and that it gives 'down' is $f_{+-} + f_{-+}$ or 0.2. In fact, for a two-state system any question is equivalent to the question 'Is the spin up along an axis in some direction?' If that direction is defined by the unit vector V with components V_x, V_y, V_z then we can say the probability that the spin is up along this direction if the condition of the electron is $++$ is $p_{++}(V) = \frac{1}{2}(1 + V_z + V_x + V_y)$. For the other conditions we have $p_{+-}(V) = \frac{1}{2}(1 + V_z - V_x - V_y)$, $p_{-+}(V) = \frac{1}{2}(1 - V_z + V_x - V_y)$, and $p_{--}(V) = \frac{1}{2}(1 - V_z - V_x + V_y)$. In the general case then where the fs give the *a priori* probabilities of each condition the probability of finding the spin up along V is the sum on a of $p_a(V)f_a$ or $\frac{1}{2}((1 + V_z + V_x + V_y)f_{++} + (1 + V_z - V_x - V_y)f_{+-} + (1 - V_z + V_x - V_y)f_{-+} + (1 - V_z - V_x + V_y)f_{--})$. In order that this always gives positive results, in addition to the condition that the sum of the fs is unity, there is the restriction that the sum of the squares of the four fs be less than $\frac{1}{2}$. It equals $\frac{1}{2}$ for a pure state.

If there are two electrons in a problem we can use classical logic, considering each of them as being in one of the four states, $++$, $+-$, $-+$, $--$. Thus suppose we have two electrons, correlated so their total spin is zero, moving into two detectors, one set to determine if the spin of the first electron is in the direction V and the other set to measure whether the second electron has its spin in the direction U. The probability that both detectors respond is $\frac{1}{4}(1 - U.V)$. Thus if one is found up along any axis, the other is surely down along the same axis. This situation usually causes difficulty to a hidden variable view of nature. Suppose the electron can be in one of a number of conditions a, for each of which the chance of being found to be spinning up along the V-axis is $p_a(V)$. If the second electron is in condition b, its probability of being found along U is $p_b(U)$. Suppose now that the chance of finding the two electrons in conditions a,b, respectively, is P_{ab}. This depends on how the electrons were prepared by the source. Then the chance of finding them along the V and U axes is $\sum_{a,b} P_{ab} p_a(V) p_b(U)$ which is equal to $\frac{1}{4}(1 - U.V)$. This is well known to be impossible if all the 'probabilities' P_{ab} and p are positive. But everything works fine if we permit negative probabilities and use for a our four states with the $p_a(V)$ as defined previously. The probabilities for the correlated states in the case that the total spin is zero are P_{ab} equal $\frac{1}{8}$ if a and b are different states, and $-\frac{1}{8}$ if they are the same.

For another example of a two-state system, consider an electron going through a screen with two small holes to arrive at a second screen (see Figure 13.1). We can say there are four ways or conditions by which the electron can go through the holes, corresponding to the $++$, $+-$, $-+$, and $--$ conditions. If we take up spin to correspond to going through hole number 1 and down spin to represent going through hole 2, then the other variable corresponding to spin in the x direction means going through the two holes equally in phase. Ordinarily we cannot say which hole it goes through and what the phase relation is (just as ordinarily we do not say which way the z-spin is and which way the x-spin is) but now we can and do. For example, f_{--} gives the probability of going through hole 2 but 180 degrees out of phase (whatever that could mean). For each of these conditions we can calculate what the chance is that the electron arrives at a point x along the screen. For example, $P_{++}(x)$, the probability for arrival at x for the condition $++$ (through 1 in phase) and $P_{+-}(x)$, the probability for $+-$ (through 1 but out of phase) are sketched roughly in Figure 13.1 as the curves (*b*) and (*c*) respectively. The independent probabilities are negative for some values of x. The functions through hole 2 are these reflected in x; $P_{-+}(x) = P_{++}(-x)$ and $P_{--}(x) = P_{+-}(-x)$. The total chance to go through hole 1, $P_{++} + P_{+-}$, the sum of the two irregular curves shown in the figure, is just the smooth bump, the solid line at (*a*), with its maximum under hole 1, not showing interference effects. But the total probability to arrive with holes out of phase, $P_{+-} + P_{--}$, shows the typical interference pattern at the bottom of the figure at (*d*).

Obviously the particular choice we used for the two-state system is arbitrary, and other choices may have some advantages. One way that generalizes to any number of holes or of states, finite or otherwise, is this. Suppose an event can happen in more than one way, say ways A, B, C, etc., with amplitudes a, b, c, respectively, so that the probability

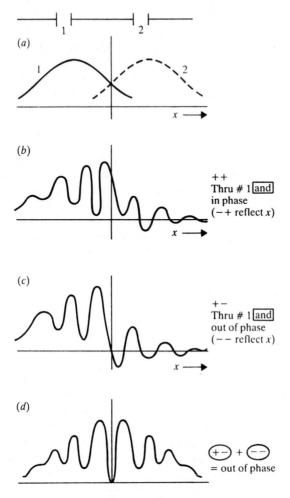

Figure 13.1 A two-state system in which an electron goes through a screen with two small holes to arrive at a second screen. (a) The total chance to go through hole 1. (b) The probability of going through hole 1 in phase. (c) The probability of going through hole 1 but out of phase. (d) The total probability to arrive with holes out of phase.

of occurring is the absolute square of $a + b + c + \ldots$ This can be described by saying the event can happen in two ways at once. For example we can say that the event happens by 'coming' in way A and 'going' in way B (or, if you prefer, by 'looping' via A and B) with a 'probability' $P(A,B) = \frac{1}{2}(1 + i)a^*b + \frac{1}{2}(1 - i)b^*a$, where a^* stands for the complex conjugate of a. The probability of 'coming' and 'going' by the same way A is $P(A,A) = a^*a$ and is the conventional positive probability that the event would occur if way A only were available to it. The total probability is the sum of these P for every pair of ways. If the two ways in P, 'coming' and 'going' are not the same, P is as likely to be negative as positive.

The density matrix, ρ_{ij}, if the states are i is then represented instead by saying a system has a probability to be found in each of a set of conditions. These conditions are defined by an ordered pair of states 'coming' in i and 'going' in j, with 'probability' $p(i,j)$ equal to the real part of $(1 + i)\rho_{ij}$. The condition that all physical probabilities remain positive is that the square of $p(i,j)$ not exceed the product $p(i,i)p(j,j)$ (equality is reached for pure states).

Finally, suppose that, because of the passage of time, or other interaction, or simply a change in basis, the state i has an amplitude S_{mi} of appearing as state m, where S is a unitary matrix (so the new density matrix ρ' is given by $S^{-1}\rho S$). We then discover we can find the new probabilities $p'(m,n)$ by summing all alternatives i,j of $p(i,j)$ times a factor that can be interpreted as the probability that the state 'coming' in i, 'going' in j turns into the state 'coming' in m, 'going' in n. This 'probability' is:

$$\tfrac{1}{2}(S_{im}^{*}S_{jn} + S_{jn}^{*}S_{im}) + \tfrac{i}{2}(S_{jm}^{*}S_{in} - S_{in}^{*}S_{jm})$$

With such formulas all the results of quantum statistics can be described in classical probability language, with states replaced by 'conditions' defined by a pair of states (or other variables), provided we accept negative values for these probabilities. This is interesting, but whether it is useful is problematical, for the equations with amplitudes are simpler and one can get used to thinking with them just as well.

My interest in this subject arose from many attempts to quantize electrodynamics or other field theories with cut-offs or using advanced potentials, in which work apparently negative probabilities often arose. It may have applications to help in the study of the consequences of a theory of this kind by Lee and Wick.

14

Gentle quantum events as the source of explicate order

G. F. Chew   *University of California, Berkeley*

Bohm[1] has introduced a notion of 'implicate order' to complement the classical Newtonian-Cartesian real-world view of separable objects moving through a space-time continuum. In the present note this classical view will be characterized as 'explicate order.' Quantum-mechanical and relativistic considerations preclude a satisfactory overall world picture based on explicate order; at the same time explicate order is for many purposes accurate and useful – being the underpinning of hard science. What is the source of such accuracy? We propose in this note that explicate order together with space-time is an approximation emerging from complex but coherent collections of 'gentle' quantum events – the emission and absorption of soft photons.

It is well known that order can emerge from complexity; the laws of thermodynamics and hydrodynamics constitute examples. We suggest that space-time and the attendant explicate order emerge from soft-photon complexity in a sense analogous to the emergence of temperature, pressure, heat content, etc., from the complexity of atomic collisions. The complexity responsible for objective reality within an apparently-continuous space-time we propose to associate with multitudes of coherent low-energy electromagnetic quanta. Immensely-large numbers, stemming from the combinatorics of soft-photon event patterns, are conjectured to be responsible for the notion of separately-moving objects. We shall identify special properties that endow the photon with unique capacity to generate explicate order.

Underlying our thinking is the Heisenberg matrix representation of quantum mechanics – which associates a complex number S_{ab} with a discrete event $b \rightarrow a$.[2] The event might be a particle decay such as that of Figure 14.1, or it might be a collision between particles, such as that of Figure 14.2. The probability that the event shall occur is given by the absolute-value squared of the complex number S_{ab}:

$$P_{ab} = |S_{ab}|^2 \qquad\qquad [1]$$

One does not speak, in the matrix picture, of space or time but only of a sudden event. There is a 'before' and an 'after' but no continuous evolution therebetween. We start with the premise that our 'world' is built from such discrete quantum events. We conjecture that our sense of continuous space-time is to be understood through collections of certain special 'gentle' events in which an initial electrically-charged particle emits or absorbs a photon and a final charged particle appears with attributes almost the same as those of the initial particle. Figure 14.3 gives an example. The events of Figures 14.1 and 14.2 are, by contrast, 'violent.' The situation after the event is totally different from that before.

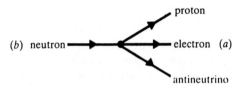

Figure 14.1   Particle decay as a discrete event.

Figure 14.2   Collision between particles as a discrete event.

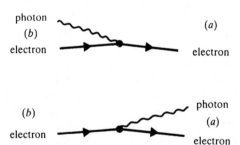

Figure 14.3   An example of a 'gentle' event.

Violent events provide no basis for the approximate continuity essential to explicate order. What endows the photon with its unique capability for gentle (almost continuous) events? The zero photon rest mass is one essential. A photon may carry an arbitrarily small amount of energy and momentum and thereby, in its absorption or emission, disturb the charged particle to an arbitrarily slight extent. Particles with non-zero rest mass lack this capability; a minimum 'kick' accompanies their emission or absorption. A second essential photon characteristic is its failure to carry any non-zero conserved quantum numbers; photon emission or absorption by a charged particle leaves the type of charged particle unchanged (e.g. electrons are not changed into protons). A third necessary characteristic involves spin; the photon is able to avoid disturbing the spin of the charged particle with which it interacts. A 'gentle event' – synonymous with 'soft-photon' emission or absorption – leaves a charged particle unaffected except for an arbitrarily tiny momentum impulse.

The classical notion of electric field corresponds to a coherent superposition of large numbers of soft photons. The language of explicate order describes a charged particle moving through an electric field as subject to a *force* which continuously changes the particle's momentum. From the quantum point of view, however, momentum impulses are discrete – associated with individual photons. The illusion of continuity stems from the very large number of gentle quantum events. What I am proposing in this note is that *another* consequence of a multitude of gentle events is the classical notion that the charged particle follows a *trajectory in space-time*.

There is no *a priori* continuous space-time in the matrix representation of quantum mechanics, but Feynman discovered that the *superposition* aspect of quantum mechanics allows the complex number S_{ab}, associated with a discrete event, to be evaluated through an infinite summation over terms, each of which associates with a graph:[3]

$$S_{ab} = \sum_G S_{ab}^G \qquad [2]$$

In this Feynman series, the symbol G stands for 'graph.' Each graph corresponds to a pattern of 'intermediate events' that might intervene between a (after) and b (before). The violent event of Figure 14.2, for example, admits the intermediate event patterns of Figure 14.4, where the wiggly lines denote soft photons. Indefinitely-large numbers of intermediate soft-photons can be emitted and reabsorbed by the charged-particle lines of a Feynman graph. Feynman's rules for the complex numbers S_{ab}^G belonging to a graph G are such that large collections of *violent* intermediate events associate with such small complex numbers S_{ab}^G as to be relatively unimportant; a multitude of *gentle* intermediate events dominates the Feynman graphical-series.[2] The problem of summing the gentle-event series has taxed the ingenuity of two generations of particle theorists.

Although Feynman-Heisenberg rules make no reference to space-

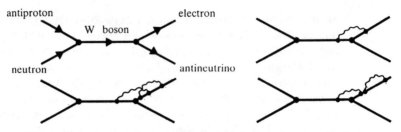

Figure 14.4   Intermediate events: the wiggly lines denote soft photons.

time, they do attribute energy and momentum to particles. Through Fourier transformation, energy-momentum variables can be replaced by *formal* space-time variables, but there is no *a priori* physical significance for these latter. It was recently discovered by Stapp[4], however, that summing the intermediate gentle-event Feynman series leads to a result interpretable through a notion of *approximate space-time localization*. Stapp shows that the coherent superposition of a multitude of soft intermediate photons can approximately place charged particles on trajectories and also approximately localize their violent events. (Stapp also makes a precise distinction between soft photons and 'hard' photons – that can change spin and deliver substantial increments of momentum in violent events.) Fourier transformation becomes physically relevant.

I propose that the space-time of explicate order arises from Stapp's mechanism. One should not accept a physical space-time continuum as an *a priori* notion but rather as an approximation emerging from large numbers of coherent but discrete gentle quantum events. My expectation is that such an understanding of space-time will allow the Copenhagen interpretation of quantum mechanics to be replaced by a quantum theory of measurement. The approximate isolation of observer from 'observed entity' will be related to the gentleness of intervening soft-photon connections. Electric 'screening' will be important – related to the photon's coupling to a conserved charge and to the tendency of complex particle systems to be electrically neutral. One will not describe measurement as occurring 'within space-time' but rather as generating an approximate meaning for space-time.

I close this note with some remarks about 'implicate order' and 'hidden variables' – terms which Bohm has invoked.[1] The foregoing speculations about explicate order have arisen in connection with an attempt to understand particle properties through the consistency of their graphically-expressed relationships.[5] Analysis of consistency depends on classifying Feynman graphs according to complexity. Photons and electrons do not occur at the lowest level of complexity, even though these particles dominate development of explicate order. At the lowest level of graphical complexity there occur 'hidden variables' (in the literature of graphical-particle theory the adjective 'inaccessible' rather than 'hidden' has been used) which have disappeared at the photon-electron level but which are responsible for the existence and properties of *elementary nuclear particles* which precede photons and electrons in the hierarchy of complexity.[6] (Graphical-particle theory[5] makes a distinction between 'elementary particles' and particles accessible to hard-scientific observations interpreted through explicate order, but explanation of this distinction will not be attempted here. Suffice it to say that there is a connection with 'hidden' variables.) An example of a 'hidden' variable is a feature of graphical order called 'color.' The property of 'color' is not exhibited by any particles accessible to the hard-scientific measurements based on explicate order, but a full picture of graphical order demands recognition of 'color' and other 'hidden' variables. At the level where such variables function there has not yet developed the degree of complexity prerequisite to the space-time on which explicate order relies. Theorists who use graphical complexity to understand particles do not employ the term 'implicate order,' but where 'color' and other 'hidden' variables occur such a term may be appropriate.

It should be apparent from the foregoing that the author envisages areas of contact between graphical particle theory and the ideas of Bohm.[1] The advantage of graphs is their providing an unambiguous and unprejudiced language – free from the semantic traps of ordinary language that stem from explicate-order roots. I anticipate graph language gradually to yield detailed understanding of how the continuity of explicate order, with the attendant space-time, relates to the discrete world of quantum events. It is furthermore not ruled out, in the author's opinion, that graphs with gentle links will illuminate the meaning of life and consciousness and also cosmology – including gravitation. Supplemented by Feynman superposition and by distinction between violent and gentle vertices, graph language has immense untapped capacity.

Acknowledgments

I am grateful to Ralph Pred for a critical reading of this manuscript.

This work was supported by the Director, Office of Energy Research, Office of High Energy and Nuclear Physics, Division of High Energy Physics of the US Department of Energy under contract DE-AC03-76SF00098.

Note added in proof:

Since this article was written, the author has come to believe that the gentle events building space-time involve quanta other than soft photons, even though soft photons are essential to measurement and objective reality. A paper now being written with H. P. Stapp describes space-building quanta which we call 'vacuons'.

References

1   D. Bohm, *Wholeness and the Implicate Order*, Routledge & Kegan Paul, London, 1980.
2   D. Iagolnitzer, *The S Matrix*, North Holland, Amsterdam, 1978.
3   See, for example, J. D. Bjorken and S. D. Drell, *Relativistic Quantum Fields*, McGraw-Hill, New York, 1965.
4   H. P. Stapp, *Phys. Rev. Lett.*, **50**, 467 (1983); preprint LBL-13651, Berkeley (1982).
5   Two recent reviews of topological particle theory have been written by F. Capra, preprint LBL-14858, Berkeley (1982) and by G. F. Chew, *Foundations of Physics*, **13**, 217 (1983).
6   G. F. Chew, *Phys. Rev.*, **D27**, 976 (1983); *Foundations of Physics*, **13**, 217 (1983).

15

Light as foundation of being

Henry P. Stapp   *University of California, Berkeley*

According to Niels Bohr quantum theory must be interpreted, not as a description of nature itself, but merely as a tool for making predictions about observations appearing under conditions described by classical physics:

> Strictly speaking, the mathematical formalism of quantum theory ... merely offers rules of calculation for the deduction of expectations about observations obtained under well-defined conditions specified by classical physical concepts.[1]

> There can be no question of any unambiguous interpretation of the symbols of quantum mechanics other than that embodied by the well-known rules which allow to predict the results to be obtained by a given experimental arrangement described in a totally classical way.[2]

> This necessity of discriminating in each experimental arrangement between those parts of the physical system considered which are treated as measuring instruments and those which constitute the object under investigation may indeed be said to form *a principal distinction between classical and quantum description of physical phenomena.*[2]

> Indispensable use of classical concepts ... even though classical physical theories do not suffice.[2]

This indispensable use of the invalidated classical concepts is a troublesome point. So is the intrusion into the theory of the scientist himself; the scientist must make a somewhat arbitrary division of a single unified physical system into two separate parts, and describe them according to mutually incompatible physical theories.

The aim of the present article is to show how recent technical developments in the quantum theory of light may allow quantum theory to be formulated as a unified theory of the physical world itself. The classical aspects of nature would then emerge automatically from the evolution of the fully quantum mechanical system, with no intrusion of observers or scientists. In this theory the electromagnetic field (i.e. light) plays a central role: it is the carrier of both classical properties and actual being itself.

The model presented here has elements of arbitrariness that render it unsatisfactory as a true model of the universe: it is a rudimentary form of such a model, not a finished product.

The technical development mentioned above arose in connection with the famous 'infrared catastrophe': the contributions of infinite numbers of very low-energy photons had led to apparent infinities in the calculation of many physical quantities. The essential feature of the resolution of this problem was discovered in 1937 by Bloch and Nordsieck: one must separate out the classical aspects of the problem. The original work[3] dealt only with simple cases, and involved approximations, but it was developed and extended in an immense collection of works by many authors. But there remained until recently the basic problem of understanding how the observed classical results emerged in all of the appropriate macroscopic limits.

This problem was resolved recently by recognizing that there was an exact separation between the classical and quantum parts of the electromagnetic current.[4] The coordinate-space Feynman path of each charged particle has one set of vertices for the 'quantum' interactions with light, and a different set of vertices for the 'classical' interaction. The radiation from each classical vertex depends only on its own location, and those of the two neighboring *classical* vertices; it is independent of what happens between these classical vertices. Furthermore, an arbitrary number of classical photons, all identical, can be emitted from each classical vertex. These classical photons, whose character depends only on the locations of the *classical* vertices can be summed. The sum is a unitary operator that creates precisely the unique coherent quantum state that corresponds to the light radiated by a classical charge moving on a space-time path defined by the sequence of classical vertices.

Before showing how this identification of the classical part of the electromagnetic field provides the basis for a unified self-governing quantum universe, with automatic emergence of classical reality, some peripheral questions will be addressed.

The first question is whether there is any need for unified formulation of quantum theory. Bohr gave convincing arguments that, in the realm of atomic physics, no theory could give predictions going beyond those attainable from his observer-based formulation of quantum theory. However, the experimental situation encountered in atomic physics is far from universal. It involves large preparing and detecting devices, which are considered to be parts of the full classically-described macroscopic environment, plus a tiny quantum system. This quantum system must be small enough so that during the interval between its preparation and detection its influence upon the macroscopic environment is negligible. For if the quantum system influences the macroscopic environment then phase information is transferred to this environment, and the Schrödinger equation fails. The macroscopic environment must then be described quantum mechanically, which contradicts the requirement that it be described classically. Consequently, as the quantum system is increased in size it must eventually reach the stage where neither the classical nor quantum description is adequate. To deal with such intermediate situations it would appear necessary to treat in a unified way the full physical system of macroscopic environment plus quantum object.

It has been claimed that most physicists accept Bohr's interpretation of quantum theory. Of course, any physicist who uses quantum theory in a practical way in atomic physics is probably interpreting quantum theory as a useful tool, in the way Bohr suggested. But at the level of basic principle the dissenters include most of the founders of quantum theory: Einstein, Schrödinger, de Broglie, Pauli, Heisenberg, Wigner, and von Neumann, to name a few. Gell-Mann said 'Niels Bohr brainwashed a whole generation of physicists into believing that the problem had been solved fifty years ago.'[5] Pauli[6] said: 'I think the important and extremely difficult task of our time is to try to build up a fresh idea of reality.'

I doubt if any physicist can be completely comfortable injecting human observers and invalid classical concepts into atomic theory, and giving up the ideal that basic physical theory should describe the world itself. The two overriding considerations are rather that Bohr's interpretation works fine in atomic physics, and that even Einstein himself, in spite of intensive effort, was unable to propose any alternative.

The present proposal is based on two results that did not exist in Einstein's day. The first is the above-mentioned development of our understanding of the classical part of the electromagnetic field, and the second is the refinement in our ideas of locality and causality that have grown out of Bell's theorem.[7]

The present proposal is in line with some ideas of David Bohm[8] and Werner Heisenberg[9] that will be described next.

Bohm-Heisenberg idea of events

The wave function of quantum theory has many similarities to the probability function of classical statistical mechanics. This latter function represents the probability for the various particles of the system to *be* in certain states at specified times. But if we were to place detectors in certain locations then it could also represent the probability for something to 'happen,' i.e. for the detectors to detect something.

The square of the absolute value of the wave function of quantum theory has an intuitive significance similar to this 'happening' or 'event' interpretation of the classical probability function, and Heisenberg was willing to say that the detection event actually occurs at the level of physical device.[9] Then the probability for 'finding' the particle can be interpreted as the probability for this physical detection event to occur, quite apart from any human participant or observer.

The difficulty with this idea is to know how to describe in a precise way what has 'happened.' If we consider the 'event' to be the observation by a human observer, then we know by education and training how to judge whether this observation conforms to certain specifications. And these specifications have, quite naturally, a certain impreciseness, which allows for the necessary quantum fluctuations. But if we are going to consider the event to be something in the external physical world itself, then we need some sort of mathematical description of what is happening. But what is the precise form of the description of device plus quantum object before and after the 'event'?

If one tries to use only the wave function and the Schrödinger equation of quantum mechanics then one finds that the 'event' never occurs. Rather, every possible event occurs: there is no singling out of the one event that actually occurs from the myriad of possible events that might occur.

The origin of this problem is precisely that the wave function has mathematical properties appropriate to a representation of probabilities, rather than actualities. For a system of n particles the wave, at fixed time, is a function in a space of $3n$ dimensions. But we live in a space of only three dimensions. Thus, the wave function, like a classical probability function, represents all things that possibly can happen; it does not single out the one thing that actually does happen.

To represent the actual thing one appears to have three options:

1   introduce object-like (or field-like) entities to represent the actual things;
2   introduce idea-like entities to fill up all the 'mindful' possibilities corresponding to the multi-branched wave function;
3   introduce action-type entities to 'collapse' (i.e. eliminate) the unrealized branches of the wave function.

The first alternative leads to the de Broglie-Bohm[8] pilot-wave idea, in which the part of the wave function representing all of the unrealized possibilities awkwardly continues to exist in an objective sense. The second leads to myriads of parallel worlds[10] that are all interpreted as objectively real, but which seem to be simply the consequence of insisting that the wave function represent objective reality itself rather than merely the probabilities for events. The third possibility is the one to be pursued here. It is in general accord with ideas of Bohr,[11] Heisenberg,[9] and von Neumann.[12] The problem with this idea has been the unavailability of any objective way to single out the various 'classically allowed possibilities.' Lacking any objective mechanism for making this selection, physicists have assigned this task to themselves.

Time and quantum process

The model to be proposed here is the embodiment of a *process* conception of nature. By *process* I mean nature conceived as a progressively growing set of things that are fixed and settled. This growing body of accumulating facts is considered to increase in discrete steps; at each step some unsettled things become fixed and settled.

Before Newton the history of the world could have been regarded as a growing body of facts, with the factual content of the region $t < T$ representing what is fixed and settled at time T, and the region $t > T$ representing the realm of the unfixed possibilities. However, Newton's laws altered this picture: they fixed the complete space-time story, once the initial conditions were fixed. Hence the idea of process was effectively banished.

This banishment of process made way for Einstein's theory of relativity. For if the entire space-time story is fixed, then choices of coordinates become purely matters of scientific convenience: there is no need for a scientist to worry about the questions of 'what exists now' or 'what has already taken place.' In a deterministic world the whole notion of 'becoming' becomes so nebulous and shadowy that it drops completely out of the physicist's stock of operative ideas.

The non-deterministic character of quantum theory reopens the whole question of the connection of space and time to the ontological categories of existence, being, becoming, etc. For if initially unsettled things can eventually become fixed and settled, then the order in which different things become fixed might have conceptual and dynamical significance. To expand the structural possibilities we go beyond the pragmatic confines of Bohr's interpretation: we distinguish human knowledge from general existence, and base physical theory on the latter.

As regards the relationship between order as defined by process (i.e. the order in which things become fixed and settled) and temporal order (as defined by space-time coordination) we are, *ab initio*, completely free. The theory of relativity says nothing at all about the order in which things become fixed and settled, because it was set in a framework in which no such order occurred.

As regards causal influences it now recognized[7] that quantum theory requires that what appears in one space-time region cannot in general be required to be independent of what is done (i.e. is chosen) in spatially separated regions. However, this necessity for 'non-local influences' need not provide any possibility for sending signals faster than light.

Coherent states and classical concepts

The model to be proposed here makes essential use of the coherent states of the quantized electromagnetic field. These states play a role in the model similar to those played by the 'observer' in Bohr's formulation of quantum theory.

These coherent states are, as is well known, the quantum-mechanical counterparts of the fields that occur in classical electromagnetic theory. I shall briefly review here this connection between coherent states and classical physics, and then describe some properties of coherent states that will be used in the model. Further details about coherent states, and their uses in quantum electrodynamics and quantum optics, can be found in articles by Kibble [13,14] and Glauber.[15]

The classical electromagnetic field in a cavity can be decomposed into eigenmodes i. Each such mode has an eigen frequency ω_i and a complex amplitude $a_i(t)$, which is related to the real canonical variables $q_i(t)$ and $p_i(t)$ by the equation:

$$a_i(t) = (m_i\omega_i q_i(t) + ip_i(t))/(2\hbar m_i\omega_i)^{\frac{1}{2}}$$

where m_i is a characteristic mass. Thus the real and imaginary parts of the complex amplitude $a_i(t)$ are associated with the canonical variables $q_i(t)$ and $p_i(t)$ respectively.

The possible free motions of the classical electromagnetic field in the cavity are represented by taking each variable $a_i(t)$ to be of the form:

$$a_i(t) = a_i \exp(-i\omega_i t)$$

Thus, the complex variable $a_i(t)$ moves with velocity $-\omega_i$ in a circle about the origin in the complex plane. The real and imaginary parts of $a_i(t)$ correspond to the magnetic and electric parts of the electromagnetic field, and the circular motion corresponds to the familiar oscillation of the energy of the radiation field between the electric and magnetic fields, both in the standing-wave modes, and in the circularly-polarized traveling-wave modes.

Upon quantization the complex amplitude $a_i(t)$ becomes an operator $\hat{a}_i(t)$. The operators $\hat{a}_i(t)$ obey the familiar commutation relations:

$$[\hat{a}_i(t), \hat{a}_j^\dagger(t)] = \delta_{ij}$$

Each mode i has a discrete set of eigenstates $|n_i>$, $n_i\in(0, 1 \ldots)$, where n_i is the number of photons in mode i. The eigenmodes of the full electromagnetic field itself are represented as products over the states $|n_i>$ of the individual oscillators.

One may, however, consider also the state $|a_i(t)>$ obtained by shifting the ground-state wave-function of oscillator *i* from its original position centered at the origin of phase-space to a new position centered at point $a_i(t)$. The equations of motion of the quantum system dictate that this state develop in time according to the classical equations of motion:

$$|a_i(t)> = |a_i \exp(-i\omega_i t)>$$

A coherent state $|A(t)>$ of the electromagnetic field is constructed as a product of these displaced ground states:

$$|A(t)> = |a_1(t) > |a_2(t)> \ldots$$

This state is defined by the set of amplitudes $\{a_i(t)\}$ for the various modes *i*, and hence by a positive-frequency solution $A^{(+)}(x)$ of the classical electromagnetic field equations. The coherent state $|A(t)>$ in the interaction representation can be labelled by:

$$A(x) = A^{(+)}(x) + (A^{(+)}(x))^* = 2 \operatorname{Re} A^{(+)}(x)$$

The expectation value in the state $|A(x)>$ of the quantum operator $\hat{A}(x')$ corresponding to the vector potential of electromagnetism is:

$$<A(x)|\hat{A}(x')|A(x)> = A(x')$$

More generally, if $\hat{A}^{(-)}(x')$ and $\hat{A}^{(+)}(x') = (\hat{A}^{(-)}(x'))^\dagger$ represent the creation and annihilation operator parts of the quantum operator $\hat{A}(x')$ then:

$$<A(x)|\hat{A}^{(-)}(x'_1) \ldots \hat{A}^{(-)}(x'_m)\hat{A}^{(+)}(x''_1) \ldots \hat{A}^{(+)}(x''_n)|A(x)> = A^{(-)}(x'_1)$$
$$\ldots A^{(-)}(x'_m)A^{(+)}(x''_1) \ldots A^{(+)}(x''_n)$$

Consequently, by virtue of the Dyson-Wick expansion, the *S* matrix in a coherent state is equal to the *S* matrix in the corresponding classical electromagnetic field:

$$<A(x)|B^{(+)}SC^{(-)}|A(x)> = <B^{(+)}S(A(x))C^{(-)} > 0$$

The right-hand side is a vacuum expectation value, the $C^{(-)}$ and $B^{(+)}$ are particle (i.e. non-photon) operators, and $S(A(x))$ is the *S* matrix in the presence of the classical electromagnetic field $A(x)$. This result consolidates the close connection between coherent states and classical fields.

A key formula for us will be the matrix element between two coherent states. For a single mode the formula is:

$$<a|b> = \exp[a^*b - (\tfrac{1}{2})a^*a - (\tfrac{1}{2})b^*b]$$
$$= \exp[-(\tfrac{1}{2})|a - b|^2 + i \operatorname{Im} a^*b]$$

where:

$$|a - b|^2 = (a^* - b^*)(a - b)$$
$$= (\operatorname{Re}(a - b))^2 + (\operatorname{Im}(a - b))^2$$

is the square of the distance between the two complex numbers, considered as points in a two-dimensional space.

This formula generalizes immediately to the coherent states:

$$<A|B> = \exp\left[-(\tfrac{1}{2})|A - B|^2 + i\Phi\right]$$

where:

$$|A - B|^2 = \sum_i (\mathrm{Re}(a_i - b_i))^2 + (\mathrm{Im}(a_i - b_i))^2$$

and

$$\Phi = \mathrm{Im}A^*B = \sum_i \mathrm{I_m}\, a_i^* b_i$$

Thus two coherent states $|A>$ and $|B>$ can be said to be separated from each other by a distance $|A - B|$, and a phase Φ, both of which vanish if $A = B$.

Observers and classical concepts

In the Bohr (Copenhagen) interpretation of quantum theory the observer plays a central role; he distinguishes between the classically distinct results of measurements. If before the measurement the state of atomic object plus measuring device is a pure quantum state ψ, then after the measurement the state must (if the environment is ignored) still be a pure state. If the experiment has, for example, two possible results then this pure state ψ' will have two 'classically distinguishable' components, which correspond to the two distinct possible results of the experiment. Thus the process of measurement produces a change.

$$\psi \longrightarrow \psi' = |\varphi_1> + |\varphi_2>$$

where $|\varphi_1>$ and $|\varphi_2>$ represent two (non-normalized) 'classically distinguishable' results.

The state ψ' can, however, be written in an infinite number of ways as a sum of two non-normalized vectors. So the problem is this: What distinguishes this particular separation from all of the other possibilities?

In the Copenhagen interpretation this separation is defined by means of 'conditions specified by classical concepts.' These conditions are reasonably well-defined in terms of what human observers can see and do, but they are not precisely defined in terms that are either completely compatible with quantum theory itself, or are objective in the sense that they do not refer in any way to human observers.

Once the decomposition of ψ' into its classically distinguishable components $|\varphi_1>$ and $|\varphi_2>$ has been specified, then the quantum rules say that observed state will be either $|\varphi_1>$ or $|\varphi_2>$ and that the probability that it will be $|\varphi_1>$ is $<\varphi_1|\varphi_1>$, whereas the probability that it will be $|\varphi_2>$ is $<\varphi_2|\varphi_2>$.

The idea of the present model is to replace the 'observer' by an objective mechanism based on coherent states. This mechanism produces 'events' with probabilities specified by the quantum formalism.

Mechanism of event generation

The mechanism of event generation is constructed as follows. Each event i corresponds to the specification of the Schrödinger state vector ψ_i on a spacelike surface σ_i. The region lying between σ_{i-1} and σ_i is a cell i that is bounded in both time and space. The spatial extent of cell i defines a cavity that specifies the modes that participate in the temporal development of the state from σ_{i-1} to σ_i.

The operator $U(\sigma_i, \sigma_{i-1})$ that takes the quantum system from σ_{i-1} to σ_i can be written [4]:

$$U(\sigma_i, \sigma_{i-1}) = \sum_P U(P)F(P)$$

Here P represents a multi-particle Feynman classical path, and $U(P)$ is a unitary operator that creates from the vacuum the coherent state corresponding to the classical electromagnetic field radiated by the charged particles moving along the multi-particle set of classical paths P.

The summation over all Feynman paths P tends to wash out these coherent states, but if there is a large-scale collective motion of matter then some of the coherent states having characteristic distances similar to those of the collective modes should remain prominent.

Suppose that in the unitary development generated in cell j the coherent states in the modes $i\in(1, 2 \dots n)$ remain prominent. Then the full Hilbert space can be separated into a product of two spaces, one, S_{j1} corresponding to the modes $i\in(1, 2 \dots n)$, and the other, S_{j2} corresponding to both the rest of the electromagnetic field plus the matter fields.

The coherent states are an overcomplete set of states: any state in the subspace S_{j1} can be expressed as a linear combination of coherent states in S_{j1}. Thus the state $\psi_i' = U(\sigma_i, \sigma_{i-1})\,\psi_{i-1}$ can be expressed as $\sum_k |A_\kappa> |\varphi_\kappa>$ with all $|A_\kappa>$ in S_{i1}. The corresponding density matrix is $\rho_i' = |\psi_i'> \cdot <\psi_i'|$ where the dot is placed between a ket and a bra to indicate no summation.

The mechanism of event generation is represented as follows. Let $|A>$ represent a coherent state in S_{i1} (a Schrödinger state on σ_i). Then define:

$$\rho_i(A) = |A> \cdot <A|\rho_i'|A> \cdot <A|$$

The ith event is then represented by the following transformation:

$$\rho_i' \rightarrow \rho_i = \rho_i(A)/\mathrm{Tr}\rho_i(A)$$

The probability density for this event is:

$$P(A) = \mathrm{Tr}\rho_i(A)$$

This probability density is defined relative to the measure that appears in coherent state theory:

$$\prod_{i=1}^{n} d(\mathrm{Re}\ a_i)d(\mathrm{Im}\ a_i)/\pi$$

Relative to this measure the coherent states satisfy a completeness property:

$$I = |a><a| = \sum_a |a> \cdot <a|$$

where the sum over a means an integral over $d(\mathrm{Re}\ a)\ d(\mathrm{Im}\ a)/\pi$. This completeness property entails that:

$$\sum_A P(A) = \sum_A \mathrm{Tr}\ |A> \cdot <A|\rho_i'|A> \cdot <A|$$

$$= \sum_A \mathrm{tr}\ <A|\rho_i'|A>$$

$$= \sum_A \mathrm{Tr}\ \rho_i'|A> \cdot <A|$$

$$= \mathrm{Tr}\ \rho_i' = 1$$

where Tr represents trace in the full space and tr represents trace in S_{i2}.

To see how this mechanism works in a traditional measurement situation consider the simple example:

$$\psi_i' = |A_1>|\varphi_1> + |A_2>|\varphi_2>$$

Here $|\varphi_1>$ and $|\varphi_2>$ correspond to the two possible results of the measurement discussed earlier, and $|A_1>$ and $|A_2>$ represent the coherent states generated by the interaction of these two states with the electromagnetic field.

The event-generation mechanism takes the normalized state ψ_i' to some normalized state $|A > |\varphi_A>$. The probability density $P(A)$ associated with $|A >|\varphi_A>$ is:

$$P(A) = \mathrm{Tr}[|A> \cdot <A|(|A_1>|\varphi_1> + |A_2>|\varphi_2>) \cdot (<\varphi_1|<A_1| + \\ <\varphi_2|<A_2|)|A> \cdot <A|]$$

$$= \mathrm{tr}<A|(|A_1>|\varphi_1> + |A_2>|\varphi_2>) \cdot (<\varphi_1|<A_1| + <\varphi_2|<A_2|)|A>$$

$$= <\varphi_1|\varphi_1> \exp - |A - A_1|^2$$

$$+ <\varphi_2|\varphi_2> \exp - |A - A_2|^2$$

$$+ <\varphi_1|\varphi_2> \exp [-\tfrac{1}{2}|A - A_1|^2 - \tfrac{1}{2}|A - A_2|^2 \\ + i\ \mathrm{Im}(A_1^*A + A^*A_2)]$$

$$+ <\varphi_2|\varphi_1> \exp [-\tfrac{1}{2}|A - A_1|^2 - \tfrac{1}{2}|A - A_2|^2 \\ + i\ \mathrm{Im}(A_2^*A + A^*A_1)]$$

If the two coherent states $|A_1>$ and $|A_2>$ are very different, so that

$|A_1 - A_2|$ is very large, then the exponential factors in $P(A)$, and the triangle inequality, ensure that A will, with very high probability, lie very close to either A_1 or A_2. Furthermore, the total probability that $|A > |\varphi_A>$ will be approximately $|A_1 > |\varphi_1>$ is $<\varphi_1|\varphi_1>$, and the total probability that $|A > |\varphi_A>$ will be approximately $|A_2 > |\varphi_2>$ is $<\varphi_2|\varphi_2>$. Thus in this case the event-generation mechanism gives results that conform to the Copenhagen interpretation rules.

Note, however, that the mechanism produces a classical state $|A > |\varphi_A>$ also in the cases where $|A_1>$ and $|A_2>$ and $|\varphi_1>$ and $|\varphi_2>$ are not very different. And it gives the probability density $P(A)$ also in these more complex situations where the Copenhagen rules would not apply.

More generally, suppose that:

$$\psi'_i = \sum_k |A_k> |\varphi_k>$$

and that the set of $|A_k>$ can be separated into N subsets such that all of the $|A_k>$ in each subset are far away from all of the $|A_k>$ in each of the other subsets. This separation of the $|A_k>$ induces a separation:

$$\psi'_i = \sum_{j=1}^N \psi''_j$$

The event mechanism will cause the state ψ'_i to jump into some state ψ_i that is 'close' to one of the state ψ''_j. And the total probability that the state ψ'_i will jump to a state close to ψ''_j is $<\psi''_j|\psi''_j>$. So the result is again compatible with the Copenhagen rules, but more general.

The essential point behind this mechanism is that, generally, linear combinations of coherent states are not coherent states. Consequently, for example, the second of the two following decompositions does not give states into which the quantum state ψ'_i can jump:

$$\psi'_i = |A_1 > |\varphi_1 > + |A_2 > |\varphi_2>$$
$$= \tfrac{1}{2}[(|A_1 > + |A_2 >)(|\varphi_1 > + |\varphi_2>) + (|A_1 > - |A_2>)(|\varphi_1 > - |\varphi_2 >)]$$

Thus the special role played by coherent states in the event-generation mechanism has the effect of specifying very special modes of decomposition of ψ'_i into its 'classically distinct' components.

To convert the properties described above into a complete theory one needs to specify the rules for determining (statistically at least) the placement of the surfaces σ_i. And one must specify the precise rule for identifying the subspace S_{i1} associated with σ_i. However, by introducing even arbitrary rules one generates at least a conceptual framework for replacing the human observers of the Copenhagen interpretation by an objective mechanism (based on light) that could give precision to the Bohm-Heisenberg idea of objective events as the foundation of classical reality.

In the specifications of the sequence of surfaces σ_i, and the subspaces

S_{j1}, it is important to recognize that the principles of the theory of relativity pertain to the general laws, and hence to descriptions of the *probabilities*, rather than the actualities: the actual situations do not possess the general symmetries. Thus one should not specify the sequence of surfaces σ_i independently of the developing actual situation; that would give preferences to certain space-time structures, independently of the actual. Rather, each σ_i should be specified by the prior actualities. Then there is no conflict with the general relativistic principle that different frames and coordinate systems are *intrinsically* equivalent.

This work was begun as a contribution to this volume honoring David Bohm. The deadline has now arrived and the task is unfinished. I hope, however, that even in its present rudimentary form the model described herein will serve to clarify and stimulate the thinking of readers of this volume about a subject that has filled a great part of the scientific life of David Bohm, and to which he has contributed immensely.

Acknowledgment

This work was supported by the Director, Office of Energy Research, Office of High Energy and Nuclear Physics, Division of High Energy Physics of the US Department of Energy under contract DE-ACO3-76SF00098.

References

1   Niels Bohr, *Essays 1958/1962 on Atomic Physics and Human Knowledge*, Wiley, New York, 1963.
2   Niels Bohr, *Phys. Rev.*, **48**, 696, p. 701 (1935).
3   F. Bloch and A. Nordsieck, *Phys. Rev.*, **52**, 54 (1937).
4   Henry P. Stapp., *Phys. Rev.*, **D26**, 1386 (1983).
5   M. Gell-Mann, in *'The Nature of the Physical Universe', the 1976 Nobel Conference*, Wiley, New York, 1979, p. 29.
6   W. Pauli, letter from Pauli to Fierz 12 Aug 1948, quoted by K. V. Laurikainen, *Wolfgang Pauli and Philosophy*, Theoretical Physics Preprint HU-TFT 83–6, University of Helsinki.
7   H. P. Stapp, *Amer. J. Phys*, **53**, 306 (1985).
8   David Bohm, *Phys. Rev.*, **85**, 166 (1952); L. de Broglie, *An Introduction to the Study of Wave Mechanics*, Dutton, New York, 1930; D. Bohm and B. Hiley, *Foundations of Physics*, **14**, 255 (1984).
9   W. Heisenberg, *Physics and Philosophy*, Harper & Row, New York, 1958, ch. III.
10   H. Everett III, *Rev. Mod. Phys.*, **29**, 454 (1957).
11   David Bohm, *Quantum Theory*, Prentice-Hall, 1951.
12   J. von Neumann, *Mathematical Foundations of Quantum Mechanics*, Princeton University Press, 1955.
13   T. W. B. Kibble, *J. Math Phys.*, **9**, 315 (1968).
14   T. W. B. Kibble, in S. M. Kay and A. Maitland (eds), *Quantum Optics*, Academic Press, London and New York, 1970.
15   R. J. Glauber, in S. M. Kay and A. Maitland (eds) *Quantum Optics*. Academic Press, London and New York, 1970.

16

The automorphism group of C_4

C. W. Kilmister   *Gresham College, London*

1   Introduction

One of the most pressing mathematical problems thrown up by the highly original work of David Bohm[1] is to construct numerous detailed examples that will help in the understanding of the important concepts of implicate and explicate order. Recently Bohm and Hiley[2] have themselves stressed the important role played by the Clifford algebras C_n here, since the automorphisms of the (even) Clifford algebras C_{2r} are all inner and 'any theory based on an algebra can always be put in an implicate order by an inner automorphism of the algebra'[3]. To make the notation precise, I am using C_n for the algebra generated by n anticommuting elements, which I usually denote by $E_i (i = 1 \ldots n)$, but in the case of quaternions, C_2, I use e_1, e_2, and set $e_3 = e_1 e_2$. Thus C_n has a basis of 2^n elements, including the unit, which I call 1. Unless explicitly stated otherwise, the algebra is over the field of reals, R.

The simplest example of this is C_2 which, since Hamilton's original paper[4], is known to fit three-dimensional space perfectly (as was intended) and in which the automorphism group $G_2 = \{T_q\}$:

$$T_q : v \rightarrow v' = qvq^{-1}$$

is exactly $O^+(3)$, the proper orthogonal group. This fact is easily proved since, on the one hand, for any vector (i.e. 3-vector) v, v^2 is minus the square of the magnitude of v, and is evidently invariant under G_2 and, on the other, G_2 is evidently a 3-parameter group and so is the whole of $O^+(3)$. But it is to some extent a surprise, and another way of looking at quaternions makes it more natural. This will be studied in the present section. In section 2 the next case, C_4, is introduced and the corresponding theorems are stated with explanations in section 3. Proofs follow in section 4 and a new geometrical picture is to be found in section 5. This second aspect of quaternions was found later by Hamilton[5] and is developed at some length in his *Lectures*[6] and in his *Elements*[7]; it is also very clearly stated by Tait[8].

The method is to look on a quaternion q as a quotient $q = vu^{-1}$ of two 3-vectors. In an obvious modification of Hamilton's original notation, I write:

$$q = q_0 + q_1 e_1 + q_2 e_2 + q_3 e_3$$

for any quaternion, with $q_0 = Sq$, $q - Sq = Vq$ and $\bar{q} = Sq - Vq$. Here $e_i e_j = -\delta_{ij} + \varepsilon_{ijk} e_k$. Two 3-vectors v, u involve 6 degrees of freedom, but since both can be multiplied by the same constant without affecting q, this number is reduced to five. Since a quaternion involves only four, there is some redundancy and this can be made explicit by asking when two quotients are equal:

$$q = vu^{-1} = v'u'^{-1}$$

Choose any u' and calculate the corresponding $v' = vu^{-1}u'$, which will usually be a quaternion, not a 3-vector. If it is to be a 3-vector, then $S.vu^{-1}u' = 0$, i.e. $S.vuu' = 0$ which implies that u' must be chosen coplanar with v, u. Any such choice gives a corresponding v'. Also, because:

$$q = \frac{|v|}{|u|}(\cos\theta + e\sin\theta)$$

where e is a unit vector and θ is the angle between u and v, any other pair u', v' contains the same angle θ. This therefore gives rise to Hamilton's representation of quaternions by arcs of great circles on the unit sphere. Since any two great circles intersect, the product of two quaternions $q = vu^{-1}$, $q_1 = v_1 u_1^{-1}$ can always be written as:

$$qq_1 = (vu^{-1})(uu_1^{-1}) = vu_1^{-1}$$

by choosing the factor v_1 of q_1 as u; hence Hamilton's representation of the product of quaternions in terms of the three sides of a spherical triangle. The connection with the orthogonal group is then hardly surprising.

2   E-numbers

As is well known, the odd algebras present certain peculiar features which can be avoided for most purposes by noting the isomorphism:

$$C_{2r+1}/R \simeq C_{2r}/C$$

Accordingly the next example to consider is C_4, the Dirac algebra or Eddington's E-numbers. To fix notation, I define the four generating elements to be normalised by:

$$E_a E_b + E_b E_a = 2\eta_{ab}$$

where η_{ab} is the usual diagonal Minkowski metric tensor and I adopt the $+ - - -$ sign convention. This normalisation is an appropriate one when E_1, E_2, E_3, E_4 are intended to correspond to four directions in space-time. (Notice, however, that this is a different use of the algebra from the quaternion example, since here the dimension of space-time is equal to the number of generators.) Again to fix notation, I write:

$$E_a E_b = \eta_{ab} + E_{ab}, \ E_{ab} = -E_{ba}$$

and $E_1 E_2 E_3 E_4 = E_5$, so that $E_5^2 = -1$. Also $E^a = \eta^{ab} E_b$, $E^{ab} = \eta^{ac} \eta^{bd} E_{cd}$ and so on, and:

$$E^5 = E^1 E^2 E^3 E^4 = -E_1 E_2 E_3 E_4 = -E_5$$

Then it is easy to see that:

$$E_a E_b E_c = \eta_{bc} E_a + E_a E_{bc}$$
$$= \eta_{bc} E_a + \eta_{ab} E_c - \eta_{ac} E_b + \varepsilon_{abcd} E^{d5}$$ where ε_{abcd} is the usual epsilon symbol. (Warning: ε^{abcd} is defined by raising suffixes in the usual definition, so that: $\varepsilon^{1234} = -\varepsilon_{1234} = -1$.)

The proper Lorentz group is now a subgroup of $G_4 = \{T_q\}$:

$$T_q: r \rightarrow r' = qrq^{-1}$$

where q, r are any two elements of C_4 (or E-numbers, for short). In fact, using the convenient notation:

$$r = r_0 + r^5 E_5 + r^a E_a + r^{a5} E_{a5} + \tfrac{1}{2} r^{ab} E_{ab}$$

If we interpret r^a as a standard space-time vector, then the proper Lorentz group is generated by the following six values of q:

$$q = \cos \theta + E_{ij} \sin \theta, \ i,j = 1,2,3$$
$$q = \cosh u + E_{i4} \sinh u$$

Under such transformations, r^{ab} is a bivector and r^5, r^{a5} are pseudo-scalar and pseudo-vector respectively, when improper transformations are permitted.

It is convenient to extend Hamilton's notation for quaternions in an obvious way, writing:

$$r_0 = Sr, \ r^a E_a = Vr, \ \tfrac{1}{2} r^{ab} E_{ab} = Br$$

when it also follows that:

$$r^{a5}E_a = V \cdot rE^5, \, r^5 = S \cdot rE^5$$

It is useful to have a brief 'symbolic multiplication table' for the parts S, PS, V, PV, B of an E-number (see Table 16.1).

Table 16.1   *Symbolic multiplication table*

	S	PS	V	PV	B
S	S				
PS	PS	S			
V	V	PV	$S + B$		
PV	PV	V	$PS + B$	$S + B$	
B	B	B	$V + PV$	$V + PV$	$S + PS + B$

3   Decomposition of *G*

From the analogy with quaternions two problems suggest themselves at once. A ratio of two vectors involves eight degrees of freedom, of which one is redundant, leaving seven – far too few for the sixteen of a general E-number, but we are concerned particularly with the Lorentz group. This is a six-parameter group, but a q representing a transformation of the group may be multiplied by a constant, making seven degrees of freedom. But counting degrees of freedom is only an indication and in fact the situation is a little more complicated, as we shall see. The other associated problem is to determine which qs correspond to Lorentz transformations. Both of these problems are solved by the following seven theorems, whose proofs follow in section 4.

Consider first E-numbers of the simple form:

$$q = s + tE_5 + \tfrac{1}{2}w^{ab}E_{ab}$$

which evidently form a sub-algebra of dimension 8. I shall call such a one 'of bivector type'. If we define:

$$\bar{q} = s + tE_5 - \tfrac{1}{2}w^{ab}E_{ab}$$

it follows at once that:

$$q\bar{q} = s^2 - t^2 + I_1(w) + 2E_5(st - I_2(w)) = A(q) + E_5B(q)$$

say, where $I_1(w)$, $I_2(w)$ are the usual two invariants of the bivector w, defined by:

$$I_1(w) = \tfrac{1}{2}w^{ab}w_{ab}, \, I_2(w) = \tfrac{1}{2}\tilde{w}^{ab}w_{ab}$$

and $\tilde{w}_{ab}$ is the dual bivector, $\tilde{w}_{ab} = \tfrac{1}{2}\varepsilon_{abcd}w^{cd}$. If $A(q) = B(q) = 0$, I shall call q *singular*, otherwise non-singular. Since E_5 commutes with q, it follows that the reciprocal q^{-1} of any non-singular E-number of bivector type is given by:

$$q^{-1} = \frac{\bar{q}}{A + E_5 B} = \frac{\bar{q}(A - E_5 B)}{A^2 + B^2}$$

We can define $A(q)$, $B(q)$ for any E-number q as the corresponding A, B for the part of q of the form above. Then:

Theorem 1

If q is non-singular, it can be factorised uniquely in the form $q = q_V q_B$, where q_B is of bivector type, and q_V has the form:

$$q_V = 1 + u^a E_a + v^a E_{a5}$$

which I shall call 'of vector type'. (There are corresponding results for a factorisation as $q_B q_V$.)

Correspondingly, any automorphism can be factorised into one which transforms E_5 into other elements (q_V) and one which leaves E_5 invariant (q_B). In what follows I shall be mainly concerned with the group of transformations of the bivector type, which contains the Lorentz group. The physical interpretation of the vector type is not completely clear. But some idea of it can be obtained by looking at two special cases.

1. Let $q = 1 + u^a E_a$, so that the automorphism:

    $$r \to r' = qrq^{-1}$$

    leaves invariant the component of Vr parallel to u^a, and rotates the component perpendicular to u^a into the part of Br satisfying $\bar{r}^{ab} u_b = 0$. The rest of Br, satisfying $r^{ab} u_b = 0$, is left invariant, as are the components of the pseudo-vector perpendicular to u^a. Finally, the remaining component of the pseudo-vector is rotated into the pseudo-scalar, r^5.

2. Similarly, if $q = 1 + v^a E_{a5}$, the conclusions are similar, with u, v interchanged and $\bar{r}^{ab}$ written for r^{ab}.

3. Another special case forms a warning against too glib an acceptance of non-singular qs as all that concern us. The E-number $q = \cos \theta + E_1 \sin \theta$ is non-singular according to the definition, so long as $\theta \neq \pi/2$, and the decomposition is trivially:

    $$q_V = 1 + E_1 \tan \theta, q_B = \cos \theta$$

    The singular case then gives rise to the automorphism:

    $$r \to r' = -E_1 r E_1$$

    which leaves invariant the part of r commuting with

E_1 (i.e. r_0, r^1, r^{23}, r^{24}, r^{34}, r^{25}, r^{35}, r^{45}) and changes the sign of $(r^2, r^3, r^4, r^{31}, r^{12}, r^{14}, r^{15}, r^5)$. It is therefore a Lorentz transformation of determinant -1. In fact, combining it with the transformation:

$$r^a \rightarrow r'^a = -r^a$$

which is in L^+, gives a space-reversal in the x^1-direction. Similarly:

$$r \rightarrow r' = E_4 r E_4$$

is a straightforward time reversal. In other words, G_4 contains not only the proper Lorentz group L^+, but the whole group, although the improper transformations are exhibited in this analysis as singular cases.

The set of non-singular automorphisms of bivector type is a seven-parameter group G (since one can divide through by any one magnitude).

Theorem 2

G is a direct product $G = H \times L^+$, where H is the set of automorphisms produced by:

$$q = \cos \theta + E_5 \sin \theta$$

and L^+ is the proper Lorentz group.

The transformations of H may be called phase rotations. They are in fact two-dimensional rotations linked and of the form:

$$u^a \rightarrow u'^a = u^a \cos 2\theta + v^a \sin 2\theta$$
$$v^a \rightarrow v'^a = -u^a \sin 2\theta + v^a \cos 2\theta$$

It remains to determine the elements of L^+.

Theorem 3

A non-singular q of bivector type:

$$q = s + E_5 t + \tfrac{1}{2} w^{ab} E_{ab}$$

is a Lorentz transformation if and only if:

$$\tfrac{1}{2} B(q) = st - I_2(w) = 0$$

This completes the analysis of how L^+ is contained in G_4, and I turn to the question of representing elements of L^+ by ratios of E-numbers.

Theorem 4

If $q = uv^{-1}$, where $u = u^a E_a$, $v = v^a E_a$, then:

$$(v^a v_a)s = -u^a v_a, t = 0, w^{ab} = u^a b^b - u^b v^a$$

so that $I_2(w) = 0$ and so, by theorem 3, q is a Lorentz transformation. But the set of such qs has only five degrees of freedom, and does not, of course, form a subgroup of L^+. However there is a more useful geometrical picture, which is suggested by the following.

Theorem 5

Any q in G can be written as $q = uv^{-1}$, where u, v are bivectors, $u = \frac{1}{2} u^{ab} E_{ab}$, $v = \frac{1}{2} v^{ab} E_{ab}$.

This result is a very direct analogy with the corresponding quaternion result (with which, as we shall see in the next section, it is closely connected), but it does not help in the visualisation in space-time. It is more useful to consider a seven-dimensional space with homogeneous co-ordinates to represent the elements of G.

Theorem 5 immediately suggests the question of which pairs u, v give Lorentz transformations. The answer is provided by:

Theorem 6

uv^{-1} gives a transformation of L^+ if, and only if:

$$I_1(u) = m I_1(v), I_2(u) = m I_2(v)$$

i.e.:

$$I_1(u)I_2(v) - I_2(u)I_1(v) = 0$$

Of course, even with this condition, $6 + 6 - 1 - 1 = 10$, which is much greater than 7, a redundancy of 3 being indicated – in fact very much in line with the quaternion case.

Theorem 7

If $uv^{-1} = u'v'^{-1}$, then:

$$v'^{ab} = Pu^{ab} + Q\tilde{u}^{ab} + Rv^{ab} + S\tilde{v}^{ab}$$

with a corresponding result for u'^{ab}. There are four parameters rather than three because u, v may be multiplied by a common factor.

A similar result now holds for multiplication to the one in the quaternion case; that is, $(uv^{-1})(u'v'^{-1}) = (uv^{-1})(vv''^{-1})$.

4   Proofs of theorems

There are various ways of proving the results of the last section, but perhaps the shortest is to recognise them as fairly direct generalisations of quaternion results by means of the following (partial) isomorphism.

1   Since $E_{23} . E_{31} = E_{12}$ and the symbols anticommute and square to -1, we can take $(E_{23}, E_{31}, E_{12}) = (e_1, e_2, e_3)$ as a quaternion set.

2   Then $E_{14} = E_{1234}E_{23} = -E_5E_{23}$. Since E_5 commutes with e_1, e_2, e_3 it is convenient to write it as i and to set:

$$(E_{14}, E_{24}, E_{34}) = (-ie_1, -ie_2, -ie_3)$$

In this notation, the bivector part of an E-number:

$$q = s + tE_5 + \tfrac{1}{2}w^{ab}E_{ab}$$

becomes:

$$q = (s + it) + (w^{23} - iw^{14})e_1 + \ldots$$

which can be seen simply as a quaternion over the complex field C and $\bar{q}$ is then the usual conjugate quaternion. Also, as usual:

$$\begin{aligned}
q\bar{q} &= (s + it)^2 + \Sigma(w^{23} - iw^{14})^2 \\
&= s^2 - t^2 + \Sigma((w^{23})^2 - (w^{14})^2) + 2i(st - \Sigma w^{23}w^{14}) \\
&= (s^2 - t^2 + I_1(w)) + 2i(st - I_2(w))
\end{aligned}$$

To continue with this analysis:

3   Choose a generating element (the most convenient one is E_4) and set $E_4 = k$. Clearly k commutes with e_1, e_2, e_3 but not with i. Putting this in terms of the quaternion algebra over C, $qk = kq^*$, where q^* is the complex conjugate quaternion. Then the remaining elements are given by:

$$E_1, E_2, E_3 = -ike_1, -ike_2, -ike_3 = kie_1, \ldots$$
$$E_{45} = ki$$
$$E_{15}, E_{25}, E_{35} = -ke_1, -ke_2, -ke_3$$

Any E-number can therefore be written as:

$$q = a + kb$$

where a, b are complex quaternions, and a is the part of q of bivector form, whilst b is the part involving the vector and pseudo-vector. The proof of theorem 1 is then simply to notice that:

$$q = a + kb = (1 + kba^{-1})a$$

and theorems 2 and 3 re-state a well-known isomorphism between the proper Lorentz group and complex quaternions of unit norm. (Here, though, the identification is slightly different from the usual one. A standard space-time vector has the form

$$k(r_0 + ir_1e_1 + ir_2e_2 + ir_3e_3) = kr$$

where r is a physical quaternion, i.e. satisfies $r^+ = r$, where r^+ is the complex conjugate of the quaternion conjugate. Then the Lorentz transformation corresponds to:

$$kr' = q(kr)q^{-1} = kq*rq^{-1}$$

so that:

$$r' = srs^+$$

if $|s| = 1$.)

It is easier to prove theorem 4 directly, but in this notation it also follows easily since $q = (ku)(kv)^{-1}$ where u, v are physical, and so $q = -u*v^{-1}$. Since $\bar{q} = -\bar{v}^{-1}u^+$, $q\bar{q} = |v|^{-2} \cdot |u|^2$ and since u, v are physical, $|u|^2, |v|^2$ are real. On the other hand, theorem 5 is much easier in the quaternion notation, since it is indeed the direct extension of the result of section 1 to the complex case. Here u, v are general complex 3-vectors. The condition (theorem 6) for a Lorentz transformation is $|u|/|v| = m$, a real number, so that:

$$\frac{I_1(u) - 2iI_2(u)}{I_1(v) - 2iI_2(v)}$$

is real. Finally, in the same way as in the real case, theorem 7 is a restatement of:

$$v' = fv + gu$$

where f, g are complex numbers.

5   Another geometrical picture

These results are more transparent in a different geometrical interpretation, in the formation of which I have had considerable assistance from J. A. Tyrrell. The condition:

$$st - I_2(w) = 0$$

on an E-number of bivector type, for the automorphism which it generates to be a Lorentz transformation has a ready geometric interpretation in terms of the seven-dimensional projective space V_7 of co-ordinates:

$$(x_1,x_2,x_3,x_4,x_5,x_6,x_7) = (s,t,w^{23},w^{41},w^{31},w^{42},w^{12},w^{43})$$

For the condition is exactly that the point x lies on a certain quadric hypersurface, Ω, of rank 8 and signature zero:

$$x_0x_1 + x_2x_3 + x_4x_5 + x_6x_7 = 0$$

Now a quadric in three dimensions contains (two systems of) generating lines, real if the signature is zero. Consider then a quadric hypersurface in five dimensions. A tangent hyperplane cuts it in a three-dimensional cone, lying therefore in the surface. Such a cone is the join of a quadric surface to a point outside its 3-space. This quadric has generators and so the cone, and therefore the original quadric, contains the planes which arise from joining the vertex to them. Finally, then, the quadric Ω is cut by a tangent hyperplane in a five-dimensional cone; that is, the join of a four-dimensional quadric to a point not in its 5-space. This quadric contains planes and so the cone, and therefore Ω, contain solids; that is, three-dimensional linear spaces lying altogether in the surface.

The existence of these linear spaces is a new aspect of the Lorentz group. They are not, in general, subgroups, though in one or two well-known cases they happen to be so. For example, the group of spatial rotations, generated by $\cos \theta + E_{23} \sin \theta$, and similar terms in E_{31}, E_{12}, has the general member:

$$q = q_0 + q^{23}E_{23} + q^{31}E_{31} + q^{12}E_{12}$$

or, in terms of the representation, it is the solid:

$$x_1 = x_3 = x_5 = x_7 = 0$$

Similarly the group generated by, say, terms in E_{24}, E_{34}, E_{23}, which could occur in an investigation of the electron's Thomas precession, is the solid:

$$x_1 = x_3 = x_4 = x_6 = 0$$

In terms of this geometrical picture, consider now the expression of a Lorentz transformation q as a ratio, $q = uv^{-1}$. Here u, v are bivectors satisfying:

$$I_1(u)I_2(v) - I_2(u)I_1(v) = 0$$

As bivectors, u,v lie in the five-dimensional subspace, V_5, say,

$$x_0 = x_1 = 0$$

and so the ratio expression represents a (many:one) mapping of pairs of points, U,V in V_5 on to points $Q = Q(U,V)$ in V_7. In fact the redundancy discussed above means that a solid of possible Us, each with its appropriate V (and these Vs also forming a solid) give the same Q. For any U in V_5 the condition on u,v represents a quadric hypersurface Ω_U on which V must lie, in order that the resulting Q should lie on the quadric Ω. And every such Ω_U contains planes, as noted above ... and all of this comes out of David Bohm's astonishingly fertile idea.

References

1   D. Bohm, *Wholeness and the Implicate Order*, Routledge & Kegan Paul, London, 1980.
2   D. Bohm and B. J. Hiley, *Revista Brasileira de Fisica*, July, 1984.
3   D. Bohm, *Foundations of Physics*, **3**, 139 (1973).
4   W. R. Hamilton, *Proc. Roy. Irish Acad.*, **2**, 424–34 (1844).
5   W. R. Hamilton, *Proc. Roy. Irish Acad.*, **3**, Appendix, xxxi–xxxvi, 1847.
6   W. R. Hamilton, *Lectures on Quaternions*, Dublin, 1853 (see especially pp. 60–1 of the preface).
7   W. R. Hamilton, *Elements of Quaternions*, Longmans, London, 1866 (Book II, Chap. I, especially sections 3–6).
8   P. G. Tait, *Quaternions* (second ed.), Oxford, 1873 (especially paras. 53–62).

17

Some spinor implications unfolded

F. A. M. Frescura and **B. J. Hiley**   *Birkbeck College, London*

1   Introduction

One of the more puzzling features of contemporary relativistic quantum mechanics is the enforced retreat into the concepts of 'external' and 'internal' spaces that are locally independent. Here the elementary particles are not thought of as extended structures in space-time but are regarded primarily as point objects with 'internal' variables such as spin, isospin, hypercharge, charm, etc., together with the usual 'external' space-time properties like momentum, mass, etc. This way of proceeding seems inescapable and is forced on us, not so much by physical considerations, but by technical difficulties arising from the mathematics itself. Nevertheless, this approach has received considerable impetus with the realisation that the mathematical theory of fibre bundles, a theory developed for very different reasons, provides a natural descriptive language for these ideas.

The question of spin is particularly puzzling since it arises most naturally in the Clifford algebra, a geometric algebra constructed from space-time itself. Yet spin is most easily handled through the spin bundle which, of course, treats spin as an internal variable, independent of the local space-time structure itself. Although we do not deny the fruitfulness of this approach, we feel that it is worth investigating another which arises essentially from an algebraic study of spin.

This alternative approach was stimulated by the general considerations from David Bohm's notion of the implicate order. Consequently the ideas presented will differ in many respects from those used in the fibre bundle theory even though there is a good deal of common ground. In fact, we shall be guided at least part of the way by results obtained in that theory. The fundamental difference arises because we do not give a basic role to field-in-interaction on a space-time manifold. Rather we start by taking the notion of process as fundamental; not a process in space-time, but a process from which we hope eventually to abstract basic relationships that will allow us to reconstruct our present notions of space-time. Thus, space-time can be regarded as an order of relationships. Such an idea is not new. It was proposed, *circa* seventeenth century, by Leibniz, who regarded space as the order of coexistence and time as the order of succession.

In relationship theory of space-time, the notion of locality should not be given *a priori*, but it too should emerge from a distinguished relationship. Bohm [1] has already indicated how this particular feature can be understood in analogy with the hologram, which stores non-locally in itself information defining local relationships. Of course, in this case, the notion of a local order is provided by the material object being hologrammed. In the more general situation that we are considering, however, there are no material objects and therefore no obvious notion of locality. The reason why there are no objects in the usual sense is because the fundamental order is not a regular arrangement of objects, but rather a process in which the objects appear as quasi-stable semi-autonomous structures. These are made manifest in the explicate order which, in some approximation, corresponds to the usual Euclidean or Reimanian geometry. It is therefore in the explicate order that locality emerges. Any appearance of non-locality would then arise from the fact that not *all* processes can be made 'local' together. The total order must therefore contain within itself the relationship of locality needed to explicate this geometric order. Such a relationship will require some special principle which is at present unknown. However, a similar problem arises in Chew's [2] *S*-matrix approach and, as he shows in this volume, it is the soft photons that provide the physical basis for such a relationship.

Our own approach does not use the *S*-matrix but instead is based on the relationship between algebras and the holomovement. This relationship has already been discussed in general terms by Bohm [1] and in more detail by Frescura and Hiley [3,4,5]. In the more detailed papers, we discuss at length how, when process is regarded as a fundamental notion, the dynamical variables must be given a primary role, while the concept of a state vector as a fundamental entity must be abandoned. This does not mean, however, that the state vector disappears entirely from our view. Rather, in all the physically relevant algebras the state vectors of the usual theory can be identified with certain special entities within the algebra itself; namely, the minimum left ideals. Thus the old state is now a special kind of process by which the system transforms into itself in such a way as to change none of its observed properties.

In this paper we shall do no more than simply to illustrate this idea in terms of the Dirac theory. Here the state vectors of the system are the four-component spinors ordinarily used in the description of spin one-half fermions and can be identified with the minimal left ideals of the Clifford-Dirac algebra, C_4. However, these ideals are richer structures and have properties that go beyond those of the ordinary spinor, a feature that is briefly touched upon in this paper. It is important to realise that these ideas can be extended not only to higher-dimensional Clifford algebras, but also to the case of bosons through what we call the symplectic algebras. While the Clifford algebras carry the rotational symmetries algebraically, the symplectic algebras carry the translation symmetries.

Our discussion in this paper necessarily touches only on a limited aspect of the general approach outlined above. Nevertheless, we can throw some light on the constraints that must be placed on the algebraic relations between neighbouring ideals in order to obtain a consistent algebraic approach when curvature is present. To do this, we assume an *a priori* given locality relation. But, of course, our purpose is to find an algebraic characterisation of this relation that will allow us ultimately to drop the space-time scaffold on which the structure was originally erected and replace it with a purely algebraic prescription for a neighbourhood relation.

2   The spinor structure of the algebra

By the spinor structure of the algebra we mean the reduction of the algebra into constituent spinor spaces. The Wederburn structure theorems guarantee that the algebras of interest to us are fully reducible into spinor structures. The reduction in fact can be carried out in two distinct ways, each of which is useful in its own right and each providing a different insight into the nature of the underlying processes which it describes.

Suppose P is an irreducible idempotent of the Dirac algebra. Then we can project out of the algebra two linear subspaces $P\mathscr{D}$ and $\mathscr{D}P$. If we identify the first as the spinor space, then the second can be identified as the space dual to $P\mathscr{D}$, since we can define:

$$:P\mathscr{D} \times \mathscr{D}P \to \subset \mathbb{C}$$

$$:(P\Lambda,KP) \mapsto z$$

where $\Lambda,K \in \mathscr{D}$ and $(P\Lambda)(KP) = zP$.

Our first decomposition of $\mathscr{D}$ into a composite of spinor substructures uses this fact in 'reverse'. The set:

$$(\mathscr{D}P)(P\mathscr{D}) = \mathscr{D}P\mathscr{D} \subset \mathscr{D}$$

is an ideal in $\mathscr{D}$. But $\mathscr{D}$ is simple and so contains only the ideals $\mathscr{D}$ and $\{0\}$. However $1 \in \mathscr{D}$, so $1P1 = P \neq 0$ is in $\mathscr{D}P\mathscr{D}$, so $\mathscr{D}P\mathscr{D} = \mathscr{D}$. Hence:

$$\mathscr{D} = (\mathscr{D}P)(P\mathscr{D})$$

We shall see in fact in a moment that this product may be identified as the tensor product of the spinor spaces $S \cong \mathscr{D}P$ and $S^D \cong P\mathscr{D}$. Every element Λ of $\mathscr{D}$ can thus be considered as a rank two spin tensor $\Lambda_A{}^B$. It is this decomposition that is normally exploited when anti-symmetric tensor quantities are constructed as bilinear invariants of spinors:

$$\Lambda = \psi\bar{\psi} = \lambda + \lambda^\mu\gamma_\mu + \tfrac{1}{2}\lambda^{\mu\nu}\gamma_{\mu\nu} + \frac{1}{3!}\lambda^{\mu\nu\sigma}\gamma_{\mu\nu\sigma} + \frac{1}{4!}\lambda^{\mu\nu\sigma\tau}\gamma_{\mu\nu\sigma\tau} \equiv \lambda^A\gamma_A$$

so that:

$$\lambda^A = \pm\frac{1}{4}\,\mathrm{Tr}(\psi\bar{\psi}\gamma^A)$$

$$= \pm\frac{1}{4}\,\bar{\psi}\gamma^A\psi$$

The second decomposition is not one that has commonly been used, though some interesting suggestions have been made which depend upon it (Bohm and Hiley[6], Kähler[7], Graf[8], Benn and Tucker[9]). It relies on the fact that any given primitive idempotent $P \cong P_1$ on $\mathscr{D}$ can always be supplemented by three other primitive idempotents P_2, P_3, P_4 satisfying:

$$P_iP_j = \delta_{ij}P_i$$

and:

$$P_1 + P_2 + P_3 + P_4 = 1$$

Then each P_i generates its own spin space S_i and dual space S_i^D, and $\mathscr{D}$ can be written as a direct sum:

$$\mathscr{D} = \mathscr{D}P_1 + \mathscr{D}P_2 + \mathscr{D}P_3 + \mathscr{D}P_4$$

or:

$$\mathscr{D} = P_1\mathscr{D} + P_2\mathscr{D} + P_3\mathscr{D} + P_4\mathscr{D}$$

This means that every element Λ of $\mathscr{D}$ can be uniquely decomposed into the sum of four spinor fields. Under normal circumstances (action from the left by same operator H in $\mathscr{D}$), these spinor fields remain uncoupled. But mixing of the four fields can be achieved in more general situations. Such mixing is made essential, for example, when this algebra is globalised in a non-flat manifold. The action of gravity may then be interpreted as a coupling of four fermion fields in the manner required by this structure. Bohm and Hiley[6] have used this second decomposition of the spinor structure of $\mathscr{D}$ in their discussion of a phase space description of relativistic phenomena. The process of regarding the density matrix $\rho_{AB}(x,x')$ as a vector in a higher-dimensional vector space corresponds to treating it as the direct sum of four algebraic spinors. The introduction of a full set of operators on this higher space is the equivalent to allowing transformations of the kind:

$$\rho' = \Lambda\rho\kappa$$

in $\mathcal{D}$, which can be considered in two parts:

$$\rho'' = \Lambda\rho$$

which maintains the spinor fields distinct, and:

$$\rho' = \rho''\kappa$$

which induces a mixing of the four fields together.

3   The spinor structure in component form

The two spinor structures described in the last section are not entirely unrelated to each other, even though they look quite different at first sight. Their relationship is best understood in terms of a special class of basis that can be defined for the algebra.

In the direct sum decomposition, the primitive idempotents P_i can be used to construct the 4^2 sub-algebras:

$$P_i\mathcal{D}P_j$$

of $\mathcal{D}$. Each of these is non-trivial and so contains at least one non-zero element, E_{ij} say. In fact, the structure of $\mathcal{D}$ ensures that we have:

$$P_i\mathcal{D}P_j = \{\lambda E_{ij}\}$$

where λ is some complex number. We can use this fact to normalise the E_{ij} chosen as bases for these algebras in such a way as to obtain:

$$P_i = E_{ii} \quad \text{(no sum on } i\text{)}$$

and:

$$E_{ij}E_{mn} = \delta_{jm}E_{in}$$

We then have:

$$\mathcal{D}P_i = \left\{\sum_A \psi^A E_{Ai}\right\}$$

and:

$$P_i\mathcal{D} = \left\{\sum_A E_{iA}\varphi_A\right\}$$

Thus the decomposition of $\mathscr{D}$ into the direct sum of spinor spaces corresponds to choosing a matric basis for $\mathscr{D}$.

This same matric basis determines simultaneously also the decomposition of $\mathscr{D}$ into a product of spinor spaces. Take as the generating idempotent of the ideals $\mathscr{D}P$ and $P\mathscr{D}$ the primitive idempotent P_1. Then the P_i can be used on the ideals $\mathscr{D}P_1$ and $P_1\mathscr{D}$ as projection operators which project out a total of eight one-dimensional linear subspaces. If we choose from each of these subspaces a non-zero element, we can use these to span each of these subspaces. We thus obtain a basis for each of the two ideals. Denote the basis of $\mathscr{D}P_1$ by ε_A and that of $P_1\mathscr{D}$ by ε^A. Then for some Λ_A and Λ^A in $\mathscr{D}$, we have:

$$\varepsilon_A = P_A \Lambda_A P_1$$

$$= \lambda_A E_{A1}$$

and:

$$\varepsilon^A = P_1 \Lambda_A P_A$$

$$= \lambda_A E_{1B}$$

(no sum on A), and:

$$\varepsilon_A \varepsilon_B = P_A \Lambda_A P_1 P_1 \Lambda_B P_B$$

$$= \lambda(A,B) E_{AB}$$

The same matric basis of $\mathscr{D}$, up to a multiplicative factor, thus defines also its decomposition into the product of spinor spaces.

4 Reconstruction of the algebra from a knowledge of the spin spaces

The above process can obviously be partially reversed. A matric basis E_{ij} may be constructed purely from a knowledge of the spin space S. Suppose S has a basis ε_A. Let S^D be the linear dual of S and suppose ε^A is the basis of S^D dual to ε_A, i.e.:

$$\varepsilon^A(\varepsilon_B) = \delta^A{}_B$$

Then defining:

$$E_{AB} = \varepsilon_A \otimes \varepsilon^B$$

yields in an obvious way the desired matric basis for $\mathscr{D}$. This however is not sufficient to allow the full reconstruction of $\mathscr{D}$. What we have obtained is an algebra isomorphic to $\mathscr{D}$. But how the E_{AB} are related to the original generators γ^μ of $\mathscr{D}$ is left undetermined. Now, we must have:

$$\gamma^\mu = \gamma^{\mu AB} E_{AB}$$

for some $\gamma^{\mu AB}$. Hence $\mathscr{D}$ is fully specified by S only when the $\gamma^{\mu AB}$ are fixed for a given basis of S.

5 The effect on the spinor structure of a change of idempotents

The spinor structure E_{ij} of $\mathscr{D}$ was determined by choosing arbitrarily a complete system of mutually orthogonal primitive idempotents P_i. Suppose now that we choose a different system P'_i of idempotents. How is the new spinor structure E'_{ij} related to E_{ij}?

The structure theorems on $\mathscr{D}$ determine that any two primitive idempotents P and P' are related by an inner automorphism. Thus there is some $S \in \mathscr{D}$ such that for each P_i:

$$P'_i = SP_iS^{-1}$$

Hence the two spinor structures E_{ij} and E'_{ij} will be similarly related:

$$E'_{ij} = SE_{ij}S^{-1}$$

This brings out an important difference between the two spinor decompositions of $\mathscr{D}$ that we have considered. In the product decomposition of $\mathscr{D}$:

$$\mathscr{D} = (\mathscr{D}P)(P\mathscr{D})$$

the transformation law of the spinors becomes:

$$
\begin{aligned}
\lambda &= \sum_{\alpha}(M_\alpha P)(PN_\alpha) \\
&= \sum_{\alpha}(M_\alpha S^{-1}P'S)(S^{-1}P'SN_\alpha) \\
&= S^{-1}\left[\sum_{\alpha}(M'_\alpha P')SS^{-1}(P'N'_\alpha)\right]S
\end{aligned}
$$

The fact that in this decomposition the factor SS^{-1} can be either eliminated or retained without affecting the final answer means that we have a choice in the transformation law of the spinors under a change of generating idempotent. We can choose either:

$$\psi' = S\psi \text{ and } \varphi' = \varphi S^{-1}$$

or:

$$\psi' = S\psi S^{-1} \text{ and } \varphi' = S\varphi S^{-1}$$

The first corresponds to the usual spinor transformation law, with all its well-known properties. The second puts the spinor on an equal footing with all other quantities contained in $\mathscr{D}$ and is more a natural requirement on spinors in the algebraic framework.

The freedom of choice permitted in the product decomposition of $\mathscr{D}$ is not permitted in the direct sum decomposition. The choice of transformation law in this case has to be:

$$\psi' = S\psi S^{-1} \text{ and } \varphi' = S\varphi S^{-1}$$

For suppose that ψ is an algebraic spinor. Then:

$$\psi P = \psi$$

The transformed spinor ψ' must satisfy:

$$\psi' P' = \psi'$$

But if we put $\psi' = S\psi$, this gives:

$$S\psi SPS^{-1} = S\psi$$

which, in general, is inconsistent with $\psi P = \psi$.

6 Reflections on the algebraic spinor

The considerations of the last section virtually force on us the transformation law:

$$\psi' = S\psi S^{-1}$$

for algebraic spinors. This is rather surprising, but the implications are obvious; the notion of an algebraic spinor does not coincide exactly with the older notion of a spinor. What began as an attempt to redefine the spinor in a manner more suitable to the framework of the implicate order has produced a new entity. The task that faces us now is that of establishing precisely the overlap and the differences between the old notion of the spinor and the new, and what bearing this has on the physics of the fermion. Here we make only a few preliminary observations.

The first and most striking feature of the algebraic spinor is that the spinor space does not remain invariant under a change of idempotent (and hence also under Lorentz transformation). This is in direct contrast to the spinor space normally considered, which is defined to remain invariant under transformation by the requirement:

$$\psi' = S\psi$$

This lack of invariance makes no difference, as we have noted, when bilinear invariants are constructed from the ψS in the usual way. But if we are to give ψ a meaning in its own right, rather than through quadratic functions of its components, then the transformation of the spin space becomes an important and unavoidable feature of the system. This is especially evident in the work of Kähler[7], Graf[8], and Benn and Tucker[9].

Let us consider more closely this transformation of the spin space. Suppose we vary the generating idempotent P infinitesimally to get P'. Then writing $dP = P' - P$ and $S \cong 1 + \Omega$ we have:

$$dP = [P,\Omega] \tag{1}$$

Now, P' is still idempotent, so:

$$(P + dP) = (P + dP)^2$$

or, to first order:

$$dP = PdP + dPP \tag{2}$$

From this it follows that:

$$PdPP = (1 - P)dP(1 - P) = 0$$

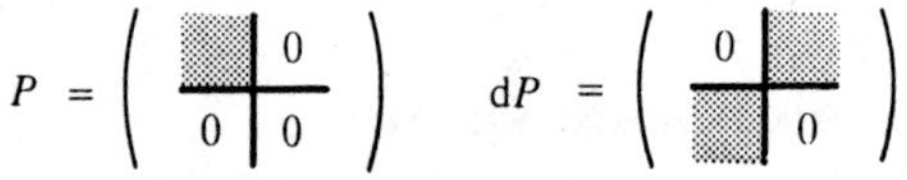

Figure 17.1   In a representation in which P is diagonal, the dP is anti-diagonal.

In a representation in which P is diagonal, this means the dP is anti-diagonal, as in Figure 17.1. This can be seen explicitly from [1] if we choose a spinor structure for $\mathscr{D}$ in which $P = E_{11}$. Putting $\Omega = \omega^{AB}E_{AB}$ we obtain:

$$P' = \begin{pmatrix} 1 & \omega^{12} & \omega^{13} & \omega^{14} \\ \hline -\omega^{21} & & & \\ -\omega^{31} & & 0 & \\ -\omega^{41} & & & \end{pmatrix} \tag{2(a)}$$

or:

$$P' = P + P\Omega - \Omega P \tag{2(b)}$$

The contribution $-\Omega P$ to dP corresponds exactly to the usual infinitesimal increment undergone by a spinor in such a transformation, but the term $P\Omega$ is not normally present. It is this that takes P' outside the original spinor space generated by P. The form of equation [2] shows that the new spinor structure E'_{AB}, when referred to the old E_{AB}, contains a mixture of all four original constituent spinor spaces. This mixing is not a problem in a flat space-time since we can use the integrability of the manifold to establish a path-independent idempotent transportation law which will enable us to identify unique spin spaces at each point. But when the manifold is not integrable, such a procedure is no longer possible and the mixing of these fermion fields becomes an inescapable feature of the system.

The fact that a 'universal idempotent' cannot be defined in general on a curved space-time forces on us yet another feature not normally present in the usual spinor theory; we must allow the spinor-vector conversion factors $\gamma^{\mu AB}$ to vary from point to point. This means that the tensor fields constructed from the ψs will have an additional variation from point to point, due to the variation of the $\gamma^{\mu AB}$:

$$dV = dV^{\mu}\gamma_{\mu}{}^{AB}E_{AB} + V^{\mu}d\gamma_{\mu}{}^{AB}E_{AB} + V^{\mu}\gamma_{\mu}{}^{AB}dE_{AB}$$

The spinor structure connection coefficients $\Gamma_{\mu AB}{}^{CD}$ defined by:

$$dE_{AB} = \Gamma_{\mu AB}{}^{CD}E_{CD}dx^{\mu}$$

replace the spinor connection $\Gamma_{\mu A}{}^{B}$ of the ordinary spinor calculus and contain all the information in them.

Another feature of the algebraic spinor not shared by the ordinary spinor is that not all spinor spaces are physically equivalent. In the usual theory, all spinor structures are allowed, subject only to the condition that in the representation of the γ^{μ} generated, we have $\gamma^{0\dagger} = \gamma^{0}$ and $\gamma^{i\dagger} = -\gamma^{i}$. This means that bases may be chosen for the spin space which are not related to each other by a Lorentz transformation. Yet the physics described by the spinors is independent of the structure generated. This of course is due to the way that the spinor is used and interpreted ordinarily. The attempt to use an algebraic spinor in the way suggested by Kähler, however, forces upon us a physical inequivalence among the spinors not present in the Dirac theory.

This is perhaps best illustrated by a simple example. Consider the ideal generated by the idempotent $P = 1/2(1 + \gamma_5)$, where $\gamma_5 = i\gamma_0\gamma_1\gamma_2\gamma_3$ *and* $\gamma_5^2 = +1$. This idempotent is not primitive and the spinors it generates are the direct sum of two ordinary spinors, but it suffices to illustrate the point in hand. The algebraic spinors of the left ideal generated by P are defined by the requirement:

$$\psi P = \psi \tag{A}$$

If we write $\psi = S + V + B + T + P$, then we obtain from [A]:

$$VS = TP$$

$$BS = BP \tag{B}$$

$$TS = VP$$

so that ψ defines a 'complex' of anti-symmetric tensor fields whose components are restricted *a priori* by relations [B]. The Dirac-Kähler[9] equation for ψ thus defines the variation of coupled tensor fields satisfying [B]. The fields in this case are obviously duals in pairs:

$$S = P\gamma_5$$

$$V = T\gamma_5$$

and B is self dual:

$$B(1 - \gamma_5) = 0$$

All spinors ψ' which are Lorentz-related to ψ will obviously have the same properties. Now consider the spinors defined by $P = \frac{1}{2}(1 + u)$, where u is a vector with $u^2 = 1$. The defining relation [A] then gives for ψ:

$$ST = B \wedge V + P \cdot V$$

$$SP = T \wedge V \qquad\qquad\qquad [C]$$

$$SB = T \cdot V$$

This defines an altogether different set of coupled tensor fields, not equivalent to the first by a Lorentz transformation.

The essential difference between the algebraic spinor and the ordinary spinor is that the algebraic spinor is in reality a spinor of rank two. This feature was forced on us through the transformation law:

$$\psi' = S\psi S^{-1}$$

that we were forced to adopt. But this does not mean that we are back to ordinary tensor physics. The point is that we have been forced to abandon the notion that only anti-symmetric tensors of given rank are relevant to the system. The algebraic spinor provides a framework for coupling together tensors of different ranks in a simple way. It also provides a framework in which this coupling may be altered by a continuous transformation.

References

1   D. Bohm, *Wholeness and the Implicate Order*, Routledge & Kegan Paul, London, 1980.
2   G. Chew, 'Gentle quantum events as the source of explicate order', this volume, p. 249.
3   F. A. M. Frescura and B. J. Hiley, *Found. of Physics*, **10**, 7 (1980).
4   F. A. M. Frescura and B. J. Hiley, *Found. of Phys.*, **10**, 705 (1980).
5   F. A. M. Frescura and B. J. Hiley, *Revista Brasileira de Fisica*, Volume Especial, p. 49 (July, 1984).
6   D. Bohm and B. J. Hiley, *Revista Brasileira de Fisica*, Volume Especial, p. 1 (July, 1984).
7   E. Kähler, *Deutsches Akad. Wissenschaften zu Berlin K. für Math. Phys. and Techn.*, No. 1 and No. 4 (1961).
8   W. Graf, *Ann. Inst. Henri Poincaré*, **XXIX**, 85 (1978).
9   I. M. Benn and R. W. Tucker, *Commun. Math. Phys.*, **89**, 341 (1983) and **98**, 53 (1985).

18

All is flux

David Finkelstein *Georgia Institute of Technology*

1 Introduction

Kepler and Einstein struggled to share in God's creative thoughts; in the early 1950s, the prevalent philosophy was more smug. The goal was a covariant renormalizable quantum field theory of each of the forces, analogous to quantum electrodynamics. By the time I finished school I was somewhat disheartened by the contrast between the ideal of physics as a branch of philosophy, engendered by many popular accounts, and the dominant practice of specialized physics. At about that time, George Yevick shared with me some notes he had brought back from a stay with David Bohm, concerning a classical guiding wave theory of relativistic spinning particles. While I have reservations about that work, touched upon below, I still recall the stimulus I derived from it, and the feeling that I was being directed towards truly fundamental questions by it, at an important time for me. I have experienced this stimulation often with Bohm's writings. In several basic matters, some of which I touch upon below, Bohm has been years or decades ahead of the rest of us in his intuition for the proper path, at least in my opinion. It is a pleasure to thank him for years of enlivenment.

2 The nature of physics

It seems to me that Bohm's conception of the goal of physics, formulated in the appendix to his book on relativity,[1] deserves more attention than it has received.

Some traditions define physics categorically; for example, as the study of matter and energy. Such definitions do not keep well. The concept of energy is itself one of the triumphs of physics, an accomplishment of the mid-nineteenth century. Newton did not study matter and energy; *ergo*, Newton did not do physics. This *reductio ad absurdum* makes the definition absurd. It is quite possible – even likely – that neither of these formerly popular concepts of matter and energy are important in the extreme conditions prevailing at the creation of the universe or in the deep core of the constituent parts of matter. So the increasingly many students of these conditions may be leaving physics behind them, according to this definition. Any definition of physics that itself uses a concept of physics may thereby limit itself to a chapter in the story. Physics is too protean to be pinned down neatly. It must be so in order to follow the even more surprising transformations of Mother Nature.

The description David Bohm gives of physics in the appendix to his *Relativity* makes physics nearly coextensive with humanity. For him, science is a mode of perception before it is a mode of obtaining knowledge of the laws of nature.

When I started doing physics I thought it was the search for the laws of nature, Bohm to the contrary notwithstanding; then, for the law of nature; and only quite lately have I been able to see it as a search for a perception of nature.

The physicist forming the concept of the electron, or any other part of matter, is extending the process by which he or she formed the concept of mother; a process of reification followed by conservation. The law of conservation of matter, still asserted in the early 1900s, is like the child's belief, 'Mommy back soon.' This belief works in a broad range of circumstances, but the maturing child eventually learns the limits of validity of this conservation law, and ultimately transcends the reification that precedes it. Bohm expects that every reification and every conservation law are likewise reflections of a certain calmness of the environment, and will eventually be outgrown by the maturing human race.

Thus Bohm is sure there are no *elementary* particles or any other permanent matter. In one of his researches he studies how cooperative vibrations of electrons in a gas behave like a new non-elementary particle, the plasmon. I think that Bohm was disappointed that this work was taken so literally, and that he meant it metaphorically too; to illustrate how every particle will ultimately be found to be the reification of a collective vibration of still finer structures.

Some have faith that an ultimate law of nature exists. For example, Einstein is such a believer. Perhaps most of us are agnostics. Bohm is a skeptic. No great Enlightenment is coming to answer all our questions. The quest is endless. Though the laws of physics generally last longer than the tablets of Moses did, what might be called the Moses syndrome has now struck too consistently for physicists to ignore. Many physicists take it for granted that laws are discovered today to be broken tomorrow. Physics presently functions with many of its practitioners simultaneously seeking and doubting the existence of what they seek. I believe the antinomian position taken by Bohm yesterday will be the common sense tomorrow.

But even if the game of nature knows no Law, physics need not come to an end but may once again redefine itself. If there is no Final Answer it is simply because there is no Final Question.

3   Quantum theory

It seems that Bohm became disillusioned with quantum theory in the course of writing his well-known text[2] on the subject, in which the theory is stoutly upheld. According to Bohr, the language we use to describe our experiments must be classical physics, and, at the same time, classical physics is not adequate for this purpose. We 'cannot and should not' improve our concepts in this respect, according to Heisenberg's statement of the permanent paradox of the Copenhagen interpretation of quantum theory.

This seems like too much protest; if we cannot then the should-not is surely otiose, and if we should not then we probably can. The exhortation resembles the *'Non fingo'* of Newton: appropriate in its time, but ultimately a challenge and a signpost to seek further. The path that Bohm took, when he set out to cross this frontier, has remarkably old and honorable precedents. The idea that quanta are guided by a pilot or ghost wave has been clearly expressed, though each time with characteristic variations, by de Broglie before Bohm; by Einstein decades before de Broglie; and by Newton centuries before Einstein. Since I have not seen Newton's work on quantum mechanics mentioned lately, I would like to remind us here of how it runs.

On the one hand Newton is an expert in the interference of light; the interference rings between two glass surfaces still bear his name. On the other, he is remarkably sure that light is a stream of particles; let us call them photons. (One wonders how he knew; the argument he gave, that light does not 'bend into the shadow,' could not have convinced him for more than a minute, since it merely sets an upper bound on the wavelength. I suggest that the phenomenon of vision itself, combined with the kinetic theory of heat, makes a wave theory of light intuitively unacceptable. Territoriality may also be at work: Newton ruled over the particles, Descartes over the waves; perhaps Newton made light corpuscular to make it his.)

In his *Opticks*, he proposes that besides photons there are guide waves, much faster than the photons, which on striking a partially reflecting surface, cause it to have 'fits' of easy and difficult transmission. The same guide waves are held responsible for the other quantum superposition phenomena confronting Newton, such as the splitting of a polarized beam of photons when it strikes a second polarizer in general position. His polarizers are 'Island crystals,' Iceland spar. As

Einstein fits his guide waves into a unified field theory, Newton fits them into a particle theory. Each to his own. Newton's ether is buzzing with faster-than-light particles and the guide waves are density waves in this gas of invisible tachyons.

Bohm's quantum potential is the furthest refinement of the pilot wave doctrine, and the cause still seems hopeless. There is first the technical many-body problem. Each of the electrons in a uranium atom requires its own individual guide wave. In unified field theories, which have progressed amazingly since Einstein, we add fields to go from one to many particles (or solitons, or kinks, or the like.) The field gets more complicated but still depends on the same three variables x, y and z. But the psi waves of quantum theory combine like probabilities. They multiply, each keeping its original variables. The guide field for the electrons of uranium is a field in a space of thrice ninety-two coordinates. It is not an occupant of our time space.

A second difficulty with all such programs is that a quantum system does not have a unique wave-function according to quantum theory. At the very least, every experiment is symmetrically described by two wave-functions, one describing the initial preparation of the system and one the final detection. For example, they may describe the initial polarizer and the final analyzer on an optical bench. At any instant during the experiment we may equally well ascribe two wave functions to the system, by propagating the initial one forward in time or the final one backward. Neither is specially the property of the quantum system.

I would like to add some of my own thoughts about wave functions. To speak about 'the wave function of the system' is a syntactic error. A wave function is not a property of the system in any classical sense, but gives far more information about the experimenter. For example, a wave function representing vertical polarization conveys only one bit of information about the photon, that it passed through a certain tourmaline crystal in the ordinary way, not the extraordinary. (The number of bits is the logarithm of the number of possibilities to the base 2; two possibilities make one bit.) But it gives infinite information, ideally, about the orientation angle of the tourmaline crystal. Indeed, the wave-function may be taken to *be* the orientation vector of the crystal. This information has no counterpart in classical physics, where we imagine one complete experimental set-up capable of making all possible measurements at once. With only one significant choice for the experimental arrangement, no matter how complex, the number of bits is zero. The new kind of information about the experimenter provided by the wave function is the result of complementarity, which forces us to choose which measurements we make. A wave-function tells us more about the *act* of measurement than about the result. It is a verb, not a noun; to treat it as a thing is a mistake in syntax. Having committed this error, one is forced to follow it with another, the idea of the collapse of the wave function. It is not that 'the' wave function 'collapses.' It is, rather, that first we do one thing, and then another.

The attempt to replace a theory of the quantum kind by one of a more classical kind seems at odds with Bohm's Heraclitean tendencies. He has, for example, suggested a language of verbs. Moreover, the role of the law of nature is taken in quantum theory by a kind of gigantic wave-function, the Feynman amplitude, giving a probability and phase for each possible history. The quantum philosophy suggests that, being a wave function, the Feynman amplitude too is more descriptive of the environment of the system, including the experimenter, than of the system; and thus that there is no place in quantum theory for an absolute law of the classical kind. The quantum kind of law is so much closer to the lawlessness that Bohm sees in the universe than is the classical kind, that one expects him to seek still more quantum anomalies beneath the ones we already know. This is the tendency of his later work on the foundations of quantum mechanics, to which I turn now.

4   Quantum time space

Bohm may have been the first physicist to take seriously the possibility that the world is not a continuum but a simplicial complex. An *n*-dimensional simplex or *n*-simplex is a figure defined by $n + 1$ vertices. A concrete *n*-simplex consists of the vertices and all the points between them in an *n*-dimensional linear space. An abstract *n*-simplex is defined merely by the vertices, which may be objects of any kind; the points 'between' them being weighted statistical mixtures of the vertices, defined by assigning a probability to each vertex with total probability 1. A subset of the vertices of a simplex defines a simplex called a face of the given simplex. Finally, a simplicial complex is a collection of simplices intersecting only in faces of the same simplices.

The operations of the differential and integral calculus, particularly the ones entering into Maxwell's equations, have exact counterparts in simplicial complexes. Moreover, one may think of a simplex as a kind of multiplication of its vertices and set up an algebraic theory of simplicial complexes which turns out to have an uncanny resemblance to the quantum theory of a Fermi-Dirac ensemble. Thus simplicial complexes may be the natural language for a quantum theory of time space itself. Regge's later translation of Einstein's theory of gravity into substantially the same language has undoubtedly led other physicists to take up this possibility, though Regge presents it as an approximation technique, not as an approach to a more exact theory.

We may regard the points of the abstract simplex already described as incoherent or classical mixtures of the vertices, and introduce a quantum simplex, whose points are coherent quantum superpositions of its vertices, in order to quantize the theory. The fundamental quanta of time space may be such quantum simplices, and the topology we usually assign to time space may be a coarse approximation to one defined by the relations of mutual incidence between such quantum simplices. Most likely, what corresponds to a point (or cell) of time space with all its fields is a simplex of the quantum complex; to a vector at a point, the product of two simplices that share a face; to a spinor at a point (paraphrasing a well-known theory of Leonard Susskind), the product of a simplex with one of its faces; and to the operation of taking a derivative (more precisely, a curl, an anti-symmetrized derivative), the (dual to the) operation of taking the boundary of a simplex. Bohm's strong intuition about this interesting line of exploration may yet be justified.

References

1   D. Bohm, *The Special Theory of Relativity* (Benjamin, New York, 1965).
2   D. Bohm, *Quantum Theory* (Prentice-Hall, New York, 1951).

19

Anholonomic deformations in the ether: a significance for the electrodynamic potentials

P. R. Holland   *Institut Henri Poincaré, Paris,*   and
C. Philippidis   *Bristol Polytechnic*

1   Introduction

It is now generally accepted that the Aharonov-Bohm (AB) effect [1] demonstrates that in quantum mechanics the electromagnetic potentials A_μ play a much more significant role than the one they occupy in classical physics. Wu and Yang [2] have emphasized this by pointing out that while the field strengths $F_{\mu\nu}$ underdescribe electrodynamic processes (quantum mechanical), the phase factors $\exp{(ie\int A_\mu \mathrm{d}x^\mu)}$ give a more complete description.

The question we wish to raise in this paper is whether the potentials A_μ are irrevocably subordinated to $F_{\mu\nu}$ in the classical domain, acquiring an active role only in the quantum domain, or whether they have fundamental significance in both domains. It seems that the latter possibility is worth considering seriously since in the AB effect the structure of A_μ is not affected by quantization. This follows from the fact that in the first quantized theory of a charged particle in an electromagnetic field, the field itself does not undergo any alteration. It would thus be surprising if quantization of the particle trajectory alone introduced new structural properties into the potentials. Rather, we feel that these properties must be, in a perhaps primitive form, already in existence in the classical regime.

In attempting to discover the classical significance of the A_μ we have at our disposal several clues. Bohm [3] has suggested an analogy between the AB effect and the dislocation of a crystal lattice. In this analogy the potentials A_μ define sets of parallel planes which can be dislocated, the line integral of A_μ representing the dislocation strength. By representing the phase of the particle wave function as a super-lattice, Bohm was able to show how a dislocation in the base lattice would produce AB type shifts of the super-lattice.

The close parallel between the AB effect and dislocation theory was later noted in a different context by Kawamura[4]. In developing a Schrödinger equation for scattering off a dislocation in a discrete lattice, Kawamura obtains the same equation as for the AB effect but with the dislocation strength in place of the flux parameter. A similar result has been found by Berry *et al.*[5], who show that the phase of the AB wave function exhibits singularities which are analogous to dislocations of atomic planes in crystals.

Now, in addition to these clues from the quantum theory, it has been known for a long time that there exist deep analogies between the continuum theory of dislocations and classical electromagnetism. Yet, to the authors' knowledge, no work has been produced which takes these analogies as a foundation on which to build a theory of electrodynamics. Rather, they have been proposed in order to elucidate dislocation theory by reference to the more familiar electromagnetic case. Consequently, the observations alluded to above, though useful pointers to an alternative understanding of the relationship between charges and fields and the role of the potentials, remain confined to the level of comparisons. We propose in this paper to develop a re-interpretation of the theory of a classical charged test-particle moving in an external electromagnetic field through the differential geometric language of continuous dislocation theory. Our aim is to bring out the fact that, even in the classical theory, if this is suitably formulated, the potentials have an important physical significance. In particular we begin to see why the above analogies work, although they only have observational significance on the level where the phase is meaningful.

In order to do this in a physically natural and intuitive manner we make the hypothesis that the Hamilton-Jacobi phase function is a real physical field and introduces into space-time a medium (or ether) the deformation states of which are determined directly by A_μ (rather than $F_{\mu\nu}$, say). The appropriateness of this notion is reinforced by the fact that our theory has the mathematical form of the continuum theory of defects, in particular in the appearance of the anholonomic mapping of frames.

That the assumption of an ether may be compatible with the principles of relativity was pointed out by Einstein[6], who noted that special relativity does not compel us to deny the existence of an ether altogether, only that we must give up ascribing a definite state of motion to it. In general relativity space-time itself, insofar as it is endowed with physical dynamical qualities, may be treated as a medium (refraction of light), albeit one to which the notion of motion is inapplicable (see also reference 7). Later Dirac[8] showed how an ether which at each point has a distribution of velocities which are all equally probable would be consistent with relativity, and alternative approaches to the quantum theory by Bohm[9,10] and Vigier[11,12] have indicated that a suitably fluctuating ether can contribute to an understanding of the microdomain.

We recall that much effort was expended in the nineteenth century in trying to understand electromagnetic processes in terms of stresses set up in an ether treated as an elastic solid [13]. However, what may have prevented an adequate ether theory being developed (aside from problems of invariance) was, firstly, that an analogy was set up with a theory (elasticity) too limited in scope to deal with the complexity of the physical process and, secondly, that attention was fixed primarily on the fields which tended to exclude consideration of particles as being relevant to the analogy.

The main point we make in this paper is that the context in which the significance of the potentials becomes manifest is actually one which involves a quite different picture of electrodynamical processes to that of the Maxwell-Lorentz point of view (for which the ether is not a relevant concept). Our method raises questions which could not be coherently understood in the usual approach (e.g. electrodynamic Burgers vector) and forces us to abandon a rigid distinction between field and particle in favour of notions more akin to those of the wholeness of the quantum domain.

2 The role of the frame in the theory of deformations

It was shown in the 1950s by Kondo [14,15,16] and by Bilby [17,18] (see also references 19–22 for reviews) that if the granular structure of an imperfect crystalline material can be neglected and the material approximated by a continuum, then the tensor which defines the density of dislocation lines is precisely the differential-geometric torsion tensor which is associated with the continuum when considered as a manifold.

Let x^μ, $\mu = 1 \ldots n$, be the holonomic co-ordinates of a material point of a continuum embedded in a space whose structure is, for example, Euclidean. The *a posteriori* standpoint is adopted so that all fields are functions of the final co-ordinates of a material point *after* deformations have set in (for a comparison with the *a priori* point of view see Kondo [23]). To study the nature of the deformation we should note firstly that there is no invariant way of uniquely mapping the deformed state as a whole back to some perfect state from which it may be presumed to have come. Rather, following Kondo, we must tear from the medium a deformed element dx^μ, which is then allowed to relax so that all strains vanish and the element coincides with a perfect lattice. The failure of many torn local elements, so relaxed into this 'natural state', to mesh to form a global perfect lattice is then a manifestation of the deformed state. We have now an amorphous collection of small pieces of perfect lattice which cannot be patched together to form a continuum of perfect lattice in the embedding space.

Attached to each material point is a local tangent space with a reference-vielbein basis of 1-forms $h^i(x)$, $i = 1 \ldots n$, i.e. a local perfect lattice basis. When a small element is torn from its environment and relaxed we have a linear Pfaffian relation:

$$h^i = h^i_{\ \mu} dx^\mu \tag{1}$$

where the frame coefficients are functions of the final co-ordinates. For the reason just outlined, equation [1] is non-integrable and this 'local natural frame' defines a set of anholonomic functions.

Further details of the theory of defects will be introduced as we need them. We shall now explain the relevance of such notions to the electrodynamics of a charged particle.

3   Electrodynamic deformed and natural states

In considering electrodynamics the notions of medium and deformed and natural states have to be defined in a way which is consistent with the physical system under discussion and its accepted theoretical description. Our treatment of the ether is based on the following consideration.

We start by supposing that the classical Hamilton-Jacobi phase function associated with the system is a real physical field (limit of the quantum phase when the quantum potential[9,10,11,12] vanishes) and note that it defines a line element. In order to study the deformation structure of this wave, we require for the purposes of comparison two space-time metrics at a point[24] (cf. bimetric general relativity[25,26]).

Consider a flat space-time which is a four-dimensional manifold whose points are labelled by holonomic world co-ordinates x^μ, $\mu = 0,1,2,3$. Such a manifold endowed with a metric $\eta_{\mu\nu}$ (a general co-ordinate version of the Minkowski metric $\eta_{ij} = (1, -1, -1, -1)$) will be denoted M_4 and this plays the role of an 'embedding space' for the wave. Referring to section 2, we suppose that the medium has already been brought to a state of deformation so that any infinitesimal element dx^μ of it is of length $ds = (\eta_{\mu\nu} dx^\mu dx^\nu)^{\frac{1}{2}}$ since the medium inherits the metric of the space in which it lies. It is our task to uncover the nature of the deformation. This we do by defining the natural state in terms of the line element:

$$dS = ds + kA_\mu dx^\mu \equiv L d\lambda \tag{2}$$

where L is the Lagrangian per unit mass of a test particle in the field A_μ in M_4. (We shall not be concerned here with the source of A_μ or Maxwell's equations, and we treat only the one-body problem.) L is a homogeneous function of $\dot{x}$ of degree one, given by:

$$L(x,\dot{x}) = (\eta_{\mu\nu}\dot{x}^\mu\dot{x}^\nu)^{\frac{1}{2}} + kA_\mu\dot{x}^\mu \tag{3}$$

where $k = e/m$ and $\dot{x}^\mu = \dfrac{dx^\mu}{d\lambda}$ lies in the tangent space at each point of space-time (λ being an arbitrary parameter). Thus there exists a Randers line element [27]:

$$\mathrm{d}S^2 = g_{\mu\nu}\mathrm{d}x^\mu\mathrm{d}x^\nu \tag{4}$$

which can be understood as arising from cutting out locally from the deformed medium in M_4 an element $\mathrm{d}x^\mu$ and allowing it to relax, thereby changing its length from $\mathrm{d}s$ to $\mathrm{d}S$. This is of course a fully relativistic procedure in that the infinitesimal time displacement $\mathrm{d}x^0$ is relaxed concurrently with the space displacements. Equation [2] thus expresses the elastic properties of the medium. That a plastic deformation is also implied by equation [2] will be shown in section 4.

The functions $g_{\mu\nu}$ represent the metric associated with the natural state referred to the world frame and we see that space-time with such a geometry (denoted F_4) is a Finsler space [28] so that the metric is a function of both particle and field parameters: $g_{\mu\nu}(x,\dot{x})$. The deformation of the ether therefore depends not only on where we are in the field but also on which direction is singled out *by the particle* in the tangent space at each point.

A consequence of equation [2] is that the Lorentz force law trajectories in M_4 obtained by varying the right-hand side, that is:

$$\eta_{\mu\nu}\frac{\mathrm{d}u^\nu}{\mathrm{d}s} + \begin{bmatrix} \mu \\ \nu\sigma \end{bmatrix}u^\nu u^\sigma = kF_{\mu\nu}u^\nu, \; u^\mu = \frac{\mathrm{d}x^\mu}{\mathrm{d}s} \tag{5}$$

where $\begin{bmatrix} \mu \\ \nu\sigma \end{bmatrix}$ are the Christoffel symbols of $\eta_{\mu\nu}$ and $F_{\mu\nu} = \partial_\mu A_\nu - \partial_\nu A_\mu$, may be written equivalently as geodesics in F_4 (on varying the left-hand side):

$$g_{\mu\nu}\frac{\mathrm{d}V^\nu}{\mathrm{d}S} + \begin{Bmatrix} \mu \\ \nu\sigma \end{Bmatrix}V^\nu V^\sigma = 0, \; V^\mu = \frac{\mathrm{d}x^\mu}{\mathrm{d}S} \tag{6}$$

where $\begin{Bmatrix} \mu \\ \nu\sigma \end{Bmatrix}$ are the Christoffel symbols of $g_{\mu\nu}$. This result shows clearly how the disparate elements of orthodox electrodynamics ($\eta_{\mu\nu}$, A_μ, $\dot{x}^\mu$) may be united in a single geometrical description in F_4. The relative acceleration of neighbouring trajectories in M_4 is expressed in F_4 by the equation of geodesic deviation.

Note that unless otherwise stated the geometrical structures studied in the remainder of this paper exist independently of the *extremum* assumption [5] or [6].

The unit tangent vectors u^μ and V^μ associated with the deformed and natural states respectively satisfy the following relations:

$$\left.\begin{aligned} u^\sigma &= (\eta_{\mu\nu}\dot{x}^\mu\dot{x}^\nu)^{-\frac{1}{2}}\dot{x}^\sigma, \; u_\mu = \eta_{\mu\nu}u^\nu, \; u_\mu u^\mu = 1 \\[2mm] V^\mu &= (1+Y)^{-1}u^\mu, \; V_\mu = g_{\mu\nu}V^\nu, \; V_\mu V^\mu = 1 \end{aligned}\right\} \tag{7}$$

where $Y = kA_\mu u^\mu$.

The metrical coefficients of a Finsler space are defined by:

$$g_{\mu\nu} = \tfrac{1}{2}\frac{\partial^2 L^2}{\partial \dot{x}^\mu \partial \dot{x}^\nu}$$

from which we deduce equation [4] by homogeneity. Equation [3] then gives:

$$g_{\mu\nu} = \eta_{\mu\nu} + k^2 A_\mu A_\nu + k A_\mu u_\nu + k A_\nu u_\mu + Y(\eta_{\mu\nu} - u_\mu u_\nu) \tag{8}$$

The strain tensor of the deformed ether is defined by:

$$e_{\mu\nu} = g_{\mu\nu} - \eta_{\mu\nu} \tag{9}$$

and vanishes if, and only if, either $A_\mu = 0$ or $k = 0$. Thus if the potentials are pure gauge ($A_\mu = \partial_\mu \varphi$ and $k \neq 0$) so that the trajectories (equation [5]) reduce to geodesics in M_4 (and $g_{\mu\nu}$ and $\eta_{\mu\nu}$ are 'equivalent' from this perspective) there is nevertheless a non-trivial strain (equation [9]) present in the medium.

The covariant vector $P_\mu = mV_\mu$ in the co-tangent space associated with the natural state is given by equation [8] as:

$$P_\mu = mg_{\mu\nu}V^\nu = mu_\mu + eA_\mu \tag{10}$$

in accord with the usual definition of canonical momentum $P_\mu = m\dfrac{\partial L}{\partial \dot{x}^\mu}$,

using equation [3]. Note that, unlike the case of a Riemanian space, one cannot find at a point in F_4 normal co-ordinates (in the sense of Rund[28]) for which the Christoffel symbols in equation [6] vanish. These symbols are not present solely to maintain general covariance (rather they reflect an absolute property of the deformed ether) and we have not discovered a 'principle of equivalence' for electromagnetism.

4   Anholonomic local natural frames

In the previous section we have established that the notions of deformed and natural states in an electrodynamic context arise naturally when one formulates the theory in terms of line elements (equation [2]). Our introduction of the natural state was carried out locally by considering the deformed and natural separations between two infinitesimally close points. In order to examine the global structure of this state, we have to find out the manner in which the flat local naturalizations fail to fit together globally to form a continuum. For this purpose we require local natural frames whose distribution will determine properties like the torsion of the natural state.

Now, as shown by one of us elsewhere[24], the existence of such natural frames is guaranteed by a structural property of the Finsler metric, no separate hypothesis as to their existence underpinning the F_4-geometry being necessary. That is, the metric (equation [8]) factorizes as:

$$g_{\mu\nu} = \eta_{ij}h^i{}_\mu h^j{}_\nu, \eta_{ij} = (1,-1,-1,-1) \tag{11}$$

where the $h^i{}_\mu(x,\dot{x})$ are the components of a field of Finsler tetrads, $i = 0,1,2,3$ labelling each Lorentz vector and $\mu = 0,1,2,3$ the component with respect to the world frame. Explicitly:

$$h^i{}_\mu(x,\dot{x}) = u^i(u_\mu + kA_\mu) + (1 + Y)^{\frac{1}{2}}(\bar{h}^i{}_\mu - u^i u_\mu) \tag{12}$$

where $\bar{h}^i{}_\mu = \dfrac{\partial z^i}{\partial x^\mu}$ and z^i are global Lorentz co-ordinates in M_4 and:

$$u^i = \bar{h}^i{}_\mu u^\mu, u^i u_i = 1, u_i = \eta_{ij}u^j \tag{13}$$

so that u^i is a Lorentz vector tangent to the deformed manifold. It follows from equation [11] that:

$$h^i{}_\mu h_i{}^\nu = \delta^\nu_\mu, h_i{}^\mu = \eta_{ij}g^{\mu\nu}h^j{}_\nu \tag{14}$$

Thus the factorization (equation [11]) of the metric introduces a field of local Minkowskian natural frames given by the Pfaffian (equation [1]):

$$h^i = h^i{}_\mu \mathrm{d}x^\mu \tag{15}$$

so that the naturalized separation (equation [4]) is given by:

$$\mathrm{d}S^2 = \eta_{ij}h^i h^j \tag{16}$$

When the element $\mathrm{d}x^\mu$ lies along the direction $\dot{x}^\mu$ these frames are proportional to u^i, as may be verified by substituting equation [12] into equation [15] to find:

$$h^i = u^i \mathrm{d}S \tag{17}$$

Equation [17] is intuitively obvious in that u^i is a unit vector lying in the tangent space with metric η_{ij} at a point in the deformed manifold, and naturalization merely consists in 'removing' this vector and allowing it to relax. We continue to denote by F_4 the geometry having an underlying field of such frames.

5 Parallelism in the natural state

The h^i frames given by equation [15] constitute an amorphous ensemble of elements of the medium rather than a congruent field. The reason for this is a two-fold indeterminacy: first, in the orientation of the natural frames; and, second, in their location.

The orientational indeterminacy arises from the invariance of the natural metric $g_{\mu\nu}$ under local Lorentz transformations of the Finsler tetrad; that is, given equation [12], the general solution to equation [11] is:

$$h^{i'}_{\ \mu} = L^{i'}_{\ i}(x, \dot{x})h^{i}_{\ \mu} \tag{18}$$

On the other hand the locational indeterminacy is a consequence of the non-integrability of the Pfaffian equation [15]. These indeterminacies are the fundamental expression of the existence of internal deformations in the ether.

It is well known[14-23] that the indefiniteness due to equation [18] is responsible for the curvature of F_4 while the anholonomy of h^i gives rise to torsion. The former is associated with defects such as disclinations and the latter with dislocations. In this article we shall concentrate on the study of dislocations only by supposing that the affine curvature vanishes. This has the effect of restricting the theory by eliminating the orientational degrees of freedom implied by equation [18]; that is, we fix the relative orientation of the h^i frames to yield distant parallelism in F_4, choosing to work with the solution (equation [12]) to equation [11].

A world vector $X^\mu(x, \dot{x})$ at a point in F_4 has a covariant derivative[28] (note that the connection transformation laws given by Amari[29] do not appear to be correct):

$$DX^\mu = dX^\mu + \Gamma^\mu_{\ v\sigma}X^\sigma dx^v + D^\mu_{\ v\sigma}X^\sigma d\dot{x}^v \tag{19}$$

(d includes derivatives in both x and $\dot{x}$.) The two sets of linear connection coefficients appear as a result of displacements dx and $d\dot{x}$ in both x and $\dot{x}$. The components of the world vector with respect to the natural frame at a point are:

$$X^i = h^i_{\ \mu}X^\mu \tag{20}$$

World vectors at two neighbouring points x (with associated direction $\dot{x}$) and $x + dx$ (with direction $\dot{x} + d\dot{x}$) are parallel if their world scalar components (equation [20]) in the natural frames at the two points are equal, i.e. if:

$$DX^i \equiv dX^i = h^i_{\ \mu}dX^\mu + dh^i_{\ \mu}X^\mu = 0 \tag{21}$$

Then comparing with the condition $DX^\mu = 0$ for parallelism referred to the world frame, we deduce that the connection coefficients for the natural state represented in the world frame, under the imposition of distant parallelism, are:

$$\left. \begin{aligned} \Gamma^\mu_{\ v\sigma}(x, \dot{x}) &= h_i^{\ \mu}\partial_v h^i_{\ \sigma} \\ D^\mu_{\ v\sigma}(x, \dot{x}) &= h_i^{\ \mu}\frac{\partial h^i_{\ \sigma}}{\partial \dot{x}^v} \end{aligned} \right\} \tag{22}$$

Observe that $D^\mu{}_{\nu\sigma}$ is a tensor and that $\Gamma^\mu{}_{\nu\sigma}$ does not transform with the usual law of connection coefficients.

In general a Finsler space has associated with it three curvature tensors. It is straightforward to confirm that these all vanish when evaluated using equation [22] and so parallel displacements are independent of path [30]. The torsion vector of F_4 on the other hand is non-vanishing and gives rise to closure failures which we examine in the next section.

It follows from equations [11] and [22] and the Leibnitz rule that:

$$Dg_{\mu\nu} = 0 \qquad [23]$$

i.e. lengths are preserved under parallel transport in F_4, as is equation [11]. The length of an arbitrary vector $X^\mu(x, \dot{x})$ in the natural state is defined to be $(g_{\mu\nu}X^\mu X^\nu)^{\frac{1}{2}}$.

For related work on the geometry of electrodynamics see also references 30–4.

6 Electrodynamic torsion and Burgers circuits

The connection coefficients (equation [22]) of the natural state imply the presence of torsion in F_4. This may be seen by considering the parallel transport of two infinitesimal 1-form displacements dx^μ, dx^ν along each other to form a parallelogram which it is found fails to close. Using equation [19] with equation [22] we find that the closure failure is given by:

$$b^\sigma = D^\sigma{}_{\mu\nu}d\dot{x}\lambda dx^\nu + \Gamma^\sigma{}_{[\mu\nu]}dx^\mu \lambda dx^\nu \qquad [24]$$

which is Cartan's torsion vector generalized to a Finsler space. Despite its appearance, the object $F^\sigma{}_{\mu\nu} \equiv 2\Gamma^\sigma{}_{[\mu\nu]}$ given by:

$$F^\sigma{}_{\mu\nu} = h_i\nu(\partial_\mu h^i{}_\nu - \partial_\nu h^i{}_\mu) \qquad [25]$$

is not a world tensor, although it is a tensor under linear transformations. In the case that $h^i{}_\mu$ is independent of $\dot{x}^\mu$, equation [25] reduces to the 'object of anholonomity', which is a world tensor. Noting that $d\dot{x}^\mu$ is not a vector element, we see that equation [24] is a non-covariant decomposition. We can rewrite b^σ as a sum of tensor quantities by substituting for $d\dot{x}^\sigma$ in terms of $D\dot{x}^\sigma$ from equation [19], or in terms of dx^μ if the geodesic law (equation [6]) is imposed, although we shall not do this here.

The procedure leading to equation [24] coincides with that which defines the local Burgers vector for a continuum [18]. Here we execute an infinitesimal closed Burgers circuit of lattice steps in the real medium and pursue the corresponding steps in a perfect reference lattice to discover the real Burgers vector. Since the lattice bases (i.e. the natural frames) are everywhere parallel, the resultant displacement is the algebraic sum of the components of dx^μ with respect to the lattice bases, i.e. $\int h^i$. Recovery of equation [24] then requires using Stokes' theorem and letting the circuit area tend to zero. Our coefficients of torsion thus describe the local density of lines of dislocation and their components can be classified into edge and screw dislocations.

In order to clarify fully the nature of this closure failure, and also to arrive at a correct application of Stokes' theorem, it is convenient to take a broader view and suppose that the Finsler space F_4 is a subspace of relativistic velocity phase space when the latter is endowed with a suitable geometrical structure (which we denote V_8). Let us first show that such a construction is possible. Suppose that $x^A \equiv (x^\mu, x^{\bar\mu})$ are co-ordinates in velocity phase space where we have written $\dot x^\mu \equiv x^{\bar\mu}$ and $A,B,C \ldots = 0 \ldots 7$; $\mu = 0,1,2,3$; $\bar\mu = 4,5,6,7$. Introduce into this space a vielbein field:

$$h^I{}_A(x^A) = \begin{bmatrix} h^i{}_\mu & h^i{}_{\bar\mu} \\ h^{\bar\imath}{}_\mu & h^{\bar\imath}{}_{\bar\mu} \end{bmatrix} \tag{26}$$

where $i = 0,1,2,3$; $\bar\imath = 4,5,6,7$ with inverse $h_I{}^A(x^A)$. The covariant differential of a vector X^A in this space V_8 is given by:

$$DX^A = dX^A + P^A{}_{BC}X^C dx^B \tag{27}$$

with $dx^A = (dx^\mu, d\dot x^\mu = dx^{\bar\mu})$. If we suppose V_8 admits distant parallelism then:

$$P^A{}_{BC} = h_I{}^A \partial_B h^I{}_C \tag{28}$$

with $\partial_B = (\partial_\mu \ \partial_{\bar\mu} = \partial/\partial \dot x^\mu)$ and a 'supertorsion' tensor exists:

$$T^C{}_{AB} = h_I{}^C T^I{}_{AB} = (\partial_A h^I{}_B - \partial_B h^I{}_A) h_I{}^C \tag{29}$$

Choose the following form for equation [26]:

$$h^I{}_A = \begin{bmatrix} h^i{}_\mu & 0 \\ h^{\bar\imath}{}_\mu & h^{\bar\imath}{}_{\bar\mu} \end{bmatrix} \tag{30}$$

where $h^{\bar\imath}{}_\mu$ and $h^{\bar\imath}{}_{\bar\mu}$ are undetermined but non-vanishing in general. We wish to show that in the resulting geometry the subspace spanned by the set of four V_8 $1-$forms $h^i{}_A$ is F_4. F_4 has as invariance group the following co-ordinate transformations which are a sub-group of the V_8 general co-ordinate substitutions $x^A \to x^{A'}(x^A)$:

$$x^{A'} = (x^{\mu'}(x^\mu), (\partial x^{\mu'}/\partial x^\mu)\dot x^\mu) \tag{31}$$

which yields:

$$dx^{A'} = \begin{bmatrix} \partial x^{\mu'}/\partial x^\mu & 0 \\ \dfrac{\partial^2 x^{\mu'}}{\partial x^\mu \partial x^\nu}\dot x^\nu & \partial x^{\mu'}/\partial x^\mu \end{bmatrix} dx^A$$

Under equation [31], h^i_μ and $h^{\bar{i}}_{\bar{\mu}}$ transform as space-time vectors, $h^{\bar{i}}_\mu$ transforms inhomogeneously, and equation [30] maintains its form. For the metric g_{AB} in V_8 we make the assumptions $g_{\mu\bar{\nu}} = g_{\bar{\mu}\nu} = g_{\bar{\mu}\bar{\nu}} = 0$, these conditions being invariant with respect to equation [31]. Assuming that:

$$g_{AB} = \eta_{IJ}h^I_A h^J_B, \; \eta_{IJ} = (\eta_{ij}, 0) \tag{32}$$

the length of an infinitesimal element becomes:

$$g_{AB}dx^A dx^B = g_{\mu\nu}dx^\mu dx^\nu$$

with $g_{\mu\nu}$ given by equation [11]. Similarly, substitution of equation [30] in equations [28] and [29] yields:

$$\left.\begin{aligned} P^i_{\mu\nu} &= \Gamma^i_{\mu\nu}, \; P^i_{\bar{\mu}\nu} = D^i_{\mu\nu} \\[6pt] T^i_{\mu\nu} &= F^i_{\mu\nu}, \; T^i_{\bar{\mu}\nu} = D^i_{\mu\nu}, \; T^i_{\mu\bar{\nu}} = -D^i_{\nu\mu} \end{aligned}\right\} \tag{33}$$

where we have used equation [22] and $\Gamma^i_{\mu\nu} = h^i_\sigma \Gamma^\sigma_{\mu\nu}$, $D^i_{\mu\nu} = h^i_\sigma D^\sigma_{\mu\nu}$. There are analogous relations for P^i_{AB} which we shall not be concerned with here. Applying equation [31] to equation [28] then gives the expected transformation laws for the right-hand sides in equation [33].

It is clear how the apparently distinct distant parallelism connections $\Gamma^\mu_{\nu\sigma}$, $D^\mu_{\nu\sigma}$ associated with F_4 are actually just components of a superconnection P^A_{BC} in a higher dimensional non-Riemannian space (V_8) with distant parallelism. To complete our demonstration that F_4 is a subspace of V_8 under the restriction of equation [30] we show how the F_4 torsion vector arises. To this end define the infinitesimal supertorsion vector in V_8 to be:

$$b^I = \tfrac{1}{2}T^I_{AB}dx^A \wedge dx^B \tag{34}$$

where $b^I = (b^i, b^{\bar{i}})$. Substituting equation [33] in equation [34] then yields:

$$b^i = D^i_{\mu\nu}d\dot{x}^\mu \lambda dx^\nu + \tfrac{1}{2}F^i_{\mu\nu}dx^\mu \lambda dx^\nu \tag{35}$$

which agrees with our previously derived result equation [24], where $b^i = h^i_\mu b^\mu$.

Note that the supertorsion tensor in V_8 obeys Bianchi identities $db^I = 0$, i.e. $\partial_{(C}T^I_{AB)} = 0$, and these induce the following identities in F_4:

$$\left.\begin{aligned} &\partial_{(\sigma}F^i_{\mu\nu)} = 0 \\[6pt] &\partial_{\bar{\sigma}}F^i_{\mu\nu} + \partial_\nu D^i_{\sigma\mu} - \partial_\mu D^i_{\sigma\nu} = 0 \\[6pt] &\partial_{\bar{\sigma}}D^i_{\mu\nu} - \partial_{\bar{\mu}}D^i_{\sigma\nu} = 0 \end{aligned}\right\} \tag{36}$$

It should be clear that our notion of a space-time ether can be consistently extended to relativistic velocity phase space, and that is what we shall do. The geometry V_8 described above is then interpreted as the natural state of a deformed eight-dimensional continuum, the vielbein coefficients defining an anholonomic map between deformed and natural states ($h^I = h^I{}_A dx^A$), the supertorsion defining a density of dislocations (see below), etc.

We now discuss the application of Stokes' theorem in the phase space ether. Following our remarks above concerning the Burgers circuit, we define the Burgers vector of the natural state to be:

$$B^I = \int_{\partial\Sigma} h^I{}_A dx^A \qquad [37]$$

where $B^I = (B^i, B^{\bar{i}})$ and $\partial\Sigma$ is the boundary of a surface Σ in the deformed state of the phase space ether. Stokes' theorem then yields:

$$B^I = \int_{\Sigma} \tfrac{1}{2} T^I{}_{AB} dx^A \wedge dx^B \qquad [38]$$

and letting the circuit become infinitesimal we deduce equation [34], showing that the supertorsion tensor represents the density of dislocations threading an infinitesimal area in velocity phase space. Note that although the vielbein field may be subject to local super-Lorentz transformations $L^{I'}{}_I(x^A)$ which leave the phase space metric (equation [32]) invariant, in equation [37] we have fixed the frame (so that this relation is globally super-Lorentz covariant and generally covariant).

Returning to our space-time subspace we find by substituting equation [35] in equation [38], or using equation [30] in equation [37], that the Burgers vector associated with a finite closed circuit in the deformed ether is given by:

$$B^i = \int_{\partial\Sigma} h^i{}_\mu(x, \dot{x}) dx^\mu \qquad [39]$$

If we utilize the relation [17] we obtain finally for our electrodynamic Burgers vector:

$$B^i = \int_{\partial\Sigma} u^i dS \qquad [40]$$

Consider the case where the Burgers vector vanishes for all circuits in phase space, i.e. the case of no dislocations. Then from equation [29]:

$$h^I{}_A = \partial_A \varphi^I(x^A)$$

and if there are no topological obstructions (all cycles are bounding) this holds globally (de Rham's theorem). In the F_4 geometry (equation [30]) this means:

$$h^i{}_\mu = \partial_\mu \varphi^i(x^\mu)$$

i.e. the tetrad is independent of the particle characteristics. One may show from the vanishing of the dislocation density $D^i_{\mu\nu}$ that $A_\mu = 0$ or $k = 0$ and so the strain tensor (equation [9]) vanishes. The converse is also true, so that we have the result: there are no dislocations if and only if there are no strains, the necessary and sufficient condition for this being $A_\mu = 0$ or $k = 0$. In this case we see from equation [12] that $g_{\mu\nu} = \eta_{ij}\bar{h}^i_\mu\bar{h}^j_\nu$ and the φ's above are a constant translation from the global Lorentz co-ordinates z^i. It is not possible for the ether to support a pure strain without a corresponding distribution of dislocations. Note that pure gauge potentials ($A_\mu = \partial_\mu\varphi$) therefore generate both kinds of deformation (see section 7).

We make two further remarks. Firstly, we may deduce from condition [23] the following expressions for the F_4 connection coefficients:

$$\Gamma_{\sigma\mu\nu} = \{\sigma,\mu\nu\} + \tfrac{1}{2}(F_{\sigma\mu\nu} + F_{\mu\sigma\nu} + F_{\nu\sigma\mu})$$

$$D_{\sigma\mu\nu} = C_{\sigma\mu\nu} + \tfrac{1}{2}(D_{\sigma\mu\nu} - D_{\nu\mu\sigma})$$

where $C_{\sigma\mu\nu} = \partial g_{\mu\nu}/\partial\dot{x}^\sigma$ is a totally symmetric tensor. These formulae show how the affine properties of the natural state are determined by the distribution of dislocations and strains. Secondly, the analysis of this section can be just as readily carried out in (x, p) phase space if we make a Legendre transformation in the usual way. A contact tensor calculus has been developed by Yano and Davies[35].

7 On the physical conception of classical electrodynamics and the significance of the potentials

We have revealed a considerable amount of geometrical information which is latent in the Lagrangian (equation [3]). Indeed our approach may be seen as a means of bringing out the significance of the Lagrangian method, which goes deeper than just the Euler-Lagrange relations.

If we treat the Hamilton-Jacobi phase as a real field, or continuous medium, permeating the background space-time M_4, the presence and interaction of field and particle in M_4 may be represented by the natural state F_4 of the medium. This idea makes sense since we have available to us two metrics at each space-time point which allows a comparison to be made between two states, a notion that is essential to the theory of deformed media. We emphasize that it is not that the field and particle are in some way embedded in a medium so that they bring about its deformation in a direct physical sense but rather that the state of deformation *represents*, or is an alternative way of thinking about, their interaction. Moreover, the deformation representing the potentials only occurs if there is a test particle present. Conversely the test particle may also potentially be represented by a deformation, but only when the field is present. Thus, *the actual* *deformation representing A_μ depends irreducibly on the presence or absence of a particle acted on by the field and cannot be thought of in any other way.* It is in this way that we treat the interaction which in the ordinary theory is expressed through the velocity dependence of the Lorentz force. This conception is rather close to the notion of wholeness introduced by Bohr, and elaborated by Bohm[36] in terms of real physical processes, in the quantum theory. Here a complete account of physical phenomena requires not only consideration of the 'observed system' (e.g. a particle) but also detailed knowledge of the environment, the 'observing apparatus', and these two aspects form an irreducible whole – it would be meaningless to think of one without reference to the other. The implications of the present theory for quantum mechanics will be considered elsewhere, but we consider it significant that our approach readily generalizes to the notion of continuously dislocated phase space, as described in section 6. We already have built into our theory therefore the idea of irreducible closure failures in phase space, which may imply a geometrical basis for the uncertainty relations.[37]

On the level that is testable (Lorentz force law) our theory is experimentally indistinguishable from the Maxwell-Lorentz theory. However we have achieved more than a mere mathematical rewording of the Maxwell-Lorentz scheme. Rather, by slanting our perspective towards geometry, we have brought to light the following facts.

1   A new approach to electrodynamics is possible based on entities (h^i) which have no counterpart in the Maxwell-Lorentz view.

2   This new viewpoint depends on an irreducible coalescing of field and particle attributes and it is in this context that the potentials play a central role in classical electrodynamics.

The situation is analogous to the relation between the causal and Copenhagen interpretations of quantum mechanics[38], which are mathematically equivalent. However, the causal approach is able to account for quantum phenomena in terms of real physical processes whereas the orthodox view denies such an attempt. Such an alternative physical perspective may then suggest changes in the formalism and hence domains where the competing theories lead to different predictions.

We now examine the above two points. The uncovering of the natural frames effectively increases the degrees of freedom of electrodynamics. Thus we may think of our scheme as replacing the potentials and velocity by tetrad coefficients, the field strengths by torsion tensors and the scalar electromagnetic flux integral by a vectorial quantity, the electrodynamic Burgers vector (equation [40], with equation [2] substituted). Correspondingly there is a change in concept, the reduction of force to geometry entailed in the transformation from equation [5] to equation [6] being equivalent to dropping Faraday's notion of lines of force in the background space-time M_4 in favour of the notion of lines of dislocation in the space-time ether.

Whereas we would normally think of $F_{\mu\nu}$ as the density of electro-magnetic lines of force threading an area which a particle may traverse and be acted upon, this idea is replaced by that of a density of electro-dynamic lines of dislocation, which do not act in the sense of exerting a force on some particle but whose distribution represents the particle along with the field. Identities [36] state that 'lines of dislocation never end'.

Each of the entities of the Maxwell-Lorentz theory can be obtained from our new functions by a kind of 'averaging' process which yields them as a result of contracting the internal Lorentz index along a tangent vector. Thus:

$$u_i h^i = dS \tag{41}$$

$$u_i h^i_{\ \mu} = u_\mu + kA_\mu \tag{42}$$

$$u^i h_i^{\ \mu} = (1 + Y)^{-1} u^\mu \tag{43}$$

$$u_i F^i_{\ \mu\nu} = kF_{\mu\nu} + [1 - (1 + Y)^{\frac{1}{2}}] (\partial_\mu u_\nu - \partial_\nu u_\mu) \tag{44}$$

$$u_i D^i_{\ \mu\nu} = (\eta_{\alpha\beta} \dot{x}^\alpha \dot{x}^\beta)^{-\frac{1}{2}} [1 - (1 + Y)^{\frac{1}{2}}] (\eta_{\mu\nu} - u_\mu u_\nu) \tag{45}$$

where equation [41] follows from equation [17], equation [42] is essentially the canonical momentum equation [10] and equation [43] follows from equation [14]. Relations [44] and [45] indicate the manner in which Faraday's lines of force are in a sense included in our theory but in a way that is related to the particle characteristics – dislocation lines represent their presence on equal terms with the field. The magnitude of the Burgers vector measures the total number of lines of dislocation linking a surface in the space-time ether.

Within the framework proposed here we have shown that treating the field strengths as the only physically meaningful entities would be analogous to attempting a description of a dislocated medium by treating its natural frame field as incidental. In reality the latter is the carrier of all the relevant structural properties. To bring this out more clearly, let us consider the classical system which is relevant to the experimental set-up of the AB effect. From the point of view of M_4, which we now describe with the aid of a global system of Lorentz co-ordinates $x^\mu (\eta_{\mu\nu} = (1, -1, -1, -1))$, consider a multiply-connected region in which $F_{\mu\nu} = 0$ so that $A_\mu = \partial_\mu \varphi$ locally. It follows from equation [5] that in this region the particle velocities u^μ, i.e. the tang-ent vectors in the deformed state, are constant along trajectories (which, of course, are geodesics in M_4). From the standpoint of the dislocated ether model in the natural state F_4 the implications of these conditions are the following: the tetrad frame and metric are given by equations [12] and [8] respectively, with $u^\mu = $ constant, $A_\mu = \partial_\mu \varphi$ and $\bar{h}^i_{\ \mu} = \delta^i_\mu$; the Lorentz torsion tensor (equation [25]) is given by:

$$F^i_{\ \mu\nu} = \tfrac{1}{2} k (1 + Y)^{-\frac{1}{2}} u^\beta [(\delta^i_\nu - u^i u_\nu) \partial_\mu A_\beta - (\delta^i_\mu - u^i u_\mu) \partial_\nu A_\beta]$$

the torsion tensor $D^i_{\mu\nu}$ is a non-differential function of A_μ which we do not give; and there is a non-vanishing Burgers vector (equation [39] or [40]). We thus have strains, dislocation densities and a non-vanishing Burgers vector in the ether where, throughout the relevant region in the deformed state, the potentials are locally pure gauge and the velocities constant.

This implies that the present theory considerably over-determines classical electrodynamic processes. We have shown in section 3 that the Lorentz law may be interpreted as a gauge-independent example of ether observability through the strain tensor (equation [9]). We might speculate that the structures we have revealed may provide a broad enough perspective to anticipate effects observable only in the quantum domain. Also, it is even possible that there are effects which go beyond those conceivable within the current quantum theory. We might suggest that the element in the present theory most relevant to the quantum theory is the line integral:

$$\int_{P(x,\dot{x})}^{Q(x,\dot{x})} h^i_{\ \mu} \mathrm{d}x^\mu$$

and that the Burgers vector (equation [39]) may imply gauge-invariant (or even gauge-dependent) effects. This would generalize Wu and Yang's[2] contention that electromagnetism is a gauge-invariant manifestation of a non-integrable phase factor.

Having been motivated by the AB effect we have in this article concentrated on analysing the dynamics of a particle in a given field. We shall discuss elsewhere Maxwell's equations which, according to the present approach, will be related to field equations in the tetrad coefficients, and also the implications of relaxing the condition of distant parallelism imposed on F_4, thus allowing non-vanishing affine curvature.

Acknowledgments

The authors wish to thank Professors G. S. Asanov, H. Rund, E. Kröner and H. J. Treder for valuable correspondence. One of us (P. R. Holland) acknowledges the financial support of the SERC and the other (C. Philippidis) the partial support of the SERC.

References

1   Y. Aharonov and D. Bohm, *Phys. Rev.*, **115**, 485 (1959).
2   T. T. Wu and C. N. Yang, *Phys. Rev.*, **D12**, 3845 (1975).
3   D. Bohm, *Proceedings of VIII International Congress on Low Temperature Physics*, Butterworths, London 1962.
4   K. Kawamura, *Z. Phys.*, **B29**, 101 (1978).
5   M. V. Berry, R. G. Chambers, M. D. Large, C. Upstill and J. C. Walmsley, *Eur. J. Phys.*, **1**, 154 (1980).

6   A Einstein, *Sidelights on Relativity*, Dutton, New York, 1922; repr. Dover, New York, 1983.
7   L. Jánossy, *Found. Phys.*, **2**, 9 (1972).
8   P. A. M. Dirac, *Nature*, **168**, 906 (1951).
9   D. Bohm and J.-P. Vigier, *Phys. Rev.*, **96**, 208 (1954).
10 D. Bohm and B. J. Hiley, *Found. Phys.*, **14**, 255 (1984).
11 N. Cufaro Petroni and J.-P. Vigier, *Found. Phys.*, **13**, 253 (1983).
12 J. P. Vigier, *Astron. Nachr.*, **303**, 55 (1982).
13 E. T. Whittaker, *History of the Theories of Aether and Electricity: The Classical Theories*, Nelson, London, 1962.
14 K. Kondo, *RAAG Memoirs*, **1**, D-1 (1955).
15 K. Kondo, *RAAG Memoirs*, **1**, D-5 (1955).
16 K. Kondo and M. Yuki, *RAAG Memoirs*, **2**, D-7 (1958).
17 B. A. Bilby, R. Bullough and E. Smith, *Proc. Roy. Soc.*, **A231**, 263 (1955).
18 B. A. Bilby and E. Smith, *Proc. Roy. Soc.*, **A236**, 481 (1956).
19 S. Amari, *RAAG Memoirs*, **3**, D-9 (1962).
20 B. A. Bilby, *Prog. Solid Mech.*, **1**, 329 (1960).
21 E. Kröner, in R. Balian (ed.), *Proc. Summer School on the Physics of Defects*, Les Houches, North-Holland, Amsterdam, 1981.
22 E. Kröner, *Int. J. Engng, Sci.*, **19**, 1507 (1981).
23 K. Kondo, *RAAG Memoirs*, **3**, D-10 (1962).
24 P. R. Holland, *Phys. Lett.*, **91A**, 275 (1982).
25 N. Rosen, *Phys. Rev.*, **57**, 147 (1940).
26 N. Rosen, *Found Phys.*, **10**, 673 (1980).
27 G. Randers, *Phys. Rev.*, **59**, 195 (1941).
28 H. Rund, *The Differential Geometry of Finsler Spaces*, Springer, Berlin, 1959.
29 S. Amari, *RAAG Memoirs*, **3**, D-15 (1962).
30 G. S. Asanov, *Finsler Geometry, Relativity and Gauge Theories*, D. Reidel, Dordrecht, 1985, problem 2.14.
31 G. S. Asanov, *Rep. Math. Phys.*, **11**, 221 (1977).
32 G. S. Asanov, *Ann. der Phys.*, **34**, 169 (1977).
33 G. S. Asanov, *Rep. Math. Phys.*, **13**, 13 (1978).
34 H. J. Treder, *Ann. der Phys.*, **35**, 377 (1978).
35 K. Yano and E. T. Davies, *Ann. Mat. Pura Appl.*, **37**, 1 (1954).
36 D. Bohm, *Wholeness and the Implicate Order*, Routledge & Kegan Paul, London, 1980.
37 P. R. Holland, 'The Geometry of Dislocated de Broglie Waves', IHP preprint (1986).
38 D. Bohm, *Phys. Rev.*, **85**, 166 (1952).
    J.-P. Vigier, C. Dewdney, P. R. Holland and A. Kyprianidis 'Causal particle trajectories and its interpretation of quantum mechanics', this volume p. 169.

20

Can biology accommodate laws beyond physics?

H. Fröhlich   *The University of Liverpool*

We assume that the laws of physics are never broken in biology. Basic statements beyond physics can, therefore, be made only in situations in which physics does not offer a definite answer. Such situations can arise in systems that are far from thermal equilibrium, as is the case in active biological systems.

Modern physics offers two basically different possibilities. One is connected with quantum mechanics, where individual processes are predicted with certain probabilities only. The other arises in open systems to which energy is supplied and where configurations connected with so called bifurcations arise where two or more possibilities for the development of the system exist.

Consider in quantum mechanics the transmission of a beam of electrons through a metal foil. This gives rise to the well-known diffraction patterns. For a single electron this pattern represents the probability of being deflected through a particular angle. Experimental test of quantum mechanics thus requires many electrons; the experiment with single electrons thus must be repeated many times, keeping the general arrangements unchanged. This experiment can be carried out successfully, although strictly speaking the arrangements will not remain the same owing to their interaction with the surroundings. Nevertheless the relevant features, distances, potentials, etc., can be kept unchanged.

Consider now, however, a biological system and assume that single processes may lead to big consequences. Assume, for instance, that a proton in the brain has two possibilities for tunnelling, as a consequence of which far-reaching nerve processes are initiated, different for the two possibilities. Quantum mechanics, in principle, can predict the relative probabilities of the two, but the experiment cannot be repeated as the initial structure may have basically been changed by the nerve processes.

We might now postulate that an agent exists that influences the tunnelling probabilities. In the present experiment this would not lead to a contradiction with quantum mechanics as it cannot be repeated. If such an agent would be assumed to exist, then one would be tempted, of course, to assume that it also can act on single electrons in the transmission experiment mentioned above, which can be repeated. In this case, however, the statistical predictions of quantum mechanics must not be influenced by the agent, which would require its influence to have properties that are non-local in time. The action of the agent could then be described as a fluctuation that in the long run is evened out if the non-local property of the agent would prevent it from repetitious action. The agent would then influence higher-order fluctuations only and thus be hardly noticeable.

A more radical hypothesis would restrict the possibilities of such an agent to living systems only. In that case one would be tempted to connect it with the possibility of the existence of free will. Experiments of a completely new type would have to be devised to establish the existence and properties of such a concept. This might be a task for David Bohm.

21

Some epistemological issues in physics and biology

Robert Rosen *Dalhousie University, Halifax*

Madness in great ones
Must not unwatched go.
        Hamlet

I am very pleased to have been invited to contribute to this Festschrift in honor of David Bohm. Although I have never personally met or corresponded with Dr Bohm, his writings were well known to me since I was a graduate student. Moreover, the epistemological struggles into which he has been drawn as a theoretical physicist have their counterpart in epistemological struggles into which I have been drawn as a theoretical biologist. I would like to address some of these latter in the considerations which follow, especially as they bear on the material basis of biological processes.

The fact is that the relation between theoretical physics and biology has, historically, never been close. For a long time, theoretical physics has concerned itself with the articulation of universal and general laws. From that perspective, biology seems limited to a rather small class of very special systems; indeed, *inordinately* special systems. Clearly, then, organisms were not the sort of thing that physicists seeking universal principles would look at. To a physicist, what makes organisms special is conceived as a plethora of constraints, initial conditions and boundary conditions which must be superimposed upon the true general physical laws and which must be independently stipulated before those laws bear directly upon the organic realm. Physicists rightly felt that the determination of such supplementary constraints was not their job. But no physicist has ever doubted that, since physics is the science of material nature in all of its manifestations, the relation of physics to biology is that of general to particular.

This view, which is a weak form of reductionism, is so commonplace that it is almost banal to state it explicitly. To suggest that it might not be true is viewed as a retreat to the most primitive kind of vitalism or animism. And yet, the facts are these.

1   At present, even in these days of 'molecular biology,' there is not one single inferential chain which leads from anything important in physics to anything important in biology, despite decades of concerted effort by some very clever people.

2   In every direct confrontation between universal physics and special biology, it is physics which has had to give ground.

Facts of this kind have led me to the position I am going to develop in these pages: that the basis on which theoretical physics has developed for the past three centuries is, *in several crucial respects*, too narrow and that, far from being universal, the conceptual foundation of what we presently call theoretical physics is still very special; indeed, far too much so to accommodate organic phenomena (and much else besides). That is, I will argue that it is physics, and not biology, which is special; that, far from contemporary physics swallowing biology as the reductionists believe, biology forces physics to transform itself, perhaps ultimately out of all present recognition.

Let me give a few examples to illustrate the assertions made above.

1   The open system

Biological phenomena of morphogenesis, especially in embryology, but also even at the molecular level, as in the folding of proteins into their active conformation, have always been deeply troubling to physicists. The inexorable emergence of successive waves of increasingly organized structures from an initially rather featureless zygote seems perversely to go 'the wrong way,' and flies insolently in the face of all physical intuition. Indeed, contemplation of the regulatory processes involved in even the earliest phases of embryonic development led the celebrated embryologist Driesch to deny that purely physical laws could ever comprehend them, and to embrace a rather vivid form of vitalism.

In the middle 1930s, von Bertalanffy and others noticed that the dynamics of open systems exhibited, of themselves, many parallels with the morphogenetic phenomena of biology. The stable steady-states of such systems manifested many inherent regulatory properties (e.g. equifinality), quite different in character from the equilibria of the closed systems which were the habitat of thermodynamics. In 1942, Rashevsky showed explicitly how a combination of chemical reaction and mechanical diffusion could make a spatially homogeneous steady state unstable; in such a system, any deviation from homogeneity would grow autocatalytically to generate spontaneously a gradient where none had been before, something which absolutely cannot happen in a closed system. In 1952 Turing proposed an independent and simpler version of the same basic situation. In the mid-1960s the physicist Prigogine, among others, realized how such perfectly plausible and commonplace physical situations transcended available physical theory, and had to set furiously to work extending the *physics* in order to accommodate them.

Although the *dynamical* study of such open systems is presently of great interest (variously called stability theory, bifurcation theory, catastrophe theory, etc.), the physical basis of the phenomena they manifest is still, in my opinion, in an extremely unsatisfactory state. This is largely because, in physics, the closed system is still taken as primary, and opening the system is regarded as some kind of perturbation. But a closed system is, in dynamical terms, so extremely non-generic that there is not much which can be said in general along this line. It seems much more reasonable, rather, to regard the closed system in its proper light, as an extremely degenerate case of open ones. But if we do this, all the conventional theoretical tools, both of thermodynamics and statistical mechanics, fail irretrievably, and we must start anew. So we see here how the most elementary situations can transcend the concerted power of centuries of accumulated physical law, without being in any sense 'unphysical' or vitalistic.

With protein folding, the situation is even worse because, in physical terms, the folding of an initially-random polypeptide chain into an active conformation seems to be nothing more than a simple free-energy minimization. Unfortunately a typical polypeptide chain may involve hundreds of individual amino-acid residues, and each of these involves ten atoms or so, so the writing of an appropriate free-energy function and, even more, its minimization, is technically very difficult. It is known, from denaturation–renaturation experiments, among other things, that the free-energy surface for such a system *should* have a single deep minimum; the transition from random to biologically active (folded) structure is rather fast and very accurate. On the other hand, the more refined the free-energy computations become, the flatter are the surfaces so generated, with many local, shallow minima in which the structures get trapped. If this discordance is not resolved, once again a most serious challenge will be presented, not to biology but to physical theory.

2   Active sites, specificity, recognition

Let us stay at the molecular level, for it is here that one would expect physical theory to have its most immediate direct impact on biology. And yet even here the most elementary considerations force us outside the reach of the most powerful theory physics knows – quantum mechanics.

In some of my own earliest published work [1] I considered the problem of what the microphysical basis for specificity would have to be like. In that work (which considered explicitly the vehicle for carrying primary genetic information) it was straightforwardly supposed that such an information-carrying active site would consist of a family of quantum-mechanical observables in a standard way. The mathematical properties of this family are constrained by the biological prerequisites for the stability and accessibility of the information; basically a form of the measurement problem with which Dr Bohm has dealt at such great length. Under these conditions it turned out that this family of observables, which in an abstract sense describes a perfectly good microphysical system, does not have a Hamiltonian; hence no Schrödinger equation, no wave functions, etc. It is thus immune to study by conventional theoretical means. We may interpret the relation of this sub-system of observables to the entire molecule in which it is embedded in the following way; the active site is an example of a sub-system which is *not physically fractionable* from the molecule. That is, there is no physical procedure which can separate the molecule into two parts or sub-systems, one of which is the active site and the other of which is 'everything else'. We can describe the whole *molecule* in standard quantum-theoretic terms (at least in principle; in fact, I believe the hydrogen molecule is still technically unconquered), but we cannot recover the site from this description. In this connection it is ironic to note that, long ago, the famous chemist Willstätter refused to accept the conventional identification of enzyme with protein; it was his contention that protein was simply an unavoidable contaminant of enzyme. In a sense, the above considerations support this view; enzyme is active site, not entire molecule, but the site is not fractionable from the molecule in which it is embedded.

The idea that every sub-system is fractionable is basic to a stronger form of reductionism common among biologists (especially molecular biologists). It is an embodiment of an analytical philosophy going back to the idea that 'mixtures' or heterogeneous phases could always be resolved into 'pure phases,' and that the properties of any mixture could be inferred from those of the constituent pure phases. This idea, in the form of 'superposition,' survives in an essential way even in modern quantum mechanics. The above very elementary considerations indicate that it is generally false and, thus, theory based upon it is at best of circumscribed validity.

Before leaving this subject, let us consider another of its practical implications. In a certain sense, the importance of a Hamiltonian is that, knowing it, the dynamics of *any* arbitrary observable α is also known, through a classical or quantum version of the relation:

$$d\alpha/dt = [E, \alpha]$$

where E is the Hamiltonian and $[\ldots]$ is the Poisson bracket. If there is no Hamiltonian, then the dynamics of arbitrary observables is decoupled from any *a priori* principle; in particular, there is no reason any more to believe that the observables which characterize, say, the specificity of an active site are related to, or functions of, any of the conventional observables used in physics, or directly measurable by means of the physical instruments we conventionally use.

This point, although tangential to the considerations which follow, is worth pursuing a bit further. We may illustrate by means of a simple and artificial example, of a purely classical kind. Consider the Hamiltonian:

$$H(x, p) = p^2/2m + kx^2/2$$

i.e. the classical one-dimensional harmonic oscillator. In this situation, an observable $u = u(x, p)$ is any numerical function of phase. Thus, $u = x^5$, to pick something simple at random, is an observable. It inherits an equation of motion:

$$du/dt = [E, u] = 5x^4p/m$$
$$= v, \text{ say}$$

Here $v = v(x, p) = 5x^4p/m$ is just another observable. It too inherits an equation of motion, which can be readily verified to be:

$$dv/dt = [E, v] = 4mv^2/5u + 5ku$$

That is, if we were to measure the observables (u, v) of the harmonic oscillator, instead of the conventional observables (x, p), we would see a very different system, of the form $du/dt = f(u, v)$, $dv/dt = g(u, v)$.

Thus, the observables of even an apparently simple system, like the harmonic oscillator, can realize many different kinds of dynamics, depending on which observables we interact with. There are even simple Hamiltonian systems which are *universal*, in the sense that they possess observables which inherit *any arbitrary* prescribed dynamics (cf. reference 2); that is, among the observables of such a system we can find *anything*. Such a system possesses, in a sense, an infinity of natures, and which one we see depends entirely on how we look at the system. Universal systems thus are ready-made universal simulators or analogs.

Mathematically, the above can be looked at as simply applying some non-canonical transformation to the 'true' variables of phase. But in a system like an organism, or even an active site, we have no idea of what the 'true' variables are, or even if there are any. The important thing in understanding specificity is to determine how the systems involved see each other, and there is no reason to believe that this is simply related to how we see them individually. In short, such considerations suggest that biological recognition mechanisms (which, as we noted previously, manifest a form of the measurement problem) may involve observables quite different from those with which physics has conventionally dealt. Once again, there is nothing unphysical about them, except that physics has unduly neglected them.

3   Relational biology

This was the name given by N. Rashevsky to a kind of holistic approach to organisms which he initiated in the early 1950s. Rashevsky, himself trained as a theoretical physicist, had spent the preceding quarter-century pioneering the idea that there could be a theoretical biophysics, related to experimental biology in the way theoretical physics is related to experimental biology. He did this by constructing explicit physical model systems for biological phenomena. We have already mentioned one; his model for the autonomous generation of a gradient on the basis of reaction and diffusion of chemical species. This in turn was a corollary of his general approach to cytokinesis (cell division). He had also developed the first workable theory of excitable tissue, culminating in the first comprehensive theory of the brain and of brainlike behavior (memory, learning, discrimination, and the like). He developed, together with his many students, pioneering approaches to the physiology and architecture of cardiovascular dynamics, the forms of organisms, and literally dozens of other topics.

But, around 1950, Rashevsky himself became dissatisfied with what he was so successfully doing. As he himself had realized, somewhere along the line he was taking he had lost the organism. To get it back he recognized that something radical would have to be done. What he did, basically, was to invent a whole new approach to the theory of biological systems, which was the inverse or dual of the one which he had been using as a physicist. As a physicist, he had abstracted away all organizational, integrative aspects of organic phenomena, leaving behind only a material system, to be treated in the same way as any other material system. The faith was that such an abstraction was only apparent; that the organizational properties would re-emerge from the underlying physics. But this seemed to be at best only partially true.

So Rashevsky asked, in effect, what would happen if we were to throw away the physics and keep only the organization. This is not as strange a thing to do as might first appear. We recognize an unlimitedly large number of different kinds of material systems as being organisms; between an amoeba and a man, say, there is hardly a molecule in common. If we persist in taking an overly simplistic material view, we must confront the basic question of how material systems of such vastly different kinds can behave so similarly, while at the same time being doomed to do biology an organism at a time.

Similarity of organization, of function, is indeed at the root of what we really want to know and understand about organisms, as it is at the basis of our deeply-held conviction that we can recognize an organism when we see one. This subjective conviction is what underlies biology as a separate science, and it has always resisted a facile reductionistic characterization. That is why all attempts to 'define life' have failed, and that is how we know that they have failed. So what Rashevsky sought was a kind of universal *bauplan* of functional organization, which must be manifested by anything we would want to call an organism, but which could be executed concretely, or physically, in many different ways. Thus, instead of starting with a particular organism as a material system and trying to discover its organization from its physics, Rashevsky suggested starting with an abstract organization, and recovering the physics through material *realizations* of this organization. That was what he called relational biology.

Behind these apparent simplicities lies a plethora of the deepest and most profound epistemological questions. Starting from a conviction that relational descriptions of organisms are equally valid, and equally real, as conventional physical ones, the fundamental problem was how to fit the two together. By their very nature, relational descriptions fall outside conventional physics. So once again, in a different way from before, we find that the most elementary biological considerations force us to do things that physics has never done, and thus cannot provide the merest hint how to proceed. Indeed, it was the attempt to provide a material basis for my own early work in relational cell models that forced me to confront epistemological problems of this kind. More than that, it forced me to the conviction which I have tried to motivate above; that biology has infinitely more to tell the physicist than physics presently has to tell the biologists. In the remaining pages, I will try to sketch a few of these things.

I have stated above that, in my opinion, the conceptual framework within which physics has historically developed is too narrow to accommodate organic phenomena. Indeed, it is inadequate in several distinct and independent ways. I shall briefly discuss two of them; the first, while of basic importance, is not truly radical; the second is both important and radical.

Both of the problems I shall discuss go to the very heart of theoretical science. No one, be he observer, experimentalist, or theoretician, can do science at all without some conviction that natural phenomena are orderly; that they obey laws which can be, at least in part, articulated and grasped by the intellect. This basic belief is generally summed up in a single word: *causality*. But there is more to it than this. In brief, we also believe that this *causal* order relating events in the external world can be imaged formally, in terms of purely *logical* relationships between propositions describing these events. Indeed, this is precisely what 'natural law' means; that causal relations in the external world can be made to correspond precisely to implications in some appropriate logical (i.e. mathematical) system.

Attention is thus drawn to the logical or mathematical systems which can image events in the external world. It is the main task of theoretical science to construct and interrogate such images. The deepest parts of theoretical science are all concerned, at root, with the class of mathematical systems which can be images of physical reality, and with the relations which exist between such images. The thrust of mechanics, either classical or quantum, is to construct canonically such classes of images, and to establish homomorphisms between them which are mainly interpreted reductionalistically. On the other hand, the thrust of the laws of thermodynamics, or of relativity, is to circumscribe the class of mathematical systems which can be images of physical reality.

The most familiar kind of mathematical image of physical events is that of a mathematical function or relation involving a sequence of arguments belonging to some manifold or set. Let me consider a particular example, which clearly illustrates the points I wish to make; the relation:

$$(p + a/v^2)(v - b) = rT$$

This is an *equation of state* describing the equilibrium points of a class of non-ideal gases (the van der Waals equations). Here p, v, T are the state variables of the gas (pressure, volume, temperature), and a, b, r are parameters.

Mathematically, this is a single relationship:

$$\Phi(p, v, T, a, b, r) = 0$$

among six arguments. There is thus nothing available mathematically to distinguish any of these arguments from any other; the distinction we have informally drawn between state variables and parameters has no mathematical counterpart. And yet, intuitively, there is the greatest possible distinction between them; the parameters determine for us the *species* of gas we are dealing with, while the state variables determine the 'secular' features which this species manifests under given conditions.

Even the state variables must be given differing interpretations. Basically, the van der Waals equation says that if two of them (p, T, say) are specified, then at equilibrium the volume v is determined thereby. But these values of p, T are set by the nature of the external world; they are determined by processes which do not obey the law (i.e. the van der Waals equation) governing the system itself. Thus, their values are determined, not by the system law, but by the system *environment*. Once these are set, the law says that, at equilibrium, the remaining argument v must have the value mandated by the law.

Thus we have partitioned the undifferentiated arguments of the van der Waals equation into three utterly distinct classes:

1   the system *genome* (a, b, r);
2   the system *environment* (p, T);
3   the system *phenotype* (v).

I have deliberately chosen this rather provocative terminology to suggest a biological parallel I wish to stress.

As noted previously, the above distinctions disappear if we interpret the van der Waals equation simply as a mathematical relation involving six arguments. The mathematics has abstracted away these distinctions and, to recapture them, we must augment the mathematics. We will do this in two stages.

First, let us rewrite the van der Waals equation, formally, as:

$$\Phi_{abr}(p, v, T) = 0$$

This is now a three-parameter family of relations, each involving three arguments. The distinction we have informally drawn between parameters and state variables is now reflected mathematically as follows: the parameters a, b, r now act as *coordinates in a function space*; they identify or pick out a particular function from a family of functions. The state variables are now the common arguments of the functions of this family.

The distinction between environment and phenotype must now be embodied mathematically. We will do this by rewriting the three-parameter family of relations as a genome-parameterized family of mappings *from environments to phenotypes*:

$$\Phi_{abr} : (p, T) \rightarrow (v)$$

We claim[3] that every linkage between physical observables, every equation of state, can (and in fact must) be written in this way.

The apparently straightforward rewriting we have exemplified with the van der Waals equation is far from trivial, either mathematically or epistemologically. From the mathematical standpoint, we have turned the arena of discourse from a six-manifold into a more structured mathematical object; something like a fiber space (for the van der Waals equation, exactly a fiber space) with a base space of genomes, and a fiber of state variables. In our special case, the equation of state (i.e. the van der Waals equation) defines a family of cross-sections which, physically, are *corresponding states* for every different species of gas; we have shown elsewhere how general questions of similarity and scaling are posed in terms of the stability of the genome-parameterized family $\{\Phi_{abr}\}$, and how they bear on major biological problems of evolution and development, but we cannot touch on this matter here.

Epistemologically, there are two issues raised by the above considerations. First, the rewriting shows explicitly that we never construct mathematical images of single systems, but of classes or families of systems, with the same states but different genomes. For each individual system in the class, the entire class creates a *context*; different ways of embedding a single system into such a class create different such contexts. By concentrating on individual systems and forgetting the context, the mathematical images we have been using have become too abstract; they have neglected or forgotten certain crucial features of physical reality. By considering a system devoid of any particular context, we have in effect identified such a system with a whole class of contexts; in mathematical terms, we have identified a space of states with the class of all fiber spaces of which it can be a fiber. Naturally, much is lost in this process.

Let us see exactly what is lost. The partition of the arguments of an equation of state into genome, environment and phenotype turns out[3] to be closely related to the old Aristotelian categories of causation; genome can be identified with *formal cause*, environment with *efficient cause*, and state itself with *material cause*. These categories are distinct and non-interchangeable; neglect of this fact has been responsible for endless mischief in theoretical biology and elsewhere. Our rewriting, then, serves to re-introduce a definite causal structure into the mathematical description of a system; a causal structure which disappears when we revert to the standard description. That is, our familiar way of describing physical reality in terms of relations on manifolds uses the same mathematical object to describe distinct systems of entirely different causal structures; it cannot therefore discriminate these structures. This is just another way of saying that the old language can only describe equivalence classes and that, to probe these equivalence classes, we must introduce more mathematical structure from the outset; change our epistemology at the very root.

Let us give a single illustration of the importance of making these causal distinctions. In his attempts to construct a 'self-reproducing automaton,' von Neumann[4] argued that, because a universal computing machine must exist[5], a universal *constructor* must also exist. Basically, his argument was that since construction (following a blueprint) and computation (following a program) are both algorithmic processes, whatever is true for computation must be true for construction. However, in the terminology we have been using, it is not hard to show that computation involves *efficient* cause, while construction (if it is to mean anything at all) involves *material* cause. The inequivalence of the categories of causation invalidates this argument, and indeed makes it very risky to extrapolate from computer models to anything in biological development or evolution (as is often done).

We may note a parallel between the considerations sketched above, and the idea of 'hidden variables' in quantum theory. Essentially, both argue that a certain level of mathematical description of physical reality only characterizes equivalence classes. In our case, however, what is needed to penetrate the classes is more mathematical structure, not more variables.

The above considerations are important, in my opinion, but not truly radical. In my concluding remarks I will in fact suggest something which is radical indeed. Once again, I will be concerned with the class of mathematical or formal systems which can be images of physical reality, and with the epistemological significance of choosing such a class.

At the moment, every mode of system description which we possess in physics, biology, human sciences, technology, or anywhere else, is at heart the same as the one which Newton propounded in the seventeenth century. However much these modes of system description differ technically among themselves, they all share a fundamental dualism, which can be thought of as a separation between *states* and *dynamical laws*. In some sense, the states represent what is intrinsic about a system, while the dynamical laws reflect the effects of what is outside or external.

In terms of the Aristotelian categories of causation, which were mentioned earlier, the separation into states and dynamical laws amounts to a corresponding segregation of causal categories. This state, which as we have argued, corresponds to material causation, is partitioned off as an independent chunk from formal and efficient cause; if we look more closely at the concept of dynamical law, we will see that in writing equations of motion the categories of formal and efficient cause are likewise fractionated from each other. I would in fact argue that the paradigm of system description which we inherit essentially unchanged from Newtonian times is at heart precisely this: that *each category of causation is reflected in a logically independent aspect of system description.*

It has always been taken as absolutely axiomatic that systems must necessarily be described in a dualistic language of states plus dynamical laws. However, when this axiom is expressed as in the preceding paragraph, in terms of the independence it imposes on the categories of causation, it perhaps no longer appears so self-evident.

I would like to suggest that the class of material systems which can be described in this way is in fact a limited class, which I have called the class of *simple systems,* or *mechanisms.* Thus, in this language, a simple system is one to which a notion of state can be assigned once and for all; or more generally, one in which the Aristotelian causal categories can be independently segregated from one another. Any system for which such a description cannot be provided I will call *complex.* Thus, in a complex system, the causal categories become intertwined, in such a way that no dualistic language of states plus dynamical laws can completely describe it. Complex systems must then possess mathematical images different from, and irreducible to, the generalized dynamical systems which have been considered universal.

Let me briefly suggest a candidate for such a language, originally suggested by an attempt to provide a physical basis for certain ideas of biological information (for fuller details, cf. reference 6) using concepts of stability. Suppose for the sake of argument we are given a dynamical system description of the form:

$$\mathrm{d}x_i/\mathrm{d}t = f_i(x_1 \ldots x_n, \alpha_1 \ldots \alpha_r)$$

where the x_i are state variables, the α_j are parameters. From these, we can form the observables:

$$u_{ij} = \partial/\partial x_j(\mathrm{d}x_i/\mathrm{d}t)$$

If this quantity is positive in a given state, it means that a (virtual) increase in x_j will increase the rate of change of x_i (or equivalently, that a virtual decrease in x_j will decrease the rate of change of x_i). It thus makes sense to say that x_j *activates* x_i in the given state. Likewise, if u_{ij} is negative in a state, we can say that x_j *inhibits* x_i in that state. We can form analogous quantities using the parameters as well, but we will omit this for the time being.

The n^2 functions u_{ij} constitute what I have called an activation–inhibition pattern. The terminology suggests an intrinsically informational significance for these quantities; at the same time, they are closely related to the stability properties of the dynamical system from which they came. The question we may pose now is: suppose we know the quantities u_{ij}; that is, suppose we know the pairwise informational interactions between the state variables which these quantities represent. Can we reconstruct the dynamical equations themselves?

The way to do this is obviously to construct differential forms:

$$\sum_{j=1}^{n} u_{ij}\mathrm{d}x_j$$

For each i, this form must be $\mathrm{d}f_i$, the differential of velocity or rate of change of the state variable x_k. Thus we recapture the original dynamics by putting f_i equal to $\mathrm{d}x_i/\mathrm{d}t$.

However, this works only if the differential form $\mathrm{d}f_i$ is exact. And exactness is a highly non-generic situation. By presupposing that we must always start with states plus dynamical laws, we place an incredibly severe restriction on what an activation–inhibition pattern can be.

The necessary conditions for exactness of the differential forms $\mathrm{d}f_i$ are:

$$\frac{\partial}{\partial x_k}u_{ij} = \frac{\partial}{\partial x_j}u_{ik}, \quad \text{all } i,j,k$$

Now a quantity like $\partial/\partial x_k(u_{ij})$ also has an informational significance; it represents the effect of a (virtual) change in x_k on the degree to which x_j activates or inhibits x_i; that is, it expresses the degree to which x_k *agonizes* or *antagonizes* the effect of x_j on x_k. In this language, the conditions for exactness of $\mathrm{d}f_i$ become: the agonist–antagonist relation and the activator–inhibitor relation are interchangeable or symmetric or commutative. Once again, this is a most non-generic situation. Thus, if we characterize a system in terms of its informational interactions of which we have in effect only specified two layers so far, we are most unlikely to find that these arise from a dynamical system.

By iterating considerations of this type, we can provide a new class of candidates for the mathematical images of physical reality, which contain the conventional dynamical systems as a very special case. There are good reasons for believing that many material systems have images in this extended class, and are hence *complex*. From this perspective, what we now call physics is seen as the special situation it is; it is the science of simple systems or mechanisms.

There are many corollaries of adopting this point of view. Let us mention a few of them.

1   Traditional modes of reductionism, or of mathematical modelling of biological activities, have among other things the effect of replacing a putatively complex system by a simple sub-system. It can be shown, using the above considerations, that a complex system describable by a web of informational interactions as above can be approximated, but only locally and temporarily, by such a simple system. Indeed, this is apparently why we have been able to do so much science in the conventional dynamical framework. But as we watch a complex system over long times, our approximating simple systems become increasingly inadequate. Depending on the circumstances, this appears to us as emergence, or error, or a variety of other similar phenomena traditionally associated with complexity.

2   If organisms, say, are in fact complex systems, and if physics is in fact the science of simple systems, it follows that the relation of physics to biology is not that of general to particular. This reinforces the point made earlier; that to encompass organic phenomena it is physics which will have to be modified, perhaps in ways even more radical than can now be imagined. Indeed, one can even question whether there are any simple systems at all; if there are not, then our traditional universals evaporate entirely.

3   Complex systems can allow a meaningful, scientifically sound category of final causation; something which is absolutely forbidden within the class of simple systems. In particular, complex systems may contain sub-systems which act as predictive models of themselves and/or their environments, whose predictions regarding future behaviors can be utilized for modulation of present change of state. Systems of this type act in a truly anticipatory fashion, and possess many novel properties[7] whose properties have never been explored.

My intention, in the above discussion, has been to give some idea of the epistemological issues raised when we consider seriously how to attack the material basis of organic phenomena. I have tried to touch on a great many issues in a short space. I hope that the resultant telescoping and abbreviation have not resulted in any appearance of dogmatism; although I believe the problems I tried to raise are real and basic, all possibilities remain wide open. In a certain sense, my contribution is only an elaboration of a remark which Einstein made to Szilard: 'One can best appreciate, from a study of living things, how primitive physics still is.' I have often found myself wishing, in fact, that Einstein's uncle had given him a beetle instead of a magnet.

References

1   R. Rosen, 'A quantum-theoretic approach to genetic problems', *Bull. Math. Biophysics*, **22**, 227–55 (1960).

2   R. Rosen, 'On analogous systems', *Bull. Math. Biophysics*, **30**, 481–92 (1968).

3   R. Rosen, 'The role of similarity principles in data extrapolation', *Amer. J. Physiol.*, **244**, R591–9 (1983).

4   A. Burks, *Theory of Self-Reproducing Automata*, University of Illinois Press, Urbana, Illinois, 1966.

5   A. Turing, 'On compatible numbers', *Proc. London Math. Soc.*, Ser. 2, **42**, 230–65 (1936).

6   R. Rosen, 'Some comments on activation and inhibition', *Bull. Math. Biology*, **41**, 427–45 (1979).

7   R. Rosen, *Anticipatory Systems*, Pergamon Press, Oxford, 1985.

22

A science of qualities

B. C. Goodwin   *The Open University, Milton Keynes, UK*

This work did not belong to the class of austere, strictly objective enquiry; it was of that fantastical kind which often gropes far ahead into the future and which originates in some stimulus outside the scope of everyday scientific activity. However, it was built on sound foundations and there was much plausibility in its deductions, which pointed to there being a unity of experience hidden behind the ultimate nebulosity of our feeling and perception.

ROBERT MUSIL, *The Man Without Qualities*

Introduction

One of the more curious aspects of the history of Western science is that the dominant scientific world-view of the sixteenth century assumed a deep unity between nature and gnosis (knowledge), hidden but accessible to imaginative thought and feeling; whereas what emerged in the seventeenth century was a science based upon a profound division between mind and the nature it contemplates, so that an 'ontological gulf exists between consciousness and its object such that the real is, for the mind that relates to it cognitively, truly an object, that which stands over against the thinking mind, appearing *to* it but not *in* it'[1]. This dramatic change of perception emerged from a fierce and fateful struggle for legitimacy and power between the members of groups championing radically different programmes of development and reform in Europe at the end of the sixteenth and the beginning of the seventeenth century. Francis Yates identified the monk Mersenne as a key figure in the demise of what he saw as a threatening, reforming and transforming Renaissance conception of the cosmos: 'Mersenne attacks and discards the old Renaissance world; his Universal Harmony will have nothing to do with Francesco Giorgi, of whom he strongly disapproves'[2]. Giorgi, the Franciscan friar whose *De harmonica mundi* of 1525 had incorporated the unifying themes of the thirteenth-century philosopher and mystic, Ramon Lull, was one of the major figures in developing and articulating the tradition of Renaissance nature philosophy. Within this tradition, 'all of reality was a single co-ordinated domain, every region of which was intrinsically related to every other region, so that to know the region called nature entailed knowing the whole sphere of Being within which nature was embedded'[1]. Furthermore, this union of the knower and the known had the consequence that a change in one resulted in a co-ordinated change in the other, mind and nature therefore undergoing a co-operative transformation. But to achieve this knowledge and insight, the seeker had to make a commitment to spiritual enlightenment so as to experience gnosis, knowledge that transforms both self and other, mind and nature then simultaneously changing to states of greater harmony and unity. In alchemy, this dual transformation was described as golden illumination for the mind (or soul) of the practitioner of the art; while gold emerged in the crucible, nature undergoing simultaneous transmutation with spiritual illumination. Neither could occur without the other.

It was to this process of unified and unifying change that the Renaissance magi such as Francesco Giorgi, Johannes Reuchlin, John Dee and Giordano Bruno were committed in their science; while in social and political action, it involved them in commitment to radical change and reform. Mersenne correctly perceived this powerful sixteenth-century movement as a threat to what he considered to be the path of intellectual and political rectitude and stability. The science which he helped to shape in the seventeenth century, and which has come down to us as the dominant tradition of Western scientific and philosophical thought, is based upon dualisms which split the unified world of the Renaissance magi into separate domains of power, particularly that between mind and nature, and the threads of these dualisms can be found running through individual sciences as well as through our social and political structures. The struggle for unification continues against the power of established interests and habits of mind. I tend to see David Bohm's efforts to bring intelligibility and experiential unity into physics as a part of this struggle; and his intellectual and spiritual vision continues the tradition of the Renaissance magi, a tradition that has never died despite the apparent victory of Mersenne and Bacon in the seventeenth century. In this essay I shall briefly describe the roots and the main characteristics of this tradition, following closely Frances Yates' lucid and illuminating treatment[2], and the ways in which it still lives in biology, where it continues to challenge received dualist wisdom. Science, committed to unification and intelligibility, achieves its objectives in bizarre and historically tortuous ways.

The science of union

The Catalan philosopher and mystic, Ramon Lull (1232–1316) worked out a theory and practice of astral science and medicine which was based upon common components of the three dominant cultures of thirteenth-century Iberia – Moslem, Jewish and Christian. The common scientific principle was the theory of the elements (earth, air, fire, water) on which he based an astral science of correspondence between different levels of being – terrestrial, celestial and super-celestial. These were linked by their possession of similar elementary properties, developed in the principle of correspondences such that the near and the far, and three levels of being, were united by virtue of sharing basic characteristics. However, Lull rejected the one-way determinism of astrology, for his system involved active participation by the practitioner of his art in mounting the ladder of creation to, potentially, the greatest heights of insight and knowledge. Here was an early articulation of what was later expressed in the Renaissance as the miracle of humanity, capable of prodigious development within the appropriate context of ethical and intellectual effort. The religious basis of the art was also common to the three religious traditions, namely the nine divine attributes or dignities of God: *bonitas* (goodness), *magnitudo* (greatness), *eternitas* (eternity), *potestas* (power), *sapientia* (wisdom), etc. To these Lull assigned letters, A being the ineffable absolute, while B to K (without J) signified the nine manifest qualities. Since God's attributes are manifest on all levels of creation, we have here another unifying principle which allowed the practitioner to ascend and descend with the letters of the art throughout the universe. Lull linked the elements, designated ABCD, to the letters of the attributes, suggesting a kind of algebra which was connected also to a symbolic geometry in the form of triangle, circle and square for each of the levels of being, from top (super-celestial) to bottom (terrestrial), respectively. These abstract symbols assist the artist in moving through the complex levels of being and organization which are to be explored and experienced through a contemplative method which owes much to the mystical traditions associated with the different religions, particularly Sufism (Moslem) and cabala (Jewish). What Lull created was a remarkable culturally synthetic art-science, a precursor of scientific method which had an immense influence in Europe for centuries. It was a major stimulus to the great radical, reforming movements of the Renaissance.

One of the earliest manifestations of this influence appeared in the brilliant circle associated with the Medici court in Florence, where what is known as Renaissance neoplatonism was developed. This was a synthetic product of ancient wisdom and modern insight which incorporated both hermetic and cabalistic teaching. The great German humanist, Johannes Reuchlin (1455–1522), also known as Capnion, travelled in Italy as a young man and absorbed this teaching, developing it in his most famous work, *De arte cabalistica* (1517), the first full cabalist treatise by a non-Jew. It takes the form of a conversation between a Pythagorean, Philolaus, a Moslem, Marranus, and a cabalist, Simon ben Elieser, who meet in an inn in Frankfurt. From their discussion emerges a synthesis of cabalistic numerology, Pythagorean mathematics, and Moslem mysticism, a structure allowing the discovery of all that can be known which aids the co-operative transformation of mind and nature.

However, social and cultural synthesis is not so easily achieved as synthetic vision. The growth of Catholic power in Iberia in the fifteenth century led to a simpler form of religious unity than that envisioned by Lull, with the expulsion of the Jews in 1492 and of the Moors in 1505. And Reuchlin was the focus of a fierce anti-Semitic attack in Germany because of his espousal of Jewish scholarship and cabalistic teaching as elements in his transformational system of knowledge and action. German humanists succeeded in turning this attack against the perpetrators by the publication of a brilliant satirical work, *Letters of the Obscure Men*, and the wave of anti-Semitism subsided. The forces of reaction and division had nevertheless made an ominous appearance, and the witch-hunts against those seeking transforming experiential insight, labelled black magic or illicit knowledge, broke out repeatedly in the sixteenth century. Reuchlin was a reformer, seeking a mystical resolution of religious problems. Luther, his contemporary, sought a political solution. The fragmentation that followed Luther's attempts at reform in religion was matched by an equivalent fragmentation of scientific knowledge which followed upon the establishment by Mersenne and Bacon of science from which the astral linkings of Giorgi's universal harmony were banished, 'cutting off at the roots the connection of the psyche with the cosmos'[2]. Bacon was deeply suspicious of the active, imaginative mind, advocating the superiority of the disciplined mind as the surer way to scientific truth, which was to be patiently collected as objective knowledge from empirical data.

That the radical impersonalism of Bacon's method applies as well to Galilei, Descartes, Newton, and Leibnitz, for example, is clear once one recalls the essentially deductive and intellectualistic character of the methods espoused by those four. Their focus on rigorous discursive reasoning as the medium for the articulation of truth eventuated in a universe whose atomic constituents were only extrinsically correlated with one another, obeyed generic laws of interaction that made no provision for individual characteristics, and was held together by a mysterious yet clearly non-anthropomorphic force: gravity. In startling contrast to this world-picture, the world-picture of the Renaissance nature philosophy was of a Cosmos composed of intrinsically correlated elements, hierarchically ordered in accordance with anthropomorphic values, and held together by a force called 'love'.[1]

There was no intrinsic necessity for science to have the characteristics which it assumed in the seventeenth century, resulting in the predominantly atomistic and mechanical components that characterize scientific descriptions, and leading to a world-view in which separate identity is primary and connected relationship is secondary. A choice was made, with particular consequences regarding the relations between part and whole, between the intelligible and the 'real', among the individual and society and the cosmos. As Bohm[3] has argued:

It is proposed . . . that the widespread and pervasive distinctions between people (race, nation, family, profession, etc., etc.) which are now preventing mankind from working together for the common good, and indeed, for survival, have one of the key features of their origin in a kind of thought that treats *things* as inherently divided, disconnected, and 'broken up' into yet smaller constituent parts. Each part is considered to be essentially independent and self-existent.

However, he also points out that:

Science itself is demanding a new, non-fragmentary world-view, in the sense that the present approach of analysis of the world into independently existent parts does not work very well in modern physics. It is shown that both in relativity theory and quantum theory, notions implying the undivided wholeness of the universe would provide a much more orderly way of considering the general nature of reality.[3]

I shall now consider how the analytical tradition, resulting in a biology dominated by atomistic (molecular) fragmentation, results in problems whose resolution lies also in concepts based upon wholeness and relational order in organisms, similar in certain basic respects to those proposed by Bohm[3] for physical reality in his remarkable book *Wholeness and the Implicate Order*.

The biology of Humpty-Dumpty

Humpty-Dumpty was, before his great fall, what biology is basically all about: an egg, embodiment of the potential for reproduction with transformation, which makes the creative process of evolution possible. After the fall, which started in the seventeenth century and was completed in the nineteenth only the pieces remained to baffle all the King's horses and all the King's men. What has emerged from twentieth century biology is that there are many more pieces than anyone ever dreamed of, and more are being discovered every day; rather like elementary particle physics, one might say, only more so. How are we to make sense of this molecular profusion, to construct an intelligible conceptual unity and so to understand organisms and their evolution? Following the traditional dualism of the mind–nature split, there is a strong tendency in biology to assume that organisms have an 'intelligent' controlling aspect and a passive, quasi-inanimate, controlled aspect. The controlling part embodies the essential principles of the biological state; the capacity to reproduce, to keep the parts working in relation to one another, to evolve and to adapt. The organism is thus seen as a dualistic mechanism, like a computer with its 'intelligent' software (programme) and its passive hardware which responds to instructions coded in the programme. And this is precisely the metaphor used in biology to explain the relationship between the DNA with its hereditary instructions, which are intelligently translated into proteins via the genetic code; and the organism which is made out of these proteins and their products. This computer metaphor for organismic structure and function has proved extremely useful in the analysis of the relationships between the different types of macromolecule (DNA, RNA and protein) which are distinctive to organisms, and in describing changes of molecular state during embryonic development and evolution. This is the successful face of molecular biology, based upon ingenious techniques of molecular analysis, many of which exploit basic macromolecular processes distinctive to organisms themselves, such as immunological (antigen–antibody) reactions, DNA replication (gene cloning) and DNA–RNA interactions (hybridization). There is absolutely no doubt about the extraordinary analytical power of these techniques, and the value of descriptions arrived at in relation to understanding the detailed molecular processes involved in reproduction and in evolution. However, what remains very elusive is precisely what these techniques and the associated conceptual structure are unable to address directly; namely, the nature of the integrated spatial and temporal order that gives organisms their distinctive attributes, particularly their morphology and their behaviour.

Here we face a rather subtle problem of causal analysis which is more familiar to physicists than to biologists. The situation is a bit like that arising from the following imaginary discourse. Suppose you were to ask somebody to explain why the earth travels around the sun in an elliptical trajectory; and you were told that it does so this year because last year it followed an elliptical trajectory and nothing has happened to change the situation. Now, despite the deficiency of this answer relative to the way we have become accustomed to thinking about this process, the statement is none the less correct as far as it goes, for it says that one of the components determining the trajectory of a body, namely its initial position and velocity (at some arbitrary point in the cycle if the motion is in a closed periodic orbit), must remain unchanged if the periodic orbit is to remain unchanged. What the statement ignores is the other part of the explanation, the laws governing the process (gravity and the inverse square law) which are required, together with the initial conditions, to define sufficient, rather than simply necessary, conditions for the process.

Biological explanations tend to ignore any reference to such laws of organization of biological systems, and so describe only necessary conditions. For example, one often finds statements to the effect that mutant genes 'cause' particular types of change of form or morphology in organisms. An example is a homoeotic mutant called antennapaedia in the fruit fly, *Drosophila*, in which legs appear during the embryonic development of the fly where antennae would normally arise. However, this is cause in neither a specific nor a sufficient sense. It is not specific, because the effect of the mutant gene can be produced in normal (non-mutant) flies by a non-specific stimulus, such as a transient change in the temperature to which the embryo is exposed at a particular time in its development; and it is not sufficient, because knowledge of the presence of the mutant gene is not enough to explain why the morphology changes as it does, just as a knowledge of last year's elliptical orbit is insufficient to explain elliptical planetary motion. A sufficient explanation requires a knowledge also of the way the mutant gene product acts upon the developmental process such that a particular morphological change occurs in a particular part of the organism, i.e. it requires a sufficiently articulated theory of morphogenesis to identify those changes in particular parameters which result in one morphology (leg) rather than another (antenna) in a particular region of the organism. Such a theory must obviously be a field theory of some kind, since we are dealing with functions with space as one of the variables. Once such a field theory of reproduction and morphogenesis is articulated (and there are promising developments in this direction[4,5]), the laws of organization of developmental processes will be embodied in the field equations in terms of the particular relational order in space and time that characterize developmental dynamics, and the organized context ('the organism') within which genes and environmental stimuli act as partial causes of particular developmental trajectories will become evident. The space-time organization of the morphogenetic field will then define some constraint on the set of possible morphogenetic trajectories and transformations which are possible, just as Newton's equations define the set of trajectories which are possible for bodies acted upon by gravitational fields. (More detailed treatments of this type of description in relation to specific morphologies can be found in Goodwin and Trainor [6,7,8].)

None of this is news: any exact description of a space-time process must be in terms of particles (usually molecules in biology) and fields, and biological reproduction is no exception. However, the particular metaphor that biologists have used to describe this process, namely that the reproductive process is directed by a programme 'written in the nucleic acid message' [9], has tended to have two unfortunate consequences. First, it implies that genes and the 'information' they contain constitute specific, sufficient explanations of reproduction, in the sense that a computer programme explains the behaviour of a computer (i.e. knowledge of the programme is sufficient to explain the behaviour of the computer), so that biologists seek solutions to the problem of reproduction in terms of hierarchies of regulator or control genes, and the 'sub-routines' they control, i.e. in managerial, instructional and information-flow terms. This splits the organism into genotype (instructions) and phenotype (the form produced by the instructions). The second consequence is that this metaphor not only divides organisms into a dominant controlling part (a mind or a soul) and a subordinate controlled part (a body), as did Weismann in 1894 [10], the originator of this dualism; it also makes it look as if biology is in some sense basically different from physics, being primarily a science of information processing and transmission rather than one characterized by particular types of organization of matter and distinctive fields of force.

It seems clear that the time has come to pass on from what was a useful metaphor in deciphering the genetic code and the processes of DNA replication, RNA transcription and translation of the nucleic acid message into protein, the great and enduring achievements of molecular biology, to a more rigorous and exact theory of the reproductive process, without which there can be no satisfactory theory of evolution. The failure of molecular biology, the science of biological particles, to solve the problem of biological form and transformation (reproduction and taxonomy) is not simply due to a lack of sufficiently detailed molecular knowledge; it is a failure to conceptualize reproduction in appropriate terms. This requires a unitary treatment of the process in terms of the space-time dynamics of morphogenetic fields and their ordered transformations. These fields are made out of gene products, organized spatially in particular ways (cytoskeleton, membranes, extracellular matrix) and diffusing over domains defined by permeability barriers, ion fluxes generating electrical currents, cells and cell sheets and adhesive, viscous and elastic properties, and other characteristics which, when taken together, define space-time behaviour distinctive to the living state. The study of this state and its transformations may be described as either biology or physics. It can be divided for convenience in various ways, according to spatial or temporal dissections. But the revolution in molecular genetics of the 1970s and 1980s, which has demonstrated that there is no stable molecular organization (site of the instructions for the genetic programme) carrying invariant packets of information through the developmental process from fertilization of the egg to the adult organism, means that the genotype/phenotype dualism has broken down and been replaced by the concept of a fluid genome that participates dynamically, and equally, with the rest of the developmental process in the generation of the organism from the egg. And in general, the eggs of the next generation are not separated out from the dynamics of the developmental process, as Weismann described in his germ plasm concept (although some species do follow this strategy); rather, the gonads and their reproductive cells are generated as part of the same developmental process that the rest of the organism undergoes. There are no privileged parts; everything undergoes flux, flow and transformation, though it is all organized. And the continuity of the living state from generation to generation, via this organized dynamic, results in a view of evolution as also a field of flow and transformation subject to both internal and external perturbation. This image is consonant with Bohm's concept of 'undivided wholeness in flowing movement', which he proposes as the primary state from which entities may be considered to arise, like vortices in a stream. This image of flow, movement and transformation as the essence of the living state, with various forms or morphologies as transient expressions of an on-going process, was forcefully described by Goethe, who introduced the term 'morphology' in the eighteenth century and gave an enormous stimulus to the study of living form. 'What has been formed is immediately transformed again, and if we would succeed, to some degree, to a living view of Nature, we must attempt to remain as active and as plastic as the example she sets for us.'[11]

Thus we return to the vision of the Renaissance magi, in which subject and object, the known and the unknown, can relate and participate in an appropriate unity, made possible by the fact that reality is a single co-ordinated domain. As Bohm[3] has put it:

> There is a universal flux that cannot be defined explicitly, but which can be known only implicitly, as indicated by the explicitly definable forms and shapes, some stable and some unstable, that can be abstracted from the universal flux. In this flow, mind and matter are not separate substances. Rather they are different aspects of one whole and unbroken movement.

References

1   S. L. Goldman (1984), 'From love to gravity: Renaissance nature philosophy versus modern science', unpublished manuscript.
2   F. A. Yates, *The Occult Philosophy in the Elizabethan Age*, Routledge & Kegan Paul, London, 1979.

3   D. Bohm, *Wholeness and the Implicate Order*, Routledge & Kegan Paul, London, 1980.

4   Odell, G. F. Oster, B. Burnside and P. Alberch, 'The mechanical basis of morphogenesis', *Devel. Biol.*, **85**, 446–62 (1981).

5   H. Meinhardt, *Models of Biological Pattern Formation*, Academic Press, London, 1982.

6   B. C. Goodwin and L. E. H. Trainor, 'A field description of the cleavage process in embryogenesis', *J. Theoret. Biol.*, **85**, 757–70 (1980).

7   B. C. Goodwin and L. E. H. Trainor, 'The ontogeny and phylogeny of the pentadactyl limb', in B. C. Goodwin, N. J. Holder and C. C. Wylie (eds), *Development and Evolution*, Cambridge University Press, 1983, pp. 75–98.

8   B. C. Goodwin and L. E. H. Trainor, 'Tip and whorl morphogenesis in *Acetabularia* by calcium-induced strain fields', *J. Theor. Biol.*, **117**, 79 (1984).

9   F. Jacob, *The Logic of Living Systems*, Allen Lane, London, 1974.

10 G. C. Webster and B. C. Goodwin, 'The origin of species: a structuralist approach', *J. Soc. Biol. Struct.*, **5**, 15–47 (1982).

11 R. H. Brady (1984), 'Form and cause in Goethe's morphology', in *Goethe and the Sciences: A Reappraisal*, Boston Studies in the Philosophy of Science, Reidel, Boston, 1986.

23

Complementarity and the union of opposites

M. H. F. Wilkins *King's College, London*

The main tradition of thinking in the West has concentrated attention on distinct things of fixed nature which are separable from each other. From this, basic science has grown. But there has been a less well-recognised philosophical tradition which has concentrated on the relations between things, and how these relations produce changes in things and in their relations. Thus Heraclitus in ancient Greece and, at about the same time, philosophers in China saw the essence of reality in change and renewal. Opposition was the relation which produced change. Thus opposite principles such as yin and yang pervaded everything, and change came about by opposed things forming a unity. As Pan Ku said in the first century AD 'Things that oppose each other also complement each other.' In the West these ideas were kept alive by thinkers like Nicholas de Cusa (who saw God as the coincidence of opposites), Giordano Bruno, the mystic Jacob Boehme, and also the alchemists who saw in chemical reactions the union of opposites giving rise to new substances. These ideas were developed into a philosophical system by Hegel. He argued that if one thought about opposed concepts, for example being and not-being, one was led to think of their unity in the concept of becoming. To define being one has to refer to not-being, and vice-versa; logically the two concepts are interdependent, inseparable and, in many respects, the same. But to say that being and not-being are the same is a contradiction. To avoid this, thought makes a leap and resolves the contradiction by thinking of the higher-order concept of becoming, which contains and unites both being and not-being. This type of argument – thesis, antithesis and then synthesis – is reasonable enough, but Hegel went further. As an idealist, he saw ideas as the primary reality which gave rise to all phenomena. He therefore

338

extended the idea of the unity of opposites from the world of thought to all aspects of the natural world and of human life, especially history. Thinkers today are more doubtful about this extension, especially to the natural world; and the fact that Hegel was obscure adds to the uncertainties. In any case, I shall make use of a very simplified[1] view of Hegel.

In his lifetime Hegel's ideas were widely accepted in Germany, but afterwards his philosophy was little used, with the notable exception that Marx and Engels, though materialists, enthusiastically took up his ideas which provided them with a dynamic philosophical basis for their revolutionary political ideas. Marxism is of special interest because it is the clearest example we have of an attempt at practical application of Hegel's philosophy[2]. Marx saw historical change arising primarily from the opposition of social economic classes in society. Thus it was historically inevitable that the opposition between the capitalist and working classes would ultimately lead to the unity of a classless society. Lenin emphasised that the transition from a state of inherent continual opposition to the unity of opposites only took place under suitable conditions. Thus, under the right conditions, opposition ceased to be negative or destructive and, instead, gave rise to positive construction. This view gave a somewhat different emphasis to that of Hegel, who seemed to imply that unity of opposites was achieved almost automatically by the movement of thought; he saw 'in contradiction the negativity which is the inherent pulsation of self-movement and vitality'[2]. Lenin[3] emphasised that 'the most essential thing in Marxism [is] the concrete analysis of concrete situations' and stressed the need for Marxists to study with great care and objectivity the particularities of the contradictions at each stage in a process of change. Thus Lenin, like Hegel, saw opposition in things themselves and not merely in abstractions created by the mind.

C. G. Jung, the analytical psychologist, has used somewhat similar ideas about the unity of opposites in describing processes which take place during psychoanalysis; a destructive opposition between mental functions may, as a result of psychoanalytical work, be replaced by positive healthy complementarity[4]. Jung drew a parallel between these therapeutic processes and those which alchemists described as taking place in their work. He regarded the symbols of alchemy as corresponding to aspects of the psyche: for example, in alchemy the incestuous union of God the Father and the Son (the supreme union of opposites)[5] gave rise to the dove which represented the Holy Spirit; and, if I understand Jung correctly (his writings are at times obscure), this holy union corresponds to the complementary union of the intellect and feeling. Jung and the Marxists both claimed to be working in a scientific manner and both stressed that, in order to achieve a union of opposites, it was necessary to make careful objective observation and detailed analysis of the phenomena involved.

I first became interested in complementarity as a result of contact with Jung's ideas. Later, in teaching molecular biology, I had to consider the relation of symmetry and asymmetry in macromolecular assemblies. I concluded that it was useful to regard this relation as an example of complementarity, and I began to look for other examples of complementarity and to compare them. Hegel considered all kinds of different 'pairs of opposites' as being basically similar, e.g. pairs of concepts like being and not-being, geometrical opposites like left and right, the physical opposites of positive and negative electricity, opposed social classes in society, or the highly asymmetric pair of seed and soil which unite to give rise to a new plant. Is a similar principle of opposition or contradiction operating in these very different situations and giving rise to particular forms in the natural world (for example, as the opposition of symmetry and asymmetry in a crystal can give rise to forms like dislocations)? Or is one, as some philosophers imply[6], merely playing with words when one uses terms like contradictions, conflict, antagonism, opposition and mutual exclusion in very different situations?

Even if we do accept that it is valid to apply the idea of the unity of opposites to a very wide variety of situations, we may still ask the question: How useful is it to do so? Marxists and Jungians are convinced of the usefulness of such ideas, but many others do not think that way. Clearly, the best way to find an answer to this question is to consider practical examples and see, in that context, to what extent the idea of unity of opposites is illuminating. In the present study I take examples from physics, molecular biology, psychology, music and visual arts. I also consider the nature of human creativity and have been especially interested to see if any new light can be cast on the problem of human conflict. I have used complementarity to mean the same as unity of opposites. To complement means to form something complete, whole, perfect, fulfilled or consummated. This implies a specific interaction between the parts (two in our case) which gives rise to the wholeness or perfection, and I have taken this interaction to be the creative interaction which gives rise to the unity of opposites. I have not, as is often done, used complementarity in the sense of completing but not interacting; for example, it is often said that art and science are complementary without meaning that they interact significantly.

What I have written is best regarded as a report on work in progress. Possibly it will help to stimulate interest in this subject, or will readers agree with Jantsch, in his account[7] of the important new ideas about order developing through fluctuations, where he dismisses unity of opposites as a 'clumsy western attempt at making a rigid structure of notions move...'? I would be glad to have comments. (Since this was written I have found relevant ideas in the very practical study of negotiations[8].)

Niels Bohr and complementarity in modern physics

Niels Bohr was an outstanding scientist with a strong philosophical interest which focused on problems of paradox, ambiguity and limits to knowledge. Before he met complementarity in physics, Bohr was, for example, interested in the complementary relation between the strictness of definition of a word and its practical usefulness. The meaning depends on context and can be defined more clearly if the context is limited; but, in limiting the context, the word loses some of its usefulness. In classical physics such limits do not exist; for example, the motion and position of a body can be measured independently of each other and, in theory, without limit to the accuracy. But when very small particles of matter such as electrons are studied, it is found that they behave differently from everyday bodies, such as billiard balls, which obey classical laws. It was found that an electron, depending on how it was observed, behaved either like a particle or, in another experiment, like a wave. It thus appeared that an electron had two, seemingly contradictory, natures which combined to form a complementary whole. The nature of this paradoxical whole can only be comprehended in terms of quantum mechanical theory. Roughly speaking, one could say in Hegelian terms that the opposite concepts of particle and wave have united to produce wave mechanics, though, historically, wave mechanics did not arise simply from opposing the two concepts.

The complementarity implicit in wave mechanics expressed itself in another way that particularly interested Bohr. In contrast to the classical case, the measurement of the motion (or momentum) of an electron cannot be made independently of measuring its position. The two measurements are inextricably connected. This is a consequence of the fact that observing the electron alters its momentum. To try to see the exact position of an electron we shine light on it. But, in line with quantum mechanics, light behaves both like a train of waves and like particles which possess momentum. When the light meets the electron, it behaves like a particle and the collision alters the motion of the electron. To reduce this effect so that we can determine the momentum of the electron more exactly, we can use light of longer wavelength and less momentum, but the result is that the position is then seen less clearly. Depending on how we make the measurement, we can either measure position accurately and motion inaccurately, or position inaccurately and motion accurately; if we focus on one the other becomes blurred. In fact, if we measure motion very exactly, the electron appears to extend over all space; that is, it has no position. Thus momentum and position are mutually exclusive. This mutual exclusion is defined by Heisenberg's indeterminacy principle, which expresses the fact that the total information in terms of momentum and position is limited. Bohr regarded the mutually exclusive momentum and position measurements as forming a complementary limited whole. Because momentum and position are mutually exclusive, we can regard them as opposites; but we cannot recognise in the complementary whole a set of relations other than mutual exclusion.

With our present thinking we cannot distinguish in these phenomena a Hegelian pair of opposites which leads to a unity of opposites. I have found no evidence that Bohr ever referred to Hegel either in writing or in conversation. Possibly this is because Bohr never dealt explicitly with change arising from opposition, though he chose the motto 'opposites are complementary' and the taigitu (yin–yang) sign for his coat of arms[9] when he was awarded the Danish Order of the Elephant.

It is also not possible to distinguish a pair of opposites from a unity of opposites in the relation of exactness of meaning of a word and its usefulness. The same applies to the complementary relation of compassion and justice[10] which Bohr mentioned, and the relation of 'thoughts and sentiments' as presented by Bohr[10]. However, this last example can be put into Hegelian terms. Bohr regarded thoughts and sentiments simply as mutually exclusive. Looking at this in more detail we see that thought is by no means autonomous; it requires sentiments, emotion or feeling to motivate it and to help decide in what direction it goes. It would seem that thought and sentiments are never completely separable but are always to some extent interdependent – even a series of deductive thoughts requires some motivation to keep it going, and sentiments are always associated with some kind of thought. The idea of mutual exclusion derives from the fact that strong emotions like anger obstruct clear thought, leaving only simple repetitive angry thoughts. And, vice versa, concentrated clear thought drives out all sentiment except cool quiet intellectual enthusiasm. Thus, like the momentum–position complementarity, the opposition of mutual exclusion does not seem capable of being transformed into a unity. However, Jung's ideas[4] about thought–feeling relations are different. According to Jung the state of mutual exclusion and opposition is not the optimum state, because thinking and feeling are then upsetting each other; for example, a neurotic person might find that thought was disturbed by the upsurging of uncontrollable emotions or, alternatively, intense intellectual activity could suppress all feeling and concern for others. Jung sees the optimum state of the mind as being a complementarity in which thinking and feeling interact constructively and form a unity. With such an optimum state of mind one could act with great energy, being both fired by strong feeling and guided by clear thinking; or one might react to a work of art by fusing incisive intellectual analysis with the strongest emotion. Probably, human limits will always leave us with some degree of mutual exclusion of thought and sentiment, but we can distinguish between a state of marked opposition and a state of partial co-ordination and unity. By making such a distinction, Bohr's complementarity of thoughts and sentiment acquires a Hegelian form of unity of opposites.

Bohr emphasised that the analysis of what happens when an electron is observed – the fact that the observer (including the means of observing) interacts with the observed electron – has the important implication that no clear demarcation can be made between observer and observed [10]: one has to recognise an essential unity between them. By analogy, one could argue that this suggests that there is an essential unity between self and non-self and therefore between self-interest and altruism. There is no record that Bohr made this ethical speculation specifically, but I suggest that his deep interest in philosophy which had holistic tendencies, was connected with his unusually strong concern that scientific knowledge should benefit humanity.

Bohr spent much time and energy trying to ensure that nuclear energy would not become a threat to the future of humanity [9]. His efforts did not succeed and, as a result, he was most concerned about the dangers of international tension. When Bohr compared complementarity in different areas, he wrote: 'We are not dealing with more or less vague analogies, but with examples of logical relations which, in different contexts, are met with in wider fields.' But of human conflict Bohr wrote [10]: 'The mutually exclusive character of cultures, resting on tradition fostered by historical events, cannot be immediately compared to those met with in physics, psychology and ethics, where we are dealing with intrinsic features of the common human situation.' He goes on to say that 'contact between nations has often resulted in the fusion of cultures retaining valuable elements of the original national traditions', and he refers to the 'most serious task' of promoting mutual understanding between nations. Evidently Bohr did not see resolution of the opposition between nations as involving inevitable logical barriers of the kind he saw in the examples of complementarity he described.

L. Rosenfeld, a close collaborator of Bohr, has presented [11] a rather different view of Bohr's philosophy from that gained from Bohr's limited writing on the subject. Rosenfeld brings Bohr more into line with Hegel. For example, he claims that Bohr's interest in complementarity began with his father emphasising the complementarity of seemingly irreconcilable approaches in biology; that is, those in térms of function or purpose and in terms of physical and chemical analysis. Similarly, Rosenfeld attributes the view to Bohr that, when people hold seemingly irreconcilable points of view, the concept of complementarity can help them to get rid of prejudices which could foster intolerance. Rosenfeld also describes a discussion with Bohr about the guidance people sought in religion: 'Bohr declared with intense animation, that he saw the day when complementarity would be taught

in the schools and become part of general education; and better than
any religion, he added, a sense of complementarity would afford
people the guidance they needed.' It would seem that Bohr had something in mind which he felt was very important and went beyond
what he had written about ambiguity and limits to communication.
Bohr is said to have regarded his philosophy as being at one with
that of ancient China. I cannot avoid the thought that Bohr saw the
paradoxical aspect of complementarity having an importance in the
same way as the paradoxes of Zen Buddhism. This relates ethics and
unity of opposites as discussed in my last section.

Complementarity and molecular biology

The rapidly developing new science of molecular biology exhibits
many complementary features. The great challenge – to make a
synthesis of the physical and biological sciences – required uniting the
seeming opposites of the non-living and the living. For example, this
science has revealed structures which combine the properties of
crystals, which epitomise static non-living matter, with the properties
of micro-organisms which, of all living things, proliferate with the
greatest rapidity. Evolution involved the relation of the opposite properties of inheritance of defined characteristics and the capacity of these
characteristics to be modified.

How could evolution and inheritance be interpreted in terms of
physical sciences? The main idea, often considered by biologists, was
that the gene, the unit of inheritance, had to possess a material basis.
But what was the structure of this material gene? The quantum
mechanics physicist Erwin Schrödinger answered[12] this question in
1944 when he suggested that the gene was an 'aperiodic crystal or
solid' in which a defined arrangement of atoms encoded the genetic
message which passed from one generation to the next. Schrödinger's
use of the term 'aperiodic crystal' could suggest that regularity and
irregularity were combined in one structure, but he probably did not
mean that. However, this is what one *does* find in the actual genetic
material, the DNA double helix.

In this structure there is a regular arrangement of atoms along the
outside of the two helix chains, but inside there is an irregular arrangement of chemical groups. These groups join one chain to the other
and are of four different kinds, each with a different shape and size.
There is a complex sequence of these groups along each chain. This
sequence encodes the genetic message and constitutes the basic
structure of the genes. But how can the DNA double helix, which is a
tightly-packed structure, be very regular on the outside when the
inside is irregular? This paradox was brilliantly resolved by the idea
of Watson and Crick of the so-called complementary[13] pairing (the
complementarity being both geometrical and chemical). They dis-

covered that the four different groups in DNA could be joined together to form two pairs which had the remarkable property that the exterior dimensions of the pairs were exactly the same, and the positions of the chemical bonds at the ends of the pairs were exactly equivalent. As a result, if the two chains were joined by the pairs, the outer parts of the chains would be exactly regular and independent of the sequence of groups along the inside. The exact geometrical and chemical relations in the pairs enabled the two parts of DNA to come together to form a well-defined whole. Since different groups are in special relation in this well-defined structure or whole, we may properly describe it as complementary. In Hegelian terms we could say that the opposites of regularity and irregularity have formed a unity, this unity involving a special, specific relation of the opposites. Recently, other relations of regularity and irregularity have been found in DNA. For example, the double helix is not rigid; it can stretch, compress, bend and twist. It is possible that this flexibility of the double helix may take special forms which are related to its functioning. It has also been found that the irregular sequence of groups inside the double helix produces slight irregularities on the outside. These are not so great that they hinder the processes which depend on the outside being regular, but they seem to provide a guide to protein molecules which need to find particular sequences of groups inside the double helix.

The double helix is regular on the outside probably because of biological requirements, though evidence on this is not yet clear. If the outside is regular, the double helix could fit into various kinds of molecular machinery and pass through them with mechanical regularity. Thus DNA would be like a cine film which has regularly-spaced holes on its sides (which engage with sprockets) and yet carries on it a complex sequence of pictures.

In molecular biology one is studying interacting components which do not contain a very large number of atoms. As a result, the variety of different forms is somewhat restricted. It is not surprising, therefore, that the components interact in much the same way as clockwork which, for simplicity of design and manufacture, also has a restricted variety of forms and which, like most machinery, operates in a regular repetitive way. In the DNA double helix the complementarity appears mechanical; even so, the unity of opposites in the double helix structure seems to illustrate Hegel's thinking.

Does the complementarity in the DNA structure give rise, as one might expect, to some special new property? Watson and Crick immediately saw that the structure provides a mechanism[13] for self-replication of genes. If the two chains are separated, each can act as a template on which a new double helix, identical with the original, can be constructed. In theory, genes might be replicated by a group on one chain pairing with an identical, rather than a different, group on the other chain. But the geometrical and chemical possibilities of linking like with like are very restricted indeed compared with the possibilities of complementary linking of like with unlike. In fact, almost invariably, the highly specific binding of one kind of biological molecule to another – a phenomenon fundamental to living processes – is somewhat complementary in nature. Such mechanical complementarity is not of great interest; it is almost unavoidable because the molecules must, for energy reasons, fit closely together.

Very precise replication of DNA is necessary in order both to preserve the structure of those genes which function satisfactorily and to avoid damaging mutations. On the other hand, some capacity for modifying or mutating genes is required so that living things can survive by adapting to changing environment, and also so that evolution of improved forms can be possible. Originally, it was believed that a single 'mistake' in forming one pair of groups in DNA would be the main mechanism of mutation; but recently it has been found that most genetic changes are produced by a much more radical change. Breaks are produced in the DNA chain and whole sections of chain containing large numbers of chemical groups are removed bodily and reinserted in a new position in the chain. This natural process of breaking and reforming of DNA chains is carried out by the same chemical means as are used by genetic engineers in their artificial rearranging of genes. Thus we have a relationship between opposites: the precise replication of genes and their extensive rearrangement. Such a relationship is biologically necessary, and is an example of complementarity which characterises life.

DNA acts as a store of biological information. With the aid of complicated molecular machinery, this information is 'read' and used to build protein macromolecules which form the main structure of living things and perform the multitude of special actions which keep us alive. Most proteins are compact structures which are highly specific, both in their shapes and in the arrangements of chemical groups on their surfaces.

In the case of muscle, one kind of protein forms filaments which interdigitate with filaments composed of another protein. Bridges form between the two kinds of filaments but the bridges have mobile ends which can travel along the filaments so that the filaments slide between each other. This sliding increases the interdigitation and thus shortens the length of the muscle. When many filaments lie side by side, the most efficient arrangement will be one in which the optimum relation between neighbouring filaments is repeated throughout the structure. It is not surprising, therefore, that most muscles have a highly periodic, almost crystalline, structure. On the other hand, for motion to take place, the bridges apparently move asymmetrically. In somewhat the same way, the human body is symmetrical from side to side, but the symmetry is destroyed in walking.

Asymmetry in crystals

Let us consider the relation between symmetry and asymmetry in the apparently simple case of crystals. The chemical and physical forces between the molecules in a crystal cause the molecules to arrange themselves in a regular periodic way, the symmetry corresponding to the state of minimum energy. Thus a crystal exists in a symmetric form, but can it grow symmetrically? In the best known way that crystals grow, the answer is no. A crystal grows by molecules attaching themselves to its surface. But the attachment of a molecule to a flat surface is less strong than the attachment to an indentation or crevice which can partly surround the molecule. Such an indentation exists at the edge of a single layer of molecules which spreads as the molecules deposit on the flat crystal surface. Thus we can understand why crystals grow by deposition of molecules at the edge of such layers; but such growth would stop as soon as the layer covered the whole face of the crystal. However, if there is a local break in the regular structure of the crystal, distortion in the crystal can be such that the growing edge of the layer can gradually rotate, thus building up a continuous spiral succession of layers. Apparently the energy loss produced by the break in symmetry is outweighed by the gain in attachment energy at the edge of the layer.

Even when they are not growing, crystals always have an asymmetric aspect; though they may be very regular indeed, they can never be perfect. Breaks in symmetry give metals greatly increased strength and contribute to many of their special properties, and local imperfections in insulating crystals give rise to many very important and special electronic properties, e.g. those of semiconductors and transistors, which are the basis of microelectronics. Where there is irregularity in a crystal, the symmetry and asymmetry do not just 'add together' or oppose each other in an unorganised way. Energy requirements cause special new structural forms to develop; for instance, special types of dislocation or disinclination which retain some regularity but also have specifically related breaks in regularity. This is an example of Hegelian interaction of opposites which give rise to new higher-order forms. Schrödinger knew that the coming together of symmetry and asymmetry in a crystal could give rise to special new phenomena. I have wondered whether this was why he suggested that genes were aperiodic crystals, but probably this is not so because he also likened the gene to a very large molecule, and he may have used the term crystal merely to express the stability of the structure. However, Schrödinger's use of the term aperiodic crystal stimulated me, as a solid-state physicist, to become interested in studying gene structure; and, of course, I was by no means the only physical scientist who was stimulated by his writing to move into biology.

Symmetry and breaking of symmetry in the self-assembly of simple living systems

Many biological structures are, like muscles, built up from assemblies of sub-units which are identical protein molecules of one type or a small number of types. This is economical in that a large structure may be built using only the relatively small amount of genetic information required to define the few types of protein. However, the sub-units need to be very cleverly designed if they are to fit together to build a unique structure, unless that structure is very simple. Providing the structure is symmetrical, the assembly of the whole structure can proceed automatically by a process which is essentially the same as crystallisation. As is the case with crystals, symmetry aids assembly and provides stability. Spherical virus particles are a simple example; they may contain only one type of protein. This forms a spherical shell which surrounds and protects the nucleic acid (like DNA) which carries the genetic message which codes for the virus protein. In such simple cases the form of the whole is determined by the properties of the parts. Tubular shells formed from a helical array of identical sub-units are also common, tobacco mosaic virus studied by Klug and Butler[14] being an interesting example. In this case, assembly proceeds in ordered steps separated by a break in symmetry. First the protein sub-units crystallise to form discs – circular, flat, symmetrical assemblies of thirty-two sub-units. Next the nucleic acid interacts with the discs; it does not interact with unassembled protein. The nucleic acid interaction causes the individual protein molecules in the disc to change their shape so that the circular flat assembly is no longer stable; it breaks, changes its symmetry and curls up into a short segment of helix. Then other discs interact with the nucleic acid and the resulting helical segments join together to build up the completely helical assembly. The length of the whole assembly is limited by the length of the nucleic acid molecule which fits inside it. An advantage of this rather complex mode of assembly is that the nucleic acid does not have to be added separately to the assembly and the protein shell cannot be assembled completely without the nucleic acid being in it. Also, assembly should be faster if pre-assembled protein discs are used instead of single protein molecules. It is important to note that the breaking of symmetry during assembly is not random; it gives rise to a specific dislocation at a particular stage in assembly. It seems proper, therefore, to describe the relation of regularity and irregularity as a complementarity. We may note that the change of symmetry results from the individual molecules undergoing a structural or conformational change which, in similar cases, is often an abrupt change from one well-defined conformation to another.

Molecular switching with change of symmetry is probably also the key to how much more complex bacterial viruses assemble themselves. These viruses, if greatly magnified in the electron microscope, look like little creatures, their various parts being called, head, tail, middle piece, collar, etc. Each main part is composed of a fairly small number of different proteins, but there are about forty different kinds of protein in the whole virus. At first all these proteins may float about separately in solution. Then, in the first step of assembly, one type of protein aggregates to form one part of the virus, e.g. a disc, tube or shell. When this assembly is completed, the constituent protein molecules become able to bind to a second type of protein. By analogy with the assembly of tobacco mosaic virus, it would appear that the molecules which aggregate undergo a change in structure when the assembly is completed, this change being switched on by the completion of the assembly. The second protein cannot assemble or bind to the first protein until the first protein has completed its own assembly process. We get, therefore, an ordered sequence of assembly steps. This sequence is self-generating. In the same way, the main parts of the virus, such as head and tail, cannot join together until the assembly of both head and tail is complete. Clearly, the constituent proteins are very cleverly designed indeed, so that they can switch their structures and thereby themselves control the assembly process, presumably by changing or breaking symmetry.

The way in which these viruses assemble suggests that, at the molecular level, life necessarily involves both symmetry and breaking of symmetry. This is an expression of the fact that in life there is not only order, but also change and mobility; the breaking of symmetry can introduce mobility which may correspond to Hegel's 'pulsation of self-movement and vitality'.

There is also a combination of symmetry and asymmetry in the static structures of many virus particles and other biological assemblies of protein molecules. In the case of a virus protein shell there is a geometrical limit to the number of protein molecules which can be arranged in an exactly regular way. In order to build larger shells, an irregular small group of molecules (e.g. three molecules) is repeated exactly over the surface of the shell. Furthermore, a greater variety of forms is possible when asymmetry is introduced; for example, the head of a bacterial virus may be longer than it is broad. As well as helping structures to be stable, symmetry can provide a basis for amplification of biochemical changes. Enzymes, which are biological catalysts, often consist of a number of protein molecules arranged symmetrically in a group. If one of these molecules receives a chemical signal which produces a conformational change in the molecule, the enzyme activity of the molecule can be switched on. As a result the group of molecules becomes asymmetric. The forces between the molecules then cause the other molecules in the group to change their conformation so that symmetry is restored. Thus one chemical signal switches on the activity of all the molecules in the group.

Breaking of symmetry in music and art

The emergence of special qualities from the interplay of symmetry and the breaking of symmetry is seen in many fields of art. In music and dance the powerful, even hypnotic, effect of regular beat is related to bodily rhythm – heart-beat, breathing and walking. The breaking of the regularity, the unexpected and surprising element, has a further higher-level impact and introduces a more complex level of expression, syncopation of rhythm being a simple example. It is the same with harmony and discord, and also with the building up of a theme and breaking or modifying it. The basic rhythm, harmony or theme is a reference system which is an essential part of the higher structure; and, therefore, the breaking of symmetry must not go so far that one loses contact with the reference system. In the same way children enjoy playing games which scare, but the scare must not go too far. It is important to note that music will not result from mere mixture or addition of regularity and irregularity. The composer needs to create a meaningful combination of both; in fact, a complementarity. Then, quoting Arnold Schöenberg, 'Dissonances are only the remote consonances.'[15]

In visual arts regular periodicity produces very strong effects. Regular flashing lights intoxicate at discotheques and, as riot control agents, severely disorient. Soldiers marching, e.g. slowly at a funeral or goose-stepping aggressively, have a strong effect on those who watch them. The marching together gives the soldiers a feeling of comradeship and, of course, an obedient uncritical mechanical attitude of mind. The strong effect of the marching derives from the complementary relation of the machine-like aspect of the body and its opposite, the unique nature of an individual. Similarly, the impact of a chorus line of dancers is strengthened when one can recognise dancers as individuals. The inhuman/human complementarity is also, presumably, the basis of fascination with automata and puppets, and the strong and strange effect of masks in theatre and ballet. The coming together of the mechanical and non-mechanical evidently gives rise to new qualities.

Human creativity as a complementary process

Creativity is concerned with the bringing into being of something new. Since something new must be essentially unpredictable we cannot hope to follow the whole process of creation. If we could follow each step precisely it would mean that the product was not new but merely a rearrangement of previously existing components. An example of an elusive step in the process of creation, outside logic, is the inductive leap in science. But even though creativity has its mysterious side, we can expect that many aspects of creativity may become fairly clear.

Many thinkers, in line with a long tradition, have claimed that all innovation derives from complementarity. For example, Jung wrote 'every creative person is a duality or a synthesis of opposite or contradictory attitudes'[15], and Coleridge[16] saw that the power of the poet 'reveals itself in the balance or reconciliation of opposite or discordant qualities'. Similarly it has been claimed[17] that the basis of poetry is in paradox, and that metaphor is based on verbal opposition. Recent studies by psychologists of creativity often refer to dualities of some kind being involved in creativity, and sometimes these are complementarities, for example the duality of convergent and divergent thinking. A fair proportion of studies, however, do not refer at all to complementarity or to related ideas, although in view of the obscure nature of creativity we may expect many psychologists to be reluctant to speculate about it.

Psychologists who believe that creativity is based on complementarity agree that it involves, on the one hand, the intellect, which corresponds to activities in the cortex of the brain and, on the other hand, mental functions such as intuition, emotion and instinct, which correspond to activities in parts of the brain which are sometimes regarded as developmentally more primitive and animal-like. Henri Bergson believed that the mental function which complemented the intellect was intuition, which could provide knowledge by direct immediate perception independent of reasoning. Intuition, somewhat instinctive and empathic, gave a broad, rather unspecific, overall impression or feeling which would then be refined and articulated by the intellect. This idea is supported by Einstein's impression that he was guided by his 'nose' (like an animal)[18], and that he became aware of a solution to a scientific problem at first in the form of visual or muscular images[19] which he then had to transform into mathematics.

Many scientists seem, like Einstein, to be guided by hunches. But others have found that, following much careful study, a clear idea suddenly appears in the mind. It would seem then that two levels of the mind interact. A thought which moves in the unconscious mind passes into the upper levels, which Freud called the preconscious, and then into consciousness[20]. There it has to be selected and recognised by conscious thought. When that has been done, a flash of insight is completed. Probably there is no unique pathway for creativity; it may differ from person to person. Jung believed that, in the creative fantasy of the artist, intuition was not necessarily dominant[4] and that the fantasy could partake of any of the four basic mental functions that he recognised. But, whether it is in science or art, the creative person must make the most careful, thorough and intent study of the world, becoming immersed in it empathically and yet keeping some objective detachment.

One of the greatest barriers to creativity is the existence in the mind of firmly embedded conventional patterns of thought from which one cannot escape. This inability to escape and to explore other possibilities may be due to the very existence of the pattern not being recognised (does a goldfish recognise the existence of the walls of the bowl which confine it?), or it may be due to inability to question the correctness of the pattern because it is seen, not as thought, but as reality itself. Psychic regression from cortical activity may provide a way to escape from domination by such patterns. Thus, some psychologists see free reversible regression as important in the creative process. But such regression may alarm the subject because the intellect is no longer in control and there may be a feeling that, like a psychotic, he is losing touch with reality, whereas in fact he may be moving closer to reality. Thus the subject may retreat from creativity. Frank Barron[21] noted that creative writers are 'friendly to the unconscious'. Schiller[22] wrote of a non-creative man: 'You are ashamed or afraid of the momentary and passing madness which is found in all creators.'

Thought patterns are very important because they can provide real practical security; but they can also produce illusions of psychological security. As a result, to think of questioning or giving up patterns may produce strong feelings of insecurity and fear – if I give up my beliefs what will remain of me? Such fear may be a major obstacle to creativity. Added to it can be fear of failing, which gives rise to rationalisations that a creative approach would be *unreasonable*. Brainstorming is a technique for overcoming such fears. There is also the fear, possibly unconscious, of adopting an unconventional approach which may lead to our becoming socially isolated. We are, in effect, exposed to the anxieties of brainwashing which is applied by ourselves and by society. As a result, it is only courageous people who will seek out and accept a great creative challenge; most people prefer the safety of mediocre conventionality. Einstein[23] said 'I have little patience with scientists who take a board of wood and look for the thinnest part and drill a great number of holes where the drilling is easy.' Einstein had not only the audacity to seek the thick parts, but also the ability to choose those thick parts which were drillable and, moreover, the energy to persist and find the ways to drill them.

Arthur Koestler suggested[24] that the basis of creativity is the 'perceiving of a situation or an idea in two self-consistent but habitually incompatible frames of reference'. Here again we have the complementary union of opposites; the mind vibrates, so to speak, on two wavelengths. The main obstacle to creativity then lies in the fact that the mind finds it much easier to operate at one time in one frame rather than in two.

Although conventional thinking is an obstacle to creativity, convention can also play a role in creativity. For example, Thomas Kuhn[25] has made clear how commitment to convention aids exchange of ideas between scientists and provides a framework in which anomalies may be recognised by open-minded scientists. He described the complementary relation of commitment and open-mindedness as an 'essential tension' which led to creativity. Clearly, in this complementary union of commitment and uncommitment, we are not guided by Aristotelian logic (A cannot be not-A) which would lead to the scientist being in a mere state of partial commitment. Such a state would not provide creative energy. Instead, an apparently paradoxical logic permits the scientist to combine strong commitment with questioning and open-mindedness. Similarly, when a creative scientist explores an unconventional idea, passionate faith in the idea must be combined with the energy and humility to question it.

According to the discussion above, the creative state of mind has several main characteristics. We must be prepared to accept the limitations of conscious thought and to seek guidance in the depths of the mind. We need to look and listen with total attention, making the fullest use of all our faculties. We must be prepared to persist in the face of all kinds of discouragement, anxiety and fear. As a result, we have the possibility of becoming free from domination by conventional patterns of thought and images. Seen in this way, the creative state is needed, not only in special areas like art and science, but in all forms of living. Those who lead a virtuous life will be frequently making creative acts, often small ones, which are added to the inevitable background of mechanical reflex actions which are much of living. For example, in human relations we need to pay the closest attention to the needs of others, and of ourself, by observing how a living being is constantly changing and giving signs, however small, of some new potentiality. In these terms, love is a creative human relationship.

Thinking more broadly, we may relate creativity to the general nature of life itself. Life has two opposite aspects, one of homeostasis and regularity of routine established patterns, the other of exploration and successful breaking of routines. Thus an amoeba is filled with homeostatic mechanisms, but needs to explore to find food and a good environment in which to live; and a human being needs the security of the familiar, but also seeks the tonic effect of variety and change. And, at the simplest level of life, genes need to copy themselves repeatedly and exactly but also, from time to time, need to mutate. Thus human creativity is a special, extreme, example of the ability of life to transcend its repetitive nature.

The creative state, though it is most evident at special times, is in fact present always in some degree in all living. For example, a scientist may become most aware of the creative process when there is a flash of insight; but that flash has not come out of nothing, it has come out of a mass of experiences and thoughts assembled and related by the scientist during years of work. During that preparative work the scientist has often been in a continuous state of creativity, observing carefully, selecting and rejecting facts, choosing and rejecting directions to follow, and all the time keeping an open and enquiring state of mind. As a result, observations and ideas are woven together to form somewhat new relationships. These may dissolve away, but, at a critical stage, they may reach the point where they suddenly click together to a much greater degree than before.

Mechanical and non-mechanical aspects of the human mind

The comments about music and art relate to the way the human mind works. On the one hand, the mind works like a machine, and we need that, e.g. when we drive a car or, rather differently, when we engage in simple logical thought. But, on the other hand, life is full of situations where a mechanical, robot-like response is quite inappropriate – we need a non-mechanical, creative response which not only includes thinking but also emotion, feeling, intuition and sensation. The robot and non-robot mental activities can be regarded as complementary, each being dependent on the other. Jung saw the activities of the mind as consisting of the conscious and unconscious parts which, in the healthy integrated psyche formed a complementary synthesis; additionally, the mutually exclusive complementary functions of thought and feeling, and of intuition and sensation, were fused together in balanced relationship and activity.[4]

Because the human mind has a well-developed mechanical aspect we have little difficulty in dealing with well-defined situations of a kind we have already experienced. Our minds have been programmed by that experience and we can meet the situation with a suitable mechanical response. But what can we do when we face a situation which is difficult to define or has unprecedented aspects? If the difficulty and newness of the situation are small, we may have sufficient energy and creative courage to face the problem – we may, in fact, enjoy the challenge. But if the challenge is great, it is easy for us to be overwhelmed by it. We may lack the courage to face the fact that we do not understand the situation. The unknown can be frightening and we may not have the energy and ability to think new thoughts. As a result, we may regress psychologically and unconsciously seek comfort and security by adopting without question some ready-made thought pattern such as that of convention or authority (e.g. the belief that Soviet disarmament proposals cannot be trusted). Such regression is negative and compulsive and differs from the positive free exploratory regression involved in creativity. The regression may also prevent us thinking clearly, with the result that we deceive ourselves and force the situation into a well-known category, although we really should see that it does not fit (e.g. like the general who always prepares to fight the next war like the last).

Thus our minds become fixed and narrow; we are, like Shakespeare's man, 'most ignorant of what he is most assured' (or vice versa). If we are intellectual people we may try too much to solve problems by logical thought, because we have the feeling that logic is reliable and gives security. Thus we try to solve complex social economic problems by a technological approach, e.g. we may think that more efficient crops will solve the problem of Third World starvation (they do not). And governments may seek to stabilise society by using science-based force, or try to resolve or contain international tensions by military technology of mass destruction. And, of course, if we fail to persuade ourselves that conventional attitudes can solve the serious problems we face, we may simply retreat into a feeling of helplessness, which is the state of very many people today, e.g. in relation to nuclear war. Alternatively, if we do not retreat into apathy, our fear and frustration may be converted into hatred and aggression. This, in the context of conflict, gives rise to the greatest dangers.

Psychology of human conflict resolution

Let us consider in what specific ways the principle of unity of opposites can operate in human conflict resolution. The psychological factors involved are much the same for all kinds of human conflict. Therefore, although I shall refer to conflict between two individuals, I shall also use the East/West confrontation to illustrate principles.

The main characteristics of confrontational conflict are as follows. Each party in the conflict of course regards his own behaviour as reasonable, but the behaviour of each mutually reinforces in the other the unreasonable and psychologically regressive tendencies which, as described above, develop in difficult and threatening situations. There is a lack of ability to observe the opponent objectively. Threats and fears cause each side to exaggerate the faults of the other. By projecting one's own faults on to the other, the faults in one's own system seem less important; and by condemning others one feels virtuous. Each party forms a fixed image of the other and of the certainty of op-position between them. Also, fixed ideas develop about what appear to be final self-evident principles of freedom, justice, democracy, socialism, etc. Thus illusions of certainty instilled by society set limits to thinking. Accordingly, people in the US have a simplified and distorted picture of the USSR as being opposed to freedom and threatening the US, which they see as the bastion of democratic liberty. And, like a mirror image, the USSR sees itself as the stronghold of socialist justice which is threatened by an unjust aggres-sive US. Dependence on a simplified stereotyped image of the partner in conflict leads to misperceptions of his attitudes and intentions.

With such firmly-established confrontation we are not likely to resolve the conflict by merely appealing to reason and pointing out that both sides have many interests in common. Strong emotions have created unreasonable attitudes which prevent the opponents observing the whole situation with care and objectivity and analysing it productively. For reason to prevail we need to remove the blocks of unreason. To do this we need the same frame of mind as is needed for creativity. In fact, we have to be creative. So long as the blocks operate, intellectual analysis merely strengthens rigid defensive attitudes. We need to achieve a creative freedom where the mind can explore new possibilities and where a creative regression replaces the negative regression which locks the mind in confrontation. This creative freedom involves complementarities like the unity of opposites of commitment and non-commitment which we discussed in relation to scientific creativity.

The basic difficulty in conflict resolution is that each opponent concentrates attention on his own requirements and does not have the freedom of mind to put himself in the other's shoes and be objective about the other's requirements. How to transcend such unreasonable self-centredness is, of course, an age-old problem to which religions have given much attention: How can human beings free themselves from undue attachment to self and learn to behave altruistically? The problem is often seen as one of choosing between attachment to self or to non-self or choosing between being either self-centred or helping other people. This is a false separation because, as Spinoza emphasised, we cannot, in the wider sense and longer term, separate the interests of ourselves from those of others. We need to pay attention to the total situation, thus including ourselves in a unity of opposites of self and non-self. This is especially necessary in a conflict situation. In Christian terms this is made clear by Meister Eckhart[26]: 'He is a . . . righteous person who loving himself loves all others equally.' Thus we should love ourselves as we should love others or, in a more limited form, we should treat others as we would have them treat us. This is in recognition of the fact that we and our opponent have the same basic psychology, share the same joys and sorrows and the same fundamental human needs. It will not help therefore to resolve the conflict if, instead of being self-centred, we direct attention away from our own needs and towards those of our opponent. We must pay attention to both, and this requires that we are practical and effective in asserting and articulating our own interests.

In practice it is difficult to focus on both sets of needs. This is partly because the mind finds it easier to follow one train of thought than to follow two, or to operate in one mode rather than two (for example, thought and emotion tend to be mutually exclusive). But probably the most important difficulty arises from the fact that when we focus on our own needs, fears and anxieties arise which tend to run out of control, and we then see our opponent as providing a threat which reflects our fears. Since most of our fears are unconscious it is difficult to resist their effects. By not recognising the basic similarity between ourselves and our opponent we create opposition. In this respect, a unit of opposites would be achieved if we quite simply recognised our essential similarity, though in practice that can be very difficult. But opposition also arises because we and our opponent have differences as well as basic similarity. For example, we may have opposed economic interests or ideologies. In that case, much patient persistent creative work would be needed to resolve the conflict.

In such work we need to hold two points of view in one mind at the same time. But that alone will not necessarily lead to creativity; it may instead give rise to destructive mental conflict, indecision or mere sitting on the fence. An active open-mindedness coupled with intelligent discrimination is needed to help the opposition of views to produce a creative tension. We may gain some idea of the state of mind needed if we recognise in conflict resolution a unity of opposites in the way the mind works.

For example, consider the way in which we make moral judgments in a conflict. Such judgments can either add to conflict or help to resolve it. Clearly we need, as always, to have a strong moral sense (for the moment I shall ignore conflict of moral values); we also need to observe closely the behaviour, not only of our opponent but also of ourselves, and we need to recognise in what ways that behaviour is moral or immoral. We cannot do any of this properly if we are made unreasonable by our emotions about our self-interests. If we are unreasonable in that way we are likely to make self-righteous moral condemnations which have a finality about them which lacks compassion and which discourages improved behaviour in the future. Self-congratulatory or self-apologetic judgments can have similar inhibitory effects. What we need is a unity of opposites of judging and not judging. This unity is achieved when we are able to make suitable discriminations in how to judge. The capacity to discriminate requires that we have a realistic image of ourselves and not an image which is unrealistically good or bad.

We can also perceive a unity of opposites in the way in which we should provide encouragement and opportunity to our opponent and to ourselves to behave well, but should, on the other hand, not impose our expectations so that we put unreasonable trust in the ability of either party to behave well. Further, the encouragement to behave well may not be only a matter of providing positive encouragement and opportunities, but also of discouraging and restricting behaviour. For example, it is desirable that we establish mutual understanding of how certain behaviour will raise the level of conflict rather than reduce it, that understanding being likely to discourage such behaviour. Thus in conflict resolution we may need to adopt attitudes which are both hard and soft; while we may overflow with generosity in certain respects, we should not allow ourselves to be swept away indiscriminately by a naive sense of the goodness in all things. In line with this, it has been said that St Anthony of Egypt regarded prudence as the greatest of the virtues.

What I wish to bring out in this discussion is the need for an essential duality or paradoxical quality in the way our minds work. We need to develop the capability to move freely out of one kind of mental operation into another and to engage in two (or possibly more) mental processes at the same time. In that way we can avoid mental blocks and achieve a free and open state of mind. This desired state of mind presumably resembles that engendered by studying the paradoxical koans of Zen Buddhism.

If we can escape from our emotional blocks we can begin to pay attention to all aspects of the conflict situation. As Sun Wu Tzu said in the fifth century BC: 'Know the enemy and know yourself.' Such close attention is often described as objective, which is correct in that we should not be swayed by prejudice. But our discussion of creativity showed that creative attention involves empathy – we need to feel ourselves into the situation. Thus our state of mind may be described as a union of the opposites of subjectivity and objectivity.

We need to observe and analyse all aspects of the conflict. For example, in the East/West confrontation there is a whole spectrum of factors ranging from material facts, e.g. military, geographical, etc., to psychological and spiritual factors which include our ideals and values and those of our opponent. To examine critically our own ideals and values is especially difficult because we depend on them so much to give meaning to our lives. It is also important, though not so difficult, to recognise what we have in common with our opponent; for example, in the international case, both sides have similar needs for economic and cultural co-operation.

The possibility of resolving conflict depends very much on the general way the opponents think about the conflict. Can they grasp the possibility that there may be a resolution which benefits both sides but which cannot yet be conceived? In the East/West confrontation the opposing governments and the majority of their people see the conflict continuing, with consequent danger and economic waste (possibly alleviated by *détente* and arms control), or ending either in war or economic collapse of the opponent. The idea that the conflict might be ended by agreement or reconciliation is unattractive because it is only thought of in terms of a degrading and impractical compromise with evil. Such attitudes are the result of mechanical thinking. We see the world as being like a giant mechanism of parts which interact but remain fixed in nature. But if we see the components of the world changing their nature as they interact, and changing their mode of interaction, creative and unforeseen possibilities may be opened up. It is not easy to keep our minds open to such possibilities of something new emerging, because our minds tend to slip back into established lines of thought which rule out such possibilities. In the same way the majority of physicists would have ruled out the possibility of a credible relativity theory before Einstein had actually created it. Scientists create new ideas not only by observing natural phenomena very closely, but also by playing about freely with ideas so that new ideas can grow and sort themselves out. When the leaders in the governments of the US and USSR face each other with the almost unimaginably destructive threat of nuclear war hanging over them, it might seem too much to ask of them that they should play about freely with ideas. None the less, this is what has to be done if the future of the world is to be made safe. We need to escape from the clear, but somewhat limited, thinking which takes place in the cortex and to let the mind regress creatively into intuitive and imaginative activity. Then, as in all creativity, the results of such free play can be examined critically by the intellect.

Dialogue encourages a free movement of mind and is, of course, essential in conflict resolution. In dialogue each mind learns from the other. The thinking of both parties unites and helps to create, in effect, one common mind which can achieve more than two separate minds. Empathy is then replaced by sympathy; opponents are transformed into partners who work together to solve what they have come to regard as common problems.

Let us not be deterred if new possibilities and new ways of thinking seem strange; the new is at first almost always strange or even alien. But I. A. Richards[27], describing complementarity in metaphor and poetry, wrote; 'It can seem to be the most peace-bringing liberation ever.' And Heraclitus said 'Out of discord comes the fairest harmony.' This harmony, which may seem strange at first, is not a static or passive harmony but is filled with creative potential and life. Thus creative potential may arise from the transformation of destructive potential. But how are we to survive as the destructive potential of science-based weapons comes nearer to being enough to destroy all life on earth? The Russell-Einstein manifesto said that to avoid nuclear doom humanity needed a 'new kind of thinking'. In facing this gigantic and horrific challenge let us have courage. If we have the courage to make creative dialogue between East and West, we may then achieve a 'new kind of thinking'.

Acknowledgments

This article is a development of a lecture I gave at Wichita State University as Watkins Visiting Professor in 1982. I am grateful for helpful advice from David Bohm and Basil Hiley, especially on Bohr's philosophy, and from Barrie Paskins, especially on Hegel and on conflict. Mistakes are, of course, mine.

References

1   M. C. Sturge, *Opposite Things*, Burleigh, Bristol, 1927.
2   R. Norman and S. Sayers, *Hegel, Marx and Dialectic*, Harvester Press, Brighton, 1980.
3   V. I. Lenin, *Collected Works, Vol. 38, On the Question of Dialectics*, Lawrence & Wishart, London, 1961.
4   J. Jacobi, *The Psychology of C. G. Jung*, 5th edition, Routledge & Kegan Paul, London, 1951, p. 43.
5   C. G. Jung, *Collected Works, Vol. 14, Mysterium Coniunctionis*, Routledge & Kegan Paul, London, 1963, p. 465.
6   H. B. Acton, *The Illusion of the Epoch*, Cohen & West, London, 1955.
7   E. Jantsch, *The Self-Organising Universe*, Pergamon, Oxford, 1980.
8   R. Fisher and W. Ury, *Getting to Yes*, Hutchinson, London, 1983.
9   S. Rozenthal (ed.), *Niels Bohr*, North-Holland, Amsterdam, 1967.
10   Niels Bohr, *Essays 1958–62 on Atomic Physics and Human Knowledge. The Unity of Human Knowledge*, Interscience, New York, 1963.
11   L. Rosenfeld, *Physics Today*, **16**, October (1963) p. 47.
12   E. Schrödinger, *What is Life?*, Cambridge University Press, Cambridge, 1944.
13   J. D. Watson, *The Double Helix*, Atheneum, New York, 1968.
14   P. J. G. Butler and A. Klug, *Scientific American*, November (1978).
15   A. Rothenberg and C. R. Hausman (eds), *The Creativity Question*, Duke University Press, Durham, NC, 1976.
16   S. T. Coleridge, 'Fancy and imagination', in A. Rothenberg and C. R. Hausman (eds), *The Creativity Question*, Duke University Press, Durham, NC, 1976, p. 61.
17   Monroe Beardsley, 'On the creation of art', in A. Rothenberg and C. R. Hausman (eds), *The Creativity Question*, Duke University Press, Durham, NC, 1976, p. 305.
18   Einstein, *A Centenary Volume*, ed. A. P. French, Heinemann, London, 1979, p. 31.
19   A. Einstein, *Ideas and Opinions*, Alvin Redman, London, 1954, p. 26.
20   Frank Barron, 'Creativity', in *Encylopaedia Britannica*, Vol. 6, 1972, p. 709.
21   Frank Barron, 'The psychology of creativity', in A. Rothenberg and C. R. Hausman (eds), *The Creativity Question*, Duke University Press, Durham, NC, 1976.
22   Morris I. Stein, *Stimulating Creativity, Vol. 1*, Academic Press, New York, 1974, p. 25.
23   Einstein, *A Centenary Volume*, ed. A. P. French, Heinemann, London, 1979, p. 23.
24   A. Koestler, 'Bisociation', in A. Rothenberg and C. R. Hausman (eds), *The Creativity Question*, Duke University Press, Durham, NC, 1976, p. 108.
25   T. S. Kuhn, *The Essential Tension*, University of Chicago Press, Chicago, 1977.
26   *Meister Eckhart*, trans. by R. B. Blakeny, Watkins, London, 1955.
27   I. A. Richards, *Complementarities*, Carcanet New Press, Manchester, 1976.

24

Category theory and family resemblances

Alan Ford   *University of Montreal*

The particular aim of this paper is to draw attention to the epistemological importance of a well-established but sadly neglected principle
of semantics which finds its origin in the thinking of Ludwig Wittgenstein [1]. The principle, which I will henceforth refer to as the 'family
resemblance principle' because of the example chosen by Wittgenstein
to illustrate its existence, can be stated as follows.

> In order for two members of the Jones family to be typical
> Jones, it is not necessary for them to have anything at all in
> common; in fact they may be totally different in every respect; they
> must merely each have something in common with another Jones.

The principle becomes semantic when we make the analogy between
family resemblances and words. It then becomes 'semantic principle
no. 1':

> In order for a word to be used in a particular way there must
> be a precedent in the family to which it belongs, i.e. there must
> be some word in the same category that is already used in this
> way.

1   Following the pragmatists' tradition, I will refrain from the temp-
    tation to use the word 'meaning' when referring to aspects of
    semantic interpretation and instead refer only to a set of inter-
    pretive strategies known as 'uses', thus respecting Wittgenstein's
    advice: 'Don't look for the meaning, look for the use.'
2   The word 'category' is here being used in the way that I hope will
    be interpretable after reading this article.

This principle is particularly well illustrated in semantics in the field
of naming, which is a fundamental aspect of the use of language in
the expression of ideas. When one extends the referential field of a

word by using it to refer to a newly (first time for the speaker) named object B, one follows a general principle which holds that 'X may be used as a name for B if B has something in common with A, a unit which X is already used to name.'

Let me illustrate the application with the way in which the word 'hold' is used in English. 'Hold' is used to refer to a particular sort of manual contact with an object: 'Having the object in the hand.' An extension of the use of the word 'hold' is its use to refer to bodily or even mental contact in general illustrated by the use in expressions like 'holding an opinion or an idea.' A further extension from this use is to go beyond physical or mental contact completely and to refer only to physical proximity or location. This is how we understand 'holding a dinner', 'holding a party' or 'holding a meeting.' This is the sort of reasoning that led Wittgenstein to the conclusion that the search for meaning was illusory, to the extent that the hope of finding a common property for three different uses of the same word was not necessarily a logical possibility.

Suppose now we apply the family resemblance principle to categorization, for the latter implies necessarily the act of naming; you can't, I would think, invent a category cognitively without giving it a name.

In fact according to the emphasis that I would like to get across here, categorizing is simply a cognitive extension of the process of naming. It may seem to some readers that I have got this relationship back to front, but it is a feeling among contemporary semanticists that the classical idea that language is a portmanteau for meaning 'la vision ferroviaire du langage,' as Fauconnier[2] so aptly names it, is an obstacle in semantics, in the same way that David Bohm[3] has suggested that the mind–body distinction has inhibited the growth of scientific thought in general.

Once it has a name, then the word that designates the category takes on life and goes on naming related concepts. Inevitably the category that sparked its existence continues to be associated with its name, but it is easy to see how all the objects to which the name applies haven't necessarily the property which may at the origin have given birth to the category. Perhaps I can illustrate this with an example from the field of syntax, a good example being the category referred to as 'adverb.'

'Adverbs,' we are told at school, often not without an etymological reference in support, are words used to modify or qualify verbs. Thus we achieve the effect of communicating something more than the fact that 'John ate the porridge' when we say 'John ate the porridge slowly.' But 'John ate the porridge twice' or 'Only John ate the porridge' or 'Amazingly John ate the porridge' don't tell us more about John's way of eating his breakfast unless we are particularly flexible in our use of 'way.' Yet 'amazingly,' 'twice' and 'only' would all generally be classified as adverbs. If we try to find a satisfactory definition of adverb in terms of sufficient or necessary conditions that 'slowly,' 'amazingly,' 'twice' and 'only' would all meet, we run into the family resemblance problem that Wittgenstein first alluded to. It is quite easy to show that all four members of the set have, individually, at least one property in common with another member but it is not necessarily the same one in each case. It is thus perhaps equally conceivable that they do not in fact have any properties in common at all.

The family resemblance principle is also active when words are borrowed or transferred from one language to another. For example a speaker of English learning French may learn at one stage that an object which in English he would refer to as 'ball' is referred to as 'balle' in that language. He immediately proceeds do refer to all objects called 'ball' in English as 'balle' in French, running into all the difficulty one can imagine when he is trying to refer to 'boulette' (meat balls, 'ballon' (balloons and other inflatable balls), 'couille' (testicle), and so on.

The fundamental aspect of the fact that categories are in fact designated by words is that they are believed to be basic to reasoning. At least argument structure in formal debates, and certainly a lot of informal ones as well, can be reduced to the general structure of a syllogism:

1   Token *a* must have property *A* because it is a member of category *X*.

There are also often many conclusions of the general form:

2   Token *a* is not a member of category *X* because it does not have property *A*.

The latter in particular is often rendered more palatable by making the same demonstration for several properties.

Principally for this reason there has been a lot of linguistic discussion over categories and this is probably true of many other sciences as well.

Curiously, in contemporary linguistics the nature of categories and their properties have not been of interest or concern. They are simply assumed and attention, which largely reflects the syntactic preoccupation that has dominated the subject since the publication of Chomsky's *Syntactic Structures* in 1957[4], has been focused upon their internal ordering and relationships in what has been offered as a hypothesis concerning the cognitive level.

What is to my mind of greater interest is the status of the category as a form utilized in thought or reasoning and the influence of its formal properties upon the latter. It is of course difficult to pursue this because of the particular status of the category in occidental thought, a status which it continues to occupy today despite the decline of the syllogism. The work in generative linguistics in particular bears witness to this fact.

The whole question is, do we reason with the aid of categories, i.e. is the establishment of a cognitive categorial level a prerequisite to abstracting information via reasoning, or are they in fact something which in the wake of Aristotle we have learned to impose upon reasoning in order to give it some formal weight. I would like to offer some non-category-based arguments in favour of the latter hypothesis.

Pragmatists, ergotherapists, writers of detective novels and the scripts for whodunnit films are all concerned, in part at least, with this question.

Experience has taught us all that doors won't necessarily open if we have the key, yet this same 'experience' makes us aware of the fact that they usually do if we do. How many potential suspects are eliminated by Sherlock Holmes readers because they didn't have access to a critical key and so could not have been on the scene of a particular crime, even though they could have got through the window like any imaginative burglar? How many potential scientific discoveries are not made because a prerequisite postulate was unavailable? There is something about the 'usually' or the 'could' which leads me to think that human reasoning is inevitably linguistically conditioned and that the use of categories is indelibly impregnated with the quality of the name which has all the properties of a family resemblance.

References

1   Ludwig Wittgenstein, *Philosophical Investigations*, German with English translation, Basil Blackwell, Oxford, 1953; 2nd edition (revised), 1958.
2   Gilles Fauconnier, *Espaces Mentaux*, Editions de Minuit, Paris, 1984.
3   David Bohm, *Wholeness and the Implicate Order*, Routledge & Kegan Paul, London, 1980.
4   Noam Chomsky, *Syntactic Structures*, MIT Press, Cambridge, Mass., 1957.

25

The implicate brain

K. H. Pribram   *Stanford University*

Initiation

At Christmastime 1975 the issues of quantum physics became relevant to my explorations of how the brain works. I had come to an impasse with regard to two aspects of brain function. One impasse was the dilemma of whether to think about the events which occurred at the junction between, and in the fine branches of, nerve cells as wave forms or as statistical aggregates. This dilemma appeared to me to be similar to that faced in quantum physics where electrons and photons – particles – at times displayed the characteristics of waves.

The second impasse had to do with perception. Evidence was accumulating to show that the nerve cells of the part of the cerebral cortex connected to the retina responded to a transform of the retinal image, a transform which yielded what Fergus Campbell and John Robson of Cambridge University[1] called 'spatial frequency.' Since the same transformation also occurred in the formation of the retinal image by the pupil and lens of the eye, the question arose as to whether the 'spatial frequency' domain also characterized the physics of the visual world which we perceive.

I took these issues to my oldest son, a physicist and superb teacher, who gave me an intensive course in quantum physics over the Christmas holidays. Toward the end of his really excellent briefs, and having completed some of the essential readings such as *Physics for Poets*[2] and the like, I remarked how happy I was to be a neuroscientist and not a physicist; we have our problems but, by comparison to what seems to be the conceptual muddle of quantum physics, we're doing all right.

My son replied, as have many other physicists (and also Karl Popper the philosopher when I faced him with the same issue) that modern physics is not interested in concepts; the mathematical formulations are so precise and have had so much predictive value that conceptualization is not only not necessary but gets in the way. 'However,' he added, 'there are a few physicists who don't agree to this. They are far out types who would appeal to you.' And he gave me some names such as Max Jammer and David Bohm, and references to the books they had written.

Synchronicity

Back at Stanford, not a week had elapsed before I was asked whether I had heard of David Bohm. My reply was professional. Had I not just 'graduated?' Of course I had heard of David Bohm. Despite my hubris, I was gently advised of two papers which Bohm had written and which had been published in *Foundations of Theoretical Physics* in 1971 and 1973 [3, 4].

This was on Friday afternoon. Saturday morning I awoke early and read the two papers. Bohm, in simple clear language, declared that indeed there were conceptual problems in both macro- and microphysics, and that they were not to be swept under the rug. The problems were exactly those which my son had pointed out to me. And, further, Bohm suggested that the root of those problems was the fact that conceptualizations in physics had for centuries been based on the use of lenses which objectify (indeed the lenses of telescopes and microscopes are called objectives). Lenses make objects, particles.

Should one look through gratings rather than lenses, one might see a holographic-like order which Bohm called implicate, enfolded (*implicare*, Latin to fold in). He pointed out that in a hologram the whole is enfolded into every portion and therefore the whole can be reconstructed from each and any part.

I was exuberant. Bohm held the answers which I had been seeking. I had for years [5, 6] maintained that part of the puzzle of brain functioning, especially the distributed aspects of memory storage and the transformation into the spatial frequency domain, resembled the process by which holograms are constructed. My hunch that perhaps the physical input to the senses shared this transform domain seemed to be sufficiently realistic to be shared by one of the major contributors to theoretical physics.

That Saturday morning I was performing some surgery and my secretary had asked to be present since she had never seen me perform a brain operation. During the surgery (which went without difficulty) I explained not only what I was doing to the assembled team, but also told them of the good news contained in David Bohm's two theoretical articles. My secretary asked 'Is this the same David Bohm who has invited you to a conference at Brockwood Park to meet with Krishnamurti?'

I had not registered that invitation in my memory, but we looked it up later that morning and indeed there was my third encounter with David Bohm that week! Obviously we were meant to meet.

Meet we did and often over the next decade. I went to London even before the Brockwood Park conference and have returned there often to hash out specific problems with David Bohm and his close associate, Basil Hiley. Always, both were gracious and patient in the face of my ignorance, and explained everything to me in great detail.

Only once did Bohm become impatient. I challenged him when he expressed the belief that the universe was all 'thought' and reality existed only in what we thought. I expressed dismay with such nonsense. Why, if that were so, would I need to perform experiments and why would they so often come up with results contrary to what I had been thinking? Bohm answered that that was because my thoughts were probably muddled – to which I unfortunately had to agree. But then I noted that the experimental results were usually very clear and not muddled at all, and therefore reality seemed not to reflect my muddled thoughts.

The argument became somewhat heated and I decided that, since Bohm had not been feeling too well, I had better not push too hard – but none the less Bohm had to go to hospital to have heart bypass surgery a few weeks later. Since I did not win the argument, I seem not to bear responsibility for this turn of events. After all, my thoughts could not have determined David's difficulties with his heart since I was not aware of them. Bohm has recovered fully, and neither he nor Hiley have blamed me for the episode.

The plenum

Are the events occurring at the junctions between, and in the fine dendritic branches of, nerve cells to be considered as waves or as statistical aggregates? What makes electromagnetic energy manifest as particles under some circumstances and as waves under others? Is Niels Bohr's complementarity formulation[7] the best we can do?

An answer to these questions took the following form and was reached in several steps. Bohm indicated to me that it was inappropriate to ask these questions in the form that I did. The question could not be framed in terms of either/or; rather, waves and particles (statistical events) mutually imply each other. In this formulation, Bohr's complementarity was replaced by implication, an entirely different conception. Bohr had invented complementarity to indicate that at any one moment, with any specific technique, only one aspect of a totality could be grasped. Heisenberg[8], addressing the same issue, proposed the uncertainty principle: we can never be completely objective in our knowledge because knowing involves the techniques by which we make our observations. As Wigner, Heisenberg's pupil, has pointed out[9], modern physics no longer deals with observables but with observations.

Bohm's alternate conceptualization of the wave/particle implication demonstrated that indeed both aspects of the totality could be grasped in one setting. I noted that physics had made conceptual sense in the days of Clerk Maxwell when the universe was filled with an ether and particular events made waves in that medium. The modern era of conceptual confusion seemed to arise with the abandonment of the ether by Einstein in his special theory of relativity, and by Michelson and Morley[10] on the basis of their failure to demonstrate a distorting drag on the presumed ether produced by the earth's rotation.

So why not reinvent the ether? Perhaps give it a new name so as not to confuse the concept with the one now discredited. Dirac[11] and others had already made the same proposal. In fact, Bohm had suggested this solution to Einstein in 1953 and Einstein had replied that such a solution was a cheap shot, meaning that it simply replaced one set of problems with another. None the less, Bohm and Hiley pursued the idea and proposed[12] the existence of a medium which they called the 'quantum potential.' Events, particles, perturbed the medium in such a way as to account for the wave aspects of quantum mechanics.

Philippidis *et al.*[13] then demonstrated in a computer simulation how to account simultaneously for both the particle and the wave aspects of the single- and double-slit experiments. These experiments had epitomized the conceptual dilemma of quantum physics as expressed in the infamous Schrödinger's cat (which seemed to be both alive/dead) and the collapse of the wave function (which indicated that when the cat was actually observed, the observer decided that the cat was indeed dead or alive).

The mutual implication of particle and wave was thus demonstrated. True, the quantum potential as a medium had to have some special properties. It certainly could not produce drag. It had to be a potential which was manifest to observation only when perturbed (by a particular event). But is this any worse than ignoring infinities in equations when it is necessary to do so in order to make predictions?

The concept of a quantum potential does indeed rationalize not only quantum physics but also cosmology. When a plenum composed of electromagnetic energy and plasma rather than an empty vacuum characterizes the universe, there is no longer any need for someone with a pea-shooter on Andromeda to shoot particles (photons) toward the earth so that we might see them. Rather, a perturbation of the quantum potential occurs on Andromeda, the perturbation is transmitted as a wave form to us, where it reaches the shores of our visual receptors. Here the wave breaks into particles and the breakers are perceived as light.

Non-local processes in the brain

Non-locality was one of the basic issues which had stimulated my initial foray into physics. When patients suffer damage to their forebrains they do not lose particular memory traces: they may not be able to speak or to identify objects visually or tactilely; they may even lose the ability to recall a whole mnemonic category[14]; but individual specific memories seem to be sufficiently distributed so that they may be recalled despite extensive damage. The memory traces may, of course, be located elsewhere in the brain than in the damaged part, but then the mechanism by which the traces are recalled must to some extent be distributed or else there would be at least an occasional instance where some single isolated memory loss would be produced.

The invention of holography seemed to hold the key to understanding this distributed non-local aspect of memory storage and retrieval, as well as the constructive aspects of perception. If indeed the input to the pupil of the eye came in the form of wavefronts of electromagnetic potentials, such potential orders had the distributed non-local enfolded characteristics which were also captured in the process of holography. As well, certain aspects of brain physiology, such as the fact that single cells in auditory somatosensory and visual cortices resonate to limited bandwidths of the energy spectrum, appeared to share the attributes of the holographic process[15]. These tuning curves reflect the dendritic non-propagated slow potentials – the hyper- and depolarizations – which characterize the dendritic patterns in receptor surface and cortex which are constituted in response to the sensory input.

On the basis of Bohm's conception, it is the wrong question to ask whether these slow potentials (hyperpolarizations and depolarizations) occurring in the receptors and in the nerve cell structures of the brain are to be conceived as statistical events or as waves. Polarizations occur in a medium provided by such cells as the Mueller fibres in the retina and the oligodendroglia cells in the brain (cells which envelope the fine branches of neurons). This medium can be conceived as a manifold within which the polarizing events are produced.

Mutual implication, rather than either/or, best describes the microneural relationship. Thus the mathematical formulations which have been developed for quantum field theory should go a long way toward explaining such phenomena as the saltitory effects which occur in dendritic networks and are responsible for influencing nerve cell output in an apparently non-local fashion.

Space-time and the implicate order

An equally important step in understanding came at a meeting at the University of California in Berkeley in which Henry Stapp and

Geoffrey Chew of the Department of Physics pointed out that most of quantum physics, including their bootstrap formulations based on Heisenberg's scattermatrices [16, 17], were described in a domain which is the Fourier transform of the space-time domain.

This was of great interest to me because Russel and Karen DeValois of the same university had shown that the spatial frequency encoding displayed by cells of the visual cortex was best described as a Fourier transform of the input pattern [18]. The Fourier theorem states that any pattern, no matter how complex, can be analyzed into regular waveform components of different frequencies, amplitudes and (phase) relations among frequencies. Further given such components, the original pattern can be reconstructed. This theorem was the basis for Gabor's invention of holgoraphy [19].

At a subsequent meeting Bohm agreed that in his concept of an implicate order (at least at a first level) the enfolding was of space and time, and that at this level the implicate and the explicate (space-time) domains were related by a Fourier transform.

Sensory experience is in space-time. When we say that we wish to make sense of something we mean to put it into space-time terms – the terms of Euclidean geometry, clock time, etc. The Fourier transform domain is potential to this sensory domain. The waveforms which compose the order present in the electromagnetic sea which fills the universe make up an interpenetrating organization similar to that which characterizes the waveforms broadly cast by our radio and television stations. Capturing a momentary cut across these airwaves would constitute their hologram. The broadcasts are distributed and at any location they are enfolded among one another.

In order to make sense of this cacophony of sights and sounds, one must tune in on one and tune out the others. Radios and television sets provide such tuners. Sense organs provide the mechanisms by which organisms tune into the cacophony which constitutes the quantum potential organization of the electromagnetic energy which fills the universe.

Coda

This is my understanding, thanks to my son John; to Henry Stapp and Geoffrey Chew; and to Basil Hiley and to Eloise Carlton, who often served as creative interpreter for our deliberations. But above all, I am indebted to you, David Bohm, for providing the inspiration to pursue these ruminations and to give substance to them.

References

1   F. W. Campbell and J. G. Robson, 'Application of Fourier analysis to the visibility of gratings', *J. Physiol.*, **197**, 551–6 (1968).

2   R. B. March, *Physics for Poets*, McGraw Hill, New York, 1978.
3   D. Bohm, 'Quantum theory as an indication of a new order in physics. Part A. The development of new orders as shown through the history of physics,' *Foundations of Physics*, **1**, 359–81 (1971).
4   D. Bohm, 'Quantum theory as an indication of a new order in physics. Part B. Implicate and explicate order in physical law', *Foundations of Physics*, **3**, 139–68 (1973).
5   K. H. Pribram, 'Some dimensions of remembering: Steps toward a neuropsychological model of memory', in J. Gaito (ed.), *Macromolecules and Behavior*, Academic Press, New York, 1966, pp. 165–87.
6   K. H. Pribram, *Languages of the Brain: Experimental Paradoxes and principles in Neuropsychology*, Prentice-Hall, Englewood Cliffs, NJ, 1971; 2nd ed., Brooks/Cole, Monterey, Ca., 1977; 3rd ed., Brandon House, New York, 1982.
7   N. Bohr, *Atomic Theory and the Description of the Universe*, Cambridge University Press, 1934.
8   W. Heisenberg, *Niels Bohr and the Development of Physics*, McGraw Hill, New York, 1955.
9   E. P. Wigner, 'Epistemology of quantum mechanics: Its appraisals and demands', in M. Grene (ed.), *The Anatomy of Knowledge*, Routledge & Kegan Paul, London, 1969.
10 G. Holton, *Thematic Origins of Scientific Thought*, Harvard University Press, Cambridge, Mass., 1973, Chap. 9, pp. 261–352.
11 P. A. M. Dirac, 'Is there an aether?', *Nature*, **168**, 906 (1951).
12 D. J. Bohm and B. J. Hiley, 'On the intuitive understanding of non-locality as implied by quantum theory', *Foundations of Physics*, **5**, 93–109 (1975).
13 C. Philippidis, C. Dewdney and B. J. Hiley, 'Quantum interference and the quantum potential', *Nuovo Cim.*, **52B**, 15 (1979).
14 E. Warrrington and R. McCarthy, 'Category specific access dysphasia', *Brain*, **106**, 859–78 (1983).
15 K. H. Pribram, M. Nuwer and R. Baron, 'The holographic hypothesis of memory structure in brain function and perception', in R. C. Atkinson, D. H. Krantz, R. C. Luce and P. Suppes (eds), *Contemporary Developments in Mathematical Psychology*, W. H. Freeman, San Francisco, 1974.
16 H. P. Stapp, 'S-matrix interpretation of quantum theory', *Physics Review*, **D3**, 1303 (1971).
17 G. F. Chew, 'The bootstrap idea and the foundations of quantum theory', in T. Bastin (ed.), *Quantum Theory and Beyond*, Cambridge University Press, 1971.
18 R. L. DeValois and K. K. DeValois, 'Spatial vision', *Ann. Rev. Psychol.*, **31**, 309–41 (1980).
19 D. Gabor, 'Theory of communication', *J. Inst. Elec. Engrs.*, **93**, 429 (1946).

26

Three holonomic approaches to the brain

Gordon G. Globus   *University of California, Irvine*

The relation between technology and thought has been penetratingly discussed by Bolter[1]. Technology shapes thought. Pottery, for example, was a 'defining technology' for the Greek philosophers. The potter holds an ideal image of the pot to be produced – the *eidos* – and molds the clay accordingly to produce an imperfect approximation of the ideal. Plato's doctrine that ideal *a priori* forms *are* the true reality, which the manifest things of the world but imperfectly realize, reflects this technology. The clock was a defining technology for pre-twentieth century physics. Thus Laplace conceived of the entire universe as a mechanistic clockwork following completely deterministic Newtonian laws. Descartes thought of animals and La Mettrie included man as clock-like. The contemporary 'Turing's man,' as Bolter calls us, takes the computer as defining technology and even conceives man in the image of the computer. Similarly, the technological achievement of holographic image production, based on Gabor's Nobel-Prize-winning work in microscopy (reprinted in Stroke[2]), has played the role of defining technology for late-twentieth century holistic thinkers.

As applied to brain science, holography suggests this rough line of thought: 'The brain somehow produces images, constructs the perceptual world. Maybe the brain produces these images something like the holographic system produces images.' [Direct realists, of course, would deny that the brain produces images (see, e.g. Gibson[3,4] and Neisser[5]). For them the brain supports direct perceptions of the world without any mediating images. For some difficulties with this view, see my discussion of methodological

372

solipsism[6].] The holographic line of thought is a highly revolutionary notion (see, e.g. van Heerden[7], Pribram[8], Westlake[9]), since the ardent mainstream belief was – and remains – that the brain is a wet computer, a biological instantiation of a universal Turing machine. (In this mainstream belief we have the brain scientist as 'Turing's man.')

I want to carry forward this rough line of thought by considering two alternatives to the holographic model of brain functioning. I think alternatives are worth considering: perhaps the defining technology of holography has held our imaginations captive – holography may be but one technological exemplar of holonomic principles – and it might prove salutary to consider other possibilities, pursuant to the fundamental idea that the brain *qua* image-producing system follows the law of the whole. So my strategy is broadly 'holonomic' rather than narrowly 'holographic.' This strategy roughly goes: 'The brain somehow produces images. Maybe it follows holonomic principles in so doing.'

I briefly summarize the main theme of what follows. In the holographic version of image-producing system the system is initially empty, like a *tabula rasa*, and information is loaded in by input (through 'experience'). This is a 'weak' holonomy in that the enfolded whole – the 'implicate order' (Bohm[10]) – is entirely derivative of input, not the primary reality. In a second 'strong' version, the holonomic system initially is full with existence; there is an *a priori* plenum of enfolded *existentia* that is the fundamental reality. In the third 'very strong' version, the holonomic system is initially full with all possible worlds; there is an *a priori* plenum of enfolded *possibilia* that is the fundamental reality. So for the three versions of brain functioning, the *a priori* plenum is empty, full with existence, and full with possibility, respectively. I especially focus on the third version in what follows.

The originally empty plenum

We recall that in holography the apparatus is set up initially with *blank photographic film*. Order is then loaded into the blank film in a special way, such that the whole order is (to use Bohm's terminology) 'enfolded' or 'implicated' to each and every region of the film. Then when the developed film (the 'hologram'), or even a small piece of it, is illuminated in a certain way – *voilà!* – out pops the original order (with loss of resolution and decrease in window of observation as the piece gets small). So each point of the film *becomes* full when the holographic apparatus enfolds the whole order of some object to the film, or enfolds the order of many objects to it, but initially the film is blank. Thus in taking holography as technological exemplar of holonomic image-producing systems, the system must be considered initially empty, a kind of holonomic *tabula rasa*. The holographic brain retains traditional roots.

Holographic theories of brain follow holography closely (see especially Pribram, Nuwer and Baron[11]). The essential idea is that the brain performs a Fourier (or Fourier-like) transformation on input which enfolds the input order into the neural equivalent of the wave interference pattern recorded in the hologram. In the case of perception the enfolded order is then processed in enfolded form. Finally, the order is unfolded by inverse Fourier transformation into perceptual information. For this theory the perceptual system is an indelible *tabula rasa*, awaiting order to be loaded in along the world line of experience.

I say this holographic version of holonomic image production by machine or brain is based on 'weak' holonomy because the implicate order does not have primacy, but is *derived* from the explicate order inputed to the system. As we shall see, the other two versions of holonomic image-producing system give primacy to the implicate order, but for the holographic system the whole is not primary creator of images but is dependent on input.

The holoplenum of *existentia*

The existentially full system is best understood against the background of Bohm's strong version of holonomy. (Bohm's *Wholeness and the Implicate Order*[10] provides a profound and wide-ranging development of the holonomic paradigm.) He begins the last chapter by stating:

> Throughout this book the central underlying theme has been the unbroken wholeness of the *totality of existence* as an undivided flowing movement without borders . . . In the implicate order the totality of existence is enfolded within each region of space (and time). So, whatever part, element, or aspect we may abstract in thought, this still enfolds the whole and is therefore intrinsically related to the totality from which it has been abstracted. Thus, wholeness permeates all that is being discussed, from the very outset. (p. 172, emphasis added)

Again, with regard to the interference pattern of the light that is present in each region of space:

> In each such region, the movement of the light implicitly contains a vast range of distinctions of order and measure, appropriate to a whole illuminated structure. Indeed, in principle, this structure extends over the whole universe and over the whole past, with implications for the whole future. (p. 148)

> Such movement of light waves is present everywhere and in principle enfolds the entire universe of space (and time) in each region (as can be demonstrated in any such region by placing one's eye or a telescope there, which will 'unfold' this (content). (p. 177)

So there is a plenum that contains *existentia*, the totality of what is. To emphasize that *existentia* are in enfolded form, I shall call this plenum the 'holoplenum.'

This existentially full holoplenum that enfolds the totality of existence is the primary reality for Bohm. Objects are secondary, derived by unfolding from the enfolded totality. More precisely, there is a continuous movement of enfolding and unfolding. Bohm uses here the image of 'a turbulent mass of vortices in a stream' (p. 18). The flowing stream *qua* plenum 'creates, maintains, and ultimately dissolves the totality of vortex structures.' (p. 19). Similarly:

> The things that appear to our senses are derivative forms and
> their true meaning can be seen only when we consider the plenum,
> in which they are generated and sustained, and into which they
> must ultimately vanish. (p. 192)

So the totality of existence is primarily enfolded; and recurrent, stable and separable forms of existence are secondarily unfolded, like vortices in the stream of total existence. The totality of reciprocal enfoldings and unfoldings is called by Bohm the 'holomovement' or the 'holoflux.'

It should be noted that it is not the enfolding–unfolding process that gives rise to the implicate order carried in the holomovement. The enfolding–unfolding process has to do with world creation and nihilation, where the world is generated from and sustained by the holoplenum and ultimately vanishes into the holoplenum. The implicate order in contrast arises from total existence, or better, the implicate order *is* total existence. So the fundamental reality is the implicate order carried by the holomovement, and the explicate order is derivative of the implicate order. The fundamental case of real existence is total interpenetration, complete convolution, which is the ground for everyday *existentia*, the ground that generates the ordinary world.

Bohm's (briefly presented) discussion of the brain, seen against this background, expands the holographic model. (Bohm does not seem especially concerned with the brain theory quoted just below, since it does not come up in his discussion of the 'enfolding–unfolding' universe with Renée Weber [12]. When Weber asks him about holographic brain theory at the start of the interview he advises her, 'You should really do an interview with Pribram for that' (p. 44). I think Bohm's conjecture about the brain is not crucial to his larger theory.) The body, Bohm says, 'enfolds ... in some sense the entire material universe' (p. 209).

> Various energies such as light, sound, etc., are continually
> enfolding information in principle concerning the entire universe
> of matter into each region of space. Through this process, such

information may of course enter our sense organs, go on through the nervous system to the brain. More deeply, all the matter in our bodies, *from the very first*, enfolds the universe in some way. Is this enfolded structure, both of information and of matter (e.g. in the brain and nervous system), that which primarily enters consciousness? (p. 197, emphasis added)

So there is information coming in through the senses as in holographic brain theory, but also, in a deeper sense, the entire universe is enfolded 'from the very first.' Thus, the brain is always already filled with the order of universal existence prior to input. *The totality of* existentia *are* a priori *implicate to brain matter.*

What distinguishes Bohm's suggestions about the brain in the final chapter of *Wholeness and the Implicate Order*[10] from holographic brain theory is the idea that the brain might directly unfold the *existentia* of the holoplenum from its own matter. Now, all matter in principle enfolds total existence for Bohm; the brain is nothing special in this regard. But for Bohm's conjecture to go through, there has to be a mechanism by which the brain, unlike the stone, can unfold *existentia* from the holoplenum both brain and stone share. However, this would violate a basic principle of Bohm's holonomy, for the following reasons.

The fundamental law of unfolding lies within the holomovement. Out of the primordial holomovement, the perceptible world is continuously unfolded. The holomovement has ontological primacy over the world in virtue of generating the world. ('The things that appear to our sense are derivative forms and their true meaning can be seen only when we consider the plenum' (p. 192).) It is the holomovement itself that exclusively determines what is to be unfolded. The world is hoist on the holomovement. But then, to give the power of unfolding to the brain would be to put the holonomic 'cart before the horse.' The brain is no more able to get at the information enfolded within each of its small regions than the rock is able to get at the same enfolded orders. Unfolding is the sovereign province of the holomovement, and not of the holomovement's secondary derivatives, lest the ontological primacy of the holomovement be sundered. Thus Bohm emphasizes that '*what is* is the holomovement.'

> It is the implicate order that is autonomously active while, as
> indicated earlier, *the explicate order flows out of a law of the
> implicate order*, so that it is secondary, derivative, and appropriate
> only in certain limited contexts. Or, to put it another way, the
> relationships constituting the fundamental law are between the
> enfolded structures that interweave and inter-penetrate each other,
> throughout the whole of space, rather than between the abstracted
> and separated forms that are manifest to the senses (and to our
> instruments). (p. 185, emphasis added)

The fundamental law of unfolding is of the holomovement, not the abstracted and separated brain. It is the holomovement that is un folder and enfolder; the world is unfolded and enfolded. Thus:

$$\text{Holomovement} \underset{\text{enfolded by}}{\overset{\text{unfolds}}{\rightleftharpoons}} \text{World}$$

But then a worldly brain that has the power to unfold would be completely anomalous, tearing the fabric of the theory. So the brain cannot get at information enfolded to its matter any more than a stone can, for if so the fundamental law of unfolding would be taken from the holomovement and given to its derivatives.

Furthermore, the role of input to the system now becomes problematic. On the one hand, the input's information is *redundant*, since the brain's matter always already enfolds the totality of *existentia*. (Or the holistic totality is irrelevant, since input tells existence specifically.) If input's role is determinative rather than informative on the other hand, i.e. if explicate input functionally selects from the totality enfolded to the brain matter, selects order for unfolding, then the whole loses primacy with respect to the power to unfold, and holonomy is thereby severely weakened. A problem of 'levels' also arises: the input order is at the level of the system, whereas the implicate order is 'at' the level of the system's components, yet these vastly disparate levels are supposed to come together in consciousness. So Bohm's conjecture regarding brain functioning does not seem to be viable.

The holoplenum of *possibilia*

We recall that in the first version of holonomic image-producing system the enfolded order was originally dependent on, derivative of, input. Holonomy here is 'weak,' in that the whole does not have primacy. The explicate order of input is more fundamental than the implicate order, which does not exist in the absence of explicate input. In the second version, the enfolded order was *a priori* implicate. Here the enfolded whole does have primacy, but a number of problems arise, as just discussed. For the third version (Globus [13,6,14]) the enfolded whole is neither primary nor secondary to explicate input, but is ordinarily of complementary status to it. This third version of holonomic image-producing system will next be elaborated.

Enfolding and unfolding here become cooperative processes. The enfolding process that creates the holoplenum is non-specific; there are randomly-generated 'waves' of all frequencies, phases and amplitudes which are superposed. There results an interference pattern of infinite richness, all possibilities of explicate order being enfolded to it by random mechanisms. So the non-specific process generates a 'holoplenum of *possibilia*.' The unfolding process, on the other hand, specifically selects a possibility for actual explicate existence. Brain action thus includes a continuous indiscriminate generative process and simultaneously a discriminate selection process. The selection process unfolds particular orders to explicate existence and the generative process provides all possibilities of enfoldment.

The enfolding process can be thought of as in a certain sense 'passive' and the unfolding process as 'active.' By 'passive' I mean that the process has no discrimination, no order, only blind random activity that generates the holoplenum of *possibilia*. The 'active' process in contrast discriminates, selects specifically. Ordinarily these processes are cooperative, but extraordinarily, as in meditation, the active selection process ceases operation, the unfolded world accordingly collapses, and there remains the 'passive' non-dual void, a holoplenum of *possibilia*.

Now I have argued above that the brain cannot unfold the *existentia* enfolded to its matter any more than a rock can, and by parity of argument the same would hold true for *possibilia*. What we are to conceive instead is that the brain in its unsurpassed complexity generates its own holoplenum of *possibilia* – a virtual holoworld of possible worlds. The holoplenum of *possibilia* is thus a system property. The brain matter might enfold a plenum, like all matter, as Bohm says, but also, and uniquely, the brain system upholds, constitutes, generates its own plenum.

To unpack this idea, consider the immensely rich, continually fluctuating, electrochemical field in a small brain region. The natural mathematical description of this field of fluctuating points utilizes complex numbers, treating the field as if a number of waves of different frequency, phase and amplitude are interfering. This electrochemical field would be a function of spontaneously generated neural activity coursing through densely interconnected neural networks, whose wiring logic is such as to create an electrochemical interference pattern of such richness that all possible world orders would be enfolded to it. Whatever the brain's matter enfolds (whether *existentia*, or even *possibilia*) at its highest level the brain generates its own plenum governed by the law of the whole, a virtual holoworld of enfolded possible worlds.

At the same time that the brain continuously generates a holoworld, there is a holonomic mechanism for unfolding particular worlds from the holoworld. The concept here is that the brain generates neural filters on input that are mathematically complex and continuously tunes these filters; that is, the battery of complex filters on input is tuned, moment to moment, to pick up this or that. Thus the tuned filter on input physically realizes certain abstract specifications or concepts, sets up abstract 'conditions of satisfaction.' (On intentionality and conditions of satisfaction, see Searle[15].) On passing the suitably transformed input through such a complex filter, an instantaneous cross-correlation is performed. (Holonomic systems are especially adept at instantaneously computing cross-correlation, autocorrelation and convolution (see Stroke[2]).) When the abstract conditions of the filter are matched by abstract properties of the input flux – when 'reality' satisfies the filter conditions as indicated by the high correlation – those abstract conditions attain a special status, and specify unfoldings of particular worlds from the autonomously generated holoworld. So enfolding and unfolding are cooperative, *simultaneously generative of all* possibilia *and selective of particular* existentia.

The reciprocity in the holographic system, rather than cooperation, is striking; there is a Fourier transformation that enfolds order to the hologram, and inverse Fourier transformation unfolds that same order. Again, in Bohm's several illustrations of ink drops in turning glycerin[10], the glycerin is turned and the ink drop is distributed to the whole medium; on reverse turning, the ink drop is unfolded out of the medium. In Bohm's stream illustration, vortices are created (unfolded) from the stream and dissolved (enfolded) into the stream. In all these illustrations, the dominating image is that of back-and-forth-within-a-primary-whole. But these images do not fit the third version of holonomic image-producing system; that which is unfolded for this version is not again enfolded. Instead all possibilities are continuously enfolded and one actuality is continuously unfolded. The 'passive' principle governs enfoldment and the 'active' principle governs unfoldment. The brain indiscriminately generates a holoworld of all possible worlds and, based on the match between the abstract specifications of its continuously-tuned holofilters on input and the abstract properties of the input flux, worlds are discriminately unfolded from the holoworld.

The difference in conception between the holoplenums of *existentia* and *possibilia* is reflected also in the theory of mind (as applied to perception, in the present discussion). For Bohm, both mind and matter are unfolded from a 'common higher-dimensional ground' (p. 209). This is Spinozan in spirit, the common ground providing a neutral monism ('a nature beyond both') from which both mental and material aspects are unfolded.

> The more comprehensive, deeper, and more inward actuality is neither mind nor body but rather a yet higher-dimensional actuality, which is their common ground and which is of *a nature beyond both*. Each of these is then only a relatively independent sub-totality and it is implied that this relative independence derives from the higher-dimensional ground in which mind and body are ultimately one (rather as we find that the relative

independence of the manifest order derives from the ground of the implicate order). (p. 209, emphasis added)

For the holoplenum of *possibilia* version, in contrast, mind is not unfolded like matter, but *mind is the very action of unfolding.* In the case of perception, mind is a process of selecting worlds from the holoworld constituted by autonomous processes. (Or we might say in phenomenological terms that 'intentional action' is selective unfolding.)

To summarize the third version of holonomic image-producing system, there are complementary neural processes at work under ordinary conditions. The randomly functioning 'passive' process continuously generates a neural holoplenum of *possibilia*, a holoworld of possible worlds, a plenum filled indiscriminately. The discriminative process continuously selects the perceived world by unfolding from the holoworld. The two processes thus complement each other in generating the world. The world's status is accordingly derivative and is illusory (as in a kind of holonomic rendition of the doctrine of *maya*). Under extraordinary conditions, in great contrast, the discriminate process ceases, and there remains the indiscriminate process that generates the holoplenum of *possibilia*, a dynamic distinction less void that enfolds all *possibilia*.

Discussion

We have seen that the strong holonomy of Bohm's conjecture regarding the brain runs into difficulty. The alternatives are either reversion to the weak holonomy that looks to holography as defining technology or modification to a very strong holonomy with its holoplenum of *possibilia*. The alternative weak and very strong versions are next considered with respect to the empirical findings of brain science. Since available data is not rich enough to discriminate them, my discussion of this point is limited to the general prospect for holonomic brain functioning.

There is excellent evidence that the brain Fourier transforms input, which means that the brain has the capacity to deal with wave forms and follows, as Pietsch[16] says, a 'wavy logic,' or what Yevick[17] calls a 'Fourier logic.' (For a review of this evidence, see Kent[18] (4.I and 5.VI) and DeValois and DeValois[19].) The evidence suggests that:

The brain employs Fourier analysis in the domain of spatial frequencies in its analysis of visual input. Thus, visual exposure to a square wave grating fatigues the brain's ability to respond to odd harmonics of the square wave grating, even when these are subsequently presented individually in the form of pure spatial sine wave gratings. Even harmonics are not affected. The only easy explanation of this is that the brain processes the spatial

> frequency components of the spatial square waves by some
> Fourier-like process which separates them into independent
> frequency channels. (Kent[18], p. 114)

So the brain perceptual system is doing the right kind of thing if the brain is to be considered a holonomic system at a fundamental level.

It should be noted in this regard that the brain might compute a Fourier transform in the cumbersome serial fashion that the computer does. (Cf. the Blackman and Tukey[20] algorithm for calculating the fast Fourier transform.) But it is also conceivable[11,18] that an instantaneous Fourier transform might be gracefully accomplished, as in optical information-processing systems[21]. The available data is not rich enough to resolve this issue.

When we turn from the lower-level processing in the perceptual system to higher brain functions, such as conscious perception, there is even less data. Higher brain functions remain a vast *terra incognita* for brain science. The mainstream has confidently *assumed* that the brain is a 'wet' computer, a biological instantiation of a universal Turing machine, and mainly ignored the alternative holonomic version put forward by Pribram[8] and others. There has been little felt sense of 'crisis' about the brain model that takes the computer as technological exemplar, and accordingly little motivation to embrace scientific revolution. As already mentioned, the computer is a 'defining technology'[1] for the contemporary 'Turing's man.' Turing's man just shrugs off the brilliant existential, essentially Heideggerian, critique of artificial intelligence by Dreyfus[22], who argues in effect that computers can't do what *Dasein* does.

To summarize the empirical situation, in so far as we know, the data available is consistent with the brain's functioning significantly at lower levels according to holonomic principles (Fourier logic), in addition to or rather than functioning according to analytic principles (Boolean logic). The data is not yet in with regard to higher levels of brain functioning. Holonomic speculations accordingly remain of heuristic value.

It must be admitted that holonomic theories of brain functioning 'sound implausible,' and especially so for the *a priori* holoplenum of *possibilia*, but this might be said of any revolutionary paradigm in relation to the consensus paradigm. There is, however, biological precedent for *a priori* theories.

As Jerne[23] has discussed, an analogy can be drawn between the central nervous system and the immune system. (See also Conrad[24], Young[25] and Edelman[26].) The immune system is faced with the task of matching antibody to an infinite variety of antigen, including antigen produced technologically. It was once thought that antigen somehow instructed the immune system to produce matching antibody, but it is now known that there is an *a priori* set of antibody, and antigen *selects* the best matching antibody for amplified production. There is a many-to-one mapping of antigen on to antibody such that *a priori* antibody covers the entire *a posteriori* antigen domain. Thus the immune system, implausibly to traditional belief, continuously generates what I have called an *a priori* plenum of *possibilia*. Jerne[23] argues that there is a basic principle of biological nature at work here which is relevant to brain functioning. The *a priori* holoplenum of *possibilia* embodies this principle.

There is another line of evidence that bears on the alternative versions of holonomic image-producing systems. (See Globus[13] for a more extensive discussion of this evidence.) It appears that under special circumstances ('altered states of consciousness') human beings have the creative capacity to constitute *de novo* perfectly authentic worlds in the absence of input, worlds which have never previously been experienced. If this is so, then the weak version cannot account for it, since the world for this version is derived from input. The very strong version, in which all worlds are *a priori* implicate, is consistent with this creative capacity, however; in altered states of consciousness novel worlds (Castaneda's[27] 'separate realities') might be unfolded from the holoworld.

The 'special circumstances' in which this creative capacity becomes manifested include both ordinary dreaming and extraordinary sorceric practices. In the latter[28,29], the sorceric adept has the waking ability to hurl himself or herself (or the disciple is hurled by the master sorcerer's power) into the *nagual*, where strange yet fully authentic worlds are constituted. For example, a well-timed shove by 'Don Juan' pushes 'Carlitos' from the *tonal* into the *nagual*, and Carlitos immediately finds himself removed from an airline office to a marketplace miles away where there are some bizarre goings on[29]. In ordinary dreaming, the same kind of authentic novelty occurs. We dream worlds we have never before seen, and the 'lucid dreamer' can do so at will.

It is of course true, per Freud[30], that the dream world somehow resembles past worlds, indeed specific past worlds pointed to by the dreamer's free associations. This led Freud to consider the dream world to be second-hand, a composition of memory traces of past experience. Since the second-hand dream world is dependent on past input, this would be consistent with the holographic model. I have argued elsewhere[31] however, that the resemblance between the dream world and past waking worlds is entirely abstract, and not based on concrete memory traces. Concepts operative during various waking experiences become simultaneously re-operative during dreaming, where the concepts generate their own fulfillments.

Another kind of 'evidence' relevant to the alternative versions of holonomic image-producing system comes from the mystical tradition (the 'perennial philosophy'). (For a wider discussion of holonomy and mysticism, see the Weber interview of Bohm on the physicist and the mystic[12] and also my defense of Bohm against Wilber[33].) It is clear that in the perennial philosophy the non-dual whole (the Godhead, *Brahman*) has ontological primacy over *existentia*. The Godhead is an infinitely full plenum, the original source of all explicate existence. This is inconsistent with the holographic version, where the plenum is originally empty, but consistent with the idea of the *a priori* holo-plenum of *possibilia*.

To illustrate further, consider the succinct paradox formulated by Sri Ramana Maharshi (discussed by Wilber[31] (p. 250)):

> The world is illusory.
> Only Brahman is real.
> Brahman is the world.

Interpreted holographically, the 'illusory' world is the world unfolded by the brain, a world that models the true reality (Brahman). But the claim that joins the paradox ('Brahman is the world') must remain paradoxical on the holographic interpretation, since a model is not the same as that modeled.

Interpreted according to very strong holonomy, the world is 'illusory' in the sense that the primary reality (Brahman) is a holoworld from which the world is secondarily derived by unfolding. That 'Brahman is the world' is interpreted to mean that Brahman enfolds all possible worlds. Thus the paradox is resolved: the true reality of brain is an *a priori* holoworld enfolding all possible worlds and from which particular 'illusory' worlds are unfolded. When unfolding action – which is tantamount to 'intentional action' – ceases, there remains the void of the holoplenum that enfolds all possibilities. The resolution of the mystical paradox in terms of very strong holonomy, and that paradox's persistence in terms of weak holonomy, supports the very strong version of holonomic image-producing system.

Summary

Three versions of holonomic brain theory have been discussed. The first version[11] takes holography as defining technology. Here the holoplenum is originally empty, and loaded by explicate input, and accordingly holonomy is 'weak.' The second version, based on a conjecture by Bohm[10], has the holoplenum originally full with *existentia*. This version's strong holonomy is flawed, since the explicate brain system is anomalous, having the power to unfold what otherwise belongs to the holomovement. The third version[13,14,32] finds the holoplenum originally full with *possibilia*. This version is supported by consideration of altered states of consciousness and the perennial philosophy.

References

1   J. D. Bolter, *Turing's Man*, University of N. Carolina Press, Chapel Hill, 1984.

2   G. W. Stroke, *An Introduction to Coherent Optics and Holography*, 2nd edition, Academic Press, New York, 1969.

3   J. J. Gibson, *The Senses Considered as Perceptual Systems*, Houghton Mifflin, Boston, 1966.

4   J. J. Gibson, *The Ecological Approach to Visual Perception*, Houghton Mifflin, Boston, 1979.

5   U. Neisser, *Cognition and Reality*, W. H. Freeman, San Francisco, 1976.

6   G. Globus, 'Can methodological solipsism be confined to psychology?', *Cognition and Brain Theory*, **7**, 233–46 (1984).

7   P. J. van Heerden, *The Foundation of Empirical Knowledge*, Royal Van Gorcum, Netherlands, 1968.

8   K. Pribram, *Languages of the Brain*, Prentice Hall, Englewood Cliffs, NJ, 1971.

9   P. R. Westlake, 'The possibilities of neural holographic processes within the brain', *Kybernetik*, **7**, 129–53 (1970).

10 D. Bohm, *Wholeness and the Implicate Order*, Routledge & Kegan Paul, London, 1980.

11 K. Pribram, M. Nuwer and R. J. Baron, 'The holographic hypothesis of memory structure in brain function and perception', in R. C. Atkinson, D. H. Krantz, R. C. Luce and P. Suppes (eds), *Contemporary Developments in Mathematical Psychology, Vol. II*, W. H. Freeman, San Francisco, 1974.

12 R. Weber, 'The physicist and the mystic – is a dialogue between them possible? A conversation with David Bohm', in K. Wilber (ed.), *The Holographic Paradigm and Other Paradoxes*, Shambhala, Boulder, 1982.

13 G. Globus, 'Science and sorcery', (in German) in H. Duerr (ed.), *The Science and the Irrational, Vol. I*, D. Reidel, Dordrecht, Holland, 1981.

14 G. Globus, 'Holonomic theories of brain functioning', *NIMHANS Journal* (Bangalore), **3**, 1–6 (1985).

15 J. R. Searle, *Intentionality: An Essay in the Philosophy of Mind*. Cambridge University Press, 1983.

16 P. Pietsch, *Shufflebrain*, Houghton Mifflin, Boston, 1981.

17 M. Yevick, 'Holographic or Fourier logic', *Pattern Recognition*, **7**, 197–213 (1975).

18 E. W. Kent, *The Brains of Men and Machines*, New Gran Hilo, New York, 1981.

19 R. DeValois and K. DeValois, 'Spatial vision', *Annual Review of Psychology*, **31**, 309–41 (1980).

20 R. B. Blackman and J. W. Tukey, *The Measurement of Power Spectra*, Dover Publications, New York, 1958.

21 L. J. Cutrona, E. N. Leith, C. J. Palerno and L. J. Porcello, 'Optical data processing and filtering systems', *IRE Trans. Inform. Theory*, **6**, 386–400 (1960).

22 H. Dreyfus, *What Computers Can't Do*, Harper & Row, New York, 1979.

23 N. K. Jerne, 'Antibodies and learning: selection versus instruction,' in G. C. Quarton, T. Melnechuk and F. O. Schmitt (eds), *The Neurosciences: A Study Program*, Rockefeller Press, New York, 1967.

24 M. Conrad, 'Evolutionary learning circuits', *Journal of Theoretical Biology*, **46**, 167–88 (1974).

25 J. Z. Young, 'Learning as a process of selection and amplication', *Journal of the Royal Society of Medicine*, **72**, 801–14 (1979).

26 G. Edelman, 'Group selection and phasic reentrant signaling; A theory of higher brain function', in F. O. Schmitt and F. G. Worden (eds), *The Neurosciences: Fourth Study Program*, MIT Press, Cambridge, Mass., 1979.

27 C. Castaneda, *Separate Realities*, Simon & Schuster, New York, 1971.

28 C. Castaneda, *Journey to Ixtlan*, Simon & Schuster, New York, 1972.

29 C. Castaneda, *Tales of Power*, Simon & Schuster, New York, 1974.

30 S. Freud, *The Interpretation of Dreams* (trans. J. Strachey), The Hogarth Press, London, 1953 (1900).

31 K. Wilber, '*Reflections on the new-age paradigm: a conversation with Ken Wilber*', in K. Wilber (ed.), *The Holographic Paradigm and other Paradoxes*, Shambhala, Boulder, 1982.

32 G. Globus, *Dream Life, Wake Life*, State University of New York, New York, 1987.

33 G. Globus, 'Physics and mysticism: current controversies', *Re Vision*, **8**, 49–54 (1986).

27

Wholeness and dreaming

Montague Ullman, M.D.

It is a decade since my first encounter with David Bohm and his way of thinking about reality. My concern then, as now, is with the nature of our dreaming experience. His views set up a certain resonance that subtly, but insistently, helped me move to a new way of looking at dreams. I say new because it departs radically from the views I held as someone brought up in the psychoanalytic tradition. To mention one such radical departure, to which I will come back later, I no longer look upon dreaming primarily as an individual matter. Rather, I see it as an adaptation concerned with the survival of the species and only secondarily with the individual. I refer to this as the species-connectedness aspect of dreaming. In this presentation I will try to relate two aspects of Bohm's thought to dreaming; namely, the notion of unbroken wholeness and his concept of the implicate order.

Bohm postulates an underlying order, not directly knowable, but constituting the ground of all being, the implicate order[1]. Out of this a manifest order arises. Through the way we perceive this manifest order we ourselves create a perceptual order, otherwise known as consensus reality or middle-order reality[2]. As a result of long conditioning our perceptual order takes discreteness as the primary given, despite our ever-deepening understanding of field interrelationships. Bohm suggests, and I think rightly so, that this approach to understanding the nature of reality has played an important role in fostering the degree of alienation and fragmentation that now exists among the members of the human species.

Bohm's contributions offer some leverage to set in motion a counter-force. What if we were to turn things upside down and emphasize connection and wholeness instead of discreteness? And if each of us were to re-examine the givens in our individual disciplines? Might the perceptual order we arrive at then move closer to the manifest order and, in so doing, become more attuned to the implicate order? In what follows I will try to illustrate what I mean by re-formulating a way of looking at our dreaming existence.

There are two ways of knowing the world and our relationship to it. They are quite different and serve different needs of the organism. The first is the way of scientific knowledge, with its down-to-earth counterpart, common sense. This is knowledge of the world as object. Its function is to separate, compartmentalize, fragment, analyze the world into bits and pieces small enough for us to handle and use for our own ends. This mode of knowledge has resulted in mastery but not wisdom. It is incomplete and therefore false. Despite the heroic proportions to which it has evolved it can no longer stand alone as the measure of man's potential.

Whatever dreaming is, and we are far from understanding its true nature, it is a regular feature of the sleep phase of our existence. Properly appreciated, our dream life can be seen as an example of a second mode of knowledge that stands, not in opposition to, but in a complementary relationship to what we ordinarily regard as knowledge. I am referring to the aesthetic-creative approach to knowledge which is probably older than our strivings for mastery. It seeks to create and maintain meaningful contact between men. It helps man to transcend himself and experience himself as part of a larger whole. In the formulations of Andras Angyal[3] it serves man's *homonomous* need, the need to connect with a larger supporting environment, just as the mastery over objects serves his *autonomous* need, the need to maintain one's own boundaries. In its manifestations it is immediate, sensuous, ineffable and infinite. It is the wave counterpart to the particulate notions of science. It serves man's need for unity, togetherness and harmony. When scientific knowledge is developed in a one-sided way it results in the separation of subject and object and becomes divisive in character. When the creative-aesthetic way of knowing is misapplied it results at best in the cult of an aesthetic élite, at worst in impractical arrangements. Regardless of which mode is used, a poor fit between the mode of knowing and the context to which it is applied will result in misfiring and unintended consequences. We are all familiar with the unintended ecological consequences of the indiscriminate application of the first mode of knowing and the misuse of art for political purposes in the case of the second mode.

Our dreams relate to the aesthetic-creative mode and in that sense have something in common with art. The task of the artist is to enter into the life of another human being and, working with the residual plasticity that exists, to come up with the most aesthetically pleasing result. The fund of knowledge in the world has not increased objectively but the world has become a better place in which to live.

Before I examine this question of fit and context more specifically around the issue of dream consciousness I want to call attention to something we often pay lip service to but fail to appreciate fully; namely, that we are all much less separate than we think we are. The preoccupation with separateness has come about by the way our personal lives have been booby-trapped by the failures of history. We go about our daily tasks with a limited and often expedient view of our connection to *all* other members of the human species. Were we to allow a truer vision of this underlying state of interconnectedness we would be more inclined to remedy rather than increase the fragmentation and separateness among members of the human species that has been our heritage and that we so blindly perpetuate.

Dreaming

Our dreams provide us with an accurate and reliable way of monitoring the mishaps and difficulties we experience in maintaining collaborative and affective bonds with others. Throughout our lives we fight a war on two fronts. On the one hand are the personal assets and limitations shaped by our unique life history that we bring to this issue of connectedness. On the other hand we are caught up in the mix of both supportive and destructive fallout from the way our social institutions and arrangements relate to this issue.

The play of these forces provides the battleground that appears in our dreams. Failures and frustrations in maintaining positive bonds form the subject matter of our dreams. It is as simple as that. It becomes more clear if we disengage from the way we have been taught to look at our dreams and review them with freshness and curiosity. The little knowledge we have acquired, in its emphasis on the personal, has obscured the essence of what dreaming is all about. If we were to take dreams seriously we would have at hand a reliable monitoring system that informs us in a precise way just where our unifying trends were at. Few of us are fortunate enough to fulfill our creative, loving, relating needs in the course of our day. Our failures and shortcomings, as well as our successes in these areas, are what we dream about.

Dreaming is an example of the sensuous, immediate, embracing mode of knowing that we spoke about earlier. Dreams are expressive, visionary and ineffable. They lead us from the present to infinity without seeming to traverse either time or space.

Our dreams arise out of recent and remote feeling residues. That part of us which is linked to others through feeling is more real, more enduring and more significant than other dimensions of our existence. It compels belief. It dissolves distance, creates unity and links us to the real world. This is the stuff of reality. On the surface our dreams are a seemingly anarchic play of images that descend upon us uninvited. As metaphorical expositions, however, these images reflect the core of our being and the place we have made for ourselves in the world. I use the term descend advisedly because, for too long, we have been misled into thinking that dream content ascends into consciousness from a primitive substratum of our personality. I believe the opposite to be the case.

We live our lives as fragmented individuals, seeking self-realization through our connections to a larger whole. By the feelings they generate and by the information they contain, our dreams can further our effort to live in harmony with a universe of which we are only a very small part and to which we are connected or disconnected by very small acts. Dreams come to us uninvited and unannounced. They involve us whether we want to be involved or not. They are to be reckoned with, providing we allow ourselves to recognize their importance and do the work necessary to transform information mobilized while dreaming into information useful to us in the waking state. Our waking mentality sometimes finds it difficult to encompass certain truths about ourselves, about others and about society at large. When awake our need for security and concern with our discreteness sometimes results in a protective cocoon that obscures our vision. Dream work can prod us into facing issues a bit more honestly. Such work has a way of confronting us with our blind spots and enhancing our capacity for involvement.

Dreams deal with facts, but facts of a most particular kind. They can be recognized later as facts, even though they are expressed in a strange language that is borrowed from the realm of our visual experiences. This can best be illustrated by a simple analogy. If you were working with an array of colours and wished to convey the impression they made to someone else and had the choice of describing them in words or presenting them visually, the likelihood is that you would choose the visual form as the more effective. The dreamer is in much the same position. He deals with an array of feelings that have not yet been clearly sorted out and that defy verbal expression. They do lend themselves to visual display where their source in life experience and their connections can be seen at once. The visual metaphor is a most natural and effective mode of expression of feelings. For the dreamer the visual metaphor is best suited to his need to say a great deal in the limited time available during active dreaming.

What is the agency that provides this unending source of unerringly apt visual presentations? I think that we honestly do not know the answer. It is easy to gloss over our ignorance by attributing the source to some reified internal demon variously known as primary process, the unconscious or, simply, the Id. The basic question has to do with the nature of the process involved in the selection and organization of the visual images with which we build the content of our dream consciousness. If we look at this without allegiance to deeply embedded theoretical biases we seem to be involved in a rather intriguing process. We bring together a selected array of bits and pieces of past data pertaining to our lives. We rearrange these in a spatial and temporal ordering that bears no relationship to their original time-space frame of reference. The rearrangement enables us to express precisely, dramatically and effectively the particular interplay of feelings mobilized by a current unresolved life situation.

Socially available images provide us with the special kinds of building blocks needed to capture and express one or another aspect of our subjective life. It takes a rather high level of creative and organizational ability to tap our internal computer for the appropriate bits of information with which to achieve this end and then to rearrange them in a way that can be used as emotional templates to highlight a current significant aspect of our life. In this respect the powers displayed by our dreaming selves seem to exceed the scope of our waking faculties. The comparison is unfair, of course, since each is supreme in its own domain. Each is a useful way of grasping different aspects of our existence. However, we do tend to pay more attention to the one than to the other.

This view of dreams suggests that we are capable of looking deeply into the face of reality and of seeing mirrored in that face the most subtle and poignant features of our struggle to transcend our personal, limited, self-contained, autonomous selves so as to be able to connect with, and be part of, a larger unity. As someone once remarked, our eyes are the instruments that nature created in order to see itself. So may dreams be seen as an instrument that enables us to view our human nature and the vicissitudes it has been subjected to in the course of our unique life history. In the interest of reaching out toward a sense of unity each of us tunes our psyche to an exquisitely sensitive pitch in order to store and use what we have seen, heard and learned about the world and our place in it. At night we draw upon this store and shape it to our immediate purposes. There is a level and range of creativity in our dreams, which for some of us come out only at night, but for all of us are more discerningly honest at night.

This point of view is congruent with the basic phenomenologic aspects of dreaming. Put simply, these have to do with our ability, while dreaming, to realign our waking view of ourselves and others to bring it more in line with the reality of our historical existence. Our dreams confront us with what is. They offer us a deeper insight into the truth about ourselves.

This approach to knowledge gives us powerful tools with which to effect change and transformation. Any system, including a given personality system, becomes more than it conceives itself to be when, in fact, it is shown to be more by the exposure and identification of these connecting channels to a larger reality.

Dream work

What I should like to consider next are those features of dreaming that I have come to know and appreciate through the group dream work I have been engaged in since the mid-1970s. A description of the process has been given elsewhere[4]. In brief, it consists of structuring a small group arrangement so that it can be of maximum help to the dreamer without being intrusive. Eschewing the theoretical and technical strategies of formal therapy, its sole purpose is to help the dreamer appreciate, to the extent of his own readiness and desire, all that the images can convey about the current emotional context of his life. The members of the group are oriented to meeting the two basic needs of the dreamer. The first need is to feel safe. In order to feel free to share the dream with others and to engage in the self-disclosure necessary, an atmosphere of trust and safety has to be generated. This is brought about in a number of ways. The control of the process lies completely in the hands of the dreamer. No one in the group assumes the role of the therapist and the dreamer is the final authority as to what in the dream fits into the context of his life. The process respects the dreamer's privacy as well as his individuality. There is no imposition of any *a priori* system of symbolic meanings so that there is respect for the dreamer's ability to use any image in highly idiosyncratic ways. Trust is further generated by the sharing that goes on at several different levels. In the course of ongoing dream work everyone, including the leader, has the option of sharing a dream and, in due course, everyone becomes known to each other at this deeper level of communication.

The dreamer has another need which the group must fulfill; namely, to help him make discoveries about himself that are difficult for him to make alone. Various strategies are pursued toward this end. The first involves the group members making the dream their own, projecting their own feelings and thoughts into the images and thus creating a reservoir of possibilities in the hope that some may have meaning for the dreamer. At a later stage the group, through its questions, helps the dreamer reconstruct the emotional climate that led to the dream. Then, working with the context thus elicited, they help the dreamer build further bridges between the images in the dream and his life situation. The questions are put in an open-ended way that leaves the dreamer free to deal with them in any manner he chooses. The dreamer is helped to contextualize the dream, i.e. to relate the imagery to those aspects of his life and personality that they metaphorically point to. The group is functioning as a catalytic agent in trying to make explicit what is implicit in the imagery. The reality captured in the dream is explicated into the waking mode through a social process that offers both support and stimulation to the dreamer. This leads to significant and helpful readjustments in the perceptual order. By sharing their own projection, the group adds to the mutuality of the process and deepens the feeling of safety and trust.

Dreaming and wholeness

Dreams offer an opportunity to set in motion a natural healing process, providing the dreamer has a supportive, stimulating and non-intrusive social milieu in which to explore the connections between dream imagery and life context. The essence of this natural healing potential derives from the dreamer's ability, while dreaming, to produce imagery that reflects recently exposed areas of *dis-connection* with others or with himself. By this I mean that the dreamer concerns himself with any ongoing events or experiences that, in significant ways, impinge on his felt sense of connectedness to others. Some vulnerable area is touched off by a recent happening. This, in turn, sets off reverberations at different levels. It is the recent event that defines the issue to be explored in the dream.

The quality of connectedness emerges clearly in the course of group dream work. In the presence of a safe atmosphere generated by the non-intrusive nature of the process, social defenses melt away or, at any rate, don't interfere with the deep-level sharing and sense of communion that is generated. Group members are able to respond at a feeling level to someone else's imagery. This is understandable in terms of sharing a similar social milieu, but it may also point to a deeper way that imagery has of linking people together; something more akin to a shared aesthetic response.

While dreaming we affect a figure ground reversal. Awake and tied to the perceptual order we allow ourselves to see things in their discreteness. The important part played by connectedness, Bohm's notion of the unbroken wholeness, is like an insistent Greek chorus, dimly heard or not attended to at all. The reversal that takes place while dreaming brings aspects of that unbroken wholeness, at least as it applies to our relationships with others, more closely to our attention. We confront ourselves with the state of our connections, the strategies we use to undermine these connections and the social pressures that place obstacles in the way of connections.

This ability to reflect the dreamer's concern with the maintenance of connections has led me to the speculative notion that, while asleep and dreaming, we engage with a much broader aspect of our human nature, one that goes beyond the concern of the individual. Group dream work discloses an agency that works against fragmentation. Trust, communion and a sense of solidarity develops rapidly in a dream-sharing group. This concern with connections links dreaming to a larger issue; namely, the survival of the species. There has been an unfortunate emotional fallout from the fragmentation of the human race that has come about historically, that continues into the present and to which we continue to contribute. It is as if, while dreaming, we are displaying this from our personal and immediate point of view. If unchecked this fragmentation carries within it the seed for the potential destruction of the human species. Only through constructive and effective bonding can this fragmentation be overcome and the species endure. It is in this sense that dreams may be looked upon as that part of our nature that is concerned with the survival of the species. The individual's concern with the maintenance of his sense of connectedness to others is part of this larger concern; namely, that of species-connectedness. The preservation of the individual is necessary, of course, for the preservation of the species but, while dreaming, we seem able to transcend individual boundaries to move toward our place in a larger whole.

How do these considerations about dreaming enter more specifically into the constructs emphasized by Bohm? In a general and analogous way the view of dreaming presented here is more intrinsically related to notions of inter-connectedness and unbroken wholeness than are dream theories designating reified psychic entities at war with each other. Awake, we are mired in our own discreteness and, by the language we use, trapped by the seeming discreteness of all else about us. Asleep and dreaming, we forsake linguistic categories as a primary mode of expression and risk feeling our way back into an underlying connectedness. While dreaming we explore both internal and external hindrances to flow and unbroken wholeness.

Dreaming and the implicate order

The concept of the implicate order and the concept of other orders that follow from it provide us with some admittedly speculative ideas about the relationship of dreaming to the question of species-con-nectedness. The implicate order represents in a sense an infinite in-formation source. The manifest order represents the way things are, free of perceptual and conceptual limitations and distortions. The perceptual order represents our limited grasp of the manifest field and, in turn, our indirect tie to the implicate order. Might our dreaming experience, with its capacity to zero in on a more real or truthful version of ourselves, be closer to the manifest order? Might it be, in effect, a bridge between the perceptual and the manifest order and be closer to the natural transformation of the implicate into the ex-plicate?

As Bohm points out we need a new language to talk about these transformational processes. Might the language of the dream, its direct sensory approach as a way of expressing the nature of our existence at the moment, be closer to such a language than our reliance while awake on more abstract ways of talking about our relation to the world? Might it be a way of bringing us back to our connection to the manifest order? Our senses have the ability to bring us into direct contact with the manifest order but our personal and cultural conditioning have set up a perceptual screen separating us from the manifest order. The language of the dream is unique in that it is expressed in a sensory mode primarily but without any loss of our remarkable and creative abstract abilities. It is the language of the sensory (predominantly visual) metaphor. Dreaming may be a way of monitoring our distance from the manifest order, from the reality behind the way we look at ourselves, at others and at the social order in which we live our lives. When, awake, we invest the time and energy to retrieve the information in those images. We are, in effect, closing the gap between the perceptual and the manifest orders. We come closer to the actuality of our historical existence and, in that way, free it of some of the perceptual and conceptual distortions that have accrued to it.

When we realign an aspect of our perceptual order with its middle-order correlate, we are simply replaying this selected aspect of our life, using a different operator. The result is strange and unfamiliar to the program we are immersed in while awake. What makes dream work rewarding is the promise it holds for enriching that program through this exposure to the manifest order. It is as if our dreams have brought us closer to a deeper sense of connectedness than comes through in the perceptual order.

Using these concepts the task becomes one of defining where the position of the dreamer is in relation to each of these three orders of reality. What has been called condensation (the ability of a single image to have many references), for example, may be viewed as a superposition[5] arising in an order not directly comprehensible in the waking state. The ability of the dreamer to link past and present into a sense of the immediate present may also derive from the more temporal and spatial fluidity that characterize these more basic orders. Imaging is therefore not simply a primitive mode. It is a necessary mode of staying closer to manifest-order reality.

By bringing us closer to the manifest order our dreams may bring us closer to the mystery of the implicate order. It is interesting to further speculate about this possible connection and the light it may shed on the nature of paranormal phenomenon. But that is another story.

References

1   D. Bohm, *Wholeness and the Implicate Order*, Routledge & Kegan Paul, London, 1980.
2   A. Comfort, 'The implications of an implicate', *J. Social Biol. Struct.*, **4**. 363–74 (1981).
3   A. Angyal, *Foundations for a Science of Personality*, The Commonwealth Fund, New York, 1941.

4   M. Ullman and N. Zimmerman, *Working with Dreams*, Delacorte/
Eleanor Friede, New York, 1979; reprinted J. P. Tarcher, Inc., Los
Angeles, 1985.
5   A. Comfort, personal communication.

28

Vortices of thought in the implicate order and their release in meditation and dialogue

David Shainberg, M.D.

According to Bohm[1] there is an underlying order in the universe which he calls the 'implicate order.' The universe is filled with energy and light and electromagnetic waves travel throughout the whole of it. These waves are constantly crossing and interrelating with each other. As these waves each encode information, their interweaving creates contrasts and connections that generate further information. Matter is also energy, encoded waves; it is the 'same' as the energy and it reflects it. All forms of matter-energy affect each other through their participation in the whole. The implicate order is articulated in the movement of this energy which unfolds and enfolds information. The explicate order is what we see as form. Thus the flowing unfolds into the explicate order which expresses the implicate which has unfolded what was enfolded in it.

In this new paradigm mind is implicated because it is an expression of the ordering implied in the whole. Mind is not in the brain – it is enfolded over the whole of matter. Consciousness and language, like will and attention, are movements of the whole, parts of the explicate reflecting that implicate. The order is expressed in the fact that there are minds – and in the fact that these minds organize reality. It is also expressed by the fact that matter *is*. Its existence is organization of energy. The unity of this order is displayed in the core processes we know as the relationship between mind and matter. Both mind and matter are projections of a higher order of reality. Briggs and Peat[2] write:

> Thus as these energies enter consciousness through the sense organs, it is, in each instant, the whole which consciousness encounters, which consciousness (and perception) *is* . . . and

processes of the brain are a holographic imprint of the whole. Therefore both the order of consciousness and the order of matter, observer and observed, are projections and expressions of the implicate order where the two are one and the same. Each is a mirror reflecting itself. Mind is a subtle form of matter, matter is a grosser form of mind.

The essence of the implicate order is an enfolding and unfolding movement of the whole which Bohm calls the holomovement. It is happening in the invisible movement that produces all forms in the universe and it is seen in the particular forms we see with our naked eye. There are trees and birds and microorganisms, as well as millions of other forms. Bohm refers to these particular forms as 'relatively autonomous subtotalities.' By this he means forms that persist in themselves despite changes in their surroundings. But they continue to be in relationship to the greater order. Human consciousness and language are relatively autonomous subtotalities, but we find that they also create fixed points in this universal forming which block further transformations. We see the blocks in the inner conflicts of human beings and the difficulties of human relationship on both the personal and the group levels. As a result of these fixations in consciousness, relationships between human beings don't seem to unfold or enfold in the manner that Bohm's ideas of the implicate order imply. Instead these points become like rocks around which the stream of life moves. By definition these fixations are part of the explicate as well as the implicate order. Therefore we need to take a look at how such blocks relate to the essential movement that is supposedly characteristic of the implicate order.

From the moment of its appearance on the earth, the human organism has a connection with the many different processes on the planet. Consider, for example, the process of respiration. The lungs are structurally capable of taking in oxygen and excreting carbon dioxide. The hemoglobin molecule is able to carry the oxygen molecule from the alveoli of the lungs to the muscle tissues. The oxygen that the lungs incorporate is produced by the photosynthetic process of the plants, which make use in turn of the carbon dioxide the lungs excrete. When the oxygen taken in by the lungs reaches the muscle tissues in the blood stream that carries the transformed hemoglobin molecule, the muscle tissue is able in turn to receive that substance and to incorporate it into the adenine triphosphate molecule. That molecule is capable of operating in the Krebs cycle which will break down the glucose molecule, which in turn transmits energy in a form that the protein actinomysin is capable of using in order to contract. The glucose has been obtained from the foodstuffs in the environment. The contraction of muscles expresses and transforms the relationship of the organism with other material forms in the universe.

We could analyze many different systems in the human organism and other biological forms and find that they also are functioning in an integrative network with what is 'outside' the individual and with what is 'inside.' The kidneys, for example, adjust the fluids in the body so that they can continue to do their tasks in the brain and other organs. But they are also adjusting the fluids so that the balance of electrolytes is favorable for oxygen consumption and muscle contraction. The kidney is a form that establishes its definition by what it does. What it does is relationship. In fact all the forms that appear in our universe express relationships; their shape signifies a specific connection to 'others,' and in their process they define their position – their meaning. Griffin [3] has written:

> A 'thing' in the basic sense is an occasion of experience. Each occasion of experience *begins* with a whole host of prehensions or feelings of other things (previous occasions of experience). It creates itself out of this web of relations. Hence, the relation to other things is *constitutive* of the very essence of a thing. Far from needing nothing but itself, it needs *everything* else – God and the entire past universe. It pulls some aspect of everything into itself as the raw material out of which it creates itself.

Form, which we distinguish as a separate object with our eye, is not an isolated definitive outlined thing which relates to other such objects. Its structure is the active process, a structuating event, that is making a relationship to all other active processes. That seems like an obvious point, but I think we pass over it much too quickly. We look at forms as the things we, the well-defined subjects, observe as if the thing is there in its pristine completeness; as if it is only what we see, and when we don't see it it remains as we think of it until we return to see it again. In this process we lose sight of the fact that our observations delineate only particular kinds of relationships and that we do not see the different levels in the relationships of any one thing to everything else in the universe. When we delineate our level of observation we have found the meaning for us of the thing we see. That meaning fits our level of perception. If we look at a tree under a microscope we find a whole different set of meanings. If the poet looks at the tree he finds a meaning that is different from the wood-cutter's meaning. Each form, however, is a complex set of processes, each of which is in connection to everything else in the universe. The relationships to other things are expressed by the very nature of the form itself.

But when we come to the human brain we come upon a more mysterious and complicated 'occasion of experience.' As a thing it is a set of relationships. But it is also a process of making more relationships. It is part of the human organism but its part is specifically to make connections to all the other parts as well as all other aspects of the universe. For example, when the brain registers a perception of a tree the neurological impulses are the result of the interrelationship between the energies of the tree that have become matter and the energies that have become matter in the form of the structure of the brain. There is a compatibility in those processes and forms so that the brain can register the response. It displays the nature of what it is when it registers perceptions and forms an image of tree which it compares to other images that it has labelled as tree.

When we register that we have seen a tree that image has been assembled out of the several different responses; the proprioceptive resonance with another standing object, the sensations of vision, touch, smell, taste and hearing in the wind. We repeatedly have these same sensations when we are in the arena of the energy that is arranged as a tree. The form of the tree stays the same thru storms, changes of season, and it often regrows after its destruction by fire. We see it again and again in the same place so we assume that what we are seeing is really there and then we share these sensations with others who seem to have similar images. When we see the tree again we remember the previous response. So the responding process seems to have stayed the same, despite the fact that we have had many different experiences. We assume then that we are a continuous being, a capacity to respond, which we think of as our 'self.' This 'self' we feel to be in connection with the other continuous forms like the tree.

This brain also connects different images that appear out of memory. It creates images such as paintings or books which it projects into the world in material forms which other brains respond to. The response of others to forms that are projected by our brain demonstrates that other brains make similar connections. This adds to the sense that we share a communal reality with other brains.

While the lungs and other such tissues are forms of relating like the brain, they are more specific in their kind of connection to the rest of the body and the universe. The lung tissue, for example, organizes to perform a definite task, the transport of oxygen and the excretion of carbon dioxide. We might say that we change our ways of breathing, fast, slow, depending on the needs of the tissues for oxygen, but breathing has a well-defined kind of relationship in the reality of physiological process. The brain, however, does something different from other organs when it connects different perceptions and when it sets up new realities; while using the repetitive neuronal mechanism it uses those repetitions to make relationships between many different forms. It is responsive both to the relationship between its own memories and its creations and to the relationships between those creations and perceptions. It is the active process by which the organism is known to be an extended relationship beyond its contiguous boundaries.

These extended relationships of the human organism, along with its flexibility, make it capable of participating in the flow of ordering that seems to reach beyond the defined states of much of the explicate order. As a structure it is light energy, like all other forms in the universe. As light energy it interacts with and is responsive to the emanating light energy of other forms. It is like a photographic plate, responsive to the ambient light in the universe; its process also involves a transmission of its own waves of energy which interact both with what it interacts with and within its own energy system. The movement of the brain unfolds these new connections in a reality that is greater than itself and enfolds others back into their place in a memory where there is a hierarchy of relationships as well.

Despite the apparent flexibility in the brain and nervous system of human beings we find, however, that there are numerous conflicts in human beings. These conflicts raise the question as to whether there is something about the human brain which creates blocks in the flow of ordering that is inherent in the implicate order. Certainly human beings are not alone in nature in showing conflict. Trees 'fight' for space and light, animals kill each other over territory, weeds suffocate other plants. Yet, there appears to be a balance in the system. Perhaps the conflicts that we note in human beings and between human beings are the same sort of process. But in our case at least two factors are different. First, we are aware of these conflicts and engage in various activities which would appear to want to reduce them, although these activities could in a wider perspective be seen to be part of the same overall movement of nature where organisms in conflict find co-operative connections in response to their difficulties as well as more violent ones. But the second factor is that we have developed the capacity to extinguish our species and perhaps the planet itself. This makes our conflict more ominous and spurs us on to try to understand how conflict happens and how we can find more adequate solutions to our situation. We know that numerous species have not survived in the course of evolution because they were unable to integrate in a changing environment[4]. But the new question of our species is whether we can live through the environmental changes brought on by our own thought.

The obstructions in human process seem to be part of the basic problems that our thought creates. Thought is at the core of our response in reality and out of those thoughts come all kinds of further ramifications. For example, the responses and recognitions of the brain are often stored in memory. When we meet a new situation we usually take that part of it we perceive and make a quick test to see which category in memory it fits. Then we project that old model on the present to see if it is indeed the same kind of experience. Comparing and adjusting the two models, consciousness arrives at its image of the new situation and then checks that image against the image in memory of how similar such situations have been met in the past.

This basic process of consciousness is a moderately flexible response to new moments. But built into its structure is a less flexible feature; it becomes fixed on ideas or images of good situations that have occurred in its experiences. It then attempts to replay them in the present because they worked (gave pleasure) in the past. A perception is compared to the memory but the perception is not given the weight of past experience because the latter is more comfortable, fits into whole systems of concepts, or has a program of action which we know and do not want to change. In a human relationship we might meet someone who reminds us of someone in our past and we instantly assume that this someone is exactly like the other and we react to him as if he were exactly like him. Thus when consciousness meets new situations and checks with memory for help in defining the nature of the new situation, it often depends more on memory for determining what is in front of it than it does on the perception of reality.

This tendency to live in terms of memory is most serious in human beings whose life since childhood has been tense and conflicted, and who have not been able to integrate the uncertainties of their reality. These people continue to focus on an image that once in childhood they were completely satisfied and filled. This may be a memory from the earliest days when as infants they were without language and were primarily sensory motor organisms. Perhaps they knew a feeling of bliss in the state of physical closeness to their mother in which they were merged with her in a symbiotic oneness. Then when they come into their daily life and realize its imperfections, trials and uncertainties they are driven by the desire to recover that fulfilment they had when they were infants. To secure that security they have in their minds they will do whatever is necessary. They will kill, steal, build nuclear weapons, try to accumulate as much money as possible in order to assure themselves of what they think will be security. Operating in that way consciousness becomes a block to the unfolding-enfolding movement of the brain that connects the explicate order to the implicate.

While thoughts, images and feelings are processes which connect 'things' in the movement of relationship, they can also fix the relationships into specific old forms. In this they seem to be doing what nature does when it repeats itself by making the same form over and over. It makes many trees, many dogs, many insects and many human beings. It makes many different individual varieties of those species. The implicate order seems to unfold templates which are as uniquely different as trees and humans but these templates are unfolded into the explicate order in a repetitive way. The fixation into repetitive behavior that is characteristic of human beings is part of what we might think of as the *form of repetition* in nature. We observe that the repetition forms in consciousness when it consistently meets the present with the past. Whether it is in the form of repeating an old relationship or attempting to obtain the goal of a particular desire, consciousness uses the same mechanism to engage the present. And that mechanism is itself a repetition of a past event. So, at many levels, and among them human consciousness, nature is expressing the form of repetition.

When compared to the uncertainty of the present and all that might unfold from a spontaneous response, these events of consciousness appear to be quite conservative. The basic uncertainty of life calls for a brain to respond, but the brain seems to prefer the security of its old plans and programs. The explicate form – the memory image – becomes a nodal point which demands that a new situation becomes like an old one. In the case of our daily activity and the necessities of conducting our life this is an extremely useful function, but in our human relationship it seems to be an obstruction.

Human relationships are a new form of process in evolution because they bring together two or more of the potentially most flexible processes in nature. The human brain is able to move beyond the repetitious structure of nature into novel interactions in which new events occur. At those moments the way of nature is extended, for the human process involves a relationship to what is greater than the isolated units of self that consciousness had previously defined. But when a particular thought or focus in consciousness dominates a person's behavior, this flow in human relationship is inhibited. Such foci force relating processes into a vortex by insisting that the movement of relationship stay in its orbit. Look at the nuclear arms race as such a vortex arising out of the greed of human beings who are isolated in their separate selves and do not feel the connection to other human beings. In their isolation they are also feeling a peculiar emptiness and they become greedy for everything they can get to fill themselves. Hence nuclear industries proliferate because they provide large amounts of money and the greed is so extensive that such people do not care about the ways they obtain their money or what might happen from their actions[5].

The matrix of thoughts creates a focus around which there are relationships that form a vortex and make up a fragmented subsystem, a 'relatively autonomous subtotality' which, in contrast to other subtotalities, brings about conflict with the larger whole. The vortex fragments off from the movement that is occurring in the other aspects of the universe. It is not receptive to information from those aspects. The fixed ideas organize the relationships in the present and bring about a system of relationships that keep the vortex operating in a way which, to some extent, separates the system from the larger whole. A particular way of relating to other human beings does not separate the human being from his organic connections to oxygen and carbon dioxide, but it may curtail his capacity to share the symbolic communications with the rest of the world. For instance, professional groups who do not recognize they are part of the whole human enterprise are cut off from their connection to the creative process that comes with their relationship to what is beyond themselves.

In this response of the brain it repeatedly unfolds a form which restricts the movement in the implicate. But why doesn't this restriction get communicated back to the brain and why doesn't the brain respond to the disorder between itself and the ordering of the implicate? We might guess that if this form were connected with the flow of the implicate its characteristics would be transformed by the integration with that flow and the block would be released and more open relationships would unfold. But that doesn't happen with much regularity. More often than not the form maintains itself and there is no action by the brain to create a more harmonious relationship with reality. Apparently the agreement brought about by this subsystem has provided pleasure and security which is communicated to the brain as more satisfactory than the alternatives memory promises beyond the repetition of these safety measures. Despite psychological conflicts or psychosomatic illnesses the security in the repetition is read as preferable to any change.

To gain some purchase on this difficulty, consider the development of the human child. He is faced with a wide range of responses in his newly-developing nervous systems; often he has difficulty in bringing them together in adequate relationship to each other and to the other forms in the world. Unless he is exposed to the process of interaction in which these responses are sifted out, his nervous system does not develop properly[6]. If his mother is respectful of her own participation in the flow of such responsiveness he develops a capacity for that kind of ordering in himself. If, however, the mother, as so often happens, is caught up in some fixed form herself, his vitality throws her into anxiety by demanding that she face every new situation. He isn't yet caught up in repeating the remembered forms and is able to respond in a more flexible manner. His aliveness expresses the essence of the unfolding-enfolding order, but at the same time he is faced with the mother's encouragement toward a more focussed organized form. In a sense she is a welcome assistance as it provides him with an aid in ordering. But if she makes it seem that such a focus will protect him from the uncertainty that she finds in the implicate order, and which she thinks everyone needs to be protected from, she blocks his participation in that larger order.

As part of his organization in reality every child comes to his own focussing[7]. Indeed he naturally forms a self, a center, which focusses his relationships. But that focus naturally dissolves when each ordered condition opens new relationships to other foci around him. That changing moving process of relating is after all the essential insecurity of human existence. The self is then a relatively autonomous subtotality that unfolds in the implicate and is displayed in the explicate, only to be dissolved again into the implicate. The child's brain is another subtotality and the responses that flow thru it are part of the explicate order as well. The thoughts and images construct the self but, as we have said, that flow of responses in the brain includes the seductive offering which comes with the promises of security in the repetitions of memory and the mother's support for his identifying with some fixed way of living. The propaganda of consciousness seems to be that if he chooses one identity, one self, one set of plans for how to be in the world, he might find security and pleasure. Under the influence of the mother, the child takes up with the offering and assumes that the self will be a haven of security from the insecurity which is inherent in the implicate order movement.

Many people describe the fact that during the early phases of their life, when their mothers could not understand their flowing responsiveness, they felt alone and isolated and thought the world a hostile place. The anxiety of their mother made them feel that something was wrong with their responding and therefore something was wrong with their self. As a result of that inner feeling in their life they could not develop a well-grounded faith in their own capacity to respond spontaneously to the world, moment to moment. Meanwhile they observed that if they acted in certain ways, their mother responded to them in ways that made them feel better. Although they knew they could not trust their mother to comprehend their essential being they found that if they acted in these ways the anxiety would, at least, be lessened. The forms of behavior which pleased the mother and others in their family became an image in their mind for how to find what little solace they could in a world that was not geared to the appreciation of the flow that their brain expressed. They dedicated their lives to the realization of this state of being which promised, if achieved, to give a measure of relief from their uncertainty[8].

The dedication to the achievement of that image fixes a person's relationship in the explicate order and in some sense curtails his flow in the implicate order. This fixation occurs in the explicate order when genetic programming repeats itself in the formation of trees, turtles, or whatever organism. But most such fixations maintain a balance with the whole movement of the implicate order and its connections. Operating in that fixation, however, the human being will assume that he *is* a perfect lover or a great writer. But paradoxically he feels he *should* be doing certain things so he can prove that he is what he assumes that he is. And he expects other people to treat him according to that image. He is no longer open to the flow of whatever new connections appear. Instead he has definite ideas of what he needs to do for his life to be perfect. When those ideas fail to achieve the predicted results there are intrapsychic repercussions in which self-hate and self-contempt are his main thoughts. As he thinks that he is already in a state of being equivalent to the image, he is enraged at any evidence that he is not. For example, one man felt that he was a gifted writer and that he could write a good paper with only a first draft. When he found that his first drafts were not what he wished he would become enraged at himself and say he was an idiot. Clearly he assumed that he was, in fact, that brilliant person who could write a perfect first draft because otherwise he would not have been humiliated by the difficulties of the writing. He was not interested in learning different ways of working on his writing. Nor was he interested to know why he did not communicate with his audiences. When he received a rejection of a manuscript he railed at the editors because they could not understand that his work was profound. He focussed on the limitations of the editors and what he was entitled to from them.

So the life process of people caught in such an image is a circular form that operates inside its own criteria and does not connect with the elements of the reality outside of its defined fragment. In this form the human being is an explicate focus and the relationships that occur in the carrying out of the program of this focus create a vortex between the explicate and the implicate ordering.

What is most astounding in this image process is the way the individual commits himself completely to the virtues of thought. Moreover, in much of his other cognitive operations he not only gives great weight to his thoughts, he believes the thinking process to be the central reality. When he names and describes something he feels that he has grasped its essence. He has more respect for what he organizes in thought or what thought offers him than for his direct sensations. The repetitive use of thought acts like a rock in a stream. The vortex is formed as a result of forces exercised by the form of repetition in consciousness. The pull to repeat the desirable memories draws all other relating processes of the implicate order into the orbit of the explicate focus. The man who is absorbed by the fixation of his image responds to those aspects of reality which will enable him to execute that image.

But individuals who are caught in the repetitive process that makes a vortex do occasionally become aware that their fragmented condition is inadequately related to the greater whole of the implicate order. Responding to the contrast between the constriction of their prison and the flows of enfolding and unfolding that they find in some relationships with other human beings, or in art or nature, they are stimulated to try to find more freedom. Some seek this freedom in perverse behavior. Generally in perverse states relationships are less well-defined and offer different connections from the image's programs. They also offer a diversity of form that moves more freely than the image with less which is bounded. They do not have the necessity that their images had and they feel that they can move into realms that are not controlled by thought. In that form their fixation on one image is dissolved when their behavior opens into relationships of a more formless nature. Such perverse states are sought after and found through the use of drugs, sex of certain kinds, masochistic practices, alcoholism, and other perversions.

When we talk to people who have acted perversely we often find that they feel their life has not been what it should be. They felt trapped in a vortex which was based on the premise that their image would give them certainty and security. But the contradiction between their attempt to realize a fixed image of what life should be and the movement of the implicate order created a deep strain at the core of their being. They wanted to be relieved of that strain.

In the perverse state they feel that they have achieved an image of a state that they had projected as a relief from the strain. That image they have had in their memory as a wonderful way to be and the relationships projected by that image promised them the recreation of the time when they were infants and felt organized in their merger with their mothers in a kind of connecting that obliterated all separations, differentiations and tensions of being. The goal of the perversion was to bring them back into the state of being which once existed before they became fixated in the vortex created by the self and its images. Whereas they had some glimpse of moving into a freer realm in which they would be able to flow, in the sense of the implicate order, into many different relationships, they are actually caught in another image and another vortex.

People who use perversion to deal with the dilemma of the vortices of thought are forced to keep repeating the same behavior again and again. They have to keep repeating their efforts to relieve themselves of the tension because they do not understand the image-making process and the way they are still cutting themselves off from the enfolding and unfolding of the larger order.

Sometimes, however, the people who are trapped in the necessities of realizing their image understand the wider implications of their narrowed frame of mind. They know that they are fragments that have broken off from a relationship to something larger. They sense that their actions are always getting caught up in the image process and that they must somehow find a way to change the situation, but that it must be a way that doesn't get caught in the tangle of their own 'doing.' They see that the fixation must be dissolved or they must be transformed by something that is larger than their self.

Some people will take a trip to the seashore, others to the mountains or to some other natural setting that enables them to see the difference between their fixation in the vortex and the flow of movement in nature. For people who live in cities, where the buildings and houses are all man-made and permanent, nature offers a contact with change and variety of movement that is more flexible and clearly flowing than is the explicate in the city. In the city the lines are mostly vertical and horizontal, while in nature there are curves, diagonals and other unusual shapes. In nature there is a direct sense of the cycles of organic growth: the flowers bloom; leaves change color and come out again in the spring; fish move in the pond; the variety of living processes shows the diversity of form in nature and the continual movement of its producing of forms.

There are many different ways in which human beings sense the limitations of their thought and manage to find connections to the implicate order beyond, but here I want to focus on two processes which seem to me to point at some of the essential ways the fixation in the vortex of the explicate in human relationship moves to the openness of relating that is possible in the implicate. These two activities are models for how that process works.

Perhaps a person has experienced moments when his mind was quiet. Perhaps he has been with another person in a particular way and knows that quiet of connection. Perhaps he reads a book about the ways to quiet his mind, but in one way or another he gets a whiff of the knowledge that he is trapped and that there may be a way to get beyond these limitations. Perhaps encouraged by someone who seems to him to be free, or as a result of other influences, he decides to start watching his thoughts. There are many ways to do this in various techniques of meditation. As a model consider zazen, Zen meditation.

In Zen meditation a person is told to watch his breath with his thought[9]. Attentive to that breathing, he is not trapped by thoughts or the vortex around them because the thinking just keeps coming and going and there is a flow of observations which seem to come without his holding to his self as the observer. In the midst of this insight a person finds that a quiet acceptance comes over him. He knows somehow, without being a he that knows, that the responses of thoughts, feelings, breathing are all that he has thought of as himself and that they are his self so much as the happening that is a continual event in nature. They simply appear. His body itself seems to appear continually as energy turned into matter which will disintegrate back into energy (nothingness) so he 'knows' he isn't his body. It is a mass, a presence in an unfolded order; the responses seem to originate in the domain of that order which is not graspable by any thought or image because they are all in a different realm. Yet they too seem to be part of that larger order, which' we would call the implicate order. He feels that he is some-thing that has been enfolded into the implicate order as part of the vast energy domain and has unfolded as a material form which is the explicate relationships he perceives. But then he knows too that his perception of thingness and the conceptualization of his self as enfolded-unfolded is itself part of the explicate order and he suspects any of his attempts at formulation. In the totality of his events in meditation the meditator breaks out of the fixations that had been happening within his thought and knows his relationship to the implicate order.

As he watches what happened with his breath the meditator is also becoming more aware that his thought process is quite fragmented and that it develops first one theme and then another and another. It creates scenarios with causes and effects and identifies with images of self that are agents of self in these scenarios. He sees too that, as these thoughts appear, there is a basic identity of the observer and he thinks of himself as this observer and that observer owns all the thoughts and feelings he observes. But then he wonders; if all of these thoughts come and go, seemingly without his thinking them, what is this thought that he is the observer? Is that not just another thing that is coming and going? If that thought is also a coming and going thought, who is he? Just another phenomenon playing across his brain? As he watches, indeed the observer appears to be just that, a thing, a conception, that is repeated from moment to moment and without that he is nothing. As that insight hits the meditator he sees too that his breathing goes on without his 'doing' or 'thinking' anything. It is a direct responsiveness in the world. It is.

> Dogen-zenji became interested in Buddhism as a boy as he
> watched the smoke from an incense stick burning by his dead
> mother's body, and he felt the evanescence of our life. This feeling
> grew within him and finally resulted in his attainment of
> enlightenment and the development of his deep philosophy. When
> he saw the smoke from the incense stick and felt the evanescence
> of life, he felt very lonely. But that lonely feeling became stronger
> and stronger, and flowered into enlightenment when he was twenty-
> eight years old. And at the moment of enlightenment he
> exclaimed, 'There is no body and no mind!' When he said 'no
> body and no mind,' all his being in that moment became a
> flashing into the vast phenomenal world, a flashing which included
> everything, which covered everything, and which had immense
> quality in it; all the phenomenal world was included within it, an
> absolute independent existence. That was his enlightenment.
> Starting from the lonely feeling of the evanescence of life, he
> attained the powerful experience of the quality of his being. He
> said 'I have dropped off mind and body.' Because you think you
> have body or mind, you have lonely feelings, but when you realize
> that everything is just a flashing into the vast universe, you
> become very strong, and your existence becomes very meaningful.
> This was Dogen's enlightenment, and this is our practice.
> (Reference 9, page 103.)

When human beings come together they have the opportunity for a group meditation on the way their common consciousness creates restrictions on their movements in the implicate order. All of them are in the implicate order and appearing as explicate phenomena inasmuch as they are identified with their individual selves. As they are together they can see this flow of the unfolding of the forms as it manifests in their individual being. Often, however, when individuals come together in a group they try to justify their identities and they repeat themselves endlessly; they want the other to know who and what they are. They express and defend the opinions with which they came into the encounter. They often don't allow for those fixed positions to dissolve and therefore they do not allow for a mutual experiencing which might occur if they were to share with others what they experience in their presence. The vitality in human relationship is drained of its dramatic presence and it becomes a dulled encounter in which the talk is meaningless drivel given over to continuing in the vortex of relationships which the fixed images have created.

In a true *dialogue* between people, however, a different ambience pertains. A true dialogue promotes trust between people. Where there is trust the individuals are more willing to see the frozen condition of the relationships imposed by the conditions of thought. The members of a true dialogue pay attention to this fixation and its vortex and are aware of the limitations it imposes on the group communion. Their dialogue seems to have originated in some awareness of the limits imposed by these kinds of restriction on the relationship in the implicate order. So the members of the dialogue discover that their commitment is attentiveness to what consciousness is, rather than an attempt to continue the forms into which they have lapsed. As they are together they find that the other people in their group dialogue are examples of what it means to be a human being like themselves. All of them have come into the dialogue because they sensed that they are trapped in a self-orientation and suspect that being with another who is equally caught up will give them a chance to see into self-deception. This face-off shows each person the fixation in the self that is characteristic of thought and consciousness in all of them. If they are all thinking of themselves as separate others, they are also not different in that they are all doing that. Then they can all become aware that the particular opinions of each are focusses of relationship and as focusses they are organizing forces, but if those foci become fixation points they have blocked the contact between individuals and therefore prevented the group as a whole from knowing its relationship to the larger order in which humanity participates.

When one person holds that his perspective is the only one, he reflects the way another person thinks that he too holds the special perspective on reality. In a discussion where people reveal their beliefs that they each have the absolutely correct perspective there is a unique opportunity to discover the nature of the process in which such conviction takes place. Of course such a group could freeze into the opposition between opinions, but in a dialogue group, where people are attending to the movement of thought, it is possible to see how the certainty comes into being and get a glimpse of the rigidity in such frozen points. With that the group begins to expand its awareness and to look at how consciousness narrows down on particular structures and loses sight of how the foci emerge.

When the dialogue partners see that thought gets into a frozen state the insight dissolves the state and the oscillation around the vortex stops. Then they talk more freely in discussion with each other, sharing and connecting in their relationships in a more vivid way; they relate in the freer way that ordering in the implicate order offers. In one instance one member of the group was expressing how deeply he felt that all relationships were lacking something. He said that he always felt that any two people are locked into their particular content and perspective. But as he talked about this he noticeably loosened up and started smiling. He said that he had, as he talked, begun to feel that a connection was established with the group and that there was no lack in that moment. He said he knew that we all came out of the same perceptive events, the same window, and that made him aware of how he had become stuck in his ideas about each person only being his particular content. He somehow knew better about the way in which all of our perspectives were generated and connected to our common generativity. At that moment the dialogue fell into a flowing discussion in which there was a juxtaposition of different views. Each individual could see that his ideas were but one perspective on the whole of any process. Each person knew that his perceptual activity was the movement which made a reality at every moment. We shared images, feelings and other not-quite-formed views and, as we tossed around some of the different ramifications of these images and feelings, new connections and references came forth. The discussion moved from talk about particulars to more general and even cosmic relation-ships and then circled back to the particular in an ever-widening circle of connections that linked to our personal past, present and future, as well as to the past, present and future of humankind.

In that movement of the implicate in the dialogue, each individual discovers his connections to the other people in the group and to other human beings in general. More accurately put, we should say that the dialogue is an active connecting in which relationships are made and dissolved, and remade again in new forms each second. Then the person in the dialogue feels that being together with the group is a harmonious process and often begins to think of how he could also be in other places in his life in a similar manner if he would but pay attention to the blocks that occur in thought. Some-times one person reminds another of himself in a more exciting way; this time the reminding is a resonance or a knowing that he is part of the movement of the one consciousness he shares with everyone in the group. He discovers that he shares images and feelings that the other is having but is not talking about and that shows him that he is registering responses of other people that the other people may not have articulated to him. Perhaps they don't even realize they are having such feelings until he speaks of them. But from this resonating he senses their connection in an ambient movement which is finding forms they share in making. They know they are people who make connection to all parts of the explicate order and, as people who connect, they are part of the implicate order as well. The dialogue is a dramatic example of the way human life expresses the unfolding of the implicate order into explicate forms. From the perspective of a brain scientist, Mackay writes [10]:

> Perhaps the most characteristic conscious human activity is that reciprocal interaction with others which we call *dialogue*. I am not now referring to the non-committal alternating monologue that sometimes passes for dialogue in our sophisticated society, but the deep-going relationship of mutual vulnerability through which another in a special way becomes 'Thou' to me and I to him. The distinction between the two seems to have an illuminating parallel at the level of information-flow analysis. As long as someone communicating with another is able to shield his own evaluative system from the address of the other, he can in principle treat the other as an object, a manipulandum, open in principle to full scientific specification like another physical object. Once the barriers to fully reciprocal communication are down, however, a specially interesting configuration becomes possible, in which the information-flow structure that constitutes each supervisory system *interpenetrates* the other, and the lines of flow from each return by way of the other, so that the two become one system for purposes of causal analysis.
>
> In this relationship, each conscious agent becomes indeterminate for the other . . . as well as for himself. Each is mysterious to the other, not merely in the weak sense that the other cannot gain the necessary completely determining information, but in the strong sense that *no such information exists*, either for him or for his interlocutor, until after the event. There are 'interaction terms,' as a physicist would say, in the joint state-equation, which prevent it from a uniquely determinate solution for either, even if the physical systems concerned were as mechanistic as pre-Heisenberg physics pictured them.

One of the central features of dialogue is that it makes apparent that discussion between human beings is an important part of the natural order of life on earth. Human response and articulation of that response, feedback of reactions to that response and the clarifying of the relationships between different responses, are the way human beings participate in the flow of the implicate order. The dialogue unfolds the different forms that are established in the interaction between people and those forms are enfolded back into different meanings of their relationships to other people. The movement itself is the articulation of the implicate order in the human domain [11].

Perhaps what we are also revealing here is that points of order or centers of organization are inherent to the implicate order as it unfolds into the explicate. These points always create something of a vortex around them as they provide for interactions and further relationships in that flow. Perhaps some are more restrictive than others. Lower animals do not have as wide a relationship in the implicate order as the human being, with his extensively connected human brain. The fixed images in consciousness, however, are themselves only a relatively fixed point as there are numerous relationships intertwining and unfolding from them, even if they do form a vortex. Even in that condition the human brain is more extensively related than a paramecium. Any form, any organism, is always changing and is in relationships that bring about movements and change. Certainly throughout our universe these relatively fixed points are in interactions that allow for dissolution and transformation from focus to focus. In meditation and dialogue human beings become aware of their larger relationship to the implicate order and it enables them to see the limitations of the point of fixation. In that awareness they outgrow the restrictions in their relationship in the implicate order and extend their participation in that greater order.

Acknowledgment

I want to thank Catherine de Segonzac for her assistance in the preparation of this paper.

References

1   David Bohm, *Wholeness and the Implicate Order*, Routledge & Kegan Paul, London, 1980.
2   John Briggs and David F. Peat, *Looking Glass Universe: The Emerging Science of Wholeness*, Simon & Schuster, New York, 1984.
3   David R. Griffen, *The Need for a Post Modern Paradigm*, unpublished manuscript, 1984.
4   N. Eldredge and I. Tattersall, *The Myths of Human Evolution*, Columbia University Press, New York, 1982.
5   David Shainberg, *Nuclear Arms, National Sovereignty, and Consciousness; Comprehensive Psychotherapy, Vol. 6*, Gordon & Breech, New York, 1984.
6   D. H. Hubel, 'Effects of distortion of sensory input on the visual systems of kittens', Eleventh Bowditch Lecture, *Physiologist*, **10**, 17 (1967).
7   Jerome Bruner, *In search of Mind: Essays in Autobiography*, Harper & Row, New York, 1983.
8   Karen Horney, *Neurosis and Human Growth*, Norton, New York, 1950.

9   S. Suzuki, *Zen Mind, Beginners Mind* (Trudy Dixon, ed.), John Weather-
    hill, New York, 1970.
10 D. M. Mackay, 'Conscious agency with unsplit and split brains', in B. D.
    Josephson and V. S. Ramachandran (eds), *Consciousness and the Physical
    World*, Pergamon Press, New York, 1980.
11 David Shainberg, *The Transforming Self: New Dimensions in Psycho-
    analytic Process*, Intercontinental Medical Book Corp. N.Y., 1973.

29

Reflectaphors: the (implicate) universe as a work of art

John Briggs   *New School for Social Research, New York City*

A number of years ago I was quite surprised to discover an uncanny resemblance between an approach I was pursuing into the underlying structure of works of art and David Bohm's visions into the underlying construction of matter. The coincidence between these two ideas continues to surprise me, but Bohm himself added an even stranger twist one afternoon some years later when I had the opportunity of interviewing him for a radio show. The show focused on the possible relationships between the arts and science and, in the course of the interview, Bohm offered that he didn't see why great works of art couldn't also have something important to teach us about the laws of nature.

The possibility he raised that day is curious and haunting and in the next pages I will try to catch a glimpse of its ghost by outlining the hypothesis I found so startlingly mirrored in David Bohm's implicate order.

The hypothesis in question is a way of conceptualizing both the structure of works of art and some aspects of the process which goes into creating them. Specifically, it describes the global interaction of what I call 'reflectaphors.' Reflectaphors are created in the dynamics that takes place among the elements that comprise a work of art. In the visual arts, reflectaphors emerge in the interactions of elements like shape, line, color and negative space. In literature they appear in such techniques as irony, pun, motif, symbol and metaphor. Through reflectaphors are displayed an artwork's subtlety and its ability to astonish: they are the intersection between its parts and the whole; seedbeds of its 'truth'; the nexes of the mind apprehending and the thing apprehended; and they remain both unchanged and in process. They are the artwork's hidden order.

To illustrate the interworkings of that order, I propose first to look in detail at its appearance as metaphor.

X/Y: two sides of a mirror

Metaphor is traditionally defined as an unusual or non-logical assertion of identity between two terms. Some aestheticians view metaphor (including simile) as the backbone of poetry. Aristotle claimed that 'it is the greatest thing by far to be the master of metaphor.'

A sample poetic metaphor will illustrate why. In his well-known *Ars Poetica*, Archibald MacLeish sets out to tell his readers what a poem is by writing one. His strategy is to identify the abstract concept 'a poem' with a series of sensuous images, creating a string of stunning metaphors. Through these metaphors the poet *evokes* rather than prescribes an understanding of what a poem is. Consider one of MacLeish's figures: 'A poem should be wordless as the flight of birds.'

The metaphor is conventional in that it is composed of two terms – X, 'a poem,' and Y, 'a flight of birds' – asserted to be at least potentially (i.e. 'should be') identical. And the mind is given pause.

Behind that pause lurks the secret of poetic metaphor – a peculiar equation of tension between terms. For in the same mental space X and Y are convergently compared and contrasted.

On the contrast side, $X \neq Y$ because the reader knows very well that a poem is not a movement made out of flesh, blood, feathers and the instinct to negotiate currents of air. Applying 'wordless' to the equation heightens this contrast almost to the point of paradox.

On the comparison side, the asserted $X = Y$ compels the mind to stretch out to connect the terms. For the metaphor to do that there must be enough felt similarity between them. For example, we might see in the flight of birds an orderly activity, a free and lyrical quality, a living and ultimately unutterable meaning that might be appropriate to a poem.

Might be – but, of course, anyone attempting to give an account of all the meanings of this metaphor would immediately run head-on into two problems. First, the analyzable meanings here are both complex and multiplex because the number of discernible similarities and shades of similarities between the wordless flight of birds and a poem is limited only by human imagination. Second, to delineate fully even one meaning would require actively ignoring the contrast side of the metaphor – for to include that would effectively undercut *any* meaning by making us aware that a flight of birds is basically *not* like a poem. Moreover, the fact that it is not like a poem creates still further meanings which are, themselves, not fully analyzable. Not surprisingly, therefore, the interpreted meanings of metaphors often turn out to be paradoxical or self-contradictory. The movement which produces this effect bears connection to Bohm's implicate order.

According to Bohm, matter and energy continually unfold and enfold, appearing in particular (explicate) forms like photons and mountains and then disappearing into the (implicate) background. For Bohm this primordial unending movement from implicate to explicate and back again implies the whole. He calls it holomovement and considers it primary to all natural law. In a metaphor, an analogous sort of thing seems to happen with meaning.

Recently one of the many subtleties of the often paradoxical movement of meaning through metaphor surfaced during a class discussion of the MacLeish lines. I was explaining that I personally experienced the image as a flight of birds in formation very high up and silent, wordless. Then someone in the class pointed out that birds in flight often make quite a bit of noise, also not words, but probably communication of some sort – and we realized such an image could also fit MacLeish's metaphor. Obviously, taking that angle on the metaphor alters and broadens – in Bohm's terms unfolds and enfolds – one's conception of its meaning. In the movement through the mind of the old conception and the new, one gets a taste of the whole.

This suggests the metaphor is meaning as an ongoing process and perception rather than meaning as the conclusions of knowledge. To illustrate, consider the difference between the MacLeish metaphor and the statement 'A poem should be made of rhymed couplets.' Evidently, the statement is conclusive and logical. There is no sense of movement from the two terms, no hint of the kind of activity created by the provocative ambiguity of the metaphor. The statement may be arguable, but it can be quickly assimilated and filed away by the mind. MacLeish's metaphor, however, invites neither agreement nor disagreement, and despite its stipulative syntax, the sentence leaves the mind in a state more like that of hearing a question than understanding an assertion.

Perhaps that is the metaphor's point. Certainly it was MacLeish's point. 'A poem,' he says at the end of *Ars Poetica*, 'should not mean but be.' The metaphor should move the mind beyond the conceptual confines of the X and Y terms, from meaning (which is paraphrasable and analyzable) to an implicate-explicate-implicate movement of meaning or being (which is not). Amazingly, if the metaphor strikes the right chemistry between X and Y, even repeated encounters with it will not inhibit this movement.

How can this be? The answer may lie in understanding how consciousness perceives a metaphor.

At present, neuroscience is only beginning to grapple with the immensely intricate questions of how consciousness works. But whatever the specific mechanisms, it seems plausible to generalize that a great deal of conscious processing (including layers of the unconscious and perception) relies on some form of comparison and contrast activity[1]. For example, a sound is 'heard' against a background of other sounds (the voice of a friend shouting above the crash of the sea) by a process which separates out, abstracts, by contrast, the pitch, volume, rhythm of one sound (the voice) from that of the background (waves) and compares and contrasts it to patterns (of words, the friend's voice) recorded in memory.

Memory, whether genetically acquired as instinct or experientially acquired as learning, lies at the root of the brain movement in which the complex mix of reason, emotion, brain states, perceptual regimes and immediate environmental influences unfold in conscious (explicate level) awareness as a stream of comparing and contrasting. These comparing and contrasting activities then refold into the background (implicate) levels of the brain to set the stage for further comparisons and contrasts.

In the appendix to his 1965 book *The Special Theory of Relativity*, Bohm considers theories of perception by Piaget, Gibson, Held, Ditchburn and others and conveys his sense of them through an elegant hypothetical illustration which I will modify and simplify to make the point here about metaphor.

Suppose you are walking along a road in the obscure light of the moon. You see an unknown shape in the distance (contrast: the figure to its background). Initially you think you are seeing a person (comparison: of that shape to the complex memories of human shapes in various positions), but as you draw closer you notice features unlike human ones (your comparison has disclosed elements in contrast) and you then formulate a new image of what you see as an animal (comparison) until this comparison too reveals a contrast. At this juncture, still retaining elements of your comparisons of human-like and animal-like features, but confronted by undeniable contrasting elements which make this conclusion unlikely, you may compare your information to some idea you have of a monster and begin to panic. Finally, trembling on the edge of flight, you press ahead enough to recognize the shape as a bush (comparison of features of the object with features in the memory-abstraction 'bush').

Sequences of comparison-then-contrast-then-comparison unfold with neuronal rapidity and flow indistinguishably into one another. Nevertheless, it is obvious that consciousness does *not* see the shape simultaneously as background, person, animal, monster and bush. That would be absurd, if not actually psychotic. Instead, what is perceived in the advance toward the shape is a series of advancing conclusions or abstractions, each held successively as a theory (and one of the roots of 'theory' is the Greek *theâsthai*, 'to see'). At any moment the comparing and contrasting sequences yield apparent knowledge of what is being seen.

In poetic metaphor, however, comparisons and contrasts between the X and Y terms don't alternate; they remain in dynamic X/Y tension or balance. The metaphor's dynamic appears to engender the perception that the metaphor means all the possible similarities between its terms and none of the similarities. The categorical or conclusive mind set which is the staple of our consciousness is momentarily cancelled out. We have the vivid and immediate experience that our meanings may be viable but they are horribly limited. Indeed, it isn't far-fetched to imagine a poet writing a piece in which he approaches an object and reveals in metaphor that it is a man, an animal, a monster *and* a bush. Moreover, he might suggest there are also other possibilities he senses are present in the object but cannot quite discern, and that all of these, in turn, reflect his own existential condition and the very act of his observing so that, in the end, he is finding himself in the object. Meanwhile he could be revealing that his experience is more than any of this because it is none of these things. Such coalescences and twists occur in literature all the time. It is what William Empson meant by his use of the term ambiguity [2].

Something like this happens, for example, in Robert Frost's poem 'The Road Not Taken.' The narrator in the poem tells about stopping at the place where the single road he had been traveling on diverged and how he decided which of the two alternative paths to take. In the course of four stanzas, each road is described in such a way as to suggest that every feature of the roads is also a feature of the narrator's dilemma in living his human life (e.g. 'I looked down one [road] as far as I could/To where it bent in the undergrowth'). Meanwhile, though he is at pains to tell the reader how similar the roads were, the narrator also asserts that they were different (e.g. 'the passing there/ Had worn them really about the same' yet 'I took the one less traveled by'). This comparison/contrast, similarity/difference ambiguity is central to our experience of the roads as a metaphor.

'The Road Not Taken' might be called a central one-term metaphor because the narrator never says explicitly that the activity of a man choosing roads X, is metaphorically equated with any Y. But the tone and weight of the narrative suggests that such an unstated Y-term is present. Indeed, the fact that the reader can never say for sure that a Y such as 'choosing one's path in life' is meant at all adds considerable energy to the X/Y, comparison/contrast tension. (Actually it's more a harmony than a tension, in the musical sense of the word harmony.) When asked to respond to the various meanings that people had given to this poem, Frost himself insisted rather sharply there was no ulterior meaning at all. It was about a man in the woods choosing roads. In a sense, his reaction could have been expected. Artists typically become sullen or hostile when asked what their work means. Why? Because it's the wrong question. To want to 'know' the meaning of a metaphor indicates you're bent on missing its meaning. By not falling victim to the lust for a meaning, Frost kept his metaphor alive.

There are many varieties of poetic metaphor. Some metaphors

appear as images, as in poet Richard Hugo's line 'The sun bruises the oats gold' which is formed from three compressed metaphoric juxtapositions–

1 (X) sun $=$ (Y) a being or physical object capable of bruising;
2 (X) the act of bruising $=$ (Y) natural processes which engage photosynthesis; and then
3 this strange bruising, as an action (X) implicitly equated in the metaphor with (Y) making the oats valuable (like gold).

Compression of several different metaphoric elements in interlocking X/Y tension is typical of artistic structure.

In other cases, a central X-term may be linked serially in a piece to a number of different Ys to produce a branching-term metaphor, as in the Emily Dickinson poem where the narrator explicitly compares 'a certain slant of light on winter afternoons' to several images and ideas, including 'the heft of cathedral tunes,' 'an imperial affliction' and 'a heavenly hurt.'

In poems, the use of metaphor as a technique is extensive and in metaphor resides all of those qualities of vitality, mystery, truth and timeless excitement we normally associate with poetry itself.

For that reason, it is important to consider why, outside of literary context, in the world at large, metaphors do not have these qualities. Though general-use metaphors have a structure which also cojoins unlikely or illogical X and Y terms, the structure in this case is superficial.

For example, calling somebody a 'rat,' claiming that a cigarette will taste as fresh as a drop of rain, or giving the name space*ship* to a vehicle which plies the regions beyond earth's atmosphere, are all forms of metaphor. General-use metaphors abound, and they can be as strikingly unusual as any poetic metaphors. But they are unlike them in one crucial respect. In the general-use metaphor the comparison and contrast between the terms can be *resolved*. The general-use metaphor stresses the *similarity* between X and Y. Such metaphors are dressed up forms of conclusion and knowledge and so they function essentially in the way ordinary communication does. A specific point is intended by the metaphor, a message – and once the point is apprehended, the metaphor is over. 'I saw Mrs Bradshaw today; she was high as a kite.' A metaphor like this is entirely empty or misleading unless the listener, who presumably has a context for Mrs Bradshaw, can draw an appropriate conclusion about what is meant (e.g. the lady has been taking drugs).

In contrast, the message of poetic or literary metaphors ('a poem should be wordless as the flight of birds') remains essentially complex and ambiguous though, oddly, literary metaphors are by no means vague ('the sun bruises the oats gold'). They are lucid despite their rigorous disavowal of message.

Literary metaphors should also be distinguished from the type of metaphor known variously as 'root' metaphor, 'conceptual archetype' or 'model'[3]. The Newtonian notion that the universe is a machine is an example of this type of metaphor. It has an 'envisioning' quality because it is more open-ended than a general-use metaphor. For instance, scientists inspired by the metaphor of celestial mechanics have been able to envision and uncover numerous mechanical-like aspects of nature. When an envisoning metaphor is created, it has meanings which are unknown at the time and this can make the metaphor hugely inviting. However, in the end the invitation is to discern what those meanings are – quite different from the invitation of a poetic metaphor.

David Bohm, of course, is probably more aware than any scientist in modern times of the traps of envisioning metaphors. Not only has he argued eloquently against the way science has explicated to distortion the Newtonian metaphor; he has tried to incorporate in his model a clear sense of the limitations of all scientific models, including his own, to provide ultimate meanings. I remember that during our radio show he said he thought scientific theories should be presented like poetry because, like poems, theories are insights, acts of perception, rather than hard and fast conclusions. In presenting his implicate order, Bohm is always careful to spell out the suggestive rather than objective value of his illustrating metaphors like the hologram or the glycerine ink-drop experiment. He is always pointing beyond, showing where his theory, vast as it is, must shade off into more subtle reaches and regions of the unknown (the super-implicate order, higher-dimensional realities, chaos as infinite degrees of order, the super-quantum potential and the super-super-quantum potential), always impressing the listener with the limitations of the mind in the face of this vast order of which the mind itself is a mirror. In this way, Bohm tries to avoid the common fate of scientific metaphors and accomplish something very like what happens in the X/Y dynamics of metaphors in poems. But Bohm's understanding is rare. The very richness of an envisioning metaphor is usually its downfall. Greedy for certainty, the mind can't resist and seeks to draw out every last ounce of the treasure until the metaphor collapses. Poetic metaphor avoids this exploitation and eventual exhaustion (though not for the lack of critics' trying) because of its X/Y dynamics and because the metaphor is set in a subtle structure of other metaphor-like devices which engender a pervasive order. This order is, as it were, especially designed to frustrate the drive of consciousness to analyze, paraphrase or constrict the movement which is that order's meaning.

Reflectaphoric order

There are a number of reasons to propose the neologism reflectaphor. While it might be possible to expand the existing term metaphor to cover the wide range of similar phenomena which occur in literary artforms, the visual arts, music and performing arts, like most other critical terms in the arts, metaphor suffers from over-use. Extending it further could inevitably result in confusion arising from the way the critical literature and common usage have conflated the general-use, envisioning and literary metaphors under the single term and have compounded metaphor indiscriminately with other critical terms like symbol, emblem and image.

Nevertheless, the X/Y dynamic of literary metaphor, as I have defined it, has so much to offer by way of illuminating what is happening generally in artistic structure, that I propose to retain an echo of this type of metaphor in a new term.

The word metaphor comes from the Greek *meta* and Aryan *medhi* which mean 'middle, between, among and beyond' and from the Greek *phore* derived from *phoros*, 'to carry or to bear.' The word 'reflect' comes from the Greek *re* and *flex* which means 'bending back or bending again.' Putting these together, a reflectaphor can be thought of as having the quality of carrying between and beyond by a constant bending back. One side of the reflectaphor is carried over to the other, but then is reflected or carried back again and, therefore, once again *beyond.* The comparison/contrast design of the reflectaphor propels this movement, bending the mind back again and beyond, giving no rest in conclusion. Between the elements of a reflectaphor there is no meaning as such; the meaning is the continual revelation – what Bohm calls unfoldment and enfoldment – of this reflective movement.

Two further important dimensions of the 'reflect' in reflectaphor will also become apparent as we probe deeper into artistic process and structure. First, a reflectaphor mirrors the apprehender of the reflectaphor so that, as Bohm would say, the observer becomes revealed as the observed. Second, a reflectaphor in the context of a particular artwork is mirroring other reflectaphors in that context and in fact is a reflection of the whole of that context.

The first step toward contacting that larger order of reflectaphors is to see that the kind of dynamic we observed in the individual poetic metaphor also appears in other artistic techniques. In literature any technique or aspect of a piece can be reflectaphoric; for instance, irony.

In 'The Road Not Taken,' as we noted, the central axis of the poem is a metaphor (X) roads like (implied Y) life. But this metaphor is itself worked out ironically. The narrator's statement that he decided to take one road 'because it was grassy and wanted wear;/Though as for that, the passing there/Had worn them really about the same' combined with his assertion that 'two roads diverged in a wood, and I –/I took the one less traveled by' create a context that causes the final statement, 'And that has made all the difference' to become ironic to a high degree. There is also irony in the fact that, although the narrator appears to emphasize the road he took, the title of the poem is 'The Road Not Taken.' In irony, the words or situation intend one meaning (X) and yet another meaning (Y) is perceived. If there is tension or harmony between the two – sometimes contradictory – meanings it creates a reflectaphor.

Even puns can be reflectaphors. 'Would he had been one of my rank!' one Shakespeare character says, and his comrade replies, 'To have smell'd like a fool.' Rank as status (X) is juxtaposed to rank as bad smell (Y). The similarity between X and Y (they're the same word) emphasizes the contrast, and the reflectaphor is formed.

What happens when these and the many other reflectaphoric techniques are brought together into a whole context? Here lies what is perhaps the most dramatic similarity between Bohm's theory of matter and the structure and process found embedded in works of art.

One of the primary models Bohm uses to illustrate the implicate order is the hologram. He focuses on the fact that in a hologram each region contains information about the whole picture which is recorded on the holographic plate. If a laser beam is passed through different fragments of the plate, this whole picture will be revealed to have been encoded in each piece, though seen from different angles. Holographic images are produced by recording on to the plate the interference patterns of light. Bohm says that since all matter-energy is composed of extremely subtle interference patterns moving continually throughout space, each particle or wave of matter and energy contains a unique image of the whole.

In artistic creation an analogous holomovement takes place through the medium of reflectaphors.

Joseph Conrad's masterwork *Typhoon* provides a brilliant example of this and shows how the artistic hologram is formed by concatenations of reflectaphors enfolded in every aspect of the story; characters, setting, plot, conflict and an array of expressive techniques.

Ostensibly Conrad's tale is about a rather dull-witted sea captain who navigates his ship through the unimaginable fury of a tropical typhoon. In actuality, the story is about the nature of a human being's relationship to his fellows, the relationship of mind to matter, fate and will, knowledge and ignorance, truth and illusion, courage, cowardice, imagination and the creative act. In short, it is a story that implicates the whole.

Conrad depicts the storm which the plot of the tale revolves around as commencing with the surprising oppressive placidity characteristic of typhoons. A puzzling calm besets the ship and turns out to be the prelude to the tempest that follows. In its context, this storm becomes a reflectaphor comparing/contrasting (X) its paradoxical placidity with (Y) its amazing energy. The typhoon-as-plot-device, in turn, stands in X/Y comparison/contrast to Conrad's rendering of the strikingly un-imaginative captain whose fate it is to ride out the storm. He is one of literature's most improbable heroes, described to the reader as an (X) absurdly placid character, lacking foresight and drive. Incongruously, however, he possesses 'fiery metallic gleams' on his cheeks 'no matter how close he shaved,' and these foreshadow (Y) the inner spark and power that allows him, for all his perplexing dullness, to take on the typhoon. Like the typhoon, the captain possesses tremendous force, at first obscured by a face of apparent placidity. The captain's name – another reflectaphor of the typhoon – is MacWhirr.

MacWhirr is also juxtaposed in reflectaphoric X/Y to his ship. The Nan-Shan has 'the reputation of an exceptionally steady ship in a seaway.' MacWhirr is described as physically 'stolid' and proves to be psychologically exceptionally steady in the distressing seaway of the typhoon. In this regard, the fiery gleams on MacWhirr's cheeks (X) are also a reflection of (Y) the fire in the Nan-Shan's boilers that keeps the stolid ship with her head to the wind.

The Nan-Shan carries a cargo of Chinese coolies and they reveal yet another reflectaphor of MacWhirr and the typhoon. Portrayed as a 'languid' (placid) lot, during the storm the coolies become anything but languid, clawing and thrashing each other in a frenzy because the footlockers they have brought with them have been battered open by the pitching of the ship, and the silver dollars which they have spent years away from home earning are flying around the innards of the cabin. At one point, the boatswain opens a hatch and witnesses this scene which Conrad clearly intends to suggest is a human typhoon. Even rolling circular dollars which the Chinese are chasing are reflectaphoric of the 'circular storm' raging outside.

All these connections are interlocking reflectaphors in which one image, theme or event is equated with another to which it is logically dissimilar. Out of the basic reflectaphor of the typhoon whirl galaxies of reflectaphoric relationships: captain to storm; Chinese to storm; dollars to storm; ship to captain; storm to ship; passivity vs activity to all of the above; and so on in manifold, swirling compressions and combinations. Taken together, these relationships make the work a kind of moving hologram, a holomovement, in which each element (e.g. MacWhirr, the ship, the dollars) reflects by implication the whole. Moreover, this hologram partakes of something analogous to what Bohm calls a 'higher dimensional reality.'

Bohm notes that in the quantum domain, because each detectable atomic particle must exist in three dimensions, an object with 10^{24} atomic particles would have 3×10^{24} dimensions of space. For him this multiplicity of dimensions is a powerful way to visualize his implicate-explicate order because it means that each object of our perceptions is an expression or display of the enfoldment and unfoldment of higher implicate dimensions into our familiar explicate three-dimensional space. One might observe analogously that each reflectaphor contains two dimensions of X/Y dynamics and numerous dimensions of meaning. With a structure such as *Typhoon*, where there are many interacting reflectaphors, it seems possible to conjecture, and perhaps to observe, that within the explicate space of the story a matrix of implicate and higher dimensional realities are enfolded.

The fact that each element and combination in the piece is in a similarity/difference relationship with a multiplicity of other elements could also help account for the feeling that a great work of literature like *Typhoon* or 'The Road Not Taken' is always turning away from closure, even at its end. Closure would be the possibility of resolving the similarity/difference dynamic – translating the reflectaphor into a conclusion such as an allegory or symbol. Instead, for the reader there is an elusive sense of the similarities in the elements of character, event and setting which emphasize their obviously vast differences. The X/Y dynamics and permeation of reflectaphors create a distinct impression that there is always something *more* or *other* than the literal elements of the piece. Those elements seem always to stand or move beyond themselves.

I propose to call this special quality of a work of art its 'this∗otherness' – a neologism intended to open up a slightly different view on the artistic process.

In a poetic reflectaphor the X-term – 'this' – is asserted to be the same as the Y-term – the 'other'. But because of the comparison/contrast dynamic – indicated here by the sign ∗ – 'this' is also vividly set off from the 'other.' For the reader, the feeling of 'this∗other' is a movement, like the buzzing, uncanny current set up by the shifting poles in an electrical device.

In the context of a literary fiction like *Typhoon*, the this∗other-ness dynamic exists throughout and is an expression of the artwork's wholeness. MacWhirr is a 'this' but he is also a great deal 'other' than this. He is the ship, the typhoon, the Chinese, etc. Each encounter with a 'this' is a discovery at some subliminal level of how that 'this' exists as an immediate and elusive embodiment of every 'other' in the piece and so the piece as a whole. At the same time, lest the reader fall into the error of taking MacWhirr as an abstraction, a symbol of something other than what he is, the dynamic ∗ bends him back. MacWhirr is MacWhirr, a 'this': the stolid captain in the story.

This∗other-ness is also the relationship of the observer to the observed and this is perhaps its major effect. In many artforms the elements of the work are fixed – words on a page, lines and colors in a painting – yet the perceiver's encounter with the reflectaphors sets in motion a profound process of unfoldment and enfoldment between the terms of the reflectaphors in the piece and the perceiver's own identity. Thus, the reader of *Typhoon* tacitly perceives the movement of similarity/difference between himself and MacWhirr, the typhoon, the Chinese, etc. He sees implicitly that in his life, in his mind and in the world there are all manner of typhoons.

In the preface to one of his stories, Conrad called the effect of discovering one's identity in a story 'solidarity:'

> The presented vision of regret or pity, of terror or mirth, shall awaken in the hearts of the beholders that feeling of unavoidable solidarity; of the solidarity in mysterious origin, in toil, in joy, in hope, in uncertain fate, which binds men to each other and all mankind to the visible world.

Finally, in its largest aspect, the reader may perceive through the story that in the this-ness of the world there is also an overall other-ness, an order which cannot be contained by our definitions – a super-implicate order.

One more example from *Typhoon* will illustrate how the unfolding reflectaphoric, holographic, super-implicate and this*other-ly order – Conrad's 'solidarity' – subtly informs an artwork's entire structure; and it may recall Thomas Mann's claim that the only way to write a novel is 'with mirrors.'

The boatswain enters an empty coal bunker just before opening the door to the 'tween deck cabin and witnessing the mayhem of the Chinese chasing their dollars. In the pitch black bunker just before reaching the door, the sailor finds himself menaced by a loose metal bar, a coal-trimmer's slice, which is being hurtled around in the blackness by the pitch of the ship. The boatswain has the distinct impression that this piece of metal is trying to catch him and kill him. Finally, as if by blind luck, his hand falls upon the slice and he is saved. A moment later, he opens the door to the 'tween deck. Here, rather than being chased by pieces of metal, the Chinese are trying to catch metal pieces (their rolling dollars) which by a seeming blind luck keep slipping from their grasp. The ostensible reasons for these cat-and-mouse chases between man and metal are manifestly different (the boatswain wants to save himself from being battered to death by an unseen force; the Chinese want to secure their possessions). Or are they so different? The scene is like a chemical solution mixing these reflectaphors with others in the story having to do with blindness, circularity and luck or fate.

This illustration and the others from *Typhoon* are far from untypical of the piece as a whole and represent only a very small sample of its total reflectaphoric connections (a 'higher dimensional' total, probably impossible to calculate). One does not need to assume that Conrad was consciously aware of these connections or that he intended them – though there is good evidence that he was well aware of the principle. Creators frequently say that in the act of creating they feel as if they participate in an order that is beyond them.

It should also be noted that not all novels have the direct mirror-type of reflectaphors exhibited by *Typhoon*. In fact every great artist finds his or her own approach and techniques for the expression of this∗other-ness so that the variety of reflectaphoric structures is an immense and fascinating subject in itself.

Figure 29.1 'Man With Umbrella,' after Kao Ch'i-p'ei (courtesy of the British Museum, London).

One should also not infer that a work of art's greatness is to be measured by the sheer complexity or quantity of reflectaphoric permutations. Even a single, simple reflectaphor can be enduring, as Matso Bashò's haiku:

One's life, a single
dewdrop.
Its lonely savor.

Umbrella terms

In the art of painting, reflectaphors exist on a number of levels and are articulated through numerous techniques. For example, reflectaphors can be created when a painting of one thing looks subliminally like another – a building that looks subtly like a face, a range of mountains that is as sensuous as a reclining body.

Reflectaphors occur most intensively, however, among the shapes, colors and lines of the painting. This can be seen readily in a relatively simple Chinese portrait, after Kao Ch'i-p'ei (AD 1672?–1734), called 'Man With Umbrella' (see Figure 29.1).

Let us begin to explore the this∗other-ness resonance in this painting with the shape which appears as the top of the man's umbrella, abstracted thus:

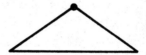

This shape is echoed reflectaphorically throughout the painting. Notice that it is in the hat strapped to the man's back; in the notch of his front pant leg; in the notch between the rear and front pant leg; in the shape of the shadow under the arm; in the top ⌃ of the bridge (where the entire figure of the man himself might be viewed as something like the dot on the umbrella peak).

Each of these variations is slightly different from the △ of the umbrella, different enough probably to pass unnoticed as reflections. For instance, note the comparison/contrast created by the △ ⌒ lines which form the bridge the old man is walking across. These shapes are a kind of *X/Y* between the Euclidian triangle composed of straight lines (like the umbrella) and the Riemannian triangle made of curved lines. This △/⌒ reflectaphoric tension is maintained throughout the piece in numerous variations. In these permutations of permutations of the basic △ shape, the viewer is no longer following actual lines but tracking lines of force created by the overall composition. This suggests another kind of visual reflectaphor at work. Look at the shape formed by the line of the man's back and rear pant leg and stomach, then up to the dark spot behind the nape of the neck – a shape that might be abstracted

Again, there is the ◺ shape, complete with curve/triangle reflectaphor and a solid spot at the buttocks' apex. Between the armpit and the nape of the neck this line is not filled in, but is suggested by the faint upward thrust in the armpit shadow which draws the eye toward the heavy dark spot at the neck. Here the line which begins at the rear pant leg and ends at the neck is itself a kind of reflectaphor; that is, though it is 'this' (a line) it is also many 'other' things – a trouser leg, a shadow, a belly and chest, an armpit and, for a while, between the arm and neck, nothing at all. Each ◺ is reflectaphorically both there and not there since each figure's lines are also lines of other triangles, other parts of the composition. Thus, while the this*other-ness spreads an implicit recognition of the ◺ everywhere, it keeps its distance so the similarities are never overstressed or conclusive. The painting cannot be resolved into a clever collection of ◺ shapes. Each variation blends into the others, appears and vanishes into the overall picture. Yet the presence of these reflections contribute to the deep sense of coherence in the piece.

These, of course, are formal elements. But there are other quite important aspects to this painting. How do they fit? One might wonder, for example, about the this*other-ness of an old man crossing a bridge hung in space. And what about the old man's character? Is that reflectaphoric, as well?

Leonardo da Vinci's 'Mona Lisa' is perhaps the most popular example of portraiture in the history of painting and can be taken as exemplary of the reflectaphoric effect of creating character by visual means. Albert Rothenberg notes that over the centuries critics have described the Gioconda smile as both 'good and wicked,' 'cruel' and 'compassionate,' 'the smile of the Saints at Rheims' and 'worldly, watchful and self satisfied,' a look of both 'modesty and a secret sensuous joy.'[4]

Leonardo evidently created in this smile a this*other-ness in which various psychological states were reflectaphorically related. In that particular remarkable smile, which is Mona Lisa's and no other's, something universal about the nature of human passion shines through. Something similar is happening with the old man on the bridge – something conveyed by his expression and the attitude of his body. Could one say what his character is in the instant of the painting? determination? resignation? sourness? humor? combativeness? Or should we say that the painting has somehow penetrated and found the common ground for the structure of all those different emotions (and more)? Yet the man with the umbrella is not an abstraction, a human generality. He is a particular, unique presence. The painter has expressed through line and simple shape the sense that this man crossing a bridge stands beyond himself, that his lines extend outward to touch the solidarity of humanity and being. It is as if his individuality were somehow founded upon his universality; as if the viewer's sense of his universality were founded upon the old man's uniqueness.

Like the narrator choosing roads in the Frost poem, the situation of the man with the umbrella is charged so that, even though we aren't told this is a reflectaphor whose terms are (X) the old man crossing the bridge with (Y) our own life, we perceive that it is. And in so far as we are disposed to assign meaning to the painting, the expression and attitude of the old man's body has something like the effect of the irony in 'The Road Not Taken.' Each time we think we've got it, we must see we haven't. With paintings, however, we generally don't assign meanings, not consciously, anyway.

In fact, in talking about 'Man With Umbrella' I have made explicit aspects which remain implicit for most viewers and were probably so for the artist in the act of making his creation. However, that's not to say either that the implicit is not real or that by making it explicit we have come any closer to understanding the actual 'truth' of the piece. That 'truth' must ultimately lie in the mysterious realm of what brought all these reflectaphors together in the artist's mind and in the poignant movement that takes place when they are encountered by a viewing consciousness. Some reflectaphors, like 'the sun bruises the oats gold,' depend upon being explicit and shocking; others, like the bunker scene in *Typhoon* and the △ of 'Man With Umbrella,' remain implicit for their effect. The relative degrees of explicitness or implicitness; the types of techniques used to express the reflectaphors and the reflectaphoric combinations (e.g. irony, metaphor, pun); the types of reflectaphors inherent in each genre and artform (the gestures of dance; contrast and tonalities in black and white photography; the conceptual quality of words) all have quite different effects on the observing consciousness. Yet they have a similar effect as well: to create a sense of a this*other-ness order, a moment of uncanniness where, as Heidegger said, one comes into immediate contact with being.

The whole issue of explicit and implicit can be illuminated by analogy to Bohm's assertion that explicate forms like electrons are also implicate and that the strangenesses of quantum mechanics – such as the puzzle that the electron can be both particle and wave – are really symptoms of the fact that implicate and explicate are two sides of the same coin. Our minds prefer to see one side or the other. The power of a great work of art is that it gives both sides simultaneously. Implicit and explicit converge. That is the meaning of the this*other-ness order and a major function of the X/Y dynamics.

In the creative mind

Modern abstract art, photography, dance, music – all artforms and styles find ways to express that order. Composer Igor Stravinsky, in his *Poetics of Music*, noted that for him 'variety is valued only as a means of attaining similarity'[5]. In his Norton Lectures Leonard Bernstein defined compositions of the Romantic era as having what he called 'extrinsic metaphor,' in that melodies and instruments are used to refer to objects or processes like birds, brooks, characters. He also noted a more general feature of composition, 'intrinsic metaphor,' where a set of notes becomes varied so that the variations are, in effect, compared to each other[6]. In 'serious' music, regardless of stylistic, cultural and historical changes, a reflectaphoric order appears. A composer once remarked to me that he thought of the notes in a musical composition as forming 'a little expanding cosmos with its own laws and forms, like our cosmos.'

But in saying this, one very much wants to avoid implying that reflectaphoric order is some subtle principle by which an artist generates, more or less mechanically, variations of the same thing. Just as Bohm says that for the physical universe it will be impossible to formulate a general law of the whole, in the reflectaphoric universe a general law for constructing reflectaphors will not be possible. This is because reflectaphoric order unfolds to undercut the very processes and machinations of thought.

An experiment in perception will help illustrate this point. It is known that if persons are subjected to a single brief tone (or touch) recurring at fixed, short intervals of, say, a second or so apart, the series of sounds very quickly becomes perceived as rhythm, even though, objectively, no rhythm exists. In the days before digital clocks people had direct experience of this – the tick tick tick sound of a clock becoming in the mind a tick-tock pattern. The brain, it would appear, is a kind of patterning device. Further evidence for this is as near as one's habits.

On the other side, research has shown how quickly a pattern, once established, falls into the background of conscious awareness in the phenomenon of 'habituation.' In habituation, brainwave responses begin to flatten and arousal diminishes until the pattern is hardly noticed at all[7], or until a trance-like state occurs in which at least some levels of the brain are dulled, as happens with patterns used to induce hypnosis and with narrowly rhythmic music (rock music, chants).

Taken together, these observations suggest what may be happening with reflectaphors. In a Beethoven symphony, in 'Man With Umbrella,' in *Typhoon* and in 'The Road Not Taken' the brain's craving for establishing a patterned order is satisfied by the constant display of similar items; at the same time arousal and alertness are maintained and habituation suppressed by the fact that these variations unfold in always unpredictable ways – that is, by the law of comparison/contrast which makes each figure (even after repeated encounters) cognitively dissimilar from the last. The reflectaphoric figures create an alertness in consciousness and, in a sense, this unfolding alertness is itself the order.

It therefore follows that such an order cannot be produced or comprehended mechanically. For example, as we noted earlier, in a poetic metaphor, to achieve the proper X/Y tension, the terms have to be close enough together for an observer to perceive their similarities yet far enough apart to create an enduring, perhaps astonishing, contrast. How could one determine mechanically what the proper distance is to achieve that spark? As Jorge Luis Borges says, the terms of a metaphor must be 'precise':

> I always remember that wonderful line in a poem by Emily Dickinson, which can exemplify this: 'This quiet dust was gentlemen and ladies.' The idea is banal. The idea of dust, the dust of death (we will all be dust one day), is a cliche; but what surprises is the phrase 'gentlemen and ladies,' which gives the line its magic and poetic quality. If she had written 'men and women' it would have failed as poetry, it would have been trivial.[8]

There is a further complication to codifying this proper distance between the terms: the effect of context. Many reflectaphors which make little sense or altogether too much 'conclusive' sense outside their literary context (poem, play, story) have exactly the right similarity/difference harmony within that context. Example: Shakespeare's lines 'This above all, to thine own self be true/And it must follow as the night the day,/Thou canst not then be false to any man.' Outside the play, this has become the most banal sort of conclusive aphorism. In the play's context, however, it is said by Polonius who is false to everybody – and so the lines are reflectaphorically ironic. To the extent that we do become habituated to great works of art, it's when we take things out of context or allow our conclusions about the piece to shut off active perception of the reflectaphoric movement.

Thus, it would be an unproductive paradox to assume that reflectaphors could be generated by some scheme or formula. If it were possible to recognize and predict the pattern, the mind would become habituated to the structure and the structure would fall from this* other-ness into conclusion. As Frost insisted, 'No surprise for the writer, no surprise for the reader.'

Creators know well that attempting to generate an artistic resonance or reflectaphor by analytically or premeditatively balancing terms unavoidably collapses into confusion and arbitrariness. Most artists are quick to point out that any choice of words, lines or notes can be 'justified' on some aesthetic, emotional, rational or other grounds, but that for each moment and position in the piece it is not the most justifiable choice which counts. It is the one which 'works.' There is about the discovery of a good reflectaphor a stochastic quality, as unexpected for the artist as if he had just fallen off a ledge (though sometimes a subtle one), but then in midair seems to remember the ledge was always there. When a creator has tumbled over the edge and finds himself flung along the iron flight-path of his 'right' choice – Wordsworth called it the 'inevitable' choice – he feels paradoxically free. Creators have long maintained that creativity is impossible to teach. Can you teach someone how always to tumble over the rules without yourself making rules which would have to be tumbled over? As Aristotle said of metaphor, it is 'the one thing that cannot be learned.'

But why do artists make reflectaphors? What is their felicity in the creative act? Many creators have said a piece begins for them in something vague, amorphous or objectively insignificant; a trivial object, a memory, silly melody, idea or a fusion of these which uncannily floods the artist with the impression that it contains somehow an immensity, perhaps all the world. Perhaps it is a vision of the whole universe and the artist's relation to it. Perhaps it is a vision of what Conrad called 'truth.' As one sculptor described it to me:

> At times there emanated from people almost palpable extensions
> of themselves, and certain objects possessed a special
> dimensionality. A small puddle iridescent with spilt oil and
> reflecting a patch of midwestern sky would suddenly expand for
> an endless split-second to encompass my entire universe.

This glance of this∗other-ness becomes for the artist a touchstone or what Henry James called a 'germ' out of which the piece evolves. The germ might also be thought of as something which serves the artist as a sudden window, opening between the explicate and the implicate. The evolution of the piece out of that germ (a process which Frost described as like ice riding on its own melting) is a reflectaphoric evolution, each element emerging in X/Y tension with others. In a peculiar and often quite indirect way, the inspiration for the creation and the thing created began to mirror each other. The initial perception is that some one element – idea, memory, melody – contained the whole, and, in the end, the creator produces a form in which each unique element reflects the whole of the piece. Then, since each element in the piece stands or moves beyond itself, the piece as a whole stands beyond itself – which, again, is in keeping with the standing-beyond quality of the piece's inspiration or germ.

The artist's biography also enters strongly into this process. As Rothenberg has pointed out[4], many elements of creative works arise out of superimposing remembered or personal experience on to the constraints of the piece. For example, in creating a character, a novelist may adopt personality traits of someone he has actually known or read about as well as his own personality traits, he then finds these traits modified, shaped and coordinated by the imagined events and other characters in his story. In the case of a photographer, a tension exists between the external scene being photographed and what Ansel Adams calls the internal or imagined 'visualization' of that scene. There is, therefore, in the creative process an ongoing similarity/difference dynamic between (X) the forces of the artist's personal experience of the world and (Y) the material of his invention. The fateful balancing of this unfolding X/Y (which can become exceedingly complex) enters into such important issues as finding the proper 'distance' on the piece, attaining an authentic 'persona' or style and achieving the appropriate voice or tone for the work.

In the evolution of the artwork, the artist doesn't make choices according to some analyzable logic or pattern, but chooses elements that feel 'right,' in harmony with the this*other-ness of the germ. In this process the particular, the individual – the puddle iridescent with oil, the two roads in the woods, Captain MacWhirr, the artist's own life – becomes the universal. The universal, in turn, is revealed as something immediately present to our senses – the place where implicate and explicate have coalesced.

(In)conclusion

Those familiar with David Bohm's theory of the implicate order may be as surprised as I was to find such correspondence between a scientific theory and a purely aesthetic one. Bohm has proposed that matter and energy are holographic – that information about the whole is enfolded in the interference patterns of the matter and energy waves which instantiate space and time. He has also proposed that the universe is multi-dimensional and flowing and that in it the observer is the observed. A reflectaphor could also be viewed as a kind of interference pattern, created by the reverberations of the colliding X/Y terms and producing an unfolding and multi-dimensional reality. However, instead of unfolding into – and as – space and time, reflectaphors unfold in holomovement to instantiate for the observer of the artwork that he is essentially what he observes – every reader is, in some sense, MacWhirr; we are all the old man on the bridge. And the artists who created them were also those figures. (But perhaps in such discoveries lies the secret meaning for us of space and time.)

Creative artists who know anything about David Bohm's work usually recognize immediately that he has envisioned a physical universe which is congenial and familiar, one which has been echoed before in aesthetic ideas like Aristotle's concept of the dramatist inspiring 'pity and fear,' T. S. Eliot's 'objective correlative,' Keats' 'negative capability,' the symbolists' 'correspondences,' Nicholas of Cusa's *coincidentia oppositorum.* It is a universe where, in William Blakes' words, one can 'see the world in a grain of sand' – or a pair of roads, a typhoon, an old man crossing the bridge with an umbrella. It is a universe that would have been recognizable to da Vinci who wrote in his journal that 'every body placed in the luminous air spreads out in circles and fills the surrounding space with infinite likenesses of itself and appears all in all and all in every part.'

Bohm brings new light and considerable force to these ancient artistic visions. But we began by asking if the artistic vision can add anything to our contemplation of the physical universe.

The question remains open. I can offer here only a few vague intimations.

The holographic and reflectaphoric perspectives are strikingly similar but by no means exactly the same. The difference raises a number of questions. Could physical reality also be reflectaphoric; that is, based on an X/Y dynamic such as is found in works of art? For example, could such natural relationships as man/other men, man/objects, objects/energy derive their vitality, perhaps even their very being, from a similarity/difference dynamic? Certainly there is ample evidence that similarity/difference is involved in the shape of the physical world: DNA unfolds the similarity/difference dynamic in all living creatures; the way ontogeny recapitulates phylogeny suggests this vital harmony and tension; matter-energy exchange suggests it. In the consciousness of human beings appreciation of this dynamic is obscured by our tendency to view things as either similar *or* different and to introduce causality to explain away the fact that everything is similar and different simultaneously. Taking a reflectaphoric approach might affect the way in which we classify natural objects and transform the meanings which we give to our classifications.

The reflectaphor is a hinge between the explicate order of our familiar reality (the grain of sand) and the implicate order (the whole implied by the sand). If we were to observe objects around us as grains of sand, as this*other-nesses, could this provide a new perspective into what is happening at the quantum level? In evolution? Should our scientific explanations of natural phenomena have a comparison/contrast dynamic between implicate and explicate; between analysis and what lies beyond analysis? Bohm himself has been an advocate of this position. If we were to take such an approach seriously, how would the universe appear to us and how would we perceive nature's laws? Might, for example, the unknown then become a vivid dimension of our experience of the known – similar to what happens in metaphor when the unknown emerges out of the junction between the two known terms? In a work of art, only when the unknown or ambiguity is present does one implicitly perceive the whole of the piece – and the whole beyond the piece. What would be the role of the observer and the observed in such an X/Y relationship? For ages artists have been portraying the physical world as a reflection of the mind, heart and soul of human beings – and vice versa (e.g. the Chinese chasing dollars are the typhoon). What if the artists are right and the world around us *is* literally a mirror of our minds? Deep within the similarity/difference of physical things is there a natural law as broad and rigorous as the law of gravity but governing what Conrad meant by the 'solidarity . . . which binds men to each other and all mankind to the visible world'?

Many people have been surprised by David Bohm's thesis for various reasons. Some have been surprised by its elegance; some by its sweeping grandeur; some by its perfect aptness to their field of interest. There are even some who are surprised at how much they dislike it. In my case, I was surprised to discover someone in science who saw the world as an artist does; a scientist who had found a creative rather than a random universe; a scientist who found in nature a continuous mystery allied with a continuous meaning. But perhaps I shouldn't have been surprised because, after all, artists and scientists do have in common a fascination with our sensual world – and both are driven to discover in its immediate and apparently chaotic phenomena some glimpses of enduring order.

References

1 David Shainberg, 'Consciousness and psychoanalysis,' *Journal of the American Academy of Psychoanalysis*, **3**, 131 (1975).
2 William Empson, *Seven Types of Ambiguity*, 1930.
3 Max Black, *Models and Metaphors. Studies in Language and Philosophy*, 1962.
4 Albert Rothenberg, *The Emerging Goddess*, 1979.
5 Igor Stravinsky, *Poetics of Music: In the Form of Six Lessons* (Arthur Knodel and Ingolf Dahl, trans.), 1970.
6 Leonard Bernstein, *The Unanswered Question: Six Talks At Harvard*, 1976.
7 David Shainberg, *The Transforming Self*, Intercontinental Medical Book Corp., N.Y. 1973.
8 Jorge Luis Borges, 'Poetry: a conversation with Roberto Alifano' (Nicomedes Suarez Arauz and Willis Barnstone, trans.) *The American Poetry Review*, Nov./Dec. (1983).

30

Meaning as being in the implicate order philosophy of David Bohm: a conversation

Renée Weber *Rutgers, the State University of New Jersey*

Weber You are more and more interested in meaning, so can we explore what meaning is; not the definitive essence of it, but why are you interested in it?

Bohm I am interested in meaning because it is the essential feature of consciousness, because meaning is being as far as the mind is concerned.

Weber Is meaning being?

Bohm Yes. A change of meaning is a change of being. If we say consciousness is its content, therefore consciousness is meaning. We could widen this to a more general kind of meaning that may be the essence of all matter as meaning.

Weber We understand the idea of meaning in the human world, but how can it apply to the non-human world?

Bohm There are several ways of looking at it. Let's take the notion of a cause. Now we know that Aristotle had four notions of causation; of these, the material and the efficient cause are still recognized by modern science. The other two, the formal and the final cause, are not. But if we could bring in this notion of the formal and the final cause, we might say that the form that a thing has is its cause and also its aim, its goal, its end. The two go together. If we think of the dynamics of the establishment of form, it requires some sort of end in view, so the formal and final cause must go together. This is also the basic essence of Rupert Sheldrake's idea of the formative cause [ed. in Sheldrake's *A New Science of Life: The Hypothesis of Formative Causation*]. The formative cause is basically very similar to meaning. Meaning operates in a human being as a formative cause: it provides an end toward which he is moving; it permeates his attention and gives form to his activities so as to tend to realize that end.

Weber So we could say, using an Aristotelian example; just as the acorn moves toward oakhood and stops growing when it reaches the oak and then continues to maintain its oakness, in an analogous way when a human purpose is achieved in an action, that action ceases and becomes something else. You are proposing this analogy?

Bohm Yes, not only to create the thing, but to sustain it. The final cause is not only to become an oak, but to remain an oak, to carry out all the activities that are required to continue to be the oak.

Weber Is meaning still applicable there?

Bohm Yes, because meaning is to sustain your existence rather than to change it.

Weber The problem is this: in giving that explanation, you are already using a teleological framework. Suppose scientists do not accept that and say that the development can be explained in terms of the first two causes only, i.e. the material cause and the efficient cause?

Bohm Well, that's a rather limited range, and it wouldn't serve to explain quantum mechanics, which is fundamental.

Weber In what way would it fail to explain it?

Bohm Quantum mechanics has no causal explanation. It is supposed to be one of its virtues that it is entirely random and statistical and therefore there is no explanation. It has no explanation of *time*, how one moment becomes another. That is, quantum mechanics is a theory of one moment, of one measurement, and there's a statistical probability of getting a certain result. Then you drop whatever you have done and start out with the next measurement, and apply statistics again. It does not explain how you get from one measurement to the other or in fact why or how any measurement produces the result that it does. It says the formula will give you the probability and that's all there is to it.

Weber But then you don't have efficient causation in quantum mechanics, or even material causation.

Bohm In a way, that's what they say. You have no causation except a statistical one or perhaps, in Heisenberg, who has put in the idea of potentiality. But that does not make the causation very clear; it just says in some vague sense that the potential is capable of acting in a certain way and gives the statistics of that action. It doesn't really discuss cause as such.

Weber Isn't that all the more reason for someone *not* to bring in the formal and final cause? If quantum mechanics says there is no justification for *any kind* of causation, why bring it in at all?

Bohm What kind of justification does one want? Simply to say that quantum mechanics has been unable to give a cause of it? I would have an explanation of the electron in the following terms: it is constantly forming and dissolving in a similar way, and what is behind it is this formative cause; that is, a formal and a final cause constantly tending to form.

Weber   How do you visualize that?

Bohm   We might think that the present wave function is the description of a very small part of the formative field of the electron, or the system. This, at any rate, is my suggestion. Quantum mechanics has narrowed down what it can discuss and says: that's all. Nothing else exists, and that's all that can possibly be studied. I'm proposing that we study something else; for example, the *succession* of events. Let us interpret the wave function differently as representing a description of the formative cause, but as having some sort of meaning which would also tie in with things like the non-local correlation. There would be a meaning connected with the whole system as well as with any one part.

Weber   Where would the formative cause and the meaning come from?

Bohm   Where does the wave function come from? It's just simply proposed by Schrödinger and a few other people and they say if you work with it it will give you an answer. Nobody explains it. There is always an assumption, in every theory, from which you derive the rest of the theory.

Weber   You're suggesting that what the formative causation, and the notion of the formal and final causes would add is explanation, meaningfulness, context and philosophical content.

Bohm   And possibly some other content, so you could handle a broader range of questions.

Weber   Can you give an example?

Bohm   Time, for example. Present quantum mechanics cannot handle time. It can only discuss one moment, compute the probability of that moment, then take another moment and compute its probability, and so on.

Weber   All of it discrete, whereas your proposal would provide a binding whole in one large context. To return to the same question, is there meaning in the non-human world, the world of nature, and in the universe as a whole?

Bohm   That's what I'm proposing; not only that there is a meaning to it, but rather *that it is meaning*. We began by proposing that human consciousness *is* its meaning, not to say *that it has* a meaning, *but it is* its meaning. According to what it means, that is what it is.

Weber   What it means to whom? To us? Or to some other context?

Bohm   Let's think about ourselves for a moment. If we say something has a meaning, who is the person to whom these meanings are being attributed?

Weber   To the individual, to the subgroup, to the culture . . .

Bohm   What is the culture but a whole set of meanings? If you change the meaning, you have changed the culture. If you change the meaning of the life to the individual, he is different.

Weber   People get around this by saying 'Meanings are subjective, they have a place in the human world, but not in the subatomic world or in the cosmological world.'

Bohm   We have a hidden meaning perhaps and we should explore meaning there too.

Weber   That's what you are saying. You're extending meaning to the large, to the small and to the in-between, which is the human scale. You say that *meaning is being.* One can see that in the psychological world and in the social world quite clearly, but less so in the physical world.

Bohm   If the electron were determined by a meaning, that would be its being. If there is a formative cause for the electron, the formative cause is what the electron *is.*

Weber   But one might question the validity of the analogy. The fact that the meaning of the human being is its being you can document, and you've done it with many good examples, from psychosomatic medicine, for example. But it is much harder to see in what way the meaning of the electron becomes its being, because the electron doesn't assign its own meaning the way a human being does.

Bohm   I don't think the human being assigns his meaning. I think it happens naturally.

Weber   *Is* its being, you're claiming.

Bohm   Yes, it is its being. To propose that we assign meaning pre-supposes another being who decides what the meanings are going to be for him. I don't think anybody functions that way. That is, he's got his meanings from the culture, from the society, or else from his perceptions, and so on. He doesn't *choose* his meanings; *he is his meanings.*

Weber   It is clear in the inner domain. What is not clear is, is it analogous? Since *we* attribute meaning to the world of nature and to the electron, does the electron also attribute it to itself? That would be the analogy carried through.

Bohm   I think the word 'attribute' is causing trouble. In a vague sense, of course, sometimes we can consciously attribute meaning. But in general we don't attribute it; we simply react with meaning, as in the example of someone who perceives a shadow as a threatening figure and whose biochemistry instantly changes.

Weber   So meaning, as you are using it, is not reserved for what is self-reflective and self-conscious in a human sense.

Bohm   For example, if a person is conditioned to look at things in a certain way, he doesn't deliberately assign meaning; he immediately *sees it that way* and has no choice about it. He doesn't even know he's doing it.

Weber   You are proposing that in the subatomic world, something like that also happens.

Bohm   It's primarily unconscious in the subatomic world. If we say that 99.99 per cent of our meanings are not conscious, we don't choose them, they just take place. That's the analogy. I would say that the degree of consciousness of the atomic world is very low, at least of self-consciousness.

Weber   But it's not dead or inert. That is what you are saying.

Bohm   It has some degree of consciousness in the sense that it responds in some way, but it has almost no *self*-consciousness.

Weber   Is it possible to state what the meaning of that kind of being is? You started to say that *time* has something to do with it, and coherence and development.

Bohm   Yes, the coherence of large systems. The formal and final cause determine fundamentally what a thing is. They determine how it acts, how it grows, how it sustains itself, where it will end, what it will become, and what it gives rise to. Therefore, that is what it is, right?

Weber   And you're saying that this is really embedded within the subatomic and cosmological world itself?

Bohm   Yes. My proposal is that everything is of that nature. The wave-function resembles information with meaning and is much more than a description of things as hard material objects. Its multi-dimensional character is a sign that it cannot be put into ordinary space but that meanings are specifically multi-dimensional. Therefore in this view space and time themselves would be some kind of meaning. We attribute meaning – our minds attribute meaning – in a certain way, even if not consciously. But that meaning infuses its *intention* and *action* towards the world. In so far as there's a consistency between these two, then that system has some stability.

Weber   So one philosophical import of this view is that *nothing in the universe*, and that includes the domain of nature, is neutral or value free in the positivistic sense.

Bohm   In so far as meaning is value, yes. There may be all kinds of implicit values, in the way things behave.

Weber   To simply describe them in the positivistic fashion is not to understand them, according to this view.

Bohm   Yes. That would be to see them outwardly.

Weber   And mechanically. In that case, the inner impulse that you are describing, the *telos*, is then overlooked and not understood.

Bohm   Yes. There is an interesting point – even in mechanics and physics – things can always be looked at in both ways. The laws of Newton, which we look at as mechanical and causal, when put into Lagrangian form, take a teleological form which is equivalent to saying that the particle now moves to minimize a certain function called a Lagrangian which is integrated over time. It has to do with long periods of time as if it had an end in view to keep its Lagrangian as small as possible. The interesting point is that not all of Newton's laws take that form. It's possible to get many equations that cannot be put in that form; all the laws having to do with the fundamental particles take that form, which suggests that that form has some importance. It has never been explained why that form should be there. Most physicists always start with the Lagrangian nowadays; 'we must find a Lagrangian,' it's a sort of universal principle. But why there should be a Lagrangian, nobody ever says, or can say.

Weber   What is the significance of this?

Bohm   It would be part of a view that says that the whole principle of movement is that it contains this end in view, so that it would be quite natural to put the laws in that form. There are some laws, when put in that form, that are indistinguishable from laws of a mechanical nature.

Weber   So that the mechanical laws can *mask* or cover up these teleological ones.

Bohm   They are a *special case* of the teleological laws. It will not work the other way round.

Weber   But to you, the teleological laws are primary and the mechanical laws may in fact be teleological, the universe's way of implementing its purpose. Is that the idea?

Bohm   Yes, that is what I am proposing.

Weber   So the cosmology you're proposing *is meaning*, inherently.

Bohm   Yes. In that sense, *meaning is the essence of reality*.

Weber   That's a marvelous thought. If someone were to try to pin you down and say 'What *is* the meaning of it: is it development, is it self-awareness through time and variety,' what would you answer?

Bohm   We have to discover that. There is no fixed meaning. That is its characteristic, that there is no *final* meaning. The whole point of meaning is that the content is in a context, which in turn is in a context, and therefore meaning is not final. We are always discovering it, and that discovery of meaning is itself a part of the reality.

Weber   The discovery of meaning, and the creation of meaning. Of course the question is: Do we discover meaning or do we create meaning?

Bohm   We can look at it both ways. We discover meaning in some sense, but whatever we discover we also create some idea as to how we are going to put it – the way it is going to be abstracted from the context.

Weber   In your earlier implicate order philosophy you proposed terms like intelligence, order and compassion when applied to the universe as a whole. Would those be a part of the meaning of the universe as it unfolds itself?

Bohm   Yes, intelligence is part of this process of the perception of meaning. In fact when you say 'I understand' you really say 'I see the whole meaning of this.'

Weber   You say that if meaning changes, being changes. Does this mean that as we understand, as this holomovement understands itself more deeply and more in detail through history, its *being* becomes clearer or fuller?

Bohm   Yes. A change of order. Any change of understanding is a change of being, at least of the creatures who are doing it and of all that they affect.

Weber   Isn't this analogous to Hegel?

Bohm   Yes, I think the point Hegel made was that analysis doesn't necessarily mean breaking things into bits, but rather unfolding the meaning. He made the interesting point that analysis is at the same time synthesis, because when you have unfolded the meaning, the being has changed and something has been added to it. It unfolds a meaning which is another order of being.

Weber   That's the synthesis.

Bohm   Yes, the analysis is at the same time a synthesis.

Weber   It also unifies things.

Bohm   There is a larger being which includes the analysis and the material analyzed. Instead of saying that the analysis is just *about* the thing analyzed, the analysis is a *change* in the thing analyzed.

Weber   So this links change, permanence, development and significance, all in one?

Bohm   Yes.

Weber   You are after all a quantum physicist. Is meaning in some way analogous to energy, or could it be like the charge on matter?

Bohm   No, information is a very condensed form of meaning that has to be unfolded. Information by itself may be irrelevant or just wrong, but information is the form *within*, virtually. But obviously that form as the meaning is not complete without the *whole* meaning and all the contexts spreading indefinitely. So the concept of information is very limited without adding and bringing in the meaning.

Weber   Concepts in particle physics, like spin or charm, would be limited and you are saying they are true, but there is more meaning than that. What would be appropriate words besides development or time that one could apply to those?

Bohm   I don't know. The point is that we think of these meanings as signasomatic, in the sense that the significance affects the soma. The spin, the significance of spin, implies some somatic consequences. The result of observation is to change the meaning and therefore change the being. There is a great analogy between how analysis, which adds further meaning, is a change of being, and the observation adds some meaning and therefore there's a change of being. It gives a good image of how the observer and the observed are one.

Weber   That's an example of the claim that the observer and the observed are one?

Bohm   Yes. The point about meaning is that once you bring in the signasomatic side of meaning you can see that meaning is the observer. Thought producing meaning is the observer, but the observer is the observed, because that meaning is inseparable from the somatic and it unfolds immediately into consequences which are observed, hence physical.

Weber It illustrates in what way the observer is the observed, but it also leaves open what being is because you are saying that being is *knowing about being.*

Bohm Being and knowing are inseparable.

Weber Exactly.

Bohm Meaning is something like the form which informs the energy, so it will actively direct the energy and shape it.

Weber This view assigns a highly active role to human beings. Isn't that the implication of what you are saying?

Bohm Yes.

Weber Every time meaning changes for us, we've changed what being is for us.

Bohm Yes, and also what it is in itself; the whole being of whatever being is, has changed. The question is: How important is the change, and we don't know that. But at first you might say because it is so small it is not a very significant change. But the size of the change is not always significant.

Weber A so-called small effect can have far-reaching consequences?

Bohm Yes.

Weber You used an example yesterday of size as a poor indicator of importance; people said, if we just split one or two atoms, that's nothing.

Bohm Yes, they might have said 'This can have very little effect.'

Weber And they were wrong!

Bohm I don't know if they said it, but if they had said it, that would have been an analogy.

Weber I was going to ask you at what level of organization meaning comes in, but that's obviously the wrong question, from what we've been saying.

Bohm Meaning organizes everything.

Weber If somebody would use meaning as a synonym for cosmic intelligence or cosmic mind or something like that, how would you respond?

Bohm Mind and matter are inseparable, in the sense that everything is permeated with meaning. The whole idea of the somasignificant or signasomatic is that at no stage are mind and matter ever separated. There are different levels of mind. Even the electron is informed with a certain level of mind.

Weber It's a beautiful and poetic metaphor, but specifically in what way can one say that the electron is somehow infused with mind?

Bohm In so far as any meaning determines what it is, how it acts and so on, it is behaving in a way similar to how a mind acts.

Weber As a philosopher I can see that this part of your work, your implicate order philosophy, relates to historical philosophy in several ways. I think the developmental side is reminiscent of Hegel, but the new concepts of somasignificance and the signasomatic really evoke Spinoza. Like him, you conceive matter and consciousness as two aspects of one being.

Bohm   Yes. We haven't penetrated that ultimately – the mystery of it may go further – but as far as I can see consciousness contains a self-awareness. This sort of process without self-awareness – it's hard to know if you would call it consciousness – but you can call it a kind of mind in the sense that the computer is almost a kind of mind. This would be far more subtle than a computer, but it would still not be self-aware.

Weber   It would be aware, but not *aware* of being aware.

Bohm   Yes.

Weber   That comes in at higher levels of organization. One can see how this works by applying it to a human organism; there it's more clear-cut. For every state of mind there's a state of body and vice versa, like in Spinoza.

Bohm   It's also very subtle levels of being, within the implicate order, which may not even be located in the body, in the sense that it may be affected, rather as Sheldrake is suggesting, by fields which are not local.

Weber   These fields affect us and we affect them; it's a mutual interpenetration and exchange.

Bohm   Yes.

Weber   Are you proposing something like a *meaning field*?

Bohm   Yes, that's exactly it. You could say (and Sheldrake seems to agree with this) that the morphogenetic field is a field of active meaning – meaning in the signasomatic and somasignificant sense.

Weber   It may sound naive, yet somebody might ask 'How did it get there?'

Bohm   One theory is that it accumulates gradually. In discussions with Sheldrake, for example, one idea that has come up is that meaning is constantly operative at different levels. It works from the implicate to the explicate, but there is also a projection out of the implicate to the explicate and an introjection back into the implicate order. If we keep on introjecting similar content, it will build up a certain meaning.

Weber   So the meaning field is the consequence both of an inner impulse which somehow it *is*, and of what it has undergone in history, and in human consciousness.

Bohm   One can see that in human beings clearly; if nature is similar to us, then it should be happening there too.

Weber   That is one of the beautiful aspects of this world view. It envisions a universal coherence and points to an all-encompassing principle that runs throughout the system; it doesn't just start at the human or organic level. You are saying that it exists on all levels.

Applied to the very large scale, what would a cosmologist say, for example, of the constant making and unmaking of galaxies and stars?
Bohm We haven't gone into it sufficiently to see how it would work there. The universe is supposed to have started from this big bang. We might say that that is the formation of a certain meaning and a certain structure of meaning which unfolds. There could be other universes, within this sea of infinite energy. Let's look at basics – meaning, energy, matter and, ultimately, self-awareness. Meaning infuses and informs energy, giving it shape and form. Now a certain from is matter, which is energy which has stabilized into a regular form, more or less stable, with some independence. But there must be a meaning that is behind it. In terms of quantum mechanics I would say there will have to be some development of the wave function beyond the present theory which is just what that is, i.e. it would be a formative cause, *a field of meaning.*
Weber The field of meaning would be displayed, to use your terminology, by the explicate or the material.
Bohm Yes, that is the display.
Weber This is the point on which people are going to have to shift in their thinking: it doesn't only have meaning when it comes *out of* the enfolded order; meaning runs through the *implicate order* as well as the explicate order, at all levels.
Bohm Yes. In fact you could think of the whole series in seeing one level of the implicate as the signasomatic consequence of the next level, which is less subtle, right?
Weber Yes.
Bohm There could be many levels, an indefinite set of levels of implication.
Weber Would the signasomatic principle function all the way through?
Bohm Yes, because something is somatic relative to something which is more subtle.
Weber So this would function in the non-human world, the subatomic world, too, and would apply at all the levels of implication, inner and outer.
Bohm Yes.
Weber It's dazzling and one can't help but draw the conclusion that you are saying: 'This is a universe that is alive (in its appropriate way) and somehow conscious at *all the levels.*'
Bohm Yes, in a way.
Weber That's what I take this to mean.
Bohm We don't know how far the self-awareness would go, but if you were religious, you would believe it in the sense of God, or as something that would be totally self-aware.
Weber You mean, as a whole. The question is: Is there a significance to the holomovement *as a whole*?

Bohm   Yes, that is a question of what proposal we want to explore. People have, in effect, been exploring notions of that kind in religions. One view is to say that the significance is similar to that of ourselves in a sense that Christians would say that God is a person.

Weber   Or, anyhow, a being.

Bohm   Well, they say three persons, the Trinity, which are one. Anyway, it's something like a human being, or rather the other way around; that man is the image of God. That implies that there is a total significance. If you say Atman, in Hinduism, something similar is implied.

Weber   Atman and Brahman, seen as identical; the micro- and the macrocosm.

Bohm   Yes, and Atman is from the side of meaning. You would say Atman is more like the meaning. But then what is meant would be Brahman, I suppose; the identity of consciousness and cosmos.

Weber   Looked at from the so-called subjective side it would be Atman; that would be the meaning. And what is meant is the objective.

Bohm   Meaning in this sense that the somasignificant and signasomatic unite the two sides. This claims that the meaning and what is meant are ultimately one, which is the phrase 'Atman equals Brahman' of classical Hindu philosophy.

Weber   It's an identity-thesis claim. To relate this again to what some of the great philosophers of the past have said: somasignificant and signasomatic – aren't they your way of working out your own creative concepts for what Spinoza meant by mind and body, and what Hegel meant by subject and substance?

Bohm   Yes, this is a way of understanding how these are related, extending the understanding, or extending the meaning.

Weber   It has plagued philosophers through the ages that there are these two ways of apprehending reality. You are proposing that *signa* and *somatic* are somehow the very fabric of everything in the universe and that this gets expressed in appropriate ways at different levels of organization.

Bohm   Yes, and that the bridge is the energy which creates the soma and regulates it and so on.

Weber   Let's pursue this idea of a bridge of energy.

Bohm   The energy which is informed with meaning.

Weber   Would it be right to call that the efficient cause?

Bohm   Yes, I think that is the nearest to Aristotle's efficient cause. The soma is the material cause.

Weber   And the signa is the formal-final cause?

Bohm   Yes. The somasignificance would be the formal-final cause. The significance is both the form and the end.

Weber   So psychosomatic implications, of which you gave examples earlier, hold true even on the cosmological scale?

Bohm Yes.

Weber Could one put into words the idea of *a* meaning or *a* purpose for all this? You once suggested greater clarity of the universe about itself.

Bohm That could be part of its end. Maybe an end of greater order, greater clarity, an end to create something.

Weber So that meaning and being become transparently clear to the organism at all the levels of itself?

Bohm That would be part of the end. I don't know how to put the end yet. The end could be said to be love, it could be said to be order, harmony, but the end could also be said to be the process itself.

Weber Spinoza would have liked that. He said that the universe doesn't have to have a reason, *it is*, and that's enough. Although you start out from physics, your view seems to be similar to that.

Bohm Yes, because it's not to say that it *has a meaning*, but it *is its meaning*. We are trying to be more clear as to what this meaning is, because then it will have changed our being.

Weber You are a physicist, yet so much of this sounds like what a mystic would say: that in the mystical experience there simply is profound and self-evident meaning, without utilitarian overtones. Isn't that what you are saying?

Bohm Yes, utility is only a small part of meaning. Utility is a meaning, but it's a rather restricted meaning. The question is: Useful for what? It always occurs in some context – without the context we cannot discuss utility.

Weber Archibald MacLeish defines poetry in that way. He says: 'A poem should not mean but be.' So the meaning is its being. To shift to another question: are time, history and development necessary for the evolution of form and consciousness?

Bohm That needs exploration. Somebody like Krishnamurti and some other people like the mystics would say that it has nothing to do with it. That is one approach. On the other hand, we have to understand the meaning of time more deeply. We have hardly touched it so far.

Weber As a human species, you mean?

Bohm Yes. We have to see more deeply the meaning of time – the relation between time and the timeless. What is called eternity does not mean all time, but what is *beyond* time. Is there meaning beyond time? That is one of the questions. Perhaps the mystic would say that there is.

Weber In fact, the mystic would say that the profoundest sense of meaning arises beyond time.

Bohm And that meaning is being beyond time.

Weber That is the classical mystical position.

Bohm But time is also meaning and the question is 'How are the two related?' I think that we have hardly begun to touch that.

Weber   Would you care to make some tentative statement about how time is related to meaning and being?

Bohm   In so far as meaning is *telos*, which we will now put in terms of time, it may be something deeper than that, beyond time.

Weber   Of which this is just the outcome.

Bohm   Yes. We haven't fully understood what time is – to see how it emerges from what is beyond time – that is one of the questions that needs exploration.

Weber   How would one even begin such an exploration?

Bohm   For example, we could consider orders that are beyond time, from which the time order might emerge; an implicate order that is beyond time that would be possible to have a sub-order of time emerging from it.

Weber   It would be beyond time, yet be the source of it in some way?

Bohm   Yes.

Weber   Would this be the super-implicate order or beyond that?

Bohm   It might be beyond that. There would have to be an implicate order from which time itself emerges. The distinction between the significance and its somatic consequences is one which we make in thought only. They merge and flow into each other. But time itself arises out of that sort of distinction because we say there's meaning and the end – in so far as the end is not yet realized – is time. If the end were immediately realized, we would not have time.

Weber   Time is like the expression of the gap between this being and its becoming, that being.

Bohm   Yes. If we say that there are enfolded in being potential ends which are not yet realized, that begins to provide the ground for time.

Weber   If we look at it cosmologically and philosophically, it brings up the question, 'Is there something incomplete or unrealized in this whole cosmos that would bring about this gap between what being is and what its becoming will be – a necessary enfoldment of it?'

Bohm   In so far as meaning is incomplete it inevitably implies time. The mystic might say that perhaps the total is complete and does not involve time, but that there is another set of meanings which is not complete which *does* involve time. Here it becomes a question of value. The mystic might place the highest and supreme value on the one that does not involve time and may tend to give much smaller value to the one that does. On the other hand, we must explore that to see if the mystic is always right.

Weber   All the more so because your whole philosophy seems to grant genuine status to the world of history and changing development as part of the meaning of the whole thing.

Bohm   Yes. See, there is a kind of meaning that is incomplete, and the question is what is its value? That's our first question. The mystic may be undervaluing that.

Weber Filtering it out as if it were an accident of the universe.

Bohm At least, a great many mystics may do that. On the other hand, in the Christian tradition, and the Jewish one probably, time and history have a very great significance.

Weber Your implicate order philosophy says that genuine understanding of the holomovement requires one to look at both the temporal and what is beyond time, together. You are suggesting a synthesis, a holist approach to this question.

Bohm Yes. If we were to take this view of Hegel's about analysis, that analysis is the *enfoldment* of what is to be analyzed, and that at the same time is a synthesis. It enriches the thing, it adds to the thing that is being analyzed. It adds meaning and therefore adds being.

Weber So concerning the question raised earlier, 'Do we discover or do we create meaning?' it is as if in discovering it we create it or create it *in us*.

Bohm Not only that, but we enrich it; we create something which has not been there.

Weber We add to it.

Bohm Yes. We are a part of it and it is part of us.

Weber Since any meaning that we grasp in it changes its being, this makes us *partners* in the evolution of the universe?

Bohm Yes, that's the proposal. Therefore if we take that complete universe of the mystics and let it unfold in time, then that unfoldment is similar to analysis. It unfolds what is implicit. As Nicholas of Cusa said, eternity both enfolds and unfolds time. We may add that unfoldment enriches what was enfolded. It adds meaning to it and therefore being.

Weber Since the point of departure of your whole philosophy is not crude materialism to begin with, being transcends the visible, the tactile and all that.

Bohm Yes, and space and time. In fact the visible and the tactile are the outcome of meaning, in this generalized sense.

Weber They are derivative, and the generative orders are these invisible realities.

Bohm Yes, at least in some sense; if we see the meaning of something, that thing has in some way been changed. But the question is: How significant is the change? That is something that needs to be explored. You say that is a small change, probably, but it may not be so small in its full implications.

Weber You are proposing that its magnitude is overlooked.

Bohm Magnitude may not be the significance.

Weber I don't mean quantity-wise, but its significance.

Bohm Its significance is overlooked. Teilhard de Chardin has proposed something like this; when you study science it gives an account and explains everything except the human being in his essence. One view of it is to say that's not a very important oversight. Or else one may say, gradually we'll take care of it. But the other view is to say that though it looks small, it may be that it reveals what is much more significant.

Weber   Is there an analogy in the world of physics?

Bohm   Just what I said earlier, i.e. those small atoms disintegrating, revealing something much more significant.

Weber   What does all this imply for the human world? Looking at the universe in this way changes our lives in what way?

Bohm   It's hard to say at first, but it will clearly imply something very different, a different attitude in the sense that we won't give that much primary weight to the external and the mechanistic side – the side of fragmentation and partiality. Also, it encourages us much more toward a creative attitude, and fundamentally it opens the way to the transformation of the human being because a change of meaning is a change of being. At present we say because of the confused fragmentary meanings we have a confused fragmentary being, both individually and socially. Therefore this opens the way to a whole being, in society and in the individual.

Weber   It also seems to bring in ethical responsibility, because if we are, or can be partners in, helping to transform being through our meanings, wouldn't that imply that what we think and feel *counts*?

Bohm   It counts. When you say responsibility, the key word is response. Nobody can be responsible who is unable to respond. If you ask somebody who is unable to respond to be responsible, you have not responsibility, but probably guilt. As long as the meaning is confused, nobody can respond to all this. His response is going to be very limited and therefore that responsibility is very limited.

Weber   To relate it to human psychology and transformation, the key seems to be the Socratic maxim 'Know yourself,' go inward, and also 'Observe.'

Bohm   And also outward. The outward and the inward are one part of one total meaning.

Weber   You are really saying *our being is meaning*. The whole world *is* meaning.

Bohm   Yes. The being of matter is its meaning; the being of ourselves is meaning; the being of society is its meaning. The mechanistic view has created a rather crude and gross meaning which has created a crude and gross and confused society.

Weber   This view, your view, would make human beings feel rooted and have their dynamic place in the whole scheme of things.

Bohm   At least they would have a chance to find it there. It's a view within which it makes sense to observe to find out where your place is.

Weber   Beautiful!

Index

451